Medgar Evers

Medgar Evers

Mississippi Martyr

MICHAEL VINSON WILLIAMS

The University of Arkansas Press
Fayetteville
2011

Copyright © 2011 by The University of Arkansas Press

ISBN-10: 1-55728-973-5
ISBN-13: 978-1-55728-973-5

15 14 13 12 11   5 4 3 2 1

Text design by Ellen Beeler

⊗ The paper used in this publication meets the minimum requirements of the American
National Standard for Permanence of Paper for Printed Library Materials Z39.48-
1984.

Library of Congress Cataloging-in-Publication Data

Williams, Michael Vinson, 1971–
    Medgar Evers : Mississippi martyr / Michael Vinson Williams.
        p. cm.
    Includes bibliographical references and index.
    ISBN-13: 978-1-55728-973-5 (cloth : alk. paper)
    ISBN-10: 1-55728-973-5 (cloth : alk. paper)
    1. Evers, Medgar Wiley, 1925–1963 2. African American civil rights workers—
Mississippi—Jackson—Biography. 3. Civil rights workers—Mississippi—Jackson—
Biography. 4. National Association for the Advancement of Colored People—
Biography. 5. Civil rights movements—Mississippi—History—20th century.
6. African Americans—Civil rights—Mississippi—History—20th century.
7. Mississippi—Race relations. 8. Jackson (Miss.)—Biography. I. Title.
F349.J13W55 2011
323.092--dc23
[B]
                                                                    201102720

*To my ancestors, to my grandmothers Grady B. "Mur" Williams
and Bell "Mama Bell" Smith, my great-grandmother Earline
"Mama" Glass, and my great-aunt Tommie Etoy Kilgore; they always
knew and demanded that I become a man of pride and principle*

*To Medgar Wiley Evers and the countless men, women, and children
whose determined and broad shoulders he humbly stood upon to
make this world a better place for my children, I say thank you*

Contents

Acknowledgments

I must first thank my parents, James and Delois Williams, who provided me with an academic foundation grounded in self-love and a respect for knowledge and one's overall responsibility to humanity; without them I could not have succeeded. I owe my undying love and gratitude to my wife, Truly, and our two daughters, Ayo and Marimba; this project took a number of years from their lives and yet they never complained too loudly. They have been and continue to be my rock of stability in all of this and for whatever is to come. I must also thank my brothers Reginald, Malcolm, and Solomon, who have stood by and for me, and my sisters Zakia, Johannah, Dawn, Angela, Tina, Jamie, and Marimba, who have kept me enveloped in the knowledge that I am loved; family is everything to me and they all continue to prove why this is so.

I could not have accomplished this project without the assistance, encouragement, and guidance of Charles Ross, Ted Ownby, Angela Hornsby-Gutting, and Ethel Young-Minor, who gave of their time unconditionally, and I continue to appreciate their dedication, scholarship, advice, and professionalism more than they will ever know. I would also like to thank the anonymous readers who meticulously poured over this lengthy manuscript multiple times and offered invaluable feedback, pointers, and scholarly advice. I want to also extend my sincere gratitude to Bob Dylan for allowing me the use of his song, "Only a Pawn in Their Game," in this work; it is much appreciated. I must also thank the staff at the University of Arkansas Press, particularly Julie Watkins and Lawrence J. (Larry) Malley, whose professionalism and belief in this project made all the difference.

This project would have also suffered without the assistance and patience of the faculty and staff of the J. D. Williams Library at the University of Mississippi. I must also acknowledge the invaluable assistance provided by the faculty and staff of the University of Mississippi Department of Archives and Special Collections, the University of Memphis Special Collections, Alcorn State University, Emory University, University of Southern Mississippi, Tougaloo College, Mississippi State University, and the Mississippi Department of Archives and History. I would also like to thank the faculty and staff of the Kenya National Archives, who were helpful beyond words. Without the assistance of the above individuals and their knowledge and willingness to share, this would have been a far more difficult project to complete.

I owe a special and personal debt of gratitude to Mrs. Myrlie Evers-Williams, Mrs. Carrie Elizabeth Evers-Jordan, and Mr. Charles Evers, whose patience, encouragement, and kindness allowed this project to go forward and heightened my sense of personal responsibility. I am also grateful for the kindness displayed by the many individuals who consented to interviews such as the late Dr. Gilbert R. Mason Sr., Mrs. Ponjola Andrews, and Mrs. Ineeva May-Pittman. Each interviewee offered himself or herself completely, which aided this process in ways that defy words; I appreciate each and every one of you. To all of the countless individuals who had a part in this project but whom I have been unable to mention by name, know that your kindness, enthusiasm, friendship, and humanity inspired this work, and so again I say thank you.

Abbreviations

ACMHR	Alabama Christian Movement for Human Rights
AFL-CIO	American Federation of Labor-Congress of Industrial Organizations
CAA	Council on African Affairs
COFO	Council of Federated Organizations
COGIC	Church of God in Christ
CORE	Congress of Racial Equality
FBI	Federal Bureau of Investigation
FCC	Federal Communications Commission
ICC	Interstate Commerce Commission
IHL	Institutions of Higher Learning
LEAC	Legal Educational Advisory Committee
LDF	Legal Defense and Educational Fund
LOC	Library of Congress
MDAH	Mississippi Department of Archives and History
MIA	Montgomery Improvement Association
MSC	Mississippi Southern College
NAACP	National Association for the Advancement of Colored People
NVS	Newton Vocational School
PCEEO	President's Committee on Equal Employment Opportunity
RCNL	Regional Council of Negro Leadership
SCLC	Southern Christian Leadership Conference
SNCC	Student Nonviolent Coordinating Committee
UDL	United Defense League
UMC	University Medical Center
UN	United Nations
UNESCO	United Nations Educational, Scientific, and Cultural Organization
WCC	White Citizens' Council
WPC	Women's Political Council

Medgar Evers

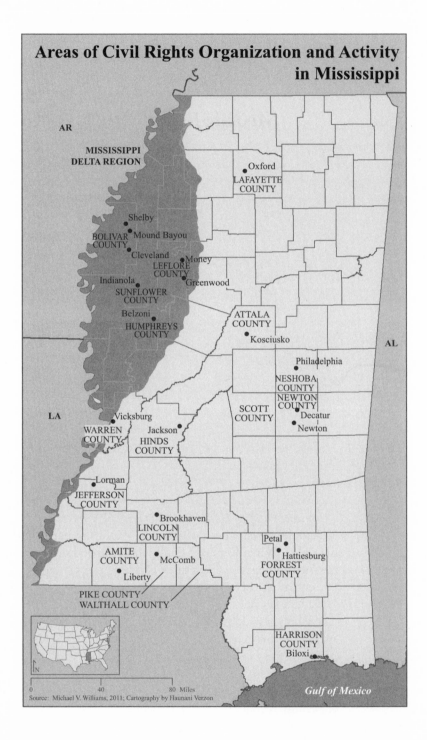

Areas of Civil Rights Organization and Activity in Mississippi

AR

**MISSISSIPPI
DELTA REGION**

Oxford
LAFAYETTE
COUNTY

Shelby
BOLIVAR   Mound Bayou
COUNTY
Cleveland   Money
LEFLORE
COUNTY
Indianola   Greenwood
SUNFLOWER
COUNTY
Belzoni
HUMPHREYS
COUNTY

ATTALA
COUNTY
Kosciusko

AL

Philadelphia

NESHOBA
COUNTY
NEWTON
COUNTY
SCOTT   Decatur
COUNTY   Newton

LA   Vicksburg
WARREN   Jackson
COUNTY   HINDS
COUNTY

Lorman
JEFFERSON
COUNTY

Brookhaven
LINCOLN
COUNTY
Petal
AMITE   Hattiesburg
COUNTY   McComb   FORREST
Liberty   COUNTY

PIKE COUNTY
WALTHALL COUNTY

HARRISON
COUNTY
Biloxi

N

0   40   80 Miles
Source: Michael V. Williams, 2011; Cartography by Haunani Verzon

Gulf of Mexico

Introduction

A PRELUDE TO MARTYRDOM

A bullet from the back of a bush took Medgar Evers' blood
A finger fired the trigger to his name
A handle hid out in the dark
A hand set the spark
Two eyes took the aim
Behind a man's brain
But he can't be blamed
He's only a pawn in their game

— *Bob Dylan*

ON THE EVENING OF JUNE 11, 1963, Myrlie Evers settled into her comfortable middle-class home and waited with anticipation for President John F. Kennedy to address the nation. Her husband, Medgar Evers, who also served as field secretary for the National Association for the Advancement of Colored People (NAACP), had left for work early that morning, and both had discussed what the president might say, particularly as it related to civil rights. When Kennedy finally took the podium, Myrlie watched the address with intensity. Their three children also watched, not knowing that their entire world would drastically change in the not-so-distant future. Myrlie had allowed the children to stay up late that night so they could greet their father when he arrived home.[1] Although Evers had not returned by midnight, this caused no alarm as his NAACP work often kept him busy well into the night. Around 12:20 A.M., Evers pulled his Oldsmobile into the yard as he had done countless times before. His son Darrell heard the car approach first and excitedly announced, "Here comes Daddy." The entire family recognized the familiar sounds that signaled his arrival, and Myrlie "wondered what Medgar would have to say about the speech."[2]

They heard the automobile engine shut off and the sound of the car door opening. This action accompanied the pause that always occurred during the time it took Evers to collect belongings, to decide what to bring inside and what items to leave behind. True to form, he chose to bring in work-related material, including the remainder of the t-shirts the NAACP had passed out earlier with the words "Jim Crow Must Go" emblazoned across the front.[3] This morning would be different; all familiarities disappeared as the early morning air filled with the unfamiliar sound of a piercing gunshot.

Medgar Wiley Evers, at the age of thirty-seven, had been shot in the back with a model 1917 .30–06-caliber Enfield high-powered rifle. Myrlie heard the shot and knew immediately what had happened. Despite being pregnant with their fourth child, she rushed toward the front of the house and heard a second shot, which turned out to be their neighbor Houston Wells firing a warning shot into the air. Although at the time she did not know whether the assailant had fired the second shot or not, she snatched open the door in hopes of being able to "get . . . [Medgar] in, or give him a gun" had they missed him.[4] Hope all but evaporated when she saw her mortally wounded husband drenched in blood. Despite the extent and severity of his injury, Evers had managed to pull himself along the carport toward the side door of the house, still tightly holding his key, "trying to come home," Myrlie recalled.[5] His movements, however, were followed by a trail of blood that snaked ominously along the carport behind him. Almost instantly members of this middle-class community rushed outside upon hearing gunfire and "members of Evers' family screaming." Surrounded by his wife, concerned neighbors, friends, and his children, whose screams of "Please, Daddy, please get up!" he undoubtedly heard, individuals present laid Medgar on his daughter Reena's mattress and placed him in the back of Houston Wells's station wagon.[6] The actions of everyone present at the scene, including the Evers family, the Wells, and the police, appeared disjointed, chaotic, and out of sync; things seemed to be happening fast and slow at once. It slowly dawned on those present that another "Negro" in Mississippi had been killed.[7]

The violence the Evers family suffered and endured during the early morning hours of June 12, 1963, was not a new experience for black Mississippians. Mississippi had a well-earned reputation for violence, oppression, and tyranny when it came to its African American population. White Mississippians had lynched Emmett Till in Money, shot-gunned to death Clinton Melton in Glendora, and kidnapped and murdered James Chaney,

Andrew Goodman, and Michael Schwerner in Philadelphia. Whispered claims that the various rivers and waterways throughout the state were littered with the bodies of "Negroes" circulated through black communities as black lives seemed to have no value. These types of quieted allegations were much more than mere accusations. On July 12, 1964, a fisherman found a severed and badly decomposed body in a back waterway of the Mississippi River and authorities believed that it might be that of Michael Schwerner. The body turned out to be that of a twenty-year-old African American named Charles Moore; the remains of his murdered friend Henry Dee later surfaced as well. Members of the local Ku Klux Klan, James Ford Seale in particular, were later implicated in their murders.[8] African Americans could be and were killed for the least offense and their bodies sometimes were never found; this reality hung over black communities like the cloud of oppression whites meant it to be. This type of environment encompassed the world Medgar Evers lived in, it illuminated the social problems that he grew up around, and it proved to be the world that eventually molded him into the person he became.

During the 1950s and 1960s, civil rights activists in Mississippi understood that the possibility existed for an immediate and untimely death. Evers and countless other activists accepted this reality and knew that there were many whites willing to murder them and personally lay the death card upon their bodies as a warning to others. In spite of this fact, Medgar Evers, in 1958, warned an audience that neither he nor Negroes as a collective could afford to "cease to press forward, relentlessly, until every vestige of segregation and discrimination in America becomes annihilated."[9] Evers faced and accepted the dangers of fighting for civil and political rights in Mississippi and as a child had railed against the inequities that served as demarcation lines between blacks and whites. As children, Medgar and his older brother Charles often fought with white newspaper boys who sold white papers such as the *Jackson Daily News* in black neighborhoods, while the Evers brothers were not allowed to sell black papers such as the *Chicago Defender*.[10] The discussion of any historical figure ultimately leads to the question of memory and the person's overall position in the collective consciousness. Medgar Evers is no exception.

Historical memory remains a significant part of the civil rights movement and, as of late, has become an important focus of historians and scholars alike. Its relevance lay in explaining how people remember the movement, events, and individuals as both victim and villain. The historians Renee C. Romano and Leigh Raiford define memory as the "process by which people recall, lay claim to, understand, and represent the past." Memories can be personal, collective, or shared but whatever form they take, Romano and

Raiford emphasize, "memories of the past are not static."[11] The civil rights movement occupies a variety of places within the public memory. Civil rights memorials are constructed for a variety of reasons (e.g., financial, personal, as indicators of city/state progress) and contain within them a window into the thought processes of the city and state as a whole.[12]

There are, of course, physical reminders of Medgar Evers's importance to the city of Jackson and the state of Mississippi. Much like other cities across the country who memorialize their civil rights activists, Jackson has several commemorative sites emphasizing Evers's contributions: there is now a Medgar Evers Boulevard, a Medgar Evers Library, Community Center, Post Office, and Museum. The neighborhood Evers lived and was murdered in while in Jackson became the city's first historic district.[13] On a much broader scale, the Medgar Evers Primary Academic Center in Ford Heights, Illinois; the Medgar Evers Fine and Performing Arts School in Chicago, Illinois; and Medgar Evers College in New York all stand as towering symbols to a man whose dedication to the power of education and overall influence transcended both county and state boundaries. Even at the legislative level, his impact on the cause of social justice has received official notice.

On May 25, 1999, the Jackson City Council voted unanimously to designate July 4 as Medgar Wiley Evers Day.[14] In addition, Mississippi senators Thad Cochran and Trent Lott spearheaded a resolution, adopted by the U.S. Senate, declaring June 9–16 Medgar Evers National Week of Remembrance.[15] The House, with House Concurrent Resolution No. 94, demonstrated the importance they placed on Evers's activism. During the 2003 regular session of the Mississippi Legislature, Resolution No. 94 publicly conveyed thanks to and respect for the work that defined Evers's life. After outlining the work of Medgar and Myrlie Evers, the resolution contained the following statement: "Now Therefore, Be It Resolved By The House Of Representatives Of The State Of Mississippi, The Senate Concurring Therein, That we do hereby commend the life and accomplishments of Medgar Wiley Evers and his widow, Myrlie Evers-Williams, and express our greatest respect and gratitude."[16] The "Mississippi Man" had now been embraced by the very state that forty years earlier had struggled to silence his voice.[17]

Future scholars will undoubtedly discover that Medgar Evers was a compassionate, stern, stubborn, driven, and complex person of determination and high character. This is not to say that he lacked faults or never made mistakes. What is certain is that his work and life deserves deeper examination in order to fully understand his contributions to the struggle for social equality. Africans maintain that it is up to the living to remember the dead, for they only die when they fail to remain active particles of thought bouncing off and interacting with the memories of the living.[18] The historical particles embodying the memories of Medgar Evers, however, have surfaced fewer times and interacted even less within our collective memory over the years since his assassination.

In order to analyze and compare contemporary historical figures to their predecessors, historians tend to organize individuals into descriptive categories. As a consequence, civil rights activists are often defined by their relationship to selected groupings. Individuals, for example, who advocate legal or economic approaches to change are placed in one category, integrationists versus separatists in another, while persons bound by a creed of nonviolence, and those willing to use violence to obtain social and political parity, are placed in yet a different group. Of course, these are only a few examples.

Evers does not fit neatly into any one category. He worked to solve economic issues, voting issues, segregation issues, political issues, murders, rapes, lynchings, and a plethora of other social and political problems using a variety of strategies and tactics. Whereas noted historian John Dittmer and prominent sociologist Charles Payne present moving accounts of the efforts of grassroots organizers to initiate struggle and change at the local level, Evers does not fit neatly within that category either. He was neither of the elite nor of the grassroots, but an effective bridge between the two that helped to strengthen the civil rights movement in Mississippi. Evers proved to be just as comfortable with speaking and organizing individuals at the local level, as he was with strategizing with renowned persons such as Martin Luther King Jr., Attorney General Warren Olney III, David Dennis, Robert Moses, and other national and civil rights figures. What was important and unique about Medgar Evers was his sincerity and the social and political fluidity he exhibited.

In the past, civil rights scholars have approached the movement from the perspective of events, individuals, categories, and results. Evers provides us with an opportunity to study all four in the life of an individual who embodied civil rights struggle while defying attempts at historical categorization. Medgar Wiley Evers represented so many different approaches and addressed such a variety of social and political issues that he does not fit easily into the paradigmatic frameworks scholars often construct. Thus, he provides a real opportunity to reexamine the meaning of civil rights struggle in Mississippi and across the nation.

The issue of struggle remains an important thread within civil rights historiography. Previous scholars have provided a limited view of Evers's contributions to the civil rights movement for a variety of reasons. This, in part, might arguably be due to a previous lack of access to his personal and professional papers. This present work makes use of recently available archival materials and thus offers a deeper analysis of both the meaning of the civil rights struggle in Mississippi and the role that Evers played in the African American struggle for social, economic, and political equality.

The choice to use biography as a medium of analysis occurred after careful thought and the realization that biography allows the telling of a complete story that does not merely analyze the outcome. A biographical approach helps to identify the nexus of events that cause individuals to become who they become and thus the reasoning behind crucial decisions made or not made. Previous scholars such as Alex Haley, Taylor Branch, Chana Kai Lee, David Levering Lewis, and David Garrow have all successfully used biography as a means of dissecting historical periods and analyzing the impact of individuals associated with social and political change. Their success in examining their subjects of focus through biography lends credence to the approach taken here. Biography provides the best means of addressing the intricacies and nuances that defined Medgar Evers and thus provides a better understanding of his commitment to sustained social activism. A secondary, but no less important, component of this examination of Evers and the meaning of civil rights struggle rests within the ever-evolving relationship between him and the NAACP. The evolution of that relationship remains a central part of the discussion and persists throughout the work. Evers's attention to the freedom struggles against colonial rule in Africa during the 1950s and 1960s were important factors in his approach to civil rights struggle in the United States. In fact, some of his strongest personality traits like defiance, self-determination, and racial pride were also reflected in the lives of some of Africa's earliest leaders.

In *The Anthropology of Slavery*, Africanist historian Claude Meillassoux writes of the Sudanese hero Sunjata. Mande tradition maintained that Sunjata, Meillassoux noted, was "destined from birth to resolve a crisis, usually political in nature."[19] In many regards, the life of Medgar Wiley Evers resembles the legendary Sunjata. From his childhood until his murder, Evers's constant awareness of the oppressed social conditions of black Mississippians bolstered his commitment to the movement for civil equality. The harsh reality of African Americans' inferior social status in Mississippi solidified his commitment to stay in the state and to struggle to change its social and political constructs rather than leave as many had done before him. For Evers, it seemed treasonous to leave Mississippi rather than devote his life to the pursuit of African American social progress in the state. "I'll be damned . . . if I'm going to let the white man lick me," Evers remarked. "There's something out here that I've got to do for my kids, and I'm not going to stop until I've done it."[20] Though his passion was evident to those who knew him, Evers more often worked behind the scenes and thus many Americans remain unaware of his overall contributions to the civil rights movement.

More than anything else, it was the social realities of African Americans that emotionally, psychologically, and geographically bound Evers to Mississippi. His determination to expose the extreme depths of the inequality practiced in Mississippi to a national audience aided the work of civil rights leaders such as Martin Luther King Jr., David Dennis, John Salter Jr., and Robert Moses. His drive and determination also inspired entertainers such as Lena Horne and Dick Gregory. Gregory readily attributed his "being in the civil rights fight" to Medgar Evers inviting him to speak in Jackson.[21] In addition, civil rights organizations such as the Southern Christian Leadership Conference (SCLC), the Student Nonviolent Coordinating Committee (SNCC), and the Congress of Racial Equality (CORE) all depended upon Evers and his work in Mississippi to aide their organizational programs in the state.[22]

At first glance, one might not have identified Medgar Evers as a civil rights activist. His physical appearance resulted from a history of athleticism and physical training that produced a muscular frame reminiscent of an athlete rather than a civil rights organizer. Evers stood five feet eleven, with a magnetic smile and an empathic personality that people discerned the minute they spoke with him. He took great pride in meticulously dressing and keeping a short sporty haircut, and thus was, as his wife, Myrlie, noted, "strikingly handsome in a non-Hollywood way . . . [but] intelligent and serious-minded."[23] For Evers, however, nothing was more important than gaining citizenship rights for African Americans, and this reality consumed his life and eventually caused his death.

Since becoming NAACP field secretary in 1954, Evers's reach encompassed every facet of the civil rights struggle. His presence was felt in voter registration drives, economic boycotts, investigatory reporting, and other direct-action tactics. The Reverend Robert L. T. Smith, a civil rights activist and friend of Evers, acknowledged to police officers Fred Sanders and John Chamblee soon after Evers's murder that "Medgar Evers was the man in power in the State of Mississippi and he was over every body [*sic*]. . . . [N]o one did anything except when Medgar Evers gave his OK."[24] Evers enhanced the struggle for civil rights in Mississippi with his presence, selfless dedication, and activism. His position of leadership in the civil rights movement often made him the target of white violence and retaliation. Yet his ability to transform fear into courage and commitment to the civil rights struggle made him all the more effective as a leader and activist. The legacy of struggle and commitment he left influenced social struggle across America as people transformed his death into a call for continued activism. By the same token, his death cemented the urgency behind the need for social change.

Despite his many accomplishments and sacrifices, the name Medgar Evers still does not ignite the pot of public memory into a furious boil. Yet his deliberate choice to fight *for* Mississippi made him effective on both the local and national level. In order to understand the man Medgar Evers became, and why he worked with such diligence and relentlessness for social and political equality, one has to employ the method of extrapolation. For, as historian Ethel Murrain has written, to "understand Medgar Evers it is important to understand his background—the economic, social and political conditions that he was born into."[25]

To fully understand Medgar Evers the man and the activist, the personal, familial, and political lives of Mississippi's first full-time NAACP field secretary must be examined. Absent such an examination, his commitment to the struggle for civil rights in Mississippi can neither be easily understood nor explained. Evers's fight for civil rights, in what could be historically termed the most racially oppressive state in America, is a testament to his unyielding courage. It also speaks to his determination to destroy a sociopolitical system that constricted the political, social, and economic opportunities of fellow blacks.[26]

Scholars interested in the civil rights movement have tended to focus on the ways movement leaders were able to organize and mobilize large masses of what Charles Payne terms "dependent and, to all appearances, apolitical people" to struggle against oppression and tyranny. A crucial objective of the civil rights historian is to ascertain the degree to which the movement affected the behavior of the people involved and the ways in which individuals changed and shaped the direction of the movement.[27] Medgar Evers proved vital in successfully encouraging local people to resist all facets of white supremacy. His ability to effectively accomplish this task proved both a remarkable achievement and a necessary skill-set for an activist in Mississippi during the 1950s and 1960s. In addition, his aptitude for transforming fear in the common man and woman into concerted activism, combined with his personal connection with the youth, solidified Evers as an important leader in the overall movement for equality in Mississippi and the nation at large.

In many ways, this work adds to the overall discussion of the civil rights struggle by chronicling an individual who, some might argue for the most part, has been largely overlooked. The objective here is neither to deify Medgar Evers nor place him upon a pedestal. It is rather to analyze his contributions so one might understand his overall impact on the movement for social, political, economic, and racial equality. Without question, Evers helped to bring about crucial changes for black Mississippians in these four critical areas. Through voter registration drives, sit-ins, boycotts, and other nonviolent tactics for change, Evers challenged Mississippi's system of white supremacy and provided African Americans with a measure of hope. He managed to accomplish this feat while exhibiting a loyalty to the state that often bordered on fanaticism. The importance of this work rests in the opportunity, aided by new source materials on Evers, to lessen the gap in the historical scholarship on Medgar Evers, the civil rights struggle in Mississippi, and the fight for social and political equality on the national level.

Throughout the following pages, the struggles Evers waged and the social, political, and cultural problems the nation shouldered during the 1950s and 1960s define his life. In many ways, they also speak to the personal and familial sacrifices Evers made and the frustrations he and countless others endured in the fight for sociopolitical parity with whites and the ways that civil rights activism forced this nation to reexamine its commitment to the American ideal. It has been my goal here to allow Evers to speak directly to the problems of his day and the strategies employed to overcome them. By doing so, it is my hope that the reader grasps a deeper understanding of the complex nature of civil rights struggle from a grassroots, organizational, and generational perspective. While this remains the story of Medgar Wiley Evers, it is my hope that in the telling, it becomes our own.

1.

"Mama called him her special child"

A LINEAGE OF RESISTANCE

Mama called him her special child.
> *—Carrie Elizabeth Evers-Jordan*

The values of any new generation do not spring full blown from their head; they are already there, inherent if not clearly articulated in the older generation.
> *—Erik Erikson*

DECATUR, MISSISSIPPI, settled in 1836, serves as the seat of Newton County. The city chose its name in honor of naval commodore Stephen Decatur.[1] Incorporated in 1840, Decatur—like most cities in the Deep South —relied upon the work of African Americans to prosper.[2] Despite Decatur's reliance upon black labor, its white residents demanded that blacks adhere to codes, written or otherwise, maintaining racial segregation. As African Americans challenged white hegemony in America, particularly during the 1920s and 1930s, whites throughout the South resorted to more brutal means of domination and Decatur proved no different. After all, it was at the Decatur fairgrounds, Medgar Evers later recalled, where "a close friend of the family got lynched . . . because he sassed back a white woman."[3] Decatur, for African Americans, proved as dangerous as any other area where black people were willing to resist dehumanization. Here is where James and Jessie Evers moved to from Scott County, Mississippi. Decatur appealed to James Evers because of the opportunity to work in the sawmill industry and thus provide a better life for his growing family.[4]

Medgar Wiley Evers was born in Decatur, Mississippi, on July 2, 1925, to James and Jessie Evers. From birth, he assumed a family heritage of social resistance within the varied social and political systems of white control, white-generated violence, and black economic exploitation. Taking into account the oppressive state in which they lived, the refusal of the Evers family to cower in the presence of segregation and white supremacy is quite remarkable. When we place that refusal in the context of a violent Jim Crow South, their resistance becomes all the more phenomenal. Although the term Jim Crow may have had its beginnings in song and dance, it eventually symbolized racial division, oppression, violence, and inequality for African Americans at the county, state, and national level.[5] Decatur, like the rest of the South, was dedicated to racial separation and white dominance.

In 1925, Decatur was still a small town having fewer than 2,500 people. Its exclusion from both the 1920 and 1930 U.S. Census, which only included "places" with populations between 2,500 and 10,000 inhabitants, verifies this assumption. In fact, in 1920 the whole of Newton County had a population of only 20,727 of which 6,957 were identified as "Negro."[6] Whites in Decatur were determined to control the black population, and their resolve stiffened during the holiday season when whites and blacks congregated more often than any other time of the year. During the Christmas season, whites came to town to light fireworks and to enjoy the holiday festivities. African Americans, however, were denied the opportunity to be a part of the fireworks extravaganza. According to Charles Evers, the "Klan had a rule: 'No niggers allowed in Decatur around Christmas.'" In 1935, the Everses challenged this ban as James, armed with a broom handle fitted with a metal cap, led his boys into town and viewed the festivities without repercussions.[7] Medgar grew up within this small-town environment of racism and oppression, and it had a profound impact upon his ideas regarding the meaning of citizenship. The Everses' close-knit family structure added to Medgar's understanding of the importance of unity and group support.

In addition to Medgar, the Everses also had six other children: Eddie, Eva Lee, and Gene, from Jessie's previous marriage, and James Charles, Carrie Elizabeth, and Mary Ruth. The Evers family lived in a quiet area of Newton County and got along well with both blacks and whites in the community. Although they "were a poor family . . . , they were never destitute," Myrlie Evers recalled, "and they managed to take care of themselves without help from anyone. They took pride in that and in the respect in which they were held by the community generally, both white and Negro."[8] The respect his father commanded from whites, combined with his refusal to cower in their presence, and the inner strength and religious devotion of his mother inspired Medgar to challenge the legitimacy of Jim Crow.[9]

James Evers believed in hard work and led by example; he, at times, could be stern, abrasive, and "mean." Like most African American families (and families in general during the Depression years), the 1920s and 1930s forced family units to depend upon multiple sources of income to survive. James Evers, or Jim as most people called him, worked at a variety of jobs while Jessie took in washing, worked in white homes, and took in boarders to help meet the family's financial needs. No matter how desperate their economic situation, Elizabeth Evers-Jordan recalled in an interview that their father never allowed his girls to work for white folks.[10] This rule of law within the Evers home served as a means of avoiding the potential for rape that dogged black women who worked under the ever-watchful eye of white men. Historian Danielle L. McGuire provides an excellent analysis of the various ways white men used rape as a horrific display of power and punishment, as well as a vile form of individual or group entertainment.[11]

The Everses were self-sufficient, which is why the daughters never *had* to work for whites. Self-sufficiency, however, did not stop Elizabeth and her sisters from looking with envy at their female friends who did work for white families and had the money to show for it. Of the many business ventures the Everses claimed, they also owned a kind of store that sold hot food and other items to black and white patrons. Evers-Jordan explained that she and her sisters were allowed money at times, and this tended to placate their need for spending cash. In addition to the store, Evers-Jordan remembered that the Evers provided space for the only black barbershop in Decatur, operated by a Jim Thomas. The Evers family managed the store themselves, with the women conducting the day-to-day operations. The barbershop and beauty salon were business ventures the family rented out and collected monies on. Evers-Jordan remembered that her mother had beauticians as far away as Meridian, Mississippi, coming to Decatur to rent work space in the beauty salon. The beauty industry has historically occupied an important role in the black community. Barbershops, in particular, were vital to establishing and sustaining a group economy and provided black barbers with status in black and white communities alike.[12] In addition to the barbershop and store, James developed several other business operations.

James Evers operated a variety of business ventures of his own. Charles Evers acknowledged that their father proved to be quite a proficient businessman who owned his own property in Decatur, built and rented out two small homes on it, and kept a small farm. He raised cows, chickens, and pigs. Had a pair of mules. Grew vegetables for himself, and cotton to sell. He was a small lumber contractor, too. . . . Daddy had lumber contracts in Hazlehurst, Union, and Decatur, making sure lumber was dried right. He worked for our small family funeral home, too. We never had a whole lot of money, but Mama and Daddy made us appreciate what we had.[13]

Medgar grew up surrounded by examples of manhood and self-sufficiency, which molded his independent character and cultivated a devotion to the welfare of humankind.

Elizabeth Evers-Jordan and Charles Evers, the last remaining of the Evers siblings, spoke often of the positive influence their parents had upon them and their siblings. Charles recalled that when it came to analyzing the character of men, their father taught him and Medgar "that most men are timid, measly, and mediocre. Be tough, and they'll fall in line behind you."[14] This helps explain Medgar's often-domineering persona, which some interpreted as meanness. This characteristic often surfaced at the first hint of weakness on the part of African Americans in the face of white opposition. Medgar drew on many of his father's lessons, and the following words of advice best seem to have defined his attitude regarding the struggle for civil rights: if "you're scared, you can't do nothing. Show a coward some nerve, and you can back them down."[15]

In a social environment that demanded meekness on the part of black people, men in particular, it was significant that James Evers stood as a man and, with consistency, maintained his dignity. As a consequence, Medgar never accepted the validity of a Jim Crow system. When he reached adulthood, Evers put into practice the aforementioned ideals of manhood and womanhood drummed into him by his mother and father. These ideals were bolstered by a family heritage of resistance, a heritage fully visible and hanging like ready fruit from the ancestral branches of both family trees.

The willingness to stand on the side of righteousness and to be self-sufficient were family traits passed down to James Evers. He, in turn, passed them along to his children. James's father, Mike Evers, had also proven to be business minded. Charles noted that his grandfather owned and "farmed two hundred acres of corn, peanuts, and potatoes out in Scott County, [which whites later took 'illegally' from him regarding an issue of unpaid taxes] just west of Decatur." He also pointed out that "Mike Evers was rough, fought a lot, and taught Daddy to have no fear. Daddy's mother, Mary Evers, was part Creole Indian, with long, straight hair and high cheekbones."[16] Although Charles admitted that he could not remember a lot about his father's family, he knew that they were hard workers and fighters.[17] In order to understand Medgar, Myrlie Evers-Williams notes, you have to go back to his mother. Medgar may have inherited his fighting spirit from his father, but his overall goodness, caring attitude, and deep concern for the welfare of others can be attributed to the influence of his mother.[18]

Whereas the Evers patriarch could be rough, tough, and confrontational, its matriarch proved quite the opposite. Jessie Wright Evers was a communal-minded religious woman who had a reputation for feeding those in need and her house was always open to the less fortunate. Evers-Williams remembered an encounter that occurred at the Evers home very early one morning. When a stranger knocked on the door, "daddy Jim" answered it to find a man looking for Jessie because he was hungry and people had told him that she would provide him with food. Myrlie noted, with amazement, that Jessie got out of bed at 2:00 A.M. and cooked him something to eat.[19] This type of human expression made an indelible impression on Medgar as a child and helped shape the type of person he became.

One cannot over emphasize the positive impact that women have on the ideological development of the boys in their family. The influence is stronger whenever a humanitarian element or devotion to community service is touted as a part of one's religious or social responsibility. The maternal grandmother of civil rights activist Andrew Young, who later served as congressman and U.S. ambassador to the United Nations, also provided food to any person in need while Young's mother, Andrew J. DeRoche notes, continued "this tradition by taking casseroles to ailing or elderly members of the church."[20] In both the Evers and Young families, religion and human expression and compassion went hand in hand.

Practiced religion was an important component of Jessie Evers's character, and it helped define her as a mother, wife, and individual. Although James remained a Baptist and served as a deacon at his church, Jessie belonged to the Church of God in Christ (COGIC). She proved a devout member of COGIC and sold the church the land to build on, Evers-Jordan recalled. She was a true servant of God.[21] In addition to her religious strength and devotion, Jessie also claimed a family heritage endowed with a fighting spirit.

Much like James's mother, Mary, Jessie also claimed a Native American heritage. One of her grandmothers had been a "full-blood Indian" and her father a mulatto who, Charles recalled, had "once shot two white men and left town in the dead of night when someone called him 'a half-assed mulatto.'"[22] In addition, one of Jessie's great-grandfathers named Medgar Wright, for whom she named Medgar, was a half-Indian slave who took no abuse from anyone nor allowed any misdeed to go unchallenged.[23] The fighting spirit existed on both sides of the Evers family, and Jessie and James through their actions made sure their children were well aware of their family's heritage and its propensity for refusing to cower in the face of oppression.

Jessie never spoke much about her first marriage, but before marrying James she had been married to a man named "Nick" Grimm and they had three children together. After marrying James, Elizabeth noted that Jessie wanted to give her husband children of his own even though he claimed her three as his and had raised them as such. Her parents had been married almost eleven years, she recalled, before the birth of Charles. Elizabeth acknowledged that their parents had indeed been married a long

> time [and] mama didn't think she [could] have any more children, but she wanted some more children—she wanted some Evers as dad said "I got you three . . . those are mine too." She said, "well I want some Everses" because they was Grimms you know. And mom said she prayed and asked the Lord to bless her to have some more children. And so here come Charles—after eleven years—then Medgar, then Elizabeth (that's me), and then Ruth. But mama said "now Lord you can stop me now." [But it seemed as if once] she started having them Everses . . . she couldn't stop.[24]

With each successive child, the Evers developed a stronger sense of unity and interfamily dependency.

James Evers served as the center of a concentric circle of family independence. While discussing the soup lines that were provided in downtown Decatur, Charles remembered his father warning the family that if "the Evers family got in that soup line, I'd kill every one of you, and then kill myself."[25] Elizabeth attributes their strong sense of self to the fact that they always had their own and never had to depend upon whites for anything. She took pride in the fact that during that time they owned about twelve acres and had "never lived on nobody's plantation."[26] As a consequence of his independence, James Evers proved very influential in shaping Medgar's views on the system of segregation and the illegitimacy of ideals touting white superiority and black inferiority. In fact, Myrlie Evers remarked that the examples of manhood provided by James Evers influenced "Medgar and his brother, Charles, . . . to test these [segregated] boundaries, to push against them, to attempt to widen them."[27] Both parents instilled in their children the importance of working for what they needed and to depend upon themselves rather than white society to supply those needs.

While growing up the Evers children were taught to always work hard. We "had to work all our lives; we weren't allowed to have anything easy," Charles remembered. "And we were taught to give respect first and then we could demand respect. . . . So that's how we came up."[28] As a means of maintaining family unity, James and Jessie demanded strict codes of personal and familial behavior from their children. Both were "very strict . . . ," Charles remarked. "They brought [us] up in, what people call now, the old ways and that was yes ma'am, no ma'am. [For instance,] you [could not] eat until the table [was] blessed." Education remained another important component of the Evers family structure. Both parents insisted that their children attend school and Charles recalled that playing "hooky out of school" meant that you would be punished when discovered.[29] He admitted, however, that Medgar proved less confrontational and more committed to educational success.

When it came to academics, Medgar Evers exemplified excellence. Medgar "was the star [of the family], he always studied hard and he knew what he was doing; he wanted to be a lawyer," Charles recalled.[30] Decatur, like the rest of the South during the 1940s and 1950s, did not provide equal educational facilities for African Americans. Decatur maintained a high school for whites but none for African Americans. White students traveled to school aboard well-equipped school buses while African American students walked to schools that were often ill equipped and in disrepair. Charles, Elizabeth, and Medgar remembered the many instances of racism they experienced while walking to school as white students threw objects from bus windows when they passed by. In addition to these assaults, Medgar noted that they would also "yell filthy things." As an added affront, bus drivers often used the bus either to dust the walking students or to splash them with muddy water.[31] Medgar later acknowledged that these abuses perpetrated against children in grades as early as first were a mild start in the dehumanizing process for African Americans. "If you're a kid in Mississippi this is the elementary course," Medgar explained.[32] Newton Vocational School (NVS), located in Newton, Mississippi, served as a high school for African Americans in Decatur. NVS boasted a capable administrator in the person of Noah Hannibal Pilate, who demanded competence in his faculty and excellence from his student body.

Noah Hannibal Pilate was a native of Warren County, Mississippi. His parents were farmers and he attended public school in Vicksburg, later earning a BS from Alcorn Agricultural & Mechanical College and a master's degree in school administration and school supervision from Tennessee A&I State University in Nashville. His wife, Dessie, received her BS and master's degree in home economics from Tuskegee Institute in Tuskegee, Alabama. They both taught at NVS and Noah also served as its principal until he retired in 1966.[33] The Pilates moved to Newton in 1928 and Newton Vocational School served the black community of Newton and surrounding areas well.

After Noah arrived in Newton, Dessie noted that "college degrees and certification were stressed for teachers in the local Negro school." By 1938, a majority of the teachers were certified and either had or were working on advanced degrees.[34] Noah required the very best from his students and stood as a symbol of strength that Medgar would have appreciated. Ponjola Andrews, a schoolmate of Medgar Evers at NVS and later Alcorn College, maintained that N. H. Pilate "was well loved, well thought of, and . . . [was one who] did an excellent job with what he had."[35] Over time, Andrews noted, school officials changed the name to Pilate High School in honor of the hard work and dedication Noah Pilate displayed throughout the years. N. H. Pilate provided that familiar strong male persona that Medgar had looked to his whole life. He would later demand that same type of strength and fortitude from the men who occupied positions within his inner circle. In order to attend high school in Decatur, Mississippi, during the 1930s and 1940s, however, African Americans had to pass an eighth-grade exit exam to determine their ability to continue the education process at the advanced level.

Elizabeth remembered that "to go into high school . . . you had to do the Constitution; you had to pass all that and everything." African American eighth-grade students, Elizabeth remembered, were required to go to the courthouse to take their final exams to determine their ability to attend high school and do the required work. If they passed the exam, their parents then had to figure out a way to get them down to Newton and to provide means of accommodation. Jessie allowed Elizabeth, Medgar, and Charles to "board with some of her friends that lived down there [in Newton] to go to high school and [the] only reason because it was segregated. We had a high school right there in Decatur, but because we was black we wasn't allowed," Elizabeth explained.[36] Other families, who also wanted their children to have the opportunity to complete a public education, were faced with the economic and physical hardships associated with boarding accommodations and many children suffered as a result. The social discrepancies resulting from this type of social system were not lost on Medgar, and the residual effects stayed with him throughout his life.

While in high school Medgar intensified his study habits and concentrated harder on academics as a whole. He would always be somewhere reading, Elizabeth recalled, or using the family dictionary to find the meaning of big words he had come across. The practice of bolstering reading comprehension by defining unknown words laid the groundwork for his extensive vocabulary. Myrlie Evers-Williams admitted that she sometimes manufactured excuses, particularly during their courtship at Alcorn, to leave the room where she would then consult a dictionary to look up a word he had used. She carefully explained, however, that Medgar "did not use the many unused words in a way that would make you feel dumb or ignorant; he didn't try to showcase his knowledge of an expanded vocabulary, it was just a normal thing that he did."[37] Evers always wanted to know the meaning of anything that he did not understand, and he never accepted things at face value. As children, Elizabeth remembered his sitting in the living room looking up words and his rebuke, when they bothered him, of "'now ya'll gon leave me alone now, I'm trying to find this'" . . . and [Elizabeth would accuse him of being] nothing but a bookworm . . . and he'd say 'gon and leave me alone—gon girl—I'm trying to pick this up.'" She added that Medgar spent a lot of time by himself thinking about things and how to change the wrongs of the world.[38]

When considering Medgar Evers's background it is not surprising that he dedicated his life to ending segregation; in many ways his entire existence had been constrained by it. Furthermore, his parents' examples of manhood and womanhood, combined with a family heritage of resistance, demanded that he challenge the very nature of a segregated system. Yet the question always remained, how far could you push before whites killed you? How best to negotiate daily encounters with whites and still maintain your self-respect? Thus Medgar, like many African Americans in the South, remained locked in a constant battle to overcome the very "two-ness" of being an American and a Negro, which W. E. B. Du Bois argued plagued blacks living within an unjust and abusive society. The potential for social and protracted violence demanded that African Americans develop a "double-consciousness": one to display in the presence of whites and the other reserved for the African American community. This type of constructed dual persona forced many African Americans into a state of functional social schizophrenia in order to cope and interact within a violent society.[39]

Medgar could be both sensitive and at the same time fiery when he believed that he, or someone he cared for, had been wronged. Elizabeth admitted that Medgar "was always a special child and mama called him her special child because . . . [it looked as if there] was always something on his mind." She also remembered that Medgar used to carve his name "Medgar W. Evers" on the trees, the wash house, the back of the house, and any other space that he could claim. She associated that practice with the belief that he always knew that something was wrong with the way that society operated and that wrong had to be challenged.[40] By writing his name upon items he encountered daily, Evers may have also been reminding himself of his value as a human being and thus the need to resist attempts to devalue that existence.

Evers's belief that things had to change affected how he behaved as a child, and specific childhood quirks lend a particular understanding to his later behavior as an adult. As a child, Evers required personal time to think, and he often physically removed himself from those around him. This behavior proved so compelling that Jessie Evers felt the need to offer her daughter-in-law an explanation for what she could expect as his wife. At that moment, she spoke to Myrlie in a voice that denoted honesty and sincerity; Myrlie understood that her tone signaled that something important would follow:

> Daughter, now my son's a little strange, I don't want you to get upset with him if he pulls away from you because it won't be because he doesn't love you, but that's just the way he is. . . . He's my strange child . . . , he needs to be by himself at times. . . . Sometimes I [would] look out the window and I see them all out there playing and I look again a few minutes later and he's nowhere to be found and I'd go out and I'd look for him and I'd find him in his favorite spot under the house. And I asked him Lope . . . what's wrong? [And] he'd say "nothing mama, I'm just thinking."[41]

Myrlie Evers took this as a warning not to take offense if and when her husband physically or mentally removed himself from her because he had practiced this behavior as a child; he was always thinking and contemplating ideas and the right and wrongs of the world. This may have proven an unusually mature approach for a young boy to have toward life, but it served as a phenomenal asset to anyone laboring to exact social change in segregated Mississippi.

As a boy growing up in Decatur, Medgar likely did not realize the important role he would play in the movement for civil equality. Childhood proved far less stressful, despite segregation, and the Evers brothers participated in the same types of games and roughhousing as did other boys in the community. Medgar loved to hunt and fish, hobbies that he continued to pursue as an adult. Charles remembered their childhood as "ordinary." He also admitted that he and Medgar "kept up something in the community, I mean like mischief; I don't mean like stealing, nothing like that. We just always doing little things—particularly bout white folks."[42] Although Medgar and Charles went after "white folks" every chance they got, Medgar also loved playing and spending time with his sisters.

Evers loved to play around, and aggravating his sisters proved a favorite pastime. He loved to box and annoyed his sisters to no end by either hitting them or trying to trip them up whenever they walked by before receiving a whipping from their mother for his continuous meddling. Elizabeth also noted the tender side he showed by playing with them constantly and helping around the house. She has never forgotten the love that her brother showed them and how generous he gave of his time. Not long after the family received electricity, Medgar built his sisters a playhouse behind their parents' home and ran an extension cord from the house that provided lights that allowed them to cook in it.[43] Despite his robust behavior, Elizabeth maintained that Medgar was "kind of a quiet person; he wasn't afraid like, but he didn't bother nobody, but didn't nobody bother him either." He was also sensitive to any injustice, according to Charles, no matter how slight, and he resented unfair treatment under any circumstance.[44]

During their childhood Medgar and Charles enjoyed the family's subscription to the *Chicago Defender,* a black newspaper, and read it every chance they got. They also decided to sell the paper in Decatur and sent off for a number of copies. Both knew that the white-owned Jackson *Clarion-Ledger* was sold in Decatur without incident. They sold the *Chicago Defender,* successfully, for a few months before those in power learned of their enterprise. Eventually they stopped selling the paper due in part to pressure from local whites and fear on the part of some blacks who believed the boys, and their paper, were lightning rods for trouble. Both brothers were angered by the situation and sought to level the playing field the best way they could. Once their minds had processed the intensity of the economic discrimination they had experienced, disappointment transformed into anger, which then led to direct action. Charles recalled that their

> attitude was if we can't sell our papers, ya'll [meaning whites] can't sell in our neighborhood, can't sell in our community. So when the white boys came down . . . one time, . . . we took the papers and . . . just tore 'em up and ran them out of our community and that was way back then [when white retribution could be deadly]. Those kind of things we'd do and we just didn't allow them to do it; didn't allow them to sell no papers round our neighborhood because we couldn't sell in our neighborhood.[45]

It is apparent here that even as a child Medgar understood the importance of protecting one's community so as to ensure that its residents were not subjected to discrimination and racism without some form of organized response.

Medgar displayed resilience and diplomacy whenever faced with issues concerning fair play and equal opportunity. In contrast to Charles's "rough, tough, don't give a damn attitude," Medgar, Charles submitted, "was the guy who would go at . . . [problems] more diplomatically." In the face of heated interactions, Medgar often tried to diffuse the situation. He would always be the one saying, "Don't do that, do it this way, [that is] not the way to do it," Charles explained.[46] Growing up in Decatur allowed Medgar to develop social and political skills that later proved beneficial in his NAACP work.

Medgar's gift for diplomacy never wavered throughout his childhood; in fact, his command of the art of diplomacy intensified with age. He later honed his diplomatic skills while working with sharecroppers in the Mississippi Delta during the 1950s. As NAACP field secretary, his skills of diplomacy proved invaluable. Although Charles labeled their childhood "ordinary," life in Decatur trained Medgar for the leadership role he commanded from 1954 until his assassination. Regardless of Medgar's tough exterior, Charles remained protective of his younger brother. Medgar did not like cold weather, and so on cold nights Charles would stand close to the heater, warming his own clothes, and then run and jump in the bed to warm it up for Medgar. When he had warmed it to his liking, Charles would call out "Lope . . . , come here and get in the bed and [he would] slide over and get in."[47] His concern for his younger brother never ceased. In fact, it deepened as Medgar's involvement in the civil rights movement intensified.

The Evers children grew up during the segregated 1920s, 1930s, and 1940s when white-generated violence happened throughout the South with mind-numbing frequency. During this period, established codes of social behavior between blacks and whites were clearly understood, and overstepping established boundaries, real or imagined, often yielded severe consequences. Without question, whites expected Negroes to show deference to any white person they encountered regardless of their age and blacks were never to suggest equality of any sort. African American children learned their racial place in society at an early age. They also learned the consequences for stepping outside of established social and political boundaries. Whites expected blacks to both know their proverbial *place* at all times and to remain within it.

When African Americans refused to adhere to their prescribed social position, violence resulted. Black Mississippians knew more than any other racial group in the South that rape and murder were more than enough reasons for whites to lynch a black person during the Jim Crow era. The propensity for whites to react violently, however, was not limited to charges of rape, murder, or kidnapping. Historian Neil McMillen shows that, in addition to accusations of rape and murder, the Mississippi

> record abounds in lynchings for lesser affronts [such as]: "insubordination," "talking disrespectfully," striking a white man, slapping a white boy, writing an "insulting letter," a personal debt of fifty cents, an unpaid funeral bill of ten dollars, a $5.50 payroll dispute, organizing sharecroppers, being "too prosperous," "suspected lawlessness," horse killing, conjuring, and, of course, mistaken identity.[48]

Lynch law reigned in Mississippi, and it made those who stood against the violence and intimidation all the more crucial to the development of an organized resistance movement.

Above all other types of punishment, lynching represented one of the most vile displays of abject control, and thus its wide and unpredictable use proved one of the many methods whites used to exercise power. African Americans in the South knew full well that their white counterparts used the rope and faggot as a means of control. They also knew, as John Dittmer points out, that "neither youth, old age, nor social class offered protection to Negroes who did not stay in their place."[49] This represented the black/white social dichotomy of the South that the Evers family confronted daily and one in which Evers learned to negotiate and, more important, to defy.

Medgar Evers grew up with a clear understanding of the social differences between blacks and whites in the South. He also knew firsthand of the ultimate punishment for those accused of crossing customary behavior guidelines. His brother Charles recalled an incident that profoundly affected the way he and Medgar viewed their place in Mississippi and the necessity for change:

> I think the thing that really hurt us, that really, really got to us, my dad had a very good friend Mr. . . . [Willie] Tingle. Mr. Tingle was very close to my dad and to the family and the white people killed him. [They] lynched him and dragged him down through the streets, through the black community and carried him down to the fairgrounds (in Decatur, Mississippi) and hanged him up to a tree and shot him and just shot him all to he fell down off the tree. Medgar and I, we just didn't understand. I and him was about eight or nine or ten maybe. I said daddy, why did they kill Mr. Tingle? Daddy's answer was "just cause he colored son" and he never give us any other reason. But the reason . . . they claimed Mr. Tingle had winked at a white woman or did something silly—stuff like that, but we knew early on that [things] just were not equal—were not treated fairly—and we always did resent it.[50]

For months Medgar passed by the remains of "Mr." Tingle's clothing while running "rabbits down near the fairgrounds" and the brutality of the incident remained fresh in his mind. After the murder "nothing was said in public," Medgar recalled. "No sermons in church. No news. No protest. It was as though this man just dissolved except for the bloody clothes."[51]

The Tingle lynching remained with Evers his entire life. This senseless murder of a family friend whose children Medgar often played with served as a catalyst strengthening his commitment as an adult to positive change and social equality. For Evers, the lynching of Willie Tingle brought to bear the absolute helplessness of the African American community when people

chose not to resist barbarism and inequality. He acknowledged that everyone "in town knew it but never a word in public. . . . They left those clothes
on a fence for about a year. Every Negro in town was supposed to get the
message from those clothes and I can see those clothes now in my mind's
eye."[52] He placed this childhood incident of brutality into a mental file—one
that grew over the course of his life.

Charles attributed Medgar's inner strength to the respect their father
commanded from blacks and whites. James Evers never feared whites, and
he made sure they knew it. On one occasion, Medgar and Charles accompanied their father to Charlie Jordan's store. While he and Medgar stood
outside, they were accosted by a group of white boys Charles remembered
to be about eighteen or nineteen years old. James approached the boys and
said, "Let me tell you crackers something, you better leave my boys alone,
you hear me . . . leave 'em alone and I mean that. Mr. Charlie, you better
come and tell these crackers something."[53] Both Medgar and Charles
watched as the storeowner ordered the boys to leave and they did. Their
father's confidence around whites had a lot to do with the confidence
Medgar developed and the bravado, in defense of justice, he displayed as an
adult.

Charles also spoke of another incident that showcased their father's
refusal to be bullied by whites. When James went to the commissary to pay
his bill, Jimmy Boware, who managed the store, attempted to charge him
more than James knew he owed. Both Charles and Medgar witnessed the
following incident. Despite Boware's insistence, James Evers reminded him
again of what he owed. Boware disputed the amount, maintaining that
Evers owed more than he admitted and that he had better pay it. James,
however, politely but sternly refuted the proposed amount and stood his
ground. He answered Boware's accusations, Charles recalled, with

> "naw sir, naw sir, naw sir, . . . this is what I owe you." And he
> [Boware] said "are you calling me a liar nigger"? And dad, I could tell
> dad was getting angry, and dad looked at him and said, "I'm not call-
> ing you a lie . . . , I'm telling you this is what I owe you cause this what
> Jessie say I owe you" . . . and see dad lived by mama and he said
> "that's what I'm gon pay you."[54]

Things escalated to the point that James broke a Coca-Cola bottle and
threatened to kill Boware if he made a move toward the area where everybody knew he kept a gun. James then backed out of the store to what must
have been a shocked and somewhat befuddled white audience.

After the confrontation, he and his sons "walked home down along the
railroad tracks," Charles recalled, "Medgar on one side of Daddy, me on

the other. We put our arms around Daddy's waist, he put his hands on our heads. We were so happy." Both Medgar and Charles would remember their father's counsel: "Don't ever let *anybody* beat you," James advised. "Anyone ever kicks you, you kick the hell out of him."[55] He also advised his boys to "never run from white folks, never turn your back on 'em or they'll kill you," Charles noted.[56] Although both Charles and Medgar believed that whites would come to the house as nightriders to harm or murder their father as a result of the incident, no whites ever came and Charles admits that to this day he has never understood why "they never came to kill my daddy."[57]

The incident at the commissary reminded Charles how much he appreciated his father. In particular, his "not running, not tucking, not paying that rascal [Boware] what he said he owed him." Instead, James paid the amount he and Jessie knew he owed, throwing the money on the counter on his way out. The event provided another crucial lesson for Medgar: stand your ground when you know you are right and be prepared to defend your position regardless of the consequences. The confrontation with Boware, Charles remarked, has "been with me my whole life . . . and I never forgot it. And I guess that's what really . . . made me and Medgar as tough as we are about fear. Have no fear, why be afraid."[58]

The confrontation at the store had a profound effect upon Medgar, and it changed how he approached activism, how he saw himself as a black man in the South, and how he dealt with white people who opposed African American progress. The entire incident, his sister Elizabeth explained, did Medgar and Charles "so much good [because] that [event] give them guts because their daddy, back in that time, dad stuck up. . . . So we was raised not to be afraid of white people."[59] The confrontation, however, had wider social and cultural implications for the Evers boys than merely their father refusing to bow to racist behavior. By facing down Boware, James also openly defended the word, integrity, and math skills of his wife against the word of a white man, and this would not have gone unnoticed by Medgar. James had also challenged the age-old practice of white economic manipulation that proved the foundation of the sharecropping system and had led to the perpetual indebtedness of thousands of African Americans.

The constant display of manhood their father exhibited helped cultivate a spirit of rebelliousness in Medgar Evers as well as a love and pride in himself. Love of the individual self, combined with personal confidence and community devotion, were and remain powerful tools of racial uplift. These were lessons that Evers received in abundance, and it shaped his belief that equality belonged to all groups. The physical model that James provided the Evers children was bolstered by Jessie's insistence that they were "just as good as anybody—it doesn't matter because you're black, it doesn't because there white—they are no better than you are and she taught us that," Elizabeth proclaimed.[60] These were ideals that Medgar took with him overseas during World War II, ideals that were enhanced by social structures often devoid of the racist practices of the South.

For Medgar, the military provided respite from the dehumanizing actions of whites against blacks in Decatur. Prior to enlistment, he had wondered just how long he could take living in Mississippi under a system of segregation and degradation. As a black male, he admitted that it pained him to have "to watch the Saturday night sport of white men trying to run down a Negro with their car, or white gangs coming through town to beat up a Negro."[61] Whites degraded African American men for sport in a variety of ways, but it seemed that after dark kicking "niggers" proved a popular form of vile entertainment. It did not matter how old or how young a black person was, Elizabeth recalled, whites would just walk up and kick them in the buttocks as hard as they could. African American men had to endure this particularly degrading form of harassment in silence and often in the presence of family members.[62] With the oppressed reality of life in Mississippi fresh in his nostrils and a desire to experience a different reality, Medgar left high school and enlisted in the U.S. Army on October 7, 1943.[63]

As a soldier Medgar Evers served in the European Theatre and his brother Charles in the Pacific. Medgar saw action in Liège, Antwerp, Belgium, Normandy, Le Havre, and Cherbourg. He served in the 325th Port Company, a segregated unit commanded by white officers, which followed the Normandy invasion into France.[64] Port battalions entered an area shortly after an assault began and delivered needed supplies to assault troops engaged in battle.[65] Medgar acknowledged that he also served on the famed "Red Ball Express [while] in France and Germany."[66]

The Red Ball Express represented a system of supply trucks that developed out of the necessity of transporting provisions to American soldiers often in the heat of battle.[67] Men such as Medgar were instrumental in making sure that supplies reached critical areas. In an interview with military specialist David Colley, John Shevlin, assistant tank driver, maintained that had it not been "for the Red Ball we couldn't have moved. They all were black drivers and they delivered in the heat of combat. We'd be in our tanks praying for them to come up."[68] Sentiments such as these attesting to the effectiveness of black soldiers underscored their intolerance for any system of inequality upon returning stateside.

Although often relegated to service details, African Americans also fought in pitched battles and many served in the Normandy campaign of 1944. In particular, the 761st Tank Battalion, the first African American armored unit to see action, landed on Omaha Beach, Normandy, on October 10, 1944, and by the end of the first week of November were committed to battle.[69] African American soldiers received a number of individual and company commendations for their service during the war, and Medgar proved no exception. He received two combat stars for service and the Good Conduct medal.[70] Military service abroad also helped broaden his views and introduced Medgar to social situations devoid of racism. While overseas, Charles remembered that

> Medgar found [that] white women liked . . . Negro soldier[s]. In France . . . Medgar met a local French family and fell for their daughter. In Mississippi, Medgar could never have touched her. In France, he walked with her, kissed her in public. . . . To a Mississippi Negro, this was amazing. To the French, Medgar was a soldier first, an American second, and a Negro third. Going with this French girl made Medgar even more sure the racism we'd grown up with in Mississippi was unnatural and could be changed. It convinced him black and white could live in peace.[71]

Myrlie acknowledged that Medgar did indeed have strong feelings for this French woman and that there were no social problems or stigmas associated with their relationship. Upon returning to the states, Medgar kept the letters and pictures of his French love in a shoebox at his mother's home until he married Myrlie. Upon a later visit to see his parents, Myrlie noted that Mama Jessie produced the shoebox and told him that it was time to destroy its contents. He asked her to do so.[72]

Despite the fact that the French often treated African American soldiers with decency, racism still existed for blacks serving overseas. There were many skirmishes between black and white soldiers, and the derogatory term "nigger" proved often to be the motivating factor behind these clashes. Although African American soldiers knew they could not strike back against white officers, they resisted in a variety of ways including arguing, talking back, fighting other enlisted men, and informing the "Negro press" of their problems. Soldiers employed the latter tactic as a means of applying pressure on military officials to address the concerns of their Negro enlisted men.[73] Black soldiers also endured racist remarks from Europeans and others while on duty and when injured sometimes did not receive the same treatment from doctors as did white soldiers.

Private Marion Alexander, stationed in Marseille, France, in June 1945, is a case in point. Alexander often expressed his anger regarding the treatment he received and, in this instance, wrote a letter providing his wife with "some more of the details of this god-damn Hospital." Since his hospitalization, Alexander maintained that not once had the ward surgeon asked him how he felt. "He come in and pass my bed, go to the white patients bed and ask them how you feel son. And when he get to me he just look at me and walk out. Is that the way to treat a patient. [*sic*] Of course I don't give a damn it is just the principle of the situation." He advised his wife to "write to every large Colored Newspaper or send a cablegram any way to let them know how the Colored men are being treated over here. I am not the only one it is thousands of us is [*sic*] catching hell, and I mean hell." His letter, as would be the case for many others, was passed on to the NAACP.[74] The discrimination black men endured were not relegated to their treatment in area hospitals; African American soldiers also faced discrimination in officer training opportunities.

Despite exemplary service, African American soldiers were denied opportunities to receive officer training. Sometimes officials glossed over the discrimination and at other times it proved quite blatant. PFC William L. Reese Jr., of Battery A, 999 Field Artillery Battalion, had been in the service since May 5, 1943, NAACP special counsel Thurgood Marshall noted. Like Evers, PFC Reese had seen action in the European Theater "on several occasions" and was currently stationed in Germany. Reese reported to Officer Candidate School, and they refused to admit him based upon his race. The letter received from Tom G. Coleman, 1st Lt. A.G.D. Asst. Class Officer, stated that the "present policies of this Training Center, with regard to Colored troops disqualify him from assignment to an Officer Candidate Class." Thurgood Marshall thought the discrimination so bold "with the signed statement by Lieutenant Coleman [,] that it would demand an investigation by the War Department."[75] For African Americans, the battle against racism and Fascism proved one and the same. It also proved to be one that Africans waged with gritty determination against European colonialism.

For Evers, his growing awareness of the ways in which Africans were challenging oppression abroad with positive results bolstered the connection blacks made between "male identity and political rights." This "historic connection," historian Jennifer Brooks has written, resulted from African Americans' military service during World War II.[76] As with other African American veterans, Medgar's participation in World War II stiffened his resolve to bring the democratic ideal into fruition at home. Evers was not alone, however, in his understanding of African Americans' connection with the independence struggles in Africa.

Historian Hollis R. Lynch argued that since "the end of the eighteenth century, at least a minority of Afro-Americans has tended to see the fate of their group as inextricably linked with that of Africa." Group organization and individual work by stalwart persons such as Martin Delaney, Paul

Cuffee, Henry McNeal Turner, and W. E. B. Du Bois, to mention a few, strengthened the link between African Americans' struggles for equality and that waged by their African brothers and sisters. African Americans' concerns for the oppression Africans faced intensified with the Italian invasion of Ethiopia in 1935. African Americans considered Ethiopia a shining example of black progress, achievement, and sovereignty. Responding to the fall of Ethiopia in 1936, Max Yergan, an African American graduate of Shaw University, spearheaded the development of the International Committee on African Affairs, later known as the Council on African Affairs (CAA). "Radical, black-led and interracial," remarked Lynch, "its goal was to enlighten the public about Africa and to promote the liberation of that continent." The council consisted of prominent African Americans such as Ralph Bunche, at the time a political science professor at Howard University; Mordecai W. Johnson, president of Howard University; and the famed singer and orator Paul Robeson. The council worked to influence U.S. policies and to draw political support away from more conservative political leaders. By the mid-1940s, conservative politicos intensified their offensive strategy against the council as evident by Mississippi senator James Eastland's verbal assault of Paul Robeson during a congressional address.[77] Although the council collapsed in 1955 due to internal schisms, investigations by the Federal Bureau of Investigation (FBI) and the Internal Revenue Service (IRS), accusations of communism, and other structural problems, the organization demonstrated the intensity with which African Americans looked toward Africa and its liberation struggles.[78]

Medgar Evers both read and heard news accounts of African nations fighting for their freedom from colonial rule. He later developed an interest in Jomo Kenyatta and the Mau Mau movement (1952–1956) for independence in Kenya. Jomo Kenyatta, a member of the Kikuyu people of Kenya, served as the leader of independent Kenya and was a reported member of the Mau Mau. In 1962, he successfully negotiated the terms that would lead to Kenya's independence from British colonial rule. The following year, he became the prime minister of an independent nation. Although Kenyatta negotiated the terms leading to Kenyan independence, his success depended on the work of the Mau Mau. As a revolutionary group, the Mau Mau advocated violent resistance to British colonialism and fought against their colonizers using guerrilla warfare and gained the support of the people in the process.[79]

Evers had great respect for Kenyatta and flirted with the notion that a Mau Mau type movement could work for African Americans in Mississippi. For a brief moment Medgar and Charles took this notion of violent resistance seriously and, according to Charles, asked themselves key questions:

Why not really cross the line? . . . Why not create a Mau Mau in Mississippi? Each time whites killed a Negro, why not drive to another town, find a bad sheriff or cop, and kill him in a secret hit-and-run raid? To avoid suspicion, one of us could drive home, the other take a bus. We thought this was how to teach righteousness to whites. We bought bullets, made some idle Mau Mau plans, but Medgar never had his heart in it, and over time we dropped it.[80]

These types of ideals were not unique to the Everses as returning soldiers and activists across the country were fed up with the way blacks were treated and looked to the Mau Mau as a group ripe for emulation.

On December 20, 1964, Mississippi activist Fannie Lou Hamer served as the primary speaker at the Williams Institutional Christian Methodist Episcopal Church in Harlem, New York. In addition to Hamer, Malcolm X also attended the program and spoke as well. While attending the National Democratic Convention in Atlantic City, New Jersey, in August, Hamer's moving testimony concerning the conditions African Americans faced in Mississippi had touched the nation. After Hamer concluded her Harlem speech, Malcolm took the podium. He argued that the Mau Mau strategy should be applied in America to bring about change and when analyzed carefully, he explained, people would "have the key to how to straighten the situation out in Mississippi." Malcolm maintained, "with no anger," that when one recognizes the successes the Mau Mau achieved toward Kenya's independence, it becomes clear that "In Mississippi we need a Mau Mau. In Alabama we need a Mau Mau. In Georgia we need a Mau Mau. Right here in Harlem, in New York City, we need a Mau Mau."[81] The discussions above demonstrate how the battle tactics for civil equality in Kenya could have turned into an all-out war for the same in America.

Although willing to consider a violent plan of resistance, Medgar did not believe in its overall practicality or effectiveness in bringing about real change. In an interview with Francis Mitchell for *Ebony* magazine, Evers acknowledged that it "didn't take much reading of the Bible, though, to convince me that two wrongs would not make the situation any different, and that I couldn't hate the white man and at the same time hope to convert him."[82] His resolve to convert whites in Mississippi, while at the same time inspiring African Americans to stand against oppression, strengthened his desire to achieve civil equality in a peaceful manner. Evers did not intend to provide any person or group with legitimate cause to attack African Americans' struggles for equality on the grounds that it advocated violence. Returning to Mississippi as a World War II veteran increased his desire for equality as well as his determination to attack the problem of sociopolitical oppression head-on. During World War II, Evers had witnessed what racism and hatred could do on a global scale, and it drove him to resist inequality in every way possible.

While military service provided Medgar with positive experiences, it also produced disturbing images he would never forget. Charles remembered that his brother "had some bitter experiences in the war." On Omaha Beach, Medgar "saw lots of dead soldiers, saw how horrible it is to kill a man. Medgar was young, and he fell in with the men around him," Charles explained. "He began swearing, took on some rougher attitudes." One white officer took an interest in him and encouraged Medgar to go to college and develop his intellect, but most were mean to him. According to Charles, "Medgar was always very proud of being a veteran, . . . but he never got over some of the racial prejudice he'd suffered in the service."[83]

Discrimination and racism were ever-present realities for black soldiers regardless of which state they hailed from. Along with Medgar, more than 85,000 black Mississippians served in the military during World War II and, as Dittmer points out, "each felt the sting of racial discrimination."[84] Also, the effects of seeing so many dead bodies strewn around the beach had to have impacted Medgar in ways that challenged any previous conception of how cruel men could be to one another. Other soldiers described the scene that often awaited their counterparts arriving in France and the impact that the sight of death could have on a person. Staff Sergeant Chester Jones recalled that when he and his group arrived, evidence of the Allied Force's June 6 landing was unmistakable. He saw "dead bodies floating on the water, laying along the shoreline, on the beach, dead soldiers strewn everywhere." Furthermore, if "you were not conditioned to seeing the dead you received an unforgettable initiation on the beach."[85]

As a consequence of his time in the armed forces, Medgar Evers underwent some substantial ideological changes. He had known the injustice that segregation represented, but his travels overseas reinforced his position as did his time in New York. His sister Elizabeth remembered that before his overseas deployment, Medgar stayed in New York where blacks and whites, he informed the family, "could stay in the same hotels . . . and eating you know, and didn't have to be segregated and he could see the difference."[86]

On April 16, 1946, Medgar's stint in the armed forces concluded with an honorable discharge. When he returned home, he sat down with the family and let them know that "he [had] seen that something was wrong," Elizabeth recalled. "He went and served his country, came back home, and couldn't even go up to a restaurant and eat. And he [said] 'something's got to be done.'"[87] He also returned to Decatur hurting from the fact that when the bus arrived in the South "he had to go all the way to the back of the bus and sit down with his army uniform on—[after he] don' went and fought for his country."[88] Prejudice, coupled with the violence exacted against African Americans he witnessed as a child and the freedoms that he experienced while in Europe, fueled Evers's desire to combat racism at home. His mother questioned what could be done about segregation since "that's just the way [things were]?" His answer: "it don't have to be though, . . . [there has] got to be a change."[89] After their stint in the military, Charles and Medgar began to seriously critique the political structure of Decatur.

At the conclusion of his military service, Medgar proved more determined that African Americans obtain not only voting rights, but all rights entitled to them as U.S. citizens. According to Myrlie, it was during his stint in the army that Medgar felt the impossibility of returning to Mississippi and continuing the life that he led before going to war. Without a doubt, "if Mississippi hadn't changed, he had. He had a whole new vision of what life could be like, of the way it was lived in other places by other people."[90]

The fact that black soldiers challenged more vigorously the unequal social position of African Americans at the conclusion of World War II was not a new phenomenon. There existed no real difference between the social and political expectations African American soldiers harbored after World War II and those held by their counterparts at the conclusion of World War I and as far back as the American Civil War.[91] In each instance, African Americans expected and demanded civil equality from the very society they fought to protect. Whites soon realized that once the genie of participation had escaped, they could not put it back in the bottle of containment. For, as Frederick Douglass declared in 1863, "Once let the black man get upon his person the brass letters, U.S.; let him get an eagle on his button, and a musket on his shoulder and bullets in his pocket, and there is not power on earth which can deny that he had earned the rights to citizenship in the United States."[92] Medgar Evers epitomized Douglass's sentiment, and the vision of equality that Evers saw as his right and the right of all African Americans as U.S. citizens was not exclusive to him. African Americans' military service in World War II emboldened their resistance as a whole and strengthened their resolve to participate in the political arena as a means of establishing justice in America for black folks.

Historian Jennifer Brooks argues that World War II had a profound effect upon African Americans' notions of manhood and citizenship. War magnified these two ideals through the success black soldiers achieved in meeting the various challenges associated with military service. Fulfilling military duties, Brooks argues, enhanced African American veterans' sense of self, "of who they were and where they fit into postwar political life. In putting a premium on the role of men as citizens—as soldiers performing the highest of civic duties—the war tended to strengthen the historic connection between male identity and political rights."[93] World War II would be an all-important war in the global struggle for independence versus stand-pat policies of racial control.

For African Americans, World War II proved to be more than a battle against Fascism and practiced atrocities abroad. It was also a battle against segregation and racism practiced and upheld at home. Of more importance to the Black Freedom struggle, as the historian Timothy Tyson notes, "World War II not only changed the landscape of domestic politics but gave African Americans an unprecedented power to redeem or repudiate American democracy in the eyes of the world."[94] For African Americans, there existed a clear connection between Fascism and Jim Crow and thus the United States had to destroy both to ensure all of its citizens the full measure of equality. Anything less than that, historian Glenda Gilmore declared, blacks considered "a hollow victory."[95] As a result, a groundswell of support developed for ending segregation and racism in America as the United States attempted to do so abroad. The *Pittsburgh Courier*, a black newspaper, led the charge for a "Double V Campaign."

In 1941, the *Pittsburgh Courier* commanded a circulation of about 200,000 and thus wielded a great deal of influence in black communities across the country.[96] It sought to use this influence to link the fight for civil equality at home with the war efforts abroad. The *Courier* also sought the support of powerful organizations such as the NAACP. W. P. Bayless, *Pittsburgh Courier* circulation manager, explained to NAACP executive secretary Walter White the objectives of the "Double V" initiative. "The purpose of the 'Double V' Campaign is not only to help this country to win victory over its enemies on the battlefield, but to win VICTORY over our enemies here at HOME." Bayless reminded White that, at present, blacks were "fighting all forms of discrimination on account of race, color, class or creed; fighting poll tax and political disfranchisement; fighting for educational equality and for equal opportunity in [the] defense industry."[97] Thus, Bayless presented the Double V Campaign as another needed weapon in the civil rights arsenal. When African American soldiers read or heard about initiatives such as the Double V, they understood that the individual battles against racism they waged across the ocean were also being fought at home from a more organized perspective.

At the conclusion of World War II, it seemed evident that the war served as a catalyst for rebellion against all forms of oppression. In fact, the very Mau Mau movement that Evers and other black soldiers respected had been fueled by individual Kenyans who fought for the British during World War II. Upon their return to Kenya, having witnessed social situations devoid of crushing racism and armed with the knowledge that whites could indeed die, these returning soldiers refused to cower under previous conditions of inferiority, oppression, and racial domination.[98] Evers's war experiences were similar to the experiences of Kenyan soldiers fighting for the British, who later became Mau Mau, and the results proved the same. Much like Kenyans who used the war experience to ignite their fight for an independent Kenya, what Medgar witnessed and endured in the armed forces assured his participation in the civil rights movement in the United States.

If World War II served as a catalyst for oppressed groups to challenge their oppressors abroad, the phenomenon continued its manifestation within the mental, spiritual, and physical bodies of returning African American soldiers. Once the challenge to white authority produced victories, however slight, it emboldened other individuals to support further moves challenging white hegemony, and again the Mau Mau served as shining examples of what a united black front could accomplish.

Whereas some African American leaders such as Adam Clayton Powell Jr. considered the Mau Mau struggle for independence a legitimate one, they condemned the violent tactics this resistance movement employed. Despite an abhorrence of the level of violence on the side of both the British and the Mau Mau, African Americans found it hard to ignore the impact violent resistance had on the colonial system. The Mau Mau's use of violence challenged African Americans' views on nonviolence as a primary tactic for social change in America. Historians such as James H. Meriwether argued that the "Mau Mau fighters [in fact] pushed black Americans to consider more fully how extensively to use violence in resisting white supremacy, and a number of people reached the conclusion that the Kikuyu had been left with little recourse." Although African American civil rights leaders such as labor organizer Asa Philip Randolph, Congressmen Adam Clayton Powell Jr., Sidney Williams, director of the Chicago Urban League, and other prominent African Americans renounced colonial brutality, civil rights leaders understood the need to separate themselves from the violent portion of Mau Mau to avoid damaging U.S. support for civil rights demands.[99] This caused divisions between the conservative civil rights leadership and its more militant activists. The Mau Mau would continue to impact the conscious of those resisting oppression around the globe.

Historian James Ranaku maintains that the legacy of the Mau Mau lay in its defeat of the British. With each defeat the British armor of invincibility shone less bright and when the Mau Mau defeated them, that invincibility collapsed, leading to further agitation throughout Kenya and other social developments.[100] With reported Mau Mau victories and inspiring speeches by Jomo Kenyatta, African Americans applied their admiration for the liberation movements in Africa to their fight at home. Again, the Council on

African Affairs "was at the forefront in publicizing the events, offering encouragement and some aid to Kenyan nationalists and demanding an end to British 'terrorist' rule."[101] African American veterans appreciated the significance of any win in the fight for sociopolitical justice and thus reveled in the victories won by Africans in their struggle for independence. They admired the tenacity of the African liberation movement and expressed their support for the end of colonial rule. Africans also expressed their respect and admiration for the Black Freedom struggle in the United States.

The Honorable Koigi Wa Wamwere, who also served as Parliamentary member and assistant minister for information within the Kenyan government, points to the connection and inspiration that both the Mau Mau movement and the civil rights movement provided each other:

> The Mau Mau inspired the civil rights movement, but in time when we came to the U.S. and listened to speeches of people like Malcolm X and Martin Luther King, but mostly Malcolm X, some of us were greatly inspired; at least for once we found people who had appreciation for the Mau Mau, people like Malcolm X, people like Franz Fanon, and they made us realize how important the Mau Mau were to us and that inspired us and in fact . . . it helped me to decide actually to come back to Kenya even before I finished my studies, [he was attending Cornell University studying hotel management,] and I just felt . . . that we needed to complete the revolution that the Mau Mau started by coming back to fight for a democratic system that would actualize our tenets and guarantee that people got what they fought for.[102]

Koigi left school during his second year and came back to Kenya to fight for equality. He maintained that "if Mau Mau inspired the Civil Rights movement, in time the Civil Rights movement actually inspired . . . the struggle for the second liberation in this country."[103]

The Mau Mau proved a formidable foe against oppression, and it is understandable that Evers found a certain level of inspiration and hope within its fight against colonialism. In the end, there proved not much difference between African Americans' fight for equality in the United States and Africans fight for equality and freedom on the continent. As Koigi observed, "the [political] system that was then in the U.S. [in the 1950s and 1960s] was some type of internal colonialism . . . , but what was internal colonialism in the U.S. was external colonialism in this country. To that extent we were the same people subjugated by the same forces and that is why the struggle of one inspired the other. We were truly . . . tied together by the strings . . . [of] destiny."[104]

Medgar Evers returned from the army with renewed convictions that African Americans claim citizenship in its entirety. Charles suggests that racism proved to be the X factor that drove Medgar to the civil rights movement. The denial of equal opportunity for social, political, and economic equality represents the foundation of racism. It was "being denied the right to participate [that angered Medgar.] He went to the army and fought for this country and came out and we wasn't enjoying the freedom we fought for," Charles noted.[105] For Medgar, the ballot represented the most tangible symbol of social and political equality. The NAACP later proved a perfect fit for Medgar, since it touted voting rights as its primary strategy for achieving social change. As field secretary, it became his job to organize African Americans to register to vote. If African Americans wanted to achieve political and social advancement, Evers noted, "Our only hope is to control the vote."[106]

As a young man, Charles had wondered how all the white sheriffs, constables, and mayors got in their respective offices. He and Medgar concluded that political power came with the ballot. Every white person in office, who received his appointment because voters elected him, legitimated the Everses' argument that voting rights equaled political power. As a consequence, Charles remembered that he and Medgar "decided, well we gon start to get our folks to vote so we can get our own sheriff of Decatur. [I was to] become the mayor of Decatur . . . and Medgar . . . the sheriff of Newton county. So the only way to do that was to register and vote. . . . I started trying to get blacks to register and Medgar did too. And that's when all hell broke loose."[107] The hell storm that Charles spoke of had its roots, however, not in Decatur, but in two legal rulings: a Supreme Court decision in 1944 and a legal decree in Mississippi in 1946.

Whites had long relied upon intimidation and the law to stifle, if not to prevent, African Americans from voting. During the 1920s, African Americans were denied membership in the Democratic Party in most southern states. Democrats used the white primary to maintain their political advantage. African Americans' denial of a political voice in the Democratic Party allowed whites political control at the primary stage, which, more often than not, led to Democratic victories in general elections in the South. This exclusionary tactic proved one of the chief and effective legal methods for denying African Americans the franchise and it allowed the Democratic Party to dominate its Republican rivals as well. The NAACP fought against this type of political terrorism and in 1927, resulting from a suit in Texas over African Americans' exclusion from voting in the Democratic primary, the Supreme Court ruled the Texas Democratic primary unconstitutional in *Nixon v. Herndon*. In 1944, the Supreme Court ruling in *Smith v. Allwright* ended the legality of the white primary system as a whole.[108]

These two NAACP legal victories cut a wide path for challenging the exclusion of blacks from voting polls. Recognizing that there were nearly 350,000 black Mississippians of voting age in 1946, whites, particularly in the South, were well aware of the social and political ramifications of the Supreme Court ruling.[109] As an additional area of concern, whites realized that the Mississippi Legislature, perhaps without forethought, had passed a law in 1946 exempting returning soldiers from having to pay their poll taxes for the past two years. This revision in the law provided over 80,000 African American servicemen in Mississippi with the economic incentive to challenge the democratic hypocrisy they charged the U.S. political system with tolerating.[110]

Many returning servicemen refused to go back to their previous position of inferiority and social degradation and headed to the polls with the intention of exercising their right to vote or their right to fight, whichever came first. Whites noted the more aggressive stance of African American servicemen in defense of political equality and fair play. Sociologist Charles Payne pointed to their tenacity in opposition of Mississippi senator Theodore Bilbo retaining his Senate seat after his reelection in 1946. Black veterans testified against Bilbo over a three-day period during the hearings held in Jackson, Mississippi, and black supporters packed the courtroom. Of more importance, between 1940 and 1947, the number of black registered voters increased from an estimated 2,000 in 1940 to 5,000 seven years later.[111]

During the 1940s, many African Americans looked to the wisdom of sociologist W. E. B. Du Bois, who in 1919, upon realizing at the conclusion of World War I that white racism would never recognize and reward black loyalty and sacrifice, called for black men to stand up and demand their rightful place in society. In a piece titled "Returning Soldiers," Du Bois made the following admonition:

> This is the country to which we Soldiers of Democracy return. This is the fatherland for which we fought! But it is *our* fatherland. It was right for us to fight. The faults of *our* country are *our* faults. Under similar circumstances, we would fight again. But by the God of Heaven, we are cowards and jackasses if now that that war is over, we do not marshal every ounce of our brain and brawn to fight a sterner, longer, more unbending battle against the forces of hell in our own land.
> We *return*.
> We *return from fighting*.
> We *return fighting*.
> Make way for Democracy! We saved it in France, and by the Great Jehovah, we will save it in the United States of America, or know the reason why.[112]

After World War II, African American servicemen returned to the South determined to "Make way for Democracy" at all costs. Medgar and Charles Evers decided to challenge Mississippi's combative environment of legality, morality, and hypocrisy by demanding voting rights—a demand that the NAACP had worked hard for since the 1920s.

In 1946, Medgar, Charles, A. J. and C. B. Needham, and Howard and Charlie Denson decided to register to vote at the courthouse in Decatur.[113] Medgar acknowledged that the registration process went over without a hitch, but it was when they returned to vote in the Democratic primary election that problems occurred.[114] Segregationist Theodore Bilbo was running for reelection. The action that the Evers brothers took that July 2 was not unique to Decatur. All over the country events such as this were taking place with startling results for conservative whites. In 1946 and 1947 alone, Gilmore notes, "black World War II veterans formed impromptu regiments to assault the polls of southern cities."[115] Thus Medgar, and those accompanying him, were not acting as individuals in a small rural Mississippi town, but rather as part of a national move to secure voting privileges in the South.

When Medgar and Charles arrived at the courthouse to cast their votes, they realized they knew the white men gathered to prevent their entry.[116] Although he could not remember all the names, Charles vividly recalled the presence of a Dr. Jack and a drugstore owner named Sleech Pennington as members of the group assembled to prevent their voting that day.[117] Both Charles and Medgar were students at Alcorn A&M College and were on campus when their parents received early warnings from area whites to prevent Medgar and Charles from attempting to vote. Charles remembered that "they'd heard we [were] coming and they told my mama and daddy 'you better tell your boys they better not come or they gon choose trouble' and Daddy nem want to know what trouble?"[118]

James and Jessie Evers never tried to talk Charles or Medgar out of going to the courthouse to vote, but they wanted them to know based upon the talk around town, what they might expect. Medgar recalled the courthouse incident in his interview with Francis Mitchell:

> The six of us gathered at my house and we walked to the polls. I'll never forget it. Not a Negro was on the streets, and when we got to the courthouse, the clerk said he wanted to talk with us. When we got into his office, some 15 or 20 armed white men surged in behind us, men I had grown up with, had played with. We split up and went home. Around town, Negroes said we had been whipped, beaten up and run out of town. Well, in a way we were whipped, I guess, but I made up my mind then that it would not be like that again—at least not for me.[119]

Medgar had resolved during the tense meeting not to surrender his life without claiming the life of some of his antagonists if need be.

In a 1962 interview with Ben H. Bagdikian, Evers shared his thoughts about the confrontation. When things started to go from bad to worse, "[I remembered that] I had a knife in my pocket and I opened it up while it was still inside. One thing I knew: if I went, I wasn't going to die alone."[120] The incident at the courthouse was one of many instances where Medgar faced the possibility of death. Although his version of the courthouse showdown seemed to lack a full accounting, Charles Evers filled in the harrowing details. "Medgar and I went on [in to vote, he recalled]. "Man it was rednecks everywhere. They . . . had guns and baseball bats and [when we walked up to the courthouse one of the men said] 'alright Charles, you know you just being smart.' One of the crackers said 'nigger you better gon back and get on out before you get hurt.'" Charles reminded the man that he had fought in the army and thus had earned the right to vote. When he and Medgar started up the steps, some of the men blocked their path. The situation grew more heated as both sides began pushing and jockeying for position. Charles remembered one individual in particular whose actions surprised him. "I looked at old Mr. Dr. Jack, I said Dr. Jack I'm surprised at you. . . . I'm surprised; you a person that brought us here and you standing in there trying to deny me the right to vote. 'Well, but see, some things that you know niggers ain't supposed to do.' That's what he told me."[121] The six men eventually decided to leave and try to vote at a later time.

Although the men had decided to leave, this did not absolve them of the mob's growing frustration and anger. Medgar remembered that upon leaving the polling place their encounter with the mob continued.

> [While] we were walking the white mob began to drive by in cars. I remember one of them, it was a 1941 black Ford. As it went by very slow a guy leaned out with a shotgun, keeping a bead on us all the time and we just had to walk slowly and wait for him to kill us. . . . They didn't kill us but they didn't end it, either. We were pretty bitter. We went home, got guns of our own and headed back in a car. We left the guns hidden in the car and tried walking into the polling place again and the mob blocked us again. We didn't pursue it. We drove back. I was born in Decatur, was raised there but I never in my life was permitted to vote there.[122]

None voted that day and accounts from Charles attributed their leaving the courthouse to the pleas of a "sincere" white woman who assured them that one day their time would come, but asked that they avoid the trouble at present. Despite the volatile nature of the event, the Evers family never received violent retribution as a result. The stand that both Charles and

Medgar took that day fueled their desire for social equality and that passion stayed with them well after they left Decatur. Former New York state senator George Metcalf observed that instead "of intimidating Medgar, the [failed voting] experience firmed his resolve" to continue fighting for equality in Mississippi.[123] Constant civil rights issues and resistance movements during the 1940s gained both traction and attention from civil rights activists who sought to capitalize on America's growing concerns about its global image.

On October 11, 1947, W. E. B. Du Bois and the NAACP released a larger document containing "An Appeal to the United Nations for Redress," which charged the United States with woeful discrimination, neglect, and hypocrisy in its treatment of African Americans. As a consequence, the NAACP appealed to the United Nations (UN) to rectify the issue. In a prepared statement Du Bois, the *New York Times* reported, charged the United States with "failing to practice what it preaches, claiming that 'while this nation is trying to carry on the Government of the United States by democratic methods, it is not succeeding because of the premium which we put on the disfranchisement of the voters of the South.'"[124] Du Bois inquired as to when "will nations learn that their enemies are quite as often within their own country as without?" As a means of further pointing to the social and political problems in the Deep South, Du Bois exclaimed that it "is not Russia that threatens the United States so much as Mississippi; not Stalin and Molotov but [Mississippi politicians such as] Bilbo and Rankin; internal injustice done to one's brothers [he continued] is far more dangerous than the aggression of strangers from abroad."[125] Toward the latter part of October, the NAACP went before the UN to file formal charges of racism.

On October 23, 1947, the NAACP "filed with the United Nations formal charges of widespread discrimination against Negroes of the United States in social and economic affairs," the *New York Times* reported. The NAACP outlined the charges in "An Appeal to the World . . ." containing some 155 pages summarizing "the history of the African Negro slave and his emancipation and of the laws and violations of law that have entered into his history." Du Bois maintained that a proper relationship between the United States and its black citizens was paramount for the continued development of the country. For, as Du Bois explained, one could find "almost no area of American civilization in which the Negro has not made creditable showing in the face of all his handicaps." He further pointed out to UN officials that the submitted "petition 'which is open and articulate and not designed for confidential concealment in your archives, is a frank and earnest appeal to all the world for elemental justice against the treatment which the United States has visited upon us for three centuries.'"[126] Actions such as these tended to force the hand of U.S. officials who were cognizant of America's global image and understood the fodder that charges of racism and discrimination against African Americans afforded America's foreign enemies. The fact that a host of nations, including "the United Kingdom, Russia, the Union of South Africa, India, Argentina, Denmark, Mexico, Poland, Pakistan, Egypt, Haiti and Liberia," all sought copies of the "Appeal," did not help quiet these concerns.[127] President Harry Truman could not have missed the snowball effect of this growing global relations nightmare.

Prior to the NAACP's "Appeal" in 1947, the National Negro Congress had presented a petition to the UN the previous June calling for an end to racial oppression and discrimination.[128] Truman, as a consequence of various meetings with civil rights leaders, social organizations, and religious groups concerning the civil rights crises, issued Executive Order 9808 on December 5, 1946, establishing the President's Committee on Civil Rights. He instructed the committee to study the racial problems facing the country and to use the data to formulate a plan of action. On October 29, 1947, mere days after Du Bois and the NAACP went before the UN, the President's Committee on Civil Rights issued its report titled *To Secure These Rights;* their report on the state of civil rights in America took the momentum out of Du Bois's UN petition.

The committee acknowledged what Du Bois and other civil rights activists already knew, that Americans could no longer "escape the fact that our civil rights record has been an issue in world politics. The world's Press and radio are full of it." It went on to suggest a series of changes designed "to strengthen the federal civil rights enforcement machinery." Of more importance, "*The United States is not so strong,*" the Committee continued, "*the final triumph of the democratic ideal is not so inevitable that we can ignore what the world thinks of us or our record.*"[129] This report received a great deal of support and Truman was heralded as one dedicated to racial progress. Although the NAACP's "Appeal" died due to U.S. pressure placed on the UN, the influences of United Nations Educational, Scientific, and Cultural Organization (UNESCO) commissioner Eleanor Roosevelt, and NAACP internal conflicts over Soviet support of the petition, the attention it received could not be ignored.[130]

Intense international scrutiny provided civil rights activist real leverage in their dealings with U.S. officials. Global attention and commentary on America's civil rights woes forced American officials to take seriously the country's civil rights problems as well as the sincerity of those fighting for social and political equality. As the historian Mary L. Dudziak has written, "American vulnerability on the race issue gave civil rights activists a very effective pressure point to use in advocating for civil rights reform. Civil Rights organizations relied on the argument that race discrimination harmed U.S. interests in the Cold War."[131] Politically astute activists such as Medgar Evers, Roy Wilkins, and others would not have missed the global impact that civil right challenges had on America's international reputation as a purveyor of democracy and egalitarianism. This understanding of the power of global and domestic attention and its strategic value, especially when it came to civil rights confrontations, was not lost upon civil rights leaders, and it became one of the major tactics used during the mid-1950s and 1960s. Medgar Evers, particularly after the failed voting attempt, paid close attention to the importance and necessity of formulating well-planned approaches to social resistance.

From 1946 forward, Medgar planned his protests with extreme care. He weighed the odds, calculated the risks, and combined his commitment to civil equality with careful thought, all of which served him well as NAACP field secretary. Before his promotion to field secretary in 1954, however, there was Alcorn Agricultural & Mechanical College, insurance sales in Mound Bayou, Mississippi, and the life altering lessons of what black oppression looked, felt, and tasted like.

Established in 1871, Alcorn College, now Alcorn State University, stands as "the oldest historically black 'land-grant institution' in the United States and the second-oldest state-supported institution of higher learning in the state of Mississippi." In 1875, former U.S. senator Hiram Rhodes Revels received reinstatement as president of Alcorn. It was under his leadership that the state legislature reorganized the institution and changed its name to Alcorn Agricultural & Mechanical College in 1878. The name change conformed to the requirements mandated in the 1862 federal Morrill Land-Grant Act.[132] The Morrill Land-Grant Act provided large tracts of land to individual states. States could either use or sell the land as a means of raising monies to construct a public educational institution dedicated to teaching courses in agriculture, mechanics, and officer training. Alcorn A&M College provided African Americans with an educational opportunity that many took advantage of to enhance their personal lives and the development of their respective communities.

The years that Medgar spent as a student at Alcorn in southwest Mississippi helped cultivate his leadership abilities. In the fall of 1946, he enrolled in Alcorn's high school program located on its campus in Lorman, Mississippi. He completed the requirements for the high school diploma and enrolled as a freshman majoring in business administration during the 1948 fall term.[133]

In 1950, he met Myrlie Beasley on the very first day she arrived on campus and was immediately taken with her. Although Myrlie admits that her grandmother Annie Beasley and her aunt Myrlie Polk had warned her to stay away from veterans, she fell in love with Medgar despite his being seven years her senior. She remembered that it was something different about him that separated Medgar from the rest of the "boys" on campus and that initial meeting continues to stand out in her mind.[134]

Myrlie Beasley was born in Vicksburg, Mississippi, on St. Patrick's Day 1933 to Mildred and James Van Dyke Beasley. Her mother was sixteen and her father well into his twenties when Myrlie arrived. The family did not stay together long, and by the time Myrlie turned a year old her mother and father had separated. Mildred decided to leave Vicksburg shortly afterward. Myrlie's paternal grandmother Annie McCain Beasley, whom she called "Mama," and her aunt Myrlie Polk assumed the responsibilities of raising her. The "fact that both of them were teachers," Myrlie acknowledged, provided her with "more than a little status in the Negro community." She went on to do well in grade school attending MyIntyre Elementary Jr. High School and later graduating from Bowman High School in May 1950. Both her grandmother and aunt were independent and strong willed and looked after Myrlie with an intensity that sometimes seemed a bit stifling. Yet they were responsible for the strong-willed woman she later became.[135]

Had it not been for Jackson State College president Jacob Reddix, Myrlie would have pursued a degree outside of the state of Mississippi. His refusal to write a letter to the Mississippi Board of Higher Learning acknowledging that Jackson State did not offer a major in music forced Myrlie to continue her academic pursuits in the state. She had already applied for scholarships at Fisk and Talladega Universities but did not receive one. She knew, however, that the Mississippi Board of Higher Learning had set aside funds to assist black students who could not pursue their desired major in the state for whatever reason. In order to qualify, students had to demonstrate that no black college in the state offered the desired major. Myrlie knew that neither Alcorn nor Jackson State offered a music major and all that she needed was a written letter from the school president of both attesting to that fact. Reddix, however, refused to write such a letter and informed the board that his institution offered "enough music education for what Miss Beasley needs to pursue her goals in life." Myrlie felt betrayed and lost any chance to receive financial assistance from the state.[136] As a result of this setback, she chose Alcorn A&M College, a decision that would change her life and eventually place her in the center of the civil rights struggle in Mississippi.

Evers-Williams recalled that when she first met Medgar, she thought "what a man." She remembered leaning on a light pole on campus when "a decent looking, not handsome, but decent looking" older gentleman with an unusual persona approached the group of freshmen girls of which she was a part. As she continued to lean against the light pole Medgar approached and warned that she had "better stop leaning on that pole, [because] you might get shocked." He later told her that she had tossed her hair in an arrogant manner when he said this and she admitted that she probably did. However, she could not forget him and continued to think about the man who seemed to ooze confidence from every pore of his body.[137]

For the young seventeen-year-old Myrlie, Medgar was like no man she had ever known. It "was something about the way he carried himself," she noted. It was his "class, dignity, a sense of purpose [that drew her to him both physically and intellectually]."[138] As an added attraction, Medgar always prided himself on keeping a clean and neat appearance regardless of the quality of his clothes, and he continued this practice at Alcorn. Myrlie took early notice of his devotion to both neatness and cleanliness and recalled that whenever she saw him "he [would be] clean, God he was so clean. We wore blue jeans then, but they always had to be ironed and with creases, . . . his blue jeans were always impeccable . . . and I remember the first time he kissed me how clean he was, I mean his body, his mouth, the whole bit, you know, just a cut above."[139] Medgar was also smitten with Myrlie. His sister Elizabeth remarked that he "loved his Myrlie" and would call home all excited, exclaiming that "you [all have] got to see this girl, she can sang and she got long hair." Myrlie knew that Medgar loved long hair, but his bluntness never failed to amaze her.[140]

Never one to shy away from a direct statement, Myrlie recalled that not long after meeting Medgar, he told her that she was going to be the mother of his children. With such a note of assurance, she wondered where this man was coming from since he had not even told her that he loved her yet. Evers responded with an air of confidence. He admitted to Myrlie that he had not yet told her he loved her for the simple reason that he did not yet know her, but that "when its time to tell you I love you, I will." This kind of open honesty and directness "threw a seventeen-year-old [girl] off guard," Evers-Williams said. Yet, she acknowledged that from the very beginning she saw in Medgar "the possibility of someone I could believe in, I saw the possibility of Medgar being a man that you could depend upon. The strong silent strength that I could feel there, said to me that's the kind of man you want."[141]

Evers possessed a certain air about him that made people, especially women, feel safe in his presence. Myrlie remembered that during "the last few days of his life, at a mass meeting when Lena Horne came down and made an appearance, she said a few days after that, which was a day after his assassination, that she had no fear while she was in Mississippi because she knew Medgar Evers would take care of her, he made her feel safe."[142] Lena Horne, a celebrated actress and singer, had received acclaim and national attention for her performances and social activism. After meeting Medgar Evers, Horne remained "deeply impressed" with him "and permanently inspired by . . . [his] strength and dedication."[143] That strength of character and devout commitment to the fight for equality, regardless of the personal cost, helped increase Horne's eagerness "to do more on behalf of the movement."[144] Just as Lena Horne knew immediately that she could count on Medgar, Myrlie remarked that she, too, "knew that from the very beginning."[145]

In spite of some reservations against the union from both sides of the family, Myrlie and Medgar were married on Christmas Eve 1951 at Mount Heron Baptist Church in Vicksburg, Mississippi.[146] Both knew that marriage would bring about its own set of difficulties, but they were committed to each other and believed that to be enough to see them through the rough times. Myrlie and Medgar were dedicated to academics, and Evers excelled as a student and a campus leader. Many students who attended Alcorn during this period attribute their social awareness to the school's family-like structure and demands that one become an asset to the race.

Laplose Jackson, director of Student Affairs at Alcorn and former schoolmate of Medgar, maintained that Alcorn nurtured and ingrained within its students the quality of being prepared for all things and for every situation. Alcorn graduates, Jackson noted, tended to maintain these qualities after graduation. During the time he attended Alcorn, from 1950 to 1954, instructors were really concerned with students and cared about their well-being. Yet, most of all, he believed that the teachers at Alcorn "wanted their students to be professional, have a good work ethic, and to go on to do important things."[147] Medgar, however, was never content with just learning what professors taught from the text, nor was he willing to allow them to remain campus-fixated while the community suffered.

Evers believed in application rather than theorization, and he applied this belief to every task he pursued. As a student, this often created an antagonistic classroom relationship between him and some of Alcorn's faculty members. Evers's insistence that teachers apply the full weight of the entire academic system to the task of solving the problems of the community rather than merely using it to disseminate information was the foundation of much of that antagonism. As a consequence, Medgar, Myrlie recalled,

> was a [constant] threat to the serenity of instructors, because they said he was a troublemaker you know, he challenged them to do more than teach the text and . . . they liked him to a degree, they had tremendous respect for him, but they felt threatened by him because he was shaking the foundation and they were saying, you know "go on away, you don't know what you're talking about you're a student." Heck a student, this man was a man, he fought in World War II, he was no kid coming out of high school talking about them . . . about the need to register and vote.[148]

Since childhood Evers had a penchant for looking toward the future and focusing on its possibilities. He viewed the present as a motivator for making one's visions of the future a reality. He did not consider the present to be a moment in time and space deserving of contentment. Thus he saw the possibility of Alcorn and believed that instructors should take the college into the community with the sole purpose of securing equality in all facets of everyday life. Myrlie argued that such a refusal to be self-serving can again be traced back to his mother. After all, she raised him with the idea that "you had a responsibility not just [to] your family, but the larger family. . . . And for Medgar having been in World War II, he saw it not only as a commitment to family, to community, but to state, to nation."[149] As a result, he considered his time at Alcorn as an opportunity to make a positive contribution to the college and a vital chance to develop leadership skills that would prove beneficial in the fight for sociopolitical equality.

Evers took on many leadership positions during his matriculation at Alcorn. He served as editor of the campus newspaper, the *Greater Alcorn Herald,* and as president of the Junior Class and vice president of the Student Forum. His position as vice president of the Student Forum during the 1951–1952 school term, garnered him the Certificate of Merit in 1952 "for outstanding and faithful services rendered."[150] He also served as a member of the debate team, college choir, the football team where he played halfback, and the track team.[151] In addition, he edited the college yearbook, the *Alcornite,* in 1951 and according to Ronald Bailey "participated in a monthly interracial discussion group on world affairs at all-white Millsaps College [in Jackson] as a result of his work with the campus YMCA." It was at one of these interracial sessions, the historian Dernoral Davis notes, that Medgar learned of the NAACP.[152] Although Evers graduated in 1952 with a business administration degree, it would be the opportunities that Alcorn provided to enhance his leadership skills that proved essential to his political, administrative, and communicative development.

Dr. Alpha Morris, a schoolmate of Medgar's, a professor of sociology and chairperson for the Department of Social Sciences at Alcorn, remembered that Medgar seemed to be always moving toward some goal. "Medgar was a very serious person, very business like in terms of his academics . . . very conscious about his academics [and] getting his work out." In addition, she noted that Medgar was somewhat of an activist on campus. With the school on the verge of change, in 1948 students became more assertive. At one point, students were protesting the quality of the food. They started out by leaving the food on the table and walking out of the lunchroom and later grew more aggressive and began throwing food around to garner attention to their grievances. Medgar worked to resolve various issues on campus and to build a workable bridge between the students and the administration.[153]

Alpha Morris believes that Medgar's leadership style differed greatly from his brother Charles. As a student leader Medgar had a different tactic than Charles when it came to organizing. Medgar worked through organizations rather than mass protests to bring about change. He was very much concerned with campus conditions and how to improve them, but "his demeanor," Morris recalled, "was more of a person who [opted] . . . to work within the system as much as possible to bring about a change."[154] She felt that the problem-resolution strategy that Evers employed as a student encompassed putting the issues on the table and then working to resolve them. This practice represented the cornerstone of his foundation of leadership. Myrlie pointed out that Medgar "was always, or almost always open to intelligent discussion and strategizing and putting an issue on the table, stating what he felt and if somebody felt opposite put it on the table. [He wanted to know] is there any place for common ground, and if so let's pursue it and perhaps at the end of this encounter we will have something that's workable for both of us."[155] His diplomatic approach to conflict resolution endeared him to his fellow students at Alcorn and served as a foundation for his leadership role in student government.

Evers always commanded respect from those around him, recalled Ponjola Andrews. Although a couple of years ahead of her in high school, she remembered that even then Medgar had an air of leadership about him that the students recognized and they had a lot of respect for him.[156] Andrews maintained that Alcorn students respected Medgar as a student leader as well. She categorized him as a straightforward, "sober thinking person" who was really mature and she attributed that maturity to his time in the military. She believed that by the time Evers arrived on campus "he had found himself . . . and he had a vision, and he had a goal, and he worked toward that goal and it showed and he was productive even after he finished college because he kept going to a different level." That, vision, she argued, was to help his people.[157]

Medgar, while a student at Alcorn, fought to raise students' awareness of their social responsibility and power as a student body. This proved a very important part of students' need to increase their status in the eyes of the administration. Andrews recalled that school officials often treated students as if they were small children. Medgar proved instrumental in demanding that the administration treat students as adults rather than children. Much like Alpha Morris, Andrews maintained that Medgar was a person who worked behind the scenes to bring about these changes and was not as vocal as his brother Charles, but she believes that the two were working together.[158]

Myrlie caught the first hint of Medgar's absolute dedication to equality while at Alcorn. She recalled that he was always "very concerned about the injustices that existed and often expressed to me his views as to why he should not be able to have the simple courtesy of being addressed as 'Mr.' and of being able to ride anywhere he chose to on buses, sit where he liked to in movie houses or enter any restaurant. After all, he had fought for his country in World War II."[159] Along with the various leadership opportunities Alcorn afforded Medgar, the institution also provided its students with structure, high expectations, and a personal mandate.

Ponjola Andrews, as well as the other Alcornites, believes that the structure at the school helped to nurture the leadership potential within each student; whatever qualities one arrived with on the campus, Alcorn had a way of developing them to their fullest potential. Alcorn, according to Andrews, had a very structured social system and she believes that the extended family atmosphere the school fostered made a real difference in the lives of its students. That family atmosphere served as a trusted monitor of students' behavior while simultaneously insisting that they act with common decency, that they respect themselves, that they behave as true representatives of their communities, and finally that they dedicate their lives to changing the society for the better.[160]

Myrlie also pointed out that Alcorn served as an important breeding ground for intellectual development. Alcorn "was a community that was stretching its intellect; it was a community that was influencing people who would become the next set of leaders. So [as students] you tried to inject, as [Medgar] did, the responsibility of leadership in one's community there." Students, Myrlie remarked, "had all [of] these people to pick and choose from, and minds, the exchange of ideas, the intellect, the development of the intellect and the richness of it" were all academically stimulating. Individuals understood, nonetheless, that everybody would not agree. Yet Evers did not see this as a reason to avoid discussing the problems at hand and recruiting individuals to join the movement. Medgar "used to say," Myrlie recalled, that "'if [he] could only get one out of a hundred that's one we didn't have.'" Alcorn, she continued, "was a rich ground for cultivating . . . young fresh minds who were dedicated not only to themselves and their communities, but to the larger essence of what he felt our being should be, to make [the world] a better place."[161] Evers not only believed in the ideal of selflessness, he practiced it daily.

Evers often spoke on the value of personal responsibility to the collective and the role that Alcorn played in developing that responsibility. In the foreword of the 1951 *Alcornite* yearbook, Evers advised his fellow classmates that

> The hour is nearing when we as a class shall not be a class of one hundred and fifty units combined; but rather, one hundred and fifty separate units where each unit will have to take a much greater responsibility upon him or herself to help further the progress of our great and ultra-modern civilization. . . .
>
> As the hours pass into obscurity and as our daily tasks, irrespective to their nature, become more complex, we shall realize the indispensable part that our Alma Mater has played in our development as individuals. She has provided for us the facilities and fine standards of scholarship that we have used to create knowledge in order to meet the obstacles with a considerable degree of know-how and confidence.[162]

Medgar Evers was now ready to take the struggle for equality from "Beneath the shade of giant trees" and into the everyday world of black and white America.[163] Outside of the nurturing environment of Alcorn, however, Evers knew better than most that no amount of military service or displayed patriotism would cause whites to accept blacks as equals.

Despite exemplary military service during World War II, African Americans soon realized that many white southerners were not willing to extend equality to returning Negro soldiers, or the race as a whole, no matter what blacks had accomplished overseas. In spite of African Americans' participation and sacrifice in World War II, conservative white southerners believed that blacks were to forever remain the social and political equivalent of "girls" and "boys," outcasts of society, children who needed guidance and care from their white superiors. White southerners' paternalistic ideology developed during slavery and persisted as a means of controlling blacks in the South.

Historian Joel Williamson argued that white southerners, "in the last decades of slavery began to build a stereotypical image of the black person as simple, docile, and manageable." As a result, they "labored hard to see all blacks as, essentially, perpetual children."[164] As children, this meant that whites considered themselves the parents and thus should make all-important decisions for their black charges. The ultimate objective, however, was to keep them in their respective place, and political power helped whites accomplish this goal. When African Americans stepped out of their prescribed social place, conservative whites responded by using abject power to reinforce white supremacy and justified such force as corrective punishment for wayward children gone astray; this, after all, was for their own good. Whites, as Williamson pointed out, had "used [such power] . . . in a series of riots as black soldiers came home from France after World War I, and afterward in scattered violent forays." As a means of coping with the hypocrisy of using violent repression as a mechanism for benevolent tutelage, whites, Williamson continued, "developed a method whereby they could see themselves both as the good parents of blacks and yet do the violence necessary to keep blacks in place."[165] Whites still believed they knew what was best for blacks in the 1950s as much as they thought they did in the 1850s, and violence remained a tool for control. For African Americans, however, World War II helped to combat notions of inferiority and paternalistic dogma and served to destroy the perpetual childhood syndrome label many whites assigned to blacks.

Noted psychologist Na'im Akbar argues that for African American men, the transformation from boyhood to manhood proved paramount for collective and individual development. "Boys have dreams," Akbar notes. "They dream, they think, they wonder, they build unreal worlds in their minds. Only men have visions and visions become the instrument of human collective societal transformation."[166] For Evers, that vision reflected a world based upon equality and political participation for African Americans. He threw his entire physical and intellectual self into making that vision a reality that would lead to the human collective societal transformation of which Akbar spoke.

In 1952, Dr. Theodore Roosevelt Mason Howard, an active member of the NAACP, offered Evers a job as an insurance salesman for the Magnolia Mutual Life Insurance Company. The company was a new business venture started by Howard and a group of African American businessmen. Students at Alcorn considered Magnolia Mutual to be a great employment opportunity as well as a position of status, and many used it as a steppingstone to economic independence and professional proficiency. Like many students before him, Evers considered Howard a positive influence in his life, and he, too, believed that this opportunity would lead to greater things.

At the time, Evers most likely did not fully comprehend how strong an impact his insurance work in the Delta would have upon his work in the area of civil rights. In an interview with the British writer Nicholas Hordern for the *Delta Democrat-Times,* Myrlie asserted that his dedication to fighting for civil rights strengthened during his tenure with Magnolia Mutual in the early 1950s. Selling insurance in the Delta provided Medgar firsthand knowledge of the oppressed conditions in which black sharecroppers lived under, and it strengthened his resolve to seek political change.[167] On many occasions, however, his resolve took a beating. The insurance job required that he and his new wife move to Mound Bayou, Mississippi, which, Myrlie remarked, lay "in the heart of Mississippi's Delta [region]."[168] While working in the Delta, Evers found his niche in the Black Freedom struggle as he was now able to discuss the social problems blacks faced with those most impacted by them. He also learned to harness his anger when those he met balked at the idea of openly resisting oppression. When faced with these types of individual hesitations, Evers channeled his personal frustrations toward ending the brutal system of black exploitation and oppression in the Delta that epitomized the system of white supremacy in the South.

The counties situated wholly within the Yazoo Delta, as historian James Cobb points out, consist of Bolivar, Coahoma, Humphreys, Issaquena, Leflore, Quitman, Sharkey, Sunflower, Tunica, and Washington. Counties either partially within the region or adjacent to it include Carroll, Holmes, Panola, Tallahatchie, Warren, and Yazoo. These counties, particularly the first group, served as political and economic strongholds of the white planter class that was determined to keep African American labor accessible to landowners, accountable to the landed class, and subservient to the white hierarchy.[169]

Medgar Evers was defined by his childhood, the examples his parents provided, the racism he encountered, and the freedoms he experienced overseas. Each of these life experiences helped focus his attention on combating racism and making the country live up to its democratic creed. While attending Alcorn, Evers honed his leadership skills and ability to convince people around him to buy into his program and to fight for their individual and collective rights. Upon graduation, his life would take on another change—one that would shun the comforts of a middle-class lifestyle and embrace one of struggle, confrontation, and the need to defend the defenseless. His desire to change Mississippi was not only for his wife and children but also for, in his words, "all the wives and all the kids who expect and deserve something better than they are getting from life."[170] Mound Bayou would be just the beginning with Jackson, Mississippi, waiting in the wings.

2.

The "Road to Jericho"

FROM THE MISSISSIPPI DELTA
TO JACKSON, MISSISSIPPI

You know . . . any man with an ounce of pride who works in the delta soon wants to do something.
—*Medgar Evers*

You will have to see the mass of disfranchised, frightened Negroes in the Mississippi Delta to understand what it is to be without freedom.
—*Dr. Clinton C. Battle*

You know, [in] a one-horse town, they'll do anything to you.
—*Fred Clark Sr.*

THEODORE ROOSEVELT MASON HOWARD proved to be one of the greatest political influences upon Medgar's early political development and played a prominent role in shaping the type of vocal activist he became. Born in Murray, Kentucky, on March 2, 1908, to Arthur and Mary Howard, Theodore Roosevelt Howard (during the late 1920s he added Mason) demonstrated intellectual potential at an early age. He received his undergraduate degree from Union College in Lincoln, Nebraska, and his medical degree from the College of Medical Evangelists in Loma Linda,

California, now Loma Linda University. During Howard's matriculation, historians David and Linda Beito note, the College of Medical Evangelists served as "the chief SDA [Seventh Day Adventist] medical school."[1] Much like Evers, Howard also detested segregation and abhorred the inner feelings he suffered with every report of a lynching or beating of a black person, and these experiences also drove his activism.

As a civil rights activist, physician, organizer, and local businessman, Howard held a great deal of influence with black Mississippians, and his personal wealth helped strengthen that influence. His economic holdings made him one of the wealthiest black men in Mississippi and his home reflected the level of wealth he had acquired over the years; his prosperity allowed for a staff of servants and chauffeurs. Howard raised pheasants, quails, and hunting dogs for sport, and he loved horse racing and fast cars. One look at Howard, Myrlie Evers remarked, "told you that he was a leader: kind, affluent, and intelligent, that rare Negro in Mississippi who had somehow beaten the system."[2] In January 1941, Howard accepted the position of chief surgeon at Taborian Hospital in Mound Bayou; the hospital celebrated its official opening the following February. This appointment also afforded him a great deal of respect in the African American community.[3] Historians such as David and Linda Beito point to his financial standing as one of the reasons why whites paid him so much attention.[4] Thus, when he voiced the need for African Americans to demand equal rights guaranteed them as American citizens, local whites could ill afford to ignore him or his influence in the black community.

The fact that Howard's economic livelihood did not depend upon the graciousness of local whites allowed him to challenge the segregationist system of Mississippi with much more freedom than could the average black Mississippian. In addition to advocating full citizenship rights for African Americans, Howard also fought to end police brutality. Civil rights historian John Dittmer noted that his campaign to end police misconduct led to "an unprecedented meeting with state police commissioner Colonel T. B. Birdsong to air grievances against the Mississippi Highway Patrol."[5] His ability to organize a meeting of this magnitude demonstrates the amount of influence Howard wielded in Mississippi and the importance the white leadership placed upon that influence. In conjunction with his insurance company, Howard oversaw a variety of successful business ventures that provided him with personal wealth and political influence. He founded a housing construction firm and a credit union, owned a restaurant with a beer garden and a thousand-acre farm, and raised a variety of livestock.[6] His proposal for the creation of the Regional Council of Negro Leadership (RCNL) in 1951 eventually provided him with a powerful political organization and thus a larger activist platform. The base of the RCNL consisted of influential African Americans capable of acting against segregation, fighting against racism and violence, and fearlessly addressing the economic and social concerns of African Americans in the Delta.

With the RCNL, black Mississippians now had an organization to help ward off the political and economic pressures associated with fighting inequality. Howard was the organization's charismatic leader who could command an audience. His organizational abilities and political influence allowed him and the RCNL to organize mass meetings with thousands of blacks in attendance. In May 1952, more than seven thousand people gathered in Mound Bayou to hear a speech by Democratic congressman William Dawson. In 1954, ten thousand gathered to hear from famed NAACP attorney Thurgood Marshall.[7] Since whites considered the RCNL a local organization, it avoided the stigma attached to the national NAACP and could operate with more freedom and latitude.[8] Thus, the RCNL helped lessen fears regarding civil rights organizations. In many ways, it "acted as a kind of advanced guard for the NAACP," remarked the Beitos, and "emboldened blacks to take the risk of open participation in the NAACP."[9]

Howard epitomized the power and effectiveness of the black businessman and the impact of black political organization. In light of the role black-owned businesses played in the fight for equality, their impact upon the early civil rights movement often lacks appreciation by historians. However, by "forming and joining the RCNL," David and Linda Beito have written, "these men and women were pursuing a practical, though much belated, application of Booker T. Washington's dictum that voluntary associations, self-help, business investment, and property ownership were the best preconditions for civil rights."[10] This contention is similar to arguments addressing the era of black respectability put forth by such prominent scholars as Evelyn Brooks Higginbotham and Glenda Gilmore.[11] Both Howard and the RCNL had profound influences upon the ideological and organizational development of Medgar Evers.

Medgar Evers proved an apt student of Howard and functioned as a crucial component of the RCNL by serving as its program director.[12] The fact that Howard was an astute businessman who advocated African American resistance and self-worth could not have been lost on Evers, whose own forebears advocated such actions and took pride in self-sufficiency. The skills Evers learned from Howard regarding political and grassroots organizing, strategies of resistance, and leadership ability, he later applied to his work with the NAACP. Before his promotion to field secretary, however, insurance sales in Mound Bayou, Mississippi, allowed Evers a close and personal look at the depth of black oppression.

Located along U.S. Highway 61 north of Vicksburg, Mississippi, former slave Isaiah Tecumseh Montgomery and Benjamin Titus Green founded Mound Bayou in 1887. Montgomery also served as the lone black delegate at the 1890 Mississippi Constitutional Convention where the revised state constitution effectively excluded African Americans from voting.[13] Montgomery named the town Mound Bayou "because of the large Native American burial mounds situated between two merging bayous, which ran through the town."[14] Small in comparison to other southern towns, the total population of Mound Bayou in 1950 was 1,328 of which 1,327 were "Negro." The census report listed the remaining individual only as a "Foreign born" white female.[15] Evers arrived in Mound Bayou during the summer of 1952 and initially confined his insurance sales to the city of Clarksdale before canvassing the rural areas. Myrlie also worked as a secretary for the company, thus beginning a pattern of joint employment that continued over their marriage. Once Evers extended his work circle to include more rural areas, he began working with another young veteran named Thomas Moore. Moore was a native of Mound Bayou and one of Evers's closest colleagues at Magnolia Mutual. While roaming the countryside selling insurance policies, he and Evers developed a close friendship and Evers sought to teach Moore as much as he could about selling insurance.[16]

While riding from plantation to plantation collecting premiums for hospitalization and life policies and enrolling new customers, the two men spent hours discussing their futures, offering advice and contemplating the future of Mississippi. Evers believed that the state had a real chance to grow and develop into something of which everyone could be proud and the Delta, with time, could begin that metamorphosis. He likened the Delta to a virgin country and sincerely believed that if "everything got straight here, this would be the best place in the world to live." As a means of helping area blacks overcome the Delta's social and political ineptitudes, their work-related trips often included recruiting for the NAACP.[17] Evers learned two valuable lessons while working in Mound Bayou and its surrounding areas: the need to gain the trust of those with the most to lose in any struggle for equality and the genuine extent to which the Delta culture of oppression and violence perpetuated inequality and subservience among African Americans. Evers soon found that the violent methods whites employed to ensure their control over Delta blacks made grassroots organizing difficult at best.

The Delta region represented the epicenter of Mississippi's economic power and had rightfully earned the reputation of being one of the most oppressive areas for African Americans in the state of Mississippi.[18] The sharecropping system, through economic exploitation and physical violence, victimized and shackled African Americans to the land in ways that resembled chattel slavery. African American sharecroppers often found themselves at the economic mercy of white Delta landowners who exploited their labor for cotton production without remorse. Scholars such as Nan Woodruff argue that some "of the meanest corners of the 'heart of darkness' were found in the Delta during the first half of the twentieth century."[19] Delta planters had a penchant for brutality and sought complete control over African Americans by whatever means ensured their subservience and the sharecropping system aided in this process.

The demise of southern slavery resulted in the establishment of the sharecropping system. White planters wanted not only to maintain a labor force to ensure their own economic survival, but also to keep the approximately four million black men and women who were so recently chattel property dependent and controlled. Many African Americans were forced to work the lands of white landowners because of their inability, for various reasons, to secure land of their own. The landowner provided the sharecropper with the necessary supplies in exchange for a percentage of the harvested crop at the end of the year.[20] The percentage, however, favored the interest of the landowner to a much greater degree, sometimes encompassing 50 percent or more. There were, however, other positions available to blacks working the land after emancipation. A freedman could be a renter, a tenant farmer, or a wage hand, each of which often allowed greater autonomy than sharecropping. Although the tenant, renter, and wage laborer were also susceptible to exploitation, more often than not the sharecropper suffered inescapable debt and continuous denial of opportunities to catch his or her financial breath.[21]

At the base of the sharecropping system lay a malignant system of debt. In order to receive the necessary credit for supplies to work the land, landowners required sharecroppers to sign contracts stipulating an agreed-upon rate of payment in exchange for services rendered by the landholder. As collateral for equipment, seeds, and tools, sharecroppers were often forced to secure these items at outrageous prices from stores owned by the landowner or his colleagues; the landowner or local merchant then placed a lien on the impending crop.[22] Planters left nothing to chance in their desire to keep "croppers" under thumb, and the best means of doing so rested upon tactics designed to maintain sharecropper debt.

Maximizing profits at the economic expense of the worker proved the basis of the sharecropping system. Historian Neil McMillen points out that supply "merchants, whether at a plantation commissary or country store, usually had both explicit and implicit interest charges, i.e., an annual rate and a credit mark-up." When sharecroppers settled their accounts, those with "debit entries" were "subject to an additional charge of from 10 to 25 percent."[23] If, at the end of the year, the sharecropper failed to pay off his debts, the landowner placed a secondary lien on the crop for the upcoming year. In essence, the debt continued to escalate yearly leaving the individual without much hope of escape.

As an added insult, whites exploited the reluctance or inability of black sharecroppers to challenge their economic exploitation due to their fear of violent repercussions.[24] One Mississippi sharecropper reasoned that there was no real need in challenging the amount of the debt a white man placed upon blacks whether one agreed with it or not. There "is no use jumping out of the frying pan into the fire," he noted, for if "we ask questions we are cussed and if we raise up we are shot, and that ends it."[25] The oppression of African Americans proved to be as much a mental process as a physical one. This is not to say that sharecroppers took their exploitation without objection. Some left the plantation under the cover of darkness while others, such as Mississippi civil rights activist Fannie Lou Hamer, used equalizing tactics.[26]

Hamer served as timekeeper on the W. D. Marlow plantation in Ruleville, Mississippi. As timekeeper, she was responsible for recording the number of hours workers accumulated, the amount of cotton picked, its overall weight, and the money owed to each individual. Hamer, however, saw how whites used fixed scales when weighing cotton to cheat workers out of their rightful pay. In response, whenever possible, she placed her own counterbalance on the scales to rectify the inaccuracy.[27] Whites were not ignorant of sharecroppers' resistance tactics and worked to combat them at every turn. They used intimidation, firings, and violence to keep blacks who were dependent upon them for employment in line and subservient.

As a consequence of white southerners' determination to maintain control of black labor, sharecroppers were levied higher interest rates, cheated, intimidated, and subjected to spurious bookkeeping practices.[28] With few options, each year forced the overwhelmed sharecropper to renew the ill-intentioned contract and start the process all over again. For African Americans, the economic chains of the sharecropping system effectively replaced the iron variety they had seen during slavery. The Delta region, however, stood as a living, breathing testament to the destructive nature of the sharecropping system, and the more Medgar Evers trudged through the muck of despair and brokenness mirrored on the faces of Delta residents, the more he sought to understand the reasons behind the pain and despair he witnessed.

What Evers observed disturbed him deeply and he sought to understand how one race of people could be so completely overrun by another. The more he spoke to individuals trapped in the recurring cycles of violence and despair, the more he connected black oppression with economic exploitation. He came to the heartfelt realization that every facet of the Delta economic system was either practiced, enjoyed, or suffered by each successive generation. According to Myrlie:

> As time went on and Medgar had an opportunity to probe deeper into the sharecropping system, he concluded that virtually every aspect of the Delta Negro's life was deliberately manipulated to produce the results he saw around him. The helplessness of the Negro family in escaping the system, the manipulation of the schools, the collusion between plantation owner and store manager, and the frequent resort to outright fraud all combined to give illiteracy and hopelessness an almost genetic quality. Sharecroppers begot more sharecroppers generation after generation with almost no hope for escape. And beyond all of the built-in controls, beyond the system itself, lay the iron-clad rule that no Negro, sharecropper or not, could win in a showdown with a white. . . . The law was white; the courts were white; and beyond even the law and the courts lay white violence that could be forged into a lynch mob on an hour's notice.[29]

Medgar understood that control in the Delta rested upon economic debt and the promise of physical violence if "Negroes" stepped out of line. It also held promise as an organizing oasis for civil rights activism once the oppressed masses overcame the fear attached to social resistance.

The Delta provided Evers with a deeper understanding of just how desperate the situation remained for African Americans in Mississippi. It also heightened his personal awareness of his familial responsibilities and obligations. As of June 30, 1953, those responsibilities included a son. The birth of a son proved an important event for the Evers family since all other grandchildren had been girls up to that point, and there had been serious discussions regarding the continuation of the Evers name. Medgar, however, had announced with consistency that Myrlie would indeed have a boy and when his prediction came to pass, the entire Evers clan celebrated. When it came time to name this revered son of theirs, Myrlie wanted to name him after his father, but Medgar opposed, arguing that every child should have his own name. He had the perfect one in mind and he and Myrlie named him Darrell Kenyatta.[30]

Medgar Evers chose the name Kenyatta in honor of the Kenyan freedom fighter Jomo Kenyatta who had inspired him for so many years. He and Myrlie had discussed the name for some time without Evers changing his mind concerning its appropriateness for their son. Myrlie, however, dreaded the idea of her son carrying the African moniker Kenyatta both because it had negative connotations to so many white Mississippians and because she could not reconcile with an African name which she admitted "just didn't sound right to my ears."[31] As a consequence, when it came time to record an official name for the birth certificate, she placed Darrell in front of Kenyatta making the latter his middle name. The birth of a healthy and happy child elicited feelings of relief and happiness for both parents since their first pregnancy in 1952 resulted in a miscarriage. In fact, it ended in what doctors then termed a "spontaneous abortion," a phrase that Myrlie had not heard of before waking up in the hospital on that fateful day. The traumatic event of a miscarriage had rendered them both emotionally wounded, but the birth of Darrell was much like a soothing balm over their pain and it stimulated their parental drive.[32] The leadership skills and abilities Evers developed as a soldier and student allowed him to rise up the company ladder at Magnolia Mutual at a rapid pace, his ascent quickened by his desire to provide a comfortable existence for his wife and child.

In 1953, the *Mound Bayou Sentinel* publicized Evers's promotion to acting agency director of Magnolia Mutual. The article reported that since his arrival at Magnolia, Medgar Evers "has made rapid progress, and from all indications, he will soon become one of the outstanding insurance executive[s] of this age."[33] The proclamation seemed to foretell his professional future. On April 20, 1954, C. H. Webster, executive director of Magnolia Mutual, sent Evers a letter containing the following notification: "Out of consideration of the way you have served in the capacity of Acting Agency Director, I am pleased to advise you that the Executive Board has named you Agency Director, effective immediately."[34] Despite the opportunities for professional advancement afforded by Magnolia Mutual, Evers considered the existence of so much poverty and pain a constant reminder of his own social and professional fragility. Rather than frighten him, his concern for his own socioeconomic welfare reminded him of the responsibility he had to aid the people suffering around him. Thus, during his tenure at Magnolia Mutual, Evers experienced rising levels of discontent and anger regarding the social and physical condition of the sharecroppers he opined "might as well still be slaves."[35]

Although he recognized the pitiful conditions Delta sharecroppers endured, Evers never accepted the finality of it. He was determined to open their eyes to a reality that portrayed blacks as more than work animals or impoverished beings with no future or past. He spoke to them of the courage and vision of Marcus Garvey, the eloquence of Frederick Douglass, the tenacity and drive of Harriet Tubman, and the admirable qualities of other black heroes they may not have known.[36] These sessions had a dramatic effect upon him. Over a short period of time, Myrlie noted, Medgar became enamored with the black sharecroppers he met and began spending more and more time talking with them and less and less time concerned with the overall objective of selling insurance policies. The sharecroppers opened up to him and began sharing both their frustration with and disdain for their present social conditions, and these discussions often went on for hours.[37]

The detailed stories of brutality and oppression they shared with their insurance agent, combined with the horrendous living conditions Evers witnessed, seemed unbelievable even by 1953 standards. The many instances of dire social anguish that people endured daily, Myrlie maintained, snapped Medgar back to the social horrors he had endured as a child. "In a way, a horrified fascination with . . . [the violence and poverty of the Delta] drew him back again and again even as the sight of that long-ago pile of bloody clothing had drawn him to the place in the woods near Decatur where a Negro had been lynched."[38] The poverty and injustice heaped upon black sharecroppers and their families spurred Evers forward, and he developed plans of resistance with the NAACP playing more and more of a role in rallying the community to unified action.

Not long after arriving in Mound Bayou, Evers increased his activist role by undertaking a barrage of projects. As an NAACP volunteer, he revived an NAACP office in Mound Bayou and later opened a new office approximately twenty miles to the south in Cleveland, Mississippi, that eventually numbered five hundred members.[39] Here he worked closely with Amzie Moore, who was also a World War II veteran and a founding member of the RCNL. Born in 1912, Moore was a native of Grenada County in northwest Mississippi and believed that blacks should fight for their rights despite the repercussions. He also proved a proficient businessman and owned a service station and store along Highway 61, which often served as civil rights meeting places. Because of Moore's refusal to run a segregated business and his civil rights activities, whites levied heavy economic pressures against him. As a means of driving their point home, whites attempted to take both his home and businesses by demanding full and immediate loan payments.[40] Despite his financial problems, which he tried to remedy through the NAACP and Tri-State Bank of Memphis, Tennessee, Moore continued to advocate for civil equality and to increase the NAACP presence in Mississippi.

Between 1955 and 1956, Medgar Evers was instrumental in helping Moore raise the membership of the Cleveland chapter. They built its membership to 439, which made it "the second largest branch in the state," sociologist Charles Payne notes.[41] Always cognizant of the power of economics, Evers used his knowledge and business sense as a tool of liberation and resistance for the residents of Mound Bayou and its surrounding areas. The organization of an economic boycott against gas station owners who refused black customers the use of the restrooms proved to be one of Evers's earliest undertakings in the fight for social equality. George Metcalf noted that Evers "sent bumper stickers all over the state which said in large letters, 'Don't buy gas where you can't use the restroom.'"[42] Organizers feared, however, that the slogan might violate anti-boycott laws and provide whites with the legal excuse to wage an all-out attack, so they later modified it to read "We Don't Buy Gas Where We Can't Use the Washroom."[43] Here is where the RCNL showcased its economic importance to the movement for civil equality by providing Evers and other local leaders with the resources and economic support for maneuverability, community leadership, and organized resistance within a hostile environment.

By participating in the boycott, African Americans demonstrated that when properly motivated, they were quite willing to put their lives on the line to achieve a common goal regardless of the consequences. Participation in the boycott also illuminated the extent to which the enthusiasm and perseverance that Evers exhibited daily had caught on and inspired the black community to act in its best interest. Myrlie Evers recalled that as "time went by, Medgar and I would see little bumper stickers with those words on the usually beat-up automobiles of Delta Negroes. It may sound silly, but even that sort of protest required a considerable amount of courage."[44] The boycott proved an effective strategy and brought about some concessions. As a result of the economic protest, David and Linda Beito note that most "white stations began to install restrooms for blacks, both because of the falloff in customers and pressure from national suppliers and chains."[45] Myrlie maintained that the Mound Bayou boycott signified the first of many boycott campaigns that her husband would initiate, oversee, and participate in.[46] Evers, by all accounts, considered Mississippi his home and believed that injustice and intolerance demanded a continuous wave of struggle. Historians such as Vincent Harding argue that there has always been a river of resistance that has symbolized the Black Freedom struggle from the roots of the past to the current day.[47] Evers was determined to tap into that well of resistance and to channel it toward the destruction of segregation and all forms of inequality.

Spurred forward by constant tales of abuse, Evers worked to stimulate inactive NAACP chapters. As NAACP field secretary, he continued this line of activity while focusing more on creating new branches such as the one he organized in Florence, Mississippi, on April 26, 1955, "with fifty-seven (57) new members." By May 25, the branch had increased to about seventy members.[48] Working from a voluntary basis, in the Delta, however, Evers set his heart to convincing local blacks of the importance of joining the organization. The NAACP required a minimum of fifty members in a single location before they could file for a charter as a new branch. Due in large part to Evers's work, Myrlie noted that the first such request for a charter came from organizers in Shelby, Mississippi, a Delta town north of Mound Bayou, and this caught the attention of the NAACP.[49] The conditions Evers witnessed in the Delta pushed him to forgo his own comfort and that of his family, to eliminate the problems of those he came to know. The more Evers investigated the depth of black impoverishment in the Delta, the more he understood the nature of the sharecropping system and the intensity of African American exploitation. In the Delta region of the 1950s, cotton was king and black labor, much like black lives, proved time and time again to be expendable.

The thought of destroying a political system of oppression that had dogged his life and that of countless African Americans in Mississippi for hundreds of years incited Evers to fight and to organize. His commitment intensified with each horror story he encountered. The murder of a share-cropper, the rape of a black woman, or the beating of a black child by some drunken or enraged white brute, all pushed Evers to confront racism head-on. However, he was also concerned about the role he played in this vicious cycle of exploitation. In the Delta environment, Evers explained, a person soon discovers "that the education the Negro gets is designed to keep him subservient. The poor black man is exploited by whites and by educated Negroes, too."[50] As an insurance salesman, the very thought of "educated Negroes" exploiting the oppressed bothered Evers tremendously, and he ached with each premium he collected from an impoverished poli-cyholder. Myrlie recalled the toll it took on him and the fact that as "the weeks went by, Medgar began feeling guilty about his own role in attempt-ing to sell insurance to people in such circumstances."[51] Those "circum-stances" drove him to continue organizing and attempting to convince area blacks of the need to challenge the system. In the process, he faced chal-lenges of his own.

Evers's determination to assist those fighting for justice in the Missis-sippi Delta did not exempt him from moments of personal frustration. He often cringed with anger at the lack of support some members of the black community displayed. His brother Charles remembered that Medgar "was always talking about how many more blacks in the Delta there were than whites."[52] He also recalled conversations with his brother in which Medgar expressed his frustrations with the pervasiveness of fear within the Delta. Medgar acknowledged, with a hint of frustration and annoyance, that "if we can get [blacks] from being so scared and go and get registered . . . [so] they can vote all them crackers out . . . we can be in charge," Charles recalled.[53] Charles advised his brother that if he continued working with African Americans in the Delta change would come. As time went on, civil rights activists such as Aaron Henry, Amzie Moore, Fannie Lou Hamer, and others took on a more public role in the fight for equality, so Medgar "began to see that we was getting support."[54]

The fear sharecroppers displayed regarding white violence proved the major hurdle Medgar faced in his attempt to encourage people to fight against exploitation regardless of the consequences. Although he may have wanted Delta Negroes to face their fear and rebel, Evers recognized the seriousness of what he was asking many to do. He acknowledged that hundreds "of Negroes in Mississippi, especially those living in the Delta, have suffered as a result of economic reprisals, which has created an ever constant fear among the Negro population in that section of the state."[55] The fear that African Americans absorbed and exuded in the South in general, but the Delta in particular, haunted the realm of two worlds: one being the physical and the other the psyche.

Born on the Rucker Plantation near Roxie, Mississippi, in 1908, the famed author and poet Richard Wright wrote of the power that fear of white violence produced within the psyche of African Americans in general but, of more importance, the effect it had upon him. When it came to individual acts against white oppression, Wright understood early on that the "penalty of death awaited . . . if I made a false move and I wondered if it was worth-while to make any move at all." This type of paralyzing fear plagued African Americans in areas of extreme violence, and many felt this way whether they had been victims of violence or not. "The things that influenced my conduct as a Negro did not have to happen to me directly;" Wright continued, "I needed but to hear of them to feel their full effects in the deepest layers of my consciousness. Indeed, the white brutality that I had not seen was a more effective control of my behavior than that which I knew."[56] African Americans in the Delta lived with this type of fear everyday, and it often proved crippling when it came to calls for direct and open challenges to the status quo. The fears of death and brutality that African Americans exhibited in the Delta were grounded in reality even if they were unaware of the many statistics that justified those fears.

Neil McMillen presents some disturbing data concerning Mississippi and its national standing regarding white violence exacted upon African Americans. Between 1889 and 1945, "Mississippi accounted for 476, or nearly 13 percent, of the nation's 3,786 recorded lynchings." If the starting date is pushed back to include the 1880s, the lynch count for Mississippi exceeded 600 victims.[57] African Americans were well aware of whites' propensity for violence and did not require official numbers to justify fears of lynch law that always seemed to follow on the heels of African Americans' demands for social and political change.

Both the real violence and the ever-present potential for it that Wright discussed underscored the fear that plagued Delta residents, and it produced a formidable barrier against plans Evers had for establishing a united front against racism and social and political oppression. In her work, *American Congo*, the historian Nan Woodruff presents an important analytical argument for the link between violence in the Delta and labor conflicts.[58] Just as Evers remembered the Tingle lynching, Delta blacks had similar horror stories to legitimate any fears they exhibited. Many of the violent attacks perpetrated against African Americans by whites were public displays of ceremonial pomp and circumstance, a festive occasion for unified entertainment and community jubilance. A particularly heinous display of mob lynch mentality in 1904 symbolizes the type of public personification that lynchings often took and serves to underscore the psychological damage inflicted upon African Americans in the Delta. The *Vicksburg Evening Post* described the brutal lynching of a man and woman in Sunflower County. Although Luther Holbert stood accused of killing white planter James Eastland and two blacks, his supposed "wife" was guilty of nothing more than attempting to flee the area with him. According to the report:

> [W]hile the funeral pyres were being prepared they were forced to suffer the most fiendish tortures. The blacks were forced to hold out their hands while one finger at a time was chopped off. The fingers were distributed as souvenirs. The ears of the murderers were cut off. Holbert was severely beaten, his skull was fractured, and one of his eyes knocked out with a stick, hung by a shred from the socket. Neither the man nor woman begged for mercy, nor made a groan or plea. . . . The most excruciating form of punishment, consisted in the use of a large corkscrew in the hands of some of the mob. This instrument was bored into the flesh of the man and woman, in the arms, legs and body, and then pulled out, the spirals tearing out big pieces of raw, quivering flesh, every time it was withdrawn.[59]

This account represents the type of violence in which Evers had to contend on a psychological level as area blacks understood that the penalty of death often awaited those resisting white subjugation. In order to rally support, Evers had to help area residents overcome these psychological barriers to achieve the type of grassroots commitment needed to challenge the legitimacy of segregation and the racist practices it produced. He encouraged individuals to think about the future of their children and the responsibility they had as parents to help create a different world for the next generation. Of more importance, Evers demonstrated to those around him that he was willing to suffer in the struggle for equality and to place his family and their safety on the frontlines right along with theirs and this drew people to him.

This, as John Dittmer correctly points out, does not mean that African Americans were complacent or inactive while whites trampled over them. Although Nan Woodruff acknowledges that black people in the Delta had "been engaged in a human rights campaign for an entire century, if not longer," the fact remains that the psychological toll African Americans experienced following violence in the Delta worked to stifle most forms of open resistance.[60] In addition to the fears that violent behavior engendered, Evers found that extreme poverty and ill health among African Americans in the Delta also contributed to their lack of participation in campaigns calling for direct action.

If violence proved a formidable enemy of African American progress during the 1940s and 1950s, poverty and poor health served as its chief lieutenants. Poverty encompassed many Delta area blacks to the point of crushing any thought of a better tomorrow, and by the 1960s opportunities for better healthcare were almost nonexistent. Historian James C. Cobb points out that for many of "its impoverished blacks, the Delta combined an unfavorable health care environment with a startlingly unhealthy living environment. . . . A survey of 509 families in Washington and Sunflower counties showed that fully 60 percent of them were receiving less than two-thirds of the generally recognized minimum daily dietary requirement. This figure stood in stark contrast to a national figure of only 13 percent." The high rates of infant deaths in black Delta communities were problems that offered local leaders little chance for concrete solutions. According to Cobb, the "mortality rate for black infants in the Delta was 30 percent higher than for other Mississippi blacks and 109 percent higher than that for whites in the Delta." Infant mortality rates actually increased from 40.8 deaths for every 1,000 births in 1946 to 55.1 in 1965 with the Delta counties representing "the cutting edge of this trend."[61] Although these statistics are grim, to actually witness the daily suffering proved worse and that witness prompted Evers to act.

Myrlie recounted that day after day and week after week, while working for Magnolia Mutual, her husband returned home with countless stories "of children without shoes, without proper clothing; of adults with nothing to eat; of sanitary conditions no self-respecting farmer would permit in his pigpen. He painted word pictures of shacks without windows or doors, with roofs that leaked and floors rotting underfoot." As a means of emphasizing his point, Evers often drove Myrlie past the worst of shacks that appeared empty or condemned to which he exclaimed that people "live in there. Human beings. People like you and me."[62] The horrors that Medgar witnessed in the Delta compelled him to challenge them head-on, much as he had challenged injustice in Decatur.

When dealing with sharecroppers, Evers always greeted them with respect and he often brought clothing, food, and whatever other usable items he could spare to ease their suffering. He also made up his mind that when they wished to escape the iron clutches of the sharecropping system he would help them as much as he could. Many a sharecropper fled to Memphis under the cover of darkness and then North to escape a circular system of debt.[63] Evers used a variety of covert means to help people flee the state undetected. Myrlie recalled one instance involving a witness where he put the individual "in a casket . . . and got the person out of town, out of the state, across the border to Tennessee and then north."[64] In 1953, after having worked in the Delta for one year, Evers felt the need to do more to highlight the system of inequalities that epitomized the state of Mississippi. Later that year, he volunteered to carry out a direct attack upon Mississippi's educational system, a move that propelled him to the forefront of the civil rights struggle in the state and brought him to the full attention of the NAACP.

Earlier NAACP victories regarding the desegregation of Institutions of Higher Learning (IHL) bolstered Evers's decision to challenge segregation at the University of Mississippi Law School in December 1953. In a heated conversation with his wife, Evers argued that challenges against school segregation "had been done in other Southern states, and it would be done in Mississippi as well."[65] In order to fully understand his decision to confront the University of Mississippi, it is important to consider the NAACP's background in the fight to open the doors of higher education to African Americans.

By 1953, the NAACP boasted an impressive resume in the fight to end segregation in higher education. Four prominent cases highlight its dedication to equality in education and help shed light not only on Evers's decision to seek admission to the University of Mississippi, but the legal precedents that led to the 1952 desegregation suits later known as *Brown v. Board of Education, Topeka*. The success of the NAACP in suing for equality in higher education, prior to *Brown*, also explains the attention they afforded Evers's application to the University of Mississippi Law School in 1954.

During the 1930s and 1940s, the NAACP chose not to challenge the separate portion of the "separate but equal" doctrine established by the 1896 *Plessy v. Ferguson* decision. Instead, they decided to focus their attack upon individual states that failed to adhere to the "equal" ruling in *Plessy*. By attacking the lack of equality, for which the Court had already ruled in favor, the NAACP laid the foundation for challenging the validity of segregation itself in the future.[66] Between 1935 and 1938, two NAACP cases provided the momentum needed to launch an all-out attack against segregation in the field of higher education.

Charles Hamilton Houston, who had served as both professor and vice dean of Howard University Law School, directed the legal arm of the NAACP. Thurgood Marshall, who studied under Houston and was his protégé, later replaced his mentor as the head of the NAACP legal department. Both men considered segregation in higher education the logical place to begin since there were no real provisions in place to accommodate African Americans. They also believed that the South would soon see the idea of "separate but equal," in regard to academic pursuits, as impractical and too great a financial burden. In order to accommodate the academic needs of its black citizenry, under the separate but equal doctrine, states would have to build equal facilities in areas of medicine, law, engineering, and other academic pursuits for blacks that were already in place for whites.[67] Donald Murray provided the NAACP with an opportunity to test the legal boundaries of segregation, and his case helped set into motion the legal precedence needed for future attacks on the entire system.

Donald Murray graduated from Amherst College with a bachelor of arts degree in 1934. He then applied for admission to the University of Maryland Law School and was rejected "by the appellant President of the University and the appellant Registrar solely on account of his race."[68] Thurgood Marshall had a personal interest in trying this case as his application for admission to the University of Maryland Law School had been rejected four years earlier due to racial discrimination. Marshall sued the state on behalf of Murray. In 1936, the State Court of Appeals upheld the decision of the Baltimore City Court and ordered the university to open its law school to Murray. The Court ruled that since the University of Maryland housed the only law school in the state, it had to cater to the needs of its citizens regardless of color.[69] This was a legal victory in the NAACP's fight to end educational segregation and indicated that further attacks on the legitimacy of the system were possible. The NAACP's next significant case in the fight for equality in education centered on Lloyd Gaines.

Lloyd Lionel Gaines graduated in 1935 from Lincoln University, a black institution in Jefferson City, Missouri, after which he applied to the University of Missouri Law School. Like Murray, the school denied his application on racial grounds, but offered Gaines the choice of attending a law school separate from the university or sufficient tuition funds, equivalent to the cost of attending the University of Missouri Law School, to enroll in a school of law in another state. Gaines rejected both offers and the NAACP sued the university on his behalf. Three years later the U.S. Supreme Court ruled six to two in favor of Gaines and required the state to provide a law school for blacks equivalent to that offered to whites. The school the state of Missouri constructed, however, was ill funded as well as inferior and the NAACP continued litigation.[70]

Unfortunately for the NAACP, Gaines disappeared in 1939 and it remains unclear as to what happened to him. The Gaines case represented the first NAACP directed education suit to reach the Supreme Court. Historian Daniel T. Keller argued that the significance of Gaines lay in the fact that it "provided the nation with an answer to a pressing problem, and at the same time it heightened the controversy revolving around state and federal responsibility in the fields of education and human rights."[71] Some scholars argue that Gaines holds a more significant underlying meaning, as it relates to civil rights, than merely a victory against segregation in higher education. It also indicated a growing judicial intolerance for racial injustice.

Law professor Michael Klarman argues that the Gaines case was fraught with enough inconsistencies, Court indulgences, and plaintiff errors to produce a much different verdict. The fact that the justices rendered the verdict they did says a lot about their mindset regarding racial oppression. One could legitimately argue that the Supreme Court, according to Klarman, "should have dismissed Gaines as unripe, because the plaintiff had failed to pursue all available relief under state law."[72] The fact that the Court allowed the case to proceed, however, was not due to judicial incompetence but rather an indication of the justices' growing intolerance for racial discrimination. Their "willingness to finesse the procedural problem [in Gaines]," Klarman noted, combined with ". . . their unconvincing focus on the sanctity of state boundaries in their discussion of the merits suggest a growing solicitude for civil rights litigants."[73] Both Houston and Marshall must have discerned the change in the Court's attitude toward blacks' legal challenges to racism in light of the problems associated with the case that Klarman discusses. Knowledge of this type of growing legalistic bend on the part of the Court, toward black challenges to racism, would not have been lost on Houston, Marshall, or the NAACP. Although the abrupt disappearance of Lloyd Gaines left the NAACP without a plaintiff during a crucial period when a great deal of momentum had swung their way, the NAACP did not have long to wait for its next opportunity to challenge segregation in higher education.

Medgar Evers's decision to enroll at the University of Mississippi Law School came on the heels of two key court decisions addressing the issue of segregation in professional schools. In 1950, the NAACP received two more favorable Supreme Court desegregation rulings. In 1946, Heman Sweatt, an African American mail carrier, had applied to the University of Texas Law School and was forced to attend a poorly funded law school for African Americans housed in a basement. In June 1950, the Court ruled that the law facilities for blacks were unequal and ordered the University of Texas Law School to admit Sweatt. Yet despite the Court's ruling, *Sweatt*, as Klarman points out, was almost completely nullified in the Deep South. Of more importance to Medgar Evers was the fact that a segment of conservative white Mississippians reverted to the use of violence and intimidation as mechanisms for evading the *Sweatt* decision. This would be a tactic whites employed time and time again.[74] The NAACP would continue to amass key victories in their challenge to school segregation.

In 1948, George McLaurin applied to the University of Oklahoma's doctoral program in education. The university granted him admittance but segregated him from the rest of the students. The school required McLaurin to sit in an anteroom separate from the rest of his classmates; he also had to eat in a designated section of the cafeteria and use a separate section of the library. On the same day the Court decided the *Sweatt* case, they also ruled that the University of Oklahoma had to admit George McLaurin on a non-segregated basis in order to allow him the full opportunity to succeed and to interact academically with his peers.[75] These NAACP victories provided Supreme Court policy that broke down segregation in higher education. The critical *Brown v. Board of Education* suit resulted from the earlier NAACP victories, and in 1952 Thurgood Marshall led the NAACP's all-out attack upon the entire system of educational segregation.

Thurgood Marshall proved to be a careful and concise practitioner of the law. Before taking a case, he both viewed and reviewed it from all possible angles to decide its margin for victory and if that margin fell below what he believed acceptable, he passed on it. By October 1950, both he and the NAACP believed they had established enough legal precedents to attack educational segregation head-on. As a consequence, the NAACP board dropped its emphasis on seeking equality within the system of segregation and supported Marshall's plan of a full attack on the entire system.[76] In 1952, the NAACP filed the suit that shook the very foundation of segregation and opened the doors for challenging its legitimacy at every level. Medgar Evers could not have been in the dark regarding NAACP actions as he was quite active with the organization by 1952. Myrlie noted that Medgar was a voracious reader and having just graduated from Alcorn, and working to revive NAACP branches in Mound Bayou and its surrounding areas, he undoubtedly knew what the NAACP had accomplished in its fight for educational equality and thus would have recognized the significance of *Brown.*[77]

Medgar did not make the decision to apply to the University of Mississippi in haste. Both he and the RCNL were paying close attention to developments on the national front and the *Brown* suit commanded their attention. The desegregation case known as *Brown et al. v. Board of Education, Topeka et al.* consisted of the following lawsuits: *Brown v. Board of Education, Topeka, Kansas, Briggs v. Elliot, South Carolina, Davis v. Board of Education of Prince Edward County, Virginia, Bolling v. Sharpe, Washington, D.C.* and *Belton (Bulah) v. Gebhart, Delaware.* When the cases came before the U.S. Supreme Court on December 9, 1952, they were consolidated under one heading. The Court proved unable to render a ruling before the close of its 1952–1953 June term and agreed to rehear the case in December.[78] Chief Justice Fred Vinson, however, died on September 8, 1953, and President Eisenhower selected California governor Earl Warren to replace him.

It did not take long for Warren to demonstrate his willingness to address the problems associated with segregation. In fact, justices during the World War II era were more protective of civil rights than they had been during prior years.[79] Marshall and his legal team honed in on the psychological damage that educational segregation caused in the psyches of black children and utilized the research of social psychologist Kenneth Clark and his wife, Mamie K. Clark, to demonstrate the inferiority that black children experienced as a direct result of segregation. The Clarks used black and white dolls to reveal the ways in which white supremacy created internalized feelings of low self-esteem and self-hatred within black youth. When provided an opportunity, Kenneth Clark demonstrated that a majority of the black youth he included in his research analysis intimated the superiority of the white doll over the "colored" one and thus the one they most often wished to play with. The results of the Clarks's experiment spoke volumes as to how black youth viewed themselves in relation to whites in general, and Marshall hammered this point at every opportunity.[80]

Thurgood Marshall argued during *Brown* that segregation could never be equal and that it attached a stigma of inferiority upon the psyche of African American children of which they could never fully recover. As Aaron Henry later explained, "No matter how equal the facilities, the idea of white superiority and Negro inferiority remained, and we knew it was incongruous with the American idea of democracy that we were fighting for."[81] The depth of Evers's attention to the significance of what was happening nationally manifested during a community meeting in the fall of 1953.

While attending an RCNL sponsored meeting, Medgar volunteered to submit an application for admission to the University of Mississippi Law School after Dr. Emmett Stringer, then president of the NAACP Mississippi State Conference of Branches, suggested that "the time was ripe to desegregate 'Ole Miss."[82] His decision to integrate the law school, however, had much deeper roots than what many may have considered a spur-of-the-moment decision. Charles recalled that Medgar always wanted to be a lawyer, and this opportunity allowed him the chance to further develop his intellect.[83] On January 11, 1954, Evers demonstrated his sincerity to challenging educational segregation at the state's premier institution of higher learning by sending a formal request for Alcorn to "forward to the Registrar of the University of Mississippi School of Law, the collegiate transcript of one, Medgar W. Evers, as soon as possible."[84] Yet, why was he so adamant about attending the University of Mississippi? After all, there were many law schools, some of them all white, across the nation that would have accepted his application without much fanfare. The reason lay in what the University of Mississippi represented in the South and what integrating this behemoth of racial segregation would mean for the NAACP and the overall movement for equality in Mississippi.

The University of Mississippi was established in 1848, in large part, out of white Mississippians' desire to establish an educational institution in the state for the benefit of whites. In light of the changing times of the 1800s, brought about by abolitionism and southern fears of ideological pollution associated with sending their sons outside the state for academic training, wealthy Mississippians sought to protect themselves and their social and political identities from change by creating a controlled educational institution. This desire for geographic isolation from threats to their social, academic, and political ideology consumed the hearts and minds of white Mississippians who were determined to maintain the status quo at all costs. "Those opposed to us in principle," they argued, "can not be entrusted with the education of our sons and daughters." Historian David Sansing argued that as a consequence, the "founders of the state university . . . claimed a society's right, if not its obligation, to defend itself against change. They would make the University of Mississippi a bastion in the defense of the Southern Way of Life."[85]

A step toward protecting that way of life was to charter the University of Mississippi, which occurred on February 24, 1844.[86] The university held its first session on November 6, 1848.[87] This bastion of defense, however, would have been just the type of edifice the NAACP looked to topple. The fact that it lay at the heart of the very state that many across the nation recognized as the premier symbol of segregation and the primary purveyor of racism and white supremacy could not have been lost on the NAACP or Evers. In fact, Evers saw his application to the University of Mississippi as one of many strategic moves in his overall fight for social and political equality in the state and the nation as a whole.

Although Evers's decision to challenge educational segregation had wider implications for African Americans, it did not sit well with those closest to him. Even though his sister Elizabeth acknowledged the pride she had in her brother for the attempt, the Evers family remained apprehensive about his safety. They also questioned the sanity of such a decision in light of his position as a husband and father. By the time he applied to the University of Mississippi, Myrlie was pregnant with their second child, and she took his application as a personal attack upon the economic and personal welfare of their growing family. Medgar, in return, argued that his attempt to integrate the university was a step he was taking "specifically *for* his family." Not only did Evers consider his decision "a courageous step to help his people," he believed that it would benefit his children in the long run.[88] Myrlie, her family, and Medgar's parents, nevertheless, were concerned with the safety and economic well-being of his family at present and arguments exploded on both sides. Evers, though, had made his decision and he would not be dissuaded from it. He maintained that if "there were sacrifices to be made along the way, they were necessary sacrifices." As far as he was concerned, black Mississippians depended upon his leadership and willingness to go that extra mile and both his determination and stubbornness, when it came to fighting for racial equality, demanded that he not let them down.[89]

As a result of his sincerity and devotion to the cause of equal opportunity, Medgar Evers submitted his application to the University of Mississippi Law School on January 16, 1954.[90] His announcement made headlines across the state in papers like the *Jackson Advocate,* a black newspaper, and its white counterpart, the *Jackson Daily News.*[91] University of Mississippi law students were also aware of Evers's pending application, and many had mixed emotions about a "Negro" attending Ole Miss. The *Mississippian,* the campus newspaper, interviewed students and reported that the "general consensus of opinion was this: it is only a question of time until segregation will be broken down. We must prepare ourselves mentally for this change whether we like it or not." There were some who admitted, however, that if "the Negro is qualified intellectually, he should be allowed to enter school. Color should be no barrier."[92] Yet, Evers's color was the core problem and to uphold racial separation, his application would have to be addressed.

If university officials were unaware of Evers's racial background at the beginning of the application process, they were surely tipped off when the *Jackson Advocate* reported that "Thurgood Marshall . . . [would] act as [Medgar's] attorney in any and all matters pertaining to the admission of the applicant to the University of Mississippi."[93] Regardless of the moment in which university officials attached the term Negro to the name Medgar Evers, the Mississippi Board of Trustees of the Institutions of Higher Learning rejected his application on a technicality. Evers maintained that prior to any decision on the merits of his application, however, Attorney General (and later Mississippi governor) James P. Coleman and state school officials subjected him to a series of questions to determine his motivations for applying to the university.

During the latter part of August 1954, Evers received a summons from Euclid R. Jobe, executive secretary of the State Board of Trustees of the Institutions of Higher Learning, to come to Jackson for an interview. Evers agreed and brought along Alexander Pierre (A. P.) Tureaud, a "Negro lawyer" from New Orleans, to serve "as his NAACP representative," Myrlie recalled.[94] The three men met and then went to the office of state attorney general James Coleman, who conducted the interview.[95] Evers recalled a series of questions asked during the meeting including if he was "sincere." Coleman expressed to Evers "that his concern as attorney general was whether Evers was sincere about receiving an education, or whether he was merely trying to carry out a symbolic act." If it proved the latter, Coleman assured Evers that he "would fight his admission through the courts."[96] Evers conveyed to Coleman and Jobe his sincerity and determination to proceed as planned. The motivation behind Evers's application proved of grave importance to state officials. As a consequence, they asked if he was "prompted by the NAACP," of which Evers "told them, no."[97] His response provoked a series of more probing questions.

Knowing that, if accepted, Evers would interact daily with white students, the issue of living accommodations proved a concern for those conducting the meeting. It did not take long for the line of questioning to gravitate in this direction. Evers recalled that they asked "where I would stay, and I answered 'on the campus, sir. I'm very hygienic, I bathe every day, and I assure you this brown won't rub off.'" After the meeting Coleman informed Evers that he would let him know of their decision. Evers replied that he "wanted to know then." He noted, however, that Coleman "said I would hear 'in time,' and the day after registration, they sent me a letter saying my application had been denied because I didn't have two recommendations from people in the community."[98] This was not entirely accurate as Evers had sent the required letters, which, surprisingly, were written by "two white citizens." The fact that white men had written recommendation letters for a "Negro" to attend Ole Miss must have shocked and concerned university administrators. Both university officials and the IHL understood full well what was at stake if Evers integrated the law school, and his ability to do the work was never the underlying issue. As one Ole Miss law school student admitted: "I wouldn't mind going to school with a qualified Negro. It would be okay for higher education, but once the precedent is set, it will spread to the educational levels of the secondary and elementary schools, and this would be bad."[99] In the end, Evers's application (and the "precedent" it might have set) necessitated changing the entire university admission process of state-supported institutions and the IHL led the charge.

Eight months after Evers submitted his application, the IHL finally met on September 16, 1954, to discuss its merits. Board member David Cottrell Jr. issued a motion to discuss the application, which R. B. Smith Jr. seconded. The board acknowledged, through a resolution, that the time had come to discuss "the matter of the application of Medgar Ever [sic], of Mound Bayou, Mississippi, for admission as a student in the Law School of the University of Mississippi." It had been brought to "the attention of the Board that Evers had not complied with the rules and regulations of the University Law School which require that each applicant before being considered for admission must first file two letters of recommendation from prominent citizens of his community who have known him for at least ten years (if possible)."[100] The board agreed that Evers admittedly had fallen short in this regard.

In an attempt to justify its denunciation of Evers's application, IHL members placed the blame on Evers. They pointed out that in "support of his application Evers has stated personally, in the presence of Counsel, to the Executive Secretary of this Board [E. R. Jobe], that for the past two years he has been a resident of Mound Bayou, Mississippi, and engaged in business in that locality." They acknowledged that Evers had "submitted two letters, one purporting to be signed by A. C. Mackel, Natchez, Mississippi, and one from J. M. Thames, Decatur, Mississippi, neither of the places named being the community in which the applicant has lived for the past two years." The board, however, agreed to provide Evers with another opportunity to "comply with the regulations as to letters of recommendation." When he had submitted the proper documents, they would allow his revised submission "further consideration."[101] Evers's initial application, however, prompted the board to revise the admission requirements for Mississippi's state-supported Institutions of Higher Learning. They made this decision after having rejected Evers's application and moved on to other committee business.

After addressing other pressing IHL matters, R. B. Smith Jr. issued a motion, seconded by H. G. Carpenter, to adopt a revised admission requirement which the board "unanimously adopted." The resolution "ordered that all future applications by residents of this state for admission to any of the state supported Institutions of Higher Learning shall be supported by at least five (5) letters of recommendation as to good moral character from alumni of the institutions to which application is made. Such letters," the board continued, "shall certify to the good moral character of the applicant, shall recommend his admission to the institution, and shall be based on not less than two years personal acquaintance with the applicant." The board acknowledged, however, that recommendation letters from alumni residing in counties other than the one the applicant lived in would not be accepted "unless the applicant himself has resided in the county from which he applies for less than two years, in which latter event letters from the county of previous residence may be considered." These new changes, the board stated, would "not apply to applications for admission at the September 1954 term of such institutions." The five-letter requirement also pertained to nonresidents.[102]

The new admission policy, however, necessitated further discussions and revisions. At the IHL's November 18 meeting, the board reported that the Presidents' Council had waded in on the admission issue and thus the IHL adopted the following policy providing further rejection power to state institutions. "State-supported Institutions of Higher Learning are not obligated to accept students who are not bona-fide residents of Mississippi," the policy read. "The heads of these institutions are authorized to accept or reject non-resident applicants without a stated reason." As a means of further strengthening university gatekeepers but protecting certain applicants, the board also revised its previous admission requirement regarding its willingness to consider letters from alumni outside of the residence of the applicant. Letters from alumni from other counties would be considered if an applicant, living in a county for less than two years, found that there was an "insufficient number of alumni residing in the county of residence."[103] Evers application had upset the apple cart and forced the IHL to change its whole admission system.

Evers's name again surfaced during the IHL's December 16 meeting. Here, the "Executive Secretary presented letters of recommendation in connection with the application of Medgar W. Evers to the University Law Schook [sic], and on motion by Mr. [Charles D.] Fair, duly seconded, action on this matter was deferred until the January meeting."[104] That, meeting, however, failed to take up the issue. The IHL's approach to restructuring the admission requirements sparked lively debates. The board had noted in its September minutes that it had come to their attention "that no generally established or applied rule with reference to moral qualifications of all persons applying for admission to any of the State Supported Institutions of Higher Learning is now in existence." The board attempted to use this as justification for the new admission standards, which it believed would better serve "the welfare of all such institutions." This explanation, however, failed to convince those who quickly surmised the IHL's true intent.

The United Press reported the IHL's new stringent application requirements and labeled them as a racial barrier to university enrollment. The editorial argued that the "new regulation is designed specifically at preventing racial integration in the state's undergraduate and graduate schools."[105] Others, however, provided a stronger voice on the subject and the racial intent of the board's decision. An editorial in the *Delta Democrat-Times* attacked the idea of the board for its secrecy regarding the issue. "There is little point in the people electing public officials if the officials cease to be 'public' once they are elected and go about handling the business of the citizens as a whole as if it were the business of a closed and private cooperation." The writer noted that the intent of the IHL was clear despite its secrecy. The "dictum was made for the obvious reason that there are only white alumni of the white colleges and the board assumes that there are no[t] five of them in any community who would recommend a Negro as a student." Seeing that Evers could have possibly gotten the correct letters in time for the following session, the board "went on to make its new requirement that would apparently exclude Negroes in the future if alumni sentiment for segregation prevails." The whole process, the writer admitted, "stinks to the high heavens."[106] The fact that one of Evers's letters was written by the postmaster of Decatur seems to support this analysis.

The reality that Evers had gotten two white men to vouch for his application caught university officials off guard. It must have also surprised them that one of his letter writers, whom Charles Evers called Jim Tims (the board records him as J. M. Thames), also served as the postmaster for Decatur. His willingness to support the application may have been due to the fact that Medgar's mother had worked for him as the family maid. His position as postmaster, a federal post, may have also insulated him from economic reprisals and thus helped bolster his support.[107] The IHL's decision to deny his admittance hurt and angered Medgar.

When asked about his brother's feelings regarding the board's decision, Charles recalled the incident with a bit of anger. Medgar "was hurt over it, . . . he felt like—it was a state school funded by taxpayers and . . . [African Americans have] always been large taxpayers in this state. Why shouldn't we have the right to go to school? And because he was black, Negro, whatever we were in those days, he was refused." Charles suggests that the University of Mississippi's rejection of his brother inspired Medgar to "hook up with [James] Meredith later on and got Meredith involved" in the integration struggle to open the doors of higher academia to African

Americans on an equal basis.[108] With the aid of federal troops, James Meredith successfully integrated the University of Mississippi in 1962.

Medgar's attempt to integrate the University of Mississippi helped expose the depth of inequality in the state to a national audience. In a "Report on Mississippi" dated December 1954, Evers outlined the significance of the event. For "the first time in the history of the University of Mississippi a Negro made a formal application to its School of Law," Evers acknowledged. "There had been no other formal application by a Negro to any 'white' school in the state of Mississippi since Reconstruction."[109] For Evers, applying to the University of Mississippi represented the proverbial crack in the dam of Mississippi oppression.

Yet, the IHL's revised admission policy all but assured that African Americans would not be able to satisfy the application process and thus its universities would remain segregated.[110] This hurried change in the university's admission process represented yet another means by which the state of Mississippi attempted to stifle the progress of civil rights activism. Evers, however, continued to work on the local level to ensure that African Americans continued to fight for equality and to withstand the oppression that dogged them at every turn.

Despite failing to gain admission to the law school, Evers's attempt brought him to the attention of the national officers of the NAACP who, in light of the *Brown* decision, were looking to establish a stronghold in the state regarded as a tough nut to crack when it came to racial matters. The Supreme Court aided in this effort when it rendered its unanimous *Brown* decision on May 17, 1954. The Court concluded that "in the field of public education the doctrine of 'separate but equal' has no place. Separate educational facilities are inherently unequal." The Court reasoned that segregation produced an adverse effect upon the emotional, mental, and social standing of African Americans. "Therefore," the Court continued, "we hold that the plaintiffs and others similarly situated for whom the actions have been brought are, by reason of the segregation complained of, deprived of the equal protection of the laws guaranteed by the Fourteenth Amendment. This disposition makes unnecessary any discussion whether such segregation also violates the Due Process Clause of the Fourteenth Amendment."[111] The NAACP considered this a major victory and sought to use the momentum provided by the Court to establish a more intense civil rights agenda.

After the *Brown* decision, Thurgood Marshall, NAACP special counsel, set a target date for the desegregation "of all elementary and high schools in the United States." Marshall noted that each NAACP branch would "petition local school boards and [that] state conferences of [the] NAACP will work out [the] details." The NAACP, however, was willing to negotiate with local officials but their willingness to parley was limited. Marshall announced that the NAACP would "negotiate as long as the school board will show good faith. We will insist on de-segregation by September, 1955." He wanted to work with local authorities to carry out the Supreme Court's decision but was not opposed to going back to court if need be. He maintained that the NAACP "won't go to court until we are convinced the school board won't follow the law. If that comes about in any area, . . . we will then be required to take it to court provided some . . . Negro parents [agree and] are willing." Marshall also acknowledged that after rectifying the school issue, the NAACP would work on desegregating "park facilities, intra and interstate transportation and housing."[112] The NAACP also set its sights upon providing a full-time field organizer in the state of Mississippi.

The NAACP believed that the time for concerted action in Mississippi had arrived and they needed a person who could provide the dedication and commitment needed in a society as socially and politically closed as Mississippi. In light of the *Brown* decision, Thurgood Marshall recognized that the NAACP needed someone on the ground in the most recalcitrant of places to recruit new members, report and investigate abuses, maintain current NAACP chapters and establish new ones, as well as to conduct voter registration drives. As a consequence, Thurgood Marshall recommended that paid staff be added to "the toughest place of all, Mississippi."[113]

For the NAACP, getting a permanent association official in the state proved pertinent particularly with powerful Mississippi politicians' open defiance of the *Brown* decision. Mississippi senator James Eastland had brazenly informed the Senate that it was going to "take force to bring compliance" with the Court's desegregation ruling and that attempts to enforce the ruling would meet "stern resistance and lawlessness." Eastland wanted none to underestimate his determination to resist integration at all cost. "Let me make this very clear," he added. "There will be no compromise. . . . Southern people will not give an inch."[114] As a result of these types of public and political admonitions, Marshall understood that the position of NAACP field secretary would entail a lot, and he knew that only a person with the right physical, mental, and diplomatic skills could handle it.

The bravery and commitment Evers exuded seemed to identify him as the type of man the NAACP needed in Mississippi to successfully fulfill the job requirements. After all, Evers had worked hard organizing boycotts and gathering information concerning injustices. He also possessed an obvious rapport with the grassroots segment of Mississippi's black population, an asset most vital to the position of field secretary. In short, the NAACP leadership considered Medgar Evers an ideal candidate to become its Mississippi representative. The job of field secretary also helped Evers overcome conflicting issues between thought and deed regarding his selling insurance to the poor. He felt intense guilt about selling insurance to those he knew could least afford it, but who scraped up their premiums each period anyway to avoid burdening family members with funeral expenses. Employment with the NAACP, however, would address the growing guilt he carried around with him.

Ruby Hurley, NAACP regional secretary, had spoken with Evers earlier about the field secretary position granted that his "application for the University of Mississippi was turned down." When that transpired, she notified Evers that Gloster Current, NAACP director of branches, had instructed her "to extend an invitation to you to come to Atlanta on October 20[, 1954] at the Association's expense if you are interested [in the position]." She also informed Evers that other individuals would be interviewing for positions in other states.[115] Evers understood what a position of this type would mean to his family and thus expressed his excitement about the potential post. He proved uneasy with the waiting process and on November 16 reminded Gloster Current that his application had been mailed on November 1 "and todate, [*sic*] there has been no reply as to the consequences of the application." He further requested that the NAACP notify him regarding the status of the application by December 1, 1954.[116] Shortly after this letter, Gloster Current sent a memorandum to Roy Wilkins recommending Evers to the position, noting that Evers was "not only qualified, but courageous and impressive."[117] Roy Wilkins, NAACP administrator, sent out a letter of notification on November 24, 1954, offering Evers the job of "Assistant Field Secretary assigned to the State of Mississippi at an annual rate of $4500.00, beginning December 15, 1954." Evers quickly accepted the offer, acknowledging that he would be available and requested that they "send immediately my instructions for December 15, 1954."[118]

The conflict that Evers experienced between having to make a living as an insurance salesman to the impoverished and his belief in the necessity of civil rights struggle ended in 1954 with his acceptance of the field secretary position. The job "provided employment without the worry of exploiting blacks or of neglecting a career," argued University of Mississippi alum Cleveland Donald Jr.[119] In addition to his salary, Myrlie, whom the NAACP hired as Evers's secretary, brought home a little more than $2,000.00 dollars per year. For the first time, they had a combined income of more than $6,500.00 dollars a year, which may not have allowed for luxuries, but certainly assured that they "would have plenty to eat." NAACP work also allowed them precious moments together, which Myrlie appreciated in light of the fact that opportunities for personal time between the two dwindled more and more as time advanced.[120] Working for the NAACP also provided Evers with the political muscle to intensify his probing of white oppression and brutality of African Americans. He now had the support of an organization and a national position of leadership that complemented his previous attempts at local mobilization and organization.

The time Medgar Evers spent in the Mississippi Delta had strengthened his commitment to combat racism. The poverty, economic exploitation, and fear he saw mirrored on the faces of sharecroppers, their families, and the general community altered his perception of what his personal goals in life should be. He became less comfortable with the simple notion of attaining success in the business field. While in Mound Bayou, he organized people to challenge oppression while he sought organizational support for his desire to change the social and political structure of the Delta region. He found that support in the Regional Council of Negro Leadership. Through the RCNL, Evers worked to enhance his effectiveness in organizing and instituting social and political change. His promotion to NAACP field secretary, however, seemed a more perfect fit for Evers, and he believed it would strengthen his calls for change due to its historical pedigree as the premiere civil rights organization in the country.

Evers later came to discover that working for the NAACP offered its own challenges. Yet, the organization provided him with financial stability and offered further legitimacy to his calls for change. Although his new position required that he move from the Delta to the capital city of Jackson, he never forgot about the plight of the farming class. It remained an important part of his base when it came to organizing the grassroots to challenge the hypocrisy of a supposedly democratic society.

3.

The Face of Social Change

THE NAACP IN MISSISSIPPI

When you hate, the only one that suffers is you because most of the people you hate don't know it and the rest don't care.
—Medgar Evers

Every time I think about my kids and their innocence, I wonder how whites can make the youngsters suffer so. I guess that thought keeps me in NAACP work.
—Medgar Evers

No man has come to true greatness who has not felt in some degree that his life belongs to his race, and that what God gives him he gives him for mankind.
—Quoted in Medgar Evers, "News and Views"

PRIOR TO THE BIRTH of the NAACP in 1909, there were much more radical calls for an organization devoted to establishing social and political change in America. In 1905, William Edward Burghardt (W. E. B.) Du Bois served as the chief organizer of the Niagara Movement. The twenty-nine delegates met at Niagara Falls, Canada, and outlined what would be their organizational assault on racism and inequality. The organization sought to challenge Tuskegee Institute founder Booker T. Washington's seemingly "accommodationist" ideology. In response, the organization advocated direct action in the pursuit of voting rights for African Americans, the end of segregation in all of its manifestations, and the attainment of all social and political rights due African Americans as citizens of the United States. As an organization, however, the Niagara Movement could not sustain the kind of general support needed to continue past the few years it proved viable. Many individuals, white philanthropists in particular, were neither ready to accept nor support its radical message of protest and by 1908 it had collapsed.[1] The NAACP became the next group to rise as an organizational force in the fight for civil equality.

As an organization, the NAACP began in 1909 in response to the Springfield riots in Illinois the year before.[2] Responding to a call for action by writer William English Walling, New York social worker Mary W. Ovington, working with Walling, Henry Moskowitz, and Oswald Garrison Villard, called for a conference with the purpose of organizing a body capable of standing against racial violence and injustice. Prominent African American leaders were asked to attend. These included influential clergymen such as Bishop Alexander Walters of the African Methodist Episcopal Zion Church and Reverend William Henry Brooks of St. Mark's Methodist Episcopal Church. Over the course of several meetings, organizers planned for a larger gathering, billed "A Conference on the Status of the Negro" and later the National Negro Conference, which met in New York on May 31 and June 1, 1909. The radical elements of the African American protest movement were also represented in the personages of W. E. B. Du Bois, antilynching advocate Ida B. Wells-Barnett, activist and women's club movement organizer Mary Church Terrell, and Boston *Guardian* editor William Monroe Trotter.[3] The NAACP, organized and controlled by whites in its early stages, developed out of the "National Negro Conference" and claimed as members many of those who had belonged to the radical Niagara Movement. W. E. B. Du Bois served as director of publications and research for the new organization as well as its only African American executive officer.[4]

The objectives of the new organization were clear and straightforward. Historians John Hope Franklin and Alfred Moss Jr. note that the "organization pledged itself to work for the abolition of all forced segregation, equal education for black and white children, the complete enfranchisement of male African Americans . . . , and the enforcement of the Fourteenth and Fifteenth Amendments."[5] Programmatically, the NAACP sought to challenge inequality through active opposition to racial hatred and prejudice. Historian Manfred Berg argues that the association "hoped to accomplish its objectives primarily through 'the argument of the printed and the spoken word,' and 'by individual relief of the wretched.'"[6] Medgar Evers, some forty-five years later, embodied everything the NAACP had stood for throughout its brief history: dedication, sacrifice, perseverance, and a strong sense of fair play irrevocably intertwined with an intolerance for racial injustice. If the NAACP believed that it had found its "Mississippi man" in 1954, Medgar Evers also believed that he had found in the NAACP an organization best suited to his mentality and leadership style.

The new field secretary position required that Evers move his family from Mound Bayou to Jackson, Mississippi. Despite the fact that he had to leave the poverty-stricken Delta, the strong and rigorous work ethic he developed during childhood continued unabated. Evers, however, did not receive official word from the national office confirming the field secretary position until late November 1954. By mid-December, Gloster B. Current sent a letter formally welcoming Medgar "to the National Office staff as a member of the Branch Department." Current further encouraged Evers to continue investigating abuses and to secure as many affidavits as possible to support the information he had already presented to the Southeast Regional Advisory Board Meeting. As a part of the hiring process, Evers flew to New York on January 2, 1955, to complete a ten-day orientation process. Current impressed upon Medgar that the Mississippi state office should be set up shortly upon his return, but no later than January 23, when he hoped to have an open house to commemorate its readiness to serve the interests of the African American public. Evers had things in place by the twenty-third and worked to publicize the event through advertisements and letters of invitation. He also invited high-ranking Mississippi officials including Jackson mayor Allen Thompson and Governor Hugh White.[7] In the beginning, the state office operated out of a building located at 507½ North Farish Street. During the latter part of the year, the NAACP leadership decided to move its state headquarters to the black-owned Masonic Temple building on Lynch Street. The reason for the move surrounded both a need for space and the fact that their current location resided "in a building where the landlord . . . [did] not furnish janitorial service," Gloster Current reported, "and the halls are very dirty." Evers proved grateful that his "request to move to the Masonic Temple Building was granted."[8] The request for a move to a more amiable location highlighted Evers's belief that appearance was everything and one could not ignore this fact and expect a positive result.

Although Evers welcomed the financial opportunities the position afforded, he had debts he needed to clear before he could sever ties to Mound Bayou. In a letter to Current dated December 21, 1954, Evers offered his apologies as well as the reality of his financial situation. He admitted that "starting off in the red is not good business practice for either the employee or the employer, but it is about the only course of action I can take. I have tried banks, private individuals and even the Credit Union here in Mound Bayou where I have done business since being here, but none have responded favorably." Evers needed $482.86 to pay off his debt, a pretty hefty sum for 1954. The NAACP approved his request and sent a check "in the amount of $500.00 representing an advance on . . . [his] salary" at the pay-back rate of $25.00 per salary check ($50.00/month) over a ten-month period.[9] This would not be the last time that circumstances required Evers to request a financial advance from NAACP headquarters.

Medgar Evers remained committed to fighting for civil equality regardless of the personal or financial consequences, the latter often taking a heavy toll on his family. His brother Charles maintained that of everything that Medgar symbolized, a savvy businessperson he was not. He labeled his brother as more of a communicator than a businessman. Medgar, according to Charles, was not a person who could put money aside for himself because the moment a person needed something he would give his last. This behavior may not have represented the mark of a good businessman, but it certainly indicated that of a great humanitarian.[10]

Myrlie noted that Medgar never craved recognition. In fact, he let her know that the struggle he waged was never about the glorification of the self, but rather "about the mission and the little people" suffering from segregation, brutality, and inequality. As a consequence of his devotion to the welfare of African Americans, "Money, power, and prestige were unimportant" as indicators of wealth and self-worth.[11] Although Evers understood the dire state of African Americans in Mississippi, very few persons outside of the state truly understood the extent of the repressive tactics used to retain control over Mississippi's African American population. Evers, however, was instrumental in shattering the harmonious façade that Mississippi officials insisted represented black/white relations within the state.

Nineteen fifty-four provided Evers the opportunity to assume a leadership position and align his sense of fair play with an organization boasting an impressive history of fighting for first-class citizenship. For both Evers and the NAACP, however, the year proved to be an extensive learning experience. A permanent NAACP presence in Mississippi proved a new venture without the benefit of established road maps. The job of field secretary required Evers to make quick decisions using his best judgment to get things moving in a positive direction. The position, Roy Wilkins informed Evers, included "conducting membership campaigns; conferring with branch officers and committees in shaping of local programs and interpretation of the national program; stimulating committee work; lecturing and demonstrating on procedure and tactics; filling speaking engagements on Association work and on the race problem generally with branches and other groups."[12] He would have to decide where and when to organize new branches and how to convince African Americans to join the NAACP despite the possible negative consequences of doing so. Yet the Supreme Court's ruling in *Brown v. Board* placed pressure on the NAACP to move into the South, and it is here that Medgar Evers served another important NAACP function.

For civil rights activists in the 1950s, Mississippi's history seemed to make it impervious to change of any kind. By most accounts, the state epitomized the Old Confederacy and its social and political ideals regarding race relations. The *Brown* decision provided African Americans with the legal opening to challenge Mississippi lawmakers' ability to uphold unequal practices in the future. In addition to Mississippi, Thurgood Marshall also recommended that paid staff be added to Florida, North Carolina, Georgia, and Texas. The NAACP leadership understood that, in light of the *Brown* decision, they needed a cadre of people on the ground in the South who knew the area and could navigate among its people. It would be these civil rights sentinels the NAACP charged with beginning "the fight in the schools," Nossiter explained, and who would "call attention to brutalities, . . . [and] sign up new members." Mississippi required a certain type of individual: one who was tough, unwavering, dedicated, and willing to take the system head-on despite the apparent dangers, and Medgar Evers appeared to be the right man for the job.[13] As many African Americans expected, the *Brown* decision intensified violence and white supremacist organizing across the nation, but particularly within Mississippi.[14]

Many white Mississippians were stunned by the *Brown* decision. In response, elected officials went on the defensive and rallied support for the system of segregation. The Mississippi Legislature had already attempted to show good faith, and possibly influence the Court's decision, by enacting a public school equalization program during the latter part of 1953. Mississippi governor Hugh White had already recommended "to a special session of the Mississippi legislature," a NAACP press release reported, "that schools be equalized in order to maintain 'cherished segregation traditions.'"[15] The plan promised to do away with many of the obvious disparities between blacks and whites in the field of education. The approved legislative measures allowed for equal salaries for teachers regardless of race, equal opportunities for African American students, equal transportation facilities, and a few other choice amenities. The legislature, however, did not appropriate the money needed to pay for this enrichment plan pending a favorable Court ruling. Anticipating a negative verdict, the legislature established the Legal Educational Advisory Committee (LEAC) to protect the system of educational segregation. The LEAC, according to McMillen, "would serve as the planning agency for Mississippi's defiance of the federal mandate."[16] Other individuals, though, were not willing to depend solely upon the legislative branch to protect segregation and white supremacy in Mississippi.

As the reality of integration dawned on those in the South, many whites felt the need to maintain white supremacy at all costs and no state epitomized this need more than Mississippi. President Dwight Eisenhower's lackluster position regarding *Brown* did nothing to strum up local support. He refused to publicly endorse the Court's decision or to provide the South with direction on how to best implement the decision. African Americans were not impressed with his assurances that he would enforce the ruling.[17] Claude Ramsay, Mississippi labor leader and former president of the Mississippi American Federation of Labor-Congress of Industrial Organizations (AFL-CIO), maintained that as a result of Eisenhower's lack of a strong showing of support for the *Brown* decision, "a vacuum was created and we then saw a counter force begin to develop in the form of a White Citizens Council movement, especially here in Mississippi."[18] This could clearly be seen in Sunflower County where segregation appeared absolute. Despite its totality, the historian J. Todd Moye argues that massive resistance to integration had to be manufactured.[19] Yet, many white Sunflower Countians took up the mantle of resistance with great enthusiasm.

Southern grassroots resistance movements looked to their leadership for direction in responding to the *Brown* decision. Immediately after the Court's ruling, Mississippi and Georgia politicos such as Senator James Eastland and Governor Herman Talmadge touted southern conservative ideals and railed against the Court's decision.[20] Historian Numan V. Bartley remarked that the "Border states used the interlude [between *Brown* I and II] to make constructive preparations for compliance." The "Deep South [however,] entrenched itself yet further."[21] Mississippi, Alabama, and Georgia fought desegregation attempts, and as time progressed, each proved more determined to defend the southern ideal of racial separation. Over time, Bartley continued, the "Deep South sank deeper into hysterical reaction," and "like an unstable planet, swayed between their magnetic attraction of North and South."[22]

White Mississippians considered the *Brown* decision another northern attempt to subjugate the South and to destroy the "racial harmony" that prevailed. Politically astute individuals such as Mississippi circuit judge Thomas Pickens Brady viewed the decision as a thinly veiled attempt by northern liberals, communist factions, and NAACP agents to destroy the South and institute their own amalgamation-based agenda. "The great barrier to the integration of the races has been segregation," Brady wrote in his pamphlet *Black Monday.* "It is also the greatest factor for peace and harmony between the races." Brady considered *Brown* a racial problem with larger social and political consequences: the infiltration and establishment of socialism and communism that threatened the very sanctity of true Americanism. The South, he believed, had to stand against the threat in all of its components and be willing to do so with violence if necessary. Brady warned those who supported integration that you "shall not show us how a white man 'may go through the guts' of a negro! You shall not mongrelize our children and grandchildren."[23] Southern fears that their ways of life and that the sanctity and safety of southern childhood and womanhood were under attack created a movement of massive resistance to racial progress in the Deep South. The birth of the Citizens' Council demonstrated how sincere white segregationist hardliners were in their desires to preserve southern culture and control the black population and none proved more virulent in this endeavor than the state of Mississippi.

Massive resistance in Mississippi proved to be a two-pronged beast. On one side of the divide lay influential politicians such as Mississippi governor James P. Coleman and U.S. senator John Stennis who advocated a somewhat moderate approach. This group sought to mediate the segregation issue out of the public eye and among levelheaded whites and acceptable black leaders—the goal being the institution of what Coleman coined "practical segregation" based on equalization. This plan, of course, was nothing other than an attempt to revert back to the 1896 *Plessy* decision. Other southern leaders such as Judge Brady and Senator Eastland, however, took a much harder line on the issue of segregation and favored the creation of an organized resistance movement.[24]

In July 1954, Robert "Tut" Patterson, a plantation manager in Sunflower County, gathered like-minded men together in the west Mississippi town of Indianola and created the Citizens' Council. The group organized to defy the Court's ruling, protect white supremacy, and use economic pressure to intimidate African Americans from supporting desegregation efforts. Although council members relied upon economic intimidation, many were not opposed to using violence to protect the system of racial segregation. Historian Joseph Crespino noted that the council "was, in their minds, a counter to what African Americans had in the National Association for the Advancement of Colored People." Although small in the beginning, the White Citizens' Council eventually spread to neighboring states and, in a few years time, exceeded 30,000 members. Aaron Henry, a pharmacist and active member of the NAACP, recalled that their "goals were to make it impossible for any Negro in favor of desegregation to find or keep a job, to cut off his credit or mortgage renewal, and to discourage Negro voting. It was also clear that whites who were sympathetic to civil rights would suffer the same reprisals."[25]

For white southerners in particular, the Court's decision in *Brown* indicated dire social and political changes in America's future racial hierarchy. As a consequence, many southern politicians argued that the heightened involvement of the federal government in state business amounted to encroachment upon states' rights and they sought to circumvent the work of the Court. An NAACP release announced that Mississippi senator James Eastland and congressman John Bell Williams had introduced S.J. Res. 159 and H.J. Res. 532 asking that Congress "approve a constitutional amendment which, if ratified by the States, would destroy the Court's jurisdiction in matters of racial segregation."[26] With the advent of the Supreme Court's *Brown* decision, southern states went on the defensive, and Mississippi led the way in the fight over state sovereignty and the ideology of segregation.[27] African Americans knew all too well that violence often accompanied whites' social frustrations resulting from African American resistance and group organization.

Historian Michael R. Belknap connects the escalation of violence against African Americans to the expansion of social and political rights during the 1950s and 1960s. The "drive to expand black civil rights, which accelerated so dramatically in the years following the Supreme Court's 1954 [*Brown*] decision . . . , met violent resistance from a militant minority of southern whites. Although those who committed this anti-civil rights violence were guilty of murder, assault, arson, and numerous other crimes proscribed by state law, their offenses generally went unpunished."[28] Other scholars also argue for the emergence of a white "backlash" in response to black advancement during the 1950s and 1960s.

Michael Klarman maintained that the *Brown* decision, in particular, "crystallized southern resistance to racial change, which . . . had been scattered and episodic." Furthermore, it produced a southern political climate conducive to racial extremism that continued well into the 1960s. For Klarman, "the post-*Brown* racial backlash created a political environment in which southern elected officials stood to benefit at the polls by boldly defying federal authority and brutally suppressing civil rights demonstrations.[29] For black Mississippians this came as no surprise. For, as civil rights activist John Salter Jr. noted, when it came to civil rights agitation, Mississippi operated "as a garrison state that viewed itself not only as being prepared for war but as already fighting a war."[30]

The lack of judicial support for African Americans fighting oppression angered and frustrated Evers because he witnessed the day-to-day misery of those victimized by white oppression and violence. More disturbing remained the fact that the oppression many faced was often carried out with the blessing, if not direct assistance, of local law officials. Although the May 17 Court decision represented a huge victory for the NAACP, it proved a hollow one for African Americans who soon realized that nothing had changed. As enforcement limitations of the Court's decision materialized, many African Americans internalized what Aaron Henry openly acknowledged: "The Supreme Court had given . . . [African Americans] a beautifully wrapped gift, but when we removed the shiny wrappings, the box was empty."[31] Evers and community activists had to contend with community feelings of helplessness and frustration when *Brown* failed to topple segregation right away and they had to do so with urgency in order to keep community support for organized struggle alive and viable.

Although Medgar Evers did not assume the official duties of NAACP field secretary until January 1955, he had been battling the problems associated with a rising white resistance movement and the violence it engendered well before any official appointment to the NAACP. Despite intensified resistance to black empowerment, Evers took on the role of field secretary with a gritty determination to exact progressive change. The seriousness with which he approached his position materialized as early as April 2, 1955, when Evers announced in the *Jackson Advocate* that the recruitment of two thousand new members represented their immediate goal.[32] His commitment to *voter registration* complemented the national strategy of the NAACP for attaining racial equality. As field secretary, Evers proved quite effective in directing the intense light of public opinion upon the dark face of the South.

Medgar Evers successfully aroused national curiosity regarding the treatment of African Americans in Mississippi. He personally investigated and documented crimes of physical brutality against black Mississippians as well as the emotional scars that beatings, rapes, and murders left behind. By sending documentation to New York, Evers allowed the truth of brutality and repression to escape Mississippi's iron curtain of media silence. As a direct result of his investigations and reports, George Metcalf observed, "a national campaign to combat the horrible conditions prevailing in Mississippi began."[33] The constant examples Evers provided the NAACP of the brutality and oppression blacks faced in Mississippi proved a source of embarrassment for government officials when appearing in NAACP press releases and national newspapers such as the *Pittsburgh Courier* or the *Afro-American*. Nossiter explained that for oppressed African Americans in Mississippi, this represented a significant accomplishment since prior to "Evers's advent, scores of such incidents had left no more lasting trace than a few sarcastic paragraphs in the local newspaper, or the isolated story in a northern newspaper, at most."[34] It is apparent that Medgar's investigations helped to nationalize Mississippi's previously ignored patterns of racial violence. Yet, how did these acts of violence against African Americans trigger in Evers the need to stay in Mississippi when so many others, including his siblings, chose to leave?

Part of Evers's decision to remain in Mississippi can be attributed to his "capacity for sympathizing with the underdog, the one who was oppressed, a natural instinct to help people who were in trouble."[35] Although Adam Nossiter identifies a critical component of the dogged determination Evers displayed, other explanations for his commitment to Mississippi demand attention. The religious influence his mother had on the family remains a critical component to his overall dedication to the state.

Religion has always played a primary role in the development and structure of the African American community since it supplied comfort during times of strife as well as mechanisms for revolt against injustice. The church has always been the center of the African American social movement. Whether used as meeting places for strategizing or places for spiritual recuperation, the church and African American religious services played a vital role in the struggle for social change and educating upcoming generations on their social responsibilities. As a consequence, historian David Chappell argues that "it may be misleading to view the civil rights movement as a social and political event that had religious overtones." Many individuals considered the civil rights movement as a religious event "whose social and political aspects," Chappell continued, "were, in their minds, secondary or incidental."[36] However, African Americans expected much more from their religious practices than spiritual rapture; they understood that true fulfillment meant physical work and sacrifice and none more than Martin Luther King Jr. exemplified this ideal. "The belief that God will do everything for man is as untenable as the belief that man can do everything for himself . . . ," maintained King. "We must learn that to expect God to do everything while we do nothing is not faith but superstition."[37] The church became an important mechanism for teaching young boys and girls their individual worth and value and their responsibility to resist oppression and inequality. It also became an effective platform for religious leaders such as Fred Shuttlesworth, Ralph Abernathy, T. J. Jemison, Malcolm X, and a host of others who were important leaders in the Black Freedom struggle.[38]

Both James and Jessie Evers accepted religion as a necessary part of everyday life, and the children attended church services several times a week. Noted psychologist Jacqueline S. Mattis argued that "religious socialization shapes how adults and youth make meaning of and interpret the world, as well as how they negotiate social and emotional situations."[39] Individual negotiations regarding "social and emotional situations" have often come in the form of open challenges to socially preconceived ideals of inferiority and or racial degeneration. In response to the social and political ills of the society in which she lived and raised a family, Jessie Evers drilled into the psyche of her children "Biblical precepts like the brotherhood of all men," which Medgar undoubtedly took to heart. She also instilled in her children the belief that "they were no better or worse than anyone else, and they believed her."[40] Nossiter noted that as a result of these life lessons, Medgar's upbringing, built upon a foundation of self-worth and fair play, convinced him that "Mississippi's . . . [ways of oppression] must be overturned."[41] At the very heart of individual growth lay the social, communal, and familial act of socialization.

Sociologists contend that it is through socialization that individuals learn their place in both the family and society as a whole. At the very heart of the socializing process rests the family unit. The process of racial socialization has been used over the course of America's history to uplift certain members of society while, at the same time, stifling the social, political, and cultural development of others. Historically, the educational system in America has venerated the history and social worth of white Americans while simultaneously denigrating the social worth of Native Americans, Mexican Americans, Asians, and African Americans.

Psychologists Stephanie I. Coard and Robert M. Sellers have examined the impact of racial socialization and the significance of the African American family in the overall process. Both define racial socialization "as the process by which messages are transmitted/communicated inter- and intragenerationally regarding the significance and meaning of race and ethnicity." They further contend that "racial socialization involves teaching children values and norms associated with race and ethnicity, and problem-solving skills that enable children to be flexible in their approach to race-related situations without losing a core sense of self."[42] In a southern society built upon the use of violence to control and subjugate "minority" groups, it often proved difficult for African American families to protect their children's self-esteem and sense of self-worth. One only has to revisit the results of social psychologist Kenneth and Mamie Clark's doll test to understand the psychological damage that white supremacy and Jim Crow practices created in the African American psyche and its negative impact upon the community. Sometimes parents used fear as a mechanism for protecting their children from racial violence while also attempting to protect their core sense of self.

Fred Clark Sr., a Mississippi activist, recalled that fear proved a common tactic parents used to protect their children from a hostile environment. As a child, he remembered his aunts telling the children "ghost stories during that time [of the Emmett Till lynching, 1955] to keep us off the street because the police would beat up black kids if they'd catch you out or they'd beat you up and do ever what else they want with you. So the parents and stuff feared for our lives and safety, so they would often tell us ghost stories to scare us into the house."[43] Tactics such as this had permeated the black community since the days of slavery and were used to offer both physical and mental protection for black boys and girls. Both sociologists and psychologists acknowledge the importance of an individual's core sense of self-worth to their progressive development. However, for African Americans during the Jim Crow era, the protection of that self-centered core proved both vital and yet so hard to keep alive and vibrant within the psyche of the upcoming generation.

Coard and Sellers also concur with conclusions reached by A. W. Boykin and F. D. Toms regarding the significance of racial socialization in the African American family. Coard and Sellers acknowledged that African Americans have a different experience than whites when it comes to preparing their children to interact in a world that proves nonsupportive and, at times, hostile. They contend that "African American parents recognize that being Black means that their children must prepare for a nonsupportive world and learn how to survive and cope with racial prejudice, racial discrimination, and racism." As a result, they point to parents' desire to ensure that their children understood the reality of their social position within the larger society. As a means of protecting their children as best they could, Coard and Sellers maintain that "many African American parents . . . point to the need for their children to understand the social, economic, and political forces impinging on racial equality in order to enhance their ability to cope with the realities associated with being Black in America."[44] For Medgar Evers, however, his parents' insistence that African Americans do for themselves, demand respect from all they met, and internalize the knowledge that they were as good as anybody else in the world regardless of skin color, provided a brand of racial socialization that protected and enhanced the self-centered core.

Evers's incubation period, within a family unit emphasizing complete social and political equality, produced an individual who could do nothing less than challenge any system or individual intent on stifling one's awareness of self-worth and access to equal and fair treatment as a citizen of the larger society. For Medgar Evers, the solution to defeating inequality was not merely to develop the ability "to survive and cope with racial prejudice, racial discrimination, and racism" hoping to eventually wear it down, nor was it to relocate to a place where it existed less overtly. He believed that to

stamp out injustice where one lived and then to spread that triumph outwardly in a concentric circle until social and political inequality no longer
existed as a viable system of oppression was the only real solution to the
problem of inequality.

In 1958, *Ebony* published an interview with Medgar Evers titled "Why
I Live in Mississippi." Here Evers spoke candidly with *Ebony* correspondent
Francis H. Mitchell throughout the interview concerning his love for
Mississippi. From his comments it is easy to understand his reasons for
remaining in the state. He explained to Mitchell that there was too much to
lose by leaving. Evers envisioned a better Mississippi and understood that
to leave it would be to turn his back upon what Mississippi *could* be, for an
acceptance of what it *now* was: chaotic, merciless, and uncivilized. He
maintained that Mississippi represents "home. [It] is a part of the United
States. And whether the whites like it or not, I don't plan to live here as a
parasite. The things that I don't like I will try to change."[45] Change, for
Evers, could only come with a cadre of committed people willing to struggle,
fight, work and, if need be, die to bring about social and political equality
for African Americans.

Evers made several references to his family as reasons why he chose to
fight for Mississippi's future. He compared the upbringing of whites to that
of African American youth. While noticing a young white boy during his
interview with Mitchell, Evers pointed out that the little boy was "free.
They've [white society] taught him that he owns the world. That's what I
want for my kids—freedom—right here in Mississippi. And as long as God
gives me strength to work and try to make things real for my children, I'm
going to work for it. . . . And in the long run, I hope to make a positive contribution to the overall productivity of the South."[46] Evers had been around
Delta sharecroppers long enough to understand that, as with agriculture,
social, economic, and political advancement and productivity could only
occur with careful tending and the constant weeding out of the undesirable.
For Medgar Evers, the younger generations were the most important element for combating the undesirable growth of racism. Evers affirmed that
the youth would be "the leaders in the future fight. . . . [And thus,] have a
definite responsibility to help, because much of what we are struggling for
now will benefit them directly 10 years from now—will open up opportunities that were not open when I came along."[47]

Arguably, the most influential event that helped solidify Evers's commitment to the movement and Mississippi occurred in 1954 on the night that
his father passed away. The circumstances surrounding the death of his
father left a lasting impression. He recalled:

I was in the basement of the hospital at Union, Mississippi (that's where Negro patients stayed), at my dad's bedside. He had had a hemorrhage and was sinking fast. I heard a rising murmur of voices . . . a rushing of feet, and there was an ugly crowd outside the building. A nurse called me upstairs and asked me to help. There was a Negro, with his leg bandaged. He had been in a fracas with a policeman, someone had shot him in the leg. The whites were like madmen, muttering among themselves about the "nigger," peeping in the windows to see if they could spot him. My dad died a short time later, and outside, these whites were demonstrating like animals. I've never forgotten that either. A Negro cannot live here [in Mississippi] or die here in peace as long as things remain as they are.[48]

Much like the Tingle lynching, Evers used the helplessness experienced through personal and shared tragedies, and the degrading circumstances surrounding the death of his father, as a catalyst for change and a mechanism for strengthening his resolve to eliminate oppression and racism. Myrlie maintained that as "much as anything he saw around him, I think that experience at his father's deathbed convinced Medgar that he had to continue his personal crusade against injustice and segregation."[49] In reference to the overall behavior of whites, Evers acknowledged that there "are some of . . . [their] ways that I don't care for, . . . [but] as long as God gives me strength to work and change them, I'm going to do it."[50] Thus, in order to save Mississippi, he had to stay and fight for its redemption and the NAACP proved a vital component in his growing arsenal.

For Medgar Evers, the NAACP served as a resource mechanism that could provide protection, financial assistance, and legal support for persons willing to stand against oppression. Although he maintained a friendly relationship with the NAACP leadership, Charles Evers believes that organizational leaders did not always have the best interest of his brother at heart. He maintained that the NAACP leadership "used [Medgar] . . . to further the NAACP and they wanted to use somebody who they could direct and tell what to do. And Medgar would sorta, somehow, go along with some of the things they said. I wouldn't."[51] Medgar continued to view the NAACP as his primary vehicle of support in the civil rights movement. In spite of his growing disillusionment with their lack of encouragement for direct-action tactics, he remained loyal to the organization.

Economic pressures that whites placed on African Americans proved to be one of the biggest problems Medgar had to overcome in his fight to convince African Americans to stand up and challenge discrimination and oppression. The tactic of economic repression hit farmers and businessmen harder than others because of their dependency upon loans for seeds, supplies, or start-up funds for business ventures. Both represented the socioeconomic group that Evers relied upon the most to carry out NAACP programs and mandates. The NAACP sought to deflate this type of economic tactic by working with the African American owned and controlled Tri-State Bank of Memphis, Tennessee.

By establishing an economic relationship with Tri-State Bank, Gloster Current noted that the NAACP was responding to the economic threats of the White Citizens' Council. The NAACP "met the propaganda effect of their [WCC] announcements, which was to scare Negroes, with a counter-propaganda by announcing a program to build up a financial institution in Memphis whereby a Negro institution would offer relief to those who constituted good credit risk," Current explained.[52] Tri-State Bank agreed to work with farmers who met their loan requirements but who also agreed to deposit money with the bank as a means of helping it expand. In a letter written to Reverend J. E. Johnson of Yazoo City, Mississippi, dated January 19, 1955, Roy Wilkins, administrator of the NAACP, explained the loan program established with Tri-State Bank. Wilkins assured Reverend Johnson that the "national office of the NAACP is working to see that money is available for loans to those Mississippi farmers, homeowners, business and professional men who are being denied credit by white financial institutions because of their views on civil rights." He further assured Johnson that Tri-State Bank president Dr. J. E. Walker had "agreed to give special attention to applications for loans from Mississippians if additional money is deposited with the bank in savings accounts so that it can expand its loan program."[53]

Wilkins acknowledged that the NAACP had already deposited "$20,000 of its reserve funds in a savings account at the Tri-State bank" and had also encouraged other businesses to do the same. The overall goal was to establish a minimum of five hundred thousand dollars in new accounts. The loans, however, were not free expressions of financial good will; they came with strings attached. Wilkins pointed out that all "loans will be available on regular bank terms. The whole transaction is on a strictly business basis, handled by the bank in the regular way. Each applicant must satisfy the bank's usual requirements for a loan, including the usual security. The point is that if Mississippians have difficulty in getting loans, on regular terms, from banks in the state, they can apply to the Tri-State bank in Memphis."[54] Wilkins identified Medgar as the contact person for those in need of the services Tri-State Bank provided and this presented Evers with an all-important selling point for standing against oppression: African American economic independence. The added responsibility, however, increased his workload.

Myrlie noted that the Tri-State Bank program added to the overall workload that her husband balanced each day. He was immersed, Myrlie recalled, in "passing along requests for loans from victims of economic reprisal, sending their applications . . . , answering their complaints, explaining procedure, apologizing for delay, [and] soothing ruffled feelings when a loan was turned down."[55] Gloster Current later reminded Medgar that his primary job would be to gather facts, affidavits, and financial information of discrimination that would "substantiate any charge made by the Association." Current believed that the Tri-State Bank program would eventually pressure white bank officials into reconsidering their discriminatory loan practices when learning of their loss of business to an out-of-state financial entity.[56] Evers quickly found that the role of field secretary was indeed a multifaceted one.

Evers took his role as field secretary to heart and never missed an opportunity to combat misconceptions and outright attacks upon the character of African Americans in general and the NAACP in particular. On February 8, 1955, the *Jackson Daily News* reported that while speaking before the Laurel Lions Club, Mississippi candidate for governor Paul B. Johnson Jr. assured the audience that as "a private citizen, . . . [he would] fight with every ounce of strength to maintain segregation, for the ultimate result is intermarriage." Johnson explained, however, that white Mississippians wanted African Americans "to progress within their own limitations and inherent capabilities. They will continue to advance if they are left alone by the long-hair do-gooders and neo-socialists and minority groups that do not have the Mississippi Negro's best interest at heart."[57] The following day, Evers countered with a hint of anger and an uncommon measure of biblical comparison. In defense of the NAACP, Evers issued an organizational release to respond to Johnson's comments. In the statement, Evers proclaimed that it

> should be made perfectly clear to Mr. Johnson Jr. and all who think like him that the NAACP lives by the Holy Bible and the Constitution of the United States of America and as long as those two noble documents are kept alive, the NAACP will continue to fight, here in Mississippi, for those things that they guarantee—-Life, Liberty, and the Pursuit of Happiness. Not for the White man, nor just the Black man, but for every Freedom loving American.
>
> The Bible speaks of the Savior as being no respector [*sic*] of persons— the NAACP doesn't digress from this mode of thinking and acting one iota.[58]

Johnson had also spoke on the issue of "Negro" responsibility and argued that blacks must bear some of the responsibility for the inferior position they held in society.

In conjunction with his calls for continued segregation between the races, Johnson maintained that "we hear too much talk on the Negro's right but we hear nothing about the Negro's responsibilities. . . . We have failed to hold the Negro's feet to the fire of responsibility. . . . We have been too soft in the matter of the Negro helping to pay his way."[59] Evers, in further defense of the rights and integrity of African Americans, made sure that his statement contained a stringent reply to Johnson's claims of Negro irresponsibility. He chose to use conclusions made by Johnson regarding the need for responsibility to support his argument for African American political participation on an equal basis. He insinuated that surely:

> Mr. Johnson must be aware of the fact that responsibilities normally come after privileges. If that is the case, then would it not be logical and within keeping with your idea of responsibility Mr. Johnson, that Forrest County[, Mississippi] give all citizens, black or white the same opportunity to become qualified electors so that the Negro might assume his rightful share of the responsibility of electing competent public officials?

> Such utterances bespeaks [*sic*] the underlying moral respect one has for another.

> We shall not rest until Demagogues like you are driven from the Political Arena of Mississippi.[60]

Evers translated racial attacks as personal assaults against the integrity of African Americans, and he refused to allow such attacks to go unchallenged.

The NAACP relied upon Medgar to investigate instances of abuse, physical, verbal, or otherwise, against the African American populace in Mississippi. As a result, he investigated charges of police brutality, murder, voter discrimination, economic sanctions against African Americans, and a host of other injustices. In a report to Roy Wilkins dated March 25, 1955, Evers recounted his "personal inquiry into the alleged maltreatment [of Paul Ferguson] at the hands of law enforcement officers" in the north Mississippi town of New Albany. The bus that Ferguson traveled on passed through New Albany on its way to East Saint Louis, Illinois. After his two-day investigation, March 22–23, Evers concluded that

> Mr. Ferguson's Civil Rights without question was violated. The young man asked the bus driver how many more stops would the bus make before reaching its destination, after receiving the answer he (Ferguson) made the expression "Oh Jesus!" which the bus driver did not like coming from a Negro to a white man, so the driver took a swing at the

young man [he actually hit Ferguson in the head with a ticket puncher] who at an instance had knocked the bus driver down and started beating him. A Negro woman is said to have pulled Ferguson off the driver.[61]

After the altercation, Ferguson went straight to City Hall for police protection, which they denied him. In his report, Evers recorded that when "the driver caught up with Ferguson and the police, the police told Ferguson that he did not hit white men in this part of the country and consequently held him while the driver hit him and kicked him." Ferguson recalled that while in the cell, he was kicked and beaten with a blackjack by the sheriff and when he fell from the blows, "the bus driver kicked me in the eye." Ferguson pointed out that he was dressed in his "Air Force uniform." The bus driver also assaulted Ferguson's wife, who was pregnant at the time. "After having beaten Ferguson," Evers reported, "the police locked him in a cell while his wife stood by helplessly." Although Reverend J. L. Tolbert and other members of the black community paid the $250.00 bond to have Ferguson released, it remained "the general feeling among the residents of the community," Evers remarked, "that there should be some Federal protection for Ferguson when he . . . [returned] for trial on April 5."[62] The NAACP was so dependent upon Medgar and his work in Mississippi that any mishap in sending needed or requested information to the national office elicited sound reprimands.

While preparing an NAACP statement for circulation in a daily paper in Washington, D.C., as well as for the *New York Times,* the *Pittsburgh Courier, Chicago Defender,* and the *Afro-American,* the national office received a late editorial from Jackson, Mississippi, entitled "Yes, We Defy the Law." The editorial contained the sentence "If the Supreme Court decision is the law of the land then we intend to violate the law of the land." The fact that the Mississippi office had failed to get this pertinent clipping to the national office resulted in a wordy reprimand. Although NAACP headquarters secured the story in time to issue a statement, Wilkins stressed to Medgar the necessity of getting information such as this in on time. NAACP objectives were to gather and release pertinent information regarding racism and southern defiance of federal laws as a means of applying pressure on Washington to act against the lawlessness running rampant in Mississippi. This harkens back to one of the major strategies outlined at the initial organization of the NAACP in which it sought to expose racism and inequality "through 'the argument of the printed and the spoken word.'"[63] As a means of bringing the point home, Wilkins ended the letter of reprimand with the following:

In 1930 Walter White succeeded in having the United States Senate turn down a man nominated for the U.S. Supreme Court by President Hoover. This victory was won by one vote, and Mr. White conducted the fight nation-wide on the basis of a newspaper clipping that had been sent to him from North Carolina. As a result of the 1930 fight and the vote in the Senate, Mr. White and the NAACP in the next eight years were able to defeat eight senators who voted "wrong" on the confirmation of the judge. This tremendous victory, one of the highlights in the whole NAACP history, was built on a newspaper clipping which reached the national office in time for it to do something about the situation.[64]

Evers issued a quick apology with the promise that nothing of the sort would happen again.[65] In addition to the demands placed upon him from the populous with whom he worked, Evers was besieged by the demands and deadlines imposed by the national leadership, with very little sympathy for his need to take that rare, but needed, break.

Evers rarely got a chance to get away, and when he did he remained fearful that he would miss something important and that thought often ruined any chance at rest he might have had. Myrlie recalled that he loved fishing, hunting, and sitting around the house debating current issues with close friends such as Robert Smith, Cornelius Turner, and Houston Wells; he engaged in these types of activities as often as possible.[66] Despite his need for an occasional getaway, whenever the national office needed him but could not reach him, Medgar received a message of rebuke. In a memorandum dated August 18, 1955, Ruby Hurley, NAACP southern regional director, informed Evers that she had attempted to reach him to obtain needed information for the *State Times* regarding an upcoming meeting. She stressed her failed attempts to reach him at both his office and his home. Furthermore, she offered Evers the following advice: "I would suggest that you not attempt to continue a vacation at this time while the situation is as tense as it is in Mississippi. None of us has attempted to take a full vacation at this time. It is particularly important that you be on the scene in Mississippi where the situation is more tense than it is in some other areas. I thought that you got that as a suggestion yesterday when I talked to you."[67] Despite the unrealistic expectations, combined with the impractical notion of one man being physically responsible for an entire state, Evers continued to take on more and more responsibilities and, in the process, became the official face and voice of the NAACP in Mississippi.

Medgar Evers used his position as field secretary to help provide the things that people needed on a day-to-day basis and the NAACP set aside funds for emergency purposes. The Christmas season provided Evers with a myriad of opportunities to see that people were also furnished with items that were not limited to daily needs. During the Christmas season of 1955, the NAACP wired Evers five hundred dollars for immediate operations and also sent a check for fifteen hundred dollars to help assist members who had been pressured due to their NAACP work or affiliation. Although the money covered items such as "back rent, grocery bills, medicine and doctor bills," Wilkins noted that it could also be used for candy and toys for area children. The extent to which the money could be used for the latter he left up to Medgar. Although Wilkins acknowledged that the NAACP had placed quite a burden upon its field secretary, "both physically and otherwise," they were confident that he would account for the money spent and see to it that those to whom it was intended received it. In addition to this financial responsibility, Evers also oversaw the "Mississippi Relief Revolving Fund." This financial account set aside one thousand dollars for his dispersal to victims of the White Citizens' Council and other oppressive entities.[68]

As a consequence of his constant work among the people, his comforting them, meeting with them, eating with them, and providing direct financial assistance, people were more inclined to believe in Medgar and know that he would be there when things were good as well as bad. Cornelius Turner, who was a local Jackson businessman, activist, and one of Evers's best friends, explained that "Medgar had a terrible feeling for people and he never wanted to subject other people to something he wouldn't do himself, that was the beautiful part about his whole life. He was just that way with everything. If Medgar asked you to do [it], you can just know that he would do it himself."[69] For those whom Medgar asked to risk their lives in the cause for justice, his willingness to get in the trenches alongside them made all the difference in the world.

The economic plight of farmers occupied much of Evers's attention and that of the NAACP. He had worked with sharecroppers most of his professional career with Magnolia Mutual and continued to do so as field secretary. Because of their need for credit and funds for equipment, African American farmers were the most vulnerable to economic pressures. Whites counted on this vulnerability to both frustrate and keep blacks from participating in any struggle for sociopolitical equality. Many farmers were unable to meet the requirements to obtain a loan from Tri-State Bank and thus were overwhelmed by financial hardships. The pressures associated with impoverishment forced many to acquiesce in their own exploitation just to survive. In 1956, the NAACP established the Committee on Emergency Aid to Farmers in Mississippi as a means of addressing their economic concerns.

The committee, although a separate entity, remained subordinate to the

NAACP and subject to its authority. According to organization reports, the purpose of the committee was to

> assist on [a] limited basis Mississippi landowners who because of activities or connection with the NAACP and/or the desegregation program and who were formerly considered good credit risk but at the present time unable to get loans they need at prevailing rates in their own communities from banks and other lending institutions and who are unable to qualify or secure loans from the Tri-State Bank in Memphis or other lending institutions.

Each farmer could receive no more than fifteen hundred dollars in aid and all loans were made through Tri-State Bank with donations and NAACP assurance of repayment.[70] The committee, however, conducted strict background checks to determine eligibility and credit worthiness and for this it depended upon the investigatory work of Evers and NAACP field secretary-at-large Mildred Bond.

The NAACP hired Bond on January 1, 1954. She was a graduate of New York University and Columbia University where she majored in social psychology and had also studied in Europe and Mexico. Since coming aboard, Bond had "worked with various NAACP Branches in Membership and Fundraising Campaigns, school integration problems, other Branch community projects and workshops, [as well as] State and Regional Conferences." Thus, NAACP officials believed that they were sending a person well qualified to assist Evers in addressing the needs of African American farmers.[71]

In 1956, African American farmers throughout the Delta were experiencing economic pressure at untold levels, and Evers worked to make NAACP financial coffers available to the neediest. In order to do that, he had to identify them and he and Bond worked hard to single out and encourage those wronged to accept help from the NAACP and to stand against injustice by recording affidavits detailing economic exclusionary tactics.

Mildred Bond (now Bond Roxborough) first met Medgar Evers when the NAACP sent her to Mississippi to help deal with the economic problems farmers faced resulting from their attempts, or that of family members, to vote. As a consequence, she and Medgar rode throughout the Delta amassing information from farmers who had been subjected to economic reprisals and were willing to discuss their problems and seek some type of redress. Evers was not naïve to the dangers they faced while agitating for change and proved prepared to defend himself and Bond if the need arose.

While riding through the Delta with Medgar conducting interviews, Bond remembered that she had a habit of taking her shoes off and resting her feet upon the floor of the car. On one of those occasions her feet happened to rest upon something hard and when she asked Medgar what it was he replied, to her surprise, "oh, that's just my shotgun." His admission immediately sent both her feet straight into the air regardless of how undignified the position might have appeared.[72] Carrying a gun for protection was not anomalous to Medgar's character. While riding through the Delta, he often kept a .45 pistol hidden beneath a pillow on his seat. In fact, he kept a collection of weapons at home to protect his family from danger or physical attack and, like fellow Mississippi activists Hartman Turnbow, Amzie Moore, Aaron Henry, and C. O. Chinn, Evers believed in armed self-defense.[73] Colia Liddell Clark, who served as Evers's runner and his special assistant, argued that "Medgar did not believe, I don't care who ever tells you he did, he never believed in non-violence."[74] He did, however, respect the use of sound tactics and strategies in any operation.

Evers believed in examining all strategies before passing judgment and required those working with him to do so as well. "I want you to go and study non-violence," Clark recalled Evers's instruction. "I want you to go all the way with it, I want you to study it thoroughly, I don't believe it's go'n work. I believe in . . . economic development, I believe we have to have a solid base on which to build anything and I don't believe nonviolence and preachers can do that." Evers, however, loved Martin Luther King Jr., Clark maintained.[75] Still, he worked hard to ensure that his family remained safe.

As an added precaution for protecting his family against violent reprisals, Evers taught his wife and children battlefield tactics and evasive measures for when, or if, a threat emanated from outside the house. Whether riding alone or working around the house, Evers used his military experience and training to offset the chance that his family might be harmed. He also had contingency plans to protect those within the house in case of gunfire. John Salter, a professor at Tougaloo College in Jackson, maintained that Medgar had equipped his home with bulletproof window blinds all for the sake of protection.[76] Violence proved a constant companion to civil rights activists, and many believed violent resistance to be the only way to overcome the oppressive system of segregation. Evers had struggled with the notion of violent response since his return from military service and, in many ways, he was not so much different from those who considered violence a legitimate mechanism for self-defense and achieving meaningful social change.

Weaponry has always been a part of the African American struggle for freedom, equality, and citizenship. Men and women have used weapons (standard and makeshift) to defend their communities and to protect themselves and their property. During the enslavement period, revolts were common occurrences. When runaways were captured, they sometimes killed themselves or their children rather than submit to a racist system of inequality and physical and mental degradation.[77] During the 1950s and 1960s, some civil rights activists held tight to the idea of the "right to bear arms" and integrated this right into the overall fight for civil equality and citizenship.

Robert F. Williams of Monroe, North Carolina, served as the epitome of civil rights activism and stood as a symbol of manhood, dignity, and self-respect. His actions in North Carolina inspired a generation of civil rights activists and helped mold a new style of civil rights leadership based upon armed self-defense and resistance. In many ways, Williams and Evers were a lot alike and their goals and objectives mirrored each other if their overall tactics and strategies did not.

Robert F. Williams was born on February 26, 1925, to Emma and John L. Williams in Monroe, North Carolina. Like Evers, Williams also claimed family members who had been enslaved and who believed they were just as good as any other human being. Williams also served in the military and returned to North Carolina in 1946 imbued with a sense of entitlement to full citizenship rights and thus a refusal to accept the status quo of inequality. Elected president of the Monroe chapter of the NAACP in 1957, Williams surrounded himself with individuals who believed armed resistance to white brutality was the answer to the problem of white supremacy. This idea received validation in 1946 when Williams and other black men armed themselves and faced down a Ku Klux Klan intent on desecrating the body of Bennie Montgomery, a black serviceman and a friend of Williams. Williams and the national NAACP leadership were often at odds due to his open support of armed self-defense and that divide caused the NAACP, in 1959, to suspend his presidency of the Monroe chapter. Williams, however, continued to advocate armed resistance, believing that nonviolence proved "a very potent weapon when the opponent is civilized, but nonviolence is no repellent for a sadist."[78] This realization continued to haunt men such as Evers, who constantly witnessed the brutality whites inflicted upon blacks.

In an interview with Manning Marable, Myrlie explained Medgar's belief that a racial war could occur. Medgar believed, Myrlie recalled, that "'you must always be prepared for whatever comes our way.' And we were talking about the guns, the arms, collecting what we would need to fight if by chance we ended up in a race war. Which he felt could possibly happen. . . . [If we] found ourselves in a separate part of America, how we would not be starved out, how we would be in a location where we would not be surrounded and wiped out at one time. . . . [H]e was thinking about building a nation . . . of black people."[79] As the civil rights movement progressed, white violence made it harder for the NAACP leadership, particularly Roy Wilkins, to control branch members who were leaning toward violent response to white brutality. After all, they were the ones subjected to the brutality and not Wilkins or members of the national office in New York. Despite efforts to control violent responses on behalf of a variety of organizations, such as the Deacons for Defense, there developed pockets of resistance groups across the country dedicated to community empowerment and protection from white encroachment and attack.[80]

Although Evers preferred to attain rights for African Americans in a peaceful manner, he had been a soldier and he proved quite willing to apply that battlefield mentality and readiness to the fight for civil equality. One could see his military training come to the fore in the way he approached potentially dangerous situations. He always surveyed the area in case he needed to make a quick escape. He also walked his neighborhood to familiarize himself with the way it was structured; in particular, the areas surrounding his home where an ambush would most likely occur. Despite the dangers, black Mississippians had an inner strength and fortitude that Evers tapped into, and this impressed Bond from the time she first arrived in Mississippi.

What impressed Mildred Bond the most about black Mississippians "was the willingness of [the] people to sacrifice themselves to take the chance of going to Yazoo, Mississippi for example, to register and vote after having witnessed or learned about the beating of someone who had already tried this."[81] Evers, however, understood the tenacity that people had when they came to trust you, which is why the NAACP placed so much faith in his abilities. Cornelius Turner maintained that Medgar's "honesty and his straightforwardness," combined with his willingness to put his life on the line with everyone else, drew people to him and it caused them to feel for him. With a hint of a smile, Turner added, "How can you not feel strong about someone like that?"[82]

Medgar Evers's overall sense of urgency and respect for those with whom he spoke, regardless of their station in life, made his overall recruitment efforts quite effective. Evers, much like other military veterans, connected with the downtrodden of the community and they served as his support base. This was not an anomaly as activists such as Robert Williams recruited from those who had suffered the most and thus who believed they did not have a lot to lose.[83] Evers understood the importance of the painstaking time required to help people overcome their physical and emotional fears in order to connect with them. When asked to describe his overall demeanor, Mildred Bond Roxborough thought with care and then offered the following:

He seem to me, in my judgment, . . . [to be a] very thoughtful person, restrained in terms of, he wasn't gregarious, somewhat reserved in my experience, but you got the feeling that he was a genuinely good person and that he was stubborn, determined; he had a mind of his own and when he determined that this was a goal to be reached he try to find ways of reaching it, very steady kind of a person.[84]

Evers had developed those qualities described by Bond Roxborough from growing up in Decatur under the fist of oppression, and he applied them toward the liberation of African Americans. His rapport with people made an indelible impression upon Mildred, and she remembered being taken in by the reality that the very "people who had virtually nothing were willing to risk that in order achieve the goal of being a full-fledged citizen and the privileges to which they were being denied." She asserted that individuals notified of branch meetings would come from

across fields and whatever to go to a little black church at night to a meeting. . . . Some of those people couldn't write and they were willing to sign, you know they would do an X and you would print the name beside the X on a test and that made an indelible impression on me that these people who had nothing were willing to put their lives on the line for a principle.[85]

The people "who had virtually nothing" were the very foot soldiers upon whom Evers depended, and their constant oppression kept him moving toward the overall goal of liberation. Again, the farmers made up a major part of his grassroots constituency.

The Committee on Aid to Farmers requested wide sweeping investigations to identify victims of economic repression to offset the economic pressure whites projected onto blacks. The committee budgeted a salaried position for a "full-time field officer" to collect this type of data and report back to the committee. Although no information surfaced verifying that committee officials elected Evers to that post, he did engage in the type of investigatory work that the committee required. By January 23, 1956, Evers and Bond had interviewed a total of seventy persons, logged eight hundred miles, obtained seven notarized affidavits, and filled out fourteen "detailed information sheets" on individuals willing to air their grievances in public. Throughout the process, they visited a total of ten counties and provided the following percentages of the African American population within each: Bolivar, 68 percent; Humphreys, 70 percent; Yazoo, 62 percent; Coahoma, 78 percent; Panola, 56 percent; Tunica, 82 percent; Holmes, 74 percent; Sunflower, 68 percent; Tallahatchie, 64 percent; and Jones with 26 percent. They noted, however, that information concerning economic pressure could not be obtained for farmers in Tunica, Humphreys, and Panola Counties where the workers assured them that they had received no such pressures at that time.[86]

Evers explained to Current the reasons why some of the farmers had not met the Tri-State Bank requirements for securing much-needed loans. Some "of the difficulty experienced by some farmers in attempting to secure loans from the Tri-State Bank," he relayed, "was due to the fact that in Mississippi the banks grant loans on growing crops. It is reported that in Tennessee this is not the case."[87] The amount of the loans needed for the fourteen farmers totaled $27,862.79. This financial projection did not include the seven statements submitted by a Mr. Moore of individuals who had signed affidavits, but could not be contacted. Evers stressed to Current that the "majority of the farmers indicated that they needed the loans by February 15, 1956, and at the latest by February 28, 1956."[88] Both Evers and Bond believed that their arrival had given the people hope and would help boost NAACP memberships and support for its programs.

The two field secretaries concluded in their report that their visit "came at a most propitious time." In every locale, contacted individuals expressed to Evers and Bond their "appreciation and pleasant surprise . . . as evidenced by such remarks [as] 'It is good to know that we are not alone down here:' 'We can trust the NAACP:' 'We are surrounded, not knowing where to turn:' 'We must stay here, we have no place else to go—everything we have is here, but we cannot fight without help.'"[89] Historian Pete Daniel's examination of the extreme brutality and economic intimidation tactics black Mississippians endured during the 1950s underscores the appreciation many African Americans exhibited toward the relief efforts Evers and Bond provided.[90] The positive remarks of those who appreciated Medgar and his work kept him committed to the struggle for equality, and during his darkest moments he opened his mental file containing these types of admissions and they propelled him forward.

Evers was not so naïve as to believe that he and Bond had canvassed the entire Mississippi Delta and identified all of its sufferers or that the NAACP could help every person they encountered who needed assistance. He noted that many individuals identified "were not (1) NAACP people and were in need due to other reasons; (2) had not exhausted all of their resources; (3) or could not be helped by such a plan."[91] Furthermore, there existed a host of individuals living on plantations to whom they did not have access to for various reasons and thus the extent of their needs went unidentified. Evers, however, acknowledged the foundation of their economic problem.

Evers concluded that the problem, in many instances, was "not due to the NAACP, but rather to the growing mechanization of the plantation. The owners are making day laborers out of them to avoid farming on 'fourths.'

Various tales were related to field workers how these families are being driven from plantation to plantation as each owner resorts to cutting down on the cost of labor by getting cotton picking machines, planters, etc."[92] Evers's reference to "mechanization" addressed a key point in the transformation of plantation work in Mississippi as it related to cotton harvesting. In 1944, a Mississippi plantation experienced the advantages of the mechanical cotton harvester, which saved the plantation owner a substantial amount of money over what he would have spent having the same cotton harvested by humans.[93] This conclusion proved not to be so much an issue of race as one of economics. Despite this shift toward machinery, Evers sought to address the problem and to find a solution to the continued and blatant economic exploitation that African Americans faced. His thinking revolved around the idea that if inequality could be defeated, then whatever problems plagued African Americans would dissipate over time.

Evers took the field secretary position seriously and maintained detailed reports concerning the problems black Mississippians faced when standing against injustice. Various letters between Medgar and NAACP leaders provide insight into his role with the organization. A letter dated January 11, 1956, gives a glimpse into the types of pressures exerted on individuals and the intricate role Evers played in attempting to mediate solutions and alleviate problems.

Referencing the pressure placed on George Jefferson of Vicksburg, Mississippi, Medgar wrote to Roy Wilkins apprising him of Jefferson's situation and the dire consequences that would result if whites succeeded in their intimidation tactics. He assured Wilkins:

> that my interest in this case is based purely on the fact that Mr. Jefferson is the backbone in regards to the stand taken in Vicksburg on the Civil Rights issue and that every possible amount of undue pressure, economically and otherwise, has been placed on him.
>
> The objective, as has been pointed out by some influential whites[,] is to "strip" him financially and break his influence in the community. If such is done, they (the whites) feel that the strong opposition to segregation—and all of its evils[—]will have been destroyed in Vicksburg.[94]

Evers served as a link between the realities of African Americans struggling in Mississippi and the NAACP leadership, the latter often unaware of both the extent and severity of the problems black Mississippians faced when combating southern racism. Although Evers, on a personal level, worked hard to eliminate problems caused by racial discrimination, he also considered NAACP financial coffers as legitimate mechanisms for protecting victims of Mississippi's oppressive social and political regimes.

In regard to the plight of George Jefferson, Evers requested individual financial assistance in the sum of $50,000 dollars. Jefferson had also written to Wilkins on January 10 requesting the sum and outlining a payment proposal. Evers knew the amount to be substantial, but figured the benefits, in terms of community support for the struggle against oppression in Vicksburg, would outweigh the overall cost. Evers acknowledged

> that the amount of money needed immediately to save his [Mr. Jefferson's] housing development ($50,000) is a large sum, but the boost that it would give him and the community as a whole would be tremendous.

> It is fully recognized that the transaction would be made strictl[y] from a business standpoint and that such [a] loan would be repaid within one year.

> If there is any possible help that can be given Mr. Jefferson it would be appreciated tremendously.[95]

These kinds of appeal for financial assistance underscore the pressure exerted upon black Mississippians and the pressure Evers felt to provide assistance.

Charles Evers's earlier recount of the frustrations Medgar expressed and his concerns regarding African Americans in the Delta underscored his unwavering desire to make sure that he did everything he could to alleviate the problems of individuals brave enough to step forward. In this light, his request for $50,000 to assist George Jefferson proved understandable. Not everyone who stood against southern oppression received sanctions from the white community. Regarding the plight of teachers in certain locales, Medgar informed Wilkins that he did "not have at hand information very pertinent to the teachers, except that there are numerous teachers, that I know, who have publicly stated that they were members of the NAACP, and as of this date [April 30, 1956] have not been fired or approached in any way. There are rumors, however, that in some of the Delta counties some of the teachers have been fired. I have nothing positive on this allegation."[96] Although Evers worked hard to address the economic needs of others, he often found himself in financial despair as well.

On May 4, 1956, Evers wrote to Gloster Current explaining his financial difficulties. He requested a loan "for one thousand dollars ($1000), to be repaid within a two-year period." Evers explained that Myrlie was "not working," which he acknowledged "of course is my responsibility . . . but the fact is that my wife was overworked" and "we thought it best for her sake and the children, that she devote full time at home with them." Evers needed the loan to also cover a home mortgage loan and the various "incidentals" associated with responsible home ownership. As a means of reassuring Current of his devotion to the state, Evers added, "As you can see, I do not plan to leave. I am anchoring myself here for better or for worse, (I hope better), but if worse comes, I'll be in the middle of it."[97] Six days later Current informed Evers that Roy Wilkins had approved the loan "at the rate of $40 per month," which would be deducted "semi-monthly" over a two-year period.[98] Having his financial problems taken care of, in what Evers termed, "in the nick of time," he now focused on the problems African Americans faced and Belzoni, Mississippi had proven to be problematic.[99]

Evers and Mildred Bond also investigated incidents that had nothing to do with farmers but still spoke to the overall issue of oppression and intimidation. On January 21, 1956, they spoke with gunshot victim Gus Courts of Belzoni, Mississippi. Courts was a sixty-five-year-old grocer and president of the NAACP chapter in Belzoni. He had also been close friends with Reverend George Lee, who had been murdered the previous year for advocating that African Americans register and vote. Gloster Current reported that on November 25 "about 8:30 P.M." Courts "was making change for a customer when unknown assailants drove up alongside his pick-up truck which was parked outside the building and shot through the window." Evers noted that after the shooting, Courts "was immediately taken some 80 miles to Mound Bayou Hospital where he was given the proper care and saved his life."[100] His injuries consisted of gunshot wounds to his left forearm and lower "left side of his abdomen." His wounds would have been more severe, according to Dr. Henry, "the hospital's physician," if the shots had hit him in the front of the body instead of from the side.[101] Evers reported that these "and many other acts of terror and violence are being committed against militant Mississippi Negroes." Yet, of importance to Evers's sense of responsibility, he added that "in each instance the NAACP has come to the rescue to make certain something is done along the line of justice and to prevent a reoccurrence of such a thing."[102] Mississippi legislators, however, were not standing idly by and Evers kept abreast of what was happening in the state from a political perspective.

Mississippi lawmakers proved active in their attempts to control the level of activism in the state. The one way to ensure control was to criminalize such activities and make them punishable by fine or imprisonment. The Mississippi House of Representatives fought hard against civil rights activity. Evers reported that the "Mississippi House of Representatives passed by a vote of 121–2 a bill that would make the activities of the NAACP a 'violation of Mississippi laws, customs, and traditions,' and further that 'violation could bring a fine of $5,000 and six (6) years in prison.'"

The bill, Evers remarked, was sponsored by "Representative Karl Weisenburg of Jackson County, Mississippi." Evers, however, remained defiant, adding that if "such a bill becomes a law, we are ready to spend our first day in jail."[103] Evers, much like Martin Luther King Jr., Malcolm X, and other civil rights activists across the country, paid strict attention to developments in the law and, of more importance, attempts by political groups to alter it to the detriment of African Americans.

Evers understood that sometimes individuals considered the NAACP an intimidating figure that could make certain situations worse. As a consequence, he, in some instances, requested that the NAACP hold off political action in support of the wishes of individuals under pressure from the white community. The police in Sunflower County, "more specifically of Indianola," Evers noted, placed extreme pressure on Dr. Clinton C. Battle. Battle had informed Roy Wilkins, of the NAACP national office, earlier that he had been "framed on a DWI charge by the *Indianola* Police Dept. as part of a vicious smear campaign of the Citizens Councils."[104] He later changed his mind, however, regarding desired action and contacted Medgar in an effort to prevent possible NAACP action.

In response to Battle's desire to calm things down, Evers sent a letter to Roy Wilkins on September 27, 1956, apprising him of the fact that Dr. Battle "would prefer that the National Office . . . not say anything, along the line of publicity, because it appears that they [police authorities] are trying to take his driver's license from him, which could possibly injure his practice since he is a country doctor. He appreciate [*sic*] your standing by. This, he asked me to request of you so as not to make it any more difficult for the time being."[105] This episode further indicates the multifaceted role that Evers played and the trust community members placed in him. Dr. Battle had contacted the national office on his own, but he believed that Medgar could stop the wheels of organized response that he might have placed in motion and thus save his practice. By all accounts, the position of field secretary required far more than cataloging racial incidents and filing monthly reports.

Evers continued to investigate, document, and report the problems that white supremacy produced in the African American community. On July 18, 1956, J. Francis Pohlhaus, counsel for the Washington Bureau of the NAACP, wrote Medgar regarding his "monthly report of April 25th, . . . [which] made reference to the mob killing of Carl Jenkins of Jackson." Pohlhaus requested further information regarding the Jenkins case, including whether federal officials had been notified.[106] On July 30, 1956, Evers apprised Pohlhaus of the difficulties that occurred regarding the gathering of information. According to Medgar, it proved increasingly difficult for us to get any concrete information, except for what the papers carried, and the chance to view the victim's [Jenkins's] body which had many bruises about the head, face and neck, also a bullet hole through the skull.

Since this occurred in a white neighborhood, around 11:00 p.m., with no Negro witnesses, you can imagine how difficult it might be to get information.

The incident has not been brought to the attention of Federal officials to my knowledge. . . . Thus far we have been unable to obtain information from employees who worked with Mr. Jenkins, because of reluctance, apparently as a result of possible economic and physical reprisals.[107]

These accounts were numerous. However, Evers's involvement in the movement extended beyond the investigation of physical violence.

Evers and African American congressman Charles C. Diggs Jr. of Detroit, Michigan, wrote numerous letters regarding voter discrimination in Mississippi. Congressman Diggs boasted an impressive academic and political career, having become the youngest member of the Michigan State Senate and, on November 2, 1954, the state's first "Negro" congressman.[108] On October 2, 1956, Congressman Diggs wrote Evers inquiring whether there existed "any evidence of continuation in the recent Mississippi Primary of the intimidation and other illegal means of keeping Negroes from voting?" He also asked about which congressional district, in Medgar's opinion, displayed "the most flagrant attempts to keep Negroes away from the polls?"[109]

On October 9, 1956, Evers responded in a straightforward manner. In regard to continued voter discrimination, he answered with a resounding yes. He affirmed that there remained "continued acts of intimidation and other illegal means . . . employed to keep Negroes from becoming registered voters." In reference to specific problematic counties, Evers reported that

down in Forrest County, Negroes are refused the new forms for registration, whereby they might become qualified to vote. In this particular county there are more than 12,000 Negroes, with less than twenty registered voters, and in another county, about thirty miles from Forrest County, Negroes at one time, even the first of this year, constituted thirty-five percent of the total registered voters in the county, some 1300 or more. However, in the early part of this year, a new registration was called by the county supervisors and circuit clerk, and every Negro on the books, (supposedly whites too), had to re-register under the new amendment, and with the qualifications being so rigid, less than sixty-five Negroes, to date, have qualified again to vote. Now in many cases these persons have been on the books for at least ten years, but today they are voteless [*sic*] people.

Evers concluded his response by stipulating his belief that "living in Mississippi today [1956] would compare very closely with how the Jews lived in Germany under Adolph Hitler's regime, with the only difference being that we have not witnessed a barrage of mass executions."[110] This time would not be the last that Evers compared segregationist Mississippi to Nazi Germany. In 1963, when Jackson youth protested injustice by marching along Farish Street and were arrested en masse by an army of police officers, Evers exclaimed then that Jackson was "just like Nazi Germany. . . . [and the police were the] storm troopers."[111]

More than anything else, Evers believed that communal welfare rested in the hands of its residents and that individuals should unite to fight against the degradation of their social positions. When individuals took the first step toward unifying community efforts to exact social change, they were in a better position to ask for and receive assistance. As Charles Evers recalled their father's belief that one must give respect first and then demand respect, Medgar, above all else, required that African Americans collectively demand respect since they had long been giving it. Medgar believed that only through unification would whites consider blacks' demands for equal treatment with any degree of seriousness. Correspondence during the early 1960s indicates that Evers gravitated more and more toward direct action as the primary method for achieving social and economic equality, which often put him at odds with official NAACP mandates. His shift toward direct action as a remedy for discrimination and oppression, however, had its roots in the Decatur of his youth, roots that were strengthened by and replenished with the blood spilled in 1955 and the aftermath that followed.

Medgar Evers standing with pride flanked by his oldest child, Darrell Kenyatta, on the left and his daughter Reena Denise on the right. Evers spent as much time with his family as possible but his hectic schedule often limited the time he spent and thus he considered every moment with them as a precious one. (Courtesy Mississippi Department of Archives and History)

Always cognizant of his look, here a dapper Evers poses for a formal picture. (Courtesy Mississippi Department of Archives and History)

Many celebrities were guest at the Evers home. Here Evers poses with famed writer James Baldwin. (Courtesy Mississippi Department of Archives and History)

Here Medgar and Myrlie enjoy some time together. (Courtesy Mississippi Department of Archives and History)

Sometime after Evers's assassination, the Evers family posed for a family portrait while a portrait of Medgar hangs in the background. *From left to right:* Reena, Myrlie, Darrell (*standing*), and the youngest child, James Van Dyke, seated in front. (Courtesy Mississippi Department of Archives and History)

Here Myrlie Evers takes time to display the family's dining area as James, Darrell, and Reena look on. (Courtesy Mississippi Department of Archives and History)

Dressed to impress, Myrlie Evers, Reena, James, and Darrell pose for a portrait although someone has captured the attention of Reena and little Van. (Courtesy Mississippi Department of Archives and History)

Medgar Evers and NAACP director of branches Gloster B. Current. (Courtesy Mississippi Department of Archives and History)

Alcorn Agriculture and Mechanical College had a reputation for demanding professionalism from its students and faculty. One can see that ideal reflected in this official Alcorn A&M president and faculty photograph. Note the crisp style of dress and serious but engaging demeanor. (Courtesy Mississippi Department of Archives and History)

Myrlie and Medgar Evers often worked together during his time at Magnolia Mutual Life Insurance in Mound Bayou and some of his time as NAACP field secretary. Here Myrlie Evers is diligently at work on the typewriter. (Courtesy Mississippi Department of Archives and History)

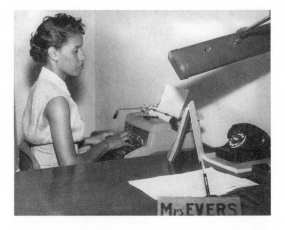

Here Myrlie Evers poses in their front yard as Darrell looks on. (Courtesy Mississippi Department of Archives and History)

Neighborhood children often gathered at the Evers home for fun and games. Here Darrell (*far left*) plays host to a number of children dressed to impress. (Courtesy Mississippi Department of Archives and History)

Here Reena and Darrell pose for the camera. (Courtesy Mississippi Department of Archives and History)

Bowman High School Class of 1950. Myrlie Evers is pictured third row extreme left. (Courtesy Mississippi Department of Archives and History)

Medgar Evers takes a break in what appears to be a public store. His military training comes to the forefront here; note that his back is against the wall. (Courtesy Mississippi Department of Archives and History)

Medgar Evers in his more youthful days. (Courtesy Mississippi Department of Archives and History)

Medgar Evers standing with a group of men in March 1963. (Courtesy Mississippi Department of Archives and History)

Evers takes a moment to relax. (Courtesy Mississippi Department of Archives and History)

Always dapper, here a young Evers sports a hat reflective of the zoot suit style of dress. (Courtesy Mississippi Department of Archives and History)

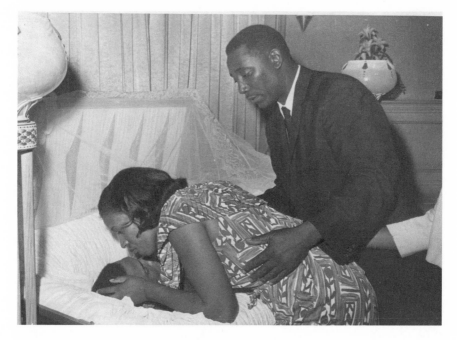

Funeral scene: Myrlie Evers bends over and kisses Evers while his brother Charles provides support, 1963. (Courtesy Mississippi Department of Archives and History)

Medgar Evers attending one of many grand openings. He is third on the left closest to the door. (Courtesy Mississippi Department of Archives and History)

Evers on stage, eighth from the left. (Courtesy Mississippi Department of Archives and History)

Medgar Evers provided a great deal of support to other organizations and often attended their functions as represented here. Medgar is fifth from the right. (Courtesy Mississippi Department of Archives and History)

From the right, Gloster Current, Myrlie Evers, Medgar Evers, and Dr. A. H. McCoy, president of the Mississippi State Conference of NAACP Branches. (Courtesy Mississippi Department of Archives and History)

Tougaloo College Archival Images

Tougaloo College proved to be a hotbed of civil rights activity and, in addition to Medgar Evers, many civil rights leaders, musicians, and social activists came to the college to speak and to lend their support to civil rights activities occurring throughout the city of Jackson and Mississippi as a whole.

From the left, Tougaloo College president A. D. Beittel, UN diplomat and Nobel Peace Prize winner Dr. Ralph J. Bunche, and respected Tougaloo sociology professor Ernst Borinski. (Courtesy Tougaloo College Archives, Civil Rights Photographic Collection)

From the left, Beittel, civil rights leader, and Nashville movement strategist
Reverend James Lawson, Southern Christian Leadership Conference president
Martin Luther King Jr., and Mississippi civil rights activist and pharmacist Aaron
Henry. (Courtesy Tougaloo College Archives, Civil Rights Photographic
Collection)

Left to right: Charles Evers,
Myrlie Evers, Ralph Bunche,
and A. D. Beittel. (Courtesy
Tougaloo College Archives,
Civil Rights Photographic
Collection)

Attendees at the funeral of Medgar Evers in Jackson, Mississippi, 1963. Some of those pictured include NAACP executive secretary Roy Wilkins (*extreme left*), civil rights activist and physician T. R. M. Howard (*third from left*), Ralph Bunche (*fifth from left*). (Courtesy Tougaloo College Archives, Civil Rights Photographic Collection)

Aaron Henry at Evers gravesite in Arlington, Virginia, 1978. (Courtesy Tougaloo College Archives, Civil Rights Photographic Collection)

Medgar receiving an award
from the Mississippi
Teachers' Association.
(Courtesy Tougaloo College
Archives, Civil Rights
Photographic Collection)

Funeral scene in Jackson, Mississippi, Reena (*second from left*), Darrell (*third from left*), Myrlie Evers, and Charles Evers. (Courtesy Tougaloo College Archives, Civil Rights Photographic Collection)

This is the famed Woodworth Chapel on the Tougaloo campus. The chapel would host many civil rights events and speakers. (Courtesy Tougaloo College Archives, Civil Rights Photographic Collection)

Martin Luther King Jr. signs autographs in Tougaloo's Woodworth Chapel. (Courtesy Tougaloo College Archives, Civil Rights Photographic Collection)

On March 27 nine students from Tougaloo College staged a read-in at the public library and were arrested. They became known as the Tougaloo Nine. *Left to right:* Joseph Jackson Jr., Geraldine Edwards, James C. (Sam) Bradford, Evelyn Pierce, Albert Lassiter, Ethel Sawyer, Meredith Anding Jr., Janice Jackson, and Alfred Cook. (Courtesy Tougaloo College Archives, Civil Rights Photographic Collection)

Julian Bond, a founding member of the Student Nonviolent Coordinating Committee and later senator, made several appearances at Tougaloo. Here, a younger Bond speaks during Tougaloo's Social Science Forum, 1967. (Courtesy Tougaloo College Archives, Civil Rights Photographic Collection)

Roy Wilkins (*left*) and Charles Evers (*right*) take some time out of their busy schedule to smile for the camera. (Courtesy Tougaloo College Archives, Civil Rights Photographic Collection)

Medgar often took trusted photographers with him to take pictures of the brutality he investigated. One of those trusted individuals was Tom Armstrong, the owner of the Farish Street Newsstand and Studio. (Courtesy Tougaloo College Archives, Civil Rights Photographic Collection)

The years Evers spent as a student at Alcorn College proved critical to his ideological and organizational development. The institution has since dedicated an auditorium in his honor. (Courtesy of the author)

Medgar and Charles Evers on the Alcorn Football team. Medgar is front row, third from the left, number 31. Charles same row, extreme right, number 29. (Courtesy of Charles Evers)

Picture of the Evers patriarch and matriarch: James Evers and Jessie Evers.
(Courtesy of Charles Evers)

Picture of Medgar and Myrlie Evers's home. Evers was shot as he exited the car.
(Courtesy of the author)

This plaque is attached to the Evers's home. (Courtesy of the author)

One of the many structures bearing Evers's name. This is the Medgar Evers branch library in Jackson. (Courtesy of the author)

Medgar Evers statue erected June 28, 1992, funded by the Medgar Evers Statue Fund, Inc. (Courtesy of the author)

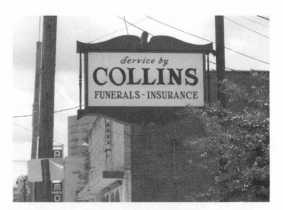

Collins Funeral Home on
Farish Street. Collins handled
Evers's funeral in Jackson.
(Courtesy of the author)

The Masonic Temple M. W. Stringer Grand Lodge erected 1955 on Lynch Street
where many of the meetings were held and which also housed Evers's office. It
would also host Evers's funeral where thousands of people gathered. (Courtesy of
the author)

4.

A Bloodied and Battered Mississippi

1955

Somebody's going to pay for this, ... And I'm not leaving. I'm going to stay here and fight until someone does the same thing to me.

           —*Medgar Evers*

Oh, what sorrow,
Pity, pain
That tears and blood
Should mix like rain
In Mississippi! . . .

           —*Langston Hughes*

We shall face each dawn and night,
With faith and courage true;
And as our goal of '63 grows near,
Strive to see our struggle through.
       —*Quoted in Medgar Evers Annual Report*

THE YEAR 1955 PROVED a trying time for Medgar Evers and the state of Mississippi as witnessed by the particular murders of two prominent civil rights activists and one fourteen-year-old boy from Chicago, Illinois. Each murder profoundly affected Evers and deepened his commitment both to the state of Mississippi and to the overturning of its oppressive regime.

117

As a result of the extreme levels of violence engulfing Mississippi during the 1950s, a number of prominent civil rights activists such as Doctors T. R. M. Howard, Clinton C. Battle, and A. H. McCoy left the state and NAACP membership suffered. Medgar Evers continued to organize and to recruit support for social struggle.[1] The events of 1955, however, took a psychological toll on Evers and challenged his belief that Mississippi could be redeemed.

Three prominent murders in 1955 illuminated white Mississippians' commitment to keeping their African American counterparts intimidated and under control. Each instance of violence brought Mississippi closer to the national spotlight and pulled African Americans further away from acceptance of the status quo. The violent events of the 1950s changed Mississippi significantly, and Evers was a fundamental part of its metamorphosis. Evers also changed during that span of time as the oppressive conditions of African Americans dramatically affected his outlook on whether voter registration drives or direct-action tactics were the proper method for obtaining civil rights.[2]

The oppressive conditions African Americans faced in Mississippi shifted into high gear during the 1950s, and every incident of violence strengthened Evers's resolve to combat Mississippi terrorism. No act of violence assaulted the sensibilities of Medgar, Mississippi, progressive whites, and the nation as did the lynching of fourteen-year-old Emmett Louis Till, who had been visiting relatives in Money, Mississippi. But prior to Till, Evers contended with the violent deaths of two Mississippians he respected for their dedication to the civil rights struggle: the Reverend George Lee of Belzoni and Lamar Smith of Brookhaven. Both murders challenged Evers's commitment to non-direct action as a viable tactic for African American progress in Mississippi and the United States as a whole.

Reverend George W. Lee was an independent businessman, minister, and active member of the NAACP in Belzoni, Mississippi, an area designated the "Heart of the Delta." Unlike most ministers during his time, Lee openly advocated voting rights for African Americans. He demanded that blacks stand against white aggression and unequal treatment, and this brand of liberation theology permeated his sermons. Lee believed that blacks had to fight for their rights on earth, in the here and now, and not be content to wait upon death to gain equality. He touted this message to the four Baptist congregations he rode circuit for: two in Jackson, one in Lexington, and one in Tchula, Mississippi.[3]

Reverend Lee owned a grocery store and printing shop. These made him less vulnerable to the economic pressures that whites inflicted upon the less economically stable.[4] His independence served him well as he labored to open the voting polls to African Americans in Mississippi on an equal basis with whites. On a personal level, Lee had accomplished a remarkable amount in terms of gaining access to the political process. George Lee, Evers noted in his 1955 annual report, "was the only Negro who had qualified himself in both County and City elections, in a county where Negroes have not voted since Reconstruction and where Negroes outnumber whites at the rate of more than two to one."[5] Myrlie asserted, however, that Reverend Lee had tried for years to vote but could not because of the sheriff's refusal to accept his poll tax payments. In 1953, Reverend Lee and "a small group of other Negroes" complained to federal authorities and only the threat of federal prosecution forced Sheriff Isaac "Ike" Shelton to agree to accept future payments.[6]

Despite constant warnings from whites to cease stirring up trouble, the many death threats he received, and the knowledge that his name appeared upon a death list, Reverend Lee encouraged African Americans to register and vote. As a response to his actions, whites warned Lee that they would kill him if he continued along this path. He ignored the warnings and continued organizing African Americans to resist intimidation and to demand the rights entitled them as citizens of the United States. On May 7, 1955, while driving home, several white men in a convertible pulled alongside Reverend Lee's car and fired two gun blasts into his automobile, one of which tore away his lower jaw. When Mrs. C. N. Gray (Pearleen), who lived in the area, arrived on the scene and "tried to get Reverend Lee to tell who did it," she realized that "the bottom of his face was shot away, blood was gushing and he was snoring real loud." He died before reaching the hospital.[7] Although disgusted by the Lee murder, Evers did not seem surprised that it had occurred. He deduced that in light of his economic independence and determination to obtain voting rights for African Americans in Mississippi, the only alternative that organizations such as the "Councils" had for stopping the minister "was to kill him."[8] Although the Citizens' Council advocated economic intimidation, some of its members were not averse to using physical violence to drive their point home.

Although investigating the murder, the NAACP sought to pressure political officials to get involved in the case. Ruby Hurley wrote to Mississippi governor Hugh White imploring that he use his political office to "offset the miscarriage of justice" surrounding the Lee murder investigation. Furthermore, she hoped that he would "lead the good, decent, and law abiding citizens of Mississippi to help other citizens who by accident of birth are colored Americans to live without fear of being shot down or otherwise killed because they dare to want to walk in human dignity as children of the one God to Whom [sic] we all pray." White, however, refused to get involved in the case stating that it was "a matter for local authorities to check."⁹

Both Medgar and regional NAACP director Ruby Hurley drove to Belzoni to investigate the Lee murder. Evers understood that, where blacks were concerned, Mississippi had a well-deserved reputation for covering up its violent actions. As a consequence, he and Ruby hurried to Belzoni to gather as much information as possible before things settled and the intimidation process took hold. After investigating the circumstances surrounding the ambush and speaking with local blacks, Evers soon discovered that witnesses to the shooting could not be located and had apparently been ordered to leave town. One witness to the event was later located and provided the FBI with his account.

Alex Hudson told FBI agents what he had seen; he provided this information from East St. Louis, Illinois, as he had left Mississippi a week after the killing. He reported that he and Angie Wellsby were sitting on the porch of Hattie Miniefield when they saw "a 1953 black Buick coming down the street from our left from town." Hudson remembered that the Buick was not traveling very fast but that "a convertible, light top, . . . [that] seemed to be two-toned" trailed the Buick. According to Hudson, the Mercury caught up to the "black Buick" passing on the right when he heard a shot and soon realized that they "was shooting at the black Buick behind them," which turned out to be the car Lee was driving. The car then crashed into the home of Katherine Blair before coming to a stop.¹⁰

In response to the murder, Mississippi officials went out of their way to keep the Lee killing a secret from the outside world as a means of avoiding federal intervention. Scholar Jack Mendelsohn remarked that "Within an hour after the shooting, a mysterious malady afflicted Belzoni's telephone system. Operators informed Negro customers that all long-distance lines were in use." Friends of Reverend Lee, however, drove to nearby Mound Bayou and contacted T. R. M. Howard (who then contacted Congressmen Charles Diggs) while a second group drove to Jackson and notified Dr. A. H. McCoy, who also served as the president of the Mississippi State Conference of NAACP Branches. The covert method utilized by the Mississippi's "Negro riders" allowed the news of Reverend Lee's murder to escape the iron curtain of media silence.¹¹

The coroner's office and police officials attempted to suggest that Lee's death resulted from a traffic accident and not murder. There were also rumors circulating that a woman might be involved, and thus the shooting may not have had anything to do with racial agitation. All of this aside, many were disheartened when the coroner suggested that the lead pellets found in the mouth of Lee were possibly fillings from his teeth. This insinuation was quickly denounced by physicians such as Dr. A. H. McCoy who were present at the coroner's inquest on May 8. McCoy reported that the "mandible (lower jaw) [of Lee] was shattered into multiple pieces, too small to be reassembled, from the tempo-man-dibular articulation to the upper third of the ramus on the opposite side." He also reported that "the region of the carotid artery and jugular vein, all soft tissues gave the appearance of having gone through a hamburger grinder." McCoy announced that it was clear to him that Lee had been killed by "blasts from a shotgun. Lead," he continued, "is not used for filling teeth." McCoy was in a position to know what dentists used to repair teeth since he maintained a successful dental practice with established offices.[12] The funeral for Reverend Lee proved to be an emotional one.

The funeral was held on May 12, 1955, in Belzoni and many individuals attended the open-casket services. Evers acknowledged that regardless of the intimidation tactics employed to stifle the investigation, "on the day of the funeral . . . there was unanimity on the lips of the residents of that immediate area that there were gun shots [sic] just before Reverend Lee's car crashed into the house." Evers believed that the black population of Belzoni was growing tired of the intimidating tactics of the White Citizens' Council, and the large presence of people at the NAACP organized memorial service on May 22, 1955, bolstered this belief. Evers stated that the memorial service for Lee would be "a day Belzoni and Mississippi will remember for years to come, for against the whims and wishes and even threats of the Citizens' Council, NAACP members and sympathizers from all over the state of Mississippi swelled this little Nazi-like town by five hundred or more."[13] As a means of increasing the pressure on those responsible for the Lee murder, Evers announced that the "NAACP would jointly sponsor with the Regional Council of Negro Leadership a one thousand dollar ($1000) reward for information leading to the arrest of the guilty party in the case of Reverend G.W. Lee."[14] Evers often attempted to link with other organizations to strengthen the Mississippi movement, a tactic that later caused problems between him and the national NAACP leadership. NAACP leaders were kept abreast of these types of linkage attempts. Regarding this incident, "R. Hurley" (Ruby, no doubt) expressed that "Evers seems to have too much of the [T. R. M.] Howard influence." Furthermore, he "has a tendency to speak out in groups saying things that just shouldn't be said." A reference was also made regarding his mentioning the possibility "of a merger between NAACP and Howard's council."[15]

Although Evers worked hard to uncover evidence in the murder of Reverend George Lee and to expose the crime to a national audience, in private the minister's execution haunted him and often elicited outbursts of rage. The fact that Evers recognized Lee as one dedicated to empowering blacks in his community intensified his distress over his murder. Myrlie acknowledged that as the investigation proceeded, the weight of it all wore on Medgar and it showed. She remembered that Medgar reacted to Reverend Lee's murder "with anger and long periods of deep brooding silence. Alone in the bedroom, at his desk in the office, or seated at the breakfast table, he would sit with a deep frown on his face. Then, suddenly, he would boil over, striking the table with his fist as though he were striking someone."[16] Evers carried each murder, lynching, rape, and beating he heard about or investigated with him psychologically as a constant reminder of the necessity to struggle to protect upcoming generations. The 1950s tested his ability to hold the pain within and to keep it from spilling over into his home.

The murder of George Lee signified how bloody 1955 would be for the African American movement for equality. John Dittmer maintained that the "most blatant political execution in that bloody year occurred in broad daylight on a busy Saturday afternoon [August 13] on the crowded courthouse lawn in the southwest Mississippi town of Brookhaven." Lamar Smith, a sixty-three-year-old farmer had been encouraging blacks to utilize the absentee ballot as a means of ousting political incumbents. As a result of this type of continued agitation, Smith was gunned downed for urging African Americans to vote.[17] In light of whites' propensity for violent reaction to black advancement, it is not surprising that Evers kept a gun with him while traveling and slept with one near his bed. This protective measure proved both taxing and stressful. As Amzie Moore explained, until you experience the fear and knowledge that each day may bring about your demise, one cannot "know what it's like to have to sleep with your gun in your hand, where every passing car might bring Death!"[18] In actuality, it meant that one felt the ever-present sense of impending tragedy, and sometimes the potential for violence created an environment for such to happen.

Myrlie recalled that one night she and Medgar "had a terrible fright" in the house, which woke them up. Medgar immediately got his rifle. Moments later, she "found him standing at the bedroom door, his rifle in his right hand, his left hand at his forehead. Opposite him, across the hall, I could dimly see [our son] Darrell using the bathroom." She recalled that "Medgar turned as I touched him and said in a voice as close to despair as I had ever heard, 'My God, what am I doing?'"[19] The fear associated with civil rights activism had placed their son in danger of being shot by his father. This had a profound impact upon Evers and reiterated the dangers associated with resisting white subjugation. Individuals who took up the mantle of resistance often experienced sleepless nights and accepted the possibility of an early death. On far too many occasions, however, those who advocated voting rights met violence head-on in the most public of places. Brookhaven resident Lamar Smith would tragically add to those numbers.

Lamar Smith was a registered voter who had voted in the primary election a few weeks prior to his murder. Thus, his political participation stood as an example to the many "Negroes" he had convinced of the importance of fighting for their right to participate in the political process.[20] Within hours of Smith's murder, Evers arrived in Brookhaven to find out what had transpired and what mechanisms were in place to apprehend the killer or killers. He discovered that Smith had "kept an unknown political appointment" that day and had been shot in broad daylight around 10:00 A.M. on the busy courthouse square with no apparent witnesses.[21] District attorney E. C. Barlow later announced that the murder of Smith was "politically inspired . . . because he was campaigning against the incumbent supervisor, J. Hugh James, whose office was up for grabs in Brookhaven's 'Democratic primary.'"[22] News reports from the *Jackson Daily News* and the *State Times* (Jackson) identified Noah Smith, a white farmer, as the shooter. Barlow issued a warrant for his arrest. He ordered the warrant after Sheriff Robert Case refused to arrest Smith, even though he supposedly saw him run to his truck with blood-spattered clothing after the shooting.[23] Although Evers acknowledged that eventually "Mr. Smith's assailants were apprehended, [and] placed under a $20,000 bond each . . . [, they] were not brought to trial because the grand jury had no witnesses and did not indict them." Here, when speaking of "assailants," Evers was referring to the report of several men who accosted Smith on the courthouse lawn before he was killed. The men involved in the "murder," according to *Jet* magazine reports, included Noah Smith, fifty-nine years old; Mack Smith, forty-five years old; and Charles Falvey, thirty-five years old.[24] The social and political situation for African Americans in the Deep South proved grave and, according to Roy Wilkins, Mississippi presented "the worst offender."[25]

Although vicious in nature, these two murders did not elicit the same degree of media attention as that of Emmett Till. When two white Mississippians brutally lynched the fourteen-year-old, and white Mississippians later absolved them of any responsibility for the horrible crime, people across the nation erupted with disgust and vented their frustrations through tears and massive demonstrations. The NAACP reported that on October 11, 1955, 20,000 individuals joined a "midday street rally in New York City" to protest the lynching.[26] The murder also had a psychological impact on African American youth in the state that used racial tension to maintain social and political control.

Civil rights activist and Mississippi native Anne Moody believed that the Till lynching added a deeper and more insidious component to the fear blacks harbored in Mississippi. "Before Emmett Till's murder," Moody recalled, "I had known the fear of hunger, hell, and the Devil. But now there was a new fear known to me—the fear of being killed just because I was black. This was the worse of my fears." Till's murder created psychological tensions in African American youth that were almost impossible to counter or prepare for the way one would approach more tangible concerns. Moody understood clearly, as did other youth, that once she secured "food, the fear of starving to death would leave. I also was told that if I were a good girl, I wouldn't have to fear the Devil or hell. But I didn't know what one had to do or not do as a Negro not to be killed. Probably just being a Negro period was enough," she thought.[27] Thus, the brutality and randomness of the Till lynching caused many African Americans to weigh their fears against their anger and, in many instances, anger won out.

As a response to the Till murder, many African Americans who were previously advocates of patience and perseverance in Mississippi and surrounding areas joined the civil rights movement and demanded more direct approaches to resisting oppression and obtaining equality.[28] The murder of Emmett Louis Till hurt Medgar Evers as a black man, a husband, and most importantly as a father. He believed that something had to be done. He had to make sure the world knew of the brutality whites imposed on blacks in Mississippi.

Emmett Till arrived in Money, Mississippi, in 1955 to spend the summer with relatives. This proved a common occurrence as many parents who had moved to northern cities often sent their children back south during the summers to keep in touch with the southern half of the family tree. On August 24, Till, along with some cousins and friends, went to a neighborhood store owned and operated by Roy Bryant. Bryant was out of town that day, leaving his wife, Carolyn, to run the store. There exist several accounts of what took place in the store between Carolyn Bryant and Till, with some saying that he "wolf-whistled" at her, and others reporting that he asked her out on a date or touched her hand in some manner. Whatever allegedly happened, Roy Bryant eventually found out about the supposed incident and on August 28, he and his half-brother J. W. Milam went to the house of Till's great-uncle, Mose Wright, around 2:30 A.M. The brothers took Till from the house, beat and pistol-whipped him repeatedly, and later shot him in the head with a .45-caliber pistol. Bryant and Milam then used barbed wire to tie a heavy cotton gin fan, weighing about seventy-four pounds, to his neck to weigh him down and threw the badly disfigured body of Emmett Till into the Tallahatchie River. A fisherman discovered the body three days later.[29] Pictures of the swollen waterlogged body of this teenager shocked the nation and forced many to try and figure out how and why this could have happened. Some individuals pointed to the *Brown* decision as a reason why violence against blacks intensified in Mississippi and why punishments whites meted out for social infractions increased in severity.

White Mississippians considered the *Brown* decision an all-out attack upon their ways of life. This court-sanctioned attack on the tenets of racial separation required whites to maintain control over their communities by instilling fear in a black population that many believed were advancing at the expense and welfare of white Mississippians. Whites were most concerned that integration would lead to miscegenation, and many saw the *Brown* decision as an attack on the sanctity and virtue of the white family structure. After all, it allowed black and white youth to mingle in a learning environment of which parents had no control or input. Thus by 1955, an increased desire to control blacks through violence proved evident, and both whites and blacks throughout the state recognized the shift in intensity.

White Tougaloo chaplain Edwin (Ed) King believed that had the Till incident happened "earlier that Emmett Till would not have been murdered for whistling at a white woman, he would have been whipped." Yet one must keep in mind that whites had indeed murder_ _ _ and brutalized black children prior to *Brown* for the smallest infrac_ _ _ _ _ merely heightened white agitation and invited closer racia_ _ _ _ r the *Brown* decision, as indicative of the Till lynch_ _ _ _ _ _ _ _ _ _ _tions of any degree produced greater scrutiny, particularly _ _ _ _ _ _ _ _ were the so-called offending party. Mississippi officials _ _ _ _ _ _ _ to effectively counter any attack upon the status quo that *Brown* invited. As a result, King noted that the "interracial meetings between schools like Tougaloo and Millsaps or even Ole Miss and Mississippi State through the YMCA, the YWCA, interracial meetings between church women . . . those kinds of things all collapsed by 1955, 56." Dittmer stretches the social ramifications of *Brown* even further. "From 1954 to the early 1960s," he exclaimed, "the Mississippi State Legislature enacted a series of statutes aimed at the enemies of white supremacy, a category so broad it encompassed literally every attempt to modify the status quo in race relations."[30] The Till murder brought Mississippi national attention as people outside of the state and throughout the world watched to see what would happen.

The Till murder hurt Evers tremendously. Myrlie Evers recalled that "Medgar cried when he found that this had happened to Emmett Till." He cried "out of frustration and anger."[31] Evers played a large role in investigating the Till murder and sending accounts of events to NAACP headquarters for publication in northern newspapers. In fact, NAACP field representative Howard Spence argued that had "it not been for Medgar Evers . . . asking me to go investigate, . . . [the Till lynching] would have just been another 'case' that's been forgot." While internal investigations continued, Evers made sure that news groups outside of the state knew what was happening to blacks in the Magnolia State.[32] On one occasion, Spence returned to Jackson to provide Evers a report of his investigation of the Till murder. Spence found a reporter from Detroit already in the office speaking with Evers. The reporter, Spence recalled, told Evers that "never before has a case of this kind been able to escape the borders of Mississippi. 'Now we're gonna see that this one gets out: because the report that you have given us will be in the Detroit press tomorrow.'"[33] Evers's role in the investigation proved to be both multifaceted and interweaving.

Regarding Evers's involvement, Mamie Till-Mobley, Emmett's mother, acknowledged that she "was grateful for his commitment and his compassion. He had been really moved by Emmett's murder. He was the one who had done the initial investigation to brief the NAACP head office." Charles Evers also recalled the added responsibility that his brother took on in searching out witnesses.[34] In the final analysis, however, Medgar noted the futility of the work the NAACP put into solving Till's murder, as far as a guilty verdict was concerned. "During the trial the NAACP was able to secure two additional key witnesses to the kidnapping and beating of Till," Evers exclaimed. However, after "having successfully gotten the additional witnesses, the new evidence proved futile in an already hostile court. The minds of the jury had already been set into a fixed 'not guilty.'"[35] Roy Wilkins had also informed the Justice Department in September that the "NAACP urges the Federal Government, through the Justice Department, to delay no longer in calling a halt to jungle fury unloosed in Mississippi. Every moment of delay compounds the national shame."[36]

In addition to the leg work Medgar Evers put into investigating the Till lynching, Tougaloo archivist Minnie White Watson, of Jackson, and long-time friend of Medgar's, believed that he was instrumental in "talking Mrs. Till into having . . . [an] open casket funeral" for her son.[37] While the Till case garnered national attention, *Jet* magazine immortalized the lynching with its publication of the brutal image of a swollen and seemingly inhuman cadaver that bore no resemblance to the fourteen-year-old child.[38] The funeral pictures of a slain Emmett Till enraged the public and brought to bear upon the nation the severity of Mississippi's brutality against African Americans. When asked why she felt that Medgar advocated an open casket, Watson asserted that it helped to solidify what was happening to blacks in Mississippi, for "a picture is worth a thousand words" and up until that point words hadn't helped that much.[39]

The murder of Emmett Till was a disturbing occurrence that pulled at the very fabric of racism at the state, national, and international level. For many African Americans, the fact that Till was a child visiting from Chicago who did not fully appreciate southern mores regarding race underscored the barbarity of his murder. Sure, Lee and Smith had been killed, but they understood the risks associated with their actions, whereas Till was a child first and a foreigner to Mississippi culture second. Regardless of the severity or the end result, the three murders heightened Evers's personal awareness that unless someone stood firm and demanded change, no black person would be safe in Mississippi or any other place where racism operated freely.

More than anything else, the murders of Lee, Smith, and Till took a tremendous toll on Evers. Their murders required justice and he believed that only by remaining vigilant in the fight for social equality, could these senseless deaths translate into something positive.[40] As a consequence, Evers traveled to Washington, D.C., as a part of an NAACP delegation to discuss the "three lynchings" with assistant U.S. attorney general Warren Olney, III.[41] Evers noted after the meeting that he, and other NAACP officials, had "made it clear to the Department of Justice official of the need for Federal intervention into the State of Mississippi for the assurance that the Civil Rights of Negroes of that state would not be abridged." They received a promise "that 'appropriate' actions" would be forthcoming from the Justice Department.[42] Evers had hoped that the Justice Department would get involved in the Till case. Olney later apprised Roy Wilkins that there was "no evidence of a violation of the Federal Kidnapping Statute in this case. Therefore, we are without jurisdiction to proceed in this matter."[43]

Following on the heels of the Till murder, Evers investigated the killing of Clinton Melton in the town of Glendora, in northwest Mississippi. Melton worked as a gas station attendant for his employer Lee McGarrh, who was identified as the owner of the gas station. On December 3, 1955, a white customer named Elmer Kimball pulled into the station to get gas. McGarrh told Melton to fill Kimball's car and he complied. When Kimball returned he argued that he had only wanted $2.00 worth of fuel to which Melton explained that McGarrh had instructed him to fill it up. Kimball then labeled Melton a "smart nigger" and threatened to kill him. Evers noted that McGarrh advised Melton to go on home to avoid any trouble. As soon as "Clinton started to get into his car," Evers reported, "he was blasted two or three times in the face with shotgun blasts which killed Clinton Melton instantly." Kimball, Evers reported, was traveling with John Henry Wilson, a "Negro," who begged Kimball "not to 'shoot that boy he ain't done nothing.'" Wilson later ran into the service station asking McGarrh "to 'save' him from" Kimball. Kimball was also a supposedly good friend of J. W. Milam, one of the killers of Emmett Till, and was reportedly driving Milam's car the day he killed Melton.[44] Evers reported that Melton left a wife and four small children ages five, three, two, and five months old who "were left fatherless by this fiendish killing." He noted that the "experience [of this investigation] shall be of long memory."[45]

Evers investigated such events with a two-fold purpose: first, to find out what happened and to obtain justice for the victim; and second, to get the news of what had happened to the national media and expose the brutality of Mississippi. Sometimes he faced resistance from the victims who did not want NAACP involvement. Beulah Melton (Clinton Melton's widow) notified Evers that "she did 'not want the NAACP to come into the case.'" When Evers pressed for a reason why, she responded with "that is why they did Mrs. Bradly like they did." Here she meant the eventual acquittal of Bryant and Milam and thus the futility of pressing the issue in light of the danger of doing so.[46] Evers, however, reminded her that "whatever we do [NAACP] for her would help all of us."[47] When Gloster Current asked Evers, "How is the family fixed?" he responded, "They are not fixed too hot; not well at all." Their financial situation also bothered Evers, although he admitted that she had received some monetary assistance from local groups such as the Lions Club and Glendora Methodist Church.[48]

Despite such hesitations, he hoped that national publicity would pressure the federal government to intervene. When investigating acts of brutality, Evers often brought a photographer he trusted to provide stirring images to bolster his written accounts. Tom Armstrong, owner of the Farish Street Newsstand and Studio, proved to be one such individual. Again as a father, Melton's death, and the faces of his now fatherless children, disturbed Evers on many levels. In response, he continued to apply pressure on white Mississippians to get involved in the struggle for civil rights and to oppose members of their race who wanted to keep Mississippi in the dark ages of segregation and wanton violence. Events in Montgomery, Alabama, however, provided Evers with additional pressure points for convincing whites to cooperate and added inspiration for blacks to continue struggling in Mississippi.

Prior to 1955, many African Americans considered Montgomery, Alabama, a progressive city. The city could point to black political participation, its hiring of black police officers, the opening of high school education for blacks, a hospital for blacks, and a host of other progressive measures. Many African Americans saw this as an indication of the city's willingness to move forward on race relations. Then came the *Brown* decision and many black Montgomerians believed there would be a smooth transition, one that would provide even greater opportunities. Yet many were not satisfied with the way things were and sought to openly challenge the segregation practiced throughout the city's bus system. The Women's Political

Council (WPC), an organization comprised of black professional women, proved important in attempts to rid the city of segregated seating in public transportation.

In 1953, the WPC met with the city commission, remarked historian J. Mills Thornton III, and presented three specific complaints: "that because of the reservation of the front ten seats for whites, blacks sometimes had to stand even though empty seats were available; that black passengers were compelled to get on at the front door to pay their fare and then get off and reboard at the back door to a take a seat . . . ; and that buses stopped, when requested, at every corner in white neighborhoods but only at every other corner in black neighborhoods." Only the last issue was resolved and on May 21, 1954, Jo Ann Robinson, WPC president and Alabama State College professor, sent Mayor W. A. Gayle a letter warning that if the bus issue could not be resolved, the city could expect blacks to protest. Protest measures, she forewarned, could also include a general citywide boycott of the bus system.[49] The seriousness of the points raised by the WPC, as well as its warnings, became painfully apparent to city officials after a seemingly routine arrest on the first day of December 1955.

On December 1, 1955, Rosa Parks, a little-known department store seamstress and NAACP member, boarded a Montgomery city bus, paid her fare, and moved to the back of the bus as required by law. Since all seats were taken on this particular day, Parks sat down in a vacant one near the middle of the bus in a section known as "no-man's-land." African American riders could lawfully sit here as long as there were no whites left standing. However, the understood rule remained that when a white person boarded the bus blacks normally relinquished their seat. When bus driver J. P. Blake realized that a white man was left without a seat, he ordered four blacks, including Parks, seated behind the white section to relinquish their seats. Drivers had the discretion, Parks recalled, "to adjust the seating in the middle sixteen seats."[50] "Having to take a certain section [on a bus] because of your race was humiliating," Parks admitted, "but having to stand up because a particular driver wanted to keep a white person from having to stand was, to my mind, most inhumane."[51] On this particular day, Parks refused to yield her seat and officers Fletcher B. Day and Dempsey W. Mixon, who arrived shortly after Blake notified police, placed her under arrest.

It was dangerous to challenge Alabama's segregated seating laws governing public transportation. Parks recalled that the bus drivers "carried guns and had what they called police power to rearrange the seating and enforce all the other rules of segregation on the buses."[52] Despite the dangers, defying bus segregation was not new to Parks as she had done so on many occasions. She had challenged the system earlier because, as she recalled, "I didn't see fit to pay my money into the front and then go around to the back. Sometimes bus drivers wouldn't permit me to get on the bus, and I had been evicted from the bus." One of those events had included an altercation with Blake in 1943 resulting in her removal from the bus. Her arrest remains a pivotal moment in the civil rights movement as it brought national attention to racism occurring in the Deep South.[53] Furthermore, Parks believed that had she "just been evicted from the bus and [if] he [the bus driver] hadn't placed me under arrest or had any charges brought against me, it probably could have been just another incident."[54]

The arrest of Rosa Parks sparked a bus boycott that lasted 381 days (of which the WPC played an integral part), united 50,000 African Americans in Montgomery, ended segregation on buses in the city, and catapulted Martin Luther King Jr. into national prominence.[55] African American riders wanted nothing more than humane treatment from a service that prospered because of their patronage. As a means of both spreading the word of what organized actions were taking place as well as a means of uniting African Americans, an advertisement in the *Montgomery Advertiser* announced that the "duly elected representatives of the people have the approval of the bus riders to present three proposals." The proposal, in part, required:

1. That assurance of more courtesy be extended the bus-riders. That the bus operators refrain from name calling, abusive language and threats.
2. That the seating of passengers will be on a "First-Come, First-Served" basis. . . .
3. That Negro bus drivers be employed on the bus lines serving predominately Negro areas. This is a fair request and we believe that men of good will, will readily accept it and admit that it is fair.[56]

The Montgomery Bus Boycott strengthened the men and women of Montgomery and instilled pride in their defense of their right to be treated with respect. The Montgomery Bus Boycott, however, had wider social and political ramifications for the civil rights movement than desegregating buses in Montgomery. As the historian Simon Wendt pointed out, the Montgomery movement also "marked the beginning of a surge in black activism" that spread across the country with nonviolence as its banner.[57] The boycott also transformed Martin Luther King Jr. into a national figure as he became the nationally recognized leader of African Americans. He also served as president of the newly formed Montgomery Improvement Association (MIA), whose function was to oversee the logistics, strategies, and organization of the boycott. The media followed King wherever there appeared a hint he might lead some type of mass demonstration or protest.

The leadership of Martin Luther King Jr. and the entire Montgomery movement impressed Evers, and he took a real interest in what had developed there. He believed that the successful use of nonviolent direct action in Alabama could also work in Mississippi, and thus he set about developing organizational relationships. As a consequence, he traveled to Montgomery on December 9, 1956, for "the closing session of the 'Institute of Non-Violence and Social Change.'" Evers's arrival happened during the height of the boycott, as it would officially end some eleven days later. In actuality, the Supreme Court ended bus segregation in Alabama on November 13, 1956, when it submitted its *Gayle v. Browder* decision. However, since legal technicalities prevented an immediate end to segregation, King and other MIA leaders decided to keep the boycott going until the Court's integration orders arrived; this did not occur until December 20.[58]

While in Montgomery, Evers met religious leaders such as Dr. Joseph H. Jackson and the famed and fiery Dr. Vernon Johns at the revered Holt Street Baptist and Dexter Memorial Avenue Baptist Church; the latter was King's pastoral church. Evers admitted that Jackson's Holt Street sermon was "really food for one's soul." His "only regret was that all of Montgomery, white and Negro, were not there to hear it, and for that matter all of the South, where it is so badly needed, particularly is it true in 'our state' (Mississippi)." His purpose, however, was to obtain a working partnership with Montgomery leaders to provide assistance with the Mississippi movement.[59]

As a means of obtaining support, Evers requested that Jackson, among other things, urge "all of our Baptists ministers in the State of Mississippi to take a more active part in this struggle for dignity." He also asked the minister to urge "influential laymen" to participate more fully "in our struggle for first-class citizenship" and for "each pastor, during 1957 and succeeding years, to take up collections to be turned over to the NAACP." Evers also extended an invitation for Reverend Jackson to come to speak at a mass meeting in Jackson the following year.[60] Evers's participation and meetings with various Alabama leaders was successful as evident by Martin Luther King's letter to Evers admitting that it "was a real pleasure having you in Montgomery yesterday. Your presence added much to the success of our meeting. You have my prayers and best wishes for continued success as you continue your struggle against the forces of evil and injustice in the state of Mississippi."[61]

In 1957, Evers reiterated his belief that the strategies used in Montgomery could work in Mississippi. He exclaimed in a speech at Mount Heron Baptist Church in Vicksburg, Mississippi, that those "Christian people in Montgomery have really demonstrated cooperation, and how effective it can be in a community. Certainly Reverend King and others demonstrating through actual practice that . . . they preach from the pulpit can be used in other forms of protest, such as registering and voting."[62] In 1955, however, the NAACP had been reluctant to endorse the direct-action strategies Montgomery activists practiced.

Despite the NAACP's reluctance to endorse the Montgomery Movement, individual NAACP members in Alabama did. On June 26, 1956, San Francisco, California, hosted the NAACP's 47th annual meeting. King attended the meeting where he delivered a major address and convention delegates, including Evers, welcomed him excitedly. Evers was inspired by King's speech touting the positive impact of direct action and its creation of a "new Negro" in Montgomery no longer willing to accept an inferior position. In response to King's leadership, Evers invited a contingent of "insurgent delegates" to his room the first night of the convention to discuss King's address and the benefit of direct-action strategies. The group hammered out a three-page resolution supporting the Montgomery Bus Boycott and the leadership of Martin Luther King Jr. Much to the chagrin of NAACP executive secretary Roy Wilkins and NAACP legal counsel Thurgood Marshall, they learned the delegates planned to deliver the resolution to the convention floor the following day. Both men met King in his hotel room to gauge his leadership and to discuss the overall boycott. As a means of preventing a "runaway convention," Wilkins finally agreed to the NAACP Legal Defense and Educational Fund (LDF) assuming litigation responsibilities associated with the boycott.[63] In many ways, the hand of the NAACP had been forced as Wilkins presented a resolution the following day indicating that "the NAACP Board of Directors and the national staff," according to NAACP reports, would "'give the most careful consideration' to nonviolent resistance as carried out in Montgomery, Alabama and Tallahassee, Florida 'for possible inclusion in our expanding program for civil rights.'" The delegates, including Medgar Evers, demonstrated their excitement with cheers and celebratory exchanges.[64]

In less than a year after the Smith and Till murders, Evers had met Martin Luther King Jr. and convinced a contingent of NAACP delegates to formalize their support for direct action by a resolution. Evers had organized this group despite knowing that the NAACP leadership had not yet approved of this type of strategy. The fact that Evers chose the NAACP meeting to intensify his move toward direct action is important. The NAACP convention allowed Evers access to 1,000 delegates with a variety of ideals and tactical leanings representing thirty-eight states. This potential for spreading a message of direct action among the NAACP leadership would have excited Evers. His brother Charles acknowledged that "Medgar wanted the NAACP to use marches, boycotts, and sit-ins" in the freedom struggle.[65] In 1956, there may not have been a better place (and with King present a better time) for Evers to assemble NAACP support for a shift in tactics. His aggressive push to marshal NAACP support seemed to indicate his awareness of this reality. The fact that the Montgomery Bus Boycott had generated national attention was not lost on Evers, who desired to utilize King's leadership stature to help focus national attention on the Mississippi struggle. He hoped that he could get King to come to Jackson to help address the social and political problems of the state thereby strengthen the Mississippi movement as a whole. Evers respected the type of commitment King's leadership garnered from those who adhered to his message of nonviolent direct-action protest. Despite its nonviolent program, armed resistance was not a foreign concept to Montgomery movement leaders.

The Montgomery boycott had undercurrents of armed resistance from the very beginning. During the early boycott phase, King had guns all about his home as individuals offered protection and armed guards. This came in response to the bombings that had accompanied blacks' resistance to segregation and racism. On January 30, 1956, while his wife, Coretta, Mary Lucy (the wife of Dexter Baptist Church member Roscoe Williams), and two-month-old daughter Yolanda (Yoki) were home, someone tossed a bomb that exploded a few feet from the house. Although no one was injured and the bomb resulted in minimum structural damage, it was strong enough to shake the house and to fill the front room with smoke and broken glass. In response to the bombing, King, Ralph Abernathy, and Reverend H. H. Hubbard went to the sheriff's office on February 1 and applied for a gun permit. King explained that he wanted the permit for the reason that his home had been bombed two days earlier and because of the hundreds of threatening phone calls he received. Despite the logic behind his request, they denied him the permit and, as James Haskins has written, "gleefully notified the news media that the 'great' advocate of nonviolence had sought to acquire a weapon of violence." King later approached Alabama governor James E. ("Big Jim") Folsom requesting that he provide King a permit to keep a gun in his automobile. Folsom informed King that he would have to discuss it with the sheriff.[66] The fact that the Montgomery Bus Boycott gained national attention, particularly with the bombings and gun permit controversy, could not have been lost upon Evers, who later proved to be a master at manipulating media coverage.

As a means of connecting the civil rights struggle in Mississippi to the national movement, Medgar Evers wrote King on July 31, 1956, and invited him to speak to the Jackson Branch of the NAACP. Evers did not attempt to hide his admiration for King and, in no uncertain terms, let King know that the NAACP in Jackson believed that his "presence would do more to bring together . . . [the] ministers and the people of Jackson than any other person or incident conceivable." Evers sought to get King to come to Jackson on other occasions as well. He extended an invitation again in November but King, because of other obligations at the time, wrote Medgar to let him know that he could not accept. However, he asked that he write him again around February where he could better apprise him of whether visits to Jackson were possible.[67]

The NAACP national leadership often was reluctant to support attempts by other civil rights organizations to work in Mississippi. Evers received pressure from NAACP officials not to participate or assist in the efforts of other organizations to mobilize in the state. Evers walked a fine line between what he believed and what NAACP leaders such as Roy Wilkins demanded regarding other organizations. This may explain why he had written Wilkins on April 10, 1956, apprising him of the fact that the Regional Council of Negro Leadership was attempting to employ the "services of such men as Rev. M. L. King or [Ralph] Abernathy" and other noteworthy individuals such as Adam Clayton Powell as speakers. Evers expressed his concerns in that he believed that "the bringing of national figures down here will tend to confuse the people and make them more gullible to the 'hog wash' of the Regional Council." He told Wilkins that if he wished to prevent the group from speaking that he could rest assured that "we the N.A.A.C.P. stand 100% with you."[68] In this particular instance, however, Wilkins did not react negatively regarding the mobilization of other organizations in Mississippi.

On April 16, Wilkins wrote Evers stipulating that he had already assured T. R. M. Howard "of our good will. I do not know who will be speaking for [t]his meeting in Jackson but I don't think our people will be confused. Please give me a report on the happenings, as full as you can get."[69] Although Evers may have provided lip service to what Wilkins and Gloster Current might have preferred, his actions in California underscored his desire to incorporate the tactics of other groups and thus cast doubt on the sincerity of the sentiments expressed in the above letter. In fact, his friend Cornelius Turner noted that Medgar was not totally satisfied with the NAACP's dedication to the courts as the primary means of achieving equality.[70] Thus, it came as no surprise that Evers kept a close watch on other organizations and the methods they employed in the fight for civil equality.

Despite Evers's disapproving letter to Wilkins, he kept the lines of communication open with Martin Luther King Jr. and participated in events sponsored by the Southern Christian Leadership Conference, the organization King and others established in 1957 to continue organized nonviolent protests. Despite being a field secretary for the NAACP, on February 14, 1957, the SCLC leadership elected Evers to the post of assistant secretary to the Reverend T. J. Jemison of Baton Rouge, Louisiana. Evers accepted the position but later received pressure from Roy Wilkins to resign because of the supposed conflict of interest with his NAACP work. When Current first became aware of Evers's election to the SCLC, he suggested that he advise Roy Wilkins of his election "as a matter of policy."[71] It proved to be more than a conflict of interest that concerned NAACP officials. They did not want the divisions a new organization might pose regarding memberships and financial contributions. As a consequence, the SCLC went out of its way to assure NAACP officials that it did not plan on undercutting their programs. Despite proposed good will between the two groups, having two civil rights organizations operating in the same geographical area created tensions, suspicions, and conflict. Historian Adam Fairclough maintained that the "NAACP's national officials immediately perceived SCLC as an unwelcomed competitor and a threat to its Southern base." The NAACP also feared that the SCLC planned on using NAACP staff and branch members to build up the SCLC at the NAACP's expense.[72] This sheds light on the reaction of NAACP officials upon hearing that Evers had accepted the SCLC assistant secretary post.

Having accepted the position, the advice to then resign posed a dilemma for Evers. He sought to rectify the situation with his superiors. Evers attempted damage control by contacting Roy Wilkins for advice as well as to explain the motivation behind his actions. "While I was completely unaware of the fact that I might have been violating the policy of the NAACP for having taken such a responsibility," Evers admitted, "I was nevertheless sincere in trying to do what I possibly could to bring first-class citizenship to our section of the country as hurriedly as possible. However, it is not my intention to run counter to the policies of our organization."[73] Evers's admission that he was working "to bring first-class citizenship to our section of the country as hurriedly as possible" underscored his belief that the NAACP was now moving too slowly and that the Mississippi movement needed to employ new strategies and tactics in the civil rights fight. However, he immediately sought Wilkins's "opinion on the matter" of his election. In response to his request for advice on what to do, Wilkins advised Medgar to "quietly ease out of service at a convenient time on the excuse that your duties with the NAACP require that you not be committed to specific duties with another group."[74] On August 20, Evers wrote King regarding the position. First he told King that he was highly honored to have had the opportunity to serve, for the past recent months, as assistant secretary to the conference, however, because of my manifold duties as a staff member of the N.A.A.C.P., and the policies of the N.A.A.C.P. regarding staff members functioning officially in other prominent organizations, I hereby request to be relieved immediately of my official position as assistant secretary to the Southern Christian Leadership Conference.

I hope that you will understand my position, and be assured that I will be happy to cooperate in whatever way possible to gain for our people first-class citizenship.[75]

King accepted Evers's resignation with the acknowledgment that "we hate to lose you from the conference . . . but I can well understand the reasons why you find it necessary to resign."[76] The whole ordeal made Evers extremely uncomfortable and irritated.

The NAACP's forbidding Medgar to work with the SCLC made him quite angry, Myrlie recalled. Of more importance, she remembered that from time to time the lack of support from the national office "hurt him so deeply [and as a result] I'd see tears at times. I saw the shoulders sag, I heard the sighs that came from him, deep sighs [and more often] I saw the look of hurt on his face . . . [when the NAACP leadership let him down.]"[77] Although no longer an official member of King's "prominent" organization, Evers still believed in the validity of the tactics King employed and their usefulness in the struggle for equality in Mississippi. Also, to have worked under Reverend Jemison would have appealed to Evers, who knew of his successful ten-day application of direct action in Baton Rouge, Louisiana, in 1953.

Theodore J. Jemison moved to Baton Rouge in 1949 to assume the vacated pastorship of Mt. Zion Baptist Church, one of the largest churches in the city. He later served as president of the local NAACP chapter. This, in itself, is somewhat interesting given his later implementation of direct action, something the NAACP tended to shy away from. In 1953, Jemison headed the newly formed United Defense League (UDL), which consisted of several community organizations. In response to African Americans' unequal treatment on area buses, Jemison helped organize a boycott against the bus company. As the leadership of the bus boycott in Montgomery later found, African Americans' economic significance to business enterprises could not be ignored for long. In Baton Rouge, African Americans accounted "for at least two-thirds of the bus company's revenue," remarked sociologist Aldon Morris. Despite realizing their economic strength, challenging segregation would not be easy.[78]

Bus drivers, with the support of state attorney general Fred LeBlanc, refused to enforce *Ordinance* 222; the ordinance allowed patrons to sit on a first-come first-serve basis. Instead, bus drivers sought political support to uphold segregation. The boycott, however, had the full support of African Americans. Fairclough pointed out that a "fleet of more than a hundred private vehicles . . . sustained the protest, with three gas stations providing fuel at wholesale prices." After intense economic pressure, city leaders presented a compromise to end the boycott. Jemison suggested that the group accept the compromise and, after a spirited debate, the UDL Executive Council presented the compromise to the people at a mass meeting where they eventually accepted it. The boycott ended on June 23 when the council adopted *Ordinance* 251. This ordinance, Fairclough noted, modified *Ordinance* 222 to the reservation of "the two short front seats for whites and the longer rear seat for blacks." Jemison maintained that he considered the compromise a temporary measure and reserved the right to challenge the entire segregation system later through the courts, but many believed they were missing a prime opportunity to overturn segregation in the city.[79] Jemison explained that his "vision was not anywhere, at that particular time, other than to see that Negroes could sit down when they paid the same fare."[80]

Although not the success that African Americans had hoped for and certainly not the result Montgomery boycotters would experience, the Louisiana Bus Boycott was a demonstration of black folks' ability to come together and exact social change. Building on this experience, leaders of the Montgomery Bus Boycott, particularly Martin Luther King Jr., sought advice from Jemison, who suggested that the group set "up a volunteer car pool."[81] Despite the role Jemison played in the movement, as well as his previous NAACP service, Medgar Evers had no choice but to resign from the SCLC. This issue bothered him tremendously.

Days prior to his resignation, speaking to a crowd at Mount Heron Baptist Church in Vicksburg, Mississippi, Evers offered the following admiration for the leadership and outcome of the Montgomery Bus Boycott and its potential ramifications for Mississippi. He informed the crowd that the

> Reverend Dr. Martin Luther King and others in Montgomery, Alabama, have to me set an example of cooperation that has been unexcelled in my lifetime and possibly yours. Those Christian people in Montgomery have really demonstrated cooperation, and how effective it can be in a community. Certainly Reverend King and others demonstrating through actual practice that that [sic] they preach from the pulpit can be used in other forms of protest, such as registering and voting.[82]

This speech was only one of many instances in which Evers sought to link the Mississippi movement with the national civil rights struggle. His constant reports and public documentation of Mississippi's brutal nature forced the federal government to take notice of what was happening in Mississippi and across the country concerning African Americans' struggles for equality. If Medgar Evers saw the potential for change that civil rights struggles during the 1950s promised, so did the state of Mississippi. As a result, it put in place mechanisms designed to stop the internal hemorrhaging that the civil rights struggle caused within the body of segregation.

Although the 1950s proved a violent decade for African Americans, it also underscored the strengthening of Mississippi's political arm of segregation and its covert tactics for maintaining the status quo. Medgar Evers had established himself as a capable leader within the community, and state officials considered him a danger to the system of segregation. Whites who occupied positions of political importance, such as Jackson mayor Allen Thompson, believed that Evers was the type of person who needed to be quieted. The Sovereignty Commission, a state-supported entity organized to protect and uphold racial segregation, seemed just the organization to accomplish this task. By the late 1950s, Evers "had become one of the most disturbing eyesores for the state agency," the historian Yasuhiro Katagiri proclaimed.[83] Although Evers may have shunned the spotlight, he took center stage in the orchestrated drama directed by the Sovereignty Commission; its surveillance of Medgar Evers provides a glimpse into the dangerous atmosphere in which civil rights activists worked, lived, and sometimes died.

Mississippi lawmakers recognized the severity of the attack upon segregation and sought ways to undercut the protracted effort to end the practice in Mississippi. As a means of weakening the effectiveness of civil rights activists, Mississippi lawmakers created a tax-supported organization to protect and enforce racial separation. On March 20, 1956, fifty-eight state representatives introduced House Bill No. 880, which provided for the creation of the Mississippi State Sovereignty Commission.[84] State representatives maintained that the protection of the sovereignty of the state of Mississippi reflected the true purpose of the Sovereignty Commission. Section 5 of Bill 880 reads:

> It shall be the duty of the commission to do and perform any and all acts and things deemed necessary and proper to protect the sovereignty of the State of Mississippi, and her sister states, from encroachment thereon by the Federal Government or any branch, department or agency thereof; and to resist the usurpation of the rights and powers reserved to this state and our sister states by the Federal Government or any branch, department or agency thereof.[85]

Although Bill 880 did not explicitly address the issue of race, its pro-segregationist stand rang clear, and on March 29, 1956, Mississippi officially instituted the Sovereignty Commission. Segregationists considered the commission the perfect weapon in the battle against integration. The state legislature confirmed its support for the creation of the "segregation watch-dog agency" by providing the commission with a two-year $250,000 appropriation within a week after its establishment. Under Mississippi governor Ross Barnett, the state legislature increased the commission's biennial appropriation by $250,000.[86]

As a political entity, the Sovereignty Commission organized around a small, yet powerful center comprising twelve members including four ex officio members: Governor James Coleman, Lieutenant Governor Carroll Gartin, House Speaker Walter Sillers, and Attorney General Joe T. Patterson. By mid-April, Governor Coleman, who also served as agency chair, announced the appointment of three prominent Mississippi attorneys to the commission: Will S. Henley of Hazlehurst, Hugh N. Clayton of New Albany, and George J. Thornton of Kosciusko. Thornton later resigned to accept a position with the "State Oil and Gas Board" and school superintendent H. V. Cooper of Vicksburg replaced him. After meeting with Governor Coleman, Gartin and Sillers appointed Senators Earl Evans and William G. Burgin Jr. of Columbus, and Representatives George Payne Cossar of Charleston, William H. Johnson Jr. of Decatur and Joseph W. Hopkins of Clarksdale, Mississippi, respectively. Governor Coleman selected Representative Ney Gore as the first director of the new surveillance organization.[87] Thus, prominent and powerful politicos staffed the commission who both supported and backed its agenda.

Financially supported with both state monies and private donations, Gregory Crofton noted that "the commission set out to defend segregation on a national level." It began the process by "quietly deploying its 'eyes and ears' throughout Mississippi to squash the civil rights crusades."[88] To effectively accomplish this goal, state senator Henry J. Kirksey recalled that an "Interesting operation of the Sovereignty Commission was to find Blacks whom they could pay, as they had paid Percy Green[e] [*Jackson Advocate* editor] to make statements in favor of voluntary segregation of the races in the state."[89]

est Commission officials kept a close eye on persons they deemed of inter

and sent activity reports to the state legislature. Agents also recruited and utilized the services of paid white and black informants to monitor civil rights activities and organizations such as the NAACP. Black Baptist minister Reverend H. H. Humes of Greenville served as one of the commission's principal informants in the black community.[90] Whenever Medgar Evers conducted meetings in Greenville or surrounding Delta areas, Katagiri maintained, Humes shadowed him "to collect 'full information' on those gatherings for the Sovereignty Commission."[91] Humes's connection with the commission would not go unnoticed by the black community or unchallenged.

In 1957, when accusations of Humes's connection with the commission were publicized, Humes threatened to file a libel suit, naming Evers as one of the defendants. His anger stemmed from a public report from the Ministerial Interdenominational Improvement Association of Mississippi denouncing Humes, Percy Greene, and others, for "having received money from the State Sovereignty Commission."[92] Evers reported that the organization developed "in an effort to imbue our ministers with more courage and knowledge of the Negro's constitutional rights, so as to become more actively engaged in our struggle for first-class citizenship in the state of Mississippi." Here Evers notes that the July 16, 1957, Ministerial meeting produced a "resolution condemning the actions of certain Negroes, who received funds from the State Sovereignty Commission." This resolution, Evers continued, "was the highlight of the meeting."[93] Humes's counterattack proved to be a problem that Evers needed to quickly address with his superiors.

Evers quickly wrote Ruby Hurley to add some clarity to a situation that appeared to be snowballing with each passing day. He readily admitted that possibly, "it was unfortunate that my name was attached to the resolution that criticized those persons who received funds from the Sovereignty Commission. I was called upon, by the ministerial group, to work with them in drafting the resolution. However, I am not a member, nor did I sign the resolution." He further noted that the libel suit was against him "(not the NAACP)" and other individuals "for a whopping sum of $325,000," which Humes maintained he would file by July 29.[94] Regardless of the infighting among black groups, the commission acquired the information needed and put it to good use.

The commission used the acquired information to identify individual activists and target them for harassment and intimidation. Commission officials also provided financial assistance to other pro-segregationist agencies such as the Citizens' Council, which, in 1960, received $20,000 "to fund the *Citizens' Council Forum.*" The *Forum* consisted of a series of radio and television programs touting the age-old states' rights argument and the conservative southern view on such issues as civil rights, black inferiority, and the inherent social and cultural dangers associated with interracial relationships.[95] In response to the commission's financial support of the WCC, Evers urged each NAACP branch to launch an immediate protest "against

the action of the Sovereignty Commission." NAACP branches in Clarksdale, Greenville, and Jackson "responded with mass protest meetings."[96]
The Sovereignty Commission, by far, epitomized the type of political muscle
that Evers and other civil rights activists faced daily.

The Sovereignty Commission kept Medgar Evers under close surveillance and logged anything that helped gauge any threat he posed. As a consequence, the commission cataloged programs where he spoke, recorded the
content of his public addresses, and filed correspondences between him and
association members. They also compiled multiple NAACP memorandums
written by Evers or by others whose ideas he supported. One particular
memorandum, dated May 13, 1963, underscored the type of rhetoric that
concerned commission officials. In this particular letter, Evers and NAACP
youth council advisor John Salter called for "an end to all forms of racial
segregation in Jackson." The group further avowed that the NAACP was
"determined to end all state and government sponsored segregation in the
parks, playgrounds, schools, libraries and other public facilities. To accomplish this we shall use all lawful means of protest—picketing, marches, mass
meetings, litigation and whatever legal means we deem necessary."
Information such as this sparked commission interests and heightened organizational surveillance of Evers and his social and political activities.[97]

Mississippi officials put in place obstacles designed to quiet dissent or
to at least make it difficult for activists to speak to large and diverse audiences. In an "Extraordinary Session" of the Mississippi Legislature in 1955,
state representatives adopted Senate Concurrent Resolution No. 6, which
made it easier to silence opponents of segregation.[98] Although the resolution
does not identify particular persons or organizations, its meaning is clear.
The resolution pointed out that it had "come to the attention of the Senate
and House of Representatives" that certain individuals had "addressed
audiences at several of the State Supported Institutions of Higher Learning,
and other State Supported Institutions." This proved a concern for Mississippi officials who put forth explicit language to prevent these speaking
engagements.

People throughout the city knew that Evers had spoken at several institutions of higher learning and had subsequently recruited many students to
the civil rights struggle. The resolution sought to prevent such efforts, and
its wording proved clear and straightforward:

> That it is the consensus of the Legislature of the State of Mississippi that
> individuals who are members, or endorse the theories, of organizations
> dedicated to the overthrow of our way of life and the spirit and intent
> of the laws of the State of Mississippi should not be invited to address
> audiences at any State Supported Institution in Mississippi; and

BE IT FURTHER RESOLVED, That the governing authorities of our State Supported Institutions are urged to carefully investigate and consider the background and character of persons proposed as speakers to audiences at such Institutions, to use caution and discretion in extending invitations to speakers, and to refrain from extending such invitations when the investigation discloses the probability of the proposed speaker's endorsing such alien theories; and

BE IT FURTHER RESOLVED, That the governing authorities of other Institutions operating in the State of Mississippi are hereby requested to apprise themselves of the consensus of the Legislature. . . .[99]

Mississippi authorities had now put in place legal methods to deal with those who verbally expressed discontent. The interpretation of their dissent, in terms of the danger to state security, lay entirely in the hands of Mississippi officials. Deep within this matrix of legalese lay the commission and its informants who kept tabs on all *persons of interest* to the state of Mississippi.

Although the Sovereignty Commission took an interest in all civil rights activities, Medgar Evers generated particular concern and the commission gathered and catalogued everything they could regarding his past and present actions. It then passed along any relevant information to local law enforcement officials, who then disrupted NAACP meetings and intimidated participants. On April 30, 1956, Evers informed Roy Wilkins that "there were more than 25 Highway patrol, local police officers, and detectives, in and around the Masonic Temple Building on the 27th [of April] whose objective, apparently, was to create a psychological fear in the people."[100] The Commission also published in local newspapers the names of activists attending rallies and their employers as a means of bringing economic pressure on them.

By the time the Sovereignty Commission perfected its segregationist tactics, lynchings of black Mississippians were common occurrences, and Evers was determined that these acts of violence receive national attention. With the power and influence of the Sovereignty Commission backing the actions of segregationists, however, the political and social atmosphere in which civil rights workers labored grew deadlier. Despite the growing risks, Evers continued to push for civil equality and, as a consequence, his file at the Sovereignty Commission grew, containing hundreds of pieces of documentation. Some of this proved repetitive but still underscores the level of scrutiny Evers's activities garnered.

As a result of Evers's defiant attitude, a trait both his siblings Charles and Elizabeth maintained he inherited from their father, members of the white community were well aware of his movements as well as his political activities throughout the state. As a consequence, by 1956, a host of individuals were willing to provide information and assistance to help the Sovereignty Commission prevent Evers from maintaining a local following. The commission proved quite effective in using its resources to both monitor and frustrate the progress of civil rights activism in Mississippi. This may help to explain the 1956 falloff in NAACP memberships. Gloster Current informed Evers that the "membership in Mississippi . . . [had] declined from 4,639 in 1955 to a total of 1,716 to date in 1956." The drastic decline in NAACP memberships concerned association leaders.[101] Despite the decline in NAACP memberships in Mississippi, the association's total membership increased from 305,589 in 1955 to 350,424 in 1956.[102] Regardless of the reasons why the numbers plummeted in Mississippi, the NAACP leadership expected Medgar to halt the downward spiral.

The community support that Evers sought sometimes proved elusive, particularly within rural areas where blacks often suffered from a plantation mentality of subservience and fear. In a letter to Roy Wilkins, Evers spoke of the hopelessness he felt encompassed areas such as Yazoo City in regard to the fight for civil equality. Due to fear and intimidation, he explained, the "Negroes [in Yazoo City] will not come together. . . . I would say it is worse than being behind the Iron Curtain[, a reference to the Soviet Union]. You can't possibly imagine how cruel the white element is to the local Negro citizens, however, it is the result of the Negroes not sticking together."[103] Although Evers understood the reasons people were afraid to challenge white supremacy, he believed that individuals had to overcome that fear, if not for themselves, then for the benefit of generations to come. Thus, while he worked harder with those who would stand against oppression, NAACP membership numbers continued to plummet and the decrease concerned the national office.

Gloster Current apprised Medgar of his concerns and quantified just how dire the situation in Mississippi had become. In particular, he pointed out the fact that a part of the membership "decline . . . [lay] in Jackson where the state office is maintained." Current advised Evers that it was imperative that he "sit down at once and forward us a complete review of the 1956 activities in the state."[104] Evers understood the significance of the drop in numbers as well as the underlying meaning behind Current's emphasis upon the membership decline in Jackson. In addition to the day-to-day battles that Evers engaged, he also remained accountable when things collapsed or did not go as members of the national office believed they should. In response to the drop in membership, Evers wrote Current on October 2 to offer an explanation:

The membership picture for this year isn't looking too good to me either. I have worked up plans for membership campaigns in two of our major cities, Jackson and Vicksburg, and in neither case were we able to get more than fifteen (15[)] persons to actively engage in our campaigns. I personally wrote sixty-one (61) members for the Jackson Branch, but it is quite difficult to even get our members to cooperate and actively engage in the campaigns, and again I say, it is not the lack of interest, but fear.[105]

Evers often found himself caught between what the national office required of him as field secretary and what the people were willing to do while living in fear and frustration. Compounding this problem, he had to deal with constant personal attacks upon his character by angry whites bent on preserving white supremacy; the many harassing phone calls threatening his life and that of his family; and minute NAACP concerns such as the possibility of litigation connected to his vehicle.

Evers kept detailed financial receipts and records, many of which document the preventive maintenance measures taken to keep the personal vehicle he used for investigating, recruiting, and providing assistance to victims of brutality across Mississippi in excellent running condition. The amount of miles Evers logged were often substantial and, according to his 1955 annual report, he traveled a total of "13,372 miles by car" between December 11, 1954, and November 9, 1955.[106] His need for a vehicle in superb running condition had everything to do with reliability. After all, African Americans carrying out civil rights work did not want their vehicle breaking down along the back roads of Mississippi or to be less than perfect when evading a group of angry whites who wanted "agitators" out of town at best and dead at worse. The dangers were real and fellow activist Samuel Bailey pointed out that Evers "knew they were after him. They had threatened him and he knew it." Evers often rode through the state with Bailey and advised him to never "let no cop pass ya [keep them]—behind ya—" due to the possibility of attack. Bailey noted that sometimes you had to move through some areas at high rates of speed. Myrlie supported this observation, remembering that once Medgar "was trailed out of a little Mississippi town and he drove better than 100 mph to escape."[107] As a testament to the need for vehicle reliability, Evers submitted at least three vehicle maintenance receipts to the national office during the months of June and July of 1956 detailing various work completed. The totaled amount exceeded over three hundred and fifty dollars.[108] However, the NAACP had legal and procedural concerns regarding the maintenance receipts and passed them along to Medgar.

On December 18, 1956, Roy Wilkins wrote Evers a stern and somewhat threatening letter of reprimand concerning the vehicle receipts Evers had submitted. He argued that the receipts appeared to be "chiefly for ordinary maintenance such as any car owner is expected to assume." Wilkins added that his first reaction "was to instruct our accountant to deduct the entire amount [$382.00] from your salary in installments." Wilkins, in consideration of Evers's "record of service," decided that the NAACP would "assume one-half the amount," leaving Evers the responsibility of paying the remaining balance. He added that this had never been done before "for any other field staff member."[109] Having addressed the procedural concern, John Morsell, NAACP assistant to the secretary, wrote Medgar two days later regarding the expenditures applied to the upkeep of his car. Morsell, adding to what Wilkins had written Medgar earlier, noted that Marshall (Thurgood most likely) relayed that the expenditures Evers had sent in regarding the upkeep of the car "could, in litigation, be used as evidence of Association responsibility for the car itself. He says that in similar circumstances organizations have been found liable for sizable damages in suits resulting from accidents in which cars were involved."[110] Evers responded to the charges and presented a plan of his own.

Although Evers accepted the reprimand in full, he admitted that it did "not feel good receiving one." He then explained to Wilkins that he did not consider himself anymore privileged than "any of the other Field Secretaries" and thus requested that he be allowed to "assume the entire responsibility of repaying the full amount [of $382.70] since it was incurred by me." Wilkins, however, refused the request reminding Evers that due to "peculiar circumstances and the difference in the atmosphere from that of other areas, we would be justified in the arrangement I outlined to you." He further added, "I hope you will let it rest on that basis."[111] There existed a real disconnect between what the national office believed things were like in Mississippi and the realities local NAACP branch officers faced concerning the everyday problems of recruitment, retention, and organizing. Whereas the work Evers had done on his car was for reliability and his eventual safety (as he had broken down before and found himself at the mercy of local whites to fix the problem), Wilkins could not see this and attributed it to "ordinary maintenance such as any car owner is expected to assume." He failed to realize, however, that the role the NAACP expected Evers to fill placed him outside of the boundaries of the responsibilities that "any car owner" was expected to "assume." These types of miscues between the national office and Evers grew more tenuous over time. Concerns such as these added to the stress Evers internalized on a daily basis, stress that the tactics of intimidation and surveillance employed by the Citizens' Council and the Sovereignty Commission heightened.

For Medgar Evers, the Sovereignty Commission proved a formidable adversary. While speaking at an NAACP meeting in Jackson, Evers reminded the crowd of "250 to 300 negroes [*sic*] present" that "the State Sovereignty Commission had many paid negro [*sic*] informants over the State and had plenty of money to pay such informants." The Sovereignty Commission file also noted that Evers warned the crowd that "it was up to the NAACP members to contribute money to the NAACP in order to combat the work of the Sovereignty Commission."[112] In response to Evers's increased notoriety, commission officials consolidated organizational memorandums to ensure that collected information on Medgar Evers proved readily available to investigators. The organized memorandums included personal and public statements made by Evers at various events. The files also contained a "list of names, automobile license numbers, and makes of automobiles which were recorded by the Jackson Police Department at a NAACP meeting at Anderson Methodist Church" in Jackson on April 3, 1960.[113] Those who associated with Evers were also targeted and their license plate numbers and personal activities recorded. Individuals who attended various mass meetings where Evers spoke were also subjected to investigations and surveillance tactics.

The Sovereignty Commission proved quite adept at keeping up with Evers's whereabouts within and outside of the state of Mississippi and maintained an array of newspaper articles written about and by him. Commission officials also sent out investigators "to check the livelihood and general information of" individuals listed and considered a possible threat to the social order.[114] As a consequence, Evers was under intense scrutiny by the Sovereignty Commission and its various agents and paid informants. Commission surveillance was not relegated to Evers alone. The Sovereignty Commission also catalogued information on the Evers children, including birth certificate records and school enrollment information. The sheer volume of catalogued information underscores just how well documented Evers's movements and speeches were. They also demonstrate the lack of privacy he and his family suffered due to his political activities. The commission believed that both his political actions and community mobilization efforts threatened the very sovereignty they sought to protect.

For example, a newspaper clipping within a commission file documented Evers as having assured "a crowd of more than 300 Negroes . . . that the walls of segregation in the South . . . [were] beginning to crumble before the efforts of both white and Negro citizens." Comparing the South to the North, he further noted that there existed "[definite] laws in the

South which . . . [made] the fight against segregation difficult but mark[ed] the path clearly. In the North . . . the problem . . . [of racism prove] more difficult because of unwritten codes in housing and business."[115] In this address, Evers not only suggested that white Mississippi was losing control over its African American population, but that its rigid segregation laws made the fight for civil equality easier to direct. Evers, nonetheless, remained aware of both the organizational difficulties that lay ahead and the political entities that represented the greatest threat to social equality for African Americans.

Because of his awareness of the activities and agenda of the Sovereignty Commission, Evers made public statements concerning its methods of operation. In memo number 2–72–34, commission investigator Zack J. Van Landingham recorded the details of an NAACP meeting that took place in Jackson, Mississippi, on November 6–8, 1959. The memo acknowledged Evers as one of the major speakers to a crowd of "about 250–300 negroes [*sic*]." The purpose of the memorandum, according to Van Landingham, was "to consolidate in one place all the information . . . [gained] on the above named individual."[116] Despite knowing that he was under constant surveillance, Evers increased his work in Mississippi and expended more of his time toward connecting the Mississippi struggle with the national struggle for civil and political equality. Again, registering African Americans to vote proved a crucial part of his daily regiment.

Medgar Evers believed that the ballot represented one of the key symbols of citizenship. Without this basic right, African Americans could neither defend their political interests nor effectively select those who would represent them. As a consequence, Evers worked with other groups to keep the voting campaign center stage in the minds of black Mississippians. The more African Americans pushed for political equality around the nation, the more Mississippi officials took serious blacks' push for voting rights in the state. As a consequence, Mississippi maintained a culture of voter intimidation and instituted a series of obstacles to deny its black populace access to the polls.

Evers reminded Roy Wilkins of the varied obstacles that hindered the black vote. Evers pointed out that "Mississippi is one of the last 'Frontier' states that is still holding on to the poll tax system as a subterfuge to voting." As a means of countering this subterfuge, the NAACP, Progressive Voters Leagues, Elks, and American Legion, "launched a 'Pay Your Poll Tax Campaign' to get as many persons to pay their poll tax as possible so as to take advantage of the 'present forces' in the office of the registrar." Here Evers identified "Hinds County Circuit Clerk, Registrar H.T. Ashford," who appeared opposed to the implementation of voting obstacles. Ashford had made it known, Evers noted, that he was "going to register anyone that comes up here who can read and write." This proved important to Evers, who reported that there were, according to the circuit clerk, a total of 32,697 voters in Jackson on November 6, 1956, of which 3,946 were "Negro." However, there were "47,000 or more" blacks in the city of Jackson whom Evers and the other groups sought to target in their voting campaigns. In addition to using radio, television, telephones, and letters to reach the masses, they were also planning to use "Register Now" bumper stickers that would be placed "on some 5,000 or more automobiles in the city," Evers noted. This proved grueling work, but the atmosphere had changed for the better, and Evers believed there now existed a need to strike while the iron was hot. He advised Wilkins that contrary "to the southern pet expression 'the time ain't ripe,' the time is ripe, for in this particular area we can get even our ultra-conservative Negroes to voice a positive reply when you ask them to pay their poll tax and register. Even our city teachers are getting into the act, generously without reservations."[117] With this seemingly new change in attitude, Evers also witnessed more rebellious activity from the youth, a development he viewed with great excitement.

In March, Alcorn students rebelled in response to a series of articles written by Alcorn College history professor Clennon King. Evers reported that King's first article had "ridiculed and castigated the NAACP, Supreme Court justices, etc., which lead [sic] to a complete boycott of the school's facilities by its 570 students." The board demanded that the students end the boycott and return to their classes or face expulsion. The students refused "on the grounds that Professor King had not been dismissed" and on March 8, Ernest McEwen, president of the student body, "read a statement that the entire student body had approved agreeing unanimously to withdraw, rather than be expelled." The students packed their belongings and many left for home. The students' public revolt, Evers recalled with excitement, "shocked the very foundation that the white supremacists thought they had reinforced so very substantially. (Imagine Negro students defying an ultimatum issued by a Board of Trustees in the State of Mississippi who happened to be white!)" Although, many of the students were allowed to return, the leaders of the boycott were "denied the privilege to reenter." With assistance from the NAACP national office, scholarships were provided for seven of the expelled students "for the remainder of the 1956–57 school term." The students attended Virginia Union University in Richmond, Virginia, and Central State University in Wilberforce, Ohio.[118] Evers had also met McEwen, by accident, while at a Trailways bus station and arranged a meeting between the two in Jackson.[119]

Evers took what had happened at Alcorn as an indication that the climate was rapidly changing. In conjunction with the ongoing investigation of abuse and prison conditions at the Hinds County jail, Evers considered these events as indicators "that everything is not as tranquil as the Governor and others would have the nation to believe." He now considered Alcorn A&M College a "smoldering inferno . . . that could possibly be repetitious of foregoing events." The only hindrance he saw to that process was "the fact that [Clennon] King will not permit himself to return to campus, which would undoubtedly activate any dormant feeling of tranquility."[120] With this type of encouragement, Evers worked harder to connect the Mississippi struggle for political and civil equality with the growing national movement.

Medgar Evers struggled to get Mississippians to understand that the movement for equality was a national movement and the sooner black Mississippians connected their struggle to the national one, the stronger the Mississippi movement would become. His constant work among African Americans in Mississippi paid off. His reputation for honesty and dedication produced individuals willing to travel to Washington, D.C., to tell their stories of brutality and violence. Here, Reverend W. D. Ridgeway and Beatrice Young would testify before the civil rights hearings conducted by the U.S. Senate Subcommittee on Constitutional Rights. Evers admitted that he "spent a great deal of time in preparing these witnesses for this hearing."[121] He learned quickly that their participation did not come without a price.

On April 4, 1957, Evers wrote to John A. Morsell alluding to signs of pressure being applied upon "our most recent witnesses, who testified in the civil rights hearings of the Senate Subcommittee in Washington, in the person of Mrs. Beatrice Young and Rev. W.D. Ridgeway. Presently, we do not know to what extent pressure will be applied."[122] Although Evers was not sure of the possibility of pressure on April 4, that was no longer the case by April 10 when he received pertinent information regarding Reverend Ridgeway. In a second letter to Morsell, Evers relayed that

> shortly after he [Rev. Ridgeway] returned from the Congressional Hearing—even before he returned open threats had been made on his family to the extent that the Negroes of the Hattiesburg community guarded the house nightly to prevent any unnatural occurrence until he had returned. As soon as he was home an agent from the Commercial Credit Corporation came out to repossess his car, though he was only three days overdue with his payments, and he had previously run two or three weeks overdue. About a week later his son-in-law was refused a loan that he had made arrangements to get for a home. The refusal came as a result of Rev. Ridgeway's appearance in Washington.[123]

Young also experienced intense economic sanctions from the white community due to her testimony. Once again, Evers worked to provide assistance. Young had a negative experience with the police prior to 1957 and the beating she endured at their hands on November 26, 1956, proved so severe that it resulted in the loss of her unborn child a week later.[124]

The NAACP's strategy for obtaining equality for African Americans centered on voting rights. The association, however, had a history of shying away from direct-action tactics. Mrs. Ineeva May-Pittman, an active member of the NAACP and Evers's neighbor, disagrees with this assertion.[125] Although Evers, by and large, adhered to NAACP guidelines for political action, at times he went against them. In a letter to Thurgood Marshall, dated June 3, 1957, he admitted that:

> We realize that voting in Mississippi is our number one target and that all efforts should be centered in that particular direction, but just recently three young men came to our office, here in Jackson, [Mississippi] and asked that we represent them in a legal move to enjoin the city of Jackson against the erection of segregated signs at the bus and train terminals, and continued enforcement of segregation in the public parks and playgrounds. They are most interested in immediately attacking this phase of our problem here in Jackson.
>
> The young men are: Mr. Albert Powell, Commander of the local American Legion Post (Negro), Mr. Joseph Broadwater, President of our local branch N.A.A.C.P., and Mr. Samuel Bailey, also a member of our local branch. These men are in an economic position to make the effort a successful one without economic sanction materially effecting them. Again I repeat, they are interested in immediate action, more especially since the recent Skelly Wright's decision in New Orleans, Louisiana.[126]

In regard to the Skelly Wright decision, Evers was more than likely referring to Judge Wright's ruling on May 24, 1957, rendering all state laws in New Orleans requiring segregation on public transportation unconstitutional and thus invalid.[127]

Medgar Evers understood the importance of bringing to the attention of governmental agencies the extreme racial and social inequalities happening in Mississippi. Whenever possible he put the issue of voter inequality before Washington legislators and appropriate civil rights committee members. However, Evers considered African Americans' inability to register to vote as the paramount issue in the battle for the ballot. On October 7, 1957, Evers acknowledged in the *Hattiesburg American,* according to a Sovereignty Commission report, that the denial of the right to register, not the right to vote, could be the first occasion for our calling on . . . the Civil Rights Commission for aid. We will not hesitate to call upon the commission for aid in those counties where our people are continuously denied the right to register and become first-class citizens. We hope, of course, that men of good will are willing to see the benefits of our constitution applied to all people.[128]

Men of "good will" of course included the president of the United States, Dwight D. Eisenhower, whose administration, from an international perspective, could ill afford to ignore sustained organized protests touting America's refusal to apply the "benefits" of the American Constitution to all of its citizens. Reports such as these hurt the country's international reputation, particularly since the Eisenhower administration had to deal with the social, political, cultural, and military aspects of the cold war.

International press groups weighed in on America's civil rights ineptitudes. French press outlets such as the *l'Humanite* and *Liberation* had openly condemned the Emmett Till murder and acquittal, and other countries expressed their disdain as well. In 1956, a correspondent writing for the India newspaper the *Hindu* had "expressed the view that [the Montgomery] 'bus boycott may well turn out to be an epochal event in the history of the Southern Negro. If it succeeds, it is bound to be copied by other Negroes all over the south where the Whites are fighting a last-ditch battle to preserve segregation of the races.'"[129] As the United States delved deeper into global politics, its racial problems took center stage and the White House realized that racism was no longer a domestic issue but a problem with international implications. The ever-growing number of dignitaries of color coming to America to conduct business and who were then subjected to racism and Jim Crow enhanced this realization. The opportunities for an international incident abounded and this worried American officials.[130] Thus, international pressures proved a real problem for the Eisenhower administration as it had for previous administrations, and Evers added another voice to the serenade of disenchantment aimed at the White House.

Evers looked to the Eisenhower administration for support in the struggle for social equality, and in 1957 it offered hope in the form of civil rights legislation. President Eisenhower, however, was not a strong proponent of the civil rights struggle. In the grand scheme of things, Eisenhower did not "see the necessity for the enforcement or passage of laws designed to protect the civil rights of blacks in the South or elsewhere," wrote historian Stephen Whitfield. Nor did he speak out against white racist violence. Furthermore, he "believed that the racial question in the United States was emotional rather than rational, that 'arbitrary law' could not be strong enough to solve it."[131] Although he was reluctant to come out in full support of the *Brown* decision, Eisenhower believed African Americans should have the right to vote and that the use of , in his words, "political or economic power to enforce segregation based on race, color, or creed . . . [was] morally wrong."[132] In 1956, he proposed legislation that became the Civil Rights Act of 1957, the first such legislation since the end of Reconstruction. Evers and other civil rights advocates hoped the act would lead to real protection and enforcement of voting rights for African Americans.

The 1957 Civil Rights Act established a Commission on Civil Rights to investigate instances of intimidation and voter denial. It also established a special division in the Justice Department to handle civil rights issues and provided federal courts with the authority to enter injunctions to protect the right to vote and to punish those who denied it. However, African Americans were less enthused with the weakened version Majority Leader Lyndon Johnson presented to ensure southern support. Johnson removed Part III of the proposed civil rights bill, which invited greater federal intervention regarding civil rights violations. His version, the historian Robert Burk remarked, "limited the jury-trial amendment to voting-rights cases alone and reduced the maximum statutory penalties for contempt convictions to $300 or a forty-five-day imprisonment."[133] The weakened version lacked real teeth to combat southern resistance and African Americans considered this a major problem with any defensive measure. The law ignored segregation and provided no real answer to voting obstacles in the South or the terror strategies of groups seeking to prevent African Americans from voting.[134] As a consequence, African Americans were doubtful as to whether the Eisenhower administration would enforce the act. A few weeks after its passage, however, the eyes of the nation turned to Little Rock, Arkansas, and the integration crisis surrounding Central High School.

Responding to the High Court's ruling in 1955, which ordered school districts to proceed with integration with "all deliberate speed," Central High School was set to implement integration in 1957. Virgil T. Blossom, Little Rock, Arkansas, School District superintendent, had developed and sold whites on an integration plan. The plan bore his name, and many believed that the citizens of Little Rock would go along with desegregation and the *Brown* decision even if they did not agree with it. Blossom, above all, wanted to ensure that the schools remained open, and he feared that if integration did not go over smoothly, the state legislature might abolish the public schools. Thus any attempt to desegregate, he believed, would have to occur slowly as white Arkansans would only accept integration in small quantities. Hence, he explained to the NAACP board in Little Rock that upon the completion of two new high schools, integration would begin at the high school level. School integration would then spread to all four Little

Rock high schools and finally to the junior high school and elementary schools. The Blossom plan, as the historian John Kirk has written, effectively "divided members of the Little Rock NAACP's executive board."[135] This plan quickly lost both support and traction when Arkansas officials realized the amount of leeway that *Brown II* allowed regarding desegregation.

It did not take long for civil rights leaders to realize that Little Rock school officials were no longer determined to integrate Little Rock's school districts with any real sincerity. The NAACP, and state president Daisy Bates in particular, believed that the Blossom plan was now designed to maintain as much of the system of segregation as possible by limiting the number of black students admitted to white schools. Bates and others soon realized that neither school officials nor Blossom supported immediate integration even when African Americans adhered to the law. Black parents had attempted to do just that by trying to register their children at white schools on January 23, 1956, and were turned away.[136] With support for integration lacking from state and federal political officials, grassroots resistance intensified and nine black students faced the brunt of the growing hostilities.

Conservative grassroots resistance groups interpreted the lack of explicit support for *Brown* exhibited by their state and national leadership as support of their disdain for school integration. President Eisenhower had been reluctant to endorse the *Brown* decision, remarking, as Klarman points out, that his duty "was to enforce Court decisions, not to approve or disapprove of them." He adhered to this type of approach in his dealings with the desegregation issue in Little Rock. Eisenhower's approach to the *Brown* decision was not unique. In 1953, Arkansas governor Francis Cherry "refused to comment on the upcoming decision." Much like Eisenhower, Cherry acknowledged that the "matter is under advisement by the Supreme Court . . . ; it doesn't *matter* what I think . . . [but] we will abide by the decision of the Supreme Court because that's the law of the land." These were hardly ringing endorsements for desegregation, and those opposed to integration interpreted the lack of verbal support from powerful state and national leaders as the wink-and-nod needed to resist any break in the segregation system.[137]

Most white parents were against integration and by 1957, they had the full support of Arkansas governnor Orval Faubus, who used Arkansas National Guard troops to prevent Minnijean Brown, Elizabeth Eckford, Ernest Green, Thelma Mothershed, Melba Patillo, Gloria Ray, Terrence Roberts, Jefferson Thomas, and Carlotta Walls from entering the school. In the beginning, "Two hundred black children had initially been eligible to attend Central High School under the Blossom Plan, because they lived in that attendance zone," historian Elizabeth Jacoway wrote. The numbers of eligible students were whittled down to thirty-seven, and then seventeen and then nine.[138] Although the students, with federal support from President Eisenhower in the form of protective military details, succeeded in integrating Central High, white flight and other combative tactics prevented a smooth transition into an integrated school system.[139] What transpired in Arkansas regarding integration did not go unnoticed by civil rights activists in Mississippi who kept a close eye on both the strategy and progress of those engaged in the civil rights struggle.

Black Mississippians paid close attention to the events transpiring in Arkansas and hoped they would inspire individuals to act in Mississippi. Mississippi civil rights activist Lillie Jones thought events in Little Rock would inspire black Mississippians to struggle harder. As a result of the actions of Eisenhower and those in Little Rock, Jones believed that "the people in Mississippi, would see that was the eyewitness of what was done there, and they knowed the same thing could happen here."[140] Evers, was disappointed with the NAACP's role in the fight in Little Rock and made his disappointment known to those around him.

Evers's friend John Salter Jr. argued that the NAACP made a conscious decision to pursue a less aggressive stance regarding the school desegregation crisis in Arkansas, a decision supported by the Eisenhower administration. Salter maintained that Medgar informed him, as well as other individuals, that "after the Little Rock situation, the National NAACP entered into basically a gentlemen's agreement with the federal government, then Eisenhower, to the effect that nothing of direct action, and in that sense they would be thinking even in terms of a school desegregation effort, would be made in Mississippi until other parts of the South had been brought into line." In essence, "the National NAACP had promised the administration that things would go slow in Mississippi." Although Gloster Current denied this, Ed King, Tougaloo College chaplain, seemed to support Salter's assertions while discussing NAACP proposed strategies regarding Mississippi. He maintained that the NAACP, through Wilkins and others, believed "that Mississippi should be left alone until the rest of the deep [sic] South had been touched." This put Evers at odds with Wilkins and the national office as he and others such as Aaron Henry believed the fight in Mississippi should go forward despite the financial cost. Salter argued that the NAACP's hostility toward the 1961 Freedom Rides and the Student Nonviolent Coordinating Committee, made up of young civil rights activists, legitimated Medgar's contentions regarding the national NAACP's strategic emphasis.[141] Salter remembered that Medgar was extremely angry about the position the NAACP took in Little Rock, and his anger showed in the more militant stance he assumed throughout the late 1950s.

Prior to the Freedom Rides of 1961, Evers solicited NAACP approval to help conduct challenges to the segregated bus system in Jackson. He looked for consent from NAACP general counsel Robert Carter to support three men seeking to move forward in this endeavor. Evers reported that three "men of good reputation, Negro, came into my office and said their plans were to ride the buses unsegregated [*sic*] here in Jackson." He asked that Carter send along a reply, by September 9, 1957, of support or denial.[142] This call for support proved interesting as Evers later challenged the system himself. The 1950s also witnessed Mississippi activists engaged in activities, regarding voter registration, which SNCC popularized during the 1960s.

Evers outlined the NAACP's program regarding voter education. During the month of September, he acknowledged that "city wide committees on registration and voting" had been instituted in seven Mississippi cities, including Columbus, Oxford, Mound Bayou, and Greenville. "These committees," Evers noted, "composed of ministers and laymen will be responsible for the conducting of citizenship schools under which the application for registration and voting, as it applies to the citizens of Mississippi, will be thoroughly taught." The committees were also responsible for duplicating themselves in adjoining counties. This, Evers believed, was prevalent now, as there seemed to be "a heavy concentration of Negro potential electors [in the first, second, and third congressional districts] who seem eager to take advantage of the new civil rights bill that was recently enacted by Congress."[143] This move indicates that Evers helped to create a sound political foundation in Mississippi that involved more direct-action strategies, a foundation that SNCC and other organizations built upon during the 1960s. Evers also sought to prod the national NAACP into moving forcefully to help offset its waning influence in the state.

The Regional Council of Negro Leadership, through its first midwinter conference on December 8, 1957, pressured the NAACP to be more aggressive. At least three hundred persons attended the workshop in Clarksdale, Mississippi, which raised over five hundred dollars. Although Evers argued that the council was "not too influential presently," that might not be the case in the near future. Despite the fact that many of the NAACP's influential "members in the Delta . . . [were] key members of the Council," Evers found it troubling that the RCNL had used the conference to challenge the NAACP's effectiveness.[144]

Most troubling for Evers was the following admonition prevalent throughout the meeting clearly challenging the association and offering alternative leadership. Spokesmen during the conference pointed out that "the N.A.A.C.P.'s statements about what we are going to do 'in Mississippi,' [are apparent] but not a single legal case having been filed in the state, and that they, (the Council), planned to take some positive action, legal and otherwise, to accomplish the job of registration and voting." This proved problematic as Evers admitted that his personal observations revealed "that the influence and persuasion that we [NAACP] have once had in the state have tended to recede because many feel that of all the legal action that have taken place in other states certainly one suit should have been filed here in Mississippi." In light of African Americans calling for more direct-action strategies, Evers felt it prudent to suggest that if the NAACP could "bring a suit in the State of Mississippi on registration and voting, transportation or education, we would enhance our cause here greatly—for most people now are interested in some type of positive action, even here in Mississippi, especially with regard to these segregation laws and this new voter amendment."[145] White Mississippians had a reputation for using extreme violence in response to civil rights activism and this fact tempered Roy Wilkins's support of the use of greater direct-action strategies. This would not be the last time Evers felt the need to challenge the actions of competing groups.

Martin Luther King Jr. understood the problems black Mississippians faced and he and the SCLC sought inroads into the state. Evers received notification from NAACP members that King was attempting to organize in Jackson. He then notified Ruby Hurley that attempts were "being made by Rev. Martin L. King and the Southern Christian Leadership Conference to establish a movement here in Jackson." Evers explained that their "contacts, thus far, have been N.A.A.C.P. officials who have in turn come to our office for advice. We have naturally discouraged, 'tactfully,' any such movement here in Jackson." Evers made it clear that he had things in place and did not want them disturbed by other groups moving into the area organizing without an understanding of the nature of the environment. Our strategy, Evers outlined, is to work "through the N.A.A.C.P. and the Progressive Voters League, of which our leaders are in key positions, to control the present state of affairs."[146] The increase in pressure from competing organizations, combined with his own desires to move forward, pushed Evers closer to a commitment to nonviolent direct-action strategies.

During the latter part of the 1950s, Evers was increasingly interested in direct means of attacking the injustices found in Mississippi. His endorsement of direct action meant that he had to take an active role. He had earlier attempted to integrate the University of Mississippi, and in March 1958 he again placed himself in direct confrontation with the segregated mores of the South.

In a personal statement, Evers recounted the events of March 11, 1958, in which he purchased a "Trailway[s] bus ticket from Meridian to Jackson."

He sat directly behind the operator and refused to move when driver G. V. Shelton ordered him to the rear of the bus. His refusal resulted in a call to the police and subsequently they ordered Evers off the bus and questioned him at a nearby police station "for some ten minutes," but afterward allowed him to re-board:

> Returning to the bus I again took my seat in the front. At this instance the bus driver pulled off with no further words, however, after having traveled approximately four blocks a cab driver, driving a black 1954 or 1955 Ford, flagged the bus to a halt, where upon having succeeded in stopping the bus, the bus driver opened the door, allowed him to come in and at this instance the cabbie, with a powerful blow, struck me on the left side of my face or head, with such severity that it was instantly numb. His attempt to further molest me ceased after the bus driver told him he would have to get off the bus. My only action was an attempt to ward off the blows.[147]

After the assault, the bus continued without further incident and Evers, upon arriving in Jackson, went to see his doctor for x-rays. Following the incident, Robert L. Carter, chief counsel for the NAACP, wrote to Roy Wilkins on April 9, advising that Medgar "has an action for damages against the bus driver, the bus company and the man who assaulted him— but what purpose would such an action accomplish since it would have to be tried in Mississippi and decided by a Mississippi jury?" Although Carter's advice must have seemed bleak to Evers, Carter did offer an alternative strategy but warned against the NAACP taking this action as well. He explained that the "other possibility is a suit attacking the constitutionality of the Mississippi bus segregation laws, but we have always felt that it was not a good idea, from the point of view of public relations, for our officials to be engaged in the direct prosecution of civil rights litigation."[148]

Although Evers was willing to pursue the matter in court, the NAACP did not share his willingness to proceed. When asked later as to why he remained stoic throughout the attack, Myrlie Evers-Williams recalled his explaining that "I really don't believe in turning the other cheek but it was to my benefit and everyone else's at that time that I simply took that blow and used it for fuel to approach all of these problems in another way."[149] On April 21, 22, and 24, Evers was interviewed "by representatives from the Interstate Commerce Commission" (ICC) regarding the incident.[150] The ICC, formed in 1887, served as the nation's first independent regulatory agency. It is important to note here, that Evers's defiance in the face of Jim Crow seating places him in the tradition of challenging transportation segregation in the same vein as noted civil rights activists such as Rosa Parks, E. D. Nixon, and Martin Luther King Jr.

Evers's determination to stand in the face of discrimination did not go unnoticed in the African American community. As field secretary, Evers received countless requests for assistance from African Americans in various Mississippi counties. Some requests came from individuals no longer living in Mississippi, but who wished for the NAACP to fight racism within their native counties. Responding to just such a request for assistance in Batesville, Mississippi, from James E. Johnson, residing at the time in California, Evers stated quite bluntly that "as soon as the Negroes of Batesville and Panola County become interested enough to want to do something to help themselves we can better, up to a point, be of service."[151] This letter emphasized Evers's understanding of the powerlessness of the NAACP to provide effective assistance without the full cooperation, participation, and support of community members. His declaration of "up to a point" reveals that he probably did not intend for the NAACP to become a permanent stand-in for black manhood and womanhood in the African American community. He sincerely believed that black men and women had to get up off their knees and stand upright if the foot of oppression were to be permanently removed from their necks. When it came to the dignity and sanctity of black manhood and womanhood, Evers could be both passionate and fiery.

Myrlie had only seen Medgar in "an almost uncontrollable rage" on two occasions, she explained, and both had to do with African Americans and their relations with whites. Evers had a fierce pride in black people in terms of their place in history and what they had overcome since enslavement. Of more importance, since returning from the war, he had developed a strong intolerance for both cowardice on the part of African Americans and white/black sexual exploitation. Thus, whenever he witnessed either a black man cowering in defense of his manhood or in defense of the virtue of black womanhood, something snapped within him and anger or, on some occasions, rage resulted.

Myrlie recalled one occasion while driving home they happened upon a black woman and white man "embracing in a parked car," and they both knew that the woman had recently separated from her husband. Evers slammed the car door and began cursing, an act that she knew to be out of character for him. When she pressed him about what had made him so angry, his reply was filled with venom and disgust. "That slut!" Medgar screamed, "That foul, no-good woman! Lowering herself to make love with a white man!. . . . I ought to get a gun and blow their brains out!" Although he did not follow through with this threat, he believed that the woman was "a traitor to her race!"[152] The second time his wife witnessed this level of rage resulted from the rape of a black woman at the hands of her white employer.

As field secretary, Evers witnessed and investigated the rape of countless individuals, children among them, and this always bothered him. On one occasion, however, the level of apathy proved more than he could handle and he lashed out in frustration, giving the husband of the victim the full brunt of his anger. While at the Jackson office, a young black couple came in to file a report with the NAACP regarding a rape. The young woman recounted the event with such detail that Evers not only believed her, but grew angrier with each passing moment, while the woman's husband sat quietly. At the conclusion of the meeting, Evers asked the two to follow him to the police station to file a report, but the husband refused.

The husband believed that nothing would be done and that, at best, they both would lose their jobs and at worse would be beaten up or killed. Evers reminded him that the man had raped his wife and that something had to be done, to which the husband countered that nothing could be done and that both of their jobs were in jeopardy if they pressed the matter. At this point, Evers recovered from his disbelief at the young man's reaction and shouted, "To hell with your jobs!. . . . To hell with getting beat up! If a white man touched my wife, I'd fight back or die in the attempt! They'd have to kill me to stop me! I'd be less than a man not to fight back!. . . . That's what you are. You're less than a man!"[153] To Evers, the thought of not fighting in defense of one's own family was inconceivable. As a consequence, he lashed out against those who felt so dejected and defeated that they could overlook acts of harm against their immediate family. Evers, however, was not alone in witnessing these types of frustrating and disheartening encounters.

Aaron Henry, who worked closely with Evers on many occasions, also recalled families in Clarksdale, Mississippi, wanting to get on with their lives after a rape rather than report it to authorities. Henry noted that this often proved a common occurrence when, out of fear, family members simply wanted to move past the event rather than stir up "trouble" for themselves by initiating legal action.[154] Rape, as historian Danielle McGuire argues, proved another brutal tool white men used to intimidate African Americans and thus protect white domination and racial control. It also served as a vile form of entertainment, a display of sexual power, and an emasculation of black manhood.[155] These were typical incidents of fear and self-doubt that civil rights activists dealt with on a daily basis. Although rape served as a brutal form of racial domination, whites used lynchings to underscore the permanency and finality of white power.

The lynching of Mack Charles Parker in April 1959 brought Medgar Evers to a low point regarding his hope for Mississippi's future and he came close to a breaking point. Poplarville serves as the county seat of Pearl River

County and is located in the Picayune metro area in southeast Mississippi. In 1959, Poplarville epitomized the small southern town where whites and blacks knew their respective places and the latter understood that his or her life often rested on the whims of their white counterparts. Poplarville is located approximately 77 miles north of New Orleans and 129 miles southeast of Jackson, Mississippi.[156] It was here that white citizens summoned up the worst side of human nature in their dealings with African Americans. Evers later noted that the mob carried out an act of barbarity that rivaled anything one may have heard about the uncivil traditions within a foreign country. He noted that the "savagery dealt Mack Charles Parker, [by fellow Mississippians] in a 'civilized society', makes a mockery out of [the] so-called cannibalism in the most remote areas of the world."[157]

On February 23, 1959, a white couple named Jimmy and June Walters, along with their four-year-old daughter Debbie Carol, were driving from Bogalusa to their home in Petal, Mississippi. About 11:30 P.M., the engine in their 1949 Dodge quit and the vehicle coasted to a stop a mile south of the Lamar County line. Realizing that he could not fix the problem, Jimmy decided to leave his pregnant wife and daughter with the car and to walk the seven miles to the nearby town of Lumberton to obtain assistance. The same evening Mack Charles Parker, an African American, and four of his friends had been seen drinking and having a good time. At some point during the early morning hours a car pulled up behind the stranded vehicle; June and her daughter were kidnapped. They were then driven to another location where June's assailant raped her.[158]

Once reported, law enforcement officials from both Mississippi and Louisiana set up roadblocks and roused any black male fitting the general description provided by June Walters. She remembered her attacker as a middle-aged black man weighing 160 to 170 pounds, approximately thirty-nine to forty years old and approximately five feet, ten inches tall. Officers took Parker into custody and placed him in a police lineup. On February 24, June picked Parker out of a police lineup and identified him as her attacker based upon his repeating the words, "You white trash bitch, I'm going to fuck you," which the rapist had allegedly uttered.[159] From that point on, Parker and his family understood that he might be lynched because of the nature of the accusation. On the night of June's identification of Parker, according to historian Howard Smead, highway patolman Bud Gray offered Jimmy his personal .38-caliber revolver to shoot Parker then and there provided that Jimmy had not brought a gun of his own.[160] The black community quickly realized that Parker was in deep trouble.

Medgar Evers hurriedly arrived on the scene to investigate the incident. On March 7, he spoke with Eliza Parker, Mack Charles's mother, "and discovered that no lawyer in the area had agreed to defend her son." Evers recalled that it was then "suggested that there were Negro lawyers in Jackson who would possibly be happy to defend her son because of the apparent innocence she had expressed in her son's case." She eventually chose R. Jess Brown.[161] It was not long before talk circulated around town that Parker's fate would not be decided in a court of law and the fact that he was now defended by two Mississippi lawyers, R. Jess Brown of Vicksburg and Jack H. Young Sr. of Jackson, only served to antagonize matters.

As Parker's trial date approached, certain white townspeople developed fears that with all of the civil rights legislation that had recently passed, Parker might get off. As a consequence, "twin sentiments developed—that . . . [Parker] not escape punishment because of a ruling in another case," Smead remarked, "and that . . . [his] two black attorneys not be permitted to affront the white community by cross-examining June Walters on the witness stand."[162] Despite the fact that June warned authorities that she could not be absolutely certain that Parker had raped her as the night had been dark without the benefit of moonlight, in the minds of those whose decisions mattered in these instances, his guilt was never an issue.[163] It is important to note that Parker had been arrested despite June's admission that she was not certain of his guilt.

Although jailed and awaiting trial, on April 24 "a white mob in Poplarville abducted . . . [Parker] from his jail cell, beat him, [with both intent and rage,] drove him to the Louisiana border, shot him twice in the chest, and dumped his body into the Pearl River."[164] As soon as the body was recovered, Evers and a "free lanced photographer were able to get exclusive pictures of the body in its gruesome state," Evers reported.[165] Myrlie remembered that Medgar was emotionally drained behind the news of Parker's murder. His pain was most certainly deepened by the fact that "it was all but admitted that the FBI report named the persons who were responsible for . . . [Parker's] kidnapping and lynching," the NAACP reported.[166] One of the more important individuals named in that document, however, would be Christopher Columbus Reyer.

Christopher Reyer of McNeil, Mississippi (south of Poplarville), provided FBI agents with detailed information surrounding Mack Charles Parker's abduction. His information also included the names of those possibly involved such as Arthur Smith, his "nephew by marriage," and the details of a meeting Reyer attended prior to the abduction. During this meeting, the men pondered about what they "were going to do with Parker." Reyer admitted to FBI agents that he then mentioned to the group that "the river was up as . . . [he] had crossed it recently. I said this because," he explained, "someone had just remarked or asked what we were going to do with Parker if we got him, and someone else said the river would be a good place for him." The men demanded to use Reyer's 1957 Oldsmobile and when he could offer no excuse they would accept he relented; they returned it later with bloodstains.[167] Evers used Parker's lynching to strengthen his resolve and to renew his commitment to stay and fight in Mississippi. Defiantly, he told his wife, "Somebody's going to pay for this . . . . And I'm not leaving. I'm going to stay here and fight until someone does the same thing to me."[168] Due to threats upon her life, Eliza Parker relocated to California.[169] In 1959, while in California, Evers chose to discuss the issue further.

On Sunday May 31, 1959, Evers delivered an address at the mass meeting of the Los Angeles branch of the NAACP. He spoke about Mississippi's negative image and the social problems that plagued it. Throughout his speech Evers never suggested a desire to leave Mississippi; his commitment was solid. He used this meeting to articulate publicly his true feelings about specific murders during the decade and their impact on the Mississippi movement.

Evers argued that the murder of Reverend George Lee "was probably the beginning of an intensified campaign of violence and economic pressure against Negro citizens who wanted the right to vote and be respected by their fellowmen."[170] He recounted the coroner's attempt to claim that the lead pellets found in Reverend Lee's jaw were "filling[s] from his teeth." Because of sustained calls for further investigation, the coroner's initial findings were later disproved.[171] This validated Evers's belief that if African Americans did not stand and demand justice in Mississippi, whites were capable of suggesting anything, at anytime, about any situation. He also addressed the lynchings of Emmett Till and Lamar Smith. Evers used their murders as proof that during the 1950s, Mississippi was lawless and blacks were dispensable. In other words, the end result of the Till lynching was that the "men responsible for the crime were apprehended, brought to trial, and as is typical of Mississippi justice, were released, and today are free."[172] In addition, nothing happened to those responsible for the Smith killing.

As a trained soldier, Evers viewed the struggle over civil rights in Mississippi in terms of strategies and tactics, those for civil equality versus those who denied it. Thus, he intimated that these "acts of violence, coupled with economic pressure, have been the chief tactics used to discourage Negroes from seeking justice and equality in Mississippi. . . . However, despite these and other acts of intimidation, people around the world have an unquenchable desire to be free men and women, even in the State of Mississippi."[173] Medgar Evers's commitment to both the state and the

African American population within it continued to define his actions as well as the dedication he demanded from those around him. But the events surrounding Clyde Kennard, whom he respected and considered a personal friend, bore a hole into his soul and therefore made it harder for him to fathom Mississippi's continued recalcitrance, or to believe in its ability to change by any measurable degree.

Clyde Kennard was born on June 12, 1927, in the southeast town of Hattiesburg, Mississippi. He moved to Chicago at the age of twelve to live with his sister. Kennard was a decent, law-abiding citizen who enlisted in the military in 1945 and served in Germany and Korea as a paratrooper.[174] Kennard lived in Chicago for some time and had attended the University of Chicago, but before he could attain his degree his stepfather fell ill and he returned to Hattiesburg in 1955 to help work the family farm. In addition, Kennard was also involved with the local NAACP where he attended meetings and attempted to register to vote. Mississippi Southern College (MSC; now the University of Southern Mississippi) was located only a short drive from where Kennard lived, and he decided to apply to finish the courses needed to complete his political science degree. Above all, he believed that as an American citizen he had earned the right to attend Mississippi Southern and that race should never be a determining factor as to whether a person received the opportunity to better his station in life; he expressed as much in the *Hattiesburg American*.

In December 1958, Kennard wrote to the editor of the *Hattiesburg American* in support of integration and emphasized his belief that race should not be the basis on which one received opportunities. "What we request," Kennard explained, "is only that in all things competitive, merit be used as a measuring stick rather than race."[175] Of course, "all things competitive" included enrollment in Mississippi's segregated Institutions of Higher Learning, and it became quite clear to all that Kennard was headed in this direction.

In 1958, Governor J. P. Coleman, in response to Kennard's impending application, invited him to a meeting where MSC president William D. McCain also attended. It was an election year and the whole integration problem proved an issue no politician wanted on their political plate. As a consequence, journalist Ronald Hollander reported that those assembled informed Kennard that "he could select any college in America that would accept him, and that the state of Mississippi would pay his expenses." Kennard refused as his home situation prevented his leaving Mississippi. Governor Coleman, however, convinced Kennard to put off his application "until after the primary in 1959," to which Kennard agreed.[176] Underestimating Mississippi's policy on school integration, Kennard believed that if his application caused no controversy, Mississippi officials would recognize his right to pursue an education and grant his request to attend Mississippi Southern. He believed that school officials at MSC were more progressive than other academic institutions in the state and that he would not require a court order to enroll. "These people at MSC," Kennard proclaimed, "are more liberal. They're not like the old ones. I'll get in without the courts."[177] Mississippi officials had other ideas and were determined not only to deny Kennard the chance to attend the college, but to make sure that he could not continue the application process in the future.[178]

In September 1959, Kennard received the news that MSC had rejected his admission application and he met with McCain to discuss the reasons why. Sovereignty Commission investigator Zack J. Van Landingham was also present. Landingham had been put in charge of investigating Kennard and had received advice from Dudley Conner, the head of the Hattiesburg Citizens' Council. Conner had advised Van Landingham that if he wanted Kennard gone, this could be arranged. When Van Landingham pressed for clarification, Conner explained that "Kennard's car could be hit by a train or he could have some accident on the highway and nobody would ever know the difference." This proved too much for even Van Landingham, who later talked with FBI agents in New Orleans about the discussion.[179] This type of conversation serves as a prime example of what civil rights activists and everyday individuals were up against when challenging the system of segregation. Kennard was in great danger and this became apparent rather quickly at the conclusion of his meeting with school officials. He likely understood the danger; yet his belief in the qualities of freedom and democracy dictated that he act, if not for himself, for future generations.

Kennard thought that the meeting might yield positive results. It did not. Upon his leaving the campus, constables Charlie Ward and Lee Daniels arrested him on trumped-up charges of reckless driving. At the police station, one of the constables returned with a paper bag containing "five half-pints of liquor" he claimed had come from beneath the front seat of Kennard's Mercury station wagon. Officers then booked Kennard and added illegal possession of alcohol to the reckless driving charge; he was then jailed and his car impounded. Many suspected the liquor had been planted as a cousin of Kennard's reported that he neither drank (including soft drinks) nor smoked. On September 25, 1960, a nineteen-year-old African American named Johnny Lee Roberts stole five bags of chicken feed from the Forrest County Cooperative warehouse and later pointed to Kennard as the mastermind behind the crime. Kennard received a seven-year sentence in Mississippi's infamous Parchman prison, while Roberts received five years probation.[180]

Evers worked hard to gain Kennard's freedom and made public his disgust at the conviction in a news release issued on November 22, 1960:

> The Greatest mockery to Judicial Justice took place Monday, November the 21st in the Forrest County Court house [*sic*] when despite the overwhelming evidence in Clyde Kennard's favor, he was convicted and sentenced to seven (7) years in the State penitentiary for alleged burglary. In a court room [*sic*] of segregationists who apparently resolved to put Kennard "Legally away." The all white jury found Kennard guilty as charged, in only ten minutes.[181]

The *Hattiesburg American* also printed his statement on its front page, and this public criticism of the Court's decision came with consequences as Evers soon found himself in court defending his own freedom.

During the trial, James Finch, district attorney in and for the Twelfth Circuit Court District of the State of Mississippi, outlined the case against Evers. Finch reminded the court that the *Hattiesburg American* had a wide circulation in Forrest County and thus large segments of the population were exposed to Evers's malicious statements. Evers made the statements, Finch charged, "with the intent contumaciously to impede, degrade, obstruct, embarrass, interrupt, defeat or corrupt the administration of justice in the Honorable Circuit Court of Forrest County, Mississippi, and said statement being an expression of contempt for this Honorable Court." This proved important to Finch because, he argued, Kennard had been "given the full benefit of a fair and impartial trial before a jury of twelve good and lawful men . . . who after hearing and considering all of the testimony both for the prosecution and the defense, arrived at what they considered a lawful and proper verdict of guilty." Finch noted that the state was acting within its authority to prosecute Evers based upon the "provisions of Section 1656 of the Mississippi Code of 1942." The court, Finch continued, had the power to punish anyone convicted of "a constructive contempt while the Court is then sitting in regular session."[182] Evers's attorneys quickly responded.

Jack H. Young Sr. and R. Jess Brown presented a motion to dismiss petition to the court regarding the charge. Both charged that Evers's "comments on the trial of Clyde Kennard constituted a valid exercise of [the] defendant's right of freedom of speech." They further noted "that the publication of [the] defendant's comments was an exercise of the right of freedom of the press, all of which are protected against interference, restraint and punishment by the State, including punishment for contempt, under the guarantees of the due process clause of the Fourteenth Amendment to the Constitution of the United States."[183] During the trial, Finch went after Evers attempting to demonstrate his guilt by examining key witnesses who could attest to Evers's statements.

Douglass Starr, reporter for the Associated Press, proved an important witness for the prosecution. Starr acknowledged that the *Hattiesburg American* was a news outlet of the Associated Press and that Evers had called his office on November 22 between "nine and nine-eighteen A.M." When asked about portions of Evers's statement to the *Hattiesburg American,* Starr admitted that he did not "remember all of the words" but that the sentences Finch presented "looks like the two sentences that I wrote." When asked, Starr acknowledged that Evers's statement went not only to the *Hattiesburg American,* but all Associated Press news outlets in Mississippi including television and radio. In a further attempt to demonstrate the impartiality of the Kennard trial and thus no reason for Evers's statements, Finch called Jack H. Young to the stand, who, although now defending Evers, had defended Kennard earlier. Finch asked Young if during the Kennard trial he had "expressed to the Court and to the jury your appreciation for the fair, courteous and impartial manner in which you had been received in this Court?" Young admitted that he had and when asked, noted that he had meant what he said and still felt that way.[184] At the conclusion of Young's statement, the state rested its case against Evers. It was now time for Young and Brown to present their case.

Attorney Brown dictated a motion to the court, moving that the court "enter a verdict for the Defendant." Brown argued that the state had failed to "prove a prima facia case in accord with the allegations of the affidavit." The court overruled the motion and when Evers's attorneys had no additional testimony to present, they rested their case as well. Judge Stanton A. Hall, after reciting Evers's statement in the *Hattiesburg American,* announced his verdict.[185]

On December 2, 1960, Medgar Evers sat in the courtroom awaiting the verdict. From the bench, Judge Hall told Evers to "come around" and he announced that "it is the judgment of this Court that you be found in contempt of this Court. I sentence you to a one hundred dollar fine and thirty days in jail." Young and Brown immediately submitted a motion for a new trial, which Judge Hall overruled.[186] Evers had an opportunity to lighten his sentence with an apology, but was so indignant at the audacity of the state and its lack of judicial prudence that he refused to entertain the idea. He made it clear that he had no intention of apologizing nor would he change his mind. In a *Jackson Daily News* report, Evers announced that he had "no apology to make even if it means six months in jail. It appears that our freedom of speech is becoming similar to that which prevails behind the iron curtain."[187] Newspaper editorials in the *State Times* (Jackson) and the *Delta Democrat-Times* (Greenville) also spoke against the curtailment of citizens' right to free speech.[188]

The fact that Evers knew Kennard and respected him for his courage, strength, and NAACP work made the whole event emotionally troubling. Kennard, Myrlie remarked, had been active in the NAACP while in Hattiesburg and thus Medgar "came to have an enormous respect for him."[189] On October 17, 1958, Kennard had also accompanied Reverend J. M. Barnes of Hattiesburg to the circuit clerk's office in an attempt to register to vote. Although Kennard informed the circuit clerk that he was not a member of the NAACP, both he and Barnes were denied an opportunity to register.[190] Kennard's arrest eventually caused Evers to display an emotional side he had worked so hard to keep hidden from public view.

In 1961, while attending a NAACP Freedom Fund banquet, Evers rose to speak to those gathered. He focused on the Kennard case. Evers had just returned from Hattiesburg where he had spoken with Leona Smith, Kennard's mother, and believed that he should now provide those assembled with a case update. His friend and fellow activist John Salter Jr. attended the dinner as well. In addition to holding a professorship at Tougaloo College, Salter served as the advisor to the NAACP Jackson Youth Council. Salter had always known Medgar to be "a very stable, very cool person. The only time that I ever saw him break down," he remembered, "came in the Fall of 1961, at an evening dinner session of the annual convention of the Mississippi NAACP." He remembered that as "Medgar talked on about the Kennard case, his voice shook and, in what was obviously deep sorrow and frustration, he wept openly. With one accord—and with many others weeping by this time—all arose and began singing 'We Are Climbing Jacob's Ladder.' When the song was over, Medgar continued, outwardly calm."[191] Colia Liddell Clark remembered the emotional aspect of the event as well as the toll it took on her. To "see a man cry in a room with four [or] five hundred people was something, I couldn't handle at that time, and I thought I was grown and matured and I could handle anything."[192] In many ways, by shedding tears in public, Evers displayed a vulnerability that others shared, respected, and accepted as proof of his sincerity when it came to civil rights struggle.

His emotional outburst proved to be a pivotal moment for Evers, who had previously equated crying with weakness where men were concerned. "Over and over," Myrlie recalled, "he had told [our son] Darrell, 'Men don't cry.'"[193] Yet, here he stood in public bearing his soul. During this vulnerable and yet very much public moment, Evers did in the open what he had done numerous times within the privacy of his own company; he let his emotions flow freely. His feelings regarding the countless and senseless murders came flooding out onto that banquet stage and all present felt his pain and sorrow. The memories of Reverend George Lee, Lamar Smith, Emmett

Till, Mack Charles Parker, Clinton Melton, and many others who preceded them were represented in the tears of a man who was overcome with emotions. In that brief moment, Evers needed to hear those around him offer words of comfort and support. He must have received some consolation when a woman from the audience called out, "That's all right, son. We all feel the same way."[194] Evers used every opportunity to publicize Mississippi's attempts to deny its African American population their right to free speech. Nineteen sixty-one also brought Evers news regarding his appeal to the contempt of court conviction.

Jack H. Young Sr. and Robert Carter of New York handled Evers's appeal. The appeal challenged the legitimacy of Judge Hall's earlier ruling as well as the basis of district attorney Finch's main reason for introducing the contempt charge from the beginning. Since Finch had painted Evers's statements as malicious and intended to dishonor the court and "obstruct" or "impede" justice, Young and Carter attacked that premise head-on. They argued that when Evers made his statement to Starr on November 22, "the case was over, Kennard had been tried, convicted and sentenced on the previous day . . . and a motion for a new trial had been overruled. Therefore, the court below had no further jurisdiction in the matter." This proved important to Evers's appeal because, his attorneys reasoned, since the trial had concluded Evers's "statement could not have possibly have tended to embarrass, degrade, impede, obstruct, defeat or corrupt the administration of justice." This had been the very basis of the prosecution's case in 1960 resulting in a guilty verdict. They did not deny that Evers's statement had been "highly critical and a harsh appraisal of the trial, but that does not suffice to constitute constructive contempt. After all[,] judges as persons and the courts as institutions are certainly entitled to no greater immunity from criticism than any other person or institution."[195]

On June 12, 1961, Medgar Evers won on appeal and the court reversed the initial conviction. Kennard, due in large part to the publicity that his imprisonment created, and to his debilitating health, gained his freedom in 1963. Kennard had cancer and the disease had ravished his body. His mother relayed to Evers that upon her visit in January, her son "had to be assisted (by other inmates) in getting dressed, as well as, walking around." After such a report, Evers contacted R. Jess Brown "and impressed upon him the urgency of getting medical attention for Mr. Kennard."[196] Brown "immediately, petitioned the Mississippi Supreme Court for a transfer of Mr. Kennard to the hospital," Evers noted, "pointing out the medical neglect which he . . . had received during his confinement by penitentiary officials." Evers noted that Governor Ross Barnett granted Kennard an "executive clemency" on "January 28" and he "was permitted to leave the hospital, January 29, for his home in Hattiesburg, Mississippi while diagnostic tests were being analyzed relative to his condition."[197] Kennard, however, died in July from colon cancer. Prison authorities had known that Kennard had cancer but refused to provide him with sufficient medical treatment or remove him from hard-labor detail until it was too late.[198]

Myrlie Evers-Williams noted that Kennard's arrest and conviction devastated Medgar in ways that both disturbed and concerned her. According to Myrlie, one moment stands out in her mind that really "shows that in all of his strength and wisdom he was vulnerable, he was very human, that he was weary but very strong in that weariness." The senselessness of the Kennard saga nearly pushed Medgar over the edge and underscored both his vulnerability and dedication to the struggle for human decency:

> Medgar came home from his office that night of either Kennard's arrest or his death (that has to be clarified) he was extremely withdrawn, very very quiet . . . I didn't say anything to him. I went into the kitchen to heat up the food so he could eat. I came back into the living room . . . and he was sitting at a place that we had told our children and each other never sit at night, and that was on the sofa where the back of it was to the large window there because we was cautious that someone might shoot into it and he sat down on the arm of the sofa, which was right in line of fire, . . . he had his head in his hands and I began to see his shoulders just shake uncontrollably and these sobs just like a heaving kind of thing just poured out . . . ; [which] I had never seen before and all the pain and the vulnerability and anger that poured out, . . . I was stunned . . . , and he took his fist and hit the wall, put a hole in it. So to me I saw a man who was so hurt . . . so weary, so tired, so depressed by it all and yet so angry that he put a hole in the wall. . . . That was unusual because I never saw a physical side [of this magnitude] to him.

She remembered that when she finally reached out to him he fell into her arms and cried.[199]

Kennard's imprisonment in Mississippi's infamous Parchman penitentiary devastated Evers on many levels and pulled at the very essence of his commitment and belief in the overall goodness of mankind. Despite the proceedings that had both violated Kennard's civil rights (and would later contribute to his death), Evers did not condemn Mississippi as a whole. He sincerely believed there were whites within the state who truly wished for justice, law and order, and equality for all. His speech in California demonstrated his commitment to continued resistance against social and political inequality. He also challenged whites who were sitting on the fence of segregation with legs hanging on both sides of the issue to rethink their position. He acknowledged the existence of a predominance of white citizens of Mississippi who believe in law and order, justice and semblance of fair play. However, this group does not have the christian [*sic*] courage to stand up against the lawless elements of Mississippi and demand that the laws be complied with as moral human obligations placed upon our democratic society. There is a tendency toward allowing the irresponsible to occupy high positions of public trust, which has nothing less than a disastrous affect in a state as backward as Mississippi.[200]

Evers hoped that with continued struggle, eventually decent elements of the white community could be persuaded to follow their hearts and refuse to allow "the irresponsible" to continue dictating policy in Mississippi. His liberal use, throughout the address, of the inclusive word "we" ("*we* have been patient; *we* believe; *we* will achieve victory; If *we* work with sufficient dedication, *we* will be able to achieve") demonstrated his commitment to stay in Mississippi and fight for its future.[201]

Although Evers believed in the proverbial "we," there were more tangible reasons related to the murders of the 1950s that explain his commitment to stay in Mississippi. Adam Nossiter observed that "more than any other man in the history of Mississippi, . . . [Evers] had exposed himself to white supremacy's most jagged edge." Medgar Evers "had literally inspected the mangled bodies" of Mack Charles Parker and Emmett Till.[202] This reality, combined with what Myrlie described as her husband's ability to feel "the deprivation of every Negro as though it were his own . . . [and suffer] with every Negro whose suffering he knew," bound Medgar to Mississippi and made leaving the state impossible.[203]

Evers spent the next few years intensifying calls for social and political change. He also put in place strategies and tactics that directly challenged white authority in the state and produced combative interchanges between black activists and conservative whites. Although the 1960s produced heartaches, violence, and social and political setbacks for civil rights activists across the nation, the first few years of the decade also offered hope for Medgar Evers. The thought of hope provided him with a measure of victory within itself. He needed the power of hope and perseverance as the Mississippi movement for social and political equality intensified between 1960 and 1963, with many in the community looking to Evers for leadership, guidance, bail monies, and support. He worked hard not to disappoint them.

5.

The Black Wave

CONSERVATISM MEETS DETERMINISM

The NAACP believes that Jackson can change if it wills to do so. If there should be resistance, how much better to have turbulence to effect improvement, rather than turbulence to maintain a stand-pat policy.

—Medgar Evers

Let it not be said of us when history records these momentous times that we slept while our rights were being taken by those who would keep us in slavery and by those who say that we are doing alright.

—Medgar Evers

Race had plenty to do with it [regarding James Meredith's integration of Ole Miss]. It was the overruling, overriding factor. We just had a Little Rock ten years behind time.

—Former Mississippi governor J. P. Coleman

I learned a long time ago from Martin King that peace is not necessarily the absence of turmoil; but peace is the presence of love and justice. And there ain't going to be no peace until love and justice prevail.

—Aaron Henry

To live . . . [is] actually to be free and you cannot want to be alive and not want to fight for freedom.

—Koigi Wa Wamwere

THE TRAGIC EVENTS of the 1950s made an indelible mark on Evers. As a result, his anger and frustration with the status of "Negroes" in Mississippi intensified during the 1960s. Correspondence during the early 1960s indicates that Evers leaned more toward nonviolent direct action as a primary method for achieving social and economic equality. He must have considered the possibility that with violence directed against African Americans intensifying throughout the state, nondirect tactics would take too long to achieve the desired result. His appeal for more direct action against the system of segregation was neither new nor unfamiliar to those who knew him. It was also apparent that Evers had not given up his dream of attending law school.

In 1954, Medgar Evers had gained the attention of the NAACP by attempting to integrate the University of Mississippi Law School. Five years later, the NAACP was considering the benefits the association could reap if he obtained a law degree. Gloster Current apprised Robert Carter "that Medgar Evers [still] has ambitions of studying law." Current inquired whether it was possible for Evers to continue his NAACP work and attend classes at "Baton Rouge, Southern University or Loyola during the week and work for us on weekends with a reduced schedule?" Current added that he "thought we [NAACP] would be better off if we had a home grown lawyer down there serving as field secretary."[1] Carter, however, believed that "it would be very difficult for him to study law in New Orleans or Baton Rouge and do the kind of job which you need him to do." Although Carter did not seem optimistic that the plan would work, he suggested to Current that if Evers could "work it out and give you some idea of how it can be done," they would be in a better position to evaluate the possibility of his succeeding.[2] Thus, as late as 1959, Evers still desired to become an attorney and thus acquire another means of combating inequality but, again, leaving the state was not an option.

Medgar Evers, at all cost, wanted to remain in Mississippi and use the law as another means of resisting the state's oppressive regime, which was grounded in and founded upon oppressive legalities. Evers notified Gloster Current that he wished to "begin such study in September of 1959." He admitted, however, that he did not wish to leave the state to attend law school. "I feel that since I have an application already on file with the University of Mississippi Law School (since January, 1954 and before employment with the NAACP)," Evers noted, "I would like to pursue that application to the fullest extent." Although Evers understood that by pursuing this path his chances of acceptance dwindled, the process itself proved to be of greater importance to him. Thus, Evers proclaimed that the "attempt would be made to open the university to Negroes." Furthermore, he believed that the publicity that would accompany such an endeavor might benefit NAACP membership in Mississippi by increasing "financial and moral support from such professionals, as teachers, who desire to go to the University of Mississippi, or some other state school, rather than leave the state. Any sacrifice of me," he added, "would not be too great."[3]

Again, Evers worked to increase his own productivity in the fight for civil rights while also working to increase the notoriety and prestige of the NAACP throughout Mississippi. Mississippi officials were quite aware of the growing influence of the NAACP in the state and the role that Evers played. As a consequence, the political leadership sought to prevent any opportunity for increased exposure of the NAACP and its programs. Sometimes, in the effort to prevent an NAACP media bonanza, state agencies found themselves pitted against local white organizers, court orders, and segregationist organizations.

On May 17, 1959, the NAACP hosted its "Fifth Anniversary Celebration" of the *Brown* decision. The meeting convened in Jackson and Roy Wilkins served as the keynote speaker. Unbeknown to those attending the gala, plans were in motion to discredit the celebration and place in handcuffs two of the NAACP's most prominent figures. "The highlight of our meeting," Evers acknowledged, "was the fact that there were officers sitting in the vast audience with warrants for Mr. Wilkins and the Field Secretary, Medgar W. Evers." The warrants for their arrest stemmed from an obscure 1942 Mississippi code preventing attacks against the system of segregation. What is of more interest than the fact that the warrant was initiated by a Citizens' Council member, was the rush by city officials to prevent the arrests from taking place.[4]

In 1942, Mississippi politicians were quite clear regarding their desire to maintain segregation and prevent the intermingling of the races. Mississippi Code 2339 read:

> Any person, firm or corporation who shall be guilty of printing, publishing or circulating printed, typewritten or written matter urging or presenting for public acceptance or general information, arguments or suggestions in favor of social equality or of intermarriage between whites and negroes [*sic*], shall be guilty of a misdemeanor and subject to a fine not exceeding five hundred dollars or imprisonment not exceeding six months or both fine and imprisonment in the discretion of the court.

Although quite explicit, Mississippi officials amended Code 2339 to address a wider range of possible challenges. In part, Code 2056 warned that if "two (2) or more persons conspire . . . [to] overthrow or violate the segregation laws of this state through force, violence, threats, intimidation, or otherwise . . . such persons, and each of them, shall be guilty of a misdemeanor, and, on conviction, shall be fined not less than $25.00, or shall be imprisoned not less than one month or more than six (6) months, or both."[5] The legal codes were clear and Citizens' Council member Elmore Greaves argued Wilkins and Evers were operating outside of the law.

While Evers and Wilkins prepared for the NAACP celebration, Greaves went before Justice of the Peace Terry Hughes (Fourth District) and filed an affidavit for their arrest. Hughes then issued arrest warrants based on the affidavit and Hinds County deputies converged on the NAACP meeting "with warrants in hand." Once tipped off of the impending arrests, the *Jackson Daily News* reported that "State officials moved in shirt-sleeved haste . . . to prevent the local arrest of Roy Wilkins." Powerful politicians, such as Attorney General Joe Patterson and Sovereignty Commission chief investigator Zack J. Van Landingham, were involved in preventing the arrests. A high-profile arrest of this type, Van Landingham maintained, would be "just what the NAACP wants. . . . I imagine they would pay thousands of dollars to get Wilkins arrested here." Van Landingham also went to the Masonic Temple, the site of the NAACP meeting, and spoke with the "warrant-carrying deputies Raymond Bonner, Bill Shuttleworth, and Lloyd Gatewood" in an attempt to prevent the arrests.[6] Although the arrests were averted, they created divisions in the ranks of the two dominant segregationists organizations: the Mississippi State Sovereignty Commission and the White Citizens' Council.

The entire event created instant tension between state agencies and local segregationist groups surrounding the attempted arrest fiasco. Elmore Greaves immediately posted a verbal assault on all involved in preventing the arrest of the two NAACP officials. He admitted his surprise to learn that the warrants had not been carried out due to "the direct and personal intervention of a cast of characters including our governor, the attorney-general, the mayor of Jackson, the district attorney, the chief of police, and sundry other nervous minions of the law." In addition, Greaves charged the Sovereignty Commission, in this case, with being "organized to wet-nurse visiting negro [*sic*] dignitaries." His verbal assault against those in political power also included Mayor Allen Thompson, whose "chief talent," Greaves charged, "lies in the field of playing both ends against the middle, and that his coat of arms is a bowl of milk toast."[7] This battle between segregationist groups demonstrates the intense pressure the NAACP and Evers were placing upon the state of Mississippi and its capitol in particular.

Medgar Evers reveled in the infighting between the two segregationist groups and their leadership. He pointed to the amount of press coverage the whole episode garnered, including the fact that his and Wilkins's photographs appeared "on the front pages of some of the Jackson papers. The effect this had on the Negro community," he noted, "was favorable to the NAACP."[8] Evers used events such as these to help showcase the growing cracks in the wall of segregationist unity on the question of civil rights organization in the state of Mississippi and how best to combat it. As a consequence, he continued to speak to the need for "Negroes" to take their destiny, and that of their race, into their own hands despite the consequences. Of more importance, Evers attacked those black leaders who profited from segregation and inequality.

Evers made no apologies for his admonishment of those he labeled "Uncle Toms." He considered them more dangerous to the movement as they had the potential to cool down the fires of resistance he was struggling so hard to stoke. In an address before the Los Angeles NAACP branch, Evers pointed out that so "often we find Negroes of means who could well afford to lead our people out of our present state but are nevertheless content with things as they are, because of the personal profit they receive from segregation and human misery." He readily pointed to those with positions in the school system as particularly problematic. "Many of these 'Uncle Toms' are given high educational posts, such as principals, superintendents, and even college presidents," he remarked, "to bolster their community prestige." Those entities, Evers argued, worked against the best interest of the black community and used their positions to repress the actions of the "more aggressive students" who challenged the status quo.[9] As a means of challenging those resistant to change, Evers increased the intensity of his rhetoric and the frequency and breadth of his speaking engagements.

In October 1959, Evers spoke during the Vesper services at J. P. Campbell College in Jackson, Mississippi. In a speech titled "Our Need for Political Participation," he warned a captivated audience that black people were the only ones who could ensure that freedom and justice rained down upon the race. He argued that political participation represented the foundation of citizenship and thus it was the responsibility of the disfranchised to fight against political inequality. Evers acknowledged to all those assembled that the

> future of the Negro voter is very large in the hands of the Negro citizen and voter. The burden of improvement rests primarily with the Negro himself. Negro citizens must prepare to present themselves in numbers to be qualified, and that preparation is their responsibility. There is no attempt here to underestimate the forces of resistance, the ignorance, trickery, fear, threats, and physical assaults that have been employed and will continue to be employed. But their eradication will not be accomplished by some miracle out of the sky, some wished-for relief

from a far-off place: it will be downed primarily through the intelligence, diligence, persistence and courage of the population presently disfranchised.[10]

Evers believed that to bring this about, the oppressed had to become more actively involved in a struggle that demanded more acts of nonviolent direct action to succeed. For many of those around Medgar, the 1960 birth and nationalization of the sit-in movement legitimated his transition to more vocal expressions for the necessity of direct confrontation.

Evers considered 1960 as the beginning of a decade of change. Yet it also continued to remind him of the need to press forward. The lynching of Mack Charles Parker had not yet produced a conviction. Evers proclaimed that the second grand jury failed to produce an indictment despite the "persons named in the 378 page F.B.I. document, which further emphasizes the need for an anti-lynch law and other strong federal civil rights legislation to protect Negro citizens from those who would take the law into their own hands." With this FBI report, Evers admitted that the "pressure being brought to bear on the Federal Government to enact needed legislation is heartening indeed." However, civil rights activists hoped that Congress would work to make it a reality.[11] By 1960, it became apparent that young people were no longer willing to wait upon their elders to lead the way.

The actions of the youth involved in the Little Rock desegregation battle had a profound impact upon young people across the country. Joseph McNeil, who would later help initiate a sit-in movement in Greensboro, North Carolina, remembered that he "was particularly inspired by the people in Little Rock . . . . I was really impressed with the courage that those kids had and the leadership they displayed."[12] In part, what happened in Greensboro came as a result of the extreme slow pace of school desegregation and the inspiration individuals took from the Little Rock Nine.[13] Once the youth took on a leadership role in the civil rights movement, and that role received national media attention, it inspired others to increase their involvement. As far as southern conservatives were concerned, by 1960 they, as the United States would be in Vietnam, were dealing with their own domino theory as fear and passivity on the part of African Americans fell in one southern city after another.

By the beginning of the 1960s, North Carolina Agricultural & Technical College, established in 1890, stood as a beacon of academic stability and progress in the African American community. African American students at various academic levels were exposed to teachers who spoke of black pride and introduced them to historical figures who advocated black responsibility and leadership. Dudley High School proved one such institution and three of the four original student sit-in demonstrators in 1960 had been students there. Strong faculty, immersion in lessons on racial pride and responsibility, and a lack of social and political progress proved a recipe for direct-action protests.[14]

On February 1, 1960, Ezell Blair Jr., Joseph McNeil, Franklin McCain, and David Richmond, four African American A&T freshmen, entered a Woolworth variety store in Greensboro, North Carolina. They purchased a few items, sat down at the segregated lunch counter, and demanded service. Blair ordered a cup of coffee but the waitress refused to serve him or the group, announcing that "We do not serve Negroes." If they wanted to eat, she reminded them, they could go to the end of the counter where there was a take-out stand "where blacks could get their food." Blair, a little bewildered, pointed out that "you just served us at [that] counter. Why can't we be served at the [food] counter here?" Although denied service, the students continued to sit-in and each day more students joined the demonstration. The resistors eventually included white students from Greensboro College and the Woman's College of the University of North Carolina (now the University of North Carolina, Greensboro). African Americans were committed to the protests as demonstrated by members of the football team who, as escorts, provided protection for the protestors by serving as barriers against the actions of agitated whites. The students also received support from outside of the state. Students in Nashville, Tennessee, had already planned to stage local sit-in demonstrations and when student protests took off in North Carolina, these Nashville counterparts began days later. By July, due to economic losses, negative attention, and continued pressure, Woolworth conceded and management quickly developed an integration plan they could control.[15]

On July 25, 1960, three African American women sat down at the now-integrated Woolworth counter in Greensboro and had a meal. The three were well dressed, well mannered, and respectful as was intended. What was significant about the three, and unknown to most in the dining area, was that Geneva Tisdale, Susie Morrison, and Anetha Jones were all Woolworth employees who worked in the kitchen. Management had selected the three to be the first African American diners under the new system "to show that we were serving" white waitress Irma Jean Edwards explained. Kitchen manager Rachel Holt had earlier informed the three to bring a change of clothes because, as Geneva Tisdale recalled, "she didn't want people to know who we *were*." The white waitresses also knew about the ruse and Mabel Bozart waited on Tisdale. After their meal, Tisdale noted that she got up and "cut a beeline" out as the three went back "upstairs, [got] back in our uniforms, [and] came back down" to work.[16] The social and economic pressure students placed on the Woolworth franchise had successfully forced the company to abolish its segregationist policies here and students across the country took up the mantle. As a consequence, this new type of resistance tactic spread to a number of cities across the country, and over the next year an estimated 70,000 students participated in sit-in demonstrations with 3,600 resistors serving jail time.[17]

The students' decision to *sit* infused into the civil rights struggle an effective strategy of resistance headed by a cadre of dedicated young activists. Student participation in sit-in demonstrations had a profound impact upon their sense of self. "I probably felt better that day [of the sit-in] than I've ever felt in my life," Franklin McCain remembered. "I felt as though I had gained my manhood . . . and not only gained it, but had developed quite a lot of respect for it."[18] This feeling of empowerment spread across the country, and young Mississippians were not impervious to the growing sense of personal importance and their ability to exact change. Medgar Evers maintained that the "unrest of young people throughout the southland and the nation has had its influence on the young people at Tougaloo College and Campbell College here in the Jackson area." He used the excitement of area youth as an opportunity to negotiate with Campbell College administrators on the possibility of establishing an NAACP chapter there.[19] After the student-led initiatives had taken hold, the NAACP leadership came out in support of the sit-in movement. Roy Wilkins announced that the demonstrations were the direct result of desegregation having proceeded "at the supersonic speed of *one percent* a year" since the Supreme Court decision in 1954.[20] However, as sociologist Kenneth Andrews pointed out, Mississippi remained impervious to the sit-in movement engulfing the South.[21]

Evers was well aware of the changes in tactics activists used across the country and became excited when that fire spread among Jackson area youth. He noted that the "southwide [*sic*] student protest has generated a [great] deal of activity on the part of Mississippi Branches, we have begun to get more activity out of branches that were on the verge of collapsing."[22] Although ecstatic about every civil rights victory, regardless of its origin, Evers was discouraged by the fact that change seemed to be happening everywhere except in Mississippi. In 1955, the bus boycott in Montgomery, Alabama, took center stage; two years later the eyes of the nation were upon the battle over school integration in Little Rock, Arkansas. By 1960, Evers could feel the opportunities for social change fast approaching Mississippi. His connection with the youth placed him within the center of a concentric circle of resistance that inspired the very youth he depended upon to continue the struggle and, in many ways, to lead it. Despite the winds of change, Evers often found himself at odds with other NAACP members who were advocating that the NAACP in Mississippi avoid participating in direct-action programs.

Again, the national NAACP was concerned about the possibility of extreme white violence in response to aggressive black resistance. Also, the NAACP leadership remained cognizant of the fact that racial violence weakened NAACP chances of securing needed political support from state and federal politicians and key business interests. This fact could be seen in the NAACP's working with President Kennedy in 1962 to defeat Rule 22. This congressional mechanism was designed to promote the dreaded filibuster— a bane to civil rights agendas. Here the NAACP focused its efforts on securing the support of key senators who would assist in defeating this measure. Historian Gilbert Jonas has written that in this instance, "JFK had . . . warned the civil rights leaders to avoid threatening these senators by demonstrations in their home states or in Washington itself, on the grounds that such would backfire because the senators would regard such demonstrations as 'a gun to their heads.'"[23] Here Kennedy was basically advocating that the NAACP accept a tradeoff. Hold off on demonstrations or run the risk of losing political support in an area that would benefit civil rights legislation in the future. Of even greater concern to NAACP leaders than losing political favor, was the fear that African Americans would resort to violence that would lead to an all-out race war. African Americans would, undoubtedly, catch the worse end of this type of open skirmish with their white counterparts and NAACP leaders such as Roy Wilkins wanted to avoid this scenario at all costs. Evers, however, often went head-to-head with other NAACP members who wanted the association to maintain a moderate approach to civil rights activism.

Evers developed a tense relationship with C. R. Darden, president of the NAACP Mississippi State Conference of Branches. Darden had written Gloster Current complaining that "Medgar Evers is too much of an antagonist in the board meetings to be tolerated. He took his American Legion of Jackson, Mississippi, took over the Jackson Branch of NAACP and there has been nothing in the Jackson Branch but confusion since that election of American Legion to NAACP Branch officers." He then requested a meeting to further discuss the issue.[24] Evers exclaimed in response that Darden was the one who was antagonistic and, at one meeting, had verbally attacked him, Ruby Hurley, and Gloster Current. Darden, according to Evers, had openly stated "that 'Gloster B. Current has no right to tell Mississippi what to do.'"[25] The divide between these two leaders hinged on Evers's desire to move the NAACP toward a more aggressive approach to combating inequality in the state and Darden's argument that this type of approach would produce devastating and, most likely, violent consequences.

As the sit-in movement spread throughout the Upper South, some members of the Mississippi NAACP Youth Council were eager to carry out demonstrations of their own. Older stalwarts of the movement such as

C. R. Darden discouraged this strategy. Evers noted that Darden, in his own "words, [argued that] 'It would create more hate by whites for the NAACP.'" Although Evers admitted that Darden's "wishes prevailed," the resulting disagreement continued to create divisions in leadership. In a personal attack, Darden had earlier informed Evers that his actions had "proven that this old adage is true, 'It is human to error, but to persist is devilish.'"[26] As a consequence, Medgar had no choice but to alert the national office of this critical development.[27] Evers, however, understood the necessity of taking an active stance in light of direct-action protests sweeping the country.

Although he acknowledged that sit-in demonstrations in Mississippi were not yet advisable, the "general attitude in Mississippi, especially among our Branches on the coast and in the Delta, is that the State Conference is being too precautious." He further noted that this hesitation on the part of Darden and others created "a situation which would make it difficult to get a desired number of members or more participation in general, financially, etc."[28] Evers informed Current that he had explained to Darden that it was imperative that the NAACP initiate "some form of brief protests to indicate to the rest of the nation that [Mississippi's] Governor Coleman's pronouncement that negroes [*sic*] are satisfied would not be augmented by complete silence, while everyone else is protesting Jim Crow." He reasoned that if the rest of the country believed that black Mississippians lacked the will to struggle at this critical juncture, the perception alone would hurt the Mississippi movement more than anything else.[29] A little more than a month after the sit-in movement began, individuals in Jackson made plans for direct-action protests against area businesses.

In a report to NAACP secretary Ruby Hurley on April 13, 1960, Evers discussed the origins of the boycott that later crippled stores along Capitol Street in Jackson. He also noted the role that students played in its success. On March 28, 1960, Evers and other community leaders, including Dean Charles A. Jones of Campbell College, held a meeting and discussed the possibility of an economic boycott during the Easter season. Evers recalled that after "a number of encouraging meetings with civic leaders, students, businessmen, clergy and others," they decided a boycott would be an effective strategy and scheduled it to begin April 10. African Americans were encouraged to refrain from purchasing anything from white merchants during the boycott. Evers noted that students from Jackson State, Campbell, and Tougaloo College proved invaluable in getting out "some ten thousand . . . handbills to the sixty-one thousand . . . Negro citizens urging them to cooperate with the boycott." Evers acknowledged, however, that there would be no demonstrations associated with the boycott and that blacks simply "won't be in their [whites'] stores except to pay bills. We won't be downtown at all." Accounts from African American leaders such as Dean Jones, who reported that approximately 70 percent of African Americans had participated in the boycott, bolstered its reported success. As chaplain of Campbell College, Dean Charles A. Jones played a critical role in the Mississippi movement by providing leadership and organizing support for the civil rights struggle in Jackson. In 1960, he also helped found the Citizens Committee for Human Rights. This organization worked closely with the NAACP and provided support for the student boycott movement in Jackson.[30]

The boycott increased the overall sense of power African Americans internalized in the city of Jackson and its surrounding communities. Evers measured the success of the boycott on two fronts: the economic loss to white merchants and increased support for black businesses. He argued that the "Definite proof lies in the fact that Negro businesses, particularly groceries and millineries witnessed tremendous increase in cash sales." This development harkens back to the ideas of educator Booker T. Washington, who argued for the importance of African Americans creating a self-sustaining and generational replicating group economy.[31] Evers also pointed to the fact "that on Easter Sunday many of the Church [*sic*] ministers made comments to the effect that this was the first Easter in recent years to see so many female members of the congregation in their seeming 'old' clothes, bears witness of a favorable end to Jackson's 'Negro Boycott.'"[32] The Sovereignty Commission responded to the overall Easter boycott by gathering information on organizers and participants and dispatching informants to ascertain the likelihood and possibility for success that a boycott of this nature posed.

In addition to the surveillance work of the Sovereignty Commission and despite the enthusiasm of the youth, Evers's sister Elizabeth Evers-Jordan recalled that overcoming the sometimes lack of assistance from African Americans in the community was one of Medgar's greatest sources of frustration.[33] Sometimes African American participation worked against the very movement Evers labored to build. On April 6, 1960, a Captain Bennett, of the Detective Bureau for the Jackson Police Department, contacted commission officials and reported "that he had received a telephone call from a Mrs. Slaughter, a white woman, who reported that her negro [*sic*] maid stated that a number of college students were going around to the various negro [*sic*] high schools and elementary schools soliciting their support for the Easter boycott of white merchants." On that same day, the commission received information from an informant identified as T-1 that Medgar Evers had visited Tougaloo College to drum up support for the boycott.[34]

The report also acknowledged the amount of pressure applied to individuals identified as boycott leaders. On April 8, 1960, Jackson police chief Meady Pierce reported that the Tougaloo College Board of Trustees suspended Reverend "Mangum [*sic*] [a probable reference to Tougaloo chaplain Reverend John H. Mangrum] . . . who had spoken at the NAACP meeting in Jackson on April 3, 1960." The board "also called the Dean of Tougaloo College . . . before them and had let him know in no uncertain terms that they did not want Tougaloo College mixed up in the boycott or any type of racial agitation in Mississippi." The report noted that Evers had made it clear that the NAACP did not organize the boycott, but rather "it was a community project."[35] This statement heightened commission surveillance as informants continued to provide the Sovereignty Commission with information.

Commission informant T-2, identified as an African American, notified the Sovereignty Commission "that he had been keeping a close check on the negro [*sic*] areas in Jackson and [that] it was his studied opinion that the boycott would be a complete failure and would not be supported by the majority of negroes [*sic*] in this area."[36] For those "negroes" who participated, there existed the real threat of economic reprisal by whites, a threat bolstered by commission identification efforts. On April 11, 1960, the *Commercial Appeal* (Memphis) reported that the Jackson White Citizens' Council "called the use of economics in the racial struggle 'a two-way street' . . . [, a threat that many] conservative Negroes feared [meant] wholesale firings."[37] Commission reports also contain accounts from white merchants who reported that business continued as usual during the supposed boycott, while some noted that more "Negroes" than usual had come in to shop.[38] Evers challenged the report of merchants who suggested they were not feeling the economic pinch. In the *Delta Democrat-Times,* Evers acknowledged that "we aren't at all satisfied with reports by merchants [that] they aren't being affected—we know its affecting them. . . . [W]e know it, because we covered the entire city in preparing for it and we got good response everywhere."[39] Some white storeowners admitted the pinch they received due to the boycott. "One store in particular," Evers recalled, "a downtown store which caters principally to Negro trade, indicated on Monday, one day after the boycott began, that it had lost seventy-five (75) per cent [*sic*] of its trade."[40]

On April 18, 1960, commission informants T-2 and T-4 (T-4 also identified as African American) reported "that in their opinion the boycott had been a complete failure, as the great majority of negroes [*sic*] in Jackson did not cooperate with the NAACP called boycott."[41] Reports such as these contradict African American accounts of the boycott's success. The Sovereignty Commission continued to keep tabs on Medgar Evers and worked to frustrate solidarity in the black community. Commission officials took particular interest in Evers as talks of major civil rights demonstrations in Jackson surfaced.

If Evers had ever felt overworked before, the early 1960s intensified the feeling. Although he stayed busy addressing the varied social and political incidents happening in Jackson, Evers remained responsible for civil rights activities happening all over the state. By 1960, many individuals were testing the mettle of segregation and depended upon Evers for assistance. Gilbert Rutledge Mason Sr., M.D., of Biloxi, Mississippi, proved one such individual. Mason openly challenged the city's Jim Crow laws regarding African Americans' access to its "public" beaches. Much like Evers, he, too, had a fighting spirit and boasted a family heritage of resistance, and the two became good friends.

Mason was born in Jackson, Mississippi, on October 7, 1928, to Willie and Alean Mason. Education was very important to his parents and Mason recalled the premium they placed on getting an education and the expectation that their children do their very best in all educational pursuits. Mason finished high school at Lanier in Jackson and then graduated from Tennessee State University in 1949 with a double major in chemistry and biology and a "strong" minor in mathematics. After Tennessee State, he attended Howard Medical School and completed the requirements for the medical degree in 1954. After Howard, he completed a one-year internship at Homer G. Phillips Hospital in St. Louis, Missouri, and then moved to Biloxi in July 1955, becoming the second practicing African American physician on the Gulf Coast after Felix H. Dunn. Becoming a doctor fulfilled a dream Mason remembered having from at least the time he "was in elementary school or as far back as . . . [he could] remember."[42]

Mason first met Medgar in November 1955 after Felix H. Dunn, president of the Gulf Coast branch of the NAACP, suggested the two meet. Although Evers was immersed in the investigation of the Till lynching, a meeting was arranged and the two men met at the "YWCA" building in Jackson. Throughout the meeting they discussed a variety of issues, but the planning of the NAACP state conference took precedence.[43] Mason acknowledged that Evers played an instrumental role in the struggle against segregationist practices in Biloxi. Evers organized the Biloxi branch of the NAACP, Mason remarked, and their friendship grew out of this association. Evers also helped organize community members against the entrenched practice of denying blacks the opportunity to live in any Biloxi neighborhood they chose.[44] African Americans were denied access to Harrison County's twenty-six-mile long stretch of manmade "or cultivated" beach, and this proved to be the rallying point for the fight against segregation in Biloxi, which Mason led with assistance from Medgar Evers.

Mason believed the best way to tackle a problem was to take it head-on. As a result of this philosophy, on May 14, 1959, he and eight others, including his son Gilbert Jr., went down to the white-only beach and swam before a police officer investigating a car accident confronted them. The policeman ordered them downtown and informed the group that they all would "find out about it" when they arrived at the precinct.[45] When Mason and Murray J. Saucier Jr. (Saucier had also participated in the beach boy-cott) arrived at the police station, assistant police chief Walter Williams explained that a city ordinance prohibited blacks from using the public beach. Despite their request to view the document, Williams refused to show them a copy of the ordinance until the following morning. The next day, when Mason and Saucier returned to view the ordinance, as the histo-rian J. Michael Butler noted, Biloxi mayor Laz Quave asked to see them and accused both "men of using the beach to involve the Civil Rights Commission and the NAACP in the coast's racial affairs, which both Mason and Saucier denied."[46] Mason, however, had notified Evers of the planned beach action and Evers informed Mason that it was up to them to decide whether to challenge the beach laws; they also understood that if they got into trouble they should contact the national office for bond money.[47] On October 5, 1959, Mason and other community leaders filed a beach-access petition with the county board of supervisors "demanding 'unrestrained use of the beach' by blacks." This action ended in disappoint-ment for the petitioners as well as economic intimidation and loss of jobs for others.[48] Determined not to be outdone, Mason returned to the beach alone on Easter Sunday, April 17, 1960, and again was arrested for break-ing the law and "charged with disorderly conduct for the act of peaceful swimming."[49] Evers kept up with the plans in place reporting that "on Sunday, April 24th, from Biloxi through Pass Christian, which includes Gulfport, Negro citizens plan to swim in the Gulf of Mexico." The white response to African American swimmers along the beach on April 24, 1960, marked a turning point for the Biloxi movement and made Evers's predic-tion that there "will be more to report on the outcome of this situation, in the near future" a statement of prophetic proportion.[50]

After his arrest on April 17, Mason gained overwhelming support from many in the African American community and decided to organize another wade-in for April 24. Butler noted that on April 19, at a Harrison County Civic Action Committee meeting, Mason described his plans to mobilize the black community against three beach "sites on Biloxi city property."[51] African Americans had organized the Civic Action Committee of Harrison

County to protect their rights and to find solutions to the various problems they faced. Until the April 24 attack upon the legitimacy of segregation along the shores of the Gulf of Mexico, however, white reaction to African Americans swimming within restricted areas in Biloxi had been relegated to verbal abuse with no real physical violence. That day proved to be different and the extent of the white response shocked the sensibilities of the waders involved, and the country as a whole, and brought Evers and the NAACP into the center of the struggle for equality in Biloxi.

On that fateful Sunday morning, the demonstrators met at McDaniel and Son Funeral Home where Mason explained their protest objectives and methodology. He also advised against anybody carrying anything that could be misconstrued as a weapon. Mason then divided all volunteers into three groups from which they would enter the beach near Biloxi Cemetery, Biloxi Hospital, and the lighthouse near a busy intersection. He then sent each to their proscribed areas along the beach. Mason noted, however, that by the time he had reached the lighthouse "the shit had hit the fan." What he saw were hordes

> of snarling white folks . . . [pour] onto the beach at the foot of Gill [Avenue] with bricks, baseball bats, pipes, sticks, and chains and [they] attacked our unarmed black protesters. The law enforcement officers were just standing around. . . . Some of the forty or fifty blacks at the foot of Gill were already in the water with at least four or five hundred whites surrounding them and beating whomever they could lay hands on. It was too late to call it off.[52]

This violent confrontation did not remain on the beach alone; it later spilled over into the black community lasting throughout the night. As a result of this level of white resistance, Mason and community members sought to get the NAACP fully involved with their desegregation attempts. They contacted both Roy Wilkins and Clarence Mitchell and notified them of the level of violence to which they had been subjected. Both Wilkins and Mitchell suggested that Evers investigate the Biloxi crisis.[53]

Prior to the "bloody wade-in," many African American residents in Biloxi were afraid to elicit help from the NAACP or to be associated with the organization for fear of white reprisal. After the beach attacks, however, people were fed up and realized "that they needed a really big bad dog to look out for them" and Mason pointed them to the "biggest and the baddest one" he knew.[54] Because of continued differences between Mason and Gulfport NAACP president Felix Dunn regarding strategy and the city's proposal to construct a segregated beach for African Americans, Mason split from Dunn and founded the Biloxi branch of the NAACP. Medgar Evers also distanced the state NAACP from Dunn, and Butler contends that "reports of Dunn's meeting with Sovereignty Commission officials after the wade-in infuriated Evers."[55]

Medgar Evers drove down and met with Mason and Dunn on the Monday after the beach violence and immediately "began soliciting memberships to see if there would be enough interest and commitment to organize a separate new local NAACP branch in Biloxi." Mason admitted that people were concerned with a person like Evers coming into Biloxi and helping to organize the African American community. People pondered the ramifications this type of outside involvement might bring to area residents and, of more importance, what forms it would take.[56] As a community response to the beach incident, Evers showed Mason and others how to gather affidavits from victims of the riot and they, in return, decided to take full advantage of the legal assistance and experience of the NAACP.

The NAACP worked to resolve the beach issue and to support those who were now taking an active stand. The affidavits from those injured in the beach attacks were forwarded to NAACP general counsel Robert Carter. Evers noted that these "complaints, along with the insistance [sic] of our Director of the Washington Bureau, Mr. Mitchell, brought very favorable action from the Department of Justice." He further reported that the "Federal Government filed suit in Vicksburg, Mississippi against Harrison County officials charging that they had violated the Federal contractional [sic] agreement between Harrison County and the United States Government of 1948, when they refused to permit Negroes to use the Gulf Coast beaches on a non-segregated basis." Evers insinuates that the actions taken by the federal government were connected to the NAACP's announcement of its support of "Negroes'" desire to gain access to the beach.[57] Although willing to work with others to forward the cause of black advancement, the NAACP steered clear of any association with the Communist Party. The Red Scare of the 1950s, and the desire to root out communist sympathizers that accompanied it, hurt both individuals' and organizations' attempts to challenge America's racial shortcomings. The oppressive actions of Wisconsin senator Joseph McCarthy legitimated any cautionary fear individuals or organization leaders exhibited.

Senator Joseph McCarthy made communism a household word during the 1950s. His attempts to link individuals to the Communist Party ruined lives and ended careers, including his own, before his rein of terror ended in 1954. McCarthy's witch hunts caused activists and civil rights organizations to temper their activism for fear of being branded a communist or communist affiliate; the fear lingered during the 1960s.[58] Evers sought to prevent any linkage of the NAACP with communism and refused it any leeway in branch organization. He came face-to-face with communist infiltration in

Walthall County and dealt with it swiftly and decisively as NAACP mandates dictated.

The NAACP had come out strong against communism early on and sought to distance the organization from any association or connection with the group. In 1950, the association addressed the communist issue with a stringent resolution, one the NAACP, during its 1956 annual convention in California, "reaffirmed and extended." The resolution now included "a ruling that 'Communists and/or persons who are prominently identified with the Ku Klux Klan, White Citizens Councils, or Communist front or Communist-line organizations, are ineligible for membership in the NAACP."⁵⁹ Thus Evers was quite clear on the NAACP's position regarding communist members or sympathizers as his actions in Walthal County demonstrated.

On September 12, 1960, Evers attended a branch meeting at Mount Mariah Baptist Church to "further encourage membership and fund raising." There was also another NAACP member present "attempting to distribute the 'Daily Worker.' This man had apparently been working himself into the community," Evers recalled, "with his smooth line of talk." Evers questioned the individual (he does not identify him) about the *Daily Worker* and he responded that "he was one hundred per cent [*sic*] for the program and policy of this particular paper." Believing perhaps that the man had not associated the paper with the Communist Party, Evers pointed out the connection which the individual admitted he knew. Evers then announced, while the individual sat in the audience, "that we do not subscribe to the Communist Party line and that we would prefer that he leave." The individual announced that he was a paid member of the NAACP and if he had to leave he wanted his money returned. Evers reported that the "Branch immediately voted to refund his money and when his card comes it will be disposed of."⁶⁰ Although the Communist Party had a history of supporting black rights, many considered the political fallout of group association too costly. The NAACP realized that any link to the Communist Party would be devastating and they made this clear to Evers. He received instruction on how to handle communist accusations and others were employed to assist him in preparing to deal with any such charges. A letter sent to Evers's home address advised that information should be gathered "for Medgar refuting communist accusations" and that a "RW and Morsell" should be conferred "on What to Do About advising Evers."⁶¹ In this light, it is apparent why Evers took such a direct approach to dealing with the NAACP member regarding his communist leanings. Things, however, were heating up in the Biloxi area and Evers returned his attention there.

In 1961, Evers was also involved in attempts by a group of committed African American parents in Biloxi to desegregate area schools. He had begun the process, Mason recalled, by writing NAACP legal counsel Robert Carter on October 11, 1960, requesting assistance and support. Although they had the legal precedents set by *Brown,* the process dragged on for nearly three years before they entered the courts, and Evers worked closely with Mason and the other parents to integrate the school. Biloxi public schools, after the Fifth Circuit Court of Appeals decision in February 1964, began desegregating classrooms in 1964 and 1965. However, African Americans would not consider the beach controversy concluded and know that they had full and unrestricted access to the beaches until July 31, 1972, when they received a favorable ruling in the *United States v. Harrison County* lawsuit.[62] From the time he spent in Biloxi strategizing, Evers and Gilbert Mason grew closer. Whenever Evers came to Biloxi he stayed with Mason and vice versa when Mason traveled to Jackson.

Whenever Evers came to town, he and Mason would go to the Blue Note, a black nightclub, where Mason ordered vodka while Medgar just sat with him. He also noted that women were always present, but that whenever a young woman approached Medgar during those times, he never offended her, but always gave her cause as to why she should not be familiar with him. Evers's love for his wife and children and his commitment to the sanctity of marriage, combined with his dedication to the civil rights fight,· kept him focused on the task at hand with no time or desire to engage in adulterous behaviors.[63]

With regard to the ever-present issue of wanton women, Myrlie recalled informing Medgar about reports placing him in situations where a lot of women were present. Evers, somewhat irritated she recalled, warned that "you're gonna have a miserable life [Myrlie] if you let people talk to you and you believe what they say. [Furthermore, did] you ever stop to think that people might be jealous of us?" To which Myrlie replied, thinking of material wealth, "Jealous of what, we don't have anything." "But we have each other. Myrlie, if I spent my time chasing every woman that would like for me to, I wouldn't have time to do my work and my work comes first."[64] Whether it was marriage or the movement, Evers's dedication and loyalty to the struggle for equality outweighed both adversity and temptation.

This is not to say that the Everses did not experience marital problems from time to time. For many civil rights activists, family life, and marriages in particular, often suffered under the pressures of day-to-day struggles. The Everses were no exception. The stress associated with constant threats from would-be assailants, the lack of financial stability, and the enormous amount of time husbands and wives spent apart placed undue pressure on marital relationships and sometimes tempers flared.

NAACP officials, celebrities, and civil rights activists of all types were often guests at the Everses' home and Medgar would sometimes call Myrlie at a moment's notice and ask that she prepare an impromptu meal. On one particular occasion, he phoned home and requested that she fix a spur-of-the-moment lunch for NAACP officials from New York in town for the annual state conference. At this moment the frustrations Myrlie felt with the entire weight of the civil rights struggle and the lack of financial resources manifested into a heated argument. Myrlie announced that she could not fix anything because they had nothing in the house but a frozen roast. Evers, somewhat shocked at the announcement, alluded to her mismanagement of the family finances, something to which she took great offense. She abruptly ended the conversation by hanging up the phone. To her surprise, Medgar left the office and showed up at the house minutes later, "demanding an explanation for . . . [her] attitude," a conversation that escalated. She remembered that at some point in the heated discussion:

> Medgar raised his hand, his face red with anger. I thought he was going to slap me. I remembered what Daddy had taught me: Always strike first—and hard. I reached for the closest weapon I could spot— the empty cast-iron skillet on the stove—and I swung it in Medgar's direction as hard as my five-foot-six, 120- pound frame would allow.
>
> The small but heavy pan connected with Medgar's temple. Astonished, he tripped backward, his eyes wide as globes. Shocked, each of us stood there in dead silence, staring at the other. He had questioned my honesty and my abilities; I had challenged his authority. Then, suddenly, Medgar retaliated, landing a large open palm on my left cheek. Every pincurl in my hair went flying. I stumbled against the washer and dryer, stunned more emotionally than physically.[65]

Both were dismayed and shocked that they had allowed "the growing pressures and personal tension [to] reach this point." Neither would have responded in this manner without the provocation of the enormous amount of pressure placed upon them by their activism. A few nights later, Clarence Mitchell, NAACP director of the Washington Bureau, provided the two with a bit of marriage counseling along with a warning for the two not to allow "the stress of this job" to tear them apart. Myrlie let Medgar know that if they were to make it, they both would have to make changes.[66]

It was never a question that both were dedicated to the struggle for equality and to each other. What they came to realize was the need to reach an agreed-upon medium between the civil rights movement and their personal and familial relationship. With that realization, Evers apprised Myrlie that he could no longer continue to "fight White people, fight with my own people to get them to challenge the system, and then come home and fight with you. . . . Either you are with me or you aren't. That's your decision." Myrlie articulated what she needed from her husband and understood what he needed from her. At that critical juncture of their relationship, Myrlie recalled, they decided that they "would work together as a team, both of us giving and taking as we grew together."[67]

The meaning of civil rights struggle often entailed losing relationships and family connections. Many civil rights activists had to make the painful decision of whether to continue the struggle and lose one's significant other or to save one's relationship at the expense of the movement. For many, civil rights activism reflected the sword of Damocles, a powerful deadly force suspended overhead by a fragile string of patience and perseverance.[68] The decision to stay or to leave the struggle was never an easy one and not everyone could construct a proper balance between family and activism in the way that Medgar and Myrlie did. When opportunities arose, they went fishing or went on a family picnic as a means of spending family time. Stribling Lake proved a favorite fishing area for Evers and he took advantage of every opportunity to go there.[69] As the 1960s progressed, however, he found very little time for leisure as civil rights activism, and the operations of other civil rights organizations in the state, intensified.

During the summer of 1961, members of the Student Nonviolent Coordinating Committee arrived in Mississippi en masse. As an organization, SNCC developed out of the 1960 sit-in movement. On April 16–18, 1960, SCLC executive secretary Ella Baker held a conference at Shaw University in Raleigh, North Carolina. The conference was comprised of sit-in protestors, student leaders, students, and civil rights organizers. Baker made sure that the students understood the importance of maintaining their own organizational autonomy rather than coming under the umbrella of another civil rights group.[70] She later acknowledged that the "students showed [a] willingness to be met on the basis of equality, but were intolerant of anything that smacked of manipulation or domination."[71] Thus, the historian Clayborne Carson argued, SNCC's founding "was an important step in the transformation of a limited student movement to desegregate lunch counters into a broad and sustained movement to achieve major social reforms."[72] For this newly formed organization, Mississippi would be both an important target and a valuable learning experience.

Under the leadership of Robert Moses, SNCC established itself as an organizing force early on by challenging inequality in southwest Mississippi. Moses was a young Harvard educated activist who had taught in New York and became enamored by the movement for equality. Moses established crucial relationships with local leaders such as C. C. Bryant and Amzie Moore to establish a resistance movement against whites' attempts to keep African Americans from voting. C. C. Bryant was an important contact in McComb, Mississippi, and had a history of civil rights activism and organization. Bryant was also head of the Pike County chapter of the NAACP. Counties in southwest Mississippi, which included Pike, Amite, and Walthall Counties, had a well-deserved reputation for viciousness in its opposition to black equality.[73]

By the time SNCC arrived, Evers had helped C. C. Bryant establish a youth group dedicated to documenting police brutality and distributing literature advocating African Americans' fight against inequality. As a result of the work Evers had previously done to organize Mississippi youth, SNCC had a socially aware group of individuals with which to work. SNCC chairman Charles McDew acknowledged that many "of the people who became SNCC organizers really got their start with the NAACP and with Medgar Evers. . . . And everybody could tell you when they first—every black person—when they first . . . met Medgar and became involved with him."[74] As a consequence, the youth SNCC encountered were just as willing and ready to work for the cause of civil equality as the students had been at North Carolina A&T.

Young people were very important to the SNCC movement in Mississippi and many of its activists were fresh out of high school. Robert Moses remembered two in particular. "So out of the first campaign," Moses recalled, "we did get Curtis Hayes and Hollis Watkins as field secretaries, who had just graduated from high school and instead of going on to college right away decided to work for a year."[75] Watkins had been inspired by the Freedom Riders he saw on television to return to Mississippi from California. He admitted that prior to leaving for California he had attended a few NAACP meetings where Medgar Evers had been "really trying to encourage and promote young people to get involved and to take out memberships in the NAACP and look at possibly getting involved in trying to get black people registered to vote." Thus when he returned to Mississippi, organizing and social struggle were not foreign to him. Hayes had deep roots in the community as the son of a local minister and was also committed to civil rights struggle.[76]

Organizing in McComb proved a treacherous and dangerous activity. In the early stages, however, a few individuals were allowed to register without much fanfare, but as the numbers increased, so did white resistance. The registration process could take two or three weeks before one received notification of his or her voting status. During this time, the individual's name appeared in the local newspaper or any other public medium for the two- or three-week period, which provided "people the opportunity to question your character," Watkins remarked. This "character" investigation proved a process within itself. Ed King explained that the "way moral character was determined, was that your employer had a right to speak about your moral character, or anyone in the community who knew you."[77] The publication of names provided opportunities for employers to threaten people with the loss of their jobs or other authoritative figures to intimidate potential voters. This public display caused a lot of apprehension among those wishing to register but who did not want to risk their lives or livelihood in the process. With the arrival of SNCC, the civil rights struggle in Mississippi took on a more direct approach for challenging the system of inequality and racial separatism.

In 1961, black residents of McComb applied the same sit-in tactics used in North Carolina the year before, and SNCC's chairman Marion Barry was the catalyst behind it all. Watkins recalled that SNCC basically had two programs, which Barry explained to the McComb group: "voter registration . . . and direct action, and that he was primarily responsible for direct action." In response, the McComb group, which included Watkins and Hayes, formed the "Pike County Nonviolent Direct Action Committee" to identify all segregated areas and determine which ones should be targeted for desegregation attempts. Barry also taught the group strategies for challenging segregation as well as processes for protecting oneself against physical attack. After careful investigation, the Pike County Nonviolent Direct Action Committee (which boasted between fifteen and twenty members) decided to integrate the local library.[78]

The group set a date for their integration assault on the public library. Despite group support for the demonstration, on the target day for "various reasons" only two individuals were "prepared to go through with the demonstration," Watkins recalled. Rather than call it off, Hayes and Watkins decided to proceed as planned and went to the library only to find it closed. The two-man group called upon other sites identified by the committee and remembered that "Woolworth's had a lunch counter, right down the street," Watkins remarked, "—it was right in line, so we went to the Woolworth's lunch counter . . . [to] order some coffee."[79]

On August 26, 1961, eighteen-year-old Curtis Hayes and twenty-year-old Hollis Watkins, who both had attended direct-action workshops, sat down at the counter of the Woolworth store in McComb and initiated a sit-in movement. The event did not begin smoothly as there were no seats available when the two men entered the store. Watkins admitted that this fact "kind of threw us off." Once a "lady and her daughter" finished and left, the men took the available seats. The police were already in the store, which led Watkins to believe that they already knew what they were planning to do. As soon as they sat down, the police asked them to move and when they refused the officers arrested them, noting the charges would be explained to them when they got to the police station. Both men received thirty-four days in jail for their efforts, but their actions encouraged the young people of McComb to take an active role in their own liberation. As a consequence of the actions of young people such as Hayes and Watkins, African American youth realized they could be an active force in the overall movement in Mississippi and when necessary could assume a leadership role. This realization connected the youth in Mississippi with African American youth struggling for equality in other parts of the nation, and Evers emphasized this connection whenever discussing the essence of struggle with young people.[80]

By 1960, black Mississippians could also boast of a Civil Rights Advisory Committee for which Medgar Evers displayed great enthusiasm. "As you probably know from having read the newspapers or listening to television and radio," Evers announced, "we now have a Civil Rights Advisory Committee in Mississippi." The interracial committee, Evers disclosed, was made up of five Mississippians: "Rev. Murray Cox of Gulfport, Committee Chairman (White); Dr. James Lucius Allen, Druggist of Columbus, Vice Chairman (Negro); Dr. A. B. Britton of Jackson (Negro); Adm. Robert Briscoe, USN (Ret.) of Liberty (White); Mrs. Wallis Schutt, President of the Mississippi United Church Women, Jackson (White); [and] Mr. V. O. Campbel of Collins (White)." Highlighting civil rights violations represented the core of the committee's objectives.[81]

The Sovereignty Commission catalogued the memorandum in which Evers advised African Americans that the "committee [was] set up to accept complaints from . . . [individuals] who have been denied the right to vote or . . . [whose] Civil Rights have been violated in any way." He warned African Americans that the Advisory Committee would be useless "unless we have complaints to file which will be kept in total secrecy. We[, the NAACP,] are therefore counting on you to get these complaints into the Advisory Committee through our office."[82] Powerful Mississippi politicians, however, were none too happy regarding the establishment of this type of advisory committee or its encouragement for blacks to "dig up complaints against the white people." Individuals such as Attorney General Joe T. Patterson sought to discredit the committee and, in an off-handed way, link it to communism. "This is one of the most blatantly un-American gestures I have seen," Patterson announced. "One would think we are living behind the iron curtain where neighbor spies on neighbor and a man is subject to charge by any hoodlum who has a grudge." Patterson further added "that the quickest way to destroy a state or nation is to put one segment of the population against another sewing seeds of dissention." Despite Patterson's warnings, Evers informed "Negroes" that the Committee would "hold its next meeting in mid-Feb. We are expecting you to have complaints ready to file with the Committee at that time."[83] Evers also took the opportunity to gather information and to take his findings to the committee.

On September 19, 1960, Evers, representing the Mississippi State Conference of NAACP Branches, filed the following complaint with the Civil Rights Advisory Committee regarding the harassment of African Americans on public conveyances in Mississippi:

> Negro Citizens who travel on interstate buses, both Greyhound and Trailways, have recently encountered numerous threats, insults, and even violence, when they have dared to take a seat any where they chose after having paid the same fare that other passengers have paid.
>
> It has become increasing [sic] inconvenient for negro [sic] citizens passing through McComb and Winona, and most Mississippi towns.
>
> The tactics used by police when a bus arrives in one of these towns are illustrated by what happened to five (5) persons who were enroute [sic] from Jackson, Mississippi to New Orleans, Louisiana on September 11, 1960. Upon arrival in McComb the police boarded the bus, ordered all Negroes to the [rear?] and those who were slow about moving were struck with night-sticks by the police and made to move along faster. Another incident occurred in Winona, Mississippi, August 27, 1960, when a young lad by the name of Johnny Fraizier [o]f Greenville, Mississippi was beaten into a state of semi-consciousness by the sheriff and the deputy of Montgomery County because he was riding near the front of the bus.

Evers included in the complaint his personal experience aboard the Trailways bus on March 11, 1958. He notified the Advisory Committee that members of the Mississippi State Conference of NAACP Branches believed that the harassment African Americans received while riding "on interstate and intrastate public conveyances is the result of an organized effort to intimidate Negro citizens and subject them to an inferior seating arrangement on public conveyances."[84] The oppressive actions and intensified methods of direct resistance, which defined the early 1960s, amplified Evers's growing intolerance for nondirect action as the primary strategy. In the process, he became more vocal regarding the necessity for strategic changes.

Two letters Evers wrote to Gilbert Mason Sr. and Robert Carter in

1960 illustrate his growing impatience with the less-than-direct methods for challenging inequality. His having to continuously adhere to NAACP policies of nondirect action, when grassroots people were demanding and often participating in more direct challenges to segregation, placed Evers in a tough position he believed undermined his authority. He found that the younger civil rights organizations that were moving into Mississippi challenged the viability of NAACP organized programs in the state. The direct-action tactics used by organizations such as SNCC and the Congress of Racial Equality provided an outlet for the frustrations of young people and, in the process, cast a disparaging shadow over the more conservative NAACP. In his previous letter to Carter regarding school desegregation efforts in Biloxi, Evers provided him with a secondary reason for composing the letter. He apprised Carter of the following and the conflict the predicament posed to his leadership status in the community:

> you know I am a paid worker with the NAACP, and at the same time I have two school age children who are presently going to private school (segregated). Now it is rather difficult for me to reconcile to the general public the fact that I believe in what I preach, while at the same time practice something to the contrary. To be very candid I would like to be one of the three or four Plaintiffs to initiate legal action to destroy the segregated system here in Jackson, either my wife or I, or both, are ready and willing to affix our signatures authorizing such action in our behalf. I would like an immediate answer to these questions.

Evers's frustration with the NAACP's belief that it was bad public relations for their "officials to be engaged in the direct prosecution of civil rights litigation" was apparent in this letter, as well as his tone of urgency. The following correspondence sent to Mason one week after the Carter letter places an exclamation point on Evers's feelings regarding the need for African Americans to challenge the system of segregation directly:

> I am anxious to get something going here in Jackson to the point that I am willing to risk even life itself.

> We have procrastinated long enough in the state and the treatment from the whites has not lessened rather increased. My feeling is, if we are to receive a beating lets receive it because we have done something, not because we have done nothing. Let me hear from you on this right away.[85]

Both letters indicate that by 1960, Evers had grown tired of the constraints of NAACP policy and protocol and was reaching out to grassroots leaders in support of more active involvement. Many leaders and participants within the civil rights struggle considered Evers a valuable asset and gladly accepted his help when offered and sought it out when needed. Not all African Americans, however, looked upon him with admiration.

Evers understood that not all African Americans supported his actions or the role the NAACP played in local affairs. In a letter written on December 28, 1960, he displayed contempt for blacks who worked against African American progress. Although he referenced no particular individual, he noted that "Uncle Toms and Aunt Thomasenes" still plagued the civil rights movement, but he warned that "they are not the ones who scratch their heads all together, when they talk with white men, but they are PHD's [*sic*], Masters and those with BS degrees. The old type of Uncle Tom is incapable of keeping up with the situation and keeping them [whites] properly informed."[86] Despite this fact, Evers continued to push for social and political equality and to lobby for the support of the entire African American community in the fight for equality. He firmly believed that the black community remained the last bastion of defense in the fight against segregation and racism.

African Americans' right to vote in Mississippi required legislative protection because of the severity and pervasiveness of southern racist ideologies. By 1960, many African Americans believed it was no longer prudent to wait for or depend upon the federal government to enforce voting rights law. Much like the Civil Rights Act of 1957, its 1960 counterpart sought to protect the right to vote through legislative mandates and congressional oversight. The act granted the Justice Department the power to examine state voting records for proof of voting discrimination. If evidence of racial discrimination surfaced, federal courts could appoint voting referees to register African Americans in areas where the discrimination occurred. Much like its predecessor, the 1960 Civil Rights Act lacked enforcement power and relied upon the administration when challenged. Evers realized that legislation alone, evident by these two Civil Rights Acts, would not be enough to bring about real change. In order for legislative mandates to account for anything, Americans would have to demand societal adherence to the notion of equality for all and to hold the federal government accountable for its implementation. He believed that the continued tenacity of African Americans in the struggle for equality would bring about this type of transformation.

Although Evers's dedication to the civil rights struggle was never in doubt, it is important to remember that his devotion to justice was not a new development. Evers always knew the difference between right and wrong and endeavored to serve on the side of righteousness.[87] For many individuals who knew and worked with Evers, he exuded something different, something unique that those around him respected and recognized as both important and special; people trusted him and followed his leadership despite the potential dangers of doing so.[88]

On March 15, 1961, Evers penned a letter to a Mr. Carter (most likely Robert Carter) of New York expressing his jubilation regarding a commitment to direct-action tactics. "[At] long last we are about to commence direct protests against racial segregation in Mississippi, Jackson in particular. Our moves will be directed [against] public conveyances, terminals . . . public library [*sic*] and parks." Evers could hardly contain his excitement and to prevent any rethinking of the strategy, he immediately outlined what had been done already and the task he hoped association officials would complete. "Our first step has been to secure bondsmen, which we are now doing. We have contacted both Attorneys [R] Jess Brown and JacksH. [*sic*] Young, who have agreed to work with us in these cases; but have indicated a desire for legal advice as to procedure with regards to appeals when such cases are brought before them. My explanation to them was in effect that I felt that much advice could be counted on from our National Office. . . . Since the youth are planning to make their move before Easter, we would appreciate your corresponding with Jack and Jess, relative to procedure, immediately[.]"[89] It is apparent that the reality of direct action against discriminatory practices rekindled his excitement and renewed his commitment to the struggle for social and political change in Mississippi. In the struggle for civil rights in Mississippi, Tougaloo College students played a critical role.

The American Missionary Association founded Tougaloo Southern Christian College in 1869, and it remains a historically black liberal arts institution. Tougaloo was chartered under the principles that it "be accessible to all irrespective of their religious tenets, and conducted on the most liberal principles for the benefit of our citizens in general."[90] Tougaloo, during the 1960s, was an integrated school in terms of both faculty and students, both of whom understood that the school supported the civil rights fight. Civil rights activist Lawrence Guyot was a freshman at Tougaloo College in 1957 majoring in political science. The Tougaloo administration proved quite progressive when it came to civil rights issues, Guyot recalled. Dean A. A. Branch "took the position that any Tougaloo student could demonstrate in anything having to do with empowerment, education, or what have you, but they had to take their books with them when they went to jail because you'd be graded just like every other student." The students bought into this type of ideal and thus the "ability of that faculty to bring out the best instincts of freedom and liberty and justice," Guyot remarked, "was uncanny."[91] Tougaloo College president Dr. Adam Daniel (A. D.) Beittel, who happened to be white, also acknowledged Tougaloo's support of its students. Beittel maintained that Evers worked with the Tougaloo students to set up an NAACP branch on campus as the "general policy [at Tougaloo] was that students were free to organize themselves into any kind of group that they wanted to organize as long as it was within the law and this certainly was within the law. And it was this group—out of this group—that this plan came to visit the city library, to which Negro students were not expected to come."[92] The library sit-in illustrated the impact that Tougaloo and its students had on the overall Jackson movement.

On March 29, 1961, Evers informed Roy Wilkins that "nine young NAACP Members from our Tougaloo College Chapter" had been arrested for violating the segregation law of the Jackson, Mississippi, municipal library. He pointed with pride that these "young people [had] exhibited the greatest amount of courage in the face of mounting tension." He explained that the students were later "released on one thousand dollars bonds each."[93] Evers knew that the impending "read-in" was to take place and had met regularly with the students "and discussed various strategies," recalled read-in participant James C. Bradford.[94] The *Jackson Daily News* also reported that Evers had "notified some members of the press in advance of the 'read-in.'"[95]

On March 27, the students went to the Carver branch library for blacks and requested books they were sure it would not have. Upon verification that the books were unavailable, the students proceeded to the Jackson Public Library on State Street and entered the white-only facility, pulled books, sat down, and started reading. Bradford acknowledged that the group knew they would be arrested but believed "the library would be a pretty good project." After all, it "was supported by tax dollars mainly, and we could not go!" The students were approached by police chiefs W. D. Rayfield and M. B. Pierce, who later arrested them when they refused police orders to exit the building.[96] Medgar Evers had worked closely with the students to organize the read-in, and this act indicated his desire to push toward direct action and a separation from the NAACP's policy of working primarily through the judiciary. He also began working closer with other civil rights groups such as the Congress of Racial Equality. CORE was an interracial group organized by Howard University graduate James Farmer, University of Chicago students George Houser, Bernice Fisher, Homer Jack, Joe Guinn, and James R. Robinson in 1942. Of the six primary founders of CORE, only James Farmer and Joe Guinn were African Americans. The organization began in Chicago and used nonviolent direct action to combat segregation.[97] David Dennis of CORE pointed out that when things began to take off in Jackson regarding direct-action programs, "CORE became actively involved with Medgar in organizing youth and training youth because a lot of people did not understand about . . . this whole sit-in piece and nonviolence resistance."[98] Thus, Evers leaned further toward direct action and organizational cooperation, all of which caused continued problems between him and the NAACP leadership.

Medgar Evers, above all else, wanted results and it did not matter to him which tactics one used as long as it worked. As a consequence, the divide between Evers and the NAACP widened. Dr. Robert Smith remembered Evers as "a very determined young man in Mississippi who wanted to be free at all costs, and whose single focus-motive was to lead the people in Mississippi to freedom, whether it involved direct confrontation; whether it involved . . . the ballot box; . . . whether it involved getting people registered to vote; or filing suit against a public institution; breaking open the barriers of public education. . . . Medgar was ready to do it, before his death."[99] In 1961, the most logical tactic seemed to be nonviolent direct action, and Evers aligned with the youth to put it into practice.

The NAACP continued to push legal strategies as the way to achieve social change despite other groups pushing direct-action tactics. By supporting the read-in, Evers advocated a shift in strategy that emphasized direct action; a direction that he was determined to move the NAACP toward. Those observing Evers did not miss this subtle shift. A. D. Beittel understood, as did others, that the library read-in "was scarcely the NAACP approach at the time because the NAACP has traditionally and still does emphasize the legal approach—that is, doing the thing which is legal."[100] During the 1960s, Evers sought not only to push the NAACP toward acceptance and implementation of direct-action strategies but also to align himself with individuals who could provide a great deal of administrative, institutional, and organizational support for the Mississippi movement.

Over time, Claude Ramsay became an individual Evers believed could provide assistance when needed. Ramsay's position as a labor leader and union organizer placed him in a position of influence and knowledge of how the state operated both in the public sphere and behind closed doors. Ramsay also considered Evers a person of integrity, sincerity, and influence, and the two men had mutual respect for each other. "Medgar was a good friend of mine," Ramsay noted, "one of the first people that I met when I became full time president [of the Mississippi AFL-CIO] was Medgar Evers." Ramsay understood the influence Evers had and this initiated their first meeting. "I got one of my [associates to introduce us.] Ray Smithart . . . knew Medgar and I asked him to contact Medgar and arrange a meeting with him." Ramsay considered Evers "a very fine person and [argued that] all Medgar was looking for was equal opportunities, equal rights, for the black citizens of this state. He was a very calm type person, wasn't a radical kind." Despite their desire to institute change, both men were bound by the segregationist state they resided in. Because Ramsay was white and Evers black, they could not chance the white backlash a public meeting would cause so Evers came to Ramsay's office or vice versa. That, Ramsay remarked, "was the kind of thing that we had to put up with."[101]

Ramsey recalled that the two men met often and talked about what needed to happen in the state to bring about positive social change as well as the importance of developing "a political alliance between organized labor and the black people primarily to turn things around."[102] The same types of labor alliances Martin Luther King Jr. (e.g., Walter Reuther) and others were orchestrating in major American cities across the country, Evers was also constructing in Mississippi.

Medgar Evers's personal persona and ways of doing things garnered him a great deal of support from those in positions of authority. A. D. Beittel remembered Evers as "a quiet person. He came to the campus from time to time and he would come to my office and we'd have a conversation." He noted that "Medgar Evers was not a rabble-rouser. . . . He was quiet but persistent." Beittel explained that Evers had many friends among the Tougaloo faculty and held a great deal of influence among a "relatively small group of students" who had organized a NAACP chapter on campus. "Mr. Evers was instrumental with this group of students in planning this [library read-in] and carefully planning it." The students had decided that they would not talk back to the police, but they would not obey their orders to leave the library and when arrested they would go quietly. Yet "behind the whole thing," Beittel remarked, "was Mr. Evers." Once the students were arrested, Evers "then arranged for bail and got them out." Ultimately, Beittel believed that Evers "was clear in his own mind what he wanted to do and he was methodical and careful in his planning and he—I think he had the good will of a good many people who disagreed with him very much because of the kind of person that he was."[103] The arrest of the Tougaloo Nine created a sense of solidarity on the part of Jackson State College students.

Upon hearing of their subsequent arrest, students from Jackson State College refused to go to class out of sympathy for the Tougaloo students and held a mass demonstration of some "700–800 students" on the campus. The Jackson State support demonstrations resulted from organizational work by Jackson State student Ruby Magee and several "members of the Social Science Department," who "didn't think that they [Tougaloo students] had been treated right," Magee recalled, "so we decided that maybe the students at Jackson State College should show sympathy for these students by demonstrating . . . so we organized a demonstration."[104] Their demonstration, however, would have consequences outside of Student Government Association president Walter Williams's expulsion and the threat of the same for Magee.

On March 28, the day after the "read-in," Jackson State students decided again to organize a support demonstration on the college campus. Police officers converged on the school campus when approximately two hundred or so individuals gathered for the mass meeting. Not long after police arrived, a number of individuals decided to march downtown and were met by police, and the encounter received national news coverage. The *New York Times* reported, "Fifty students of Jackson State College for Negroes were stopped short of a march on the city jail . . . by the police using clubs, tear gas and two German police dogs."[105] Despite the fact that African American youth were openly attacking the white power structure in Jackson, it must have appeared to many in the city that some type of tear in the fabric of time had jettisoned Jackson back a hundred years as another march of a different sort also took place in the state's capital.

On March 28, the same day as Jackson State students were arrested and beaten by the police for a peaceful march, thousands of white Mississippians cheered, celebrated, and participated in the state's "four-year Civil War centennial celebration." The "six-mile parade," the *New York Times* reported, "hailed as the biggest in the state's history." Governor Ross Barnett watched as participants paraded past the Governor's Mansion and he reviewed "more than 3,000 Mississippi Greys, units of volunteers wearing uniforms similar to Confederate uniforms," the *New York Times* continued. The centennial boasted authenticity as participants fired cannons and sang war songs such as "The Bonnie Blue Flag" and marched in formation.[106] It proved somewhat disturbing from a progressive standpoint that in 1961, just as in 1861, African Americans were still fighting hard for their rights in Mississippi to the backdrop of Confederate soldiers, Confederate cannons, and southern war songs. The events of March 29 proved little different for those choosing to demonstrate in support of the Tougaloo Nine.

On March 29, students decided again to march in support of the Tougaloo students and they were met by a violent police force. Shortly after the demonstrators gathered outside of the courthouse, violence erupted as police officers used heavy-handed tactics to disperse the crowd of supporters for the "Tougaloo Nine." They used tactics that included heavy use of tear gas, billy clubs, and police dogs. Students from Millsaps College, a white Methodist school in Jackson, also chose to march in support of the Tougaloo students. Aurelia Young, the wife of attorney Jack Young, recalled that the "Millsaps students were turned around without incident, the White students."[107] Police, however, turned their attention upon the other protesters with intense force. Tougaloo College president A. D. Beittel maintained that this "was the first use of dogs by policemen in Jackson—they were borrowed dogs; they had no dogs of their own at the time."[108] The *New York Times* reported the incident and identified Medgar Evers as "one of those hit by the police," during the demonstration. The article also quoted Evers's proclamation that "women and children in the group were beaten unmercifully."

After the attacks, Evers called Burke Marshall of the Justice Department "explaining what had taken place and asking that the young people who were on trial be given the fullest protection of the law." The violent response from the police served to galvanize the black community. Evers noted that the violence brought about "greater unity in the Negro community and projected the NAACP in a position of being the accepted spokesman for the Negro people."[109] The tactics employed by the Jackson Police Department against the black demonstrators since March 27 were captured by reporters and dispersed nationwide through a variety of media outlets.[110]

In an interview with FBI agents on March 29, Evers provided much more details surrounding the event. Regarding his own injuries, Evers testified that during the melee he had been hit about the head with what he believed "was a revolver, by a white man in plain clothes . . . [he did not know if he was an officer] " and later struck with a billy club "across the back just above the waist" by two police officers.[111] Myrlie Evers argued that the action taken by the Tougaloo Nine, however, symbolized the "change of tide in Mississippi . . . [as] Negroes took the offensive in the struggle for full citizenship."[112] The youth led the way in this new shift toward more direct-action tactics and Evers was an instrumental part of the Jackson youth movement. Regarding the library sit-in, he announced that our "long-range goal is to make it possible for Negroes to go to the city library without difficulty. This is part of our campaign to eliminate segregation in Jackson and throughout the State of Mississippi."[113] Evers tapped into the pulse of the youth struggle and, in the process, gained their support and admiration for his dedication and genuine concern for issues important to them as students first and African American youth second.

Dr. Ivory Phillips, dean emeritus of the College of Education at Jackson State University and a Jackson State College freshman in 1960, asserted that Medgar actively backed the library sit-in and had the full support of young people in general and students in particular. There were no really good libraries blacks could attend in Jackson on par with that of whites at the time of the sit-in, Phillips explained. He believed that most young people were drawn to Medgar for two reasons: his overall personality and the fact that he was one of the few college-educated leaders in the Jackson movement. As a consequence, his support and leadership impressed them. Of more importance, Evers provided students with opportunities to play prominent roles in the overall struggle, and he sought their advice on important issues such as strategies and resistance measures. John Frazier, who worked closely with Evers in the Jackson office, supports this contention. Such confidence had a tremendous effect and drew Tougaloo students such as sisters Dorie and Joyce Ladner closer to him.[114]

Evers sought to use the excitement generated by the sit-in to increase support for NAACP activities. He quickly pointed out to Roy Wilkins that the "act of bravery and concern on the part of these nine young people has seemed to electrify Negroes [*sic*] desire for Freedom here in Mississippi, which will doubtlessly be shown in increase in memberships and funds for 1961." Evers believed that both the NAACP and the Mississippi movement would benefit further if they capitalized upon the momentum. He also wanted to inspire those involved in the read-in. It "would be an inspirational gesture for these nine young people," Evers explained to Wilkins, "if we could arrange to have them attend our National Convention in Philadelphia, July 10–16." The end result of such a gesture, Evers continued, would be "further inspiration and leadership to our cause, here in Mississippi."[115] The NAACP agreed and sent the students. James Bradford recalled that Evers loaned him eight dollars of his personal money until the vouchers arrived and he could pay him back. This gesture meant a lot to Bradford and he never forgot it. When Evers was killed, Bradford admitted that "the first thing I thought about, was, 'Gaah-h-lee, I owe Medgar eight dollars!'"[116] Both Evers's dedication to the youth and his campaign to eliminate segregation resulted in his work with Operation Mississippi.

On April 7, 1961, NAACP officers met at the national office and conceived of a six-point plan of attack on segregation in Mississippi. Operation Mississippi developed out of this meeting, and Evers viewed the program as another indication of the NAACP's subtle but noticeable shift toward direct action. The first point of Operation Mississippi was for each member to make every effort "to increase registration and voting." Students would be used to assist in voter registration, specifically in preparing voters to pass literacy tests. The program would also focus on organizing citizenship training schools, facilitating publicity to encourage registration, and gathering affidavits documenting registration attempts, which would then be sent to the office of attorney Robert Carter for evaluation and further action. In the area of public accommodations, the program called for "students and other groups to test facilities available to Negroes in waiting rooms, bus and train depots, etc. [And furthermore, the] [e]ffort[s] of Tougaloo and Jackson college students to attack waiting rooms [is] to be encouraged." The program also called for a close watch on CORE's efforts at organizing in Mississippi and for "NAACP activities to take priority."[117]

Operation Mississippi required the amassing of affidavits chronicling police brutality to be filed with the Justice Department and that a recommendation would be sent to the board requesting that a "resident counsel on retainer [be hired] to accelerate the program." In addition, members suggested a White House conference to call the attention of President Kennedy to the "Mississippi situation." Evers had the task of focusing on the larger problem of economic exploitation and the tactics whites used to deny African Americans financial security through employment. Under the heading of "Employment and Discrimination," Evers was given the task of compiling "information on industries, especially those with defense contracts and their employment practices" with the understanding that attacks would be waged upon those companies discriminating against African Americans.[118]

The emphasis NAACP leaders placed on companies "with defense contracts" dated back to President Franklin D. Roosevelt's Executive Order 8802. The 1941 order prevented racial discrimination in companies holding federal defense contracts. FDR, however, did not establish this legislation out of the goodness of his heart. Order 8802 was a direct result of the pressure labor leader Asa Philip Randolph placed on the Roosevelt administration during World War II to protect the rights and opportunities of black workers. FDR understood that if Randolph carried out his threat to lead thousands of black men and women on a march to the nation's capital, it would hurt America's global image and he could not risk the international backlash this might cause. As a consequence of Randolph's actions, the NAACP could draw upon specific legislation to bolster its challenge to this type of discrimination, and Operation Mississippi was an important part of this process.

Evers did not take his role in Operation Mississippi lightly as is evident by his speech at a mass meeting on April 20, 1961, at the Masonic Temple in Jackson. The meeting was organized in support of four NAACP college students who had been arrested "for staging the state's first ride-in demonstration against segregation on public buses, [on] April 19." Evers explained that "four members of our Inter-collegiate chapter of [the] NAACP for the city of Jackson, took seats on a city bus on Capitol Street in the section normally reserved for white passengers, they were arrested after refusing to move, when ordered to do so."[119] Throughout the speech, Evers demanded that "local factories such as Vickers and General Electric" hire black workers and that "all Mississippi plants holding government contracts" do the same, thereby fulfilling the requirements outlined in President Kennedy's executive order on employment. On March 6, 1961, Kennedy had signed Executive Order 10925 to address discrimination and racism in employment. Executive Order 10925 also created the President's Committee on Equal Employment Opportunity (PCEEO) to further address the issue of employment discrimination African Americans faced.[120] Evers, in keeping with his assigned task as an officer of Operation Mississippi, asked that blacks be hired on the Jackson police force, the local Internal Revenue Bureau, and the local VA hospital. At the conclusion of his speech, Evers used the opportunity to reiterate his personal agenda: he told "the cheering crowd that the time has come for unrestricted use of public facilities, such as parks and libraries . . . [and] that the time has also come for removal of humiliating segregation signs in train depots, and the end of segregated seating on buses."[121] The NAACP also expressed interest in increasing the pressure on the local bus company.

Gloster Current assigned Evers the task of gathering the needed information on the bus line. Current wanted information regarding ownership of the Jackson City Bus Lines, "the amount of business it did in 1960, the number of riders, and particularly the number of Negro riders using the bus daily." He also wanted an account of the "approximate [amount] of fare they spend in supporting this company." The objective was to gather the type of information that would allow the NAACP to mount the most economically damaging protest possible.[122] This move indicates that the association still regarded the tactics used in Montgomery some six years earlier as viable; it also demonstrated that the pressure Evers placed on the NAACP leadership to act more forcefully had begun bearing fruit.

The constant and public attacks Evers waged against the system of segregation and the abject oppression Mississippi afforded its black population convinced his friends that his life was in danger, but he continued to speak out and refused to limit his public appearances, the tone of his message, or the access people had to him on a daily basis. One cannot underestimate the important role that mass meetings held in the African American movement for equality. In addition to marshaling bodies for protest demonstrations, mass meetings also helped develop and sustain community ties and built relationships that often led to community support of civil rights activities.

Mass meetings could be marshaled in quick fashion and were taken seriously by community residents. The role of the mass meeting was often complex and multifaceted. Although linked to civil rights organization, mass meetings held practical value for community residents and civil rights leaders were well aware of their significance in the black community. Fred

Clark Sr., Jackson resident and civil rights activist, noted that when people heard the word "mass" they knew something important or brutal had happened and they came out to learn more about the event and what was expected of the community. Yet, people also looked to these meetings as a way to address the many personal problems they were suffering with. "If people were hungry, needed food or gas, they could come to that meeting and they could get it," Clark noted. "They would raise money right there. . . . They could get something to eat or medical attention or whatever was needed. So the mass meeting served more than just a point of organizing. It was a point of survival, whatever facility we had it in."[123] Civil rights activists used the mass meeting all across the country as a means of mobilizing, informing, and taking care of community folk. These meetings were also opportunities for civil rights leaders to fashion the grassroots into a working unit that openly resisted whites' beliefs that blacks not only accepted the status quo, but were comfortable with it.

By 1961, Evers wanted white southerners to know that the days where blacks cowered in the face of inequality had come to an end. On April 20, 1961, at a mass protest meeting held at the Masonic Temple in Jackson, Evers warned: "Let it be known to those, who say that Negroes in Mississippi are satisfied that tonight we are here to indicate to the world that so long as there is segregation and discrimination anywhere in the state of Mississippi or the United States of America, for that matter, we are not and shall not be satisfied."[124] Two years later, portions of Martin Luther King's famed "I Have a Dream Speech" delivered to over 200,000 individuals on August 28 expressed the same sentiment of dissatisfaction and continued dissatisfaction until resistance produced significant social and political changes. If Evers's message was a warning to White America, it was also directed at Black America. He wanted black Mississippians to understand that the time had come to let the nation know the depth and intensity of their dissatisfaction with the current social and political structures, and that if the federal government *would* not help, blacks would take on the struggle alone despite the consequences. For Evers, full-speed ahead required a constant watch for and a sustained vigil against the practice of inequality anywhere in the state.

Fighting against inequality required that one challenge it in whatever manifestation it took. Racism and repression were not always relegated to the familiar forms of individual oppression and denial of rights. Evers's earlier statement concerning the elimination of segregation "throughout the State of Mississippi" meant just that. Although committed to fighting for social and political equality in Jackson and its surrounding counties, he kept abreast of instances of racial biases and discrimination happening throughout the state. Mississippi's various industries were important targets for civil rights activists and Mississippi politicians sought to draw key businesses to the state and to shield them from civil rights agitation.

Mississippi governor Ross Barnett (1960–1964) played an important role in the access that industries had to state tax breaks and thus how they operated in the state. Barnett's election also troubled civil rights activists who saw his move to the Governor's Mansion as problematic for civil rights advances. Evers proclaimed that the "election of Ross Barnett for Governor, for the next four years, created a state of apprehension in the minds of many." Yet, Evers believed that there had been some positive changes in the "attitude of many of the would be 'die-hards' in the state. This is not to say, however, that the fight is won, but, rather, that we are winning it faster than I think we even realize." Although Barnett may have caused some "apprehension" for many, Evers noted that when it came to African Americans progress politically and socially, "even Barnett sees the hand writing on the wall."[125]

Ross Barnett won the election in 1959 with the support of wealthy and influential individuals in the state of Mississippi. Labor leader Claude Ramsay maintained that business interests expected to benefit from Barnett's election and men such as wealthy chicken farmer "B.C. Rogers . . . put a lot of money in his campaign." In 1960, Barnett's political program "was supposed to be designed to make the state more attractive to industry," Ramsay noted. As a means of attracting more industry into the state, Barnett's plan centered on restructuring the tax laws in a manner that allowed corporations and the wealthy the lion's share of tax concessions. His "tax breaks, [and] right to work," Ramsay argued, "weakened unions . . . [and] virtually it emasculated the state's Workmen's Compensation Act." The state "was virtually broke" in two years. Former governor James Plemon (J. P.) Coleman (1956–1960) also pointed to the financial problems the Barnett administration garnered. "I left 35 million dollars in the treasury, a surplus, when I left office," Coleman recalled. "They spent all of it by 17 cents in 6 months. Made me wish I had gone on and spent it for some worthy cause." As a means of compensating, the "legislature," Ramsay proclaimed, "the same damn Governor [Barnett] that had reduced income taxes, taxes on corporations, . . . turned around and put an additional burden on the backs of the working people in the form of a sales tax increase, to balance the budget."[126] In 1961, Barnett still projected the state as the ideal place for new industries to settle and Evers and others were quick to challenge the governor's plans.

In a telegram dated September 19, 1961, Evers voiced his concerns to William C. Smith, president of Standard Oil of Kentucky, regarding a statement made by Governor Barnett. The governor, Evers remarked, had credited

Mississippi's rigid segregation laws and practices as reasons for Standard Oil's decision to "locate a $125 million dollar Oil Refinery at Pascagoula, Mississippi." Evers's inquiry to Smith was straightforward and to the point. He informed Smith that "more than 43% of the population in Mississippi is Negro, and we suffer because of these segregation practices; therefore it would be in the interest of persons here in the state, to know if Governor Barnett expressed your company's policy as to why you are moving to Mississippi. Please confirm immediately." On September 21, Smith refuted the charges in a letter to both Evers and Aaron Henry. Smith argued that segregation had nothing to do with their decision, but rather "Pascagoula, was selected strictly on economic factors such as, crude oil and product distribution."[127] This interchange underscores Evers's inability to allow any perceived slight against African Americans' best interest to go unchallenged. It did not matter if the challenge arrived from individuals, groups, organizations, or companies, Evers's response remained consistent: speak out against, organize to challenge, and mobilize a defense against the threat. Sometimes to accomplish these goals, organizations had to employ something akin to a magician's use of the slight-of-hand technique.

The year 1961 witnessed an increased number of civil rights groups organizing in the state of Mississippi. This often brought about conflict, and civil rights leaders understood that something would have to be done to coordinate their efforts. The idea of creating a civil rights coalition gained traction in 1961, especially in light of Governor Barnett's open attempts to elicit support from African Americans on the idea of maintaining segregation. Barnett, however, proved reluctant to meet with representatives of the NAACP, CORE, or SNCC. It was this desire to meet with Barnett to discuss the ills of segregation that proved the "genesis" behind the creation of the Council of Federated Organizations (COFO). Aaron Henry acknowledged that the idea for COFO was really that of "Medgar Evers." With the establishment of COFO, the group set up a meeting with Barnett. "And before the Governor knew what was going on," Henry remarked, "he had never heard of no COFO, he sat down and talked with us and enjoyed it thoroughly." The group was able to refute Barnett's attempts at selling them on segregation and, more importantly, to warn him that until he "develop[ed] the will to be concerned about the plight of the poor, and certainly that's what most of us are, then we are going to continuously be in this bag of hostility of white against black."[128] In order to present a more unified attack against racial oppression, Henry, Robert Moses, Tom Gaither of CORE, and Evers met in 1962 to revitalize the largely defunct COFO as a means of launching "a broad attack on the problems we were facing throughout the state," Henry recalled.[129] COFO became an important umbrella organization operating in Mississippi from which various civil rights organizations and groups operated. As the year progressed, tensions mounted both in and outside of the state and the potential for violence escalated.

The NAACP shunned violence, but this did not mean that all of its members felt the same way. NAACP branch members in Monroe, North Carolina, refused to submit to racial violence without defending themselves. Whereas Evers and SNCC began to push for direct action in Mississippi, Robert Williams and the Monroe chapter were doing the same, but group members here proved much more willing to defend themselves with weapons if necessary.

In June 1961, Robert Williams and the NAACP chapter picketed the town's segregated swimming pool. Williams pointed out that this "pool, built by WPA money, was forbidden to Negroes although we formed one quarter of the population of the town." Requests from blacks to use the pool had practical reasons as two black children had drowned while swimming in local creeks. The pickets continued despite growing white violence and agitation. Attempts were made to murder Williams by forcing his car off the road and "over a cliff with a 75-foot drop," but he saved himself. Over time, the boycotters were met with increasing crowds. On one occasion when a white man backed his car into Williams's car, a white mob chanted, "Kill the niggers! Kill the niggers! Pour gasoline on the niggers! Burn the niggers!" The local police, present at the scene, did nothing until Williams drew his weapon, and then they attempted to subdue him before he turned the weapon on them. The group remained at a standoff before city councilman Steve Presson ordered the police to open "the highway up and get them out of . . . [there]."[130] Williams continued on to the local pool where the picket line had begun and they were surrounded by thousands of angry whites.

City officials kept repeating that the crowd was "getting out of hand" and that someone was bound to get hurt. They finally asked Williams what solution to the standoff would he deem appropriate. Williams demanded that the state police escort them out, and they were finally called in and the group left without incident. The pool closed for the rest of the year and the picket was withdrawn. The threat of violence had kept whites at bay and, more importantly, as a result of "our willingness to fight," Williams argued, "the state of North Carolina had enforced law and order. Just two state troopers did the job and no one got hurt in a situation where normally (in the South) a lot of Negro blood would have flowed."[131] The Monroe NAACP chapter proved to be a thorn in the side of the national NAACP leadership because Williams's advocating of violent resistance was often attributed to the national NAACP. Of more importance, Williams's strategies were getting results and some NAACP leaders feared that his tactics would be replicated by other members in other areas. Nevertheless, pressure increased on Evers and the NAACP to intensify their activist tactics in Mississippi as other civil rights organizations entered the state.

Although Evers encouraged cooperation among civil rights groups operating in Mississippi, by late 1961, he took issue with some of the strategies utilized by other groups that operated in the state without coordinating with the NAACP. This led him to sometimes be critical of those he believed were operating in a manner that caused more harm than good. In a special report to Roy Wilkins, Gloster B. Current, and Ruby Hurley, Evers relayed his concerns regarding the tactics utilized by SNCC and CORE. The report offered less than flattering critiques of attempts by these two organizations to organize in Mississippi without NAACP assistance and their eventual realization that, in order to do so, they needed the NAACP. He reported that it was not until SNCC members ran "into difficulties securing bonds for young people they had caused to be arrested" and landed themselves either in jail "or gave them severe beatings; did they ask for NAACP assistance."[132]

Within these remarks, one can see Evers's frustration with other civil rights organizations' lack of respect for the groundwork the NAACP had in place. He also made note of the large crowds that James Farmer, director of CORE, and Martin Luther King Jr. of SCLC commanded in rallies held in Mississippi (approximately 3,000 and 2,500–3,000, respectively). Evers quickly pointed out that Farmer, despite the large crowds, raised "less than six hundred dollars" and King "less than eight hundred dollars."[133] Evers had legitimate reasons to be concerned over the recruiting tactics of organizations such as SNCC and CORE. More often than not, SNCC's aggressive leadership style proved quite effective in recruiting protesters within the new atmosphere of resistance marked by the 1960s. Both organizations, however, sometimes drew members from NAACP chapters, leaving Evers with the task of reorganizing the chapters and getting them up and running again. To address the problem, Evers met with Robert Moses and David Dennis to discuss their organizational differences. Myrlie pointed out that the meeting led to "the three organizations . . . working reasonably well together."[134]

In 1962, older civil rights activists witnessed an increase in the amount of native resistance to white oppression in Mississippi. Many blacks found themselves rushing to keep up with area youth and to channel their energies in a direction that best served their common goals. Evers did not always agree with the tactics SNCC used or its practice of leaving out the NAACP regarding its operations in various Mississippi locales. He believed that unified attacks assured successes while disunity drained organizational strength, morale, and group effectiveness. His frustration often manifested in his reports to the national office.[135]

Evers believed that SNCC's head-on attitude and the violent responses it engendered, induced fear in the local African American populace, making it harder to recruit or gain support for future endeavors. For instance, on September 5, 1961, Robert Moses and Travis Britt of SNCC were beaten in southwest Mississippi by enraged whites when they "took several Negro Citizens" in Amite County to register. Two days later John Hardy, also a member of SNCC, led a group to the Tylertown circuit clerk's office in Walthall County to register and ran into trouble as well. When Hardy and his group arrived, the circuit clerk, who also served as the registrar, forced Hardy out of the office at gunpoint and then assaulted him about the head with a pistol "causing an ugly laceration." When analyzing the problems associated with maintaining black support in Walthall and Pike Counties, Evers argued that much "of the fear . . . is due in the main to the activities of members of the Student non-violent [*sic*] Coordinating Committee, who have projected un-necessary publicity; resulting in violence against themselves (Student non-violent workers) and threate [*sic*] of violence and economic reprisals against prospective registered voters."[136] Although true that Evers had invited violent reprisal in 1958 with his bus demonstration; however, unlike SNCC at the time, his was an individual protest that threatened only his safety and did not produce an atmosphere of fear that could potentially reduce future support for civil rights struggle in the community. Evers was also frustrated with CORE's, SNCC's, and other group's attempts at organizing support for the Freedom Rides coming into Jackson and its recruitment of potential members in areas with a strong NAACP presence.[137]

Nineteen sixty proved the beginning of what would be a volatile decade for the civil rights movement. Evers had avoided a jail sentence for contempt of court and in the process placed the sanctity of freedom of speech squarely on the conscience of Mississippians as a whole. Nineteen sixty-one intensified civil rights organization and challenges to racism and inequality through more direct means of attack on the national level and throughout the state of Mississippi with Jackson serving as a focal point. The Jackson movement found its wings in 1961 and spread them, producing winds of resistance throughout the capital city. Nineteen sixty-one also saw more intense challenges to discrimination in the form of Freedom Rides that later escalated violent reactions to horrifying levels and intensified tensions between civil rights leaders and federal authorities. It soon became apparent that within that tense atmosphere both black and white lives hung in the balance.

6.

Riding the Rails

FREEDOM RIDE CHALLENGES AND
THE JACKSON MOVEMENT

*Oh freedom, oh freedom, oh freedom over me
And before I'd be a slave I'd be buried in my grave
And go home to my lord and be free.*

—*Folk Song*

*There was no need for me to make out a will. I had nothing to
leave anyone.*

—*John Lewis*

ON DECEMBER 5, 1960, the Supreme Court ruled in *Bruce Boynton v. Virginia* that state laws requiring segregated waiting rooms, lunch counters, and restroom facilities for interstate passengers were unconstitutional. In May 1961, CORE, led by James Farmer, organized a series of "freedom rides" to test southern adherence to the *Boynton* decision. The objective, Farmer remarked, "was to make it more dangerous politically for the federal government not to enforce federal law."[1] The 1961 Freedom Rides were an extension of desegregation challenges in transportation CORE had conducted in 1947.

In April 1947, Bayard Rustin, a practitioner and strategist of nonviolent resistance, helped organize CORE's two-week Journey of Reconciliation. On April 9, the group, consisting of eight black men and eight white men,

213

left Washington with half boarding a Greyhound bus and the other half boarding a Trailways. The group traveled through the Upper South testing southern adherence to the Supreme Court's 1946 *Morgan v. Commonwealth of Virginia* decision. The court's mandate banned segregated services in interstate bus travel. The group's planned strategy aboard each bus was for the black men to sit up front while the whites occupied the rear. If or when they were challenged, they were to inform the individual of their rights based upon the *Morgan* decision. Much as would be the case with the Freedom Riders, members of this group were physically attacked and arrested, and Rustin served twenty-two days of a thirty-day sentence on a road gang. Whereas the Journey of Reconciliation sought adherence to desegregation mandates regarding interstate bus travel, the 1961 Freedom Rides tested adherence to desegregation mandates then extended to "all interstate transportation facilities, including terminals."[2] The challenge, however, would have to be well planned and the expectations of and dangers involved for all participants clearly explained and understood.

James Farmer required that all potential "riders have spotless reputations, to prevent one person's history from discrediting the ride in the press."[3] Once chosen, the riders were to travel upon buses to targeted cities throughout the South to see if bus terminals were integrated or not. In instances where segregation continued, they were to press for integration. "After three days training in Washington," John Lewis recalled, "we would leave on May 4, stopping at terminals in Virginia, North Carolina, South Carolina, Georgia, Alabama, Mississippi and Louisiana, before finally arriving in New Orleans on May 17." May 17 was no arbitrary date but the anniversary of the *Brown* decision and it seemed a fitting conclusion to this type of challenge. Everyone understood the seriousness involved in a trip of this nature, and some wrote out wills in case they were killed. Lewis recalled that there "was no need for me to make out a will. I had nothing to leave anyone." Although Farmer made sure all involved knew that this was a CORE operation, he required that everyone sign a waiver absolving CORE of any liability for injuries suffered or should someone get killed.[4] On May 4, thirteen Freedom Riders left Washington, D.C., aboard Greyhound and Trailways buses. The riders traveled through Virginia and North Carolina without much problem before running into violence on May 9 in Rock Hill, South Carolina.

Events in Rock Hill helped prepare the Freedom Riders for the type of individuals and the level of violence they would encounter in the days ahead. When they pulled into the station that morning, Lewis went in and immediately knew there was going to be a problem. There were agitated whites already there who grew angrier as the group approached. A group of white men told Lewis that he would have to go on the side reserved for blacks, and when Lewis challenged the validity of this based on the *Boynton* decision, one of the men punched him in the face while the others kicked him. The exchange grew more intense as Freedom Riders put themselves in the fray and finally the police broke it up and later asked if anyone wanted to press charges; the riders refused to do so because the overall problem was bigger than a few individuals.[5] Things, for the riders, would get worse in the state of Alabama. People knew Alabama was a rough place and even Martin Luther King Jr. had warned *Jet* reporter Simeon Booker, who was traveling with the group, that "You will never make it through Alabama."[6]

The Freedom Riders aboard the Greyhound bus arrived in Anniston, Alabama, on Sunday, May 14. As predicted, those aboard encountered an organized mob, some of which were Ku Klux Klan members determined to exact vengeance upon the Freedom Riders. Bus driver O. T. Jones quickly left the terminal to avoid the gathered mob's continuous attacks upon the bus, but the group, after managing to slash some of the tires, pursued them in a caravan of some fifty vehicles. The bus, as a result of the now-flattened tires, stopped just outside of Anniston. After repeated attempts to physically remove the riders from the bus, Roger Couch and Cecil Lewallyn, two members of the mob, decided to make the Freedom Riders sorry they chose to *invade* Alabama. At some point, Lewallyn tossed a "flaming bundle of rags" through one of the many broken windows of the bus. It then erupted into flames and forced the riders into the hands of the waiting mob. Unknown both to the crowd and the Freedom Riders, two undercover Alabama patrolmen, Ell Cowling and Harry Sims, were also on board gathering intelligence on the Freedom Ride project. Cowling drew his pistol in hopes of keeping the crowd at bay and thus providing an opportunity for everyone, himself included, to get off the bus. When one of the fuel tanks exploded, the mob moved back, upon which the riders took advantage of the chance to escape the burning bus. The assembled group then went on the offensive, beating as many riders as they could get their hands on before police repulsed the group. As a consequence of the beatings and smoke inhalation, many of the riders required medical attention and were transported to Anniston Memorial Hospital where the mob later assembled and continued to threaten those inside. Reverend Fred Shuttlesworth expressed his anger and announced in a radio interview that "I am going to get my people. I'm a nonviolent man, but I'm going to get my people." Shuttlesworth was wholly dedicated to civil rights activism and organization. He organized the Alabama Christian Movement for Human Rights (ACMHR) as a replacement civil rights organization in Birmingham after officials banned the NAACP following the Montgomery Bus Boycott. Although determined to get his "people" out of Anniston, James Armstrong, ACMHR's chief of security, talked Shuttlesworth out of going himself, and after a few tense hours the Freedom Riders safely left Anniston in a fleet of cars Shuttlesworth sent from Birmingham.[7] While the Freedom Riders were facing their trouble in Anniston, the Trailways group had also left, headed to Birmingham where they would soon face their own problems.

The FBI had prior knowledge that the Freedom Riders would meet violent resistance in Birmingham and that the police planned to be absent, and yet it did nothing to prevent the violence. Burke Marshall, assistant attorney general in charge of civil rights for the Justice Department, pointed out that the FBI had specific information "about what was going to happen in Birmingham" and this information came from Klan sources. In addition, the Reverend Fred L. Shuttlesworth had apprised detectives of the Riders arrival and had asked public safety commissioner Eugene "Bull" Conner to provide police protection for the group when they made it to Birmingham.[8] The level of violence escalated in Birmingham by May 14 as well when a white mob attacked the Trailways riders with lead and iron pipes and oversized key rings. There was no police interference for fifteen minutes. This attack left many of the riders with significant injuries that required hospitalization. Although no one knew the extent of the injuries Walter Bergman had suffered in Anniston when Klan riders attacked him and other Riders before the bus continued to Birmingham, the beating the sixty-one-year-old took resulted in permanent brain damage and later produced a paralyzing stoke. Bergman, however, took on Birmingham with steeled determination. After the brutal attack in Birmingham, CORE discontinued the Freedom Rides. Several members of SNCC and Nashville students such as Dianne Nash and John Lewis, however, chose to continue. They argued "that the civil rights community could not afford to let the Freedom Ride fail." Lewis believed that "in this case, the truth of the absolute moral invalidity of racial segregation and the necessity of ending it—backing away is not an option. It is simply not a choice." On May 17, eight African Americans and two white students left Nashville, Tennessee, headed to Birmingham and Montgomery, Alabama. This new group of riders consisted of six African American males: William Harbour, Charles Butt, Paul Brooks, William Barbee, Allen Cason, and John Lewis; two African American women: Lucretia Collins and Katherine Burke; and a white man and woman, Jim Zwerg and Selyn McCollum.[9]

When the Freedom Riders arrived in Birmingham, police officers kept them on the bus; after a while, the officers arrested the group. Because of the pressure the Justice Department and President John Kennedy and Attorney General Robert Kennedy placed on Alabama governor John

Patterson, the Freedom Riders were released from jail. However, during the early morning hours of May 19, police officers, including Bull Conner, transported the group by car to the Tennessee line and left them stranded by the side of the highway on the outskirts of a small town called Ardmore. After receiving some assistance from a local family, the Freedom Riders returned to Birmingham and, with a bit of difficulty, boarded a bus for Montgomery on May 20.[10]

Although Governor Patterson, after much haranguing, had provided vague assurances to the Kennedys that order would prevail in the state, he did not keep his word, and the violence the Freedom Riders encountered at the Montgomery bus terminal on May 20 dwarfed the other attacks in its brutality. The mob, made up of men, women, and children, used baseball bats, wooden boards, chains, pipes, tire irons, and a host of other makeshift weapons to attack the riders. Bob Zellner, a white student at Huntingdon and later SNCC field secretary, arrived at the bus station to find that the "area looked like it had been hit by a sudden and unexpected Category 5 storm."[11] Injuries were severe and the Montgomery Police Department proved unwilling to intervene; it was later revealed that Montgomery public safety commissioner L. B. Sullivan had promised the mob a thirty-minute window in which to act without police interference. The violence, however, only steeled the Freedom Riders' commitment and on May 23, Freedom Ride leaders and participants announced the continuation of the Freedom Rides and a bus of riders headed further South to Jackson, Mississippi.[12]

Because of the dangers that Mississippi segregationists posed to the riders, many in the civil rights struggle questioned the benefits of sending riders into the Magnolia State. The Freedom Riders were also aware that Medgar Evers hoped that they would postpone their trip to Jackson because of the dangers involved. "Evers told reporters he was against our coming," Lewis recalled. "He felt it was too soon. Mississippi, he said, was not ready for us. It was too dangerous. In his opinion, there was much work still to be done there before a confrontation like the one we might bring should be forced." The riders decided to proceed despite Evers's lack of support but his hesitancy added to their already growing apprehensions.[13] Despite the dangers, the Freedom Rides continued and on May 24 two buses left Montgomery for Jackson, Mississippi. David Dennis, one of the Freedom Riders, recalled that when they "got to Jackson, Mississippi, there was a line of police" and the Freedom Riders were quickly arrested and carried "straight to the Jackson Jail" without incident.[14] The riders eventually wound up in Parchman, the state's infamous penitentiary. Despite its reputation for violence, Mississippi avoided the brutality that Montgomery and Birmingham produced, due in large part to behind-the-scenes negotiations between the

Kennedys and Mississippi officials. Regardless of the fact that the riders were not attacked, the process took a psychological toll on the participants.

The Freedom Riders understood that what they were involved in could be dangerous at the least and deadly at the most. The events in Anniston, Birmingham, and Montgomery, Alabama, legitimated any fears they had left Washington, D.C., with. In order to go through with their challenge to segregation, many convinced themselves that death was imminent but "if you gotta die," Dennis recalled, "you gotta die for it." Mississippi had posed the biggest fear yet and when nothing happened, the fact that they were still alive had to be addressed. Dennis explained that

> we had psyched ourselves to the extent of dying, that this was going to be it. . . . And when it didn't happen, I mean, we all went through some psychological, you know, problems you might say . . . because we had not expected to survive this. And that was a very explosive kind of thing, mentally. I mean, we had . . . a lot of talking through we had to do . . . in the cells and what this meant. But there were a lot of feelings about that.[15]

This is a very important aspect of the civil rights movement: the ability to override the self-preservation aspect of human nature. It is apparent, however, that overriding the natural urge to avoid death at all cost, left many with psychological scarring that more often than not, went unresolved.

Evers reported that segregationist forces delivered a heavy blow to the Freedom Rides as a whole. He noted that to "date a total of one hundred thirty one 'Freedom Riders' have been convicted for 'breach of the peace.' There has [sic] been a total of 43 released on bond; four have paid their fines, 40 in the penitentiary and 40 remain in the jails here in Jackson."[16] The Freedom Riders did not just come to town, engage law enforcement, and go home; they intermingled with local residents, discussed area problems, and hammered the need for residents to actively resist oppression. These interactions often created tensions amid local leaders who believed the Riders did not fully appreciate local problems, issues, and strategies already in place.

While in Jackson, supporters of the Freedom Riders interacted with local activists and garnered community support. Their enthusiasm, combined with their willingness to sometimes act without consulting community activists, clashed with local civil rights and organizational leaders. Evers found some of the actions of SNCC and Freedom Ride supporters to be less than admirable in some instances and disorganized in others. He believed that building a movement in Mississippi required patience, courage, and fortitude. As a consequence, the historian Raymond Arsenault has written that Evers remained wary of "overly aggressive activists who did not seem to comprehend the racial realities of Mississippi." Evers's objections to the intensity of the Freedom Riders were understandable at the time and, as Arsenault noted, "reflected a sincere concern for the future of a statewide movement that could ill afford a serious misstep."[17]

In a "Special Report" outlining the activities of "other Civil Rights Organizations in Mississippi," Evers noted that the Freedom Rides, which ended in Jackson and arrived later than expected, sparked a frenzy of activity on the part of CORE representative Tom Gaither to facilitate support for the riders. Gaither served as the point man for the Freedom Rides and had scouted out areas, tested local environments, and sought out local and organizational support along the planned bus routes prior to the riders leaving Washington.[18] In Jackson, "released Freedom riders [*sic*] from [the] Nashville Christian Leadership Conference" set up a series of what Evers described as "hastily gotten together workshops . . . for the purpose of involving Jackson Citizens into the freedom ride movement, which had not been advocated by the NAACP." Although some tensions existed between Evers, SNCC, and CORE members, the latter needed NAACP branch support of the Freedom Rides. Political scientist David Niven argued that "NAACP chapters would be particularly important because CORE did not have any significant membership in the South, and the NAACP would be needed for logistical and financial help."[19] This situation became a major problem for the NAACP as more and more youth took direct-action tactics to the fore of the movement and landed in jails across the South. Despite their desire, the youth, of course, could not remain in jail, and it was often NAACP coffers that provided the bail money for individuals who were not always NAACP members or who were not carrying out an NAACP-approved program. In many instances, the NAACP found itself inundated with request for bail monies and attempts to accommodate the multitude of arrests taxed its financial reserves. In spite of the often-contentious relationship between organization leaders, the South proved fertile ground and SNCC's aggressive attempts to set up organizational chapters increased the tension.

In addition to the move to establish a SNCC presence in Mississippi, which CORE supported, SNCC also had plans to expand its visibility in key Mississippi areas with Jackson being a logical choice. Despite their intentions, Evers noted that SNCC had only a

> skeleton operation here in the city of Jackson; with no direct action having taken place in several months. Most of the leaders of the organization mentioned earlier have been charged with "contributing to the delinquency of minors" and [are] out on heavy bonds, or have warrants out for their arrests when they return. Their activities here in Jackson at the present time are almost non-existence [*sic*].

There was an attempt on the part of [the] student non-violent [*sic*] to organize on Tougaloo College campus, however, due to our strong NAACP Chapter there, they have not made any headway. There have also been attempts to get an organization at J.P. Campbell College, which have not met with success, there again we have a strong NAACP College Chapter.[20]

SNCC often had problems sustaining local black support as many believed that "SNCC workers were . . . 'only going to stir up trouble . . . and then leave.'" Although, in 1961, SNCC may have not been as potent a recruiting force in Mississippi as they may have liked, things would change. Historian Clayborne Carson noted that by the spring of '63, SNCC had opened six offices in Mississippi "with a staff of twenty black field secretaries."[21] Evers felt, however, that other organizations were not completely respectful of the role the NAACP had played in the struggle for equality in Mississippi before their arrival, and he resented attempts by any organization to cut the legs out from under NAACP efforts at recruitment and advocacy. SNCC, according to Evers, had a penchant for doing just that.

SNCC had accomplished many of its objectives in McComb, Mississippi, by getting individuals to register to vote and providing schools to educate the population on voter registration as well as general academics. Evers believed that the presence of SNCC in Pike, Amite, and Walthall Counties was a means of laying stake to the area for both SNCC and the SCLC. Yet, it was the residents of Amite and Walthall Counties who had asked Robert Moses "to establish voter registration schools in their areas." These types of requests placed a great deal of pressure on SNCC leaders. Although Moses knew that rural areas would be more dangerous to operate in, he felt that SNCC could not turn down requests to organize in the rough areas as locals would lose faith in the organization.[22] Yet, SNCC's presence and organizing tactics in these areas conflicted with NAACP strategies and tactics.

By spreading into Pike, Amite, and Walthall Counties, Evers argued that SNCC was making it clear to the NAACP "that this was Student nonviolent [*sic*] Coordinating Committee and the Southern Christian Leadership Conference [objectives] and they felt that the NAACP's name should not be brought in even though members of the NAACP were carrying out the operation." He reported that rather than participate in a joint operation with the NAACP, "the non violent group broke away from the local NAACP." It was not until the group ran into "difficulties securing bonds," Evers continued, that they reached out for NAACP assistance.[23] Evers later challenged the effectiveness of SNCC's efforts and tactics in McComb from an organizational standpoint.

SNCC members were determined to register African Americans in McComb, and they organized individuals with a gritty determination. Evers, however, believed that SNCC's efforts undercut the program the NAACP had quietly put in place to increase participation while decreasing individual and group fear of white reprisal. On February 1, 1962, Evers wrote Alfred Baker Lewis, national NAACP treasurer, informing him that SNCC had moved into McComb during the month of August "for the widely publicized purpose of Voter Registration schools and clinics." Yet despite their efforts and the publicity surrounding McComb and Amite and Walthall Counties, Evers noted, "a total of not more than twenty (20) persons were registered, and this was in McComb alone." The reported numbers for SNCC were a great deal less than the NAACP claimed for its efforts.[24]

Evers maintained strong feelings regarding the tactics and different approaches between SNCC and the NAACP, particularly as it related to community organizational successes. Evers had worked to ingratiate the NAACP into the local communities, which had yielded positive results within a hostile environment. Evers believed that SNCC tactics placed this work in danger. He noted that prior "to the coming of SNCC, the NAACP had quietly worked with local Voter Registration Committees in McComb to enroll more than 250 Negroes on the registration books, while in Walthall County the NAACP had worked through its branch members and had gotten them to file complaints with the Justice Department for denial of registration." In response, Evers noted that the Justice Department had "filed suit early in 1961 to forbid such discriminatory practices against Negroes." Evers believed that the in-your-face approach of SNCC caused "Negroes" in Amite County to regress. He admitted that Amite had proven a tough area even for NAACP recruitment but that progress had been made toward eradicating "the fear among Negroes" in the area. In fact, he contended, the NAACP "had gotten many Negroes to go down and attempt to register." Yet, Evers believed that the "rash actions of some of the members of SNCC and the consequential shooting (to death) of Herbert Lee, (a Negro), by a State Representative further embedded fear among Negroes that they should not try to Register [sic] at this time." Thus, Evers continued, "we are not able to get Negroes in Amite County to do what they were otherwise trying to do for themselves, before the arrival of SNCC."[25] Although working toward the same goals, there existed ideological and strategic rifts between Evers and the leaders of other civil rights organizations regarding the intensity of direct-action tactics and its application. James Meredith's enrollment at the University of Mississippi, however, provided a crucial opportunity for competing civil rights organizations in Mississippi to rally around a common goal.

The NAACP had exhibited interest in integrating the University of Mississippi since the *Brown* decision, but much like the leaders of the Montgomery Bus Boycott, they were waiting on just the right person and the right time to carry it through. In fact, Cornelius Turner maintained that a friend of his wanted to attend Ole Miss prior to Meredith, but the NAACP was not yet ready. Turner remembered that Meredith came by his office in Jackson to buy a life insurance policy and started talking about applying to the University of Mississippi. Turner organized a meeting with Medgar after speaking with Meredith.[26]

James Meredith was born in Attala County near Kosciusko, Mississippi, on June 25, 1933, to Moses and Roxie Meredith. Moses came into the marriage with five children from a previous union that ended when his wife died from an illness. He married Roxie Marie Patterson in 1931 and James was the oldest of seven children born to this marriage. Much like Evers, Meredith grew up in a household that touted pride and the importance of standing up for what was right. His father demanded respect when dealing with whites and stood his ground when challenged. Historian Charles Eagles maintained that perhaps "the most public demonstration of his courage came in the spring of 1919 when he registered to vote at the Kosciusko courthouse and became one of the county's few black voters."[27] Education also became a priority that Moses Meredith advocated for his children, and it turned out to be a lesson James never forgot.

In 1950, Meredith left Attala County to stay with his uncle in St. Petersburg, Florida. He finished school there, graduating from Gibbs High School in June 1951. In July, he enlisted (for the first time) in the U.S. Air Force and concluded his service with an honorable discharge in 1955. After his second enlistment, beginning in October 1955 and ending in 1960, he enrolled in Jackson State College (now Jackson State University) in the fall of 1960. Meredith decided during his junior year to transfer to the University of Mississippi.[28] Fellow schoolmate Ruby Magee recalled that Meredith had made it clear when he first arrived at Jackson State "that his ultimate goal was to go to the University of Mississippi at Oxford." As a result, she maintained that Meredith was never actively involved in the demonstrations happening in Jackson at the time. Meredith, however, remained aware of what was occurring and offered his advice to those demonstrating or planning to do so. Meredith deliberately avoided direct participation in the demonstrations, Magee believed, because of his plans to attend the university and thus "he didn't want to do anything that would hurt his chances anymore so for getting there."[29]

On January 21, 1961, Meredith sent a letter to the University of Mississippi registrar requesting a catalog and an application form. After receiving the requested items, he spoke with Medgar, who, according to Meredith, "was the first person, outside of the In Group, to learn of my intentions to enroll." The In Group consisted of a group of student intellectuals at Jackson State College of which Meredith was a member. Evers advised Meredith to contact the NAACP Legal Defense Fund regarding the matter and to communicate with Thurgood Marshall in particular.[30] Evers proved enthusiastic at Meredith's desire to integrate the university and promised him full access to the legal resources of the NAACP. The problem with this particular promise, however, lay in the fact that the NAACP had no immediate plans in 1961 for litigation in the realm of higher education in Mississippi. As a result, Meredith acknowledged that Medgar "had come under heavy fire from his superiors for bypassing them in this instance" in deference to the LDF.[31] As a consequence, author William Doyle surmised that Evers had in fact "been exceeding his authority when he automatically promised legal resources to Meredith."[32]

Thurgood Marshall required further discussion regarding the legitimacy of Meredith's attempt to register at the University of Mississippi and insisted on speaking with Meredith to ensure his sanity, sincerity, and credentials. Evers suggested that Meredith call Marshall but decided they should call from the Evers home instead of the NAACP office. Meredith, feeling that Marshall was somehow questioning his integrity, over the course of their conversation took offense and hung up the phone. He then threatened to go at it alone without the aid of the NAACP. Meredith later admitted that sole credit must be given "to Medgar Evers, his expert knowledge of human nature and his ability to deal with people, for the case moving beyond this point." It took some time, nevertheless, for Evers to convince Meredith to send Marshall the required information needed for the case to proceed.[33]

After reviewing his transcripts and other credentials, Marshall offered Meredith the legal assistance of the NAACP and in mid-February he assigned assistant LDF counsel Constance Baker Motley to his case.[34] Motley had proven an accomplished attorney who had also worked on the *Brown* case. Evers's ability to employ diplomacy and tact had calmed the conflict and kept the process going. Although Meredith possessed the courage needed to carry out the task and to face down the abuse waiting for him, he needed the legal support of the NAACP to help guide him through what Doyle described as "the labyrinthine legal minefield that the state of Mississippi would force him into."[35]

Regarding his choice to attend the University of Mississippi, Meredith argued that he, in fact, enrolled to accomplish much more than obtaining an academic degree. He believed that he was fighting "a war against white supremacy" with the overall goal being "the total . . . destruction of [that] system" and the University of Mississippi was a strategic battleground in that war. Evers served as an advisor to Meredith, who noted that Medgar "was a black that suffered the same consequences as every black and didn't like it and wanted to do whatever he could to change it."[36] This observation illuminated a pattern of dedicated assistance that ran through the course of Evers's life, a pattern which defined him as a man, a husband, a father, and an activist.

James Meredith successfully integrated the University of Mississippi with the aid of federal marshals in 1962 and finished his degree program the following year. His enrollment did not come without costs. It appears that university officials attempted early on to keep the situation from getting out of hand. Early arrivals for the fall term were subject to a university ruling, which, according to news reports from the *Mississippi Free Press,* specified that if "students are observing or standing by, in a mob disturbance, offenders . . . [would] be immediately dismissed from the university."[37] Despite such attempts to maintain order, the ensuing riot on September 30 caused thousands of dollars in property damage and the lives of two individuals, "a French newspaper correspondent [Paul Leslie Guihard] and . . . a local white mechanic [Walter Ray Gunter]" and took thousands of police, military, and federal troops to quell. The entire incident took the pressure off of Governor Barnett and his supposed statewide economic problems. In light of the problems Meredith's enrollment caused, Claude Ramsay argued that "Barnett seized upon the Meredith situation . . . [as] a diversionary tactic to get the people's minds off of what he had been doing to them [and the state economically.]"[38]

Despite the violence and loss of life, Evers considered the integration of Mississippi's premier educational institution a victory for African Americans not only in Mississippi but across the nation. He acknowledged, with a hint of pride, that after "approximately twenty months of continuous work James Meredith enrolled at the University of Mississippi, as the first known Negro student in the 114 years history." Meredith, however, was not the first African American to attend Ole Miss as Evers hinted to with his use of the word "known," but rather the first to do so publicly. In 1945 and 1946 Harry Saunders Murphy Jr. had attended the University while allowing those around him to believe that he was just another white student.[39] Evers, however, had worked with Meredith from the beginning and interpreted his enrollment as a sign that perhaps the state could indeed change for the better.[40]

Evers informed the public that educational integration at Ole Miss would not end the overall struggle against inequality; the battle had not yet been won. The *Washington Post* announced that Evers thought that Meredith's enrollment would "ignite voter registration again and spur other educational gains all over the State." It was those "other educational gains" that drove him and lay at the basis of the NAACP's integration battle with university officials. Evers informed black Mississippians of the importance the NAACP placed on Meredith's enrollment. Throughout this battle for school integration, he noted in the *Washington Post,* "we're going to make it known to high school and college students that Meredith's suit was designed to break down barriers in all institutions of higher learning . . . but we don't expect to win without a fight."[41] Evers expected the integration of Ole Miss to have a trickle-down effect. The event, Evers believed, would open the door for qualified blacks to enter "all other junior colleges and all the colleges supported by tax money. We can look forward to the young people applying to the various junior colleges in Mississippi."[42] Yet, there proved very little time for celebrating Meredith's enrollment as young African Americans in Jackson considered 1961 the year they, too, should actively challenge segregation.

The latter part of 1961 witnessed an increase in youth activism through-out Mississippi. Young people from around the state openly challenged Jim Crow and, in the process, forced NAACP and other organizational leaders to pick up the pace. Members of NAACP Youth Councils in Clarksdale, Vicksburg, and Greenville staged sit-ins at various points of geographical significance. The months of July and August produced a barrage of direct-action attacks against segregation practices and the youth led the push for immediate changes.

During the month of July, youth leaders intensified their attack upon segregation strongholds within the city of Jackson. Evers reported that the NAACP leadership from the Jackson Youth Council, the NAACP Inter-Collegiate College Chapter, and the Campbell College Chapter "continued their wave of sit-ins, in an effort to break down the segregation here in the parks and pools in the city of Jackson." These planned protests were led by Johnnie Barbour, president of the Campbell College Chapter; Walter Jones, vice president of the Inter-Collegiate College Chapter; and Willis Logan, president of the Jackson Youth Council. Evers acknowledged that Logan had also been involved in an earlier sit-in protest at the local zoo, which resulted in "the removal of the benches by the Mayor." Although this new wave of protesters had youth on their side, this also made them much more susceptible to court actions. In response to youth activism, the court system sought to control the actions of juvenile "offenders" with both physical and legal restraints.[43]

The court system took a hard line on NAACP members who participated in civil rights activities and sought to limit, if not control, their participation. Since Willis Logan was seventeen years old, the "Juvenile Judge," Evers reported, placed him on probation for one year. Logan was also "ordered not to attend any political meetings," during his probationary period. This, of course, included "NAACP, CORE, Student non-violent [*sic*] Committee or any similar meetings," Evers explained. "He was further instructed not to associate with any one who has been active in the fight for First Class Citizenship." Evers pointed out that this punishment also applied to Verna Ann Bailey, age fourteen, and Aaron Therese Robinson, age thirteen, who were NAACP Youth Council members. In addition to supplementary restrictions on their movement, Evers reported that the youth offenders, among other things, were required to "write a term paper on Juvenile delinquency; which if acceptable to the Judge, their six months curfew will be reduced (3) months." This punishment seemed somewhat severe and arbitrary and Evers contended that "these repressive measures [were] designed to keep our young people from being active in the Fight for First Class Citizenship."[44] Despite these draconian methods, youth leaders continued to push civil rights activism forward.

The month of August proved as eventful as July had been. The month witnessed the NAACP Youth Council in Clarksdale stage their "first demonstration," Evers remarked, when "three members of the Council attempted to buy an interstate train ticket in the 'white' Illinois Central passenger train terminal." The three individuals were arrested and charged with breach of peace. In Vicksburg, NAACP youth "picketed a segregated movie house" and police arrested them for breach of peace; police also arrested Johnnie Frazier, former president of the Greenville Youth Council of the NAACP, for picketing a Woolworth's variety store on August 28.[45] The NAACP leadership recognized the importance of supporting the youth and their efforts if they did not want to lose them to other groups, a message Evers had been preaching for some time. Gloster Current, corresponding with Aaron Henry, underscored the importance the NAACP now placed on youth activism when admitting that "the stepped up activities on the part of SCLC and CORE in Mississippi which unless we continue to be aggressive, will adversely affect our own operations. Therefore, we must be prepared to support our youth in every possible instance."[46] For young activists in Mississippi, 1962 promised an opportune time to organize and participate in the struggle as soldiers of liberation rather than spectators of fortune.

The Jackson movement began in the summer of 1962. The historian

Stephen D. Classen argues that the "Jackson Movement, as well as other direct-action campaigns, were specific articulations of impatience and dissatisfaction. For movement participants, legal and bureaucratic efforts seemed gradualist and often futile."[47] In response to the growing disillusionment, the NAACP Youth Council organized boycotts of local merchants in an attempt to end overt practices of discrimination. In the beginning, Evers had been somewhat skeptical of the proposed direct-action tactics of the youth because of a lack of organization, but he warmed up to the enthusiasm exhibited by Youth Council members and worked diligently to assist their efforts whenever and wherever he could. Civil rights leaders in Mississippi viewed the Jackson movement as a state struggle with national possibilities. After all, the civil rights struggle in Birmingham had garnered national attention for both the overall movement and the Southern Christian Leadership Conference specifically. The NAACP believed the Jackson movement could benefit it by nationalizing the civil rights struggle in Mississippi. Evers's commitment to Mississippi now placed him in a unique and highly visible position of leadership. His efforts were vital to the growth of the Jackson movement and he stood at its center organizing resistance groups, strategy sessions, and financial support for those jailed in the battle to end segregation.[48] He saw in the youth a renewed hope for change and it rejuvenated his spirit just as much as his presence bolstered theirs.

Medgar Evers had a connection with the youth that elicited trust and inspired action despite the potential consequences of fighting against the status quo. As a freshman, Minnie Watson heard Medgar speak at Campbell College in 1961. Prior to that speech, Watson admitted that she had never stopped to think of either the wrongness of racism and segregation or the fact that it could be changed. She explained that Medgar challenged students to think about the fact that they deserved the same rights granted to other citizens for just being born and that "you don't have to earn it, it is yours by birth." Above all, she recalled, Medgar Evers "made you think" and he seemed "chosen" to do what he did. Furthermore, he had a way with words and "when he spoke to you," she noted, "he would try to encourage you, he didn't try to scare you but to make you think. [He wanted] to make you understand that this was more than about you, but those coming behind you and the notion if you wanted things to remain the same for them or do you want to see the other side of the coin." Watson's description of Evers echoed the recollections shared by many others who had encounters with him. Civil rights activist Hazel Palmer recalled that when she first began attending civil rights meetings, Evers was there. "And he was really a gentleman man, and he cared about peoples to register to vote to understand what you were doing it for." Whenever she saw Evers, "he was always a handshake, and how you doing and keep up the good works, some encouraging word." He worked to ensure that people knew what they were getting into so that everything would be clear.[49]

Watson believed that Medgar was honest about everything he told people and never tried to hide the dangers associated with resistance. When Evers recruited students from various colleges to participate in the movement, he always let students and young people know what to expect and soothed their concerns, Watson remembered. He both warned and reassured individuals that by resisting their oppression "you're going to be arrested, but don't worry we're going to get you out." Medgar would tell people that they should not have to get out here and fight for rights that were theirs by birth and lose their life in the process, "but since you do . . . , you got to be committed to it, do you want it bad enough," remarked Watson. People began to think that they should challenge the system, where before they may have accepted it as the way things were and may not have thought about the possibility of changing things.[50] Constance Slaughter-Harvey, the first African American woman to graduate from the University of Mississippi Law School, proved to be one of those inspired by Evers's determination. Slaughter-Harvey was a sixteen-year-old taking courses at Tougaloo College in 1963 and Evers impressed her a great deal. "I personally met Medgar, got to know him back on June 2 or June 1, and he was killed June 12. . . . And it was because of Medgar Evers that I personally got involved and because of his death that I got involved."[51] Although she admitted that Martin Luther King Jr. was "more eloquent, Medgar spoke from his heart . . . [and you] could tell he meant everything he said. [As a consequence, you] . . . were willing to follow him." As a result of his influence and selfless dedication, Slaughter-Harvey admitted that throughout her life she has tried "in my own little way, to be a part of the master plan he (Evers) put together."[52]

Myrlie also recognized the connection that her husband had to the youth and maintained that he inspired them as much as they inspired him. The connection he had with young people was always based upon mutual respect. She was convinced that he appealed to the youth because he listened to them and "their questions were not always questions of wisdom, but how to and he set an example. [Although he was thirty-seven in 1962, Myrlie maintained that] Medgar was young, young at heart, young at mind, young in action and he showed young people that he believed in them" and this was key. They knew that they could depend on him and that he would carry their issues to the NAACP leadership, which had a history of overlooking their concerns.[53]

Evers kept the youth, particularly those who were students, aware of their responsibilities to the movement, to the race, and to themselves. The auditorium was always full when he came to speak at Campbell. Watson remembered that he constantly reminded students that as "young people you have the opportunity [to make a difference] and as young people it's your obligation. You're gonna be educators, you're gonna be educated, so its gonna be your obligation to go back to your communities and take the word back . . . because it starts with you and then it starts in your home and it spreads abroad."[54] The youth believed in Evers and trusted that he would be with them whenever they needed him. Dr. Velvelyn Foster, vice president of Academic Affairs and Student Life at Jackson State University and a Jackson State College freshman in 1961, noted that Medgar was very charismatic and people believed in his message of social and political equality and students knew that he would protect them. Medgar exuded confidence, she remarked, and was not one to suggest anything he was not willing to do himself.[55] This type of active and inclusive leadership assured Evers the loyalty of students and young people in general for, as Cornelius Turner observed, "how . . . [could] you not feel strong about someone like that?"[56]

In August 1962, Medgar and Myrlie joined a petition to the Jackson Separate School District Board of Trustees and superintendent "asking that the schools under their jurisdiction be re-organized without procrastination or evasion on a non-segregated basis." The petition was filed on August 17, and involved nine parents "on behalf of fifteen children in grades two through twelve." Evers pointed out that the petition "was not just a demonstration. . . . We are deeply concerned about having our children receive a good education. We will stay with this until they do." The petitioners pointed to the issue of citizenship and what African Americans were entitled to as taxpayers in the state. One of the petitioners (unidentified) pointed to the fact that blacks "pay high taxes—a good deal of which goes for the schools. I am glad that the money goes for education, but I want my children to get their share of the benefits."[57] Myrlie noted that during the time of the integration petition, she had remarked to a friend that due to Medgar's position, it was expected that they would join the suit. Evers overheard the discussion and later advised his wife to speak for herself. He retorted that his name was not "on that petition because it's expected to be. It's there because I want it there."[58] During this time, Evers found himself under increasing pressure to keep things going and to avoid the many death threats he received via anonymous phone calls. Over time, the violent nature of these calls intensified considerably. Although his work and stress load increased, his loyalty and dedication to the Mississippi movement received a psychological boost in 1962, as did his aspirations for bringing about positive social and political change.

During the fall of 1962, the North Jackson NAACP Youth Council, with John Salter as its advisor, initiated a "far-flung" boycott "aimed at ending the . . . rampant discrimination against Negro workers and Negro consumers in 127 different business establishments." Salter, on behalf of the Youth Council, requested the assistance of NAACP branches across the nation to support the boycott and to initiate boycotts against those chain stores targeted in Jackson with locations in other areas.[59] The boycott was aimed at the business district of Capitol Street covering "State Street to Mill Street" where seventeen major national chain stores, positioned "adjacent to the largest Negro neighborhood in Jackson . . . [, depended] heavily upon Negro trade."[60] Evers played an integral role in the Jackson boycott movement, and the support he commanded in the community aided in gaining overall support for the boycott itself.

By November 1962, Tougaloo students were committed to a boycott of Capitol Street as a means of securing employment opportunities and better treatment for black customers and eventually pressuring city officials to enact sweeping changes in how the city viewed and treated its black citizens. Unlike Evers's previous boycott of downtown Jackson during the Christmas season of 1961, there was now a committed cadre of supporters and workers who could get the word out and keep the boycott moving. This reality had been bolstered by the successful boycott of the segregated Negro fair in October, causing it to close due to low attendance. Evers noted that the boycott was "at least 80% effective" and thus was "an overwhelming success."[61] Medgar Evers, John Salter, and the North Jackson Youth Council worked to convince blacks of their purchasing power and to drum home the fact that they should segregate their money from white business owners until positive social and political changes occurred.

The boycott of Capitol Street proved an extensive endeavor, targeting well over one hundred businesses. The purpose of the boycott was to obtain the following: "Equality in hiring and promotion," "End of segregated drinking fountains—restrooms—seating," "Use of courtesy titles 'Mrs.,' 'Miss' and 'Mr.,'" and "Service on a first-come, first served basis." These objectives were then printed on some 5,000 leaflets with the heading "Don't Buy on Capitol Street," along with the "general boundaries of the downtown area" and distributed. Evers worked to secure bail money for a planned picketing demonstration of downtown areas and by doing so committed the NAACP to the youth uprising whether the national office wanted it or not.[62] However, by the time the boycott was to take place on December 3, no bail money had arrived and was unlikely to do so. Evers, who at the time was out of town on a "tour of branches in the mid-west and east," noted that the tour began in Kansas City, Missouri, on November 24 and ended in Jackson, Tennessee, on December 5, 1962. He also conducted a West Coast speaking tour beginning in Los Angeles on November 9 and ending in Topeka, Kansas, on November 18, 1962. During the West Coast tour he "appeared on some 12 different television stations, as well as an equal number or more radio stations." Although absent, Evers suggested that both Jack Young and John Salter look for individuals to put up property bonds and eventually volunteers were found and monies made available.[63] They chose December 12, 1962, as the new date for the boycott and the media, notified by New York attorney William Kunstler, played an integral role in publicizing the event.[64]

On December 12, John Salter, his wife, Eldri, and Tougaloo students Rupert Crawford, Roland Leroy Mitchell, Bette A. Poole, and Walter Robert Mitchell arrived on Capitol Street, exited their vehicle at the 100 block of East Capitol Street, and unfurled their banners calling for a boycott of area businesses. They began marching two to a row until they were arrested by police captain Cecil Hathaway. The *Jackson Daily News* reported that the banners the boycotters "carried called for Negroes to buy away from Capitol St. [Furthermore, the group] . . . also showed newsmen handbills listing several individual business firms which they sought to boycott." Each boycott participant was arrested, charged with sidewalk obstruction, and given a tentative trial date with bond set at five hundred dollars each. For many African Americans, the "18-degree weather" in which the boycott took place highlighted the determination exhibited by the boycotters.[65] The city of Jackson did not take the boycott as something to be ignored and city officials, led by Mayor Allen Thompson, instituted an immediate campaign against the movement and targeted all involved.

On December 13, Mayor Thompson made it clear that the city intended to "prosecute 'agitators, pickets, and such organizations as the NAACP and others'" with intensity and diligence. That diligence included the consideration of implementing a one-million-dollar damage action lawsuit against those groups responsible for the Capitol Street boycott. Thompson met with area businesses to reassure them that law and order would prevail and that they had the full support of the city against the boycott. As a means of underscoring his support to area businesses, Thompson announced that when outside agitators travel to Jackson and "try to destroy our city, they are going to pay." He bolstered this account by announcing that the city was more than prepared to deploy "1,000 policemen up and down Capitol street to preserve the peace" in the event of future boycotts. For protestors the boycott could not have come at a more opportune time. The city of Jackson was playing host to more than "250 supervisory and sales personnel of Mississippi Power & Light Company," who were there for the company's annual state meeting and to celebrate forty years of service. Thompson wanted to offer assurances to this group in particular that he could handle the boycotters and that business would continue as usual.[66]

While the youth were more than willing to proceed at all costs, the NAACP national office was less enthusiastic about the direct-action slant taken in Jackson and thus chose to limit its support. Salter maintained that during the boycott, the national office was split on the desirability of direct action as were key leaders within the upper echelons of the NAACP organization. Evers was caught in the middle of the growing divide between the NAACP leadership in New York and the youth of Jackson, and the growing tensions between the two groups nearly pulled him in two.

Myrlie noted that the pressures placed on Medgar at this time were crushing. It pained her to witness the strain he endured as mediator between two groups that were supposedly fighting for the same goals. According to Myrlie, during the latter part of his life, the most active individuals in the movement were the young people, the elderly, and the economically disadvantaged. These three groups came together and "brought pressure to bear on Medgar and said 'you got to get those folk in New York to understand what this is all about, they are dictating what we should and should not do; yet they are in New York and they don't set foot down here and they don't understand what's going on.'" The responsibility of being caught between these three groups and the pressure each placed upon him to rectify the problem was almost too much. As a consequence, Myrlie maintained that Evers was "caught in that last year [of his life], caught between the activists, the young people and those elders, I'll call them, and the NAACP who wanted to go the legislative route and these other people said 'no no no, that's not gonna get it!'"[67]

John Frazier, who was a close confidant of Evers's, acknowledged that Medgar considered it to be a real problem whenever he failed to get people to reason together or to work in a fashion that allowed "a balanced comprehensive solution to take place."[68] Evers, however, continued to mediate between the above factions in hopes of establishing a balance between the ideology and methodology of each for the benefit of the Mississippi movement as a whole. His efforts proved successful. Evers had made the NAACP the dominant black organization in Mississippi where it had been marginalized throughout the rest of the South. Journalists Gene Roberts and Hank Klibanoff argued that Evers had accomplished this "by bridging the gap between the old heads, who believed change would come only by persistent knocking on the door, and more aggressive young blacks, who felt the door had to be pushed down and removed."[69]

With the Jackson campaign continuing into 1963, the NAACP showed a renewed interest in events as demonstrated by Roy Wilkins's pledge of NAACP support to overcome inequality in Jackson. John Salter wondered what could have sparked such a complete turn-around since Evers had worked feverishly to wrangle NAACP support for the boycott from the beginning with less than stellar results. He surmised that the NAACP's willingness to support the Jackson campaign developed, in part, out of fear that the SCLC would move into Mississippi after completing its assault on segregation in Birmingham. This notion was based in fact as Martin Luther King Jr. extended his pledge of future support for those suffering in Mississippi. King and other civil rights leaders "promised to shift full efforts of their campaign to the Mississippi Delta after finishing a current drive in Birmingham, Ala." King noted that "'little progress' has been made in Negro voter registration in Mississippi despite recent drives. 'But activity and attempt have been stimulated . . . and this will bring federal action.'"[70] This announcement carried in the *Jackson Daily News* only heightened concerns of NAACP officials that their dominant position in Mississippi was fast slipping away.

NAACP fears of a takeover by other civil rights organizations in Mississippi had certainly proven legitimate in the past and the way things were shaping up in Jackson, SCLC had a legitimate claim to assume a leadership position. This could be seen in the types of roles certain individuals held within the NAACP. Within the organizational structure of the NAACP, Salter explained that

> Aaron Henry was usually referred to as the president of the Mississippi NAACP, but he also happened to be the Mississippi board member of SCLC. Our whole legal defense in Jackson was being handled by Jess Brown, who was not a regular NAACP lawyer, and by Bill Kunstler, attorney for SCLC's Gandhi Society. Much of our bail bond in Jackson had been put up by the Southern Conference Educational Fund, whose president was the Rev. Fred L. Shuttlesworth of Birmingham—and president of the Alabama state SCLC affiliate and national secretary of SCLC.[71]

Regardless of why the NAACP offered financial support to the Jackson campaign, its members eagerly received it, and this reality added economic and political strength to a boycott that had already gripped the city.

The enthusiasm displayed by the Jackson youth, their willingness to face beatings, jail, and death strengthened Evers's commitment to Mississippi. However, the city's response to the nonviolent protests practiced by the youth angered him considerably. On May 31, 1963, the Jackson police jailed approximately six hundred African American youth of varying ages who marched along Farish Street protesting racism. The police responded in such numbers and with such force that Evers exclaimed that the "scene [was] 'just like Nazi Germany. . . . Look at those storm troopers.'"[72] However, the youth-oriented Jackson movement stimulated Evers to work even harder to support the actions of those involved. With the advent of the Jackson movement, Myrlie argued that the responsibility "rested on . . . [Medgar's] shoulders, and he would not shirk it. Even when he sagged under its weight, there was a new spirit, a new source of energy within him: for the first time, the entire Negro community was behind him; for the first time, volunteers were everywhere."[73] Evers considered the Jackson youth movement the reward for his dedication and vigilance in fighting for social and political change in Mississippi as he looked to his own children and their future. While manning the boycott front line almost endlessly, he continued to construct bridges between the NAACP and members of other civil rights organizations. Evers also demonstrated a great deal of ingenuity in his approach to civil rights activism.

When it came to strategy and execution, Ineeva Pittman remembered Evers as being a "shrewd and very smart man." She noted that the city of Jackson attempted to preempt the boycott by making mass assembly illegal and thus subject to immediate arrest. Evers, however, got around this by printing up t-shirts with messages across them and, during one occasion, he placed one of these t-shirts on a little boy and sent him marching up and down the street and "there was nothing that [they] could do," Pittman exclaimed, "because there was no great amount of people just this little boy and Medgar would be standing off and watching him." She noted, however, that Medgar had help in his attempts to ensure that the boycotts along Capitol Street were effective. Pittman pointed to the support Doris Allison, president of the Jackson branch of the NAACP, provided Medgar during the boycott. Since the annual meeting of African American teachers was scheduled for the same time as the boycott and would last an entire week, Evers feared the boycott would take a hit. If the teachers held true to form, they would spend a great deal of money on Capitol Street and the boycott would lose momentum. Allison helped solve the problem and alleviated some of the stress Evers shouldered regarding the teachers spending money in the shops of targeted merchants. According to Pittman:

> Mrs. Doris Allison, . . . who worked close with Evers, went from church to church and whispered to a few people in the teachers' meeting, and [also] set down in the general assembly, and said "Ohh isn't it a shame how those teachers when they went downtown got beaten up by those children for coming down there and shopping" and then she

would move to another section "Ohh did you here about that teacher, those teachers getting beat up down there when they went downtown to shop . . . on Capitol street because they got it boycotted did you hear about that?" By her doing that it circulated and that kept Medgar's boycott from being broken [because those teachers were afraid of being harmed if they went down there].[74]

Medgar Evers labored hard to combat segregation and to develop a support base capable of working in the best interest of the movement in his absence. He hoped that a strong foundation of resistance, not dependent upon a single leader, would avoid organizational breakdown if a particular leader was killed. Organizational strength and group direction would win the struggle for social and political equality across racial lines. This notion of an ever-changing leadership often brought him into conflict with certain members of the NAACP hierarchy.

Myrlie maintained that leadership remained the cornerstone of Evers's political life, and it also defined him as a husband, father, and son. His leadership strategy contained a multiplicity of components but, according to Evers-Williams, one component in particular was "extremely important to Medgar and that was the wisdom to develop young leaders without children or leadership skills within our young children." For Evers, leadership was momentary with the understood objective that it be passed on as soon as possible to avoid stagnation. Medgar, recalled Evers-Williams,

believed the sooner we could pass those skills on to our children the better off we would be as a people. He was critical of those who were in leadership positions and wanted to hold on to them until death. He felt there was a need to nurture our youth so that they could step in and effectively be new leaders, he believed in the infusion of new blood, and at that time, more so than now, certainly within the NAACP, the whole thing was to suppress young voices, to never give up a position once you got it, he had great difficulty with that because his take on leadership was just the opposite; part of the responsibility of leaders was to develop new ones to come along to take your place when you are gone, or to move you out of that position. . . . He just did not see enough of that happening [at the time].[75]

As a consequence, the strain between Evers and the NAACP grew as he supported and encouraged the use of direct action, youth leadership, and the help of other civil rights leaders. The strain showed on his face as the warring factions mentioned above intensified their disagreements and looked to him to solve the issues dividing them.

As 1963 progressed, so did the psychological and emotional tension Evers endured. In 1958, paraphrasing General George S. Patton's mantra that "War is hell," Evers admonished that "Psychological, economical, and physical war is hell."[76] Although by 1963, the truth of that statement wore on his face like an overgrown beard, it did not reveal the deep scars and symptoms of collapse hiding ever so close to the surface. The continued divide between the grassroots and the leadership of the NAACP in New York hurt Evers more than many realized, and he struggled to keep the two factions working together to avoid a total collapse of the Jackson movement.

Salter agreed that Evers was caught in the middle due to his loyalty to both groups. For many years Gloster Current, Ruby Hurley, and Roy Wilkins were his only links to the outside world and so what they said "carried an enormous amount of weight," Salter explained. He admitted that on the one hand, Medgar had "the militant wing of the Jackson movement and, on the other, he had the conservatives who were trying to undercut it" and by the end he was worn out and depressed.[77] Evers-Williams acknowledged that the effects of this infighting were much more devastating to Medgar than many realized as he put on a brave front when dealing with others:

> there was so much pressure on Medgar from those two warring groups who was supposedly going after the same thing and Medgar saw that coalition being weakened and the chance of that dream, if not being destroyed, being held back for a while and that was one of the toughest things in the world for him because he had to make a decision. I watched my husband age years in a matter of weeks and I knew that at some point the phone was gonna ring and they were going to tell me that Medgar had dropped dead. I knew he was going one way or the other either somebody was go'n take him out or he was going to drop dead. The stress was just more than a human being could take. And the last time that I really saw him alive was that morning of the 11th [of June 1963] when he left and he kissed us all goodbye and he came back in the house and said "I'm so tired I can't go on, but I can't stop." And he hugged us all again and left.[78]

From May to June of 1963, Medgar Wiley Evers made the conscious decision to attack segregation head-on without reservations or apologies. "Medgar had all but made up his mind . . . to leave the NAACP and to help start his own organization," Evers-Williams noted. "He was also upset about what he thought was a narrow-mindedness of the NAACP leadership in terms of joining in joint efforts to attack this monstrous problem."[79] However, before Evers could move on to the next phase of his life, there was work yet to do in Jackson, and Mayor Allen Thompson, unknowingly, helped to elevate Medgar Evers from local organizer to national leader.

7.

Two Can Play the Game

THE GAUNTLET TOSS

You can kill a man, but you can't kill an idea.

—*Medgar Evers*

I'll be damned . . . if I'm going to let the white man lick me. There's something out here that I've got to do for my kids, and I'm not going to stop until I've done it.

—*Medgar Evers*

We declare our right on this earth . . . to be a human being, to be respected as a human being, to be given the rights of a human being in this society, on this earth, in this day, which we intend to bring into existence by any means necessary.

—*Malcolm X*

We must restore our humanity first; we will be changing the world by changing ourselves first. This might be our holy mission. It might be the legacy that we can leave for our children, and their children still unborn.

—*John Henrik Clarke*

IN 1963, IT SEEMED AS IF Evers transformed into a political icon overnight. He used the momentum gained in 1962 to heighten community activism by increasing his speaking engagements and intensifying his calls for social change. Medgar had "the ability to move beyond the present," exclaimed Myrlie Evers-Williams, "and to look into the future."[1] Statements he made in 1957, regarding the social and political expectations of African Americans in Mississippi, lend credence to her contentions. On November 8, while speaking at the NAACP annual statewide convention, Evers predicted that African Americans would achieve total integration in Mississippi by 1963. The Mississippi branch of the NAACP might appear to be lagging in progress, he admitted, "when you compare this state to some of the others . . . [, but] we are getting our feet on the ground, collecting information and making other preparations." Evers believed that intensive and consistent effort on the part of African Americans would lead to success in the overall struggle for equality and this thought kept him focused and fueled his day-to-day actions.[2]

Attacking segregation remained a focal point of Evers and inequality in public transportation commanded his attention. Whenever he saw an opportunity to challenge segregation, he took it. His desire to confront inequality in all of its forms led civil rights activist Samuel Bailey to declare that "Medgar did more for this state than anybody ever walked on earth."[3] In 1961, Samuel Bailey filed suit challenging segregation in interstate and intrastate transportation. The district court, however, refused to hear the case invoking the doctrine of equitable abstention. The case, *Samuel Bailey et al. v. Joe T. Patterson et al.*, eventually went before the U.S. Supreme Court. On February 26, 1962, the Court remanded the case back to the district court, who ruled that segregation laws were unconstitutional but denied the plaintiffs injunctive relief. Again, Bailey noted the important role Evers played in the process. "I would never even have thought about filing suit for public accommodations if he hadn't asked me to."[4] The case was finally settled on September 24, 1963, when the court of appeals issued injunctions against all appellees. Challenging school segregation also remained a focal point of Evers, one he had pushed since the *Brown* decision. Some press agencies also placed pressure on the NAACP to be more proactive in challenging school segregation.

In February 1962, the *Mississippi Free Press* asked why the NAACP was taking so long to challenge segregation in education. "Though we are grateful for what the NAACP has done," the editorial read, "we do not fully understand its plan for Mississippi as relates to the schools." Although the *Brown* decision seemed to answer the question of school integration, the *Mississippi Free Press* pointed out that, as of February 1962, "[no] one has desegregated here [in Jackson]. There is no known plan for such on the part of the State, the people of Mississippi nor the NAACP." The question, as far as the *Mississippi Free Press* was concerned, was what the NAACP would do. "The People of Mississippi know what the State will do;" the editorial exclaimed, "we will watch with interest for some sign of what the NAACP plans to do."[5] Evers was not long in answering critics of his desegregation plans in the area of education.

For Evers, there was an important difference between desegregation and integration. He explained to Charles L. Butts, editor of the *Mississippi Free Press,* that "when the NAACP filed suit against a public park because it was segregated, they were trying to desegregate it. After they win the suit they integrate it, using nonviolent, direct action techniques."[6] On March 4, 1963, Evers, along with five other families, began this process when the "Legal Defense and Educational Fund of NAACP" filed suit on behalf of "ten Negro children" requesting "a Federal Court to order the first public school integration in Mississippi, on the Elementary and High School level." Evers maintained that this "was the first such suit filed by Negro residents of Mississippi." Although the NAACP watched the case develop, Evers announced in the *Mississippi Free Press* that he was not acting on the association's behalf but was "participating only as the parent of one of the children wanting to enter a superior public school." The plaintiffs included Medgar and Myrlie Evers, Samuel Bailey, A. M. E. Logan, Kathryn Thomas, Edna Marie Singleton, and Elizabeth White.[7] Because he was willing to risk the lives and safety of his family right along with everyone else, his actions endeared him to the community and helped expand his base of support. Evers also used economic incentives in the fight to muster and maintain that support.

On March 29, he focused his attention on the plight of sixty-seven-year-old Reverend Jessie Crain of Greenwood. Reverend Crain and his family of fourteen were evicted from their residence for his refusal to remove his name from the voter role. The NAACP had sent one thousand dollars emergency fund for use in the general area and Evers contacted Aaron Henry of Clarksdale. When Henry suggested that one hundred dollars be appropriated for the Crain family, Medgar and James Farmer, of CORE, drove to Clarksdale and secured the suggested amount. Evers brought the financial gift to a mass meeting, chaired by David Dennis of CORE, where some five hundred persons crowded into the "First Christian Church." Speaking before the crowd, Evers acknowledged that as activists in the fight for equality

> We appreciate Freedom Fighters like Rev. Crain and family, and to show our appreciation for his courage for standing up like a man, the NAACP is happy to present to Rev. Crain and his family $100, in an effort to help them to make an adjustment. . . . [A]nd there is more where this came from—for those who [are] willing to stand up for Freedom.

With the audience roaring with approval, Farmer promised that the national office of CORE would send an additional hundred dollars to the Crain family on April 1.[8] Any person who stood up as a man or woman despite the consequences of doing so, Evers held up as true examples of manhood and womanhood. Increases in his recruitment efforts and activism, however, brought Evers closer and closer to a showdown with Mississippi's powerful political structure. The growing divide between Evers and conservative representatives of the state widened as a result of his response to Jackson mayor Allen C. Thompson, a response heightened by the power of television.

Medgar Evers refused to accept the idea that black people were content in their present social situation and challenged anyone who proposed otherwise. When it came to racial advancement and social progress, he was not afraid to employ tactics that others did not agree with and his leadership style reflected this characteristic. His was one of optimism and a strong belief that success was directly proportional to determination. By 1963, Evers had accepted the fact that his life was in danger, and he sought to prepare his wife and children in the event of his assassination. His televised response to Mayor Thompson brought the reality of such an occurrence to bear, and it pained Myrlie and all who knew what he meant to the city of Jackson and the movement for equality in Mississippi.

Mayor Thompson was no friend to the African American struggle for equality in Jackson, and he constantly sought to control the overall effectiveness of the movement. Thompson used the press to convey his belief that the "Negroes" in Jackson were satisfied with the way things were and that when problems arose blacks and whites worked together to solve them. On May 13, 1963, Thompson presented his defense of race relations in Jackson on radio station WJDX and television stations WJTV and WLBT. He argued that what made Jackson such a great city were its beautiful facilities, wonderful schools, libraries, parks, and an absence of slums prevalent in the larger urban metropolises. He cautioned the "Nigra" citizens to realize the good they were afforded by living in such a progressive city where they could send their "children to modern schools." He added, in his mind, a further reminder that

> You have twenty-four hour protection by the police department. Just think of being able to call the police any time of the night and say come quick! Someone is trying to get into my house, I need some help. Or suppose you need the fire department, or any other of the many services that your city provides you. And as most of you know, you are also welcome to present your petitions for improvements in your neighborhoods to the Commissioners and me. Our offices are always opened to you.

You live in a city where you can work, where you can make a comfortable living. You are treated, no matter what anybody else tells you, with dignity, courtesy and respect.[9]

Thompson added, however, that there would be no change in policy and neither he nor the city of Jackson would submit to the threats of racial agitators and subversives (descriptors he assigned to the NAACP). Thompson further warned that no outsiders from the president down could tell Jackson how to handle its business. Portions of Thompson's speech were more than likely a direct response to consistent demands by Evers and other NAACP officials for significant social change. They had also called for a group meeting with city officials to address important grievances contributing to racial division.

On May 13, Evers, John Salter, and members of the NAACP branches released a statement calling for the complete end to "all forms of racial segregation in Jackson." The statement outlined the extent the NAACP was willing to go to procure equality and the depth of its commitment:

> We are determined to end all state and government sponsored segregation in the parks, playgrounds, schools, libraries and other public facilities. To accomplish this we shall use all lawful means of protests—picketing, marches, mass meetings, litigation and whatever legal means we deem necessary.
>
> At this time, we wish to let the city, state, nation and world know that we want to meet with city officials and community leaders to make good faith attempts to settle grievances and assure immediate full citizen rights for all Americans. We earnestly hope that those who have the best interest of the city at heart will accept our offer to reach a speedy and orderly settlement.[10]

Evers and the NAACP had now gone on the offensive and broadcast to the nation their desire for immediate social change and a willingness to include political officials in the decision-making process. Regardless of whether Jackson politicians participated or not, there was no longer any doubt that NAACP strategy had changed to include some of the more direct-action tactics employed by other civil rights organizations across the nation. The *Jackson Daily News* carried portions of the statement the day of Thompson's speech, and he was, undoubtedly, aware of its existence and thus could not have missed the more aggressive stance of the NAACP and its local leadership.[11] Sovereignty Commission informants, however, suggested to commission officials that the boycotts were ineffective overall and that they should consider Evers's leadership role to be less of a threat than that of Martin Luther King Jr.

On the night of May 15, commission officials contacted a white male informant identified as 5-G.C. regarding the boycotts. Commission officials noted that he was in a much better position to gather intelligence from local blacks "and informants" than any other informant listed. 5-G.C. assigned informants under his control to monitor the boycotts and ascertain the possibility of future demonstrations. 5-G.C. concluded that a demonstration would not take place in Jackson over the next few weeks. The primary reason he provided the Sovereignty Commission was "that Medgar W. Evers . . . is a weak character and a coward." As proof, the informant reported that Evers "meets with NAACP groups, CORE groups, and other agitative groups, and attempts to persuade other local Negroes to participate in parades, picketing, marches and mass meetings, etc. But, for the several years that I have known Medgar W. Evers and studied his activities, I have never seen him in the forefront or in a position that would place him in danger of bodily harm."[12] This type of underestimation of Evers's leadership role proved a miscalculation he consistently exploited.

Although the informant did not deny the potential for trouble in Jackson or Hinds County, he doubted that it would result from the actions of Medgar Evers or other local "agitators" because of a lack of leadership ability. If trouble should arise, he hypothesized, "it will be after the Negro leaders . . . active in Birmingham and other cities in Alabama and Tennessee, complete their missions there and then come to Jackson, Mississippi to lead any demonstrations that might occur here."[13] Although Evers remained a prominent blip on the commission's radar screen, commission reports continued to label him as less of a political threat than civil rights leaders such as Martin Luther King Jr. or Malcolm X. Supreme Court justice Thurgood Marshall surmised that this was how Medgar "got so much accomplished. People underplayed him."[14]

The struggle for equality in Jackson heated to a furious boil in the days after Thompson's speech. His refusal to acquiesce to NAACP requests for a biracial committee to discuss racial problems plaguing the city only added to the animosity. Thompson, according to the *Jackson Daily News,* announced that "he would meet with responsible local Negro leaders, but would not talk to representatives of the NAACP, CORE, or agitator groups." He also called for "Negroes" to "reject any bid for leadership by outside agitators" and to support the city's segregationist stance, which he argued had resulted in successful race relations in Jackson. Because Thompson refused to meet with NAACP officials, Evers announced that "national representatives were [now here] to plan 'possible direct action in the City of Jackson provided conferences to negotiate with our city officials are not worked out.'"[15]

Evers announced that the recently organized Citizens Committee for Human Rights of Jackson, headed by local black businessman I. S. Sanders, had adopted a poignant resolution. The decree announced that the organization "resents and rejects the position stated by Mayor Allen Thompson, who claims that Negro citizens of Jackson are satisfied with the status quo." In fact, "we are indeed extremely dissatisfied with the status quo and we hereby call for an immediate end to segregation and discrimination in our community." In response to Thompson's willingness to "meet with responsible local Negro leaders," Evers charged the mayor with attempting to pick "Yes-men" with whom to meet. He warned those who would be collaborators, however, that "we consider Negroes who would sell out our program as being Uncle Tom's [*sic*] of the first order and we will deal with them economically as we are dealing with those downtown [who are enabling inequality to continue]."[16] Both the national media and civil rights activists across the nation paid close attention to what was occurring in Jackson and to the militant stance of its now-outspoken field secretary.

The backbone of Thompson's attack on the movement for equality rested on his rosy outlook on race relations and African Americans' position within the city. That perception had gone out across the nation, and Evers refused to allow a slight against the sensibilities and true racial place of blacks in Mississippi to go unchallenged. He insisted upon equal television time to respond to the claims presented by Allen and made his intentions to receive equal time public. Evers announced that the NAACP was "going to insist upon having this time because we were attacked by Mayor Thompson." He further pointed out that the "ethics of the Federal Communications Commission will require it. Whether public service time or paid time, our interest is in getting time."[17]

Fighting television networks for equal time was not foreign to Evers as he had done so, to no avail, in 1957. On October 17, during the height of the Little Rock integration crisis, Evers contacted the Federal Communications Commission (FCC) charging WLBT with presenting "only the segregationists point of view" on a program titled "The Little Rock Crisis."[18] His demands for equal televised response time were, in fact, supported by the Fairness Doctrine. The Fairness Doctrine, journalist Kay Mills notes, maintained that "broadcasters had to provide 'a reasonable amount of time for the presentation . . . of programs devoted to the discussion and consideration of public issues,' while also encouraging and enabling broadcast of all sides of controversial issues."[19] The FCC denied his request, but in 1958 Evers tested his chances regarding a television appearance outside of Mississippi when he solicited Dave Garroway of NBC for an appearance on the *Today* show. His objective was to offset the rather "distorted and slanted story" of race relations in Mississippi propagated by Governor Coleman "and other southern whites."[20] There was no indication that anything came of his efforts, but in 1963, WLBT granted Medgar Evers seventeen minutes to present a televised response to Thompson. At this point, the station felt compelled to grant him airtime because, as the historian Stephen Classen has written, WLBT "was sensing the watchful eye of federal regulators" who were already investigating the station for biased and solicited station comments regarding its coverage and reporting of the admission of James Meredith to the University of Mississippi.[21] Safety concerns made it necessary for Evers's response not to be broadcast live but taped at a secret location and then aired on Jackson station WLBT.

The NAACP took particular interest in the content of Evers's speech and wanted to make sure that he answered Thompson's charge that Jackson had no slums. They also wanted him to address the issue of unemployment among blacks and "the disparity in income between whites and Negroes" as a means of toppling the rosy picture Thompson had painted. Gloster Current underscored the newfound support of the NAACP for the direct-action tactics of the youth. Current acknowledged that the "young people are ready to go. [As a result,] $5,000 should be made available to Medgar Evers for use in posting bond."[22] For Evers, things were now moving at a rapid pace and it pleased him tremendously. He now had the financial and physical help to expand the Mississippi struggle and that momentum began with his televised response to Mayor Thompson on Monday, May 20, 1963.

Evers's televised reply to Thompson reflects both the height of his notoriety and the depth of his commitment. First, he rejected Thompson's charge that the NAACP consisted of outside agitators. Evers noted that at "least one-half of the NAACP membership, is in the South. There has been branches in Mississippi since 1918. [In fact, the] Jackson, Mississippi, Branch was organized in 1926—37 years ago. Therefore, when we talk of the NAACP we are also talking about fellow Mississippians—local home-grown Negro citizens, born and reared in communities such as Jackson."[23] In response to Thompson's claims that if "outside agitators" would leave Jackson alone things would be fine, Evers countered with historical facts. He pointed out that the ideals held by Thompson reflected the historical "position of those who would continue to deny Negro citizens their constitutional rights. . . . Never in its history has The South as a region, without outside pressure, granted the Negro his citizenship rights." After all, it was the result of organizational pressures, Evers noted, and not individual states' desire to bestow equality upon the downtrodden that had led to all the social and political gains achieved thus far.[24]

The foundation of Evers's commitment surfaced time and time again throughout his speech. He maintained from beginning to end that what whites said and what blacks experienced were two different things. He warned city officials that the world had advanced over the past twenty years and new racial concepts had emerged. Evers forewarned of the futility of trying to cordon off the Negro from the rest of the world. Of more importance, black Mississippians were constantly deriving strength from the steady stream of reports of others fighting for freedom throughout the country. "Tonight the Negro plantation worker in the Delta," Evers proclaimed, "knows from his radio and television what happened today all over the world. He knows what black people are doing and he knows what white people are doing. He can see on the 6:00 o'clock news screen the picture of a 3:00 o'clock bite by a police dog. . . . He knows about the new free nations in Africa and knows that a Congo native can be a locomotive engineer, but in Jackson he cannot even drive a garbage truck. He sees black prime ministers and ambassadors, financiers and technicians."[25] Television, for Evers, proved a source of information that allowed black Mississippians a visual internalization of the struggles waged both domestically and internationally, while also further illuminating their personal and group oppression.

Personal oppression lay at the heart of his message and thus the need to challenge it. It was not enough to look outward to understand the challenges to oppression waged by other groups. Evers warned conservative Mississippians that blacks were beginning to look about their home state and compare their problems with those abroad. This proved a powerful awakening, Evers warned, for it intensified personal and group introspection. After looking to see what types of struggles other groups were engaged in, Evers maintained that the "Negro" then began to look "about his home community and what does he see to quote our Mayor, in this 'progressive, beautiful, friendly, prosperous city with an exciting future?' He sees a city where Negro citizens are refused admittance to the City Auditorium and the Coliseum; his children refused a ticket to a good movie in a downtown theater; his wife and children refused service at a lunch counter in a downtown store where they trade; students refused the use of the main public libraries, parks, playgrounds and other tax-supported recreational facilities."[26] The time for change, Evers noted, was upon the state whether people wished to acknowledge it or not.

Throughout his speech, Evers placed Jackson within the overall movement for equality by linking Mississippi residents to the national struggle.

Advancements in communication made it impossible for state officials to keep national events out of the homes of Mississippi's black residents. As a consequence, Evers warned state officials that the social climate had changed. Black Mississippians no longer felt separate from the national movement, and they derived strength from those struggling across the country.

Evers continued comparing and contrasting African Americans' social realities with the rosy depiction of Jackson's race relations Thompson presented earlier. However, he also discussed what the "Negro" wants:

> He wants to get rid of racial segregation in Mississippi life because he knows it has not been good for him nor for the state. . . .

> The Negro citizen wants to register and vote without special handicaps imposed on him alone and we are encouraging him to do so.

> The Negro Mississippian wants more jobs above the menial level in stores where he spends his money. He believes that new industries that have come to Mississippi should employ him above the laboring category.

> He wants the public schools and colleges desegregated so that his children can receive the best education that Mississippi has to offer. He believes additional Negro students should be accepted at Ole Miss and at other colleges. He feels strongly about these and other items although he may not say so publicly.[27]

Evers readily admitted that Jackson could indeed change, but argued that if "there should be resistance, how much better to have turbulence to effect improvement, rather than turbulence to maintain a stand-pat policy." Yet whether the city of Jackson or Mississippi as a whole chose to change or not, he warned, "the years of change are upon us. In the racial picture things will never be as they once were."[28]

Evers understood that whites, in much larger numbers, would have to get involved in the struggle for equality. The following addresses both the heart of his appeal and the effectiveness of his strategy. It also chronicles his subtle but intentional strategy of linking the Jackson movement to increased calls for political and social change at the national level:

> Let me appeal to the consciences of many silent, responsible citizens of the white community who know that a victory for democracy in Jackson will be a victory for democracy everywhere.

> In the words of President John F. Kennedy, speaking at Vanderbilt University, Saturday, May 18, 1963:

"This nation is now engaged in a continuing debate about the rights of a portion of its citizens. That will go on and those rights will expand until the standard first forged by the nation's founders has been reached—and all Americans enjoy equal opportunity and liberty under law. . . . All Americans must be responsible citizens—but some must be more responsible than others, by virtue of their public or their private position[,] their role in the family or community, their prospects for the future or their legacy from the past. Increased responsibility goes with increased ability—for of those to whom much is given, much is required."

To these words, one can only say—Amen.[29]

In one broad stroke, Evers placed the moral conscience, responsibility, and patriotism of white America on the table of civil rights struggle. As a strategy, he used President Kennedy as a mouthpiece to encourage the "many silent, responsible citizens of the white community" to join African Americans' fight for the right to "enjoy equal opportunity and liberty under law." He understood the nature of the white psyche, however, and deduced that better the appeal for joint struggle come, in part, from Kennedy than a direct petition from him alone. Evers realized, as did comedian Dick Gregory while in Greenwood, Mississippi, that many southern whites "hung up" on hate could not bring themselves to do what a black person told them to do.[30]

After his television appearance, things for Evers were never the same. *Ebony* had introduced him to the nation in 1958, but his television debut made him a national civil rights leader and an organizing force in the fight for civil equality. As an added bonus, his television appearance had a positive effect upon the black population of Jackson. His appearance alone signaled a severe crack in what journalist Kay Mills argued had been "an especially effective blackout of African Americans on southern TV stations." African American civil rights activists wanted the influential medium of television to provide impartial coverage on issues of importance to the African American community. By the 1960s, blacks were engaged in a concerted effort "to challenge the rules governing television and the inertia of the agency charged with enforcing them, the Federal Communications Commission."[31] As a consequence, black Mississippians considered Evers's televised speech a collective achievement and exhibited both pride and calm during the days following his WLBT address.[32]

There were both positive and negative reactions to Evers's response to Mayor Thompson. Although many noted the positive differences they saw in the way whites looked at and treated blacks in the immediate days after his speech, the desire of many white Mississippians to hold on to the old

ways of social and political control made it more difficult for white supporters of black advancement to step forward.[33] John Salter admitted that to
"anyone rational there could be no question regarding the sincerity of
Medgar Evers, or the merit of his words." Salter warned, however, that "the
power structure of Jackson, and the system of Mississippi, were not rational
on matters such as this. There were unquestionably those in the white community [to whom Evers had appealed] who subscribed to the essence of
what Medgar had to say, but they remained silent, choked by the same mantle of fear that so long had strangled their community and state."[34]

This reality did not deter Evers's plans to stay and change the things he
did not like about Mississippi. In fact, he seemed more determined than ever
to speak for those who dared not speak out for fear of the consequences. He
considered the fight for civil equality in Mississippi a personal struggle for
the well-being of every man, woman, and child. He could not, in good conscience, abandon Mississippi and he considered it his mission to make
Jackson a better place for his children as well. He sincerely believed that if
he dedicated his life to struggling for social and political change, Jackson
could become a better place. His optimism manifested while speaking with
a reporter for the *New York Times*. One day, Evers noted, when "my sons
are grown . . . they're going to find Jackson even better than New York
City."[35]

Many argue that Evers's televised speech catapulted him into national
leadership. His friend Cornelius Turner, however, believes the speech did
much more than that. In many ways, the speech provided Medgar with "a
new sense of who he really was, and what he was all about, what he was
trying to do."[36] By putting it all on the table in a national format, Evers
increased national attention on Mississippi and the civil rights movement
expanding across the state. However, his television appearance also had a
negative side. Evers was now recognizable to all Mississippians and that
visibility made it more difficult for him to disguise his travels to various
Mississippi towns to document brutality and organize support for ongoing
projects. Fred Beard, the manager of WLBT, recalled that after Evers's
appearance the station "received numerous telephone calls." He heard
about forty of those. Some of these "calls contained threats to do bodily
harm to Evers."[37] The potential for physical violence directed against him
and his family increased dramatically after May 20 because of the recognition television afforded.

The social realities of African Americans Evers outlined in his response
to Mayor Thompson underscore both his commitment to changing the conditions in Mississippi and his belief that effective change could take place.
Death was also a potential reality and it was one that he understood and

accepted. Evers believed that the possibility of death, however, was no excuse to refrain from the struggle to make life better. As a consequence, he proclaimed that "as long as God gives me strength to work and try to make things real for my children, I'm going to work for it—even if it means making the ultimate sacrifice."[38] For Evers, death was a worthy tradeoff for having stood as a man in the cause of freedom. He attempted to allay the fears others had for his safety by acknowledging that if "I die, it will be for a good cause. I've been fighting for America just as much as the soldiers in Vietnam."[39] For Evers, Jackson had been the battleground and casualties were to be expected. Yet, he believed his fight was a just one and, in 1963, television connected blacks in Mississippi with the various struggles for equality raging across the nation. Birmingham, Alabama, showcased the extent to which white supremacists were willing to go to maintain segregation and political dominance. By highlighting the intensity of those engaged in civil rights struggle in other southern cities, Birmingham provided Evers with an additional means for encouraging black Mississippians to increase their activism.

In 1963, Birmingham could boast of its thriving manufacturing and metal industries. Although the city enjoyed industrial successes, it also had a history of violent racial turmoil. The bombing of black homes, as a means of intimidating black residents, was as much a part of the city's history as its industrial development. African Americans responded to the violence with both individual and organized resistance. Civil rights struggle had been a staple in the city and since the successful Montgomery Bus Boycott, that struggle had steadily increased.

In June 1956, a group of ministers, including the charismatic and dynamic Fred Shuttlesworth, organized the Alabama Christian Movement for Human Rights. The organization fought racism and all the physical manifestations that came with it. The ACMHR, and its direct-action tactics, altered the structure of civil rights struggle in the city. The historian Glenn T. Eskew maintained that its creation "marked a clear departure from traditional black protest in Birmingham and foreshadowed the nonviolent direct action tactics of the student sit-ins and Freedom Rides."[40] The ACMHR was central to the Birmingham movement.

By May 1963, Birmingham seemed to be in political disarray. Conservatives were divided regarding proper tactics for handling the growing African American protest movement; business elites also split over tactics and devout segregationist Theophilus Eugene "Bull" Connor lost his bid for mayor to opponent Albert Boutwell. African Americans had played a crucial role in the election and were, more than likely, responsible for Connor's loss. The mayoral race divided business and labor supporters. Despite the election results, "the legal retainers of the iron and steel industry," remarked Eskew, "told Connor and the other city commissioners to remain in office while they fought the legality of the new mayor-council form of government."[41] Regardless of the political chaos developing in Birmingham, civil rights leaders understood that the problems African Americans suffered continued, and they could not help but recognize the urgent need to push forward in the fight for full citizenship rights.

In 1963, the one thing Birmingham's white leadership did not want to occur, in fact happened: Fred Shuttlesworth again invited Martin Luther King Jr. to Birmingham to help with protests and this time he accepted. There were now two major civil rights organizations operating in the city: ACMHR and SCLC. In addition, Birmingham had been dealing with an aggressive student movement, one that had initiated a selective buying campaign the previous year. Miles College student Frank Dukes had proved instrumental in getting the boycott off the ground and the pressure placed on area businesses had brought about limited concessions (e.g., the removal of Jim Crow signs, etc.) however temporary they proved to be.[42] With King on the scene, however, protests focused the type of national attention upon Birmingham that neither Connor nor the city could control.

King and the SCLC decided that the Birmingham campaign would begin on March 14, 1963, when it was believed that Connor would have lost the mayoral race and thus would not be a factor; the date would be pushed back to April 3 when Connor placed second, forcing the runoff with Boutwell. The historian Andrew Manis noted that King assigned Minister Wyatt Tee Walker to oversee the Birmingham project and "Walker spent some sixty days in Birmingham planning the logistical details of the demonstrations."[43] He spent a great deal of that time drumming up support from area ministers and educating black residents on what to expect. Walker also carried out reconnaissance missions on area businesses so that organizers would know the layout of the land, surrounding restaurants and their floor plans, and additional targets if chosen ones fell through.

On April 3, seven African Americans walked into Britling Cafeteria and sat down at the lunch counter and requested service. This action occurred at other establishments throughout the day and individuals were either arrested or lunch counters simply closed rather than deal with what whites viewed as an increasingly growing social mess. Demonstrations continued during the month of April and expanded to include the combined use of economic boycotts, sit-ins, and marches. However, none produced the types of national attention or citywide support the ACMHR or the SCLC hoped for. Wyatt Tee Walker understood this and made plans to turn up the heat on city officials that would produce confrontation for the cameras. The April 12 arrest of Fred Shuttlesworth, Martin King Jr., and Ralph Abernathy brought additional attention to the protest movement. The men had been arrested for ignoring an injunction order signed by Judge William A. Jenkins forbidding 133 people specifically from engaging in protest activities of any kind. King's name, the historian Taylor Branch noted, "was the first-named object of . . . [this] sweeping injunction."[44] While incarcerated, King wrote his famed "Letter from Birmingham Jail," which defended the movement against its detractors and defended his campaign actions and the incessant need for continued nonviolent protest. Yet through the actions of children came an end to the race relations stalemate in Birmingham, and their participation provided a literal meaning to the phrase "and the children shall lead."

On May 2, hundreds of children, some as young as six years old, marched out of Sixteenth Street Baptist Church and took their place in the overall movement. Many individuals were against the use of children and openly castigated King for allowing it. King also seemed somewhat unsure of the turn the campaign had taken but saw no other choice at that point. For a brief moment, the sight of hundreds of children marching confused Connor, but ultimately he felt he had no choice but to arrest the students; before the end of the day they had filled the jails and rendered them ineffective. The next day students assembled and proceeded to march to Kelly Ingram Park. Connor, the surprise having worn off, was in no mood to kowtow to disruptive children and attempted to regain control of the situation. As a solution, he ordered members of the fire department to spray the marchers with high-powered water hoses and before the day ended, had provided his police force with the O.K. to turn loose police dogs on the children. News outlets caught the event on camera and the attacks received national and international news play. African American spectators also retaliated by throwing bricks and rocks at the police. In a move to avoid further bloodshed and continued economic losses, negotiations between civil rights leaders and representatives of some of the most powerful and influential whites in the state had produced social, economic, and employment concessions that King, Shuttlesworth, and Abernathy announced at a news conference on May 10. City officials agreed to desegregate lunch counters, rest and fitting rooms, and drinking fountains in downtown department stores within ninety days. They also agreed to the hiring and promotion of blacks in stores and industries as well as clerks and salesmen within sixty days. City leaders agreed to the release of jailed protestors through bond or personal recognizance and, within two weeks, the establishment of a biracial committee.[45] The compromise ended the Birmingham campaign although individuals such as Shuttlesworth were not completely satisfied with the settlement. He believed that it did not go far enough. The Birmingham movement, however, had a profound impact outside of the city and in particular on the Mississippi movement.

Dramatic protests and violent responses in Birmingham proved one of the most crucial televised events during the modern civil rights movement. King and members of the SCLC and ACMHR understood the power of television and used it to project the violence African Americans suffered to a worldwide audience.[46] If the world appeared in awe of and disgusted by the violence in Alabama, black Mississippians were also disturbed and used the televised accounts to fuel their own struggles in Mississippi. Evers proved a keen practitioner of media "spin" and used it to publicize the battle in Mississippi as much as King, Shuttlesworth, and their respective organizations were doing in Alabama.[47] However, televised or not, the revolution in Jackson continued and animosity between Thompson and the NAACP intensified.

In the immediate days after Evers's televised speech, the NAACP and the office of the mayor were locked in a battle regarding participation in a planned meeting between black leaders and the city council. Evers went on record regarding the farce that Thompson's handpicked representatives for the proposed meeting symbolized and how the general black community supported the position of the NAACP. Thompson agreed to meet with a select group, and both he and leaders of the black community compiled a list of acceptable representatives.

On May 21, Evers and other leaders such as A. D. Beittel, president of Tougaloo College, and Dean Jones of Campbell College held a mass meeting at the Pearl Street AME Church to elect representatives who could meet with Thompson and effectively convey and defend the interests of the black community. The fourteen chosen representatives included Evers, I. S. Sanders, and Salter. As many expected, Thompson rejected a majority of the representatives chosen at the Pearl Street meeting. He objected to ten of the fourteen members elected but accepted Sanders, Reverends Leon Whitney and G. R. Haughton, and funeral director E. W. Banks. To these, he added ten of his choosing, which included *Jackson Advocate* editor Percy Greene, Jackson State College president Jacob Reddix, and attorney Sydney Tharp. The others he chose consisted of individuals who either supported the Thompson administration or people he considered nonthreatening such as "Joseph Albright," the *Crisis* reported, "a public relations man who worked with the Mississippi State Sovereignty Commission." Evers acknowledged that the group could not guarantee acceptance of the mayor's selection. Of more importance, he maintained that the black community could not allow the mayor to "pick our leaders." The result, Evers argued, would be "'hit and-miss discussions with hand-picked colored citizens personally known and approved' by city officials." Although he admitted that the biracial group was ready "to begin negotiations as in other progressive cities," he warned, however, that blacks were not going to "wait a week or two weeks for him [Thompson] to make up his mind. Within the very near future we will begin to picket, to march and to sit-in." In fact, on May 24, black and white clergymen, "for the first time in Jackson," met to discuss the racial problems in the city and "agreed to devote their sermons the following Sunday . . . to this issue." After a few alterations, the group met with government officials on May 27 but could not agree and talks broke down.[48]

During the morning hours of May 28, violence erupted at a local Woolworth store when sit-in protestors demanded service. Anne Moody, a Tougaloo student and participant of the sit-in, noted that the protest had been organized down to the second. Nothing spectacular happened until students from a local white high school arrived and attacked the protesters seated at the counter. As the Tougaloo students were assaulted and yanked from their seats, other protesters, some white, quickly occupied the vacated seats. The students were supported by Tougaloo faculty Lois Chaffee and John Salter, the latter who sustained serious facial injuries.[49] Evers found out after the Woolworth incident that several FBI agents had observed the events but had done nothing to quell the violence. The success and publicity of the boycott and Evers's connection to it increased his vulnerability. Whites heard and saw him speaking publicly about its goals, strategies, justification, and the resolve boycotters had toward creating meaningful social and political change. This, of course, made it all the more difficult for those around him to provide sufficient protection.[50]

In response to the negative media coverage regarding the Woolworth debacle, it took only a few hours after the sit-in demonstrations for Thompson to agree to meet with elected representatives from the black community. He now hoped to discuss solutions that would help to bring an end to the racial issues dividing city residents. The meeting took place at City Hall where Thompson agreed to accept Negro applications for policeman and school crossing guard jobs. He also noted that public facilities would be opened to everyone and all Jim Crow signs would be removed from public buildings. The mayor announced, however, that the matter of school desegregation "was in Federal Court, and was a matter for the courts . . . [to] decide."[51] Moments after the assembly concluded, Thompson reneged on the agreement, claiming he had been misrepresented. Sit-in demonstrations began almost immediately. After Thompson's claims of "misrepresentation" went public, the NAACP held a meeting at the Pearl Street AME Church with an overflow audience of two thousand attending.

Evers addressed the crowd, apprising them of Mayor Thompson's recent act of treachery and demanded to know who in the audience stood ready to march. In response to his query, the two thousand or so individuals rose as a single unit.[52]

During the early morning hours of May 29, a firebomb was thrown onto the Evers's porch. Myrlie extinguished the flames before any serious damage was done to the home or the family vehicle. The police ruled the incident a prank and suggested the Evers were not in any real danger. Protests continued and on the following day nineteen more participants were arrested for picketing.[53] For Evers, the firebombing brought the dangers of his work home and it required a reevaluation of what family life meant in the struggle for equality in the South.

After the firebombing, Evers spent an hour teaching their children safety tactics and what to listen for in case of attack. Both he and Myrlie feared that the firebombing would cause a bit of anxiety among the children. However, Evers believed "that with all the talk they undoubtedly overheard, with all of the tension of our lives, it might actually be a relief for them to feel that there was something positive they could do to protect themselves."[54] As a consequence, he reverted to his military training and taught the children how to fall without injury and how to listen for things out of the ordinary. In the event of an attack, Evers placed the responsibility for the youngest child Van on his nine- and eight-year-old brother and sister who were to ensure his safety and security. As an added precaution, Evers had the children walk throughout the house and decide on the safest place to be if attacked. After some investigation, they all agreed that the bathtub would be the safest place in the house to hide if attacked again.[55]

Despite the violent responses directed at the boycott, sit-ins, and the Evers family, direct-action tactics intensified over the following weeks and Mayor Thompson responded. Thompson refused to be moved by the demonstrations and aired his defiance in the media, citing Tougaloo College as "the cancer in this whole thing." In an obvious reference to the previous meeting with the NAACP committee, he reiterated that "there would be no applications taken for Negro police, nor for Negro policewomen[,] school crossing guards, and added [that] 'there may be applications for 500 white policemen, though.'" Evers let the Jackson public know that "the Negro community" had called a meeting. An unidentified spokesperson announced that Roy Wilkins would give the address and would more than likely participate in "some of the direct action projects."[56] Demonstrations continued and arrests mounted. When mass demonstrations led to arrests, the protestors were taken to stockades at the local fairgrounds where two large "exhibit buildings" were used as holding pens. The safety of individuals confined there caused Evers a great deal of additional worry.[57]

The Supreme Court provided Evers hope and a renewed sense that things were about to change for the better. During the spring of 1963, the Supreme Court issued a number of key rulings addressing civil rights cases and the various demonstrative tactics employed in civil rights protests. Evers was quite aware of the change in the Court's view on social protests and had hinted to some of these changes in his televised address. Within the speech, Evers pointed out that it is in the "American tradition to demonstrate, to assemble peacefully and to petition the government for a redress of grievances. Such a petition may legitimately take the form of picketing, although in Jackson, Negroes are immediately arrested when they attempt to exercise this constitutional right."[58] He later notified Mayor Thompson by telegram that "Monday's sweeping decision by [the] Supreme Court gives additional support to our legal position and right to demonstrate peaceably and otherwise protest. We are fully prepared to do this, if necessary."[59] The constitutional right of peaceful assembly and protest for African Americans of which Evers spoke received judicial support in *Peterson v. City of Greenville.*

Much as *Brown v. Board of Education* became the key case in a cluster of desegregation cases in the 1950s, *Peterson v. City of Greenville* represented a key decision in a collection of sit-in rulings the Court issued in the spring of 1963. On August 9, 1960, ten African Americans had entered the S. H. Kress store in Greenville, South Carolina, and sat at the segregated lunch counter with the purpose of receiving service. In response, the store manager closed the lunch counter and employees called the police, who arrested the group and took them to police headquarters. The group was found guilty of trespassing and fined one hundred dollars or "in lieu thereof serve" thirty days in jail. The Greenville County Court dismissed their appeal and the South Carolina Supreme Court upheld the dismissal. The U.S. Supreme Court, however, "granted certiorari [a Court review] to consider the substantial federal questions presented by the record."[60]

On May 20, 1963, the Supreme Court, led by Chief Justice Earl Warren, ruled that the convictions were unconstitutional and set the verdicts aside. However, the nature of the language used in the Court opinion was of more importance to Evers and the civil rights movement as a whole. Regarding the issue of segregation in public facilities and the right of an individual to challenge the practice through peaceful protest, Warren noted that

> It cannot be denied that here the City of Greenville, an agency of the State, has provided by its ordinance that the decision as to whether a restaurant facility is to be operated on a desegregated basis is to be reserved to it. When the State has commanded a particular result, it has saved to itself the power to determine that result and thereby "to a significant extent" has "become involved" in it, and, in fact, has removed

that decision from the sphere of private choice. It has thus effectively determined that a person owning, managing or controlling an eating place is left with no choice of his own but must segregate his white and Negro patrons. The Kress management, in deciding to exclude Negroes, did precisely what the city law required.

Consequently these convictions cannot stand, even assuming, as respondent contends, that the manager would have acted as he did independently of the existence of the ordinance. The State will not be heard to make this contention in support of the convictions. For the convictions had the effect, which the State cannot deny, of enforcing the ordinance passed by the City of Greenville, the agency of the State. When a state agency passes a law compelling persons to discriminate against other persons because of race, and the State's criminal processes are employed in a way which enforces the discrimination mandated by that law, such a palpable violation of the Fourteenth Amendment cannot be saved by attempting to separate the mental urges of the discriminators.[61]

Here, the Supreme Court tied individual states to the practice of segregation and resisted attempts by states to suggest that segregation began and ended with business proprietors' decisions on the matter.

The key piece of testimony in the case came from the Kress manager, who stated that he closed the lunch counter and ordered the youth to leave because "integrated service was 'contrary to local customs' of segregation at lunch counters" in Greenville and violated the city ordinance.[62] Since the Court ruled that the ten sit-in protestors were justified in their challenge of segregation through direct action in South Carolina, Evers reasoned that the sit-in and boycott movement in Jackson also fell under the umbrella of the Fourteenth Amendment. Thus, the actions of the city and its police force, who were impeding legitimate forms of resistance, were illegal in the eyes of the Court. Proponents of segregation had much to be concerned about as the winds of change blew hard and fast throughout the South during the early 1960s.

In 1963, segregationists witnessed an emergence of renewed support for the African American struggle for social and political equality. Seven days after *Peterson v. City of Greenville,* the Supreme Court ruled in *Watson v. Memphis* that the city of Memphis could no longer wait to fully desegregate its parks and playgrounds (25 were open without regard to race at the time of the trial). The Court rejected any notion that desegregating the city's 131 parks (23 were undeveloped raw lands) could lead to violence or racial strife. The Court noted that the "all deliberate speed" dictum of *Brown II* did not apply to the desegregation of public recreational areas because of the lack of potential structural problems associated with school desegregation.[63] The Court reasoned that the desegregation of "parks and other recreational facilities does not present the same kinds of cognizable difficulties inhering in elimination of racial classification in schools, at which attendance is compulsory, the adequacy of teachers and facilities crucial, and questions of geographic assignment often of major significance."[64] Again, the language of the ruling proved important to Evers and the legitimacy of the Jackson movement.

The Court opinion in *Watson v. Memphis*, delivered by Justice Arthur J. Goldberg, was comprehensive in scope and explanation. In part, the Court acknowledged the significance of the *Brown* decision, but noted its limitations where issues of the current day were concerned:

> Most importantly, of course, it must be recognized that even the delay countenanced by *Brown* was a necessary, albeit significant, adaptation of the usual principle that any deprivation of constitutional rights calls for prompt rectification. The rights here asserted are, like all such rights, *present* rights; they are not merely hopes to some *future* enjoyment of some formalistic constitutional promise. The basic guarantees of our Constitution are warrants for the here and now and, unless there is an overwhelmingly compelling reason, they are to be promptly fulfilled. The second *Brown* decision is but a narrowly drawn, and carefully limited, qualification upon usual precepts of constitutional adjudication and is not to be unnecessarily expanded in application.

The Court deduced that since the city had failed to justify further delay, the "continued denial to petitioners of the use of city facilities solely because of their race is without warrant." The Court maintained that "Today, no less than 50 years ago, the solution to the problems growing out of race relations 'cannot be promoted by depriving citizens of their constitutional rights and privileges.'"[65]

The Court rejected requests from Memphis officials for additional time to desegregate its recreational facilities and, in essence, ordered immediate desegregation. Michael Klarman contends that this "was the justices' first commentary on the pace of desegregation since *Brown II*." It cannot be ignored, as Klarman points out, that the Court decision "came in the same month that Birmingham street demonstrations made civil rights the nation's top political priority."[66] Many African Americans in Mississippi, including Medgar Evers, were aware of these rulings and used them to advance their activism in the state. Evers had pointed out the legitimacy of peaceful protest on May 20 and a few days later challenged the city of Jackson to defy the edicts of the U.S. Supreme Court. In that challenge, teachers had always played an important role in Evers's resistance strategy against discrimination.

Despite teachers' important role in the black community, Evers had worked extremely hard to bring them into the movement. Since teachers were subject to employment pressures as state workers, many were reluctant to get involved with Evers and some avoided him altogether. Henry Jay Kirksey, editor and printer of the Mississippi Teachers Association Journal, chose not to avoid Evers but rather to work with him. Kirksey (who would be elected to the state senate in 1979) began working for the Teachers Association in 1961 but the job ended in June 1963. He recalled that he and Evers often met to share "some ideas about how we should go about turning things around for Blacks in the profession, particularly in teaching since that was the largest professional group of Blacks in the state." They would often meet at the Teachers Association Building located across the street from Jackson State College, which, Kirksey recalled, "disturbed the leadership of the Teachers Association who told me that if I wanted to have any kind of relationship with Medgar Evers I was going to have to go down to his office and not bring him there."[67] Despite the reluctance of some teachers to get involved openly with the civil rights movement in Jackson, students were more than willing to tackle the system head-on. In light of the Supreme Court decision on peaceful protest, the youth of Jackson dared the city to restrain their efforts. Subsequently, protests involving the youth increased.

Many young African Americans experienced the racial turmoil that had inflamed Jackson for the past few years and were now vested in the struggle for change. What was surprising in May 1963, however, was the involvement of much younger individuals and their willingness to face the police and endure their use of police dogs. On May 30, students from Lanier High School began singing freedom songs on school grounds, and before long their impromptu form of melodic protest attracted dozens of supporters who clamored out of class to join in. The large gathering attracted the attention of police officers, who responded after a few passes by the school.

The Jackson Police Department used billy clubs and dogs to drive the students back into the building. Parents who heard about the ruckus and came to pick up their children were also victimized by the police.[68] Evers contacted the Justice Department and protested the beatings at Lanier High School. It was at this point that Evers realized that to effectively bring attention to the abuses blacks suffered, area ministers would have to actively participate in the demonstrations going on downtown.[69] Despite the violence directed against them, the students were far from defeated. In fact, their efforts in the struggle stirred up the emotions of the community and its leadership.

On May 31, approximately six hundred African American high school students gathered at the Farish Street Baptist Church. Upon arrival, they received words of encouragement from Medgar and John Salter. The children had been well versed regarding the rules of boycotting and readily emptied their pockets. Reverend S. Leon Whitney, pastor of Farish Street Baptist, examined the presented contents and removed anything that police might construe as dangerous or a potential weapon. As a means of further demonstrating their loyalty to the country and their rights as citizens, each student grabbed a miniature American flag and marched toward Capitol Street. Before they arrived, however, they were met by a battery of city policemen, sheriff's deputies, and highway patrolmen.[70]

The police charged the group, shooting above their heads and beating many as they ceremoniously stripped them of their American flags. The officers placed them under arrest, the *New York Times* reported, "for parading without a permit" and transported them by "patrol wagons, canvas-covered trucks and garbage trucks" to the infamous state fairgrounds for detention.[71] Evers witnessed the entire event and likened it to Nazi Germany with the police playing the role of storm troopers. The event angered him and he told Roy Wilkins the time had come to request that President Kennedy send in federal troops. Wilkins not only disagreed with this premise, but believed that the request should not be made. In the end, they decided to ask for United States marshals.[72] The incarcerated students occupied Evers's every waking moment. He knew they depended upon him and he was determined to protect them as best he could.

Medgar Evers had promised students, like Minnie Watson, that when they were arrested the NAACP would get them out, but it was proving harder and harder to get bond money for so many jailed protestors. When considering that many of those arrested were beaten and jailed without medical attention, it is easy to understand how this situation amplified his personal worries and level of irritability. On June 1, responding to the mass arrests, Evers wired President Kennedy apprising him of the gross mistreatment of black children arrested by the police and "behind [the] hog wire confines of Jackson Concentration Camp."[73] He further reported to White House officials that "City, county, and State Law officers" were involved in the atrocities perpetrated at the fairgrounds. He urged President Kennedy to begin an "immediate investigation by Department of Justice agents of these denials of constitutional rights to peaceful demonstrations and protests."[74] Although Evers requested assistance from the White House regarding the arrests, his requests were far from spurious or meek suggestions. He, in essence, demanded that the federal government adhere to current judiciary law enacted by the recent Supreme Court rulings. The Jackson Police Department, however, was not content with just making arrests; they were determined to make a statement that required a strong and sustained show of force.

Responding to the continued protests, Thompson warned that the city would not tolerate further demonstrations and that city jails could hold up to 10,000 protestors if necessary. The earlier arrests of six girls, five African Americans and one white, who were given six-month jail sentences and fined five hundred dollars for attempting to integrate "two all-white restaurants" bolstered his staunch position on civil rights activity. The *New York Times* reported that before the student-led march to Capitol Street had taken place, Jackson police arrested seventy-five students at Brinkley High School on their way to Farish Street to join the main student body. As an added deterrent against protests, Mayor Thompson announced that if the jails reached their human capacity, the fairgrounds had been revamped to hold 2,500 individuals and any overflow "could be taken 160 miles to the state penitentiary at Parchman, Miss."[75] There was no turning back or slowing down for Evers once the children took their place in the struggle. He made it clear to all involved that he was fully vested in the outcome and that now was the time for adults to join the struggle en masse.

Evers was instrumental in planning and directing the boycotts in Jackson, and he routinely did whatever necessary to secure bond monies for those arrested. His position was much more than administrative. Evers physically participated in the boycotts, and that participation resulted in his arrest on June 1, 1963, for picketing in front of the F. W. Woolworth store. Roy Wilkins and Jackson branch member Helen Wilcher were also arrested. The arrival and participation of Roy Wilkins in direct-action activities underscored the significance the NAACP now placed on Mississippi as an area ripe for change. It also demonstrated a stark departure from the established strategic policies of the NAACP. The three had been picketing only a few minutes before they encountered a "dozen helmeted policemen." During the picket, Evers wore a placard around his neck with the words "End Brutality in Jackson—NAACP" emblazoned across the front for all to see. Despite the earlier ruling of the Supreme Court, the three were taken to the city jail and booked "under an 1892 Mississippi anti-trust law." Each received a felony charge of prohibiting "free trade and commerce" and were released after NAACP attorney Jack Young posted "an unprecedented cash bond of $1,000" each. The more serious charge of prohibiting trade levied against the three, rather than the customary charge of "obstructing the sidewalk," apparently resulted from the placard worn by Roy Wilkins, which read "Don't Buy on Capitol Street."[76]

Jackson officials had plans to stop the forward momentum of the Jackson movement. City prosecutors challenged NAACP declarations of citywide judicial misconduct and unlawful arrest of protestors who sought to integrate local restaurants. Responding to the recent court decision, prosecutors proclaimed that "the court's ruling applied only to cities where a policy of segregation was made official in a city ordinance." They pointed out that the city of Jackson had no such ordinance and thus enjoyed exemption from the court's ruling in *Peterson v. Greenville.*[77] Upon their release, Roy Wilkins and Evers went to the Masonic Temple where they met with Salter, Gloster Current, and others. Wilkins, with support from Current, announced that the marches should end at least for a while. Only after pressure from Salter and others did he agree to their continuance. Evers remained quiet throughout the discussion and again found himself caught between the desires of the grassroots who were ready for action and the NAACP leadership who wanted things to slow down.[78] His tumultuous position between the old and young leadership in the burgeoning movement took on a more ominous feel after the results of an NAACP strategy meeting.

During a June 2 meeting, Gloster Current notified all present that the "Jackson movement was entering a new phase." The new phase would emphasize smaller demonstrations and implement a planned series of NAACP court actions that promised positive results. The meeting contained a few young people and John Salter. Salter was strategy committee co-chairman but was ousted in favor of a systemized rotating chairmanship. The new direction and its de-emphasis on mass protests as a tactic hurt morale, and many individuals viewed this new direction as the end of the active phase of the Jackson movement. As a consequence, "people were withdrawing their interest, and fear and fear-based apathy were again becoming paramount," Salter recalled. The meeting also represented an intensification of factionalism within the movement itself and this distracted it from its overall goals.[79]

As if there were not enough to occupy his attention during these tense moments, Evers faced personal community problems that impacted his family life and the community structure he envisioned for them. Some community residents had objected to the Everses moving into the neighborhood from the beginning because of his affiliation with the NAACP. As social activism and retaliation in Jackson heightened, a number of residents wanted the Evers out of the neighborhood immediately and made their feelings known. After the firebombing, Myrlie noted that some of their neighbors went around claiming they "knew it was go'n happen, now all of us might get burned out, or hurt, or shot." As a consequence, the Everses faced a certain level of ostracism as the boycotts and mass arrests increased. Evers exclaimed that with things in Jackson the way they were, he did not have time to deal with a community uproar or the discomfort individuals felt because of his living within their midst. When Myrlie approached him about the way the communal tide was turning, he pointed out the irony. At the very moment that some community members were complaining about their presence in the neighborhood, Evers noted that

> our children [and] our elderly are down at the fairgrounds behind barbed wire with food being served in a tin tub and the police spitting in it before they put it down; and people losing their houses because their names have been printed in the newspapers and their bosses have called them in and fired them and the banks have said you have 24 hours in which to pay your mortgage in full, I don't have time to deal with that little stuff.[80]

During the coming days, Evers intensified his public schedule and seemed to be everywhere at once: a meeting in Jackson, a rally in the Delta, meetings with government officials, continuous dialogue with government representatives in Washington, D.C., and NAACP officials in New York, and collaborative efforts with various civil rights organizations and leaders working within the Jackson movement. Many wondered, as did Myrlie, just how long he could last at this blazing pace. The amount of stress he worked under appeared to Myrlie to be much "more than a [single] human being could take."[81] If the month of May proved busy, June offered neither Medgar Evers nor the city of Jackson respite. It did, though, suggest that positive change was on the horizon and Medgar remained at the forefront of that move toward change.

On June 3, Mayor Thompson announced that applications were being accepted for black policemen and crossing guards. Many hoped this indicated that the mayor's office was now looking to repair the relationship between blacks and city officials. Evers, along with I. S. Sanders, Charles A. Jones, and G. R. Haughton, announced that acceptance of the mayor's plan of action was "conditioned on . . . [his] agreement . . . to appoint a bi-racial committee of prominent white and Negro citizens, the Negro constituency of which must be selected from a democratically approved list as previously submitted. Without these assurances, we cannot presume that protest measures will cease."[82] Thompson failed to organize the biracial committee or to keep his word regarding the hiring of black police officers and protests continued while arrests soared into the hundreds. When the city could not break the current protests happening downtown or the organizing tactics of Medgar Evers outright, it made such actions illegal and employed the courts to support its actions.

Although Thompson claimed that the boycotts were failing due to a lack of support, city officials went to court on June 6 seeking a boycott injunction. They claimed that the boycotts increased the propensity for injuries or loss of life of the policemen attempting to maintain law and order, as well as increased the risk of significant damage to city property. The court granted the injunction prohibiting any further demonstrations.[83] Despite the court order, demonstrations continued and Evers spoke out against the contradiction of the mayor and the legitimacy of the injunction itself. His statement proved both analytical and defiant, yet it epitomized who Evers had always been: a diplomatic but determined individual committed to equality and fair play and willing to push forward rather than sit still and seek material comfort. In response to the injunction, Evers announced that

> Jackson officials once more documented their unique capacity for speaking from two sides of their mouths today by seeking to enjoin NAACP sparked demonstrations and selective buying activities currently being executed to expose Jackson's rough and rigid racial abuses. Why spank a tottering infant? Why enjoin a "faltering" movement, as they describe it.

> White leaders in Jackson gave the world the answer today. Their injunction proceedings have proven that our movement is sharp, vital and inclusive. They are hurting inside. This is their outcry.

> Our attorneys are studying the language of the injunction papers and will advise us of what action to take.[84]

Evers again used the media to uplift the movement and to keep the nation focused upon the abuses perpetrated by those determined to maintain a stand-pat policy of segregation and inequality.

Regarding the court-ordered ban on demonstrations, NAACP chief counsel Robert Carter immediately set to work to challenge the merits of the injunction. On June 7, the NAACP "filed a motion to dissolve and or stay execution of the temporary injunction." Judge J. C. Stennett denied the motion. In response to the ruling, it was averred at a press conference attended by Carter, that Jackson Negroes

> have been and are being denied free access to public facilities, equal educational opportunities, the exercise of their voting rights without discrimination based upon race and the right to lead their personal lives and to pursue their business and professional occupations free from the oneness of racial discrimination. . . .

> Denial of these constitutional rights cannot occur by state authorities of whatever description and we, therefore, regard the injunction as patently invalid and without force or effect. The Chancery Court has

been advised that peaceful activities and protests against racial segregation will continue.[85]

At this point, Evers was also involved in litigation for an injunction against the city as well.

On June 7, the NAACP filed a lawsuit in the United States District Court on behalf of Evers, Wilkins, "and others" against fourteen "city, county, and state officials" including Mississippi governnor Ross Barnett, Mayor Allen Thompson, chief of police W. D. Rayfield, and state attorney general Joe T. Patterson. The suit sought a federal injunction "to restrain the defendants from interfering with the plaintiffs and the people they represent in exercising their rights of freedom of speech, peaceful assembly and picketing." The suit also directed the district court to "compel the state officials to register the NAACP as a foreign corporation authorized to do business in Mississippi."[86] It seemed that Evers now had what he had long hoped for—an active NAACP participating in civil rights struggles at the street level while ratcheting up its litigation intensity to support direct grassroots action. As a consequence, Evers resorted to past tactics of organizing that produced massive support and brought in well-known and respected celebrities to keep the fires of resistance burning bright.

On the night of June 7, Evers attended a mass rally with more than twenty-five hundred people crowding into the Masonic Temple auditorium. It seemed as if the fear that Evers had battled for so long disappeared as people jammed the halls despite the presence of policemen patrolling inside and outside the Temple. Lena Horne was one of the celebrity speakers and her words inspired the audience to continue struggling for freedom. Horne noted that "the battle . . . being fought here in Jackson, as elsewhere in the South, is our nation's primary crisis. Let it be understood that the courage and grim determination of the Negro people in these cities of the South have challenged the moral integrity of the entire nation." The concerted challenge of African Americans had, in essence, put the nation on trial for its lackadaisical approach to civil rights. She further informed the captivated audience of how safe Medgar Evers made her feel upon arriving in Jackson and how good the people of Jackson must feel to have a leader such as him. The crowd erupted with a deafening round of applause at these words of praise for their field secretary.[87] Evers, true to form, chose to focus on the task at hand. He admonished the crowd that it is

> not enough just to sit here tonight and voice your approval and clap your hands and shed your tears and sing and then go out and do nothing about this struggle. Freedom has never been free. Those who can do nothing else can at least help to raise bail money for those who are still confined. There is something for everybody to do. . . .

I love my children . . . and I love my wife with all my heart. And I would die, and die gladly, if that would make a better life for them.[88]

The crowd respected Evers's loyalty, accepted the depth of his commitment, and understood the underlying meaning of his message for continued action. Myrlie admitted, however, that when it came to his life she "loved him too much for that kind of understanding."[89]

In June 1963, Medgar Wiley Evers had worked almost nine years as NAACP field secretary, trying to expose the nation to the extreme debauchery, lack of respect for human life, and random violence perpetrated against black people in Mississippi. During that same time he had also worked nonstop to link the civil rights struggle in Mississippi to the national struggle for equality. Over time, he hoped to overwhelm the army of segregation with an opposing force endowed with superior numbers, multiple strategies, and exceptional leaders. In the first half of 1963, Evers saw his lifelong work of fighting for social and political equality bearing rich fruit that promised a continued resistance movement in Mississippi. Whether he lived to see its conclusion or not, he was never more satisfied with the efforts of black Mississippians than in 1963, while those who opposed him and the growing movement for equality had never been more concerned.

8.

Mississippi, Murder, and Medgar

OUR DOMESTIC KILLING FIELDS

*One day we will not have to hang our heads in shame or hold
our breath when the name Mississippi is mentioned, fearing the
worst. But, instead, we will be anticipating the best.*
　　　　　　　　　　　　　　　　　　—Medgar Evers

*I may be going to heaven or hell. . . . But I'll be going from
Jackson.*
　　　　　　　　　　　　　　　　　　—Medgar Evers

*As you can see, I do not plan to leave. I am anchoring myself
here for better or for worse (I hope better), but if worse comes I'll
be in the middle of it.*
　　　　　　　　　　　　　　　　　　—Medgar Evers

*For when I fall I shall rise in deathless dedication. When I stagger
under the wound of your paid assassins I shall be whole again in
deathless triumph!*
　　　　　　　　　　　　　　　　　—Margaret Walker Alexander

*Those who do nothing are inviting shame as well as violence.
Those who act boldly are recognizing right as well as reality.*
　　　　　　　　　　　　　　　　　　—John F. Kennedy

FOR MEDGAR EVERS, June 11, 1963, proved to be just as busy a day as every other day had been during the whirlwind that would be the last two weeks of his life. As usual, he spent time at his office preparing for the mass meeting scheduled for later that evening. Gloster Current was also in town and Evers felt the added responsibility of ensuring that Current had access to whatever he needed to make his trip to Mississippi a successful one. African Americans who worked with Evers were used to his seemingly boundless energy, but by June he appeared extremely tired, haggard, and rundown. His lack of energy could be attributed to the fact that there had been mass meetings in Jackson on a daily basis since May 21, an organized regiment that had continued until June 11 when, according to police reports, they were scaled down to three per week: Tuesdays, Thursdays, and Fridays.[1] Despite lessening the number of official meetings, there was still so much to do and as usual not much time in which to do it. Added to everything he had to deal with on the eleventh, an earlier near-violent incident required that Evers notify the proper authorities in hopes of preventing future occurrences.

On June 8, Evers encountered two police officers parked along the street as he attempted to cross. He reported that after parking his car, he "got out, locked the car, and stepped off the curb between the two cars, and they jammed the police car into reverse and tried to back into me. I jumped away just in time." When speaking to Myrlie about the incident, he expressed his astonishment that this blatant disregard for human life had occurred in broad daylight and in the presence of several witnesses.[2] He took time on June 11 to contact FBI agents in New Orleans to report the incident. He also included the officers' resounding laughter as he jumped from behind the patrol car. The agents assured him they would pass along his report to the Justice Department.[3] As the day progressed, Evers could not have known that only a few hours away, the actions of two white men would offer him and the movement for equality a glimmer of hope and a measure of devastation. While the June 11 televised speech of President John F. Kennedy would offer Evers the former, the actions of Byron De La Beckwith during the early morning hours of June 12 would deliver a devastating blow with reverberating consequences. In 1960, however, no one could have predicted either of these outcomes.

In 1960, Americans prepared for the rigors of another presidential election year. African Americans, in particular, paid close attention to each candidate to determine who would best support the growing movement for equality. The Republicans chose Richard Milhous Nixon as their presidential candidate and, based on his political experience, which included a vice presidency in the Eisenhower administration, their choice appeared a strong one. Nixon was a powerful politician who had a long and influential career as both a senator and a Washington insider. The Democrats, chose John Fitzgerald Kennedy, a young politically ambitious senator who, during World War II, served with honor and distinction in the U.S. Navy. Both political parties understood the prominent role that African Americans would play in the outcome of the election and each catered, to a certain degree, to that demographic throughout the election. Kennedy, however, had a history of playing to the civil rights issue when it most suited his political ambitions.

John "Jack" Kennedy knew that in order to reach high political office he could not ignore powerful southern politicians nor could he overlook the black vote. Yet, it appears that prior to 1956, Kennedy had not visited the Deep South states that would be key political areas of civil rights contention during the late 1950s and 1960s: Mississippi, Alabama, Louisiana, and Arkansas. His lack of experience with African Americans later came back to haunt him as African American leaders charged him with being out of touch with racial issues. This could be expected, as journalist Nick Bryant pointed out, since while attending neither the Choate School nor Harvard "did he befriend any blacks, and up until his mid-twenties, the only black with whom he regularly interacted was George Taylor, his valet." Kennedy, at times, demonstrated a lack of clarity regarding the true plight of blacks, and for African Americans the fact that civil rights issues did not interest him early on only exacerbated the issue.[4]

During his early years as a congressman, Kennedy sometimes displayed a passion for supporting civil rights legislation. He supported anti-poll tax legislation, antidiscrimination provisions in the Selective Service Act, and the integration of the U.S. Women's Coast Guard, among others. He also supported the proposed civil rights initiatives outlined in Harry Truman's *To Secure These Rights*, which, among other things, called for a federal anti-lynching law. Kennedy continued to mount an impressive civil rights support record and proved tenacious with alleviating the suffering of blacks living in and around the Washington, D.C., area. However, he did not engage so much in the larger civil rights arena. During his bid for the Senate and finally the presidency, this set of circumstances changed.[5]

Kennedy decided to run for the Senate in 1952, and he understood that he needed the support of Massachusetts's black voters to defeat his rival Henry Cabot Lodge Jr. During the race, Kennedy profiled his civil rights record and continued to court the black vote. In a calculated political move, he publicly expressed his condemnation of the 1951 murders of NAACP secretary Harry T. Moore and his wife, Harriette. Their deaths resulted from a well-placed bomb that blew up their Mims, Florida, home on Christmas

Eve. Although Moore died in the blast, Harriette died a week later. Kennedy's remarks brought him a great deal of favorable press from area black news organizations such as the *Boston Chronicle*. The positive press helped garner him political support in the black community as well. Leaving nothing to chance, Kennedy also turned to African American activists such as NAACP leader Herbert Tucker and Roxbury resident and reformist Ruth Batson. Both of these individuals wielded influence in black communities around Boston and, more importantly, had access to influential contacts throughout the city. He also chose to walk black beats on a meet-and-greet that included beauty salons and pool halls, which proved successful in presenting him as a man unafraid of everyday people and who would be willing to mingle among them on their terms and within their environment. In the end, Kennedy carried the day and the lessons he learned regarding the use of civil rights issues and the support of black voters became lessons he carried to the White House.[6]

Kennedy proved quite studious when it came to politics. His experiences running for Congress and then the Senate served as political stepping-stones for a presidential bid. He decided to throw his hat in the ring after a careful analysis of the kind of political support he could garner for the 1960 election; they seemed solid and he announced his candidacy on January 2. Kennedy also knew, from previous experiences, that African Americans had been crucial to past political outcomes (his included) and would be a crucial part of this presidential race. Despite this awareness, it is doubtful that even Kennedy knew how critical the black vote would be in 1960.

Once the presidential campaign gates opened and the race began in earnest, Kennedy worked hard to shore up his weakened relationship with liberals by supporting the strongest civil rights plank of his party's platform. He understood the importance of securing the support of Martin Luther King Jr. and had met with him personally in an attempt to obtain that support. He also sought to secure the black vote by assuring both Martin Luther King Jr. and the NAACP "that he wanted 'no compromise of basic principles—no evasion of basic controversies—and no second-class citizenship for any American anywhere in this country.'"[7] Evers had to be aware of Kennedy's appeals for unequivocal equality for all since Kennedy had announced as much in a public speech to the NAACP prior to his nomination. Kennedy assured African Americans that his commitment to ending segregation was not confined to the South but one that also included ending "the more subtle but equally vicious forms of discrimination . . . found in the clubs and churches and neighborhoods of the rest of the country." In the fight against segregation he promised black Americans the full "moral" and "legal authority" of the White House to combat inequality. He also vowed to protect the rights already secured in the civil rights struggle.[8] If elected, many African Americans believed that Kennedy would be an influential ally in the White House. In contrast to Nixon, Kennedy's youth played in his favor as many African Americans reasoned that his political ideas on race might not be as rigid as some of his older counterparts. As would be evident in the televised exchange between Evers and Thompson three years later, television played a prominent role in the 1960 race for the White House.

Kennedy and Nixon agreed to a series of four televised debates over the course of the campaign. Their debate in Chicago on September 26, however, spelled the end for the 1960 presidential hopes of Richard Nixon. During the debate, Kennedy appeared relaxed and confident while Nixon looked haggard, distrustful, and lacking in self-assurance. Those who watched the debate on television believed Kennedy had won convincingly while those who heard the radio broadcast thought Nixon carried the day. Kennedy realized, more so than his opponent, just how influential the medium of television would be to the outcome of the election and he fully appreciated the role blacks played in the process. He used both to his political benefit. In 1960, Martin Luther King Jr. provided both candidates a political opportunity of such magnitude that it may have decided the election.

On October 19, King, along with other young civil rights activists, attempted to desegregate the Magnolia Room restaurant in Rich's department store in Atlanta, Georgia. The protesters were arrested and Judge Oscar Mitchell handed King a six-month prison sentence for violating his probation. King was already on probation for a dubious traffic violation earlier in the year. He was to serve his time in the state penitentiary at Reidsville. In a decision that came back to haunt him, Nixon decided not to get involved. Kennedy, however, realized the opportunity this provided and engaged in a series of behind the scenes dealings to free King. These included conversations with Georgia governor Ernest Vandiver. Meanwhile Kennedy's brother Robert, who served as his most trusted political strategist, also used his influence to help secure King's release. Robert phoned George B. Stewart, secretary for the Georgia Democratic Party, who advised him to contact Judge Mitchell. The two men talked with Robert about King's release. In the midst of these negotiations, Kennedy confidants, Harry Wofford and brother-in-law Sargent Shriver, convinced Kennedy of the symbolic capital a phone call to Coretta King would provide. Kennedy agreed and made the call expressing to Coretta his personal concerns for King's safety and his willingness to provide any assistance he could. On October 27, Mitchell freed King on $2,000.00 bond, citing the political pressure exerted to end the situation. As a consequence of this series of politically calculated moves, Kennedy bolstered his support in the black community during the few critical weeks prior to the election. His public exhortations on civil rights matters, combined with his intervention in the King affair, led individuals such as Evers to believe Kennedy was fully committed to the issue of civil rights and the overall welfare of blacks.[9]

The historian Manning Marable concludes that Kennedy's decision to get involved when King was arrested, "more than anything else, won [him] the presidency."[10] When voters went to the polls in most cities and states in November, Marable remarked, three-fourths of all African American voters cast their ballot for Kennedy. When the final votes were tallied, his popular margin of victory totaled a meager 100,000 votes out of 68.8 million total votes. This represented one of the smallest presidential victories in history and African Americans had proven the deciding factor.[11] In addition to acknowledging the role blacks played in the outcome of the election, Theodore Sorenson also provides a series of supplemental explanations for the narrow margin of victory, arguing that the following seven occurrences also contributed to the narrow margin: "Television Debates; Campaign Tactics; Party Identification; Running Mate; Negro-Southern Choices" (i.e., Martin Luther King Jr. imprisonment incident); "Foreign Policy" and the "Recession."[12]

African Americans in 1960 represented a strong voting bloc. Historians John Hope Franklin and Alfred Moss Jr. point out that in that decisive year, there were already more than a "million registered black voters in twelve Southern states. In at least six of the eight most populous states in the country, blacks held the balance of power in closely contested elections." Kennedy had carried Illinois by 9,000 votes where approximately 250,000 African Americans voted for him. He carried Michigan by 67,000 votes where again approximately 250,000 African Americans voted for him. He carried South Carolina by 10,000 votes, a tally which included "an estimated 40,000 black votes." Thus, African Americans played a pivotal role in the outcome of the election.[13]

Evers watched the election with a critical eye and considered the outcome the best political result blacks could have hoped for at the time. He believed that the election of Kennedy benefited the African American struggle nationwide. Responding to the Democratic victory, Evers announced that Kennedy's election had provided "Negroes in Mississippi more hope . . . and the endorsement of the Democratic party platform, and particularly that section which deals with Civil Rights, have given Negroes in Mississippi more hope. The abolition of the poll tax and literacy tests as prerequisites to voting . . . are long items that are uppermost in the minds of many Negro citizens of this state."[14] The true commitment of Kennedy to the issue of civil rights after the election also proved to be "uppermost in the minds" of African Americans. Although his immediate actions cast a positive light during the election process, that light tended to dim as time advanced. Nick Bryant maintained that "Kennedy's success over the course of the campaign encouraged him to believe that, using symbolism rather than substance, he could continue to achieve the same level of black support as president."[15] The rude awakening awaiting the president-elect loomed on the political horizon.

African Americans, who listened closely to Kennedy's public exhortations after the election, must have noticed that his inaugural address failed to address the civil rights issue in any detail. In fact, only a brief outlining of America's commitment to human rights, regardless of geography, could be attributed to any notion of a dedication to civil equality.[16] By 1961, many African Americans were even less enthused with the president and none proved more disappointed than Martin Luther King Jr. His earlier support of the presidential candidate had rested on the belief that Kennedy possessed the intelligence and leadership skills to do more than any other president concerning civil rights issues. His lack of commitment to a strong civil rights initiative after the election, however, led King to believe the president lacked the "moral passion" to assume the mantle of greatness in defense of civil liberties for all. Kennedy's lack of a forceful response to the problems associated with the 1961 Freedom Ride campaign helped alienate him from the African American populace.[17]

In response to accusations concerning his lack of commitment to civil equality, President Kennedy made it clear that he was willing to back civil rights policies as long as they did not threaten his overall objectives. In January 1961, Speaker Sam Rayburn announced that the president did "not plan to ask for major civil rights legislation this session. . . . He is fully aware that raising the civil rights issue would imperil his big programs for the aged and the national economy."[18] The following month President Kennedy, responding to the issue of school desegregation and civil rights, proclaimed that when he thought the most useful and "most effective" time for action had arrived, he would "attempt to use the moral authority or position of influence of the presidency in New Orleans and in other places."[19] African Americans paid close attention to Kennedy's political stance regarding civil rights issues and the problems faced by those on the frontlines.

Historian Robert Dallek points out that many "civil rights activists justifiably concluded that Kennedy simply did not have the moral commitment to their cause, that his background as a rich man insulated from contacts with African Americans and their plight made him more [of] an interested observer than a visceral proponent . . . of using federal power to cure the country's greatest social ill."[20] By 1963, however, Kennedy could no longer

ignore the need to address civil rights issues head-on, not with the 1964
presidential election looming. His presidential address on June 11, 1963,
provided African Americans, once again, with hope for the future. Evers, as
in 1960, paid close attention. On the morning of June 11, Evers could not
have known that the social and political paths separating him and Byron De
La Beckwith were steadily converging and would abruptly and violently
cross in the wake of a major civil rights address. As had been the case with
Evers, Byron De La Beckwith's childhood also proved crucial to the ideas
and beliefs he developed and ultimately the path he took as an adult.

On November 9, 1920, Byron De La Beckwith Jr. was born to Byron
and Susie De La Beckwith of Colusa, California. Byron was only five years
old when his father died, which left him and his mother financially ruined
and debt ridden. Upon the death of Beckwith's father, creditors converged
upon his mother demanding financial recourse. Susie paid what debts she
could and made arrangements to dissolve property to take care of any
additional obligations. Once she completed whatever acceptable financial
relieving transactions available, she and Byron moved back to her native
Greenwood, Mississippi. In Greenwood she sought a new life void of economic scandal so that her son would have a fair chance at life. It did not
take Beckwith long to identify the one major difference between Greenwood
and Colusa: the former had "mud people" or blacks living throughout the
area. This was both a racial group and a social phenomenon Beckwith had
not experienced in any great detail, if at all, prior to moving to Mississippi.
The experience of seeing black people on a daily basis and in great numbers
stirred his interest and excited his imagination.[21] The influence of
Mississippi's racial structure engulfed Beckwith the moment he crossed its
geographical borders.

Byron came of age in Mississippi during the political reign of Senator
Theodore G. Bilbo. Bilbo, much like Mississippi governor James K.
Vardaman, was a devout racist who believed there existed vast differences
between whites and blacks. Both Bilbo and Vardaman believed that physi-
ological differences relegated "niggers" to a position of inferiority when
compared to whites. Of more importance, both men proved quite effective
in spreading their racial ideas and thus garnering support for their political
aspirations. Bilbo's vile and brutish rants concerning race, however, had a
particularly strong impact on the idealogical development of a young De La
Beckwith.[22]

Theodore Bilbo was a master at "stump" speaking and drumming up
support for his political advancement. During one such opportunity, Bilbo
spoke at a rally in Decatur, Mississippi, in support of complete segregation.
His overall goal was to deny blacks any opportunity to challenge the social

hierarchy whites had constructed. Although nothing more than children at the time, both Medgar and his brother Charles were present for the Decatur speech. At one point during the address, Charles Evers recalled, Bilbo pointed to the Evers brothers and warned the crowd that if "we fail to hold high the wall of separation between the races, we will live to see the day when . . . those two nigger boys right there will be asking for everything that is ours by right."[23] Many African Americans could not help but notice the irony in 1947 when Bilbo died from throat cancer. Whereas the rants of individuals like Vardaman and Bilbo propelled Medgar to push forward to end segregation, they had the opposite effect on Beckwith.

Like many young Americans during the 1940s, Beckwith wanted to aid the United States in protecting democracy abroad. As a means of accomplishing this, and in large part due to his academic failings, in 1942 he enlisted for a four-year term in the U.S. Marine Corps. He was assigned to Company A, Second Marine Division, and served in the Solomon Islands.[24] On September 22, 1945, Beckwith married the former Mary Louise Williams. Discharged from the marines on January 4, 1946, Beckwith and his wife briefly stayed in Knoxville before returning to Greenwood to begin their lives together and start a family. Beckwith's development, in regard to racial ideology, seemed to have come in sectional waves ridden by political heavyweights. The first and second waves were manned by the influences of Vardaman and Bilbo. After Beckwith's return from military service, Mississippi senator James Eastland helped shape his racial views.[25]

Senator Eastland held no qualms regarding his belief that blacks were inferior to whites and that they required a firm hand of control to curb their most *base* instincts. To support his position, on June 29, 1945, he delivered a speech before his senatorial colleagues regarding the performance of blacks during World War II. During his address, Eastland used negative stereotypical rhetoric to present a false account of African Americans' performances as soldiers. "The Negro was an utter and dismal failure in combat in Europe," he proclaimed. Eastland further charged that blacks were lazy, of low intelligence, deserted their posts, refused to fight, and raped white women in Allied-occupied areas in Europe. In his final analysis, he maintained "that 'Negro soldiers disgraced the flag of their country.'"[26] For Eastland, white supremacy was the only answer to the black problem and he advocated it without apology. It is also worth noting that Senator Eastland was the nephew of the James Eastland killed by Luther Holbert in 1904 and for whom he received his name; Eastland would have been aware of the way in which his uncle died. Although some of Eastland's professional colleagues doubted his political competency, Eastland's Greenwood constituency, including Beckwith, believed he was protecting their way of life.[27]

Two significant events occurred in 1954 that provided Beckwith with the focus and purpose he had previously lacked. Both the *Brown* decision and the birth of the Citizens' Council channeled his racial development into a weapon of abject denial where the rights of African Americans were concerned. In 1954, Beckwith's son was about to enter the third grade and Byron considered the *Brown* decision a blatant attack upon his segregated way of life. Thus, he saw the federal government, the NAACP, black activists, and white southern moderates as enemies to southern existence as he knew it. Mary Beckwith recalled that during this period it seemed as if Byron "just lost his damn mind."[28] The Citizens' Council fulfilled Beckwith's lifelong need to belong. It also provided him with something he always desired: access to the powerful business elements of Greenwood.[29] As soon as he was aware of its existence, Byron joined the Citizens' Council and became a dedicated member and recruiter for the cause of white supremacy.[30] From 1954 onward, Byron De La Beckwith was totally committed to maintaining white supremacy and worked a meager ninety miles from Jackson and Medgar Wiley Evers.

By helping James Meredith navigate through the enrollment process at the University of Mississippi, Evers gained the full attention of Beckwith in 1962. Mary marked this as the moment in time she first began hearing her husband talk about Medgar Evers. When talking about Evers, she recalled, Beckwith referred to him as "'that bad nigger' or 'the NAACP nigger' or 'the head nigger.' One time he said, 'He's a bad nigger. He's got to go.'" Beckwith also took part in the harassment of local demonstrators and SNCC organizers and took particular pleasure in harassing African Americans he believed were overstepping their social bounds. Beckwith and his friends often rode through black neighborhoods taking pictures of demonstrators and heckling protestors.[31] By 1963, his drive and determination to defend segregation knew no boundaries and he was quite willing to personalize racial issues. In the process, Beckwith considered any and all opposed to the status quo as a threat worthy of eradication. On June 11, 1963, three men got ready for the day's events. In their preparation, the connecting roads that drew Kennedy, Beckwith, and Evers closer together grew narrower, with Jackson becoming the focal point and the issue of civil rights, social change, and resistance occupying the minds of all three.

By June, President Kennedy accepted the fact that only a strong civil rights bill would help alleviate the racial oppression plaguing the South. He had been pressured since his election to come out strong on the civil rights issue and although he believed that his position on civil rights spoke for itself, African Americans challenged this assumption with tenacity and vigor. As a means of clearing the air, Robert Kennedy requested a meeting with key African American leaders. Famed author James Baldwin arranged the May 24 meeting and the result shook President Kennedy's sense of civil rights accomplishment. Attended by Robert and an assemblage of influential African Americans including well-known playwright Lorraine Hansberry, the meeting took place at the Kennedy family's New York apartment. The gathering, however, grew heated when "black radical" Jerome Smith expressed his frustration at the lack of any real understanding of the African American problem on the part of the Kennedy administration. The results of this meeting, combined with the Jackson Woolworth sit-in debacle a few days later and school integration battles happening in Louisiana, pushed the Kennedy administration to act.[32]

Kennedy now believed that the time to step out full force on civil rights had come. However, it was the frequency of violent encounters between blacks and whites happening throughout the South and the eminent threat of their duplication in the North that bolstered his decision. As a consequence, he believed that a presidential call for civil rights legislation would now receive support from those in powerful positions who might oppose him on other political issues.[33]

Despite advisors' objections, President Kennedy decided to give a televised speech asking Congress for a civil rights law. This decision came on the heels of an administrative victory over Alabama governor George Wallace concerning integration at the University of Alabama. Given the president's civil rights rating up to that point, Evers had to wonder just how far Kennedy was prepared to go on the race issue or whether this address would end up another disappointment.

By June 11, Evers worked almost on autopilot to take care of daily matters. Regardless of how tired and beaten down he felt, Evers remained meticulous in his daily preparation. As the days progressed, however, his was an uneasy existence as the threat of death occupied his thoughts and those closest to him. The early days of June were filled with both political events and demonstrations as the intensity of the civil rights struggle in Jackson increased. Despite pressure from city officials, mass demonstrations continued unabated. Evers understood that the meaning of the civil rights struggle entailed sacrifice, dedication and, in many instances, death; yet he took it all in stride. The days leading up to the presidential address seemed to bring upon him much greater turmoil regarding his role in the struggle for equality. He also worried about his own mortality.

Myrlie recalled that a few days prior to June 11, Medgar publicly proclaimed his love for her on two separate occasions. She remembered thinking this to be quite odd since public displays of affection were outside of his normal character. Evers also became more safety conscious where his family was concerned. He insisted that Myrlie and the children exit the right side of the vehicle whenever they arrived home after dark. He had surveyed the position of their house from a variety of angles and noticed the possibility for concealment an empty lot across from their home afforded an individual. Exiting the car from the right side, however, provided cover between them and any person hiding in the lot. He further advised that whenever they arrived home during night hours they were to turn off the headlights and never leave the carport light on. With both the carport and vehicle lights off, Evers reasoned they would have a much better chance of entering the house under the cover of darkness. During the days leading up to the presidential address, Myrlie noticed that her husband seemed more agitated and fatigued than usual. She was also shaken by his intense denial of needing either a new suit she proposed they purchase or a number of shirts she had ironed for his use over the next few days.[34] Individuals close to Evers were also increasingly concerned for his safety and apprised him of talk regarding an imminent threat on his life.

By 1963, Evers was the face of the civil rights movement in Mississippi. A lot of that had to do with the NAACP plan of having one person represent the NAACP and control civil rights activities in the state. This went against the ideas Evers had for civil rights struggle and what he thought of his own role. CORE leader David Dennis noted that "Medgar never did want this to be [an] isolated . . . NAACP project. . . . It had been Medgar's philosophy always had been . . . that if you do that, you're targeting one person, and Medgar understood the danger of this stuff. . . . Medgar wanted . . . [it to] be broadened out . . . that they get whole groups involved, and that you don't just center on one leader."[35] When one person represents the organization's leadership, it increases the chances for tragedy.

Evers understood his life was in danger and it concerned him more from the standpoint of a husband and father than as an individual. On June 10, Dr. Felix Dunn notified Medgar concerning information about a planned attempt upon his life. Dunn received the warning from a white lawyer (he does not identify him) who acknowledged that he had no further details nor a time table for when the attack on Evers would take place. In light of this verbal warning and the reliability of the source, Dunn warned Medgar to be careful and to take all necessary precautions including placing guards around his house. Fred Clark Sr. explained that this "was just no time for Medgar Evers to be running around doing what he was doing, riding by himself."[36] Those who worked and often rode with Evers, like Clark, took notice of the dangers and believed that it was becoming more and more dangerous to be seen riding with him.

Fred Clark Sr. had worked for Evers and often rode with him but had specific conditions. "I would not ride with Medgar into town [Jackson] because I just knew they was going to get him because everybody else around me got shot, and I knew he had to be on the list. . . . Wasn't nobody else in the United States doing what he was doing. In a place like Mississippi?" Evers exhibited no real desire to curb his work regimen. When Clark asked Medgar if he were afraid to travel down certain roads, Evers spoke of "God and faith and all these other powerful words, and I was scared." Clark quit riding with Evers a few weeks prior to Evers's assassination.[37] Medgar, however, continued to go about his daily routines. He was in the process of finalizing travel arrangements to meet with Aaron Henry in Washington on June 12.

On June 11, Aaron Henry met Medgar in Jackson to discuss the joint testimony they were to present to the House Judiciary Committee in Washington the following day. Both were providing testimony in support of civil rights legislation. Henry recalled that he and Medgar were asked to appear and decided to meet the day before to make sure their statements lacked repetition.[38] Evers continued to discuss his fears of death with those within his inner circle such as Henry and they vowed to do as much as they could to protect him. Evers attended a meeting to discuss a variety of issues with Gloster Current a few days prior to the presidential address. Those at the meeting, who grew increasingly concerned for Medgar's safety, brought the issue of protection to the attention of Current but nothing came of it. Although Evers concealed a lot of his worries from his wife, Myrlie remembered that after the meeting he came home and

> he did cry that time. It was so late, it was before midnight but was still late and he sat down and just shook his head and he told me what had happened at a meeting at his office that Houston Wells, and Houston's brother, and Broadwater . . . [had attended.] Some of the other men met with Gloster Current and said this man's life is in danger, we're doing the best we can to protect him, but we need money from you to hire one person fulltime to be with him which was gonna be split in two between two people. And Gloster Current told them, and I know it's true because Medgar repeated it; [we] "have more important things to do with our money than to pay somebody to look after him." And I remember those men being so angry. Medgar came home and told me about it and he didn't sob but tears, and he said "but that's o.k., . . . cause Myrlie I don't want anybody to do that anyway . . . because I don't want anybody else to get hurt . . . when my time comes it comes, I don't care how many people are around me to protect me [it will not matter]."[39]

Despite his despair, Evers continued to go about his daily routines and to prepare for his testimony in Washington. Before he went to D.C., Evers needed to know what President Kennedy would say on the civil rights issue. Having command of that information might strengthen his position in front of the House Judiciary Committee.

President Kennedy made the decision to speak at the last minute and that decision put speechwriter Theodore Sorenson in a bind as to whether he could have a polished speech ready by the time the president went on the air. In case Sorenson failed, the president and Robert Kennedy prepared an extemporaneous address and went over what should be said and how the president should say it. The finalized speech was a hybrid of preparation: a combination of a prepared speech, which Sorenson delivered with five minutes to spare, and an extemporaneous delivery.[40] Evers called home earlier that day to remind Myrlie to watch the address and that they would talk it over when he got home. At 7:00 P.M., central-standard time, the president stepped before the national podium and addressed the nation.

For many African Americans, President Kennedy's address provided hope as he committed the nation to ending segregation and inequality on all levels. Evers had argued for years that the education system, as a whole, must cater to the needs of the population and that society must back the play of those who rightfully demand equality. On June 11, he heard the sum total of his lifelong fight for civil equality echoed in the words of the nation's leader. For African Americans in Jackson, President Kennedy's address must have seemed a familiar but welcomed plea for equality for all citizens. The major difference was that the appeal for socioeconomic parity now came attached with political influence and a congressional mandate. Evers heard President Kennedy wax poetically that as a nation we

> are committed to a worldwide struggle to promote and protect the rights of all who wish to be free. And when Americans are sent to Viet-Nam or West Berlin, we do not ask for whites only. It ought to be possible, therefore, for American students of any color to attend any public institution they select without having to be backed up by troops.
>
> It ought to be possible for American consumers of any color to receive equal service in places of public accommodation, such as hotels and restaurants and theaters and retail stores, without being forced to resort to demonstrations in the street, and it ought to be possible for American citizens of any color to register to vote in a free election without interference or fear of reprisal.
>
> It ought to be possible, in short, for every American to enjoy the privileges of being American without regard to his race or his color. In

short, every American ought to have the right to be treated as he would wish to be treated, as one would wish his children to be treated. But this is not the case.[41]

For Evers, Kennedy had summed up the obvious and, in many respects, had discussed the very problems he had outlined in his televised rebuttal to Mayor Thompson. What African Americans in Jackson, and the nation at large, wanted to know was how the president planned to put an end to the inequities that had ravaged the nation since the passage of the Emancipation Proclamation some hundred years earlier. Kennedy was not long in answering those concerns.

During his address, President Kennedy argued that the issue of segregation was neither sectional, partisan, nor legislative alone, but rather an issue of morality "as old as the scriptures and . . . as clear as the American Constitution." He further noted that the "fires of frustration and discord are burning in every city, North and South, where legal remedies are not at hand. Redress is sought in the streets, in demonstrations, parades, and protests which create tensions and threaten violence and threaten lives. We face, therefore, a moral crisis as a country and as a people."[42] He informed the nation that on the following week he would ask Congress to commit itself to the notion "that race has no place in American life or law." As a consequence, he would ask Congress to enact legislation giving all Americans access to public facilities without differences. He also promised to ask Congress to provide the necessary authorization to allow "the Federal Government to participate more fully in lawsuits designed to end segregation in public education." There would be further features requested, "including greater protection for the right to vote."[43] Although Kennedy's speech addressed a majority of civil rights concerns, how far the president would commit his administration to the cause of the civil rights struggle and how much support on Capitol Hill he could muster for his efforts were the real questions of interest to Evers. He did, nevertheless, feel a sense of hope that the civil rights struggle would achieve the objectives for which he had fought.

Myrlie felt a deep sense of pride listening to the presidential address and knew that Medgar would also take comfort in the president's approach. She also admitted that the speech had given her hope "and made what Medgar was doing seem more important than ever before."[44] Evers's workday, however, did not end with the conclusion of the presidential address as he still had things to do. As always, those who depended upon Medgar looked to him to provide what was needed before the night's end. At the conclusion of the president's speech, Evers attended a mass meeting at New Jerusalem Baptist Church, where the issues of the day were discussed at length.

The meeting at New Jerusalem did not draw a large number of participants as many individuals believed the Jackson movement was on the wane
or had been broken altogether. This belief stemmed from the new NAACP
organizational changes and a de-emphasis on mass protest that association
leaders had announced on June 2. Despite the low attendance, members from
the New York office, including Gloster Current, who had earlier announced
the NAACP's new structural and strategic direction, were present. The New
York group took the opportunity to discuss voting issues and the pending
sale of NAACP t-shirts. Evers remained cordial at the meeting, Salter
remembered, but looked very tired and quietly sad. It was obvious that he
was under a great deal of pressure.[45] His belief in the need to move forward
with direct action and his willingness to extend the hand of cooperation
with noted leaders such as Martin Luther King Jr. brought him into direct
conflict with the NAACP.

In an interview with the *Clarion-Ledger,* Reverend Edwin King described
the pressure Medgar endured and the weight of the internal and organizational conflict he suffered during the final days of his life. King, according
to Martin Zimmerman, staff writer for the *Ledger,* affirmed that "the
national NAACP, on orders from the Kennedy administration, wanted to
take the civil rights movement out of the streets and into the courts." King
recalled that:

> In Mississippi in particular, . . . the Kennedy administration wanted
> civil rights activism—including the integration of Ole Miss—to wait
> until the color barrier at the University of Alabama had been broken
> and Kennedy had been re-elected in 1964.

> [Medgar] Evers resisted. . . . Evers seemed to think [Martin Luther]
> King's methods could succeed in Jackson . . . and he was prepared to
> go ahead in defiance of the NAACP's national leadership.[46]

Evers's willingness to proceed with mass direct action protests went against
NAACP directives. His determination to employ the tactics and assistance
of other civil rights leaders such as Martin Luther King Jr. underscored his
growing discontent with the procedural constraints of the national NAACP
leadership. As a consequence, Myrlie's earlier admission that toward the
end of his life, Medgar "had all but made up his mind . . . to leave the
NAACP and to help start his own organization" further emphasized the
growing ideological strain between Evers and the NAACP. By June 11, the
stress began to take its toll, and Ed King also confirmed that Medgar
appeared "very sad and very tired" at the New Jerusalem meeting.[47]

At the conclusion of the meeting, Evers stayed for some time talking
with various individuals and finishing last-minute details. Journalists Gene

Roberts and Hank Klibanoff note that Evers took the time to chat with *Jackson Daily News* chief race reporter W. C. "Dub" Shoemaker before leaving the church. According to the *New York Times,* Evers assured a reporter present at the church that without doubt "tomorrow will be a big day." Afterward he drove Aaron Henry to the airport. Before Henry left Jackson, Evers provided him with a copy of the portion of the speech he intended to deliver before the Judiciary Committee. Henry recalled that he and Medgar talked of the demonstrations in Jackson, and Medgar apprised him of the harassment he endured, including a steady stream of threats that had grown progressively worse over the past few weeks. Aaron noted that despite Medgar's apprehensions, he "was still going about his business unescorted, and his home was unprotected at night."[48]

Evers found that the hours after Kennedy's speech were filled with last-minute work and minor details such as making sure students got back home from the meeting. Later during the evening he went to Jack and Aurelia Young's house to speak with Jack, who happened to be at his law office. Aurelia recalled that "Medgar came by, [the house,] it must have been about 10:30 or near 11:00 and he said he was hungry because he hadn't eaten all day." Young informed Medgar that she had no leftovers and so he decided that he would just "go on home." Gloster Current was also at the house and he rode with Evers back to the Masonic Temple to retrieve some mimeograph paper Jack requested in order to complete a legal brief against the city-filed boycott injunction. Evers then drove Current back to the Young's home. Before the two men departed, they shook hands and Medgar proclaimed that "Mississippi will never be the same. . . . I'm tired," he admitted. "I want to get home to my family." Afterward, he drove off into the night headed toward Guyness Street and home.[49]

Myrlie and their three children had watched the Kennedy address with intensity, and they now waited impatiently for Medgar to get home.[50] Around 12:20 A.M., an extremely tired but hopeful Medgar Evers pulled into his driveway. He looked forward to seeing his family and getting some much-needed rest. The children were particularly anxious to see their father, and when Darrell heard him pull into the driveway, their excited celebrations reverberated throughout the house. Myrlie could not help wondering what Medgar thought about Kennedy's speech and looked forward to discussing it with him.[51]

They heard when Evers shut off the engine of his Oldsmobile, and they waited for him to walk through the door. Evers, with some debate, was deciding what items to bring into the house and what to leave in the car until morning; he decided on some remaining NAACP t-shirts and a few other work-related items.[52] Yet all of the familiar sounds Myrlie had come to associate with her husband's arriving home, shattered in an instance at the sound of gunfire.

Medgar Wiley Evers, at the age of thirty-seven, had been shot in the back with a high-powered rifle. Upon hearing gunshots, Myrlie rushed to the door to help Medgar despite being pregnant with their fourth child. When she snatched open the door, she saw that her worst fears had been realized in horrific fashion. Just beyond the doorsteps she saw her husband of eleven years severely wounded, drenched in blood, and unable to speak.[53] Myrlie recalled that Medgar "fell face downward and there was blood everywhere—everywhere. I screamed and screamed and, even as I did, I fell on my knees and lifted his head."[54] The scene was gruesome and the excitement roused community residents from their sleep.

Almost instantly some members of this middle-class community rushed outside in response to hearing gunfire and "members of Evers' family screaming," the *Chicago Tribune* reported.[55] Myrlie remembered that Medgar's "heart was laboring and his mouth was moving as if he was trying to talk. He seemed to be struggling, perhaps to speak, or perhaps just to live."[56] Surrounded by his wife, concerned neighbors, friends, and his children, whose screams of "Please, Daddy, please get up!" he undoubtedly heard, individuals present laid Medgar on his daughter Reena's mattress and placed him in the back of Houston Wells's station wagon.[57]

Myrlie Evers had called Jack and Aurelia Young's house screaming, "Oh Medgar's been shot." The Young's immediately went to the Evers home and what Aurelia witnessed was hard to take in. "I never knew that there was so much blood in a human body," Young remarked. "I'd never seen anybody killed before. And I didn't know that blood was thick, it was just like somebody had poured a lot of jelly in the driveway." Myrlie constantly walked about while the women on the scene like Aurelia and Barbara Morris, of New York, tried to keep her busy. Myrlie continued to walk about gathering items but somehow managed "to step over the blood," Young remembered.[58] Although it took what seemed an eternity to get things settled during the immediate moments after the shooting, Wells rushed back to his house to call the police. He found that his wife had already made the call and the police were still on the line; he took over and directed them to the scene.[59]

After the shooting, many individuals recalled the absence of the police at the Masonic Temple earlier that evening. They also noticed the failure of the police to follow Evers home, something they routinely did, and all of these abnormal occurrences created suspicions. Evers had called FBI officials at 3:35 P.M. on June 11 to report an earlier attempt by the police to hit him with their car and during this conversation he also explained that he was being "followed by police vehicles wherever he happened to go in Jackson, Miss." FBI agents reported that Evers had also contacted FBI officials with "suspicions that his office and home phones . . . [were] being tapped . . . [dating] back to three or four years ago." His "suspicions were aroused," the report continued, "because of [an] unusual amount of static on telephone lines and a feeling as if he were listening in a vacuum."[60] Although the FBI did not have a positive track record of helping African Americans, Evers had developed a relationship with Justice Department officials such as Burke Marshall and had constantly written to Washington politicians, the president, and other federal appointees regarding the problems black Mississippians faced. Thus, it made strategic sense to contact the federal government's primary Bureau of Investigation with specific instances of abuse. This was not so much done to attain immediate assistance from the agency as to establish an official documented record of intimidation tactics and abuse that could not be denied later. However, suspicions of who or what groups were behind the assassination swirled in the days after Evers's murder.

Mississippi state senator Henry Jay Kirksey believed that the Mississippi Sovereignty Commission was behind the murder of Evers and that he "was not killed by an irate White person but by the State of Mississippi."[61] Regardless of the suspicions surrounding who or what agency murdered Evers, he knew that his life was in danger and had notified those he thought were in a position to offer assistance. And, in the end, the FBI, Mississippi officials, and the NAACP failed him.

James Evers had advised his sons to "never run from white folks [and] never turn your back on 'em."[62] Evers heeded the first warning, but on June 12, 1963, the second one escaped him. Although he could not have known that De La Beckwith lay crouched in the bushes of a vacant lot across from his home, Evers's back was momentarily turned "on 'em" when the fatal bullet ripped through him. What Charles feared most had come to pass—his brother had been killed trying to make a difference in the lives of African Americans. The personal price of his death took an additional toll on the Evers family when Myrlie miscarried within a month after the assassination.[63]

The police department was determined to act quickly and decisively in this case to avoid both the appearance of complicity in the murder and the potential for a violent African American response. At 12:45 A.M. detective captain B. D. Harrell received a call that a man had been shot at 2332 Guyness Street. He dispatched to the scene officers Eddie Rosemand and Joe Alford, who arrived at 12:53 A.M. in time to assist Wells and others in transporting Evers to the University Hospital in Jackson. Evers died there sometime between 1:14 and 1:20 A.M. The police continued questioning witnesses, including four white children who reported that they were watching television when they heard the shot. Upon hearing the noise, they looked out of the window and saw three men walking very fast but did not yet know what had happened.[64] Police detectives J. L. Black and H. B. Benton rounded up several witnesses in a house-to-house search and brought them in for questioning. According to the police report, upon arrival at Evers's home, officers

> found that Medgar Evers was shot in the back with the bull[et] coming our [*sic*] his right breast about 1 inch above the nipple. [W]ith a 30–30 Rifle bullet. This occurred as he had just gotten out of his car in the drive way [*sic*] of his home at . . . about 1240 AM. June 12th 1963. The assilant [*sic*] stood at a distance of at least 135 feet away and the bullet passing through Evers and continued on into the house. Entering a glass window in the front of the house and going through an inner wall, striking a refriderator [*sic*] and glancing off at a 45 degree angle and fell spent, on the top of the kitchen cabinet.
>
> From the best that we can determine at this point the bullet draveled [*sic*] a minium [*sic*] distance of 191.5 feet [.] This could have been further as the assilant [*sic*] could have been further back than what we have estimated.[65]

Further investigation turned up more pertinent witnesses and, more important, the murder weapon.

Later during the day of June 12, officers F. C. Hammond and S. M. Magee spoke with Betty Jean Coley and Kenneth Adcock (both white), who stated they had been walking near the area where the shot occurred and had heard someone running in the nearby woods. Officers later followed the path she showed them and discovered it led toward Joe's Drive Inn. Officers investigated the area in question and O. M. Luke discovered, half concealed within a clump of honeysuckle vines, a model 1917 .30–06-caliber Enfield high-powered rifle with an attached 6x32 goldenhawk series United Telescopic sight. The gun contained one spent shell and six live rounds identified as Super Speed .30–06 Springfields. The scope contained one latent fingerprint. This later proved to be the murder weapon. Although the police continued to investigate the murder, the African American community was at a loss both emotionally and organizationally surrounding the assassination of the most recognized leader of the Mississippi movement.[66]

June 12 sent shockwaves throughout Jackson and the nation as both learned of the assassination of Medgar Wiley Evers. *Life* magazine reported that "A Jackson policeman, speaking for most of the city's whites, said, 'We're just scared to death. And that's the truth.'"[67] For African Americans, the news produced feelings of sadness, fear, and anger at not only what had occurred, but to whom it had happened. NAACP executive secretary Roy Wilkins "immediately called for Federal protection for all Negro plaintiffs and Mississippi NAACP officials who, like Medgar Evers, were involved in pending civil rights cases in the state."[68] Despite knee-jerk reactions, the reality of the devastating event subjected many to an emotional roller-coaster ride of anguish and despair. Martin Luther King Jr. declared that "America has lost one of those pure patriots whose paramount desire was to be an American and to live as an American."[69] President Kennedy also expressed his condolences and sent a letter of sentiment to Myrlie on June 13 acknowledging that "the cause for which your husband gave his life . . . will enable his children and the generations to follow to share fully and equally in the benefits and advantages our nation has to offer." Former president Harry Truman also expressed his disgust at what had occurred, noting that Evers's killer "will undoubtedly be caught and hanged as he should be."[70] Evers's assassination drew international attention as European news agencies reported the murder and its potential ramification for civil rights activism.

The *Il Messaggero* of Rome "called the murder a 'bestial crime' which 'has stirred indignation even among persons in the South opposed to racial integration.'" The Italian newspaper *L'Unita* avowed that the murder unmasks "in a most dramatic way one of the most shameful aspects of the 'American way of life.'" The Italian newspaper *Il Secolo D'Italia* reported that Evers's murder "made the racial conflict even more dramatic[,] largely annulling the efforts which have been made in various quarters to reach goals of equity and justice." By the same token, the Finnish newspaper *Uusi Suoni* acknowledged that opinion "will have to change until a great majority of Americans regard segregation as worthless and harmful . . . this problem, which is changing to a crisis, will cause many difficulties in the United States."[71] These reports served to further tarnish America's global image. In light of the heinous nature of the murder, Kennedy sought a way to provide additional comfort to the family.

As a means of consoling the family and extending his heartfelt condolences, Kennedy invited the Evers family to the White House. During their visit, he signed a draft copy of the civil rights bill and assured Myrlie that her husband's death would make the bill possible. After the Evers left the White House, however, Kennedy admitted to Arthur M. Schlesinger Jr. that he did not "understand the South. I'm coming to believe that Thaddeus Stevens was right [about the South.] I had always been taught to regard him as a man of vicious bias. But, when I see this sort of thing, I begin to wonder how else you can treat them."[72]

Although many could have predicted Evers's murder, few were prepared to hear that it had occurred. The fact that his wife and children witnessed his bloodied and battered body drudged up feelings of anger reminiscent of the Till lynching nearly eight years prior. In spite of the despair and anger, the murder of Medgar Evers had a unifying quality that elicited cooperation. His assassination ushered forth a period of cooperation and determination among African Americans in Jackson regardless of economic background, social status, or civil rights organizational affiliation.

The killing of Medgar Evers produced in many African Americans a sense of urgency and a lack of fear. It was now a general consensus among blacks in Jackson that the time had come for direct action despite the threat of physical or economic repercussion. As a consequence, Salter recalled that area ministers joined the march and pledged their support, whereas before they had been cautious in their participation and association with the movement.[73] Students were appalled and angered by the murder of a man who had dedicated his life to the cause of equality. Many African American students were anxious to make a statement denoting their anger and determination to continue along the lines Medgar had started. The day of Evers's murder, Tougaloo College student Anne Moody decided to recruit students from Jackson State College to participate in a demonstrative march and felt sick at the apathy she encountered.

When Moody and SNCC worker Dorie Ladner arrived on campus, they were surprised to find classes still in session and let the students know of their disgust. "It's a shame, it really is a shame," Moody admonished students in a classroom she visited. "This morning Medgar Evers was murdered and here you sit in a damn classroom with books in front of your faces, pretending you don't even know he's been killed. Every Negro in Jackson should be in the streets raising hell and protesting his death."[74] The march, however, was organized despite such perceived apathy. On June 12, a mass of young and old poured out of the Masonic Temple and onto Lynch Street approximately an hour and a half after a group of protesting ministers were arrested. Jackson officials were determined to maintain order at all costs.

Salter recalled that around two hundred marchers at two and three abreast, comprised of area youth, Tougaloo students, and adults determined to make a statement of dissatisfaction with the status of African Americans, advanced toward the downtown area. They were met by some one hundred city police, Hinds County deputy sheriffs, and state police who used clubs and force to subdue the marchers and break the demonstration. The *New York Times* reported that one "girl was struck in the face by a club, deputies wrestled a middle-aged woman spectator to the sidewalk and other Negroes were shoved back roughly." The aggressive stance of the police resulted in chants of "Freedom" and "We want Freedom" from the marchers, which excited onlookers and inspired participants. By the end of the demonstration, approximately 150 persons had been arrested and transported to the fairgrounds for detention. Many believed that with the death of Medgar, there would have to be mass marches and demonstrations in the days ahead.[75]

On June 13, marchers again left Pearl Street Baptist Church to carry out organized demonstrations and were met by an armed police force of over a hundred men. The marchers had intended to march to City Hall when they were met by Jackson police and, according to the *New York Times,* "clubbed . . . into submission." Claude Sitton reported that six "Negroes were struck or choked by police nightsticks drawn across their throats." In response to the violence, NAACP officials canceled a planned demonstration for later that afternoon and indicated that no further demonstrations would take place until after Medgar's funeral.[76] Events on the day of the funeral demonstrated just how close the NAACP had come to losing control of the youth, the black community, and its position of leadership in the Mississippi struggle.

The funeral was held at the Masonic Temple on June 15 where over four thousand people jammed into the auditorium and surrounding areas to show their support and catch as much of the service as possible. Individuals were angry, upset, and fearful and thus the leadership had refused to ask city officials to use the auditorium "provided for Negroes" which would have been a much larger venue. Tougaloo president A. D. Beittel recalled that since this auditorium was "a city auditorium . . . , they would have had to get permission from the city authorities."[77] Community leaders, however, did seek and obtained permission from city officials to march along the funeral route back to Collins Funeral Home on Farish Street. Although city leaders allowed the ceremonial march to take place, James E. Jackson, news editor for the *Workmen,* observed that the "mayor had imposed brutal conditions for the funeral procession. Among the stipulations was one prohibiting any singing or shouting of slogans."[78] The police were also a heavy presence and they seemed to have no sympathy for those in mourning and this behavior angered the growing crowd. Aaron Henry noted that the "upheaval came because as you marched by the body, the guys said, 'come on move, Move. Move. Move.' Well, hell, you're talking about a guy who is your best friend, and you can't linger at his casket? And say a prayer, or whatever moves you to want to retain there just a moment. And the police are moving you on."[79]

Evers's body lay at Collins until being transported by car to Meridian and then by train to Washington, D.C., where he was buried in Arlington National Cemetery.[80] Roy Wilkins conducted one of the many eulogies and other noted civil rights activists such as Martin Luther King Jr., Ralph Bunche, Dick Gregory, T. R. M. Howard, and Congressman Charles Diggs attended the Jackson service. Wilkins reminded those in mourning that "Medgar Evers was the symbol of our victory and of their defeat. . . . In life he was a constant threat to the system, particularly in his great voter registration work. In the manner of his death, he was the victor over it."[81] Wilkins also took the opportunity to ask that people join the NAACP, which did not sit well with individuals such as Charlie Cobb. "I got pissed off and stormed out," remarked Cobb. "—He stood up there, and he said, 'The most important thing you can do for Medgar Evers is buy a membership in the NAACP!'" Cobb did not mind people joining the NAACP but felt this was not the right time or venue for Wilkins to troll for members particularly since Cobb knew of "Medgar's own difficulties with the NAACP."[82] The funeral itself, however, brought people from various socioeconomic backgrounds together.

Men and women of all walks of life attended the funeral. As a result, the poor and unknown rubbed elbows with noted dignitaries and celebrities as Evers's death brought the two groups together in sorrow and reflection. Although the larger cities were represented well enough by those in attendance, there were also people "from the Delta and from the hills in northeastern Mississippi, from the Gulf Coast area, and from the pine country down in the southwestern part of the state," John Salter recalled. "The ripples of Medgar's death and the Jackson movement in general were reaching out a long, long way—stirring people and places into which no civil rights workers had yet set foot."[83] Many felt the impact of what had been so violently taken away, and people from a variety of locales wished to share their pain and frustration with others who could understand it. There existed a need to share in the hurt and to seek hope, if only by way of a kind word or smile of assurance from those present. What happened after the services illuminated the level of frustration and its potential for explosion.

People were angry, frustrated, hurt, and looking for someone to take responsibility and blame for what had happened. People wanted to know what's "going to happen now?" The answer in many people's mind "was burn, baby, burn," Fred Clark Sr. recalled. "Burn the cities down. People were angry everywhere." Individuals were now committed to voting regardless of the dangers and they openly expressed their frustration. "'I'm going to vote, damn it,'" Clark remembered people's determination; "'I'm going to vote. Damn them white folks. They done shot Medgar now. I'm mad.' That made them old folks get up off their lazy behinds and made them drunkards get sober and go vote. Everybody was on somebody's ass about going to vote."[84]

After the march, the reality of Evers's death and the overwhelming police presence angered the now over five thousand individuals gathered along Farish Street. As a consequence of the increasing anger, many African Americans disregarded the mayor's stipulation of no singing and the spiritual "Oh Freedom," led by a young woman, stirred both pain and rage in those overcome by the severity of what had transpired. At this point, the funeral march contained all the elements needed to incite a full-scale rebellion. The gospel ballad "This Little Light of Mine," modified to address the inequities on Capitol Street, added fuel to the fire and led many to march toward downtown to vent their frustrations. The police took immediate action. Had it not been for the intervention of Justice Department agent John Doar and CORE leader David Dennis, a great many might have lost their lives as the police started beating, arresting demonstrators, and shooting out the windows in buildings above protesters' heads.[85] The police were not the only ones with guns, however. Colia Liddell Clark remembered looking "on top of buildings and . . . [seeing] Blacks lined up with guns hanging over the edge of those buildings." Clark recalled that people were on the edge and "the real brothers had decided that we tired of this little game you been playing, this brother has payed [*sic*] the real price and now either you gon' to go all the way, or we go'n [*sic*] have us a day."[86] David Dennis supported Clark's observations remembering that there were plenty people there with guns who were anxious to use them because Evers had been a man of the people. Dennis remembered that this "guy walked up. Had this dead-eye [gun] bead on him. He's getting ready to blow.—And the person he was going to blow away was John Dore [*sic*]." Dennis talked him and others out of using their guns that day as he realized that "one shot here and you've got a lot of people going to get killed."[87]

Evers would not have wanted this type of reaction and the people who had been pushed to the limit seemed to understand this and dispersed before any lives were lost. Yet the eventual capture and the two mistrials of accused killer Byron De La Beckwith stirred up old emotions of racial hatred and group despair. His trials left many wondering what had it all been for and, more importantly, had Medgar given his life for nothing.

Martin Luther King Jr. summed up the feelings of many African Americans who felt they had gone as far as they could with the current system and now demanded a strong direct stance against oppression. King avowed that African Americans were "through with segregation now, henceforth and forevermore. We are through with 'tokenism' and 'gradualism' which lead only to 'do-nothingism' and standstillism. . . . We must move from the quicksands of social injustice to the solid rock of human dignity."[88] King was not the only noted civil rights leader to point to Evers's death as an indicator of how much America needed to grow as a nation. Nine days prior to his own assassination, Malcolm X argued that the world believed that 1963 would mark "a hundred years of progress toward good race relations between white and Black in the United States," but what they witnessed was a year of brute savagery. He noted that, among the other violent deaths that year, the brutal murder of Medgar Evers was indicative of the overall social problems plaguing the country.[89] The Jackson police were well aware of the potential for a citywide explosion and worked to ensure that the public understood they fully intended to solve this murder.

The Jackson Police Department, in conjunction with the FBI, continued its investigation into Evers's murder. At 1:40 A.M. on June 23, 1963, FBI special agents Waltser Prospere and Thomas Hopkins "delivered to the [Jackson] Police Department, Byron D. Beckwith . . . to be held on charge of Violating Sec. 241, Title 10, of the U.S. Code." This was somewhat odd at this point of the investigation in that the FBI had charged Beckwith with violating Evers's civil rights rather than with murder. During the afternoon, Beckwith was placed in a five-man lineup containing two FBI agents from New Orleans. Although some witnesses such as L. S. Swilley and Mrs. Leroy Pittman could not make an identification, H. R. Speights identified Beckwith without hesitation. Leroy Pittman, viewing Beckwith at the police station, added that he was the man he and his wife saw acting in a suspicious manner a few days prior to Medgar's assassination.[90]

Leroy Pittman and his wife had a store close to the Evers's home. Both had noticed a white man who "drove up and parked near their store and got out of his car and walked back to the rear of their lot just stood and looked in the direction of [the] Evers house." The man then drove off without saying anything to anyone. The police noted that Leroy Pittman's identification of Beckwith had not been a positive identification but that Pittman believed that Beckwith was the man.[91] The police, however, had a person of interest and witnesses who had picked Beckwith out of a lineup. Officers went in search of further evidence tying Beckwith to Medgar Evers.

On June 26, 1963, officers Luke and Turner interviewed several witnesses who reported they had seen Beckwith earlier in proximity to where Evers worked as well as where he was attending a mass meeting. Lillian Louie and Alphanette Marie Bracey noted that they had seen Beckwith at the NAACP office in Jackson on June 11. Louie also remembered seeing Beckwith "talking to the police [across the street] before he came into the office." Pearlene Lewis reported seeing Beckwith at the office. Both Bracey and Doris Allison remembered seeing Beckwith on June 7 at the mass meeting where Lena Horne had spoken along with Evers. Reports such as these from eyewitness accounts excited discussions of collusion between the police department and the murderer. The thought that the police could be involved in Evers's assassination was not a difficult conclusion for African Americans to reach. Black Mississippians were well aware of the state's history of police involvement or complicity in the murder and intimidation of African Americans. Police officials were also aware of the state's history and were determined to find the killer to avoid racial violence and before long they had a viable suspect in custody.[92]

On June 25, the police linked the scope mounted on the murder weapon to Beckwith when officers John Chamblee and his partner Fred Sanders learned that the FBI Crime Lab had identified the lone fingerprint on the rifle scope as belonging to Byron De La Beckwith. FBI officials had determined that five such rifle scopes had been shipped to Mississippi and they traced each down until the shop owner of Duck's Tackle shop revealed that he had traded the scope to Beckwith. FBI agents visited Beckwith while their counterparts in D.C. linked the fingerprint to him; Beckwith's fingerprints were already on file as a result of his military service.[93]

The next day, detective W. L. Allen, assistant district attorney John Fox, and FBI agent Sam Allen traveled to Grenada, Mississippi, to meet with John Goza. During the interview, Goza, who owned Duck's Tackle Shop, admitted that Beckwith had come into his store with two .45-caliber pistols and a .22-caliber rifle he had sold Beckwith earlier. Goza informed the detectives that he had traded Beckwith the "six power golden hawk scope for these two 45 cal pistols and the 22 cal rifle." Beckwith had complained that the rifle did not work and in exchange, Goza gave Beckwith "$5.00 worth of 22 caliber ammunition." A search of Beckwith's house turned up a letter from University Hospital psychiatrist Dr. Roland E. Toms. Toms later "stated that Beckwith has been his patient and that he was in need of treatment for his mind."[94] The issue of Beckwith's sanity remained a constant concern throughout the coming trials.

Many African Americans in Jackson were edgy because of several issues regarding jurisdiction and the right of the state to force Beckwith to undergo a mental examination. As a result of this time-consuming process of legal wrangling, not much was accomplished in terms of a speedy trial and, by November, the NAACP was fed up. The *Commercial Appeal* reported that the NAACP adopted a resolution condemning the "dastardly act of the murder of Medgar Evers which has gone unattended [and urged] the immediate trial of Byron De La Beckwith and others involved in this heinous crime."[95] The trial itself, however, did not go as many African Americans expected.

The Beckwith trial began on January 27, 1964, in the Hinds County Courthouse. Presiding judge Leon Hendrick heard opening statements on

January 31. Although district attorney Bill Waller admitted he did not approve of Evers's work, he presented a well-argued case over a three-day period. Full of pomp and self-assuredness throughout the trial, Beckwith believed he would be acquitted of all charges. Former governor Ross Barnett's entrance into the courtroom and his constant exchanges of pleasantries, laughter, and his patting Beckwith on the back, did nothing to dispel the possibility of an acquittal. This open display of political support combined with the fact that Beckwith sat before an all-white jury and as Nossiter wrote, "no white man had ever been convicted for killing a black person," heightened the odds of an acquittal. Anyone following the trial could clearly see that the odds seemed heavily stacked in Beckwith's favor.[96] Hardy Lott, Stanney Sanders, and Hugh Cunningham, the latter a law firm partner of Ross Barnett, made up Beckwith's legal team. Beckwith's lawyers were determined to end the trial with an acquittal and their conduct throughout hinted at their assuredness that this would happen without much effort on their part. Over a ten-day period, spectators were treated to a vivid display of legal maneuvering and strategic jousting between the state and the defense before the case went to the jury.

On February 6, Judge Hendrick turned the case over to the jury for deliberation. Everyone expected a quick acquittal, but the jury had not reached a verdict by nightfall and on the next day reported they were hopelessly deadlocked. As a result, the case ended in a mistrial, which surprised everyone including Myrlie Evers. It was a general consensus throughout Mississippi that Beckwith would be acquitted without hesitation. At that time, no one could have fathomed that a white man would enter a guilty vote on another white man accused of killing a "nigger" in Mississippi. The mistrial, however, assured that both parties would have the chance to present their case all over again and when that time came in April 1964, the jury deadlocked once again, assuring a second mistrial. At the conclusion of the second mistrial, Beckwith made bail on a ten-thousand-dollar bond and went back to his hometown of Greenwood to a hero's welcome.[97]

Waller did not ask for a third trial, although he could have. His decision not to ask for another trial did not mean Beckwith was a free man. Beckwith left the courtroom knowing full well that he could be picked up at any moment and retried a third time.[98] In 1964, the chance of that seemed slim and African Americans felt both the pain of Medgar's loss and the anger at not being able to punish the one visible figure many held responsible for his death. Evers's murder, however, brought about some political concessions in Jackson and, for many, this affirmed Medgar's life and added some measure of value to his death.

On June 18, 1963, Mayor Allen Thompson and city commissioners met with a select group of black ministers at City Hall to discuss the racial divide engulfing the city. Among other concerns, the issue of employing black policemen and school crossing guards was a critical part of the discussion.[99] The next day Thompson announced an agreed-upon social plan that would benefit all involved. In response to the proposal, the NAACP issued a press release:

> As a first step in meeting the demands of the NAACP-sponsored desegregation drive in this capital city of Mississippi, Mayor Allen Thompson has announced the appointment of the city's first Negro policeman, 27-year-old Joe Lewis Land. . . .
>
> Another Negro will be appointed to the police force within a month and four others within 60 days, the Mayor said. Among other concessions in response to the NAACP drive were:
> —Eight Negro school crossing guards to be appointed at the opening of the school year in September.
> —Appointment of / a Negro foreman in the sanitation department and upgrading of colored workers in the department.
> —Opening up of public library [*sic*] to Negroes.
> —Provision for youth employment opportunities.[100]

Mayor Thompson swore in Joe Louis Land on June 20 and "assured the Negro leaders that Land would have full authority 'to uphold the law in the Negro section' where he will be assigned." The mayor, however, refused to appoint a biracial committee or to pressure local merchants to desegregate their facilities. He assured merchants that "they could 'deal with whomever they wanted' in conducting their business and the city would make no attempt to dictate how they should run their business."[101] The concessions the mayor presented to the committee of five, however, "were based upon the condition that further mass public demonstrations and racial agitation . . . would be curtailed."[102]

This agreement was similar to the one Evers and an earlier group had rejected, yet many accepted it now as something on which to build. Reverend G. R. Haughton, pastor of Pearl Street AME Church and spokesman for the committee, stated that "we accept this as a beginning."[103] With an estimated vote of about ten to one, blacks, who attended the Tuesday night mass meeting, agreed to accept the overall proposal. Mass demonstrations would be checked as far as the committee was concerned, but Haughton warned that we "can't guarantee that there will be no demonstrations at all."[104] For individuals such as medical doctor Robert Smith, the employment of black police officers did not bring about the change that many in Jackson had hoped.

Despite having police authority, the selected officers could only arrest Negroes and patrol black communities. They also lacked the type of people skills community residents had hoped for. Although African Americans were ecstatic at the news of the hiring of black officers, community celebrations "didn't last very long," Smith recalled, "because, uh, the guys that were picked was not the choice of the Black community." It did not take residents long to realize that community jubilations might have been premature. Smith noted that the officers "had not been trained in any personal relationship skills . . . , in fact, they was taught to go out and beat heads. In fact, 2 or 3 of those guys could slang a nightstick . . . [in a way that] would make some of the White policemen look like they were babysitters, in how they could sling that stick." After the first few years any rejoicing over the officers' appointment had ended.[105]

Despite Evers's death, the struggle for equality advanced and many continued Evers's drive to integrate Jackson's public school system. J. A. Lewis had promised Medgar that he would enroll his daughter Debra in the Leake County School when she was old enough and he kept that promise to his economic detriment. On September 1, 1964, Lewis enrolled his daughter in the first grade "of the Leake County School" and he and his wife picked her up without incident. Upon learning what Lewis had done, the lumber company he worked for fired him. Lewis's daughter was only one of nine children eligible to attend the school, but the parents of the other eight "bowed to intimidating pressures, levied by white businessmen the day before, and kept their children home."[106] Lewis demonstrated the lasting power that Medgar Evers had in the community, the trust people had in his vision and their respect for his tenacity and determination.

Many believed that in death Evers could still help bring together the races and bring about social change. His death, Claude Ramsay believed and relayed to President Kennedy, would "shock the decent people in Mississippi to the point that they are going to realize the importance and begin doing something about solving these race related problems."[107] In many ways, the youth were extensions of Evers and they carried his drive and determination wherever they went. Historian J. Todd Moye noted that Evers "was responsible for the involvement of most of the young civil rights workers from Mississippi who fanned out across the state in the early 1960s. Many if not most of them had joined the NAACP youth chapters that Evers had initiated in the state in the 1950s."[108] Evers's dogged determination to stay in Mississippi and embrace struggle rather than leave and pursue financial comfort was not unique to him. Something about *home* made it worth fighting to secure. Individuals who decided to follow James Meredith's lead, as well as those for whom race was not a barrier, and attend the University of Mississippi, also reflected Evers's commitment to changing Mississippi for the better.

David Molpus, a white student from Belzoni, Mississippi, who finished his senior year of high school in Kentucky, "thought that by returning and going to Ole Miss, he could help create a new Mississippi." After all, Molpus reasoned, "Who is going to change Mississippi . . . if Mississippians don't?" By the same token, Eugene McLemore, an African American student from Walls, Mississippi, decided to attend the University of Mississippi Law School. Journalist Nadine Cohodas suggests that this "was a decision that came from the heart rather than the mind, for there were other schools that would have been more hospitable to a young black man, but McLemore had a deep sense of home, and Mississippi was home. He wanted to come back."[109]

In a profound way, the actions of both Molpus and McLemore epitomized what Evers fought to achieve: dedication from both African Americans and whites to challenge Mississippi's status quo and work to form a new Mississippi that embraced all its citizens equally. Individual sentiments reminiscent of these had kept Evers planted in Mississippi despite opportunities to work elsewhere. Whenever offered employment opportunities outside of the state, he had consistently turned them down, arguing that his rightful place was in Mississippi. He had an opportunity to take a job in California but turned it down. Due to threats on his life, Samuel Bailey remembered that "about two weeks before he got killed, I told him he ought to go to California because somebody offer[ed] him a job out there." Despite Bailey's advice, Evers refused to leave the state, explaining to Bailey that "I want it better for my children."[110] Evers believed, Myrlie recalled, that "the South . . . [would] be a better place for Negroes to live than the North [where racism was often hidden]. . . . A Negro in the South knew where he stood. That very openness and honesty could, Medgar felt, be made to work for genuine integration once the legal bars of segregation fell."[111] Evers had considered it his moral obligation to hasten segregation's demise and he spread that ideal to all he met regardless of the personal consequences.

Evers accepted the civil rights struggle as a personal mandate to make things better for those at present but more importantly for future generations. If he could not bring about the change he sought, he could at least help lay the groundwork for future generations to succeed where he failed. This type of blind yet focused dedication allowed him to accept personal loss, familial sacrifice, and the reality of death at face value and to keep forging ahead. When *Washington Post* reporter Wallace Terry witnessed two white men attempt to run Evers over with their car, the field secretary had casually informed him that this "is what you must face to get free in Mississippi."[112]

Evers had no plans to leave the state but rather to demand that it live up to the creed of equality for all. He had boldly proclaimed to all who would listen that "I am a native of Mississippi. I doubt that I will ever live elsewhere." Furthermore, he was "determined that . . . [Negroes] can gain some equality here. One day . . . whites and Negroes will live here in Mississippi side by side in love and brotherhood. And we know each other better in the South, that's why it should work better here than anyplace else." If for no other reason than his dedication and passion for equality, Evers's murder symbolized, in the words of Dr. King, "an inexpressible tragedy and an unspeakable outrage."[113]

Medgar Evers never wanted to leave Mississippi and only death proved strong enough to take him from this place. Although he wanted to be buried in Jackson and both he and Myrlie had purchased plots in a black cemetery, the NAACP and the American Veterans Committee suggested that he be buried in Arlington National Cemetery. Myrlie, after careful consideration and discussion, reluctantly agreed. When Evers's body arrived in Washington, the FBI recorded that "some 1,000 persons . . . [had] gathered at Union Station . . . to escort the hearse through the streets of the capital." Individuals later followed the casket on "a 25-Block procession to a funeral home in Northwest Washington." Prior to Arlington, John Wesley AME Church held a funeral service for Evers. Charles Evers noted that John Wesley was a big church and that its pastor, E. Franklin Jackson, "backed civil rights to the hilt." Myrlie recalled that Medgar had once spoken here to a group of two hundred people and now twenty-five thousand mourners paraded past his coffin.[114] As the many bodies walked past Evers to look upon his face one last time, "the reason for coming was simple and poignant to all, and it was said over and over again: 'He died for us.'"[115]

Evers's meaning to the civil rights struggle was etched upon the faces of the many mourners in Washington from all socioeconomic and political backgrounds: from district court judges to taxi cab drivers all paid their respects and understood what the movement lost. Seventy-two-year-old John Coleman acknowledged that he "viewed the body and then I went out and came back. He was a wonderful man, doing wonderful work. To be cut out like that is really heart-breaking."[116] This sentiment of loss and an unwillingness to allow one's reverence of Evers to end proved a common theme. Lucille Jones admitted that she "just want[ed] to witness the body. It was the onliest way that I can show sympathy." Yet when asked why she remained behind, she acknowledged that it "seems like I just wanted to see him some more."[117] Medgar Evers touched a lot of lives and he transcended religious boundaries as indicated by his work with various denominational ministers. The active presence of members of the Nation of Islam outside of

John Wesley Church, who exclaimed to all who were present that "Brother Evers died for OUR freedom," also support Evers's ability to transcend religious denominations or affiliations.[118] The last public display of mourning came the following day when Evers's body arrived at its final resting place: Arlington, Virginia.

Medgar Evers was laid to rest at Arlington National Cemetery with full military honors on June 19, 1963. Many attended the burial and high-ranking politicians such as Robert Kennedy were also present. Roy Wilkins presented a powerful and cogent statement regarding the life of Medgar and what he represented to the civil rights struggle. Wilkins reflected the depth of that commitment in his comments. In the final analysis, he avowed, "Medgar Evers believed in his country; it now remains to be seen whether his country believes in him."[119]

The "country" seemed to answer Wilkins's emotional and potent query at Arlington in the form of civil rights legislation. The very day Evers was laid to rest President Kennedy, Theodore Sorensen remarked, "sent to the Eighty-eighth Congress the most comprehensive and far-reaching civil rights bill ever proposed." The bill guaranteed any American citizen with a sixth-grade education the right to vote and eliminated discrimination in all places of public accommodation including hotels, entertainment facilities, restaurants, and retail stores "with a 'substantial' effect on interstate commerce." The president also asked that the attorney general's office be able to initiate court-ordered desegregation in education when parents, out of fear or lack of resources, could not. In addition, the bill sought to end job discrimination and increase funding for job-training programs to help African Americans better compete in the job market. It also called for the creation of a federal Community Relations Service to improve race relations and contained "a provision authorizing the federal government to withhold funds for programs or activities in which discrimination occurred," the historian Arthur Schlesinger Jr. noted.[120] Comprehensive in scope, Kennedy's civil rights bill offered African Americans hope for a better tomorrow. Many, however, could not forget that Evers, who had worked diligently for just such an administrative commitment to civil equality, could not enjoy the moment as he lay buried amid rolling hills in a softly shaded grove across from the Potomac.[121]

In many ways, Kennedy's civil rights hand had been forced by the violence unleashed upon protesters in Birmingham. Many across the United States believed that the country was staring into an abyss of racial conflagration that threatened to engulf the entire South. Kennedy understood that something had to be done to quiet the demonstrations and to bridge the racial divide or the nation risked the possibility of a racial war. Although the proposed civil rights bill suggested a move toward social inclusion for African Americans, many hoped it would pass the House and the Senate without a great deal of difficulty; yet both Republicans and Democrats knew that the proposal itself would be the only easy part of the process. On June 20, Democratic congressman Emanuel Celler introduced to the House H.R. 7152 and the debate regarding the civil rights bill began in earnest. African Americans were not content to sit on the sidelines and wait; the NAACP brought together hundreds of members from a variety of civil rights organizations to lobby Congress for passage of the bill. The Leadership Conference on Civil Rights, which was a conglomeration of civil rights, labor, and religious organizations, resulted.[122] Kennedy feared that his civil rights plans would lose political support in the wake of the August 28 March on Washington but when he could not convince African American leaders to cancel the march, he hesitantly offered his support. However, a greater threat to the civil rights bill occurred on November 22. While visiting Dallas, Texas, Kennedy fell to an assassin's bullet and Vice President Lyndon Baines Johnson assumed the presidency. Johnson quickly took charge of the bill and after quite a bit of wrangling in the House, on February 10, 1964, H.R. 7152 passed 290 to 130 and then went to the Senate.[123]

The Senate proved a much tougher political environment to negotiate than the House had been. Here, powerful southern politicians such as Mississippi senator James O. Eastland, who served as chairman of the Judiciary Committee, had proven hostile to civil rights legislation. Opponents of the civil rights bill were also armed with the dreaded but effective filibuster and, in this battle, used it for fifty-seven days, claiming a Senate record in the process. Of significance here, the record setting filibuster, led by eighteen southern senators, ended with a cloture vote. A cloture motion to conclude a debate required a two-thirds vote of the Senate to pass and the overall vote of seventy-one to twenty-nine proved more than the two-thirds needed. Political scientist Robert D. Loevy noted that "this cloture vote was the first important limitation of debate in the history of the United States Senate." The "cloture vote gains even more significance," Loevy continued, "when it is recognized that comprehensive civil rights legislation could not have passed without it."[124] In many ways, the June 10 cloture vote indicated that Washington politicians were no longer insulated from the social and political problems African Americans faced outside of the hallowed halls of Congress.

Despite the wrangling, filibustering, and political gnashing of teeth, on June 19, 1964, one year to the day after Kennedy sent it to Congress, H.R. 7152 passed the Senate with a 73–27 vote. The bill, however, did not satisfy everyone, particularly African Americans in the South. "Though it accepted a sixth-grade education as evidence of literacy for the purpose of voter reg-istration," the historian Steven Lawson argued that "the statue continued to leave enforcement with the judiciary. . . . Furthermore, the act failed to address the improper application of literacy tests, which in the past had allowed illiterate or semiliterate whites, but not blacks, to register." It also failed to direct the administration, as Lawson pointed out, to provide pro-tection for "civil rights volunteers engaged in Freedom Summer." Despite the limitations, President Lyndon Baines Johnson delivered a brief address on a Thursday evening and then signed into law, amid cameras and televi-sion lights, the Civil Rights Act of 1964. It was July 2, 1964, when this "his-toric" moment took place and civil rights activists, black Mississippians in particular, could not have missed the irony imbedded in the celebration; had Evers lived, this day would have marked his thirty-ninth birthday.[125]

When speaking of his brother's assassination, Charles exhibited the anger and sadness that still remained. He placed some of the blame for Evers's death on his lack of protection. Yet, he noted that Medgar had no protective detail because "he didn't believe in that . . . [and] that's when he was killed."[126] In a special segment of the CBS News with Dan Rather, Charles admitted his hatred and anger for whites after Medgar's assassina-tion. He recalled, however, that it seemed as if Medgar spoke from the grave and told him that violence was not the way. Still, he felt like any other per-son whose brother had been killed—he did not feel anything for those responsible.[127] In some way, Evers's assassination legitimized his struggles for equality and individuals who had taken it for granted that he would always be around, now felt the weight of his passing. What would happen now that the "Mississippi Man" was gone?[128] What type of legacy did he leave behind and how effective was his leadership?

In addition to the abstract surrounding the life of Medgar Evers, his legacy of commitment also records tangible markers that strengthened the fight for equality. He was instrumental in resurrecting old and establishing new NAACP chapters across the state of Mississippi. As early as 1958, he reported that one "of our chapters has more than 400 members, and we have more than 20 chapters in the state."[129] Evers played a major role in getting African Americans to register and vote and was instrumental in pro-viding assistance during James Meredith's integration of the University of Mississippi in 1962 as well as Cleve McDowell's enrollment in its law school the following year.[130] His documentation of violence, racism, and the oppressive tactics practiced against African Americans helped nationalize the social, racial, and political problems that plagued Mississippi.[131]

Through the symbol of his life and selfless dedication, Evers continued to inspire and to lead those who struggled against oppression. On June 13,

1965, Clarence Mitchell, director of NAACP Washington Bureau, spoke at the memorial services for Medgar at Arlington National Cemetery. Mitchell spoke of Evers's immortality. He reminded those assembled that a man as driven and as committed to equality as Medgar Evers was does not die. But rather:

> Through his words, his deeds, his personal sacrifices and his many acts of courage, Medgar Evers is with us as we continue to press forward for final victory over wrongdoers whether they be in Mississippi, Alabama or Washington. On the day of triumph do not come to this softly-shaded grove to look for him, do not seek him in the tender earth of this bivouac of many who gave their lives at home and on foreign shores. Rather at that time when men sing the songs of triumph, listen for his voice.[132]

Those who knew Medgar acknowledged that he would have a lot to be proud of today regarding the social and political progress African Americans have achieved. At the same time, they believe that he would also be disappointed in the growing apathy and lack of civic responsibility that seems to be prevalent today.

Evers would have serious problems, his brother Charles argued, with how African Americans have organized themselves in the political arena and their failure to fully utilize the political posts they occupy. Had Medgar lived, Charles believes that "he would be [both] disappointed and proud. . . . He would be proud of the progress that's been made, but he'd be disappointed in that we are not taking advantage of the progress that we've made and blacks are not. The problem that Medgar would have with black politicians," Charles continued, "is that they won't use their authority [to help the black community,] white folks in power use their authority [to help their people]."[133] For Charles, the biggest problem his brother would have today, regarding African Americans' social, political, and economic position in Mississippi and the nation at large, is their inability to unify and work toward political self-preservation and economic strength. In many ways, these were the very issues Medgar died fighting to inspire African Americans to achieve. His assassination, however, continues to be a critical part of his overall legacy and meaning to the movement.

Mildred Bond Roxborough, NAACP consultant and former field-secretary-at-large, maintained that Medgar's legacy is encapsulated in the symbolism of his assassination. She declared that he died for what he believed in and was rock steady despite the dangers around him. Medgar's "belief in the dignity of human beings and his willingness to make the ultimate sacrifice for it, because he believed that he was entitled to this . . . , is symbolized by his ultimate assassination." His death took a great toll on the movement overall and Bond Roxborough believes that because of his death, the movement "missed the steady progress I think he would have made in bringing about changes in the state of Mississippi. I think it would have been done more thoroughly and more consistently than it was done and that it would not have been done in burst because I think he would have been a continuing instrument of change in that state." Had Medgar been alive today, she suspects that he "would be concerned about the limited involvement of the middle class blacks in this country and the minimal support, comparatively speaking, which they are giving towards the improvement of our growing and expanding underclass of black citizens."[134] Yet there were changes as a result of the work Evers put in and some of this could be measured in everyday interactions.

Samuel Bailey attributed the great many changes in the state to the civil rights movement and the role Evers played in that struggle. The greatest thing that struck Bailey remained the fact that he could now "go down to circuit clerk's office, [and] see blacks not sweepin. Behind the desk. Go to [the] courthouse, see blacks going to the jury in suits. Not just janitors. Go to Sears and Roebuck and see clerks running the cash register. Go to J.C. Penney's—Gaffer's—see guys with suits on—black." African Americans could now sit down with the mayor and chief of police. "Politicians calling you on the phone asking for your vote. White. The blacks can change any election. And every politician knows that. So, them was the great things that I saw."[135]

Dr. Alpha Morris, sociology professor at Alcorn State University, also spoke of the political turmoil that plagues African Americans today. She pointed out that Medgar's legacy rests in the fact that "he started a movement through an organized structure . . . that became a vehicle to bring about change." More important, he was brave enough to struggle for change on a state and national level. She submits, however, that Evers would be disappointed in the fact that people today are not taking advantage of the political struggles (voting) and remain so caught up in material things that they have forgotten about the good of the whole.[136] By the same token, Ineeva Pittman believes Medgar would be proud to know "that the struggle continues and that there are people who have picked up his mantle and carried the struggle forward." However, she, too, argued that Medgar would be disappointed with some of the "black elected officials and leaders who are in positions because of the movement . . . [but] who are not taking fully advantage of the power that goes along with those positions. [He would be greatly disappointed in] . . . how they are selling us out in those positions, how they are becoming a part of the problem instead of solutions."[137] Evers seemed to anticipate the problems of the future, and he spoke of the dangers of complacency with both vigor and frequency.

Myrlie Evers-Williams recalled the dangers that Medgar saw in becoming complacent with minimal forward progress. He felt that the difficult part was yet to come. She explained that Medgar believed that with complacency "we lose the gains that we have worked and died for and the next time around it will be much more difficult to get them than when it was a confrontational thing." She argued, and believes that Medgar would concur, that African Americans today "are being fooled by the glamour and the glitz of having arrived, [when] indeed we haven't."[138] In a speech delivered on August 11, 1957, Evers warned of the ramifications of complacency and inactivity for future generations:

> We, as men, owe it to our fellow man and to our children to stand firm and stand out for those things that we are entitled to. I count it a blessing from God that I am able to withstand ridicule and abuse because I am willing to stand for my fellow man though many show no appreciation for the work that we are trying to do in their behalf. But let it not be said in the final analysis when history will only record these glorious moments and when your grandchildren will invariably ask: "Granddaddy, what role did you play in helping to make us free men and free women?" Did you actively participate in the struggle or was your support only a moral one? Certainly each person here, and man in particular, should be in a position to say "I was active in the struggle from all phases for your unrestrictive privileges as an American."[139]

Activity in "all phases" of the struggle for social and political equality for African Americans underscores the legacy of Medgar Wiley Evers and that, in the final analysis, is the value of his life and his overall meaning to the civil rights struggle on the local, state, and national levels.

The life of Medgar Wiley Evers categorized the growing need for social and political change. He represented the men and women of the times who were willing to die for freedom and saw it as their duty to change the society for the benefit of upcoming generations. Evers understood the meaning of struggle and the ups and downs associated with this type of life and he accepted the consequences. It is a heavy duty to know that one will die for an ideology, yet for Medgar Evers, it became an even heavier burden to live without having attempted to institute change. In the end, however, what did it all mean? Assassinations ultimately bring about the inevitable questions of legacy, remembrance, redemption, and the societal impact of a life taken in the struggle for change and the meaning of the struggle continuum.

Conclusion

It Is for Us to Remember the Dead

We have the record of kings and gentlemen ad nauseum and in stupid detail; but of the common run of human beings, and particularly of the half or wholly submerged working group, the world has saved all too little of authentic record and tried to forget or ignore even the little saved.

—W. E. B. Du Bois

I may not have nothing, may not have bread, may not have a dine . . . [sic] but I . . . thinks and I feel like I am good as anybody on topside earth, I don't care who he is.

If I die, it will be in a good cause. I've been fighting for America just as much as the soldiers in Vietnam.

—Medgar Evers

What do I care about death in the cause of . . . redemption . . . ? I could die anywhere in the cause of liberty: A real man dies but once; a coward dies a thousand times before his real death. So we want you to realize that life is not worth its salt except you can live it for some purpose. And the noblest purpose for which to live is the emancipation of a race and the emancipation of posterity.

—Marcus Mosiah Garvey

AN ARTICLE WRITTEN IN 1989 by *Clarion-Ledger* staff writer Jerry Mitchell signaled the beginning of the end of Byron De La Beckwith's final days of freedom. On October 1, the *Clarion-Ledger* reported that the Sovereignty Commission had aided Beckwith during his second trial by investigating potential jurors. According to Mitchell, the spy agency's investigations into jurors' backgrounds were prompted by a request from defense lawyer Stanney Sanders. Based on the results of its exploration, the commission then advised the defense which potential jurors to keep and, more important, which to dismiss. The information contained in the article was explosive though not surprising to those who knew Mississippi's torrid racial history.

Public reaction to Mitchell's article was immediate and divisive because it evoked memories that many white Mississippians wanted to keep in the past and elicited hostilities from those who believed it to be just another unprovoked attack on the state. It also validated the belief held by many African Americans that the state participated in Beckwith's defense despite its prosecutorial role. Regardless of the uproar the article caused, it struck a positive chord with district attorney Bobby Delaughter. Delaughter quickly realized the legal ramifications for Evers's unsolved murder that such a pronouncement entailed and he began asking questions regarding the two previous Beckwith murder trials. These queries subsequently led to the reopening of Evers's assassination investigation and eventually placed Beckwith in front of a third Mississippi jury.[1]

After some preliminary investigation, Delaughter believed that he had enough evidence to take to a grand jury to secure an indictment against Beckwith. The grand jury convened on December 13, 1990, to hear arguments and to consider whether they warranted an indictment. After hearing the evidence, the jury returned the following evening with a signed indictment and authorities arrested Beckwith three days later. Beckwith's lawyers, however, were successful in obtaining several postponements. They also argued before the Mississippi Supreme Court issues regarding the lack of a speedy trial and the question of double jeopardy. Each legal tactic from the defense proved time consuming for the prosecution and weakened their chances of putting Beckwith on trial for murder despite their presenting successful counter arguments. In spite of defense attempts to have the charges dismissed, combined with a plethora of stall tactics, Delaughter stood before the jury on January 27, 1994, more than three years after Beckwith's 1990 indictment and delivered his opening statement. During his third and final trial, Beckwith faced a Mississippi jury with quite a different racial make up than those of his two previous trials. Of the twelve jurors in 1994, eight were African American and an African American minister served as jury foreman. On February 5, 1994, Byron "Delay" Beckwith was found guilty of the murder of Medgar Wiley Evers. After the foreman read the verdict, Judge L. Breland Hilburn informed Beckwith that "by mandate of the laws of the State of Mississippi, it is required that I sentence you to a term of life imprisonment." Three years later, the Mississippi Supreme Court upheld the conviction.[2]

Although justice had finally been administered after years of denial, the fact remained that Beckwith had lived a long life filled with fond memories, family gatherings, and time spent with friends. His actions during the early morning hours of June 12, 1963, had robbed Evers of the chance to enjoy those same opportunities. As a result, many African Americans believed that Beckwith's much-delayed incarceration as an old and broken man of seventy-three, denied the spirit of justice if not the letter of it. Beckwith served his sentence in the Central Mississippi Correctional Facility in Rankin County.

Beckwith had a long history of high blood pressure and heart-related problems. On January 21, 2001, because of illness, prison officials transferred him to the University Medical Center. Ironically, the University Medical Center was the very same hospital where Houston Wells transported Evers almost thirty-eight years earlier with a hole in his back. Hospital spokeswoman Barbara Austin acknowledged that Beckwith arrived at UMC at approximately 2:00 P.M. He was pronounced dead at 10:12 P.M. and family members reported a heart attack as the cause of death. Byron De La Beckwith remained adamant throughout his life concerning his beliefs and actions on racial issues. Upon his demise, he took to his grave an unyielding commitment to white supremacy.[3] The ideals based on equality that Medgar Wiley Evers fought to bring about, however, continued to inspire African Americans.

Evers devoted his life to establishing equality for African Americans in Mississippi and the nation as a whole. His life was one consumed by the oppressive realities of African Americans in Mississippi and this drove his relentless activism. The strength exhibited by his father, combined with the religious and moral piety of his mother, provided Evers with a deep intuitive feeling that segregation and second-class citizenship were inherently wrong. He believed that one must challenge all forms of inequality if the democratic ideal America paraded in front of the world were to become reality. For many African Americans during the 1950s and 1960s, American democracy resembled the visual perversions found in fun house mirrors. On the side reflected toward whites it appeared intact and pure, but a distorted monstrosity of the notion of equality reflected from the side facing blacks. Social experiences devoid of racism that he experienced during World War II, and the times he spent "up North," bolstered Evers's innate feelings concerning the illegitimacy of segregation. Furthermore, his exposure to the struggle of people of color fighting against tyranny and European oppression in Africa strengthened his resolve to fight for social and political equality for African Americans.

Medgar Evers never really considered leaving Mississippi and even when visiting cities such as Chicago and New York, where blacks and whites mixed more freely than in Mississippi, he did not contemplate relocation. In fact, Myrlie found that those experiences had quite the opposite effect. "Rather than incline him toward staying in the North," she remarked, "Medgar's enjoyment of the North's extra freedoms always seemed to send him hurrying back to the South with new hopes of changing it."[4] For Evers, Mississippi was home and there was no other place he would substitute for it. He considered advancements in race relations happening elsewhere as physical indicators that Mississippi could also achieve the same types of political and social advancement in its approaches to race. When asked why he chose to remain in Mississippi, Evers answered because the "state is beautiful, it is home, I love it here. A man's state is like his house. If it has defects, he tries to remedy them. That's what my job is here."[5] He believed that one should not abandon his or her home because of its flaws. Instead, one should implement solutions to make the proverbial home better, to make it a beacon of hope, an isle of tranquility amid a sea of disturbance, and an example for others to emulate. Evers often referred to the significance of land and its overall value to a people as a whole. He understood the connection between landownership and racial empowerment and the fact that he and Myrlie owned twenty-five acres of land in Mato Grosso, Brasil, stood as a testament to his forward thinking.[6]

The objective of this book has been two-fold: to understand the reasons why Medgar Evers committed to fighting for change in Mississippi and to gauge both his influence upon the civil rights movement within the state of his birth and his impact upon the national movement for equality. To the former, Evers's loyalty to family, home, and the African American community solidified his commitment to Mississippi and its population, both black and white. To the latter point, his activism, combined with his ability to explain what was happening in Mississippi to a national audience, helped to bring about social and political changes in the state and influenced civil rights activism throughout the South and the nation. The importance of his role in the movement for equality and the legacy he left will require further examination.

The legacy of Medgar Evers has yet to receive full analysis because his impact and participation in the civil rights struggle has yet to be completely explored. Over the years, scholars have examined other lesser-known civil rights leaders and argued for their underlying value to the overall freedom struggle. Historian Adam Fairclough, for example, presents a compelling argument that in Louisiana, "A. P. Tureaud's career as a lawyer and activist formed the most important strand of the complex fabric that made up the civil rights movement in Louisiana."[7] Evers played the same type of complex role in the organization and strategic effectiveness of the civil rights movement in Mississippi between 1952 and 1963. His quiet and unassuming nature, combined with his dogged determination and commitment to social equality, helped change Mississippi's oppressive climate to one conducive to political and social progress. Without his commitment to creating a more egalitarian Mississippi, without his leadership, his grassroots recruitment and organizing, and his successful documentation and nationalization of Mississippi's *de jure* and *de facto* systems of brutality, Mississippi would have remained within the shadows of barbarism much longer.

Evers considered Mississippi to be much more than the state of his birth or an area of intense repression. To Medgar, Mississippi was *home* and that feeling of belonging and responsibility for its improvement made its social and political structures *redeemable* despite the problems he faced. He acknowledged that to many "it may sound funny, but I love the South. [Furthermore,] I don't choose to live anywhere else. There's land here, where a man can raise cattle, and I'm going to do that some day. There are lakes where a man can sink a hook and fight the bass. . . . There is room here for my children to play, and grow, and become good citizens—if the white man will let them."[8]

Evers's commitment to Mississippi, however, went deeper than the beauty of its rolling hills, the depths of its lakes, or the abundance of its picturesque landscapes. "I live here [in Mississippi]," Evers explained, "to better it for my wife and kids, and for all the wives and all the kids who expect and deserve something better than they are getting from life."[9] His refusal to accept NAACP offers to relocate him and his family to another state as a means of protection underscored his commitment to the Mississippi movement. That offer, however, came only in response to Myrlie's constant demands that the NAACP provide her husband with adequate security.[10] Evers's refusal to leave Mississippi even to protect his family underscored his determination to ensure that injustice and racism collapsed under the weight of righteousness and truth.

In her article "The Developmental Years," Jacqueline Dedeaux argued that internal motivations kept Medgar Evers grounded and committed to the creation of a better Mississippi. His "love for Mississippi and her people was a motivating factor which . . . [provided] the extra drive . . . [Evers] . . . [needed] to fight the raging blazes of racism." She noted that the "desire to see Mississippi as it never was, provided the catalyst to test established limits, time and time again. Solid family ties provided the cushion needed to absorb the blows, while abiding faith in God gave him strength to keep his dream in view."[11] Evers understood the turbulent period in which he lived and the limited amount of time he had before an assassin took his life.[12] He also understood the necessity of linking the struggle in Jackson to the burgeoning national movement for social and political equality. It remained his ability to see the best possible outcome in all situations, and then to convey that positive outlook to those around him, that made Evers such an effective civil rights leader.

Although relentless in his pursuit of justice and equality, Evers was not a man without fears. His greatest fear was that he might not live to see his children grow into adulthood, Evers-Williams recalled, and that possibility remained a constant worry for him. He wanted so desperately for his children to have "the freedom to learn and to do without the pressures of race, without hatred."[13] He was also a man who respected and demanded certain unwavering qualities in the people close to him. First and foremost, Evers believed that one had to remain true to self. He considered this extremely important because he believed, Myrlie noted, that "if you can't be true to yourself, how can you be true to anybody else or anything else." Thus for Evers, self-truth was one of the most important characteristics in any struggle for equality. He also valued honesty, openness, drive, and ambition in the people he encountered, believing each to be essential to individual growth and progress. As a consequence, he had little tolerance for individuals who lacked the desire to improve their current situation. He believed that a person who did not believe in something to the point of possessing a willingness to fight to protect or bring it about was sort of lost, simply a body drifting along without direction.[14] Yet, in the final analysis, what meaning does Medgar Evers hold for the unfinished struggle for black equality?

The relevance of Evers's leadership and his ability to prepare individuals for the potential social and political problems waiting in the future were apparent during the years immediately following his murder. In 1966, Ronald Reagan was elected governor of California based, in large part, upon his stringent opposition to the 1964 Civil Rights Act and his hard line against those who took part in the infamous 1965 riots in Watts, California.[15] Two years after Reagan successfully campaigned touting a platform of political toughness, the 1968 presidential election saw Richard Nixon capitalize upon whites' debilitating fear of growing social disorder and protest. His promise to bring the social chaos to an end and to curb both the crest of protests and legislative mandates for black equality pulled both conservative and segregationist whites into his political camp. As a result, Nixon's dedication to law and order, combined with his rehashing of the "return to normalcy" exhortations of President Warren G. Harding during the early 1920s and U.S. military failures in Vietnam, won him the presidency.[16] In regard to the issue of racial and civil equality, for which Medgar Evers had dedicated and forfeited his life, the historian Harvard Sitkoff maintained that the

> Nixon Administration took every opportunity to exploit the emotions of race. It urged Congress to impose a moratorium on court-ordered school busing, nominated conservative "strict constructionists" to the Supreme Court, and pleaded before the high tribunal for a *postponement in the desegregation of Mississippi's schools.* It lobbied in Congress to defeat the fair-housing enforcement program and the extension of the Voting Rights Act of 1965. [As a whole,] . . . Nixon emasculated the Offices for Civil Rights in the Justice and Health, Education and Welfare Departments.[17]

Medgar Evers had warned of the dangers of complacency and of the personal and racial consequences that could result from not paying strict attention to the development and tactics of one's political opponents, something that he did on a daily basis.

Evers kept up with current events and was not a man that an individual could sit down with and *snow* about anything. Myrlie Evers-Williams noted that the conversations people had with Medgar were not always light, and one could expect to discuss some current event. Evers also had an eye for the significance of past events and respected the lessons they provided those who studied them with care. *Mein Kampf,* the autobiography of German leader Adolph Hitler, was the last book Evers was reading prior to his murder. When Myrlie asked why he would want to read anything about Hitler or Germany, Evers pointed to its intrinsic value. He explained that he had chosen to read about Hitler because there was so much to "learn from it, the strategies that . . . [America] used then [to defeat Nazism,] might be something we can use here in Mississippi, in the struggle."[18] His continuous search for the best ways, means, and strategies to help change society for the better remains one of the many lessons he taught. These characteristics also help define his meaning to the civil rights movement in Mississippi and the need for continued struggle. He viewed the struggle for civil rights not as a one-dimensional entity, but a multisided quandary whose solution depended upon multiple strategies.

As a consequence of his belief that thought should never be one dimensional, it is not surprising that in the battle for civil rights he would examine the life of Adolph Hitler. America's response to and the tactics utilized in defeating Germany would have held great strategic value for Evers and his struggles against racism and oppression in Mississippi. This idea further illustrates his determination to apply every available resource and learning opportunity to the struggle for equality for African Americans in Mississippi and the larger nation.

Despite the fact that a great deal of progress has been made regarding the struggle for equality since the assassination of Medgar Evers, the overall battle has not been won. Although in January 2009 the nation witnessed the swearing-in ceremony of Barack Hussein Obama, the nation's first African American president, African Americans still struggle for equity in employment, adequate healthcare, and access to better public and private schools.[19] The continued prevalence of the very social ills Evers and others fought against during the 1960s has caused academics such as Thomas Shapiro to argue for a reevaluation of how scholars talk about racial progress in modern America. He argues that any *real* discussion of race in modern America *must* include discussions of how one generation bequeaths advantages and disadvantages to the next and "how individuals' starting points are determined."[20] The issues of wealth distribution or denial, combined with the social tribulations they generated for African Americans, were problems Evers fought against while working in the Delta. He continued that fight as NAACP field secretary, and yet widespread economic inequity continues to head the list of problems contemporary activists face.

Although not as overt as during the 1950s and 1960s, racism and socioeconomic exclusion still exist and each continues to take a heavy social, cultural, political, and economic toll on those who suffer under them. While "ending the old ways of outright exclusion, subjugation, segregation, custom, discrimination, racist ideology, and violence," Shapiro argued, "our nation continues to reproduce racial inequality, racial hierarchy, and social injustice." Despite civil rights legislation, most whites and blacks continue to coexist in highly segregated communities and scholars point out that since the early 1980s, progress toward racial parity has stalled.[21]

Regardless of the obvious and real social and political gains that have occurred in America over the past forty-eight years since Evers's assassination, racial disparities still exist. As a consequence, Shapiro argued that the new political sensibility *touting* racial progress and equality "incorporates illusions that mask an enduring and robust racial hierarchy and continue to hinder efforts to achieve our ideals of democracy and justice."[22] Several statistical data sets that illuminate such hindrances to racial progress support this position.

In 2007, the Census Bureau reported that the median income for African American families was $33,916 compared to $54,920 for non-Hispanic Caucasian families. During that same year, 24.5 percent of African Americans were living at the poverty level compared to 8.2 percent of white non-Hispanics. Poverty continues to dominate the lives of many African American families, a reality that often produces negative consequences upon a child's self-perception and perceived ability to achieve success. Unfortunately, recent unemployment trends for African Americans do not suggest an end to racialized socioeconomic disparities any time soon.[23]

According to the Census Bureau, unemployment rates for African Americans in 2007 doubled that of white non-Hispanics at 8 percent and 4 percent. The Census Bureau found consistency for men at 9 percent to 4 percent and women at 8 percent to 4 percent. Although African Americans make up roughly 13 percent of the total population, they represented 49 percent of the HIV/AIDS cases in 2007 and the list of racial disparities continues unabated.[24] One of the most serious trends concerns the issue of education, a subject about which Evers cared deeply. Evers spent a majority of his life fighting to end educational segregation. Despite the efforts and progress made to desegregate schools during the 1950s, 1960s, and 1970s, educational segregation resurfaced during the 1990s and its effects continue to play out.[25]

It is important to understand the social significance of resegregation in order to fully appreciate the work, objectives, and sacrifice of Medgar Wiley Evers. In education, resegregation occurs when a white school desegregates and over a period of time, due to white flight, reverts to a minority-dominated student population. Scholars Gary Orfield and John T. Yun argued that resegregation had devastating and lasting socioeconomic effects for both African Americans and Latinos. They found that "all racial groups except whites experience considerable diversity in their schools but whites are remaining in overwhelmingly white schools even in regions with very large non-white enrollments."[26] The segregated schools whites attend more often provide better educational opportunities and are better equipped and financed than the schools attended by their minority counterparts.[27] Just as the demise of educational segregation began for Evers with the Supreme Court's decision in *Brown,* so, too, would the Supreme Court play a major role in setting the stage for the weakening of those earlier desegregation victories. During the 1990s, the Supreme Court proved far less supportive of continued federal court supervision over desegregation mandates. As a consequence, the very same inequalities in education Evers fought against during the 1950s and 1960s resurfaced during the 1990s with the courts again playing a pivotal role.

Educational resegregation described by Orfield and Yun began with key Supreme Court decisions. During the 1990s, Chief Justice William H. Rehnquist's Court took a different approach regarding the necessity for continued desegregation mandates, and their rulings on cases involving desegregation issues reflected the change in 1991. The *Board of Education of Oklahoma City v. Dowell* suit proved the first in a trifecta of these type cases during the 1990s. *Dowell* effectively eroded desegregation precedents set in the 1940s and established as law by the *Brown* decision.[28] Thus, the Supreme Court determined that dissolving a desegregation decree, once local authorities had operated in compliance for a reasonable period of time, recognized both the importance of local control of public school systems and a limitation on the regulatory powers of the federal courts.[29]

The following year, the Court ruled in *Freeman v. Pitts* that school districts could be relieved of desegregation responsibilities even if they had not met all of the requirements outlined in *Green v. County School Board Of New Kent Co., Virginia*. The Supreme Court determined that in "the course of supervising desegregation plans, federal courts have the authority to relinquish supervision and control of school districts in incremental stages before compliance has been achieved in every area of school operations."[30] As a consequence, district courts lessened their supervisory roles and educational resegregation gained momentum.[31]

In 1995, the Court determined how far district courts could go to ensure the continuation of school desegregation. The Supreme Court, in *Missouri v. Jenkins,* decided that, in many instances, the district court had indeed abused its discretion.[32] These three cases illustrate that during the 1990s the Court's attitude regarding the need for continued court-monitored school desegregation had waned. More devastating to the issue of school desegregation, law professor Erwin Chemerninsky argued that together "*Dowell, Freeman,* and *Jenkins* have given a clear signal to lower courts: the time has come to end desegregation orders, even when the effect could be resegregation."[33] One must wonder whether Evers would have experienced deja vu during the 1990s regarding African Americans' relationship to the education systems available in this country.

In light of present statistics documenting social and economic racial disparities and the incongruities that continue to exist in the education field, economist Glenn Loury appears correct when arguing that nearly "a century and a half after the destruction of the institution of slavery, and a half-century past the dawn of the civil rights movement, social life in the United States continues to be characterized by significant racial stratification."[34] Medgar Wiley Evers both saw and understood the dynamics of the struggle continuum and the role African Americans had to play within it. African Americans' struggle for socioeconomic parity continues and the life of Medgar Evers provides insight and inspiration for those involved in that struggle.

Evers worked for almost nine years as NAACP field secretary and sacrificed without self-aggrandizement or the desire to use his position to attain personal wealth or power. This fact does not mean there was nothing that he wanted as a result of his hard work. Yet when what he actually desired is examined, it supports the argument that he believed that his life belonged to the movement, and thus to the people he served. Myrlie Evers-Williams remembered that Medgar

> never wanted anything from his work in the struggle except for one thing that I heard him say more than once. . . . He hoped that one day we would have such a strong voting bloc in the state of Mississippi that he could run for office and be elected to that office and that's the only thing that I ever heard him say that he wanted as a result of his work. And knowing him . . . [he] would have been a legislator of the best kind because Medgar was not about taking bribes, he was not about getting in and selling out. He may not have lasted if he had lived long enough to have been elected, he might have been assassinated then or not reelected. He was very strict about deal making, certainly if it had a shady side to it.[35]

Evers continued to look to the future to see not only where he fit into it, but also in what position he could do the most good for African Americans. Just as Evers had wanted to become a lawyer because of its intrinsic value to the freedom struggle, his desire to work in politics could have been a means of correcting the problems and the suffering of black people from a position of political authority. Evers's life was indeed one based upon group service and a desire to ensure that the rights of the oppressed masses were protected against the whims of the powerful few.

Historian Manning Marable described Medgar Evers as a "servant-leader," one who "achieves the goals of change by transforming how oppressed people perceive themselves, awakening the sense that by and through their own energies and actions they have the capacity to both resist oppression and achieve meaningful results."[36] In light of the countless labels bestowed upon Evers since his assassination, "servant-leader" best captures the essence of the man and activist Medgar Wiley Evers embodied. It also adds to our understanding of how he accomplished so much as a civil rights leader in such a short period of time. Within that all too brief but important moment, Evers demonstrated above all that a force of one could change the hearts and minds of the many. If for no other reason than that, his contribution to social uplift *must* be honored, *must* be remembered, *must* be respected and, until true freedom and inclusion comes, *must* be emulated. Those who really knew Evers understood that he exuded something special and always sought the good in those he met.

John Frazier maintained that Evers was the epitome of humanness. "Our task is to be as God-like as possible," he remarked, "and that is how

Medgar thought, that is what he believed, that is how he lived and that is what his actions were." Medgar, Frazier continued, "was a caring person that was deeply human in the highest sense of that word and I think he would want people to be able to touch that and to know that." Frazier noted that

> Medgar had those levels of depth that he reflected in his personality all the time, everyday. He was a very warm, touchy feely kind of person. [When he] was saying something to you he always put his hand around your shoulder, always touch you as if to make a part of whatever he's dealing with, with you, a part of him and thereby equalizing whatever is going on between the two of you as opposed to expressing himself in a way that's authoritative and dictatorial and professorial, it's totally different from that.[37]

It is important to note that Medgar Evers never failed to advise those in the movement to be conscious of the role they played or did not play in the freedom struggle. For him, the importance of social and political activity or inactivity lay in the questions that future generations would ultimately lay at our feet. One day, he warned, our "grandchildren will invariably ask: . . . 'what role did you play in helping to make us free men and free women . . . ?' [For the welfare of future generations, he hoped that] . . . each person . . . [would] be in a position to say 'I was active in the struggle from all phases for your unrestrictive privileges as an American citizen.'"[38] His consistent selfless devotion to fighting inequality and oppression from "all phases" defines the legacy of Medgar Wiley Evers. No other words could provide a more fitting conclusion to this work than those spoken by Myrlie Evers when she acknowledged that it "took me years to learn what Medgar felt instinctively: that freedom has to be won, that it is worth fighting for. It was the lesson of his life. It was the lesson, if there was one, in his death."[39]

Notes

Introduction

Epigraph. http://www.bobdylan.com/songs/only-a-pawn-in-their-game (accessed May 30, 2011).

1. Myrlie Evers and William Peters, *For Us, the Living* (New York: Doubleday & Company, 1967), 299–302; Myrlie Evers, "'He Said He Wouldn't Mind Dying—If . . . ,'" *Life* magazine, June 28, 1963, 37; and Myrlie Evers interview with Nicholas Hordern for the *Delta Democrat-Times* (Mississippi), Evers (Medgar Wiley and Myrlie Beasley) Papers, Box 3, Folder 48, Mississippi Department of Archives and History (MDAH), Archives & Library Division, Special Collections Section, Jackson, Mississippi, Manuscript Collection, No. Z/2231.000/S, 4.

2. Evers and Peters, *For Us, the Living*, 302; Gene Roberts and Hank Klibanoff, *The Race Beat: The Press, the Civil Rights Struggle, and the Awakening of a Nation* (New York: Alfred A. Knopf, 2006), 340.

3. Evers and Peters, *For Us, the Living*, 302.

4. Myrlie Evers interview with Nicholas Hordern, 4. For references to pregnancy, see Myrlie Evers-Williams and Melinda Blau, *Watch Me Fly: What I Learned on the Way to Becoming the Woman I was Meant to Be* (Boston: Little, Brown and Company, 1999), 76.

5. Myrlie Evers, "'He Said He Wouldn't Mind Dying—If . . . ,'" *Life* magazine, June 28, 1963, 37.

6. Evers and Peters, *For Us, the Living*, 2, 302–303; Myrlie Evers interview with Nicholas Hordern, Evers (Medgar Wiley and Myrlie Beasley) Papers, Box 3, Folder 48; "M.W. Evers Shot Dead in Mississippi," *Chicago Tribune*, June 12, 1963, 1; and "N.A.A.C.P. Leader Slain in Jackson; Protests Mount," *New York Times*, June 13, 1963, 1.

7. Throughout this work, I sometimes use the term Negro without quotation marks when period appropriate.

8. Harry N. MacLean, *The Past is Never Dead: The Trial of James Ford Seale and Mississippi's Struggle for Redemption* (New York: Basic Civitas, 2009), 4, 97, 152–154, and John Dittmer, *Local People: The Struggle for Civil Rights in Mississippi* (Urbana: University of Illinois Press, 1994), 251–252.

9. "Address by Medgar W. Evers, Mississippi Field Secretary for the National Association for the Advancement of Colored People at May 17, 1954 Celebration of the Milwaukee, Wisconsin Branch N.A.A.C.P. . . . ," May 18, 1958, National Association for the Advancement of Colored People Records, Group III, Box C-244, Folder 2, Library of Congress Manuscript Division, Washington, D.C. (hereinafter cited as NAACP Papers, LOC), 10.

10. Charles Evers, interview with the author, cassette recording, February 4, 2005, Jackson, Mississippi. Tape in possession of the author.

11. Renee C. Romano and Leigh Raiford, eds., *The Civil Rights Movement in American Memory* (Athens: University of Georgia Press, 2006), xiii.

12. For a detailed discussion of the issue of civil rights memory, see the collection of essays in ibid.

13. "The Evers Legacy: Is NAACP leader remembered for his life or the way he died," *Daily Journal* (Mississippi), January 30, 1994, newspaper clipping, Mississippi Department of Archive and History (MDAH), Subject File "Evers, Medgar, 1990."

14. "July 4th set aside as Medgar Evers Day," *Clarion-Ledger* (Mississippi), May 26, 1999, MDAH, Subject File, "Evers, Medgar, 1990."

15. "Evers Given National Tribute," *Clarion-Ledger,* June 17, 2003, and "Medgar Evers Observance OK'd by U.S. Senate," June 13, 2003, MDAH, Subject File, "Evers, Medgar, 1990."

16. Mississippi Legislature, House Concurrent Resolution Number 94, 03/HR03/R1864, MDAH, Subject File, "Evers, Medgar, 1990."

17. "Mississippi Man" is a term used by the historian Ethel Murrain. See Ethel Patricia Churchill Murrain, "The Mississippi Man and His Message: A Rhetorical Analysis of the Cultural Themes in the Oratory of Medgar Wiley Evers, 1957–1963" (Ph.D. diss., University of Southern Mississippi, 1990).

18. The idea of the responsibility of the living to remember the dead harkens back to the African belief that the dead only die when they fade from the memories and lives of the living. See, for example, Ra Un Nefer Amen, *Metu Neter,* vol. 1: *The Great Oracle of Tehuti and the Egyptian System of Spiritual Cultivation* (Brooklyn, NY: Khamit Media Trans Visions, 1990), 236–237. Africans and people of African descent, however, are not the only racial group to express or hold this belief. Such beliefs are also held by Native American and Asian cultures as well.

19. Claude Meillassoux, *The Anthropology of Slavery: The Womb of Iron and Gold* (Chicago: University of Chicago Press, 1991), 144.

20. Medgar Evers, "Why I Live in Mississippi," *Ebony* magazine, November 1958, 70.

21. Dick Gregory, *Nigger: An Autobiography* (New York: Pocket Books, A Pocket Cardinal edition, 1965), 181.

22. In particular, Payne points to the important role that Medgar's grassroots organizing played in readying Mississippi youth for the emergence of SNCC and its more direct-action tactics in *I've Got the Light of Freedom,* 185–186.

23. Myrlie Evers-Williams with Melinda Blau, *Watch Me Fly: What I Learned on the Way to Becoming the Woman I was Meant to be* (New York: Little, Brown and Company, 1999), 51–52.

24. Supplementary Offense Report, Evers (Medgar Wiley and Myrlie Beasley) Papers, Box 29, Folder 1.

25. Murrain, "The Mississippi Man and His Message," 43.

26. The term sociopolitical is used at various times throughout the book. I use the term to describe all facets of social and political struggle.

27. These are issues that sociologist Charles Payne considers key and examines thoroughly within his work, *I've Got the Light of Freedom: The Organizing Tradition and the Mississippi Freedom Struggle* (Berkeley and Los Angeles: University of California Press, 1995), 2. See also, Dittmer, *Local People.*

1.

Epigraphs. Carrie Elizabeth Evers-Jordan, interview with the author, June 10, 2005, cassette recording, Jackson, Mississippi. Tape in possession of the author. Erik Erikson quoted in Payne, *I've Got the Light of Freedom,* 207.

1. James F. Brieger, *Hometown Mississippi,* 1980, second edition, 357. For a n account of the life of Stephen Decatur written more for the general public, see James Tertius de Kay, *A Rage for Glory: The Life of Commodore Stephen Decatur, USN* (New York: Free Press, 2004), and for a more detailed discussion, see Spencer Tucker, *Stephen Decatur: A Life Most Bold and Daring* (Annapolis, MD: Naval Institute Press, 2005).

2. The *2004–2008 Official and Statistical Register: Mississippi Blue Book,* published by Eric Clarke, Secretary of State, 2005, 372.

3. Jack Mendelsohn, *The Martyrs: Sixteen Who Gave Their Lives for Racial Justice* (New York: Harper & Row, 1966), 64.

4. Evers-Jordan, June 10, 2005, interview.

5. For a deeper discussion of history of Jim Crow and its impact upon African Americans, see John Hope Franklin and Alfred A. Moss Jr., *From Slavery to Freedom: A History of African Americans,* 8th ed. (Boston: McGraw-Hill, 2000), 290; Neil McMillen, *Dark Journey: Black Mississippians in the Age of Jim Crow* (Urbana: University of Illinois Press, 1989); Leon Litwack, *Trouble in Mind: Black Southerners in the Age of Jim Crow* (New York: Alfred A. Knopf, 1998). For personal accounts, see William H. Chafe, Raymond Gavins, and Robert Korstad, senior eds., *Remembering Jim Crow: African Americans Tell About Life in the Segregated South* (New York: New Press, 2001); for historical debates, see John David Smith, *Historians at Work: When Did Southern Segregation Begin* (New York: Palgrave, 2002); for an analysis of the rise and fall of Jim Crow, see C. Vann Woodward, *The Strange Career of Jim Crow: a Commemorative Edition* (New York: Oxford University Press, 2002), and Richard Wormser, *The Rise and Fall of Jim Crow* (New York: St. Martin's Press, 2003).

6. *Fourteenth Census of the United States Taken in the Year 1920, Vol. III, Population 1920* (Washington, DC: Government Printing Office, 1922), 538.

7. Charles Evers and Andrew Szanton, *Have No Fear: The Charles Evers Story* (New York: John Wiley & Sons, 1997), 16–17.

8. Evers and Peters, *For Us, the Living,* 15; Charles Evers, interview with the author, February 4, 2005, cassette recording, Jackson, Mississippi; and Evers-Jordan, June 10, 2005, interview. Tapes in possession of the author.

9. Throughout this work I sometimes refer to Medgar Evers by his first name. I do so only in instances where clarity is necessary as his wife, brother, father, mother, and sister are also referenced and thus using his surname sometimes lacks distinction.

10. Evers-Jordan, June 10, 2005, interview; Evers and Peters, *For Us, the Living,* 14–15; Myrlie Evers-Williams and Manning Marable, *The Autobiography of Medgar Evers: A Hero's Life and Legacy Revealed Through His Writings, Letters, and Speeches* (New York: Basic Civitas Books, 2005), 4–5; and Evers-Williams and Blau, *Watch Me Fly,* 61.

11. Danielle L. McGuire, *At the Dark End of the Street: Black Women, Rape, and Resistance—a New History of the Civil Rights Movement from Rosa Parks to the Rise of Black Power* (New York: Alfred A. Knopf, 2010).

12. Evers-Jordan, June 10, 2005, interview. For a historical discussion of the barber's profession, see Douglass Walter Bristol Jr., *Knights of the Razor: Black Barbers in Slavery and Freedom* (Baltimore, MD: Johns Hopkins University Press, 2009).

13. Evers and Szanton, *Have No Fear,* 13–14, and Evers and Peters, *For Us, the Living,* 14.

14. Evers and Szanton, *Have No Fear,* 14–15.

15. Ibid., 15.

16. Ibid., 17, and Charles Evers and Grace Halsell, *Evers* (Charles Evers and Grace Halsell, 1971), 23.

17. Charles Evers, February 4, 2005, interview.

18. Myrlie Evers-Williams, interview with the author, October 24–25, 2006, cassette and note recording, Bend, Oregon. Tape and notes in possession of the author.

19. Ibid.

20. Andrew J. DeRoche, *Andrew Young: Civil Rights Ambassador,* in Biographies in American Foreign Policy, No. 10 (Wilmington, DE: Scholarly Resources, Imprint, 2003), 1.

21. Evers-Williams and Marable, *The Autobiography of Medgar Evers,* 4, and Evers-Jordan, June 10, 2005, interview.

22. Evers and Peters, *For Us, the Living,* 15, and Evers and Szanton, *Have No Fear,* 11–12.

23. Evers and Szanton, *Have No Fear,* 11.

24. Evers-Jordan, June 10, 2005, interview. Elizabeth noted that she is not completely sure that Nick was the first name of her mother's first husband. See also, Evers and Szanton, *Have No Fear,* 11.

25. Evers and Szanton, *Have No Fear,* 14.

26. Evers-Jordan, June 10, 2005, interview.

27. Evers and Peters, *For Us, the Living,* 17.

28. Charles Evers, February 4, 2005, interview.

29. Ibid.

30. Ibid.

31. Ibid., Evers-Jordan, June 10, 2005, interview; Ben H. Bagdikian "No Longer a Secret" interview with Medgar Evers in Jack Mendelsohn, *The Martyrs,* 64; and Evers and Szanton, *Have No Fear,* 37.

32. Mendelsohn, *The Martyrs,* 64.

33. Nancy K. Williams, *The History of Newton, Mississippi 1860–1988* (Newton, MS: Nancy K. Williams, 1989), 146.

34. Ibid., 150–151.

35. Ponjola Andrews, interview with the author, September 14, 2006, cassette recording, Magnolia, Mississippi. Tape in possession of the author.

36. Evers-Jordan, June 10, 2005, interview; Charles Evers with Grace Halsell, *Evers,* 63.

37. Evers-Jordan, June 10, 2005, interview; Evers-Williams, October 24–25, 2006, interview; Evers and Peters, *For Us, the Living,* 27.

38. Evers-Jordan, June 10, 2005, interview.

39. W. E. B. Du Bois, *The Souls of Black Folk: Essays and Sketches,* 22nd ed. (Chicago: A. C. McClurg & Co., 1938), 3–5. The historian Leon Litwack further

discusses the toll that white violence placed upon African Americans leading to a projected dual persona in *Trouble in Mind.*

40. Evers-Jordan, June 10, 2005, interview.

41. Evers-Williams, October 25, 2006, interview. Charles gave Medgar the nick-name Lope after a deacon in their Mother's "Holiness Church" named Will Loper. Charles recalled that Loper "was a Sunday shouter, a dancer, a twister" and Charles called Medgar Lope as a means of teasing him and the name stuck. See Evers and Szanton, *Have No Fear,* 33, and Charles Evers and Grace Halsell, *Evers,* 30.

42. Charles Evers, February 4, 2005, interview.

43. Evers-Jordan, June 10, 2005, interview.

44. Ibid., and Charles Evers, February 4, 2005, interview.

45. Charles Evers, February 4, 2005, interview; Evers and Scranton, *Have No Fear,* 25.

46. Ibid.

47. Ibid.

48. McMillen, *Dark Journey,* 236.

49. Dittmer, *Local People,* 15, and Payne *I've Got the Light of Freedom,* 7–15. For a detailed study of lynching, see Jacqueline Jones Royster, ed., *Southern Horrors and Other Writings; The Anti-Lynching Campaign of Ida B. Wells, 1892–1900* (Boston: Bedford Books, 1997).

50. Charles Evers, February 4, 2005, interview.

51. Mendelsohn, *The Martyrs,* 64.

52. Ibid.

53. Charles Evers, February 4, 2005, interview.

54. Ibid.

55. Evers and Szanton, *Have No Fear,* 1–2; Evers-Williams and Marable, *The Autobiography of Medgar Evers,* 4–5; and Evers and Peters, *For Us, the Living,* 16.

56. Charles Evers, February 4, 2005, interview.

57. Ibid.

58. Ibid.

59. Evers-Jordan, June 10, 2005, interview.

60. Ibid.

61. Mendelsohn, *The Martyrs,* 64–65.

62. Evers-Jordan, June 10, 2005, interview.

63. Information regarding Evers's enlistment in and discharge from the U.S. military was acquired from the National Personnel Records Center, Military Personnel Records, St. Louis, MO.

64. Maryanne Vollers, *Ghosts of Mississippi: The Murder of Medgar Evers, the Trials of Byron De La Beckwith, and the Haunting of the New South* (Boston: Little, Brown and Company, 1995), 31.

65. Franklin and Moss Jr., *From Slavery to Freedom,* 483.

66. Mendelsohn, *The Martyrs,* 65.

67. David Colley, *The Road to Victory: The Untold Story of World War II's Red Ball Express* (Washington, DC: Brassey, 2000), 37, 43, 47. According to Colley, "Red Ball was a common railway term in the 1940s that had the same meaning as today's express mail." Ibid., 47.

68. John Shevlin quoted in ibid., 58.

69. Mary Penick Motley, ed., *The Invisible Soldier: The Experience of the Black Soldier, World War II* (Detroit, MI: Wayne State University Press, 1975), 149–151.

70. George R. Metcalf, *Black Profiles* (New York: McGraw-Hill Book Company, 1968), 197, and "Funeral March Finishes in White-Led Agitation," *Jackson Daily News,* June 16, 1963, 1A. The *Jackson Daily News* also reported that Medgar Evers served with both "bakery . . . and general quartermaster companies," 14A.

71. Evers and Szanton, *Have No Fear,* 48; Charles Evers, February 4, 2005, interview; and Evers and Peters, *For Us, the Living,* 25.

72. Evers-Williams, October 24, 2006, interview, and Evers and Peters, *For Us, the Living,* 25.

73. Joyce Thomas, "The Protest Against 'Insult': Black Soldiers, World War II, and the 'War' for 'Democracy' at Home," in *Black Resistance Movements in the United States and Africa, 1800–1933, Oppression and Resistance,* ed. Felton O. Best, African Studies, vol. 38 (New York: Edwin Mellen Press, 1995), 130–158.

74. Marion Alexander to Mrs. Marion Alexander, June 18, 1945, and Emory O. Jackson to the NAACP Veterans' Secretary, June 30, 1945, with the enclosed letter from Anderson, NAACP Papers, LOC, Group II, Box G2, Folder 6.

75. Thurgood Marshall to Leslie Perry, June 28, 1945, and Lieutenant Tom G. Coleman to whoever it may concern, subject "Return from OCS," April 11, 1945, NACCP Papers, LOC, Group II, Box G2, Folder 6. This series contains a variety of letters and correspondences regarding the treatment of African American soldiers.

76. Jennifer Brooks, *Defining the Peace: World War II Veterans, Race, and the Remaking of Southern Political Tradition* (Chapel Hill: University of North Carolina Press, 2004), 4.

77. Hollis R. Lynch, *Black American Radicals and the Liberation of Africa: The Council on African Affairs, 1937–1955* (New York: Cornell University Africana Studies Research Center, 1978), 17, 19, 30.

78. Ibid., 50–52.

79. For greater insight into the life of Jomo Kenyatta, see his *Facing Mount Kenya* (New York: AMS Press, 1978) and Jeremy-Murray Brown, *Kenyatta* (London: Allen & Unwin, 1979). For more on the Mau Mau, see E. S. Atieno Odhiambo and John Lonsdale, eds., *Mau Mau & Nationhood: Arms, Authority & Narration* (Athens: Ohio University Press, 2003), and David Throup, *Economic Origins of Mau Mau 1945–53* (Athens: Ohio University Press, 2003).

80. Evers and Szanton, *Have No Fear,* 76.

81. Malcolm X, *Malcolm X Speaks: Selected Speeches and Statements,* ed. George Breitman (New York: Merit Publishers, 1965), 105–106.

82. Medgar Evers, "Why I Live in Mississippi," 66.

83. Evers and Szanton, *Have No Fear,* 47–48. Myrlie Evers also discusses the negative impact that Medgar's fellow soldiers had upon him as well as the interest he drew from a white lieutenant in *For Us, the Living,* 24.

84. Dittmer, *Local People,* 17.

85. Motley, *The Invisible Soldier,* 187.

86. Evers-Jordan, June 10, 2005, interview.

87. Ibid.

88. Ibid.

89. Ibid.

90. Evers and Peters, *For Us, the Living,* 26.

91. Michael J. Klarman, *From Jim Crow to Civil Rights: The Supreme Court and the Struggle for Racial Equality* (New York: Oxford University Press, 2004), 174–182.

92. Frederick Douglass quoted in Melvin Drimmer, ed., *Black History: A Reappraisal* (New York: Doubleday & Company, 1968), 259.

93. Brooks, *Defining the Peace,* 4.

94. Timothy B. Tyson, *Radio Free Dixie: Robert F. Williams and the Roots of Black Power* (Chapel Hill: University of North Carolina Press, 1999), 51.

95. Glenda Elizabeth Gilmore, *Defying Dixie: The Radical Roots of Civil Rights, 1919–1950* (New York: W. W. Norton & Company, 2008), 348.

96. Charles A. Simmons, *The African American Press: a History of News Coverage during National Crises with Special Reference to Four Black Newspapers, 1827–1965* (Jefferson, NC: Mcfarland & Company, 1998), 75.

97. W. P. Bayless to Walter White, April 20, 1942, NAACP Papers, LOC, Group II, Box A-239, Folder 8. See also, "Should I Sacrifice to Live 'Half-American,'" by James G. Thompson, NAACP Papers, LOC, Group II, Box A-239, Folder 8, n.d.

98. Eliakim Azangu, interview with the author, July 11, 2006, cassette recording, Kenya National Archives, Nairobi, Kenya. Tape in the possession of the author.

99. James H. Meriwether, *Proudly We Can Be Africans: Black Americans and Africa, 1935–1961* (Chapel Hill: University of North Carolina Press, 2002), 125–149, and Akinyele O. Umoja, "The Ballot and the Bullet: A Comparative Analysis of Armed Resistance in the Civil Rights Movement," *Journal of Black Studies* 29, no. 4 (March 1999): 561.

100. James Ranaku, interview with the author, July 7, 2006, note recording, Western University College of Science and Technology, Kakamega, Kenya. Notes in possession of the author. For an earlier account of the impact that World War I had on the resistance efforts of the oppressed, see Joe Lunn, *Memoirs of the Maelstrom: A Senegalese Oral History of the First World War* (Portsmouth, NH: Heinemann, 1999).

101. Lynch, *Black American Radicals and the Liberation of Africa,* 45.

102. The Honorable Koigi Wa Wamwere, interview with the author, July 13, 2006, tape recording, Nairobi, Kenya. Tape in possession of the author.

103. Ibid.

104. Ibid. See also, Koigi Wa Wamwere, *I Refuse to Die: My Journey for Freedom* (New York: Seven Stories Press, 2002). For further discussions regarding African American connections to the international struggle for equality, see Michael L. Krenn, ed., *Race and U.S. Foreign Policy During the Cold War* (New York: Garland Publishing, 1998); Roderick D. Bush, *The End of White Supremacy: Black Internationalism and the Problem of the Color Line* (Philadelphia: Temple University Press, 2009); and Fred Ho and Bill V. Mullen, eds., *Afro Asia: Revolutionary Political and Cultural Connections between African Americans and Asian Americans* (Durham, NC: Duke University Press, 2008).

105. Charles Evers, February 4, 2005, interview.

106. Dorothy Winbush Riley, ed., *My Soul Looks Back 'Less I Forget': A Collection of Quotations by People of Color* (New York: Harper Collins Publishers, 1991), 426.

107. Charles Evers, February 4, 2005, interview.

108. Darlene Clark Hine, William C. Hine, and Stanley Harrold, *The African-American Odyssey,* Combined Volume, 3rd ed. (Upper Saddle River, NJ: Pearson Prentice-Hall, 2006), 469 and 549.

109. Dittmer, *Local People,* 3.

110. Steven F. Lawson, *Black Ballots: Voting Rights in the South, 1944–1969* (Lanham, MD: Lexington Books, 1999), 103; Evers-Williams and Marable, *The Autobiography of Medgar Evers,* 6, and Dittmer, *Local People,* 2–9.

111. Payne, *I've Got the Light of Freedom,* 24–25. See also, Tyson, *Radio Free Dixie,* 29.

112. W. E. B. Du Bois, "Returning Soldiers," *The Crisis: A Record of the Darker Races* 18, no. 1 (May 1919): 14.

113. Charles Evers, February 4, 2005, interview. In *Have No Fear,* Charles notes that Bernon Wansley and a man named Hudson were the other two besides the Needham brothers. See Evers and Szanton, *Have No Fear,* 61.

114. Medgar Evers, "Why I Live in Mississippi," 66, and Mendelsohn, *The Martyrs,* 65.

115. Gilmore, *Defying Dixie,* 414.

116. Charles Evers, February 4, 2005, interview, and Medgar Evers, "Why I Live in Mississippi," 66.

117. Note on spelling: The exact spelling of the name Sleech Pennington referred to in this account may not be entirely accurate; spelling based upon the interviewee's pronunciation.

118. Charles Evers, February 4, 2005, interview.

119. Medgar Evers, "Why I Live in Mississippi," 66.

120. Mendelsohn, *The Martyrs,* 65.

121. Charles Evers, February 4, 2005, interview. Portions of this account vary slightly from that offered in his books *Evers* and *Have No Fear.*

122. Mendelsohn, *The Martyrs,* 66.

123. Metcalf, *Black Profiles,* 199.

124. "Negroes to Bring Cause Before the U.N.," *New York Times,* October 12, 1947, 52.

125. W. E. B. Du Bois, "Three Centuries of Discrimination," *The Crisis* 54 (December 1947): 380.

126. Ibid., 363, and "U.N. Gets Charges of Wide Bias in U.S.," *New York Times,* October 24, 1947, 9. See also, David Levering Lewis, *W. E. B. Du Bois: The Fight for Equality and the American Century, 1919–1963* (New York: Henry Holt and Company, 2000), 521–522, 528–532. The complete title of the petition was *An Appeal to the World: A Statement on the Denial of Human Rights to Minorities in the Case of Citizens of Negro Descent in the United States of America and an Appeal to the United Nations for Redress.*

127. "U.N. Gets Charges of Wide Bias in U.S.," *New York Times,* October 24, 1947, 9.

128. Alexander DeConde, Richard Dean Burns, and Fredrik Logevall, eds. in chief, *Encyclopedia of American Foreign Policy,* 2nd ed., Volume I, Chronology A–D (New York: Charles Scribner's Sons, 2002), 6–7; "Negroes to Bring Cause Before the U.N.," *New York Times,* October 12, 1947, 52; and Lewis, *W. E. B. Du Bois,* 674.

129. President's Committee, *To Secure These Rights: The Report of the President's Committee on Civil Rights* (Washington, DC: Government Printing Office, 1947), 147, 114, 148 (emphasis in original). The committee ended by suggesting a series of recommendations; see "The Committee's Recommendations," ibid., 151–173.

130. DeConde, Burns, and Logevall, *Encyclopedia of American Foreign Policy*, 7.

131. Mary L. Dudziak, *Cold War Civil Rights: Race and the Image of American Democracy* (Princeton, NJ: Princeton University Press, 2000), 43.

132. Josephine McCann Posey, *Against Great Odds: The History of Alcorn State University* (Jackson: University Press of Mississippi, 1994), ix and 11.

133. Evers and Peters, *For Us, the Living*, 27, 32. Also see biographic description of the Evers (Medgar and Myrlie Beasley) Papers, MDAH.

134. Myrlie Evers-Williams, October 25, 2006, interview.

135. Evers and Peters, *For Us, the Living*, 34–46, and Evers-Williams and Blau, *Watch Me Fly*, 17–46. Information regarding her attendance at both MyIntyre Elementary Jr. High and Bowman High located in Evers (Medgar Wiley and Myrlie Beasley) Papers, Box 26, Folders 5, 8, 9.

136. Evers-Williams and Blau, *Watch Me Fly*, 40–42.

137. Evers-Williams, October 25, 2006, interview.

138. Ibid.

139. Ibid.

140. Ibid. and Evers-Jordan, June 10, 2005, interview.

141. Evers-Williams, October 25, 2006, interview.

142. Ibid.

143. James Haskins, *Lena Horne* (New York: Coward-McCann, 1983), 130.

144. James Haskins and Kathleen Benson, *Lena: A Personal and Professional Biography of Lena Horne* (New York: Stein and Day Publishers, 1984), 156.

145. Evers-Williams, October 25, 2006, interview.

146. Evers-Williams and Marable, *The Autobiography of Medgar Evers*, 8–9, and Evers and Peters, *For Us, the Living*, 61.

147. Laplose Jackson, interview with the author, September 13, 2006, cassette recording, Alcorn State University, Lorman, Mississippi. Tape in possession of the author.

148. Myrlie Evers-Williams, October 25, 2006, interview.

149. Ibid.

150. Certificate of Merit, Evers (Medgar Wiley and Myrlie Beasley) Papers, Box 3, Folder 43; Medgar Evers, "Why I Live in Mississippi," 67; Posey, *Against Great Odds*, 114; and Metcalf, *Black Profiles*, 197.

151. "The Herald Sports Digest," *Greater Alcorn Herald*, November–December 1948, 3; Ronald Bailey, "Remembering Medgar Evers . . . For a New Generation," A Commemoration Developed by The Civil Rights Research And Documentation Project Afro-American Studies Program—The University of Mississippi (Distributed by Heritage Publications in cooperation with The Mississippi Network For Black History And Heritage, 1988), 4.

152. Myrlie Evers-Williams, October 25, 2006, interview; Ronald Bailey, "Remembering Medgar Evers . . . For a New Generation," A Commemoration Developed by The Civil Rights Research And Documentation Project Afro-American Studies Program—The University of Mississippi (Distributed by

Heritage Publications in cooperation with The Mississippi Network For Black History And Heritage, 1988), 4; Tougaloo College Archives Lillian P. Benbow Room of Special Collections, Medgar Wiley Evers Collection unprocessed, Josephine McCann Posey, *Against Great Odds,* 113–114; Melerson Guy Dunham, *The Centennial History of Alcorn Agricultural and Mechanical College* (Hattiesburg: University and College Press of Mississippi, 1971), 136, Alcorn University Archives and Special Collections; and Dernoral Davis, "Medgar Wiley Evers and the Origin of the Civil Rights Movement in Mississippi," a part of the *Mississippi History Now* online publication of the Mississippi Historical Society, http://mshistory.k12.ms.us/articles/53/medgar-evers-and-the-origin-of-the-civil-rights-movement-in-mississippi (accessed October 8, 2010).

153. Alpha Morris, interview with the author, September 14, 2006, cassette recording, Alcorn State University, Lorman, Mississippi. Tape in possession of the author.

154. Ibid.

155. Evers-Williams, October 25, 2006, interview.

156. Andrews, September 14, 2006, interview.

157. Ibid.

158. Ibid.

159. Myrlie Evers, interview with Nicholas Hordern, Evers (Medgar Wiley and Myrlie Beasley) Papers, Box 3, Folder 48, 2.

160. Andrews, September 14, 2006, interview.

161. Evers-Williams, October 25, 2006, interview.

162. Medgar Evers, foreword to the 1951 edition of *The Alcornite.*

163. Quoted section taken from the first line of the "Alcorn Ode." For the "entire Alcorn Ode," which students and faculty often memorize and recite, see "The Alcorn Ode," http://alumni.alcorn.edu/ode.htm (accessed October 9, 2010).

164. Joel Williamson, *The Crucible of Race: Black-White Relations in the American South Since Emancipation* (New York: Oxford University Press, 1984), 22–23, 82–84.

165. Ibid., 479. For additional information regarding this subject, see Lawrence W. Levine, *Black Culture and Black Consciousness: Afro-American Folk Thought From Slavery to Freedom* (New York: Oxford University Press, 1977), and Kenneth M. Stampp, *The Peculiar Institution: Slavery in the Ante-Bellum South* (New York: Knopf, 1956).

166. Na'im Akbar, *Visions for Black Men* (Nashville: Winston-Derek Publishers, 1999), 18.

167. Myrlie Evers interview with Nicholas Hordern, Evers (Medgar Wiley and Myrlie Beasley) Papers, Box 3, Folder 48, 2. No title or date provided. Myrlie Evers discusses the opportunities afforded African Americans by Magnolia Mutual, as well as the origins of the company, in Evers and Peters, *For Us, the Living,* 72.

168. Evers and Peters, *For Us, the Living,* 75.

169. James C. Cobb, *The Most Southern Place on Earth: The Mississippi Delta and the Roots of Regional Identity* (New York: Oxford University Press, 1992), note 1, 335 and 231.

170. Medgar Evers, "Why I Live in Mississippi," 70.

2.

Epigraphs. Medgar Evers, "Why I Live in Mississippi," 67. Dr. Clinton C. Battle quoted in J. Todd Moye, *Let the People Decide: Black Freedom and White Resistance Movements in Sunflower County, Mississippi, 1945–1986* (Chapel Hill: University of North Carolina Press, 2004), 40. Fred Clark Sr., interview with Leesha Faulkner, June 10, 1994, Mississippi Oral History Program, Center of Oral History and Cultural Heritage, the University of Southern Mississippi, volume 494, 1994, 44.

1. David T. Beito and Linda Royster Beito, "T.R.M. Howard: Pragmatism over Strict Integrationist Ideology in the Mississippi Delta, 1942–1954," *Before Brown: Civil Rights and White Backlash in the Modern South,* ed. Glenn Feldman (Tuscaloosa: The University of Alabama Press, 2004), 69, and David T. Beito and Linda Royster Beito, *Black Maverick: T.R.M. Howard's Fight for Civil Rights and Economic Power* (Urbana: University of Illinois Press, 2009), 13.

2. Dittmer, *Local People,* 32, and Evers and Peters, *For Us, the Living,* 89.

3. Jennie Brown, *Medgar Evers, Activist* (Los Angeles: Melrose Square Publishing Company, 1994), 63; Dittmer, *Local People,* 32; and Beito and Beito, *Black Maverick,* 46–47.

4. Beito and Beito, "T.R.M. Howard," 68.

5. Dittmer, *Local People,* 33.

6. Beito and Beito, *Black Maverick,* xii, 48.

7. Dittmer, *Local People,* 33.

8. Ibid.

9. Beito and Beito, *Black Maverick,* 78.

10. Beito and Beito, "T.R.M. Howard," 84.

11. For further discussions regarding the issue of black respectability, see Glenda Elizabeth Gilmore, *Gender and Jim Crow: Women and the Politics of White Supremacy in North Carolina, 1896–1920* (Chapel Hill: University of North Carolina Press, 1996), and Evelyn Brooks Higginbotham, *Righteous Discontent: The Women's Movement in the Black Baptists Church, 1880–1920* (Cambridge, MA: Harvard University Press, 1993).

12. Aaron Henry with Constance Curry, *Aaron Henry: The Fire Ever Burning* (Jackson: University Press of Mississippi, 2000), 80.

13. Linda O. McMurry, *To Keep the Waters Troubled: The Life of Ida B. Wells* (Oxford: Oxford University Press, 1998), 117–118, and David H. Jackson Jr., *A Chief Lieutenant of the Tuskegee Machine: Charles Banks of Mississippi* (Gainesville: University Press of Florida, 2002), 26, 30.

14. Jackson Jr., *A Chief Lieutenant of the Tuskegee Machine,* 28.

15. *A Report of the Seventeenth Decennial Census of the United States, Census of Population: 1950 Vol. II Characteristics of the Population,* Part 24: Mississippi (Washington, DC: Government Printing Office, 1952), 24–58.

16. Nossiter, *Of Long Memory: Mississippi and the Murder of Medgar Evers* (New York: Addison-Wesley, 1994), 39–41, and Vollers, *Ghosts of Mississippi,* 41–43.

17. Vollers, *Ghosts of Mississippi,* 41–43.

18. Cobb, *The Most Southern Place on Earth,* 229, 231, and Kim Lacy Rogers, *Life and Death in the Delta: African American Narratives of Violence, Resilience, and Social Change* (New York: Palgrave Macmillan, 2006), 5.

19. Nan Elizabeth Woodruff, *American Congo: The African American Freedom Struggle in the Delta* (Cambridge, MA: Harvard University Press, 2003), 2.

20. McMillen, *Dark Journey*, 128, and Hortense Powdermaker, *After Freedom: A Cultural Study in the Deep South* (New York: Viking Press, 1939), 82–83.

21. Darlene Clark Hine, William C. Hine, and Stanley Harrold, *The African-American Odyssey*, Combined Volume, 2nd ed. (Upper Saddle River, NJ: Prentice-Hall, 2003), 324–326; McMillen, *Dark Journey*, 123–125; and Edward Royce, *The Origins of Southern Sharecropping* (Philadelphia: Temple University Press), 184–185.

22. Chana Kai Lee, *For Freedom's Sake: The Life of Fannie Lou Hamer* (Urbana: University of Illinois Press, 2000), 2.

23. McMillen, *Dark Journey*, 132.

24. Ibid., 126, and Payne, *I've Got the Light of Freedom*, 16–17.

25. Quoted in McMillen, *Dark Journey*, 134.

26. Lee, *For Freedom's Sake*, 19. For a detailed examination of the sharecropping system, see Powdermaker, *After Freedom*, 75–110.

27. Lee, *For Freedom's Sake*, 18–19.

28. McMillen, *Dark Journey*, 132.

29. Evers and Peters, *For Us, the Living*, 83.

30. Ibid., 94–96.

31. Ibid., 96, and Evers-Williams and Blau, *Watch Me Fly*, 63.

32. Evers-Williams and Blau, *Watch Me Fly*, 59–63. The birth of Darrell Kenyatta Evers is also discussed in *For Us, the Living*, 94–96, and documented by the Mississippi State Sovereignty Commission, SCR # 97–97–3–245–14–1–1.

33. The *Mound Bayou Sentinel*, vol. 1, October 3, 1953, Evers (Medgar Wiley and Myrlie Beasley) Papers, Box 3, Folder 39.

34. C. H. Webster to Medgar Evers, April 20, 1954, Evers (Medgar Wiley and Myrlie Beasley) Papers, Box 3, Folder 39.

35. Evers-Williams and Blau, *Watch Me Fly*, 61.

36. Vollers, *Ghosts of Mississippi*, 43.

37. Evers and Peters, *For Us, the Living*, 78.

38. Ibid., 79.

39. Evers-Williams and Blau, *Watch Me Fly*, 62; Metcalf, *Black Profiles*, 199; and Evers, "Why I Live in Mississippi," 67.

40. Payne, *I've Got the Light of Freedom*, 29–36; Evers-Williams and Marable, *The Autobiography of Medgar Evers*, 31; and Jay Driskell, "Amzie Moore: The Biographical Roots of the Civil Rights Movement in Mississippi," in *The Human Tradition in the Civil Rights Movement*, ed. Susan Glisson (Lanham, MD: Rowman & Littlefield, 2006), 142–148.

41. Payne, *I've Got the Light of Freedom*, 33, and Evers-Williams and Marable, *The Autobiography of Medgar Evers*, 31.

42. Metcalf, *Black Profiles*, 199, and Evers-Williams and Blau, *Watch Me Fly*, 62.

43. Henry with Curry, *Aaron Henry*, 81, and Beito and Beito, "T.R.M. Howard," 87. Although both references portray the spirit of the slogan, there exist slight variations in the wording presented in each account.

44. Evers and Peters, *For Us, the Living*, 87–88.

45. Beito and Beito, "T.R.M. Howard," 87, and Henry with Curry, *Aaron Henry*, 81.

46. Myrlie Evers, "'He Said He Wouldn't Mind Dying—If . . . ,'" *Life* magazine, June 28, 1963, 36.

47. Vincent G. Harding, *There is a River: The Black Freedom Struggle in America* (New York: Harcourt Brace Jovanovich, 1981).

48. Medgar Evers, "Report of Activities for May, 1955," to Gloster Current, May 25, 1955, NAACP Papers, LOC, Group II, Box C-346, Folder 4.

49. Evers and Peters, *For Us, the Living*, 98; Evers-Williams and Blau, *Watch Me Fly*, 62; and Medgar Evers to Johnny C. Reese, March 8, 1955. Here Evers acknowledges that he would be happy to come to "Collins and set up a N.A.A.C.P. branch" once Mr. Reese secured "fifty or more persons who are interested in the cause as you are." See, NAACP Papers, LOC, Group II, Box A-422, Folder 2.

50. Medgar Evers, "Why I Live in Mississippi," 67.

51. Evers and Peters, *For Us, the Living*, 80.

52. Charles Evers, February 4, 2005, interview.

53. Ibid.

54. Ibid.

55. Medgar Evers, "1956 Annual Report," Evers (Medgar and Myrlie Beasley) Papers, Box 2, Folder 39, 2.

56. Richard Wright, *Black Boy: A Record of Childhood and Youth* (New York: Harper & Row, 1966), 190.

57. McMillen, *Dark Journey*, 229. Also see Frank Lambert, *The Battle of Ole Miss: Civil Rights v. States' Rights* (New York: Oxford University Press, 2010), 14.

58. See Nan Elizabeth Woodruff, *American Congo*.

59. "Most Horrible: Details of the Burning at the Stake of the Holberts," *Vicksburg Evening Post*, February 13, 1904. For a deeper discussion of the Holbert lynching and the background of the Holberts, see Moye, *Let the People Decide*, 3–18. There is doubt, however, as to whether the woman fleeing with Holbert was actually his wife or merely his lover. Regardless, it appears that she was at the center of the whole incident leading up to the killings.

60. Woodruff, *American Congo*, 6.

61. Cobb, *The Most Southern Place on Earth*, 263.

62. Evers and Peters, *For Us, the Living*, 79. Dittmer acknowledges that in the wake of severe poverty, activism was not always the main priority for African Americans suffering the most. See *Local People*, 25.

63. Evers and Peters, *For Us, the Living*, 80, and Evers-Williams and Marable, *The Autobiography of Medgar Evers*, 10.

64. Juan Williams, *Eyes on the Prize: America's Civil Rights Years, 1954–1965* (New York: Viking Penguin, 1987), 46–47.

65. Evers and Peters, *For Us, the Living*, 102.

66. James T. Patterson, *Brown v. Board of Education: A Civil Rights Milestone and its Troubled Legacy* (Oxford: Oxford University Press, 2001), 14–15.

67. Jessie P. Guzman, "Twenty Years of Court Decisions Affecting Higher Education in the South, 1938–1958," *Journal of Educational Sociology* 32, no. 6, Southern Higher Education Since the Gaines Decision: A Twenty Year Review (February 1959): 247.

68. "Editorial Comment: The University of Maryland Versus Donald Gaines Murray," *Journal of Negro Education* 5, no. 2 (1936): 167.

69. *Court of Appeals of Maryland Pearson, et al. v. Murray*, 182 A. 590. 169

Md. 478, 103 A.L.R. 706 No. 53, January 15, 1936; Patricia Sullivan, *Lift Every Voice: The NAACP and the Making of the Civil Rights Movement* (New York: New Press, 2009), 208–210; and Howard Ball, *A Defiant Life: Thurgood Marshall & the Persistence of Racism in America* (New York: Crown Publishers, 1998), 45.

70. Sullivan, *Lift Every Voice*, 230–233, and Patterson, *Brown v. Board of Education*, 16.

71. Daniel T. Kelleher, "The Case of Lloyd Lionel Gaines: The Demise of the Separate But Equal Doctrine," *Journal of Negro History* 56, no. 4 (October 1971): 262.

72. Klarman, *From Jim Crow to Civil Rights*, 151.

73. Ibid.

74. Ibid., 255 and 258.

75. Ibid., 205–212, 255, and 258, and Patterson, *Brown v. Board of Education*, 16–18.

76. Patterson, *Brown v. Board of Education*, 21.

77. Portion addressing Evers's love of reading, Evers-Williams, October 24–25, 2006, interview.

78. Patterson, *Brown v. Board of Education*, 57.

79. Klarman, *From Jim Crow to Civil Rights*, 231, and Patterson, *Brown v. Board of Education*, 52–57. Also, see Ball, *A Defiant Life*, 114–147.

80. Patterson, *Brown v. Board of Education*, 21–69.

81. Henry with Curry, *Aaron Henry*, 63.

82. Dittmer, *Local People*, 49, and Beito and Beito, "T.R.M. Howard," 93.

83. Charles Evers, February 4, 2005, interview.

84. Medgar Evers to Alcorn A&M Registrar, January 11, 1954, Evers (Medgar Wiley and Myrlie Beasley) Papers, Box 3, Folder 39.

85. David G. Sansing, *The University of Mississippi: A Sesquicentennial History* (Jackson: University Press of Mississippi, 1999), 3–19.

86. Ibid., 24 and 27.

87. Allen Cabaniss, *The University of Mississippi: Its First Hundred Years* (Hattiesburg: University & College Press of Mississippi, 1971), 11.

88. Evers and Peters, *For Us, the Living*, 100–101.

89. Evers-Jordan, June 10, 2005, interview; Evers and Peters, *For Us, the Living*, 100–104; and Evers-Williams and Blau, *Watch Me Fly*, 63.

90. Evers-Williams and Marable, *The Autobiography of Medgar Evers*, 13, and Charles Eagles, *The Price of Defiance: James Meredith and the Integration of Ole Miss* (Chapel Hill: University of North Carolina Press, 2009), 72–79.

91. "Negro Applies to Ole Miss," *Jackson Daily News*, January 22, 1954, Evers (Medgar and Myrlie Beasley) Papers, Box 24, Folder 1, and the *Jackson Advocate*, "Alcorn Graduate Applies for Admission to University of Mississippi Law School," January 30, 1954, 1.

92. "Students Questioned on Negro's Recent Application," *The Mississippian*, February 5, 1954. Although there was some acceptance of a "Negro" coming as inevitable, it is significant to note that Evers's name is not mentioned in the article but rather that "a Mississippi Negro would seek admission to the University School of Law."

93. "Alcorn Graduate Applies for Admission to University of Mississippi Law School," *Jackson Advocate*, January 30, 1954, 1. The *Jackson Daily News,* the

Associated Press, and the *Commercial Appeal* also reported that the NAACP would represent Medgar in "Coleman to Decide Case of Negro Who Wants to Be Lawyer," January 22, 1954, "Mound Bayou Man Files Application at 'U' Law School," January 22, 1954, and "Negro Seeks to Enter Ole Miss Law School," January 23, 1954, respectively, newspaper clippings, Evers (Medgar and Myrlie Beasley) Papers, Box 24, Folder 1.

94. Evers and Peters, *For Us, the Living,* 114–115. For a closer examination of A. P. Tureaud and the Black Freedom struggle in Louisiana, see Adam Fairclough, *Race & Democracy: The Civil Rights Struggle in Louisiana, 1915–1972* (Athens: University of Georgia Press, 1999).

95. Evers and Peters, *For Us, the Living,* 114–115.

96. James P. Coleman, interview with Michael B. Ballard, James P. Coleman Papers, Box 2, Folder title, the "Recollection of J.P. Coleman Regarding Medgar Evers' Attempt to Integrate the University of Mississippi in 1954, June 10, 1985," Special Collections Department, Mitchell Memorial Library, Mississippi State University, 1.

97. Medgar Evers, "Why I Live in Mississippi," 67.

98. Ibid.

99. "Students Questioned on Negro's Recent Application," *The Mississippian,* February 5, 1954.

100. "Minutes Board of Trustees, Institutions of Higher Learning, September 16, 1954, Mississippi Department of Archives and History, Jackson, Mississippi, microfilm roll 36962, 379.

101. Ibid.

102. Ibid., 380–381.

103. Ibid., November 18, 1954, 391.

104. Ibid., December 16, 1954, 398.

105. "Negroes to Face Alumni Barrier to Enter Colleges," *Jackson Daily News,* September 18, 1954, 1. See also, "Ole Miss Refuses to Enroll Negro in Graduate School," *Delta Democrat-Times,* September 17, 1954, 1, and John Herbers, "Secretive College Board Failed to Reveal Graduate Student Policy Despite its Wide Public Interests," *Delta Democrat-Times,* September 19, 1954, 1–2.

106. "Public Secrets," *Delta Democrat-Times,* September 21, 1954, 4.

107. Evers and Szanton, *Have No Fear,* 12, 77, 81.

108. Charles Evers, February 4, 2005, interview.

109. "Medgar Evers, Assistant Field Secretary, NAACP, Memorandum," quoted in Evers-Williams and Marable, *The Autobiography of Medgar Evers,* 17.

110. David G. Sansing, *Making Haste Slowly: The Troubled History of Higher Education in Mississippi* (Jackson: University Press of Mississippi, 1990), 142–143.

111. U.S. Supreme Court, *Brown et al. v. Board of Education of Topeka et al.,* United States Reports, Vol. 347, US, 495.

112. "NAACP Target Date for End of Segregation Set as Sept 1955," *Delta Democrat-Times,* July 1, 1954, 7.

113. Nossiter, *Of Long Memory,* 41.

114. "Eastland Says South to Keep Segregation," newspaper clipping, May 27 (no year provided but more than likely 1954), NAACP Papers, LOC, Group II, Box A-227, Folder 4.

115. Ruby Hurley to Medgar Evers, October 14, 1954, NAACP Papers, LOC, Group II, Box C-346, Folder 4.

116. Medgar Evers to Gloster Current, "Ref: Application for Employment," November 16, 1954, NAACP Papers, LOC, Group II, Box C-346, Folder 4.

117. Gloster Current to Roy Wilkins, November 19, 1954, NAACP Papers, LOC, Group II, Box 585, Folder 3.

118. Roy Wilkins to Medgar Evers, November 24, 1954, NAACP Papers, LOC, Box C-346, Folder 4, and Medgar Evers's acceptance letter to Roy Wilkins, November 27, 1954, NAACP Papers, LOC, Box A-585, Folder 3.

119. Cleveland Donald Jr. "Medgar Wiley Evers: The Civil Rights Leader as Utopianist," in *Mississippi Heroes,* ed. Dean Faulkner Cole and Hunter Cole (Jackson: University Press of Mississippi, 1980), 220. Donald Jr. also holds the distinction of being the second African American, behind James Meredith, to graduate from the University of Mississippi.

120. Evers and Peters, *For Us, the Living,* 131, 137, 140.

3.

Epigraphs. Medgar Evers quoted in the *44th Annual Medgar Wiley Evers / B.B. King Mississippi Homecoming* booklet, May 31–June 2, 2007, 36. Medgar Evers, "Why I Live in Mississippi," 67. Quote found in "News and Views," December 11, 1958, NAACP Papers, LOC, Group III, Box C-74, Folder 1, 2.

1. Manfred Berg, *"The Ticket to Freedom": The NAACP and the Struggle for Black Political Integration* (Gainesville: University Press of Florida, 2005), 15–17, and Franklin and Moss Jr., *From Slavery to Freedom,* 350–352.

2. The Springfield riots occurred as a result of a white woman's claim that she had been beaten and raped by a black man. She later admitted that her beating occurred at the hands of a white man whom she refused to identify. Anger, however, had overtaken the senses of the white population of the city who proceeded to destroy black businesses and exact violence upon African Americans at will. Two African Americans were lynched and four whites were killed while hundreds more were injured in the riot. This incident sparked nationwide outrage and caused outspoken leaders such as Ida B. Wells to question the commitment of African Americans to the cause of justice. Wells expressed reservations regarding the depth of the overall commitment to struggle because of the lackadaisical responses and seemingly overall acceptance of the event from African Americans across the country. For an account of Ida B. Wells's take on the riots, see Linda O. McMurry, *To Keep the Waters Troubled,* 293. See also Berg, *"The Ticket to Freedom,"* 10.

3. Sullivan, *Lift Every Voice,* 5–6; Aldon D. Morris, *The Origins of the Civil Rights Movement: Black Communities Organizing for Change* (New York: Free Press, 1984), 12–16; and Berg, *"The Ticket to Freedom,"* 12.

4. Sullivan, *Lift Every Voice,* 1; Franklin and Moss Jr., *From Slavery to Freedom,* 352–353; and Berg, *"The Ticket to Freedom,"*18.

5. Franklin and Moss Jr., *From Slavery to Freedom,* 353.

6. Berg, *"The Ticket to Freedom,"* 13. For a detailed examination of the NAACP, see Sullivan, *Lift Every Voice,* and Gilbert Jonas, *Freedom's Sword: The NAACP and the Struggle Against Racism in America, 1909–1969* (New York: Routledge, 2005).

7. Gloster Current to Medgar Evers, December 15, 1954, Evers (Medgar Wiley and Myrlie Beasley) Papers, Box 2, Folder 6; *NAACP Annual Report,* Forty-sixth

Year 1954, "The Year of the Great Decision" (June 1955), 19. See also, Medgar Evers to Mayor Allen Thompson and the Honorable Hugh L. White, January 21, 1955, NAACP Papers, LOC, Group II, Box C-346, Folder 4.

8. "Memorandum to Mr. Wilkins from Mr. Current," July 15, 1955, Medgar Evers to Gloster Current, July 25, 1955, NAACP Papers, LOC, Group II, Box C-346, Folder 5, and Evers and Peters, *For Us, the Living,* 184.

9. Medgar Evers to Gloster Current, December 21, 1954, Evers (Medgar Wiley and Myrlie Beasley) Papers, Box 2, Folder 6, "Memorandum to Mr. Wilkins from Mr. Current," December 28, 1954, and Gloster Current to Medgar Evers, December 29, 1954, NAACP Papers, LOC, Group II, Box C-346, Folder 4.

10. Charles Evers, February 4, 2005, interview.

11. Evers-Williams and Marable, *The Autobiography of Medgar Evers,* xiv; Evers-Williams, October 25, 2006, interview, quoted section regarding "Money, power, . . ."; Metcalf, *Black Profiles,* 201. Sentiments regarding Evers's selflessness proved a constant theme among the various individuals interviewed.

12. Roy Wilkins to Medgar Evers, November 24, 1954, NAACP Papers, LOC, Group II, Box C-346, Folder 4.

13. Nossiter, *Of Long Memory,* 41–42, and Dittmer, *Local People,* 31.

14. The *Brown* decision directly attacked the Court's 1896 *Plessy v. Ferguson* decision, which established the separate but equal doctrine. The *Brown* decision, however, did not immediately end segregation as states sought ways to get around it, forcing the Supreme Court in 1955 to require states to submit desegregation plans. This phase of the Court's decision, commonly referred as *Brown II,* was marked by the now infamous phrase "with all deliberate speed," a desegregation instruction that created more problems than it solved. For a more detailed analysis of the *Brown* decision, see Richard Kluger, *Simple Justice: The History of Brown v. Board of Education and Black America's Struggle for Equality* (New York: Alfred A. Knopf, 1976); James T. Patterson, *Brown v. Board of Education;* and Klarman, *From Jim Crow to Civil Rights.*

15. "'Uncle Toms' Scored in Mississippi School Fight," November 12, 1953, NAACP Papers, LOC, Group II, Box A-227, Folder 4.

16. Neil R. McMillen, *The Citizens' Council: Organized Resistance to the Second Reconstruction, 1954–64* (Urbana: University of Illinois Press, 1971), 15–16, and Yasuhiro Katagiri, *The Mississippi State Sovereignty Commission: Civil Rights and States' Rights* (Jackson: University Press of Mississippi, 2001), xxvii–xxviii.

17. Robert Fredrick Burk, *The Eisenhower Administration and Black Civil Rights* (Knoxville: University of Tennessee Press, 1984), 144–145, and Klarman, *From Jim Crow to Civil Rights,* 364–365.

18. Claude Ramsay interview with Orley B. Caudill, April 28, 1981, Mississippi Oral History Program, University of Southern Mississippi, Part I, 51, 59.

19. Moye, *Let the People Decide,* 31–32.

20. Numan V. Bartley, *The Rise of Massive Resistance: Race and Politics in the South During the 1950s* (Baton Rouge: Louisiana State University Press, 1969), 67.

21. Ibid., 68.

22. Ibid., 81.

23. Thomas Brady, "Black Monday," in *Mississippi: A Documentary History,* ed. Bradley G. Bond (Jackson: University Press of Mississippi, 2003), 234–235.

24. Joseph Crespino, *In Search of Another Country*, 18–20.

25. Ibid., 19; Henry with Curry, *Aaron Henry*, 91; Evers-Williams and Marable, *The Autobiography of Medgar Evers*, 14; *NAACP Annual Report*, Forty-sixth Year 1954, "The Year of the Great Decision" (June 1955), 11–12; Pete Daniel, *Lost Revolutions: The South in the 1950s* (Chapel Hill: University of North Carolina Press, 2000), 196–197; Moye, *Let the People Decide*, 56–58, 64–65; McMillen, *The Citizens' Council*, 16–17; and Bartley, *The Rise of Massive Resistance*, 82–107. For Citizens' Council membership data for Mississippi, see McMillen, *The Citizens' Council*, 26–28, and Moye, *Let the People Decide*, 68–69. According to Myrlie Evers, Aaron Henry acknowledged that he and Robert Patterson (Henry called him "Tut") grew up together and were close childhood friends in Evers and Peters, *For Us, the Living*, 233–234. Charles Payne also references the friendship in *I've Got the Light of Freedom*, 56. The formation of Citizens' Council chapters in Alabama, Louisiana, South Carolina, Georgia, and other southern areas are also subjects that McMillen addresses. The birth of the Mississippi State Sovereignty Commission became an important part of the massive resistance movement and will be discussed later. However, Crespino provides a detailed discussion of the tenets of "practical segregation" in the first chapter of *In Search of Another Country*.

26. "Halt Proposed Bias Amendment Now, Mitchell Urges Congress," June 10, 1954, NAACP Papers, LOC, Group II, Box A-227, Folder 4, 3.

27. For a historical discussion of the impact of the states' rights issue on the South and white southerners' propensity to react militarily in its defense, see Lacy K. Ford Jr., *Origins of Southern Radicalism: The South Carolina Upcountry 1800–1860* (Oxford: Oxford University Press, 1988), and for a detailed discussion of African American responses in the midst of the battle for the South, see Armstead L. Robinson, *Bitter Fruits of Bondage: The Demise of Slavery and the Collapse of the Confederacy, 1861–1865* (Charlottesville: University of Virginia Press, 2005).

28. Michael R. Belknap, *Federal Laws and Southern Order: Racial Violence and Constitutional Conflict in the Post-Brown South* (Athens: University of Georgia Press, 1987), ix.

29. Michael J. Klarman, "How Brown Changed Race Relations: The Backlash Thesis," *Journal of American History* 81, no. 1 (June 1994): 82, 98, 101, 103, and 110.

30. John R. Salter Jr., *Jackson, Mississippi: An American Chronicle of Struggle and Schism*, rpt. ed. (Malabar, FL: Robert E. Krieger Publishing Company, 1987), 8.

31. Henry with Curry, *Aaron Henry*, 85.

32. "Local Branch of the NAACP to Start Membership Drive," *Jackson Advocate*, April 2, 1955, 1, 7.

33. Metcalf, *Black Profiles*, 202.

34. Nossiter, *Of Long Memory*, 48–49.

35. Ibid., 34; Evers-Williams, October 25, 2006, interview; Charles Evers, February 4, 2005, interview; and Evers-Jordan, June 10, 2005, interview.

36. David L. Chappell, *A Stone of Hope: Prophetic Religion and the Death of Jim Crow* (Chapel Hill: University of North Carolina Press, 2004), 87.

37. Coretta Scott King, *The Words of Martin Luther King, Jr.* (New York: Newmarket Press, 1987), 65.

38. For a detailed examination of religion and the civil rights movement, see Aldon D. Morris, *The Origins of the Civil Rights Movement: Black Communities Organizing for Change* (New York: Free Press, 1984). See also, Charles Marsh, *God's Long Summer: Stories of Faith and Civil Rights* (Princeton, NJ: Princeton University Press, 1997).

39. Jacqueline S. Mattis, "Religion in African American Life," in *African American Family Life: Ecological and Cultural Diversity,* ed. Vonnie C. McLoyd, Nancy E. Hill, and Kenneth A. Dodge (New York: Guilford Press, 2005), 197.

40. Donald Jr., "The Civil Rights Leader as Utopianist," 220; Maryanne Vollers, *Ghosts of Mississippi,* 12; and Evers-Jordan, June 10, 2005, interview.

41. Nossiter, *Of Long Memory,* 31.

42. Stephanie I. Coard and Robert M. Sellers, "African American Families as a Context for Racial Socialization," *African American Family Life: Ecological and Cultural Diversity,* ed. Vonnie C. McLoyd, Nancy E. Hill, and Kenneth A. Dodge (New York: Guilford Press, 2005), 266.

43. Fred Clark Sr., June 10, 1994, interview with Leesha Faulkner, Mississippi Oral History Program, University of Southern Mississippi, volume 494, 1994, 6–7.

44. Stephanie I. Coard and Robert M. Sellers, "African American Families as a Context for Racial Socialization," 267.

45. Medgar Evers, "Why I Live in Mississippi," 65.

46. Ibid.

47. Ibid., 69.

48. Ibid., 67–68.

49. Evers and Peters, *For Us, the Living,* 106.

50. Medgar Evers, "Why I Live in Mississippi," 70.

51. Charles Evers, February 4, 2005, interview. For a deeper discussion of the torrid relationship between Charles Evers and the NAACP after he took over as field secretary, see Emilye Crosby, *A Little Taste of Freedom: The Black Freedom Struggle in Claiborne County, Mississippi* (Chapel Hill: University of North Carolina Press, 2005), 86–90.

52. Gloster Current to Medgar Evers, January 26, 1955, NAACP Papers, LOC, Group II, Box C-346, Folder 4, 4.

53. Roy Wilkins to Reverend J. E. Johnson, January 19, 1955, Evers (Medgar Wiley and Myrlie Beasley) Papers, Box 2, Folder 8. For a detailed outline of the meeting between the NAACP and Tri-State Bank spelling out the expectations of the partnership, see "Memorandum To: Board Committee on Mississippi," December 29, 1954, NAACP Papers, LOC, Group II, Box A-422, Folder 2.

54. Roy Wilkins to Reverend J. E. Johnson, January 19, 1955, Evers (Medgar Wiley and Myrlie Beasley) Papers, Box 2, Folder 8. *NAACP Annual Report,* Forty-seventh Year, "Progress and Reaction, 1955," 10.

55. Evers and Peters, *For Us, the Living,* 169.

56. Gloster Current to Medgar Evers, January 26, 1955, Evers (Medgar Wiley and Myrlie Beasley) Papers, Box 2, Folder 6, 5.

57. "Either Segregation or Inter-Marriage, Paul Johnson Says," *Jackson Daily News,* February 8, 1955, MDAH, Subject File, "Johnson, Paul B. Jr., 1948–1962."

58. "Paul B. Johnson Jr.—Confusing—N.A.A.C.P. Says," February 9, 1955, Evers (Medgar Wiley and Myrlie Beasley) Papers, Box 2, Folder 38, 1.

59. "Either Segregation or Inter-marriage, Paul Johnson Says," *Jackson Daily News,* February 8, 1955.

60. "Paul B. Johnson Jr.—Confusing—N.A.A.C.P. Says," 1–2.

61. Medgar Evers, "Ref: Case of Paul Ferguson East St. Louis, Illinois," to Roy Wilkins, Evers (Medgar Myrlie Beasley) Papers, Box 2, Folder 4, 1; Statement by Paul and Deloris Ferguson, March 7, 1955, NAACP Papers, LOC, Group II, Box A-422, Folder 1, 1.

62. Ibid. and Statement by Paul and Deloris Ferguson, March 7, 1955, NAACP Papers, LOC, Group II, Box A-422, Folder 1, 2.

63. Berg, *"The Ticket to Freedom,"* 13; Roy Wilkins to Medgar Evers, July 14, 1955, Evers (Medgar Wiley and Myrlie Beasley) Papers, Box 2, Folder 7, 1–2.

64. Roy Wilkins to Medgar Evers, July 14, 1955, Evers (Medgar Wiley and Myrlie Beasley) Papers, Box 2, Folder 7, 1.

65. For Evers's assurance that this would not happen again, see Medgar Evers to Roy Wilkins, July 18, 1955, Evers (Medgar Wiley and Myrlie Beasley) Papers, Box 2, Folder 7.

66. Evers and Peters, *For Us, the Living,* 197–199; Charles Evers, February 4, 2005, interview; and Evers-Jordan, June 10, 2006, interview.

67. "Memorandum to Mr. Evers from Mrs. Hurley," August 18, 1955, Evers (Medgar Wiley and Myrlie Beasley) Papers, Box 2, Folder 7.

68. Roy Wilkins to Medgar Evers, December 21, 1955, Evers (Medgar Wiley and Myrlie Beasley) Papers, Box 2, Folder 7, and John Morsell to Richard McLain, February 15, 1956, Papers of the NAACP: Part 20, White Resistance and Reprisals, 1956–1965 (Bethesda, MD: University Publications of America, 1995), Group III, Series A, Administrative File, General Office File, Box A-233, microfilm reel 3 (hereinafter cited Papers of the NAACP: Part 20).

69. Cornelius Turner, interview with the author, July 12, 2005, cassette recording, Jackson, Mississippi. Tape in possession of the author.

70. "Committee on Emergency Aid to Farmers in Mississippi," January 11, 1956, Papers of the NAACP: Part 20, Group III, Series A, Administrative File, General Office File, Box A-233, microfilm reel 3.

71. "Biographical Sketch" of Mildred Louise Bond, n.d., NAACP Papers, LOC, Group III, Box C-224, Folder 8.

72. Mildred Bond Roxborough, interview with the author, July 27, 2005, cassette recording, Manhattan, New York. Tape in possession of the author.

73. Simon Wendt, *The Spirit and the Shotgun: New Perspectives on the History of the South* (Gainesville: University Press of Florida, 2007), 104–105.

74. Colia Liddell Clark and Dr. Lewis Liddell interview with Worth Long, May 23, 1983, Southern Regional Council: Will the Circle be Unbroken? Program Files and Sound Recordings, 1956–1998, Box 8, Folder 19, Manuscript, Archives and Rare Book Library, Emory University, Atlanta, Georgia, 4. (Hereinafter cited SRC: Will the Circle be Unbroken?)

75. Ibid.

76. Salter, *Jackson, Mississippi,* 24, and Evers and Peters, *For Us, the Living,* 279–280. A *Washington Post* article titled "FBI Assists City Hunt for NAACP Aide's Killer" also acknowledges the existence of the protective window blinds. The *Post* correspondent maintained that the customized Venetian blinds "were designed to deflect gunfire." See the *Washington Post,* June 13, 1963, A6.

77. For discussion regarding enslaved resistance, see Winthrop D. Jordan, *Tumult and Silence at Second Creek: An Inquiry into a Civil War Slave Conspiracy,* rev. ed. (Baton Rouge: Louisiana State University Press, 1995), and Deborah Gray White, *Ar'n't I a Woman? Female Slaves in the Plantation South,* rev. ed. (New York: W. W. Norton & Company, 1999). In addition, there are also a series of works addressing the Denmark Vessey and Nat Turner revolts in Charleston, South Carolina, and Southampton, Virginia, respectively.

78. Robert F. Williams, *Negroes With Guns* (Detroit, MI: Wayne State University Press, 1998), xv–xxix, and Tyson, *Radio Free Dixie,* 49–50.

79. Evers-Williams and Marable, *The Autobiography of Medgar Evers,* 11–12.

80. For a detailed study of the Deacons, see Lance Hill, *The Deacons for Defense: Armed Resistance and the Civil Rights Movement* (Chapel Hill: University of North Carolina Press, 2004). See also, Simon Wendt, *The Spirit and the Shotgun.*

81. Mildred Bond Roxborough, July 27, 2005, interview.

82. Cornelius Turner, July 25, 2005, interview.

83. Tyson, *Radio Free Dixie,* 81–82.

84. Mildred Bond Roxborough, July 27, 2005, interview.

85. Ibid.

86. Medgar Evers and Mildred Bond, "Economic Needs of Farmers in Delta Area," report to Gloster Current, January, 23, 1956 and "Committee on Emergency Aid to Farmers in Mississippi," both in Papers of the NAACP: Part 20, Group III, Series A, Administrative File, General Office File, Box A-233, microfilm reel 3.

87. Evers and Bond, "Economic Needs of Farmers in Delta Area," microfilm reel 3.

88. Ibid.

89. Ibid.

90. Pete Daniel, *Lost Revolutions: The South in the 1950s* (Chapel Hill: University of North Carolina Press, 2000), 210–211.

91. Evers and Bond, "Economic Needs of Farmers in Delta Area," microfilm reel 3.

92. Ibid.

93. For further discussion on the effects of mechanization on black workers in the South, see *Payne, I've Got the Light of Freedom,* 17–18, Stephen Middleton and Charlotte M. Stokes, consultants for *The African American Experience: A History,* 2nd ed. (Upper Saddle River, NJ: Globe Fearon Educational Publisher, 1999), 328–329, and Daniels, *Lost Revolutions,* 8, 39–61.

94. Medgar Evers to Roy Wilkins, January 11, 1956, Papers of the NAACP: Part 20, Group III, Series A, Administrative File, General Office File, Box A-114, microfilm reel 14. To see the actual letter written by Jefferson, see George L. Jefferson to Roy Wilkins, January 10, 1955, NAACP Papers, LOC, Group II, Box A-422, Folder 2.

95. Ibid.

96. Medgar Evers to Roy Wilkins, April 30, 1956, Papers of the NAACP: Part 20, Group III, Box A-114, microfilm reel 14.

97. Medgar Evers to Gloster Current, May 4, 1956, NAACP Papers, LOC, Group III, Box C-243, Folder 5.

98. Gloster Current to Medgar Evers, May 10, 1956, NAACP Papers, LOC, Group III, Box C-243, Folder 5.

99. Medgar Evers to Gloster Current, May 14, 1956, NAACP Papers, LOC, Group III, Box C-243, Folder 5.

100. Gloster Current, "Memorandum to Mr. Moon from Mr. Current, Re: Press Release," December 1, 1955, NAACP Papers, LOC, Group II, Box A-422, Folder 1, 1; Medgar Evers, "1955 Annual Report," Evers (Medgar and Myrlie Beasley) Papers, Box 2, Folder 39, 7; and Medgar Evers to Roy Wilkins, "Report: Mr. Gus Courts," January 24, 1956, NAACP Papers, LOC, Group II, Box A-422, Folder 5. See also, "FBI Investigates Shooting of Negro; 3d Mississippi Probe in 6 Months," newspaper clipping, NAACP Papers, LOC, Group II, Box A-422, Folder 1.

101. Gloster Current, "Memorandum to Mr. Moon from Mr. Current," December 1, 1955, NAACP Papers, LOC, Group II, Box A-422, Folder 1.

102. Medgar Evers, "1955 Annual Report," Evers (Medgar and Myrlie Beasley) Papers, Box 2, Folder 39, 8.

103. Medgar Evers, "Monthly Report," January 27, 1956, NAACP Papers, LOC, Group III, Box C-243, Folder 5.

104. Clinton C. Battle to Roy Wilkins, September 25, 1956, Papers of the NAACP: Part 20, Group III, Series A, Administrative File, General Office File, Box A-230, microfilm reel 1; Medgar Evers to Roy Wilkins, September 27, 1956, Group III, Box A-230, Papers of the NAACP: Part 20, microfilm reel 1.

105. Medgar Evers to Roy Wilkins, September 27, 1956, Group III, Box A-230, Papers of the NAACP: Part 20, microfilm reel 1. Dr. Battle was also an ardent supporter and organizer for the NAACP and received a great deal of pressure from whites because of his activities; see Moye, *Let the People Decide,* 53–55.

106. J. Francis Pohlhaus to Medgar Evers, July 18, 1956, Evers (Medgar Wiley and Myrlie Beasley) Papers, Box 2, Folder 4. For Evers's April 25 monthly report to which Pohlhaus referred, see NAACP Papers, LOC, Group III, Box C-243, Folder 5.

107. Medgar Evers to J. Francis Pohlhaus, July 30, 1956, Evers (Medgar Wiley and Myrlie Beasley) Papers, Box 2, Folder 4.

108. "Program of the Fourth Annual Meeting of the Mississippi Regional Council of Negro Leadership," April 29, 1955, NAACP Papers, LOC, Group II, Box A-422, Folder 5.

109. Congressman Charles Diggs Jr. to Medgar Evers, October 2, 1956, Evers (Medgar Wiley and Myrlie Beasley) Papers, Box 2, Folder 4. In this particular letter Congressman Diggs mistakenly addresses Evers as Medgar W. Evans. For further discussion of the various legal and extralegal methods whites used to prevent African Americans in the South from voting during the 1940s and 1950s, see Dittmer, *Local People,* 1–9, 25–28, and Payne, *I've Got the Light of Freedom,* 25–27.

110. Medgar Evers to Congressmen Diggs, October 9, 1956, Evers (Medgar Wiley and Myrlie Beasley) Papers, Box 2, Folder 4.

111. "Jackson Police Jail 600 Negro Children," *New York Times,* June 1, 1963, 8.

4.

Epigraphs. Medgar Evers quoted in Evers and Peters, *For Us, the Living,* 226. Langston Hughes, excerpt from "Mississippi, 1955 (To the memory of Emmett Till)," Magazine Section, *Pittsburgh Courier,* September 1, 1956, Papers of the NAACP: Part 20, Group III, Box A-231, microfilm reel 1. Quoted in Medgar Evers, "Annual Report for the Mississippi State Office N.A.A.C.P.," November 14, 1957, NAACP Papers, LOC, Group III, Box C-244, Folder 1, 4.

1. John Dittmer, "The Politics of the Mississippi Movement, 1954–1964," in *The Civil Rights Movement in America*, ed. Charles W. Eagles (Jackson: University Press of Mississippi, 1986), 71; Henry and Curry, *The Fire Ever Burning*, 99; and Payne, *I've Got the Light of Freedom*, 40.

2. Kenneth O'Reilly, *Black Americans: The FBI Files*, ed. David Gallen (New York: Carroll & Graf Publishers, 1994), 130.

3. Mendelsohn, *The Martyrs*, 3. For works addressing the history and concept of liberation theology, see James H. Cone, *Black Theology and Black Power* (New York: Seabury Press, 1969); Diana L. Hayes, *And Still We Rise: An Introduction to Black Liberation Theology* (New York: Paulist Press, 1996); and Dwight N. Hopkins, *Introducing Black Theology of Liberation* (Maryknoll, NY: Orbis Books, 1999).

4. Mendelsohn, *The Martyrs*, 2–3, 7.

5. Medgar Evers, "1955 Annual Report," Evers (Medgar Wiley and Myrlie Beasley) Papers, Box 2, Folder 39, 5.

6. Evers and Peters, *For Us, the Living*, 155; Mendelsohn, *The Martyrs*, 3.

7. Ibid., 155–160; Memorandum from Mrs. Hurley, "Investigation of Death of Reverend G.W. Lee Belzoni, Mississippi," May 13, 1955, NAACP Papers, LOC, Group II, Box A-422, Folder 8, 2; Pete Daniel, *Lost Revolutions*, 222–224; John Dittmer, *Local People*, 53–54; Erle Johnston, *Mississippi's Defiant Years 1953–1973: An Interpretive Documentary with Personal Experiences* (Forest, MS: Lake Harbor Publishers, 1990), 34; Berg, "*The Ticket to Freedom*," 150–151; and *NAACP Annual Report*, Forty-seventh Year, "Progress and Reaction, 1955," 23. See also, "M is for Mississippi and Murder," NAACP Papers, LOC, Group II, Box A-423, Folder 1, 4.

8. Medgar Evers, "1955 Annual Report," Evers (Medgar Wiley and Myrlie Beasley) Papers, Box 2, Folder 39, 5.

9. Ruby Hurley to "The Honorable Hugh White," May 9, 1955, 2, and "White Ignores NAACP's Plea in Death Case," n.d., NAACP Papers, LOC, Group II, Box A-422, Folder 8.

10. Affidavit of Alex Hudson, May 26, 1955 and NAACP release, "Witness to Lee Murder Located in Illinois," May 26, 1955, NAACP Papers, LOC, Group II, Box A-422, Folder 8.

11. Mendelsohn, *The Martyrs*, 6.

12. NAACP Press Release, "Jackson Dentist at Belzoni Inquest, May 13, 1955, NAACP Papers, LOC, Group II, Box A-422, Folder 8, 1–2, and Memorandum from Mrs. Hurley, "Investigation of Death of Reverend G.W. Lee Belzoni, Mississippi," May 13, 1955, NAACP Papers, LOC, Group II, Box A-422, Folder 8.

13. Medgar Evers to Gloster Current, "Report of activities for May, 1955," May 25, 1955, NAACP Papers, LOC, Group II, Box C-346, Folder 4, 2.

14. Medgar Evers to Roy Wilkins, May 24, 1955, NAACP Papers, LOC, Group II, Box A-422, Folder 8.

15. R. Hurley, "Information Re Killing in Mississippi Telephoned in by R. Hurley May 13, 1955 11:55 A.M." NAACP Papers, LOC, Group II, Box A-422, Folder 8.

16. Evers and Peters, *For Us, the Living,* 159.

17. *NAACP Annual Report,* Forty-seventh Year, "Progress and Reaction, 1955," 24; Dittmer, *Local People,* 54; Payne, *I've Got the Light of Freedom,* 39; "M is for Mississippi and Murder," NAACP Papers, LOC, Group II, Box A-423, Folder 1, 5; and NAACP release "NAACP Urges Federal Action on Violence in Mississippi," August 18, 1955, NAACP Papers, LOC, Group II, Box A-422, Folder 1.

18. Amzie Moore quoted in Daniel, *Lost Revolutions,* 209.

19. Evers and Peters, *For Us, the Living,* 273.

20. Ibid., 169–170, NAACP Release, "NAACP Urges Federal Action on Violence in Mississippi," August 18, 1955, NAACP Papers, LOC, Group II, Box A-422, Folder 1.

21. Medgar Evers, "1955 Annual Report," Evers (Medgar Wiley and Myrlie Beasley) Papers, Box 2, Folder 39, 5.

22. Newspaper clipping, "Pin Vote Slaying on Trio," n.d., NAACP Papers, LOC, Group II, Box A-422, Folder 1.

23. "White Farmer Faces Murder Charge After Lincoln Negro Killed," *Jackson Daily News,* August 15, 1955, 1; "DA Arrests Suspect in Political Killing," *State Times,* August 15, 1955, 1; and *NAACP Annual Report,* Forty-seventh Year, "Progress and Reaction, 1955," 9, 24.

24. Medgar Evers, "1955 Annual Report," Evers (Medgar Wiley and Myrlie Beasley) Papers, Box 2, Folder 39, 5–6, and "Who Slew Negro Leader in Trap," *Jet* magazine, vol. 8, no. 17, September 1, 1955, 5. Although he discusses the Smith murder in his 1955 report, Evers provided a little more clarity regarding the physical attack upon Smith and the lack of an indictment during an address before the Los Angeles branch of the NAACP on May 31, 1959. The address is located under Medgar Evers, "Address to the Los Angeles, California Branch NAACP," MDAH, Subject File, "Medgar Evers 1954–1973," 4.

25. Roy Wilkins to U.S. Attorney General Herbert Brownell Jr., August 24, 1955, NAACP Papers, LOC, Group II, Box A-422, Folder 5, 3.

26. See NAACP *Annual Report,* "Progress and Reaction, 1955," 8.

27. Moody, *Coming of Age in Mississippi* (New York: Dell Publishing, 1968), 125–126.

28. Dittmer, *Local People,* 57–58, and Payne, *I've Got the Light of Freedom,* 54–55.

29. *NAACP Annual Report,* Forty-seventh Year, "Progress and Reaction, 1955," 25; Medgar Evers, "1955 Annual Report," 6; *Look* magazine release, "Emmett Till's Bravado Led to Killing, it is Disclosed," 1–3; Papers of the NAACP: Part 20, Group III, Box A-231, microfilm reel 1; NAACP's pamphlet, "M is for Mississippi and Murder," 5–6, Papers of the NAACP: Part 20, Group III, Series A, Administrative File, General Office File, Box A-232, microfilm reel 2; and Gene Roberts and Hank Klibanoff, *The Race Beat,* 86–108. For a detailed examination of the Till murder and its affects upon individuals' desire to not allow Till's death to be in vain, see the September 1, 1956, issue of the *Pittsburgh Courier.* A Sumner, Mississippi, jury found Bryant and Milam not guilty of the murder of Emmett Till and the brothers later agreed to an interview with journalist William Bradford Huie for *Look* magazine for which they were paid. Bryant and Milam admitted during the interview that they had indeed killed Till for his

brashness and admissions that he had "had white women" before. For the interview with Bryant and Milam, see *Look* magazine, January 24, 1956. For a closer examination of the impact of the Till lynching on the civil rights movement, see Clenora Hudson-Weems, *Emmett Till: The Sacrificial Lamb of the Civil Rights Movement* (Troy, MI: Bedford Publishers, 1994), and Stephen J. Whitfield, *A Death in the Delta: The Story of Emmett Till* (Baltimore, MD: Johns Hopkins University Press, 1988). For visual analyses of the Till lynching and its significance to the civil rights movement, see *Eyes on the Prize: America's Civil Rights Movement, 1954–1985*, videocassette, executive producer Henry Hampton (Blackside Productions, 1987), and *The Untold Story of Emmett Louis Till* DVD, directed by Keith Beauchamp (Hollywood, CA: Velocity Home Entertainment, 2006).

30. Ed King interview with Worth Long, August 23, 1991, SRC: Will the Circle be Unbroken? 6, and Dittmer, *Local People,* 59. Reverend Edwin King, who many referred to as Ed, is a white minister who was an active participant in the fight to secure social and political equality for African Americans in Mississippi. He participated in the Jackson campaign and supported the boycotts. Although King notes that Till whistled at Carolyn Bryant, which put the eventual tragedy in motion, there exists a variety of accounts detailing what happened in the store between Bryant and Till with his whistling being one of the many. For further discussion of the Till case, in particular the night Milam and Bryant kidnapped the young child, see Juan Williams, *Eyes on the Prize: America's Civil Rights Years, 1954–1965,* 15th anniversary ed. (New York: Penguin Books), 39–57.

31. Myrlie Evers quoted in Henry Hampton and Steve Fayer, eds., *Voices of Freedom: An Oral History of the Civil Rights Movement from the 1950s to the 1980s* (New York: Bantam Books, 1990), 6.

32. Howard Spence quoted in Bob Blauner, *Black Lives, White Lives: Three Decades of Race Relations in America* (Berkeley and Los Angeles: University of California Press, 1989), 34.

33. Ibid.

34. Mamie Till-Mobley and Christopher Benson, *Death of Innocence: The Story of the Hate Crime that Changed America* (New York: Random House, 2003), 153–154; Juan Williams, *Eyes on the Prize,* 46–47; and Charles Evers, February 4, 2005, interview.

35. Medgar Evers, "1955 Annual Report," Evers (Medgar Wiley and Myrlie Beasley) Papers, Box 2, Folder 39, 6–7.

36. Roy Wilkins Memorandum to the United States Justice Department, "Reign of Terror in Mississippi," September 7, 1955, NAACP Papers, LOC, Group II, Box A-422, Folder 3, 4.

37. Minnie White Watson, interview with the author, September 12, 2006, cassette recording, L. Zenobia Coleman Library, Tougaloo College, Tougaloo, Mississippi. Tape in possession of the author. Watson serves as assistant in the Tougaloo College archives, curator for the Medgar Evers Museum, and registrar for the Tougaloo Arts Colony. Watson noted that she has both read materials and spoke with individuals who support the instrumental role Medgar played in convincing Mamie Till to have an open casket funeral for her son Emmett.

38. See "Will Mississippi 'Whitewash' the Emmett Till Slaying?" *Jet* magazine, vol. 8, no. 20, September 22, 1955. The disturbing photo of the murdered Till

can be viewed on page 9. For further discussion of the problems that African Americans faced in Mississippi, see *Jet: Special Report Mississippi,* vol. 26, no. 16, July 23, 1964.

39. Minnie White Watson, September 12, 2006, interview.

40. Evers and Peters, *For Us, the Living,* 158–159.

41. See the *Pittsburgh Courier* September 17 edition, "Eyes of Nation Focused in Monday Trial in Miss," 1. Also see, in particular, "The Picture Story of a Little Boy's Murder," *Pittsburgh Courier,* September 17, 1955, 9, second section, and Evers and Peters, *For Us, the Living,* 158–159.

42. Medgar Evers, "1955 Annual Report," 9–10. Evers noted that the other NAACP officials attending the meeting included executive secretary Roy Wilkins, attorney Thurgood Marshall, Southeast Regional secretary Ruby Hurley, and the director of the Washington Bureau Clarence Mitchell. For a group photograph of those attending the meeting, see *Jet,* "Will Mississippi 'Whitewash' the Emmett Till Slaying?" 7.

43. Assistant U.S. Attorney General Warren Olney, III to Roy Wilkins, December 6, 1955, NAACP Papers, LOC, Group II, Box A-422, Folder 3.

44. See, Dittmer, *Local People,* 58; Beito and Beito, *Black Maverick,* 140; and Medgar Evers, "Report: Killing of Clinton Melton, Negro, by Elmer Kimbel, White," December 13, 1955, Evers (Medgar Wiley and Myrlie Beasley) Papers, Box 3, Folder 14, 1–3.

45. Medgar Evers, "Report: Killing of Clinton Melton, Negro, by Elmer Kimbel, White," December 13, 1955, Evers (Medgar Wiley and Myrlie Beasley) Papers, Box 3, Folder 14, 1–3, Dittmer, *Local People,* 58, and Payne, *I've Got the Light of Freedom,* 39.

46. Medgar Evers, "Report: Killing of Clinton Melton," 3.

47. Medgar Evers, "Information Received From Telephone Call from Medgar W. Evers Calling from Greenwood, Mississippi Enroute [*sic*] to Jackson," December 8, 1955, NAACP Papers, LOC, Group II, Box A-422, Folder 5, 1.

48. Ibid., 1–2.

49. J. Mills Thornton III, *Dividing Lines: Municipal Politics and the Struggle for Civil Rights in Montgomery, Birmingham, and Selma* (Tuscaloosa: The University of Alabama Press, 2002), 40–47, and Robinson, Hampton, and Fayer, eds., *Voices of Freedom,* 22–23.

50. Rosa Parks with Jim Haskins, *Rosa Parks: My Story* (New York: Dial Books, 1992), 77.

51. Rosa Parks quoted in Robinson, Hampton, and Fayer, eds., *Voices of Freedom,* 19–20, and Taylor Branch, *Parting the Waters: America in the King Years, 1954–1963* (New York: Simon and Schuster, 1988), 128–129.

52. Parks and Haskins, *Rosa Parks,* 77.

53. Howell Raines, *My Soul is Rested: Movement Days in the Deep South Remembered* (New York: G. P. Putnam's Sons, 1977), 40. For a detailed examination of the Montgomery Bus Boycott, including primary discussions of the event, see David J. Garrow, ed., *The Walking City: The Montgomery Bus Boycott, 1955–1956* (New York: Carlson Publishing, 1989).

54. Raines, *My Soul is Rested,* 40. See also, Thornton, *Dividing Lines,* 57–61.

55. *NAACP Annual Report,* Forty-seventh Year, "Progress and Reaction, 1955," 10; *NAACP Annual Report,* Forty-eighth Year, "New threat to Civil Liberties, 1956" (June 1957), 7; Taylor Branch, *Parting the Waters,* 128–129;

Harvard Sitkoff, *The Struggle for Black Equality, 1954–1992,* rev. ed. (New York: Hill and Wang, 1993), 37–38; and Joel Williamson, *The Crucible of Race: Black White Relations in the American South Since Emancipation* (New York: Oxford University Press, 1984), 502. Here Williamson challenges the assumption that Parks was simply a tired seamstress who lacked the strength to move to another seat. He observed that she was an active member of the NAACP who "had been trained in leadership in an Association school near Monteagle, Tennessee." See also, Thornton, *Dividing Lines,* 59–60. The local chapter of the NAACP had planned to conduct a boycott prior to Parks's action, but the pregnancy of the young woman who was to initiate the boycott made NAACP officials hesitant because of the potential for attack upon her character. For a closer examination of the origins of the Montgomery Bus Boycott and the role that women played, see David Garrow, ed., *The Montgomery Bus Boycott and the Women Who Started it: The Memoir of Jo Ann Gibson Robinson* (Knoxville: University of Tennessee Press, 1987). For more on the history of the city of Montgomery and the bus boycott, see Thornton, *Dividing Lines,* 20–140.

56. The *Montgomery Advertiser—Alabama Journal,* December 25, 1955 NAACP Papers, LOC, Group II, Box K-18, Folder 1.

57. Wendt, *The Spirit and the Shotgun,* 9. For an examination of the civil rights movement and its impact upon historical memory, see Renee C. Romano and Leigh Raiford, eds., *The Civil Rights Movement in American Memory.*

58. Medgar Evers to Rev. Dr. Joseph H. Jackson, December 17, 1956, LOC, Group III, Box C-243, Folder 5, 1; Medgar Evers "Monthly Report," December 26, 1956, NAACP Papers, LOC, Group III, Box C-243, Folder 5, 2; and Taylor Branch, *Parting the Waters: America the King Years, 1954–63* (New York: Simon and Schuster, 1988), 193–196.

59. Medgar Evers to Rev. Dr. Joseph H. Jackson, December 17, 1956, LOC, Group III, Box C-243, Folder 5, 1.

60. Ibid. and Medgar Evers "Monthly Report," December 26, 1956, NAACP Papers, LOC, Group III, Box C-243, Folder 5, 2.

61. Martin Luther King Jr., to Medgar Evers, December 11, 1956; Clayborne Carson, ed., *The Papers of Martin Luther King, Jr.,* vol. 3 (Berkeley and Los Angeles: University of California Press, 1997), 471.

62. Evers-Williams and Marable, *The Autobiography of Medgar Evers,* 76.

63. "NAACP Opens 47th Meeting," *Washington Post,* June 27, 1956, 32; "N.A.A.C.P. Studies Resistance Move," *New York Times,* July 1, 1956, 60; David J. Garrow, *Bearing the Cross: Martin Luther King, Jr., and the Southern Christian Leadership Conference,* 1st Perennial Classics ed. (New York: Perennial Classics, 2004), 78; Taylor Branch, *Parting the Waters,* 189–190; Michael D. Davis and Hunter R. Clark, eds., *Thurgood Marshall:, Warrior at the Bar, Rebel on the Bench,* updated and revised ed. (New York: Carol Publishing Group, 1994), 201–202; and Evers and Szanton, *Have No Fear,* 93.

64. NAACP *Annual Report,* Forty-eighth Year, "New Threat to Civil Liberties, 1956," 67, and Davis and Clark, *Thurgood Marshall,* 203.

65. NAACP *Annual Report,* "New Threat to Civil Liberties," 63, and Evers and Szanton, *Have No Fear,* 93.

66. Wendt, *The Spirit and the Shotgun,* 8–9; David Garrow, *Bearing the Cross,* 59–62; Branch, *Parting the Waters,* 164–167; and James Haskins, *The Life and Death of Martin Luther King, Jr.* (New York: First Beech Tree edition, 1992), 54.

67. Medgar Evers to Martin Luther King Jr., Carson, ed., *The Papers of Martin Luther King, Jr.,* vol. 3, 330; and Martin Luther King Jr. to Medgar Evers, *The Papers of Martin Luther King, Jr.,* vol. 3, 470–471.

68. Medgar Evers to Roy Wilkins, April 10, 1956, Papers of the NAACP: Part 20, Group III, Box A-231, microfilm reel 2.

69. Roy Wilkins to Medgar Evers, April 16, 1956, Papers of the NAACP: Part 20, Group III, Box A-231, microfilm reel 2.

70. Cornelius Turner, July 25, 2005, interview.

71. Myrlie Evers-Williams, October 25, 2006, interview; Evers-Williams and Marable, *The Autobiography of Medgar Evers,* 52; and Gloster Current, "Memo to Roy Wilkins from Mr. Current," March 6, 1957, NAACP Papers, LOC, Group III, Box A-114, Folder 5. For the origins of the SCLC, see Adam Fairclough, *To Redeem the Soul of America: The Southern Christian Leadership Conference and Martin Luther King, Jr.* (Athens: University of Georgia Press, 1987), 11–35.

72. Fairclough, *To Redeem the Soul of America,* 44–45.

73. Medgar Evers to Roy Wilkins, March 11, 1957, NAACP Papers, LOC, Group III, Box C-244, Folder 1.

74. Clayborne Carson, ed., *The Papers of Martin Luther King, Jr.,* vol. 4 (Berkeley and Los Angeles: University of California Press, 1997), 259.

75. Ibid.

76. Ibid.

77. Myrlie Evers-Williams, October 25, 2006, interview.

78. Adam Fairclough, *Race & Democracy,* 159–160, and Aldon Morris, *The Origins of the Civil Rights Movement,* 17.

79. Fairclough, *To Redeem the Soul of America,* 12, 28; Fairclough, *Race & Democracy,* 158–161; and Morris, *The Origins of the Civil Rights Movement,* 18–25.

80. T. J. Jemison quoted in Morris, *The Origins of the Civil Rights Movement,* 25.

81. Hampton and Fayer, eds., *Voices of Freedom,* 26. For additional accounts of the struggle for civil rights in Louisiana, see Greta de Jong, *A Different Day: African American Struggles for Justice in Rural Louisiana, 1900–1970* (Chapel Hill: University of North Carolina Press, 2002), and John H. Scott with Cleo Scott Brown, *Witness to the Truth: My Struggle for Human Rights in Louisiana* (Columbia: University of South Carolina Press, 2003).

82. Evers-Williams and Marable, *The Autobiography of Medgar Evers,* 75–76.

83. Yasuhiro Katagiri, *The Mississippi State Sovereignty Commission,* 40.

84. Ibid., 5.

85. House Bill 880, Ed King Collection, University of Mississippi Department of Archives and Special Collections, Box 2, Folder 2, 1–2.

86. Katagiri, *The Mississippi State Sovereignty Commission,* 8, quoted section, 9, and Crespino, *In Search of Another Country,* 36. Crespino offers an excellent analysis of the struggle for the minds of the masses waged by both African Americans and whites. He also offers a detailed examination of the development of white resistance to African American progress and the social and political mechanisms behind white opposition. For a brief discussion, see Crespino, *In Search of Another Country,* 70–74.

87. Katagiri, *The Mississippi State Sovereignty Commission,* 8–9. See also, James Dickerson, *Dixie's Dirty Secret: The True Story of How the Government,*

the Media, and the Mob Conspired to Combat Integration and the Vietnam Antiwar Movement (New York: M. E. Sharpe, 1998).

88. Gregory Charles Crofton, "Defending Segregation: Mississippi State Sovereignty Commission and the Press" (MA thesis, University of Mississippi, 1985), 29. Also see, Katagiri, *The Mississippi State Sovereignty Commission,* 35.

89. Henry Jay Kirksey interview with Worth Long, (n.d.), SRC: Will the Circle be Unbroken?, Emory University, Box 8, Folder 18, 16.

90. Katagiri, *The Mississippi State Sovereignty Commission,* 40–41; Dickerson, *Dixie's Dirty Secret,* 27; Sovereignty Commission Papers, SCR # 2–5–1–13–1–1–1; 9–0–0–1–1–1–1; and 9–0–0–40–1–1–1.

91. Katagiri, *The Mississippi State Sovereignty Commission,* 41.

92. Newspaper Clippings "Medgar Evers Denies Charge He's Quitting NAACP, *State Times* (Jackson), July 18–21, 1957; "Negro Pastors Assail Trio for Anti-Mix Aid," *Jackson Daily News,* July, 18, 1957; and "Humes Says He'll Sue Accusers For Libel," *Delta Democrat-Times,* July, 21, 1957, NAACP Papers, LOC, Group III, Box A-14, Folder 5.

93. Medgar Evers, "Monthly Report," July 25, 1957; NAACP Papers, LOC, Group III, Box A-114, Folder 5, 2.

94. Medgar Evers to Ruby Hurley, July 26, 1957, NAACP Papers, LOC, Group III, Box C-244, Folder 1.

95. Daniel, *Lost Revolutions,* 226. Also see Katagiri, *The Mississippi State Sovereignty Commission,* 28, 70.

96. Medgar Evers, "Monthly Report," July 22, 1960, NAACP Papers, LOC, Group III, Box C-244, Folder 4, 1.

97. Medgar Evers et al., to Mayor Allen Thompson, Mississippi Bank Association, et al., May 13, 1963, NAACP Papers, LOC, Group III, Box E-9, Folder 8, 1.

98. An extraordinary legislative session refers to an unscheduled special legislative session. For example, after the legislative session has ended, the governor has the authority to call for a special session. If the special session has not ended in the time allotted by the governor, the session continues and is referred to as an extraordinary session.

99. Mississippi Legislature, "Senate Concurrent Resolution no. 6," Evers (Medgar Wiley and Myrlie Beasley) Papers, Box 2, Folder 8.

100. Medgar Evers to Roy Wilkins, April 30, 1956, Papers of the NAACP: Part 20, Group III, Box A-114, microfilm reel 14, 2.

101. Gloster Current to Medgar Evers, September 26, 1956, Papers of the NAACP: Part 20, Group III, Box A-114, microfilm reel 14.

102. Membership statistics taken from *NAACP Annual Report,* Forty-seventh Year, "Progress and Reaction, 1955," 15 and NAACP *Annual Report,* Forty-eighth Year, "New Threat to Civil Liberties, 1956," 11.

103. Medgar Evers to Roy Wilkins, September 12, 1956, Evers (Medgar Wiley and Myrlie Beasley) Papers, Box 2, Folder 9.

104. Gloster Current to Medgar Evers, September 26, 1956, Papers of the NAACP: Part 20, Group III, Box A-114, microfilm reel 14.

105. Medgar Evers to Gloster Current, October 2, 1956, Papers of the NAACP: Part 20, Group III, Box A-114, microfilm reel 14, 2.

106. Medgar Evers, "1955 Annual Report," Evers (Medgar and Myrlie Beasley) Papers, Box 2, Folder 39, 10.

107. Sam Bailey interview with George King, May 1992; SRC: Will the Circle be Unbroken? Emory University, 6; and Myrlie Evers, "'He Said He Wouldn't Mind Dying—If . . . ,'" *Life* magazine, 36.

108. Medgar Evers, vehicle receipts, Papers of the NAACP: Part 20, Group III, Box A-233, microfilm reel 3. This series also contains additional vehicle maintenance receipts.

109. Roy Wilkins to Medgar Evers, December 18, 1956, NAACP Papers, LOC, Group III, Box C-243, Folder 5.

110. John Morsell to Medgar Evers, December 20, 1956, Papers of the NAACP: Part 20, Group III, Box A-233, microfilm reel 3.

111. Medgar Evers to Roy Wilkins, December 22, 1956, and Roy Wilkins to Medgar Evers, January 2, 1957, NAACP Papers, LOC, Group III, Box C-244, Folder 1.

112. "Subject: Medgar W. Evers," Sovereignty Commission Papers, SCR # 1–23–0–70–3–1–1.

113. Ibid.

114. Ibid., SCR # 2–55–2–35–2–1–1. For further examples of the commission's detailed surveillance of Medgar Evers and the civil rights movement in Mississippi, see *Sovereignty Commission Papers,* SCR #s 1–23–0–70–3–1–1, 2–5–3–8–1–1–1, 2–7–0–16–1–1–1, 2–55–2–16–1–1–1, 2–72–2–41–1–1–1, 2–55–10–2–1–1–1. For examples of the information collected on the Evers children, see birth certificate records, State Board of Health, Bureau of Vital Statistics, SCR #s, 2–55–9–38–1–1–1, 97–97–3–245–14–1–1, and 2–55–9–37–2–1–1, which also contains school enrollment information.

115. Sovereignty Commission Papers, SCR # 10–35–1–122–1–1–1.

116. Ibid., SCR # 1–23–0–70–3–1–1.

117. Medgar Evers to Roy Wilkins, February 1, 1957, NAACP Papers, LOC, Group II, Box A-270, Folder 9, 1–2.

118. Medgar Evers, "Monthly Report," March, 25 1957, NAACP Papers, LOC, Group III, Box C-244, Folder 1, 2–3; Medgar Evers, "Monthly Report," April 24, 1957, NAACP Papers, LOC, Group III, Box C-244, Folder 1, 2; and Henry Jay Kirksey interview with Worth Long, (n.d.), SRC: Will the Circle be Unbroken?, Emory University, Box 8, Folder 18, 17.

119. Medgar Evers, "Monthly Report," March 25, 1957, NAACP Papers, LOC, Group III, Box C-244, Folder 1, 3.

120. Medgar Evers to Gloster Current, April 9, 1957, NAACP Papers, LOC, Group III, Box C-244, Folder 1.

121. Medgar Evers, "Monthly Report," February 26, 1957, NAACP Papers, LOC, Group III, Box C-244, Folder 1, 3.

122. Medgar Evers to John A. Morsell, April 4, 1957, Papers of the NAACP: Part 20, Group III, Box A-114, microfilm reel 14.

123. Medgar Evers to John A. Morsell, April 10, 1957, Papers of the NAACP: Part 20, Group III, Box A-114, microfilm reel 14.

124. Evers (Medgar Wiley and Myrlie Beasley) Papers, Box 2, Folder 21; Medgar Evers to John A. Morsell, April 10, 1957, Papers of the NAACP: Part 20, Group III, Box A-114, microfilm reel 14, and NAACP *Annual Report,* 1959, "The Year of Jubilee," 75; and "Statement of Mrs. Beatrice Young . . . Before the Senate Subcommittee on Constitutional Rights," February 28, 1957, Evers (Medgar Wiley and Myrlie Beasley) Papers, Box 2, Folder 21.

125. Ineeva May-Pittman, interview with the author, September 11, 2006, cassette recording, Jackson, Mississippi. Tape in possession of the author.

126. Medgar Evers to Thurgood Marshall, June 3, 1957, NAACP Papers, LOC, Group III, Box A-114, Folder 5.

127. Adam Fairclough, *Race & Democracy*, 212–213. In addition, Wright had also attacked the legitimacy of school segregation almost a year earlier, see C. Vann Woodward, *The Strange Career of Jim Crow: A Commemorative Edition* (New York: Oxford University Press, 2002), 153–154.

128. Sovereignty Commission Papers, SCR # 1–23–0–22–5–1–1.

129. Cary Fraser, "Crossing the Color Line in Little Rock: The Eisenhower Administration and the Dilemma of Race for U.S. Foreign Policy," *Diplomatic History* 24, no. 2 (Spring 2000): 236–238.

130. Paul Gordon Lauren, "Seen from the Outside: The International Perspective on America's Dilemma," in *Window on Freedom: Race, Civil Rights, and Foreign Affairs 1945–1988*, ed. Brenda Gayle Plummer (Chapel Hill: University of North Carolina Press, 2003), 21–38. See also Dudziak, *Cold War Civil Rights*, 39–42.

131. Whitfield, *A Death in the Delta*, 71. See also, Robert Fredrick Burk, *The Eisenhower Administration and Black Civil Rights* (Knoxville: University of Tennessee Press, 1984).

132. Eisenhower quoted in Burk, *The Eisenhower Administration and Black Civil Rights*, 152.

133. Ibid., 210, 226.

134. Manning Marable, *Race, Reform, and Rebellion: The Second Reconstruction in Black America, 1945–1990*, 2nd ed. (Jackson: University Press of Mississippi, 1991), 41–42, and Harvard Sitkoff, *The Struggle for Black Equality, 1954–1992*, rev. ed. (New York: Hill & Wang, 1993), 32–33.

135. John A. Kirk, *Beyond Little Rock: The Origins and Legacies of the Central High Crisis* (Fayetteville: University of Arkansas Press, 2007), 98, and Elizabeth Jacoway, *Turn Away Thy Son: Little Rock, the Crisis that Shocked the Nation* (New York: Free Press, 2007), 48–52. The school district proposed a phase program for school integration on May 24, 1955; grades 10–12 would probably integrate in the fall of 1957 with grades 7–9 following if successful and elementary schools next. See Jacoway, *Turn Away Thy Son*, 48–52. See also, Kirk, *Redefining the Color Line: Black Activism in Little Rock, Arkansas, 1940–1970* (Gainesville: University Press of Florida, 2002).

136. Jacoway, *Turn Away Thy Son*, 52–54.

137. See Klarman, *From Jim Crow to Civil Rights*, 324, 333, and Pete Daniel, *Lost Revolutions*, 36–37.

138. Jacoway, *Turn Away Thy Son*, 101–102.

139. For further discussion on the Little Rock desegregation crisis and its leadership, see Daniel, *Lost Revolutions*, 251–283; Grif Stockley, *Daisy Bates: Civil Rights Crusader from Arkansas* (Jackson: University Press of Mississippi, 2005); Daisy Bates, *The Long Shadow of Little Rock: A Memoir by Daisy Bates* (Fayetteville: University of Arkansas Press, 1987); and Langston Hughes, *Fight for Freedom: The Story of the NAACP* (New York: W. W. Norton & Company, 1962), 151–155.

140. Lillie Jones interview with Michael Garvey, December 11, 1974, Mississippi Oral History Program, University of Southern Mississippi, volume 181, 1981, 31.

141. "Interview with John R. Salter, Jr.," Congressional & Political Research

Center Digital Collections, John C. Stennis Oral History Project, Mississippi State University, December 26, 1990, 14, Ed King interview with Anne Romaine, "Mississippi Freedom Democratic Party," MDAH, Accession number OH/1981.08, Volume II, B2/R33/B3/54, August 29 (no year provided), 5–6. Regarding Gloster Current's refutation that there was ever an NAACP "policy to 'go slow' in Mississippi in the late 1950s" or that the NAACP had an agreement with the Eisenhower administration to that affect, see Adam Nossiter, *Of Long Memory,* 268 note 64.

142. Medgar Evers to Robert Carter, September 4, 1957, NAACP Papers, LOC, Group III, Box C-244, Folder 1.

143. Medgar Evers, "Monthly Report," September 24, 1957, NAACP Papers, LOC, Group III, Box C-244, Folder 1, 1–2. Here Evers is referring to the Civil Rights Act Eisenhower signed into law on September 9, 1957.

144. Medgar Evers, "Special Report," December 11, 1957, NAACP Papers, LOC, Group III, Box C-244, Folder 1, 1–2.

145. Ibid., 2–3.

146. Medgar Evers to Ruby Hurley, January 24, 1958, NAACP Papers, LOC, Group III, Box C-244, Folder 2.

147. See Medgar Evers, "Personal Statement," and "rec'd via phone from Medgar Evers . . . ," March 13, 1958, Papers of the NAACP: Part 20, Group III, Box A-114, microfilm reel 14. His statement was dictated but not signed. The incident was also reported in the *Birmingham News, Facts on Film,* 54/58, Microfilm Code No. J14 4736, "Negro Says Civil Rights Violated in Bus Controversy," and the *Pittsburgh Courier,* "Attacked on Bus in Miss.: Beat NAACP Exec," March 22, 1958, 3. Newspaper clipping, Evers (Medgar and Myrlie Beasley) Papers, Box 24, Folder 5.

148. Robert L. Carter to Roy Wilkins, April 9, 1958, Papers of the NAACP: Part 20, Group III, Box A-114, microfilm reel 14.

149. Myrlie Evers-Williams, book signing lecture, Old Capitol building, June 13, 2005, cassette recording, Jackson, Mississippi. Tape in possession of the author.

150. Medgar Evers to Clarence Mitchell, May 1, 1958, NAACP Papers, LOC, Group III, Box A-114, Folder 5.

151. Medgar Evers to James E. Johnson, January 12, 1959, Papers of the NAACP: Part 20, Group III, Box A-114, microfilm reel 14.

152. Evers and Peters, *For Us, the Living,* 126–127.

153. Ibid., 128.

154. Henry with Curry, *Aaron Henry,* 72.

155. Danielle L. McGuire, *At the Dark End of the Street: Black Women, Rape and Resistance—A New History of the Civil Rights Movement from Rosa Parks to the Rise of Black Power* (New York: Alfred A. Knopf, 2010).

156. www.maps.google.com.

157. Medgar Evers, "Address to the Los Angeles, California Branch NAACP," MDAH Subject File, "Medgar Evers 1954–1973," 7.

158. Howard Smead, *Blood Justice: The Lynching of Mack Charles Parker* (New York: Oxford University Press, 1986), 3–12.

159. Ibid., 10 and 12.

160. Ibid., 13.

161. Medgar Evers, "Monthly Report," May 21, 1959, NAACP Papers, LOC, Group III, Box C-244, Folder 3, 2.

162. Smead, *Blood Justice,* 28.
163. Ibid., 12–14.
164. Dittmer, *Local People,* 83. The criminal charge leveled against Mack Charles Parker and his lynching received considerable news coverage and was reported in papers such as the *Nashville Tennessean.* For an example, see "Parker Planned Rape, Says Pals," *Facts on Film,* July 58–June 59, Microfilm Code No. J6 2233.
165. Medgar Evers, "Monthly Report," May 21, 1959, NAACP Papers, LOC, Group III, Box C-244, Folder 3, 3.
166. *NAACP Annual Report* for 1959, "The Year of Jubilee," (July 1960), 27.
167. See FBI Files, "The Abduction of Mack Charles Parker from the Pearl River County Jail, Poplarville, Mississippi . . . ," http://foia.fbi.gov/parker/parker1bpdf and http://foia.fbi.gov/parker/parker1cpdf, 183–190 (accessed December 15, 2010).
168. Medgar Evers quoted in Evers and Peters, *For Us, the Living,* 226.
169. Medgar Evers, "Monthly Report," May 21, 1959, NAACP Papers, LOC, Group III, Box C-244, Folder 3, 3.
170. Medgar Evers, "Address to the Los Angeles, California Branch NAACP," MDAH, Subject File, "Medgar Evers 1954–1973," 3.
171. Ibid. and *NAACP Annual Report,* Forty-seventh Year, "Progress and Reaction, 1955," 23.
172. Medgar Evers, "Address to the Los Angeles, California Branch NAACP," 4.
173. Ibid., 5.
174. Dittmer, *Local People,* 79–80, and Payne, *I've Got the Light of Freedom,* 55.
175. Clyde Kennard "Letter To the Editor," *Hattiesburg American,* December 6, 1958, 2A.
176. Ronald A. Hollander, "One Negro Who Didn't Go To College," *The Reporter: The Magazine of Facts and Ideas* 27, no. 8 (November 8, 1962): 30–31.
177. Ibid., 30.
178. Ibid., 30–34, Brown, *Medgar Evers Activist,* 128–130, and Payne, *I've Got the Light of Freedom,* 55.
179. Katagiri, *The Mississippi State Sovereignty Commission,* 56–57.
180. Hollander, "One Mississippi Negro Who Didn't Go to College," 31–33; Brown, *Medgar Evers Activist,* 130–131; and Klarman, *From Jim Crow to Civil Rights,* 260. See also Timothy J. Minchin and John A. Salmond, "'The Saddest Story of the Whole Movement": The Clyde Kennard Case and the Search for Racial Reconciliation in Mississippi, 1955–2007," *Journal of Mississippi History* 71, no. 3 (Fall 2009): 191–234.
181. Medgar Evers, "Officers and Members of Mississippi NAACP Branches," Papers of the NAACP: Part 20, Group III, Box A-231, microfilm reel 1.
182. *The State of Mississippi on Relation of James Finch, District Attorney, Versus Medgar Evers,* No. 4966, NAACP Papers, LOC, Group V, Box 1177, Folder 8, 1–2.
183. Ibid., 4.
184. Ibid., 4–7, 10, and 12–13.
185. Ibid., 13–14.
186. Ibid., 15–16.
187. "NAACP Official Convicted for Contempt of Court," *Jackson Daily News,* December 2, 1960, MDAH, Subject File, "Evers, Medgar 1954–1979."

188. See, "Constitutional Right Imperiled," December 4, 1960, *Delta Democrat-Times* and "If Freedom is Enjoyed Freedom Must be Granted," December 7, 1960, *State Times* (Jackson), newspaper clippings, NAACP Papers, LOC, Group III, Box C-244, Folder 4.

189. Evers and Peters, *For Us, the Living*, 214–215.

190. "Statement of Reverend J.M. Barnes," presented "Before the House Judiciary Sub-committee, April 24, 1959," NAACP Papers, LOC, Group III, Box A-270, Folder 9.

191. John R. Salter Jr., "Medgar W. Evers: Reflection and Appreciation," http://www.hunterbear.org/medgar_w.htm (accessed November 4, 2010); Salter, *Jackson, Mississippi*, 21; and Evers and Peters, *For Us, the Living*, 224–225. Salter, part Micmac/Penobscot Native American, would later assume the name Hunter Bear.

192. Colia Liddell Clark and Dr. Lewis Liddell interview with Worth Long, May 23, 1983, SRC: Will the Circle be Unbroken?, Emory University, Box 8, Folder 19, 6.

193. Evers and Peters, *For Us, the Living*, 224.

194. Ibid., 225.

195. Medgar Evers, *Appellant v. The State of Mississippi,* on Relation of James Finch, District Attorney, No. 41960, 1961, NAACP Papers, LOC, Group V, Box 1177, Folder 8, 4, 5.

196. Medgar Evers, "Monthly Report," February 7, 1963, NAACP Papers, LOC, Group III, Box C-245, Folder 3, 6. Regarding Evers's reversal, see "In the Supreme Court of Mississippi Decisions Handed Down June 12, 1961" and Justices Ethridge and McGehee opinions in *Appellant v. The State of Mississippi, on Relation of James Finch, District Attorney,* No. 41960, NAACP Papers, LOC, Group V, Box 1177, Folder 8.

197. Medgar Evers, "Monthly Report," February 7, 1963, NAACP Papers, LOC, Group III, Box C-245, Folder 3, 6.

198. Payne, *I've Got the Light of Freedom,* 55; Evers and Peters, *For Us, the Living*, 221–223; and Minchin and Salmond, "The Saddest Story," 216–218.

199. Evers-Williams, October 25, 2006, interview.

200. Medgar Evers, "Address to the Los Angeles, California Branch NAACP," 7–8, MDAH, Subject Files, Evers, Medgar 1954–1979.

201. Ibid., 8–9.

202. Nossiter, *Of Long Memory,* 28, 29.

203. Evers and Peters, *For Us, the Living*, 159–160.

5.

Epigraphs. Medgar Evers, "The Years of Change Are Upon Us," MDAH, Subject File, "Medgar Evers Speeches," 5. Medgar Evers, "Address by Medgar W. Evers . . . to Mass Protest Meeting," April 20, 1961, NAACP Papers, LOC, Group III, Box C-245, Folder 1, 2. James P. Coleman interview with Michael B. Ballard and Connie Lynnette Cartledge, J. P. Coleman Papers, Box 2, Folder "Coleman Addition Interview, October 1, 1983," Special Collections Department, Mitchell Memorial Library, Mississippi State University, 37. Aaron Henry interview with Neil McMillen and George Burson, May 1, 1972, Mississippi Oral History Program, University of Southern Mississippi, volume 33, 1980, 16–17. The Honorable Koigi Wa Wamwere, July 13, 2006, interview.

1. Gloster Current to "Bob Carter," January 21, 1959, NAACP Papers, LOC, Group III, Box C-244, Folder 3.

2. Robert Carter memorandum to Gloster Current, January 27, 1959, NAACP Papers, LOC, Group III, Box C-244, Folder 3.

3. Medgar Evers to Gloster Current, February 24, 1959, NAACP Papers, LOC, Group III, Box C-244, Folder 3.

4. Medgar Evers, "Monthly Report," May 21, 1959, NAACP Papers, LOC, Group III, Box C-244, Folder 3, 4, and Mississippi State Conference N.A.AC.P. Branches, "Fifth Anniversary Celebration of the U.S. Supreme Courts Decision . . ." program, May 17, 1959, NAACP Papers, LOC, Group III, Box C75, Folder 7.

5. Mississippi Threatens Freedom of Speech, "The 'Law' in Mississippi,'" n.d., NAACP Papers, LOC, Group III, Box C-74, Folder 1.

6. Newspaper clippings, "State Forestalls Wilkins' Arrest, *Jackson Daily News,*" May 18, 1959, and *State Times* (Jackson), no title, May 18, 1959, NAACP Papers, LOC, Group III, Box C-74, Folder 1.

7. "J.P. Accused of Blocking Arrests," *Jackson Daily News,* May 19, 1959, newspaper clipping, NAACP Papers, LOC, Group III, Box C-74, Folder 1.

8. Medgar Evers, "Monthly Report," May 21, 1959, NAACP Papers, LOC, Group III, Box C-244, Folder 3, 4.

9. Medgar Evers, "Monthly Report," June 22, 1959, NAACP Papers, LOC, Group III, Box C-244, Folder 3, 1–2.

10. Evers-Williams and Marable, *The Autobiography of Medgar Evers,* 162.

11. Medgar Evers, "Monthly Report," January 21, 1960, NAACP Papers, LOC, Group III, Box C-244, Folder 4, 3.

12. Joseph McNeil quoted in Hampton and Fayer, eds., *Voices of Freedom,* 56.

13. William H. Chafe, *Civilities and Civil Rights: Greensboro, North Carolina, and the Black Struggle for Freedom* (Oxford: Oxford University Press, 1981), 72–79.

14. Ibid., 20, 80–81.

15. Ibid., 71–85, 98; David Halberstam, *The Children* (New York: Fawcett Books, 1998), 92–94; Clayborne Carson, *In Struggle: SNCC and the Black Awakening of the 1960s* (Cambridge, MA: Harvard University Press, 1981), 9–18; Franklin and Moss, *From Slavery to Freedom,* 526; and Klarman, *From Jim Crow to Civil Rights,* 373.

16. Alison Owings, *Hey, Waitress!: The USA from the Other Side of the Tray* (Berkeley and Los Angeles: University of California Press, 2002), 44–46. For an audio recording of an interview with Tisdale discussing the event, see "Geneva Tisdale–Greensboro Sit-Ins: Launch of a Civil Rights . . . ," www.sitins.com/genevatisdale.shtml (accessed December 17, 2010).

17. Statistics taken from Middleton and Stokes, *The African American Experience: A History,* 342.

18. Franklin McCain, quoted in Clayborne Carson, David Garrow et al., *The Eyes on the Prize Civil Rights Reader,* 115. See also, Miles Wolff, *Lunch at the Five and Ten: The Greensboro Sit-ins, A Contemporary History* (New York: Stein and Day Publishers, 1970), 39–40, 43–44, 50, and 167.

19. Medgar Evers to Gloster Current, March 9, 1960, NAACP Papers, LOC, Group III, Box C-244, Folder 4.

20. Roy Wilkins, *NAACP Annual Report,* "NAACP Report for 1960" (July 1961): 5–6, 25, and 46–47.

21. Kenneth T. Andrews, *Freedom Is a Constant Struggle: The Mississippi Civil Rights Movement and Its Legacy* (Chicago: University of Chicago Press, 2004), 44.

22. Medgar Evers, "Monthly Report," March 22, 1960, NAACP Papers, LOC, Group III, Box C-244, Folder 4, 1.

23. Gilbert Jonas, *Freedom's Sword,* 164–165, 183–184.

24. C. R. Darden to Gloster Current, March 14, 1960, NAACP Papers, LOC, Group III, Box C-244, Folder 4.

25. Medgar Evers to Gloster Current, March 14, 1960, NAACP Papers, LOC, Group III, Box C-244, Folder 4, 1.

26. Medgar Evers, "Monthly Report," March 22, 1960, NAACP Papers, LOC, Group III, Box C-244, Folder 4, 2, and C. R. Darden to Medgar Evers, March 14, 1960, NAACP Papers, LOC, Group III, Box C-244, Folder 4.

27. Medgar Evers, "Monthly Report," March 22, 1960, NAACP Papers, LOC, Group III, Box C-244, Folder 4, 2–3.

28. Ibid.

29. Medgar Evers to Gloster Current, March 14, 1960, NAACP Papers, LOC, Group III, Box C-244, Folder 4, 1.

30. "Jackson Negro Boycott Vowed," *Jackson Daily News,* Evers (Medgar and Myrlie Beasley) Papers, and "No Easter Buying: Negroes Pledge Jackson Boycott," *Clarion-Ledger,* April 8, 1960, 1, "No Demonstrations: Ask Boycott by Negroes," April 9, 1960, 1, Medgar Evers, "Sacrifice For Human Dignity," report to Ruby Hurley, April 13, 1960, NAACP Papers, LOC, Group III, Box C-244, Folder 4, and *NAACP Annual Report,* "NAACP Report for 1960," 16; Salter, *Jackson, Mississippi,* 112–113. For further discussions regarding Dean Jones, see Evers-Williams and Marable, *The Autobiography of Medgar Evers,* 188, and Dittmer, *Local People,* 161.

31. Medgar Evers Report to Ruby Hurley, "Sacrifice for Human Dignity," April 19, 1960, NAACP Papers, LOC, Group III, Box C-244, Folder 4; see also Louis Harlan, *Booker T. Washington: The Making of a Black Leader, 1856–1901* (New York: Oxford University Press, 1972).

32. Medgar Evers Report to Ruby Hurley, "Sacrifice for Human Dignity," April 19, 1960, NAACP Papers, LOC, Group III, Box C-244, Folder 4, 1–2.

33. Evers-Jordan, June 10, 2005, interview. Myrlie Evers also noted that apathy proved something Medgar had a hard time dealing with; Evers-Williams, October 25, 2006, interview.

34. Sovereignty Commission Papers, SCR # 2–135–0–22–3–1–1, 2–135–0–22–4–1–1 and SCR # 2–135–0–22–5–1–1. Commission officials used the letter T followed by a number to identify informants without divulging names.

35. Ibid., 2–135–0–22–6–1–1 and 2–135–0–22–7–1–1.

36. Ibid., 2–135–0–22–7–1–1.

37. "Southern Negroes Plan Easter Boycott," *Commercial Appeal,* Memphis, TN, April 11, 1960, 26.

38. Sovereignty Commission Papers, SCR # 2–135–0–22–12–1–1 and 2–135–0–22–14–1–1.

39. The *Delta Democrat-Times,* "Reports Differ on Boycott in Jackson," April 12, 1960, newspaper clipping, Evers (Medgar and Myrlie Beasley) Papers, Box 24, Folder 7. Evers also challenged accounts of the boycott's failure from prominent African Americans such as *Jackson Advocate* editor Percy Greene, who labeled the boycott a "complete failure." See "Boycott Complete Failure," *Jackson Advocate,*

April 16, 1960, 1, and "Boycott Flop Says Jackson Negro Editor," *Jackson Daily News,* April 16, 1960, 1.

40. Medgar Evers, "Monthly Report," April 21, 1960, NAACP Papers, LOC, Group III, Box C-244, Folder 4, 5–6.

41. SCR # 2–135–0–22–15–1–1.

42. Gilbert R. Mason Sr., *Beaches, Blood and Ballots: A Black Doctor's Civil Rights Struggle* (Jackson: University Press of Mississippi, 2000), 1–18, 26, 32–37, 49, and J. Michael Butler, "The Mississippi State Sovereignty Commission and Beach Integration, 1959–1963: A Cotton-Patch Gestapo?" *Journal of Southern History* 68, no. 1 (February 2002): 117. Mason noted that he, too, was a parishioner of Reverend George Lee (discussed earlier) while attending St. James Baptist Church in Jackson, see *Beaches, Blood and Ballots,* 50.

43. Gilbert R. Mason Sr., interview with the author, August 13, 2005, cassette recording, Biloxi Mississippi. Tape in possession of the author.

44. Ibid.

45. Mason, *Beaches, Blood, and Ballots,* 49–52.

46. Butler, "The Mississippi State Sovereignty Commission and Beach Integration," 114.

47. Mason Sr., August 13, 2005, interview.

48. Butler, "The Mississippi State Sovereignty Commission and Beach Integration," 116–118; *NAACP Annual Report, 1959,* 25.

49. Gilbert Mason, Affidavit, May 3, 1960, Papers of the NAACP: Part 20, Group III, Box A-90, microfilm reel 1. "Dr. Gilbert Mason Son of Onetime Jackson Barber Arrested in Biloxi Beach Incident," *Jackson Advocate,* April 23, 1960, 1, 7.

50. Medgar Evers, "Monthly Report," April 21, 1960, NAACP Papers, LOC, Group III, Box C-244, Folder 4, 6–7.

51. Mason, *Beaches, Blood, and Ballots,* 67; Butler, "The Mississippi State Sovereignty Commission and Beach Integration," 124.

52. Mason, *Beaches, Blood, and Ballots,* 67–68; Butler, "The Mississippi State Sovereignty Commission and Beach Integration," 126. For further commentary regarding the beach incident, see "Negro Vows More Beach Mix Moves," *Jackson Daily News,* April 25, 1960, 1, 9; "Biloxi Reported Quiet after Swimming Beach Riot Sunday," *Jackson Advocate* April 30, 1960, 1, 5; and "Racial Violence Flares on Biloxi's Gulf Beach," *Clarion-Ledger,* April 25, 1960, 1. For specific instances of violent acts against African Americans, see Butler, "The Mississippi State Sovereignty Commission and Beach Integration," 126–130.

53. Mason, *Beaches, Blood, and Ballots,* 71.

54. Mason, *Beaches, Blood, and Ballots,* 84.

55. Butler, "The Mississippi State Sovereignty Commission and Beach Integration," 137.

56. Mason, *Beaches, Blood, and Ballots,* 84–85, and Mason Sr., August 13, 2005, interview.

57. Medgar Evers to Robert L. Carter, May 5, 1960, NAACP Papers, LOC, Group III, Box A-114, Folder 5, and Evers, "Monthly Report," May 23, 1960, NAACP Papers, LOC, Group III, Box C-244, Folder 4, 2.

58. For a detailed examination of Joseph McCarthy and the Red Scare era, see David M. Oshinsky, *A Conspiracy So Immense: The World of Joe McCarthy* (Oxford: Oxford University Press, 2005.

59. NAACP Annual Report, 1956, 67.

60. Medgar Evers, "Monthly Report," September, 19, 1960, NAACP Papers, LOC, Group III, Box C-244, Folder 4, 2–3.

61. "Letter to Medgar Evers to Home Address," n.d., NAACP Papers, LOC, Group III, Box C-244, Folder 2. RW may be a reference to Roy Wilkins and Morsell being Robert Morsell, NAACP assistant to the secretary.

62. Mason, *Beaches, Blood, and Ballots,* 139–140, 147–157, and Butler, "The Mississippi State Sovereignty Commission and Beach Integration," 143.

63. Mason Sr., August 13, 2005, interview.

64. Evers-Williams, October 25, 2006, interview.

65. Evers-Williams and Blau, *Watch Me Fly,* 68–70.

66. Ibid., 70–71.

67. Ibid., 72.

68. The sword of Damocles comes out of Cicero's *Tusculan disputations.* Damocles was a flatterer of Dionysius II of Syracuse. In a conversation, Damocles spoke of the wealth of Dionysius, who offered him the opportunity to experience what he spoke so highly of. When Damocles sat upon the throne, he realized that above his head lay a sword hanging by a slender horse hair. He then realized that what he thought was a life of luxury, pleasure, and happiness could change instantly and thus the perilous nature of the happiness he thought others enjoyed so easily.

69. Evers and Peters, *For Us, the Living,* 199; Evers-Jordan, June 10, 2005, interview; and Evers-Williams, October 25, 2006, interview.

70. Clayborne Carson, *In Struggle: SNCC and the Black Awakening of the 1960s* (Cambridge, MA: Harvard University Press, 2000), 19–30.

71. Clayborne Carson, David Garrow et al., eds., *The Eyes on the Prize Civil Rights Reader: Documents, Speeches, and Firsthand Accounts from the Black Freedom Struggle, 1954–1990* (New York: Penguin Books, 1991), 121.

72. Carson, *In Struggle,* 19.

73. Payne, *I've Got the Light of Freedom,* 112–113.

74. Charles McDew interview with Worth Long, April 14, 1996, SRC: Will the Circle be Unbroken?, Emory University, Box 8, Folder 22, 8, Payne, *I've Got the Light of Freedom,* 112–113, and Daniel, *Lost Revolutions,* 227.

75. Bob Parris Moses interview with Anne Romaine, "Mississippi Freedom Democratic Party," MDAH, Accession number OH/1981.08, Volume II, B2/R33/B3/54, September 5 (no year provided), Part I, 3.

76. Hollis Watkins phone interview with John Rachal, between October 23 and October 30, 1996, Mississippi Oral History Program, University of Southern Mississippi, volume 670, 1995, 6–7, and Seth Cagin and Phillip Dray, *We are not Afraid: The Story of Goodman, Schwerner, and Chaney and the Civil Rights Movement* (New York: Nation Books, 2006), 145.

77. Hollis Watkins phone interview with John Rachal, 11, and Ed King interview with Worth Long, August 23, 1991, SRC: Will the Circle be Unbroken?, Emory University, Box 8, Folder 17, 14.

78. Hollis Watkins phone interview with John Rachal, 13.

79. Ibid., 14.

80. Ibid., 14–15; Carson, *In Struggle,* 48; Dittmer, *Local People,* 106–107; and Payne, *I've Got the Light of Freedom,* 119.

81. Charles M. Hills, "Affairs of State," n.d. 1960, NAACP Papers, LOC, Group III, Box C-244, Folder 4.

82. Sovereignty Commission Papers, SCR # 1–23–0–62–1–1–1. Here the memorandum is dated January 18, 1960, and attributed to the *Clarion Ledger* (Mississippi).

83. Hills, "Affairs of State," n.d. 1960, NAACP Papers, LOC, Group III, Box C-244, Folder 4.

84. Medgar Evers to Civil Rights Advisory Commission, September 19, 1960, Evers (Medgar Wiley and Myrlie Beasley) Papers, Box 2, Folder 5.

85. Both letters are photocopied and appear in the photograph inserts of Gilbert Mason Sr., *Beaches, Blood, and Ballots*. The portion in quotations refers to the letter written by Robert Carter to Roy Wilkins regarding Evers's desire in 1958 to file suit in response to his assault aboard a Trailways bus as presented earlier.

86. Medgar Evers to Reuben W. Rhodes, December 28, 1960, Evers (Medgar Wiley and Myrlie Beasley) Papers, Box 2, Folder 10, 2.

87. Evers-Jordan, June 10, 2005, interview.

88. Sentiments were expressed by public testimonials and individual discussions by the author with persons attending the 42nd and 44th Annual Medgar Evers Gospel Memorial Celebration at St. Luther MB Church and Pearl Street AME Church in Jackson, Mississippi, June 9, 2005, and May 31, 2007, respectively.

89. Medgar Evers to Mr. Carter, Papers of the NAACP: Part 20, Group III, Box A-232, microfilm reel 2. The first name was unreadable, but a probable reference to NAACP attorney Robert L. Carter.

90. Tougaloo College, "Mission Statement and Purpose," http://www.tougaloo.edu/content/About/index.htm (accessed November 5, 2010).

91. Lawrence Guyot interview with John Rachal, September 7, 1996, Mississippi Oral History Program, University of Southern Mississippi, volume 673, 1996, 3.

92. A. D. Beittel, "Oral History Memoir," June 2, 1965, J. B. Cain Archives of Mississippi Methodism and Millsaps College Archives, Millsaps-Williams Library, Jackson, Mississippi, 5.

93. Medgar Evers to Roy Wilkins, March 29, 1961, NAACP Papers, LOC, Group III, Box C-245, Folder 1, and Medgar Evers monthly report, April 21, 1961, NAACP Papers, LOC, Group III, Box 245, Folder 1, 2.

94. James C. Bradford interview with Worth Long, April 30, 1983, SRC: Will the Circle be Unbroken?, Emory University, 7.

95. "Tougaloo Students Arrested for Entering White Library," *Jackson Daily News,* March 27, 1961, 1.

96. Medgar Evers to Roy Wilkins, March 29, 1961, NAACP Papers, LOC, Group III, Box C-245, Folder 1; Medgar Evers, report received "via phone from Medgar Evers," May 28, 1961, Papers of the NAACP: Part 20, Group III, Box A-232, microfilm reel 2; *NAACP Annual Report,* "NAACP Report for 1961" (July 1961), 24–25; James C. Bradford interview with Worth Long, SRC: Will the Circle be Unbroken?, Emory University, 6. Also see James H. Meredith, *Three Years in Mississippi* (Bloomington: Indiana University Press, 1966), 92–93; Dittmer, *Local People,* 87–88; and "Tougaloo Students Arrested for Entering White Library," *Jackson Daily News,* March 27, 1961, 1. Meredith believed that the "impulse to act [on the part of Tougaloo students] came from Medgar Evers." See, *Three Years in Mississippi,* 92. The Tougaloo Nine consisted of the following: Ethel Sawyer

[Adolphe], Meredith Coleman Anding Jr., James C. (Sam) Bradford, Alfred Lee Cook, Geraldine Edwards [Hollis], Joseph Jackson Jr., Albert Lassiter, Amennah (Evelyn Pierce) Omar, and Janice Jackson [Vails]; Tougaloo Papers, MDAH, Series 1, Box 1, Folder 1.

97. August Meier and Elliot Rudwick, *CORE: A Study in the Civil Rights Movement, 1942–1968* (New York: Oxford University Press, 1973), 4–5; Bruce J. Dierenfield, *The Civil Rights Movement,* rev. ed. (London: Pearson Education Limited, 2008), 18; and Harvard Sitkoff, *A New Deal for Blacks, the Emergence of Civil Rights as a National Issue: The Depression Decade,* 30th anniversary ed. (New York: Oxford University Press, 2009), 122.

98. Dave Dennis interview with Worth Long, February 1997, SRC: Will the Circle be Unbroken?, Emory University, Box 7, Folder 12, 9.

99. Dr. Robert Smith interview with George King, May 1992, SRC: Will the Circle be Unbroken?, Emory University, Box 9, Folder 5, 10.

100. A. D. Beittel, "Oral History Memoir," June 2, 1965, 17.

101. Claude Ramsay interview with Orley B. Caudill, April 30, 1981, Mississippi Oral History Program, University of Southern Mississippi, Part I, April 28, 1981, 68, and Part II, 73–75.

102. Ibid., Part I, 68.

103. A. D. Beittel, "Oral History Memoir," June 2, 1965, 14–16.

104. Ruby Magee interview with Orley B. Caudill, May 18, 1972, Mississippi Oral History Program, University of Southern Mississippi, volume 33, 1980, 5–6, and Medgar Evers, report received "via phone from Medgar Evers," Papers of the NAACP: Part 20, Group III, Box A-232, microfilm reel 2.

105. "Police Halt March by Negro Students in Mississippi," *New York Times,* March 29, 1961, L-25.

106. "Mississippians March: Thousands Parade to Open Civil War Centennial," *New York Times,* March 29, 1961, L-25.

107. Aurelia Norris Young interview with unidentified interviewer, (n.d.), SRC: Will the Circle be Unbroken?, Emory University, Box 9, Folder 8, 3.

108. A .D. Beittel, "Oral History Memoir," 4, and James C. Bradford interview with Worth Long, April 30, 1983, SRC: Will the Circle be Unbroken?, Box 7, Folder 1, 12–13.

109. Medgar Evers, "Monthly Report," April 21, 1961, NAACP Papers, LOC, Group III, Box C-245, Folder 1, 2–3. Here Evers reports that he called "Burt" Marshall though it is highly probable that he made a mistake and meant Burke Marshall.

110. See *NAACP Annual Report,* "NAACP Report for 1961," 17, 25, and *The Crisis,* vol. 70, no. 6, 354.

111. "Police and Dogs Rout 100 Negroes," *New York Times,* March 30, 1961, L-19; *NAACP Annual Report,* "NAACP Report for 1961," 25. For Medgar's FBI interview, see Kenneth O'Reilly and David Gallen, eds., *Black Americans: The FBI Files* (New York: Carroll & Graf Publishers, 1994), 132–136, and "Unknown Subjects, Officers, Jackson," Federal Bureau of Investigation Papers, Part III, March 31, 1961, http://foia.fbi.gov/evers_medgar/evers_medgar_part03.pdf (accessed December 7, 2010). This section contains a host of correspondences between Evers and the FBI describing police brutality. On April 7, the NAACP reported that police dogs "on duty" with the Jackson Police Department were "trained by a former Nazi storm trooper." See "NAACP Report for 1961," 85.

112. Evers and Peters, *For Us, the Living,* 235.

113. Medgar Evers, "received via phone," Papers of the NAACP: Part 20, Group III, Box A-232, microfilm reel 2.

114. Dr. Ivory Phillips, interview with the author, December 13, 2006, cassette recording, Jackson, Mississippi, and John Frazier, interview with the author, October 23, 2010, cassette recording, Hattiesburg, Mississippi. Tapes in possession of the author.

115. Medgar Evers to Roy Wilkins, March 29, 1961, NAACP Papers, LOC, Group III, Box C-245, Folder 1.

116. James C. Bradford interview with Worth Long, April 30, 1983, SRC: Will the Circle be Unbroken?, Emory University, Box 7, Folder 1, 20–21.

117. "Program Operation Mississippi," Papers of the NAACP: Part 20, Group III, Box A-232, microfilm reel 3.

118. Ibid.

119. Medgar Evers, "Monthly Report," April 21, 1961, NAACP Papers, LOC, Group III, Box C-245, Folder 1, 4, and NAACP Press release, "Ride-in Arrests Spark NAACP's March on Bias Throughout Mississippi," April 22, 1961, Papers of the NAACP: Part 20, Group III, Box A-232, microfilm reel 3, 3.

120. NAACP Press release, "Ride-in Arrests Spark NAACP's March on Bias Throughout Mississippi," April 22, 1961, Papers of the NAACP: Part 20, 3, Group III, Box A-232, microfilm reel 3, 3. Nick Bryant, *The Bystander: John F. Kennedy and the Struggle for Black Equality* (New York: Basic Books, 2006), 225–230.

121. NAACP Press release, "Ride-in Arrests Spark NAACP's March on Bias Throughout Mississippi," April 22, 1961, Papers of the NAACP: Part 20, 3, Group III, Box A-232, microfilm reel 3, 3.

122. Gloster B. Current to Medgar Evers, April 24, 1961, NAACP Papers, LOC, Group III, Box C-245, Folder 1.

123. Fred Clark Sr. interview with Leesha Faulkner, June 10, 1994, Mississippi Oral History Program, University of Southern Mississippi, volume 494, 1994, 16.

124. Address by Medgar W. Evers Mississippi Field Secretary, NAACP to mass protest meeting, April 20, 1961, NAACP Papers, LOC, Group III, Box C-245, Folder 1. Original is typed in all uppercase.

125. Medgar Evers, "Comments On Mississippi NAACP Operations," n.d., NAACP Papers, LOC, Group III, Box C-244, Folder 3, 3.

126. Claude Ramsay interview with Orley B. Caudill, April 28, 1981, Mississippi Oral History Program, University of Southern Mississippi, Part I, 60–61. Regarding Coleman's comments, see James P. Coleman interview with Michael B. Ballard and Connie Lynnette Cartledge, J. P. Coleman Papers, Mississippi State University, 36.

127. Medgar Evers and William C. Smith correspondences, Papers of the NAACP: Part 20, Group III, Box, A-231, microfilm reel 2. In the original documents both incoming and outgoing responses are in uppercase type.

128. Aaron Henry interview with McMillen and Burson, Mississippi Oral History Program, University of Southern Mississippi, 56–57, Bob Parris Moses interview with Anne Romaine, "Mississippi Freedom Democratic Party," MDAH, Accession number OH/1981.08, Volume II, B2/R33/B3/54, September 5 (no year provided) Part II, 2, Ivory Phillips, December 13, 2006, interview, Ed King interview with Worth Long, August 23, 1991, SRC: Will the Circle be Unbroken?,

Box 8, Folder 17, 1, Payne, *I've Got the Light of Freedom*, 62, and Dittmer, *Local People*, 118–119.

129. Aaron Henry with Constance Curry, *Aaron Henry*, 115, and Dittmer, *Local People*, 118–119.

130. Robert F. Williams, *Negroes with Guns*, 6–11.

131. Ibid., 10–12.

132. Medgar Evers, "Operation of other Civil Rights Organizations in the State of Mississippi," October 12–13, 1961, Papers of the NAACP: Part 20, Group III, Box A-231, microfilm reel 2, 5.

133. Ibid., 3.

134. Evers and Peters, *For Us, the Living*, 253, and Payne, *I've Got the Light of Freedom*, 62.

135. Payne, *I've Got the Light of Freedom*, 117, 119, and Dittmer, *Local People*, 112.

136. Medgar Evers, "Monthly Report, Mississippi Field Secretary," October 5, 1961, Papers of the NAACP: Part 20, Group III, Box A-115, microfilm reel 15, 1–2; Carson, *In Struggle*, 48, Dittmer, *Local People*, 108; Payne, *I've Got the Light of Freedom*, 120; and Eric Burner, *And Gently He Shall Lead Them: Robert Parris Moses and Civil Rights in Mississippi* (New York: New York University Press, 1994), 54–56. Ruby Magee identified the registrar who hit Hardy (here it is spelled Harvey) as John Q. Woods. See Ruby Magee interview with Orley B. Caudill, May 18, 1972, Mississippi Oral History Program, University of Southern Mississippi, 9, 13.

137. Medgar Evers, "Operation of other Civil Rights Organizations in the State of Mississippi," October 12–13, 1961, Papers of the NAACP: Part 20, Group III, Box A-231, microfilm reel 2, 1–5.

6.

Epigraphs. "Oh Freedom," http://www.lyricsbay.com/oh_freedom_lyrics-unknown.html (accessed May 30, 2011). John Lewis with Michael D'Orso, *Walking With the Wind: A Memoir of the Movement* (New York: Simon & Schuster, 1998), 140.

1. James Farmer quoted in Hampton and Fayer, *Voices of Freedom*, 75.

2. Clayborne Carson, primary consultant, et al., *Civil Rights Chronicle: The African American Struggle for Freedom* (Lincolnwood, IL: Legacy Publishing, 2003), 194; Darlene Clark Hine, William C. Hine, and Stanley Harrold, *The African American Odyssey*, 3rd ed. (Upper Saddle River, NJ: Pearson Education, 2006), 534; John Hope Franklin and Evelyn Brooks Higginbotham, *From Slavery to Freedom: A History of African Americans*, 9th ed. (New York: McGraw Hill, 2011), 512; and August Meier and Elliot Rudwick, *CORE: A Study in the Civil Rights Movement, 1942–1968* (New York: Oxford University Press, 1973), 33–40.

3. David Niven, *The Politics of Injustice: The Kennedys, the Freedom Rides, and the Electoral Consequences of a Moral Compromise* (Knoxville: University of Tennessee Press, 2003), 41.

4. Lewis with D'Orso, *Walking with the Wind*, 135, 138, 140.

5. Ibid., 142–143, and Niven, *The Politics of Injustice*, 45–46.

6. Niven, *The Politics of Injustice*, 48–49, and Lewis with D'Orso, *Walking With the Wind*, 144.

7. Lewis with D'Orso, *Walking with the Wind*, 144–145; Raymond Arsenault, *Freedom Riders: 1961 and the Struggle for Racial Justice* (Oxford: Oxford University Press, 2006), 141–148; Thornton III, *Dividing Lines*, 246–247, Niven, *The Politics of Injustice*, 49–51; and Diane McWhorter, *Carry Me Home, Birmingham, Alabama: The Climactic Battle of the Civil Rights Revolution* (New York: Simon & Schuster, 2002), 210.

8. Burke Marshall quoted in Hampton and Fayer, *Voices of Freedom*, 79–80, and Glenn T. Eskew, *But for Birmingham: The Local and National Movements in the Civil Rights Struggle* (Chapel Hill: University of North Carolina Press, 1997), 156–157.

9. Arsenault, *Freedom Riders*, 154–156, 180; Niven, *The Politics of Injustice*, 52–55; Eskew, *But for Birmingham*, 153–154; Lewis with D'Orso, *Walking with the Wind*, 146–149; and Nash, Hampton, and Fayer, *Voices of Freedom*, 82.

10. Lewis, *Walking with the Wind*, 150–157; Arsenault, *Freedom Riders*, 187–201.

11. Bob Zellner with Constance Curry, *The Wrong Side of Murder Creek: A White Southerner in the Freedom Movement* (Montgomery: New South Books, 2008), 92.

12. Carson, *In Struggle*, 31–38; Payne, *I've Got the Light of Freedom*, 107; Lewis with D'Orso, *Walking with the Wind*, 153–160; and Arsenault, *Freedom Riders*, 155–158, 179–208. For a detailed discussion of the violence at the Montgomery Greyhound terminal, see Arsenault, *Freedom Riders*, 212–216, and J. Mills Thornton III, *Dividing Lines*, 118–128. For the discussion of Sullivan's promise of no police interference for an agreed-upon time period, see Arsenault, 220.

13. Lewis with D'Orso, *Walking with the Wind*, 167, and Arsenault, *Freedom Riders*, 255.

14. Dave Dennis interview with Worth Long, February 1997, SRC: Will the Circle be Unbroken?, Emory University, Box 7, Folder 12, 5–6; Lewis with D'Orso, *Walking with the Wind*, 168–174; and Meier and Rudwick, *CORE*, 139.

15. Dave Dennis interview with Worth Long, February 1997, SRC: Will the Circle be Unbroken?, Emory University, Box 7, Folder 12, 6.

16. Medgar Evers, "Monthly Report," June 21, 1961, NAACP Papers, LOC, Group III, Box C-245, Folder 1, 3–4.

17. Arsenault, *Freedom Riders*, 373. For additional discussions of the Freedom Rides and its meaning, see Derek Charles Catsam, *Freedom's Main Line: The Journey of Reconciliation and the Freedom Rides* (Lexington: University Press of Kentucky, 2009).

18. Catsam, *Freedom's Main Line*, 71, and Medgar Evers, "Special Report, Mississippi Field Secretary," October 12, 1961, NAACP Papers, LOC, Group III, Box C-245, Folder 1, 1–2.

19. Niven, *The Politics of Injustice*, 42; Medgar Evers, "Special Report, Mississippi Field Secretary," October 12, 1961, NAACP Papers, LOC, Group III, Box C-245, Folder 1, 1–2.

20. Medgar Evers, "Special Report, Mississippi Field Secretary," October 12–13, 1961, NAACP, Group III, Box C-245, Folder 1, 3–4.

21. Carson, *In Struggle*, 78–79.

22. Ibid., 47.

23. Medgar Evers, "Special Report, Mississippi Field Secretary," October 12–13, 1961, NAACP, Group III, Box C-245, Folder 1, 4–5, and Carson, *In Struggle*, 47.

24. Medgar Evers to Alfred Baker Lewis, February 1, 1962, NAACP Papers, LOC, Group III, Box A-270, Folder 9.

25. Ibid. When speaking of the "State Representative" involved in the Lee murder, Evers was referring to E. H. Hurst. Hurst would later be cleared by a coroner's jury.

26. Cornelius Turner, July 12, 2005, interview. Scholars Jonathan Rosenberg and Zachary Karabell also discuss the initial steps Meredith took and the long process he endured in desegregating the University of Mississippi in *Kennedy, Johnson, and the Quest for Justice: The Civil Rights Tapes* (New York: W. W. Norton & Company, 2003), 27–84.

27. Charles Eagles, *The Price of Defiance: James Meredith and the Integration of Ole Miss* (Chapel Hill: University of North Carolina Press, 2009), 202–206.

28. Ibid., 208–214.

29. Ruby Magee interview with Orley B. Caudill, May 18, 1972, Mississippi Oral History Program, University of Southern Mississippi, 36–37.

30. Meredith, *Three Years in Mississippi*, 54–56. Meredith admits that the In Group was very much involved in his decision to attend the University of Mississippi. See *Three Years in Mississippi*, 90.

31. Ibid., 55.

32. William Doyle, *An American Insurrection: James Meredith and the Battle of Oxford, Mississippi, 1962* (New York: Anchor Books, 2001), 31.

33. Meredith, *Three Years in Mississippi*, 56–57.

34. Sansing, *Making Haste Slowly*, 160, and Eagles, *The Price of Defiance*, 227–228.

35. Doyle, *An American Insurrection*, 31–32.

36. James H. Meredith, interview with the author, July 13, 2005, cassette recording, Jackson, Mississippi. Tape in possession of the author.

37. "Meredith to Enroll; Black Vacates Stay Circuit Court Decision Upheld Ole Miss Registration on 19th," *Mississippi Free Press*, September 15, 1962, 1, located in the *American Historical Newspapers* database.

38. Arthur M. Schlesinger Jr., *A Thousand Days: John F. Kennedy in the White House* (Boston: Houghton Mifflin Company, 1965), 940–948; Robert Dallek and Terry Golway, *Let Every Nation Know: John F. Kennedy in his Own Words* (Naperville, IL: Sourcebooks MediaFusion, 2006), 171–174; Crespino, *In Search of Another Country*, 42–43; Eagles, *The Price of Defiance*, 360, 364–365; *NAACP Annual Report*, "The March to Freedom" (July 1962), 7. For discussion regarding Barnett's take of the Meredith enrollment, see Claude Ramsay interview with Orley B. Caudill, April 28, 1981, Mississippi Oral History Program, University of Southern Mississippi, Part I, 61–62. In reference to those killed, Dallek and Golway maintain that a journalist and construction worker died rather than a journalist and a mechanic. See *Let Every Nation Know*, 173–174. For a deeper discussion of the riot, see Eagles, *The Price of Defiance*, 340–370.

39. See "Negro Attended U. of Mississippi Listed as White in Navy Program," *New York Times*, September 25, 1962, "Negro 'Passed' at Ole Miss," *Atlanta Journal*, September 25, 1962, and "White Pals Glad Negro Was Ole Miss Student in 1945–46, *Jet* magazine, October 11, 1962, William Doyle Collection, "Henry Murphy, 1st Black at Ole Miss," Box 3, Folder 5, University of Mississippi Department of Archives and Special Collections. Medgar Evers, "Monthly

Report," October 5, 1962, Papers of the NAACP: Part 20, Group III, Box A-115, microfilm reel 15, 1.

40. Medgar Evers, "Monthly Report," October 5, 1962, Papers of the NAACP: Part 20, Group III, Box A-115, microfilm reel 15, 1.

41. Medgar Evers, "Mississippi Mood: Hope and Fear," *Washington Post,* October 14, 1962, E1, E3.

42. "Meredith to Enroll; Black Vacates Stay Circuit Court Decision Upheld Ole Miss Registration on 19th," *Mississippi Free Press,* September 15, 1962, 1, located in the *American Historical Newspapers* database.

43. Medgar Evers, "Monthly Report," July 28, 1961, NAACP Papers, LOC, Group III, Box C-245, Folder 1, 2.

44. Medgar Evers to Herbert L. Wright, July 28, 1961, and "Monthly Report," July 28, 1961, NAACP Papers, LOC, Group III, Box E-9, Folder 8, and C-245, Folder 1, 2–3, respectively.

45. Medgar Evers, "Monthly Report," September 6, 1961, NAACP Papers, LOC, Group III, Box C-245, Folder 1, 2–3.

46. Gloster Current to Aaron E. Henry, October 6, 1961, NAACP Papers, LOC, Group III, Box C-75, Folder 8.

47. Stephen D. Classen, *Watching Jim Crow: The Struggles over Mississippi TV, 1955–1969* (Durham, NC: Duke University Press, 2004), 59.

48. Charles Marsh, *God's Long Summer: Stories of Faith and Civil Rights* (Princeton, NJ: Princeton University Press, 1997), 24, and Ineeva May-Pittman, September 11, 2006, interview.

49. Minnie White Watson, September 12, 2006, interview; Dr. Velvelyn Foster, interview with the author, December 14, 2006, cassette recording, Jackson State University, Jackson, Mississippi. Tape in possession of the author. Hazel Palmer interview with Worth Long, (n.d.), SRC: Will the Circle be Unbroken?, Emory University, Box 8, Folder 26, 3.

50. Minnie White Watson, September 12, 2006, interview.

51. Constance Slaughter Harvey interview with George King, May, 1992, SRC: Will the Circle be Unbroken?, Emory University, Box 8, Folder 9, 3.

52. "Evers Symbolizes Struggle, Hope," *Clarion-Ledger,* June 6, 1993, 1. Slaughter-Harvey served as the Mississippi assistant secretary of state for elections and general council to the secretary of state's office. See also, Constance Slaughter Harvey interview with George King, May 1992, SRC: Will the Circle be Unbroken?, Emory University, Box 8, Folder 9, 13.

53. Myrlie Evers-Williams, October 25, 2006, interview.

54. Minnie White Watson, September 12, 2006, interview.

55. Dr. Velvelyn Foster, December 14, 2006, interview.

56. Cornelius Turner, July 12, 2005, interview.

57. "Petition to Integrate Schools: Parents Want Equal Education for Children," *Mississippi Free Press,* August 18, 1962, 1, 4, located in the *American Historical Newspapers* database. Medgar Evers, "Annual Report," December 6, 1962, Papers of the NAACP: Part 20, Group III, Box, A-115, microfilm reel 15, 5, and *NAACP Annual Report,* 1962, 99.

58. Peters, *For Us, the Living,* 245.

59. North Jackson NAACP Youth Council letter requesting nationwide support, January 28, 1963, Papers of the NAACP: Part 20, Group III, Box A-232, microfilm reel 2.

60. Ibid. and "Memorandum" May 9, 1963, from Laplois Ashford to Gloster Current, Roy Wilkins, Medgar Evers et al. regarding the "Selective Buying Campaign, Jackson, Mississippi," Papers of the NAACP: Part 20, Group III, Box A-232, microfilm reel 2, 2; Salter, *Jackson, Mississippi,* 57.

61. "Second-Hand Fair Rejected: Thousands Boycott State Fair Silent Streets Reflect Success," *Mississippi Free Press,* October 20, 1962, 1, located in the *American Historical Newspapers* database.

62. Salter, *Jackson, Mississippi,* 57–58.

63. Ibid., 59, and Medgar Evers, "Monthly Report," January 4, 1963, NAACP Papers, LOC, Group III, Box C-245, Folder 3, 1–2, 3.

64. Salter, *Jackson, Mississippi,* 58–61.

65. Ibid., 62–64, and "Racially Mixed Group Arrested," *Jackson Daily News,* December 12, 1962, 13.

66. "Thompson Warns Picketing Group" and "Mayor Calls for Support in Community Participation," *Jackson Daily News,* December 13, 1962, 1 and 6, respectively.

67. Evers-Williams, October 25, 2006, interview.

68. John Frazier, October 23, 2010, interview.

69. Roberts and Klibanoff, *Race Beat,* 334.

70. Salter, *Jackson, Mississippi,* 94–95, Dittmer, *Local People,* 160, and "King Promises Delta Drive to Enlist Voters," *Jackson Daily News,* May 2, 1963, 11.

71. Salter, *Jackson, Mississippi,* 95.

72. "Jackson Police Jail 600 Negro Children," *New York Times,* June 1, 1963, 1.

73. Evers and Peters, *For Us, the Living,* 263.

74. Ineeva May-Pittman, September 11, 2006, interview.

75. Evers-Williams, October 25, 2006, interview, and Ivory Phillips, December 13, 2006, interview.

76. Medgar Evers, "Address by Medgar W. Evers Mississippi Field Secretary for the NAACP . . . , May 18, 1958," NAACP Papers, LOC, Group III, Box C-244, Folder 2, 5.

77. "Salter Interview, Stennis Project," 16–17.

78. Evers-Williams, October 25, 2006, interview.

79. Ibid.

7.

Epigraphs. Richard Newman, *African American Quotations* (New York: Oryx Press, 2000), 186. Medgar Evers, "Why I Live in Mississippi," 70. Malcolm X, *By Any Means Necessary* (New York: Pathfinder, 1992), 56. John Henrik Clarke, *My Life in Search of Africa,* 98.

1. Evers-Williams, October 25, 2006, interview.

2. "Integration Seen by '63, Mississippi N.A.A.C.P. Aide Finds Progress in State," *New York Times,* November 10, 1957, 135.

3. Sam Bailey interview with George King, May 1992, SRC: Will the Circle be Unbroken?, Emory University, 2.

4. Ibid., 5, 7, and *Samuel Bailey et al. v. Joe T. Patterson et al.,* December 18, 1961, 369 U.S. 31, No. 643.

5. "The People will Watch the NAACP," *Mississippi Free Press,* February 24, 1962, 2., located in the *American Historical Newspapers* database.

6. "Comments by Charles L. Butts," *Mississippi Free Press,* June 30, 1962, 1, located in the *American Historical Newspapers* database.

7. Medgar Evers, "Monthly Report," March 6, 1963, NAACP Papers, LOC, Group III, Box C-245, Folder 3, 1; "Courts to be Asked to Open P.S. Here," *Mississippi Free Press,* March 2, 1963, 1, located in the *American Historical Newspapers* database; and Sam Bailey interview with George King, May 1992, SRC: Will the Circle be Unbroken?, Emory University, 5.

8. Medgar Evers, "Special Report," April 1, 1963, NAACP Papers, LOC, Group III, Box C-245, Folder 3, 1–2.

9. Allen C. Thompson, speech, 1–5, Tougaloo College Archives and Special Collections, Lillian P. Benbow Room, Medgar Wiley Evers Collection, unprocessed.

10. "NAACP Release," May 13, 1963, Papers of the NAACP, Part 20, Group III, Box A-232, microfilm reel 2.

11. "Mayor Plans Preventive Actions Here," *Jackson Daily News,* May 13, 1963, 1, 14.

12. Sovereignty Commission Papers, SCR # 2–55–10–76–3–1–1.

13. Ibid., SCR # 2–55–10–76–4–1–1.

14. Thurgood Marshall quoted in Evers-Williams and Marable, *The Autobiography of Medgar Evers,* xxiv.

15. "Jackson Leader Pledge No Deals with Demonstrators" and "Officials Plan Talk with Negroes Here," *Jackson Daily News,* May 14 and 15, 1963, 1, 14, respectively.

16. NAACP, "Background Information on New Desegregation Drive in Jackson, Miss.," May 28, 1963, NAACP Papers, LOC, Group III, Box C-74, Folder 1, 3, and "NAACP Says Allen Seeking 'Yes-Men,'" *Jackson Daily News,* May 16, 1963, 1.

17. "NAACP Says Allen Seeking 'Yes-Men,'" *Jackson Daily News,* May 16, 1963, 16A.

18. Medgar Evers to the Chairman of the Federal Communication Commission, October 17, 1957, Papers of the NAACP: Part 20, Group III, Box A-114, microfilm reel 14.

19. Kay Mills, *Changing Channels: The Civil Rights Case that Transformed Television* (Jackson: University Press of Mississippi, 2004), 27, and Stephen D. Classen, *Watching Jim Crow,* 45.

20. Medgar Evers to the Chairman of the FCC, October 17, 1957, and Mary Jane Morris to Medgar Evers denying his request, November 19, 1957, Papers of the NAACP: Part 20, Group III, Box A-114, microfilm reel 14, and Medgar Evers to Dave Garroway, February 4, 1958, ibid.

21. Classen, *Watching Jim* Crow, 50, 60, 84.

22. "Telephone Call from Mr. Current," May 17, 1963, Papers of the NAACP: Part 20, Group III, Box A-232, microfilm reel 2.

23. Medgar Evers, "Remarks of Mr. Medgar Evers, Field Secretary . . . ," May 20, 1963, NAACP Papers, LOC, Group III, Box A90, Folder 12, 1.

24. Ibid., 1–2.

25. Ibid., 3–4.

26. Ibid., 4.

27. Ibid., 5.

28. Ibid., 6

29. Ibid., 6–7.

30. Dick Gregory and Robert Lipsyte, *Nigger an Autobiography* (New York: Pocket Books, A Pocket Cardinal Edition, 1965), 176. Here Gregory is confronted with a white man who threatens to shoot him with a shotgun, but refrains when Gregory tells him to do so.

31. Mills, *Changing Channels,* 3, 58–59; Classen, *Watching Jim Crow,* 60–62. Myrlie Evers points to the impact that Reverend Robert L. T. Smith's 1961 televised political address on WJTV had on area blacks in *For Us, the Living,* 237–238.

32. Evers and Peters, *For Us, the Living,* 269.

33. Myrlie Evers acknowledges the positive exchanges between whites and blacks after Medgar's speech in ibid., 269.

34. Salter Jr., *Jackson, Mississippi,* 121.

35. Medgar Evers, "Quiet Integrationist," *New York Times,* June 1, 1963, 8.

36. Cornelius Turner, July 12, 2005, interview.

37. "FBI New Orls . . . to Director," Federal Bureau of Investigation Papers, Part II, File # 157–901, April 15, 1964, 2, http://foia.fbi.gov/evers_medgar/evers_medgar_part02.pdf (accessed December 7, 2010).

38. Medgar Evers, "Why I Live in Mississippi," 65; Myrlie Evers, "'He Said He Wouldn't Mind Dying—If . . . ,'" *Life* magazine, June 28, 1963, 36.

39. Ronald Bailey, "Remembering Medgar Evers . . . For a New Generation," 14.

40. Eskew, *But for Birmingham,* 121.

41. Ibid., 191, Thornton, *Dividing Lines,* 290, and McWhorter, *Carry Me Home,* 352–353.

42. Eskew, *But for Birmingham,* 194–209, and Andrew M. Manis, *A Fire You Can't Put Out: The Civil Rights Life of Birmingham's Reverend Fred Shuttlesworth* (Tuscaloosa: The University of Alabama Press, 1999), 330–333.

43. Manis, *A Fire You Can't Put Out,* 332–334; Eskew, *But for Birmingham,* 211–214.

44. Taylor Branch, *Parting the Waters,* 727–728; Eskew, *But for Birmingham,* 217, 237–242.

45. Eskew, *But for Birmingham,* 259–294; Manis, *A Fire You Can't Put Out,* 369–389, Thornton, *Dividing Lines,* 318–328; and McWhorter, *Carry Me Home,* 366–374.

46. Sasha Torres, *Black, White, and in Color: Television and Black Civil Rights* (Princeton, NJ: Princeton University Press, 2003), 28–31.

47. For further discussion on the Birmingham campaign, see Bobby M. Wilson, *Race and Place in Birmingham: The Civil Rights and Neighborhood Movements* (Lanham, MD: Rowman & Littlefield Publishers, 2000), and John Walter Cotman, *Birmingham, JFK and the Civil Rights Act of 1963: Implications for Elite Theory* (New York: Peter Lang, 1989). For edited works, see Marjorie L. White and Andrew M. Manis, eds., *Birmingham Revolutionaries: The Reverend Fred Shuttlesworth and the Alabama Christian Movement for Human Rights* (Macon, GA: Mercer University Press, 2000), and David Garrow, ed., *Birmingham, Alabama, 1956–1963: The Black Struggle for Civil Rights* (Brooklyn, NY: Carlson Publishing, 1989). For a closer examination of Theophilus Eugene "Bull" Connor, see William A. Nunnelley, *Bull Connor* (Tuscaloosa: The University of Alabama Press, 1991).

48. NAACP, "Background Information on New Desegregation Drive in Jackson, Miss., May 28, 1963," NAACP Papers, LOC, Group III, Box C-74, Folder 1, 5–6; Salter, *Jackson, Mississippi*, 123–131; and *The Crisis: A Record of the Darker Races* 70, no. 6 (June–July 1963): 357–359. For newspaper accounts, see *Jackson Daily News*, "Mix Drive Talked Up," May 21, 1963; "Mayor Proposes Racial Meeting," May 22, 1963; "Mayor Sets Parley Despite Conflicts," May 23, 1963; "New Plea to Negro Group," May 24, 1963; "Race Tension Here Eases Up Slightly," May 26, 1963; and "Negro Apologizes for Walking Out in 'Wrong Group,'" May 28, 1963. See also, *Clarion-Ledger*, "Mayor Lists names for Racial Meeting," May 23, 1963, and "Thompson Vows 'No Surrender,'" May 24, 1963. Evers quotes taken from *Jackson Daily News*, "Mix Drive Talked Up" and "Mayor Proposes Racial Meeting." Also see "Ask Jackson Mayor for Bi-Racial Talks: Plan Protests Marches, Sit-ins, Picketing if Demands Not Met," *Mississippi Free Press*, May 25, 1963, located in the *American Historical Newspapers* database. For discussions on the "Failing" of biracial committees, see "Bi-Racial Committees Failing in Many Racially-Torn Cities," *Clarion-Ledger*, May 22, 1963, and for a counter argument, see "Bi-Racial Body Seeks Bi-Racial Group in City," *Clarion-Ledger*, May 22, 1963.

49. Anne Moody, *Coming of Age in Mississippi* (New York: Dell Publishing, 1965), 264–267, James C. Bradford interview with Worth Long, April 30, 1983, SRC: Will the Circle be Unbroken?, Emory University, Box 7, Folder 1, 10; "Attacked by White at Lunch Counter," *Jackson Daily News*, May 28, 1963, 1, 14; Richard Hofstadter and Michael Wallace, eds., *American Violence: A Documentary History* (New York: Alfred A. Knopf, 1970), 434; and Elizabeth Jacoway and David R. Colburn, eds., *Southern Businessmen and Desegregation* (Baton Rouge: Louisiana State University Press, 1982), 240.

50. Payne, *I've Got the Light of Freedom*, 286–287.

51. Evers and Peters, *For Us, the Living*, 270–271; John D'Emilio, *The Civil Rights Struggle: Leaders in Profile* (New York: Facts On File, 1979), 52; "Background Information on New Desegregation Drive in Jackson, Miss," Papers of the NAACP: Part 20, Group III, Box A-232, microfilm reel 2; Salter, *Jackson, Mississippi*, 137; and "Mayor Declares Made No Deals," *Jackson Daily News*, May 29, 1963, 1, 12.

52. Evers and Peters, *For Us, the Living*, 271; Nossiter, *Of Long Memory*, 59; Salter, *Jackson, Mississippi*, 137–139; "Mayor Declares Made No 'Deals,'" *Jackson Daily News*, May 29, 1963, 1, 12; SCR # 2–55–10–2–1–1–1; and *NAACP Annual Report*, 1963, 108.

53. "Background Information on New Desegregation Drive in Jackson, Miss," Papers of the NAACP: Part 20, Group III, Box A-232, microfilm reel 2; Evers and Peters, *For Us, the Living*, 273–280; and Evers-Williams and Marable, *The Autobiography of Medgar Evers*, 261.

54. Evers and Peters, *For Us, the Living*, 279.

55. Ibid., 279–280.

56. "Mix Strife Can't Win Says Mayor, Thompson Brands Tougaloo 'Cancer" in Demonstrations," 1 and "Wilkins Reported Coming to Town," *Jackson Daily News*, May 30, 1963, 11.

57. Ivory Phillips, December 13, 2006, interview.

58. Medgar Evers, "Remarks of Mr. Medgar Evers . . . ," May 20, 1963, 2.

59. NAACP, *The Crisis,* "Background Information on Jackson, Mississippi," 358.

60. *Peterson v. City of Greenville,* 373 U.S.244, 245 (1963). The *Peterson* (No. 71) case was one of five dealing with sit-ins heard by the Court. The other four cases comprised of *Lombard* (No. 58) in New Orleans, Louisiana; *Gober* (No. 66) in Birmingham, Alabama; *Avent* (No. 11) in Durham, North Carolina; and *Shuttlesworth* (No. 67) also in Birmingham, Alabama.

61. Ibid., 247–248.

62. Ibid., 246.

63. *Watson et al. v. City of Memphis et al.,* 373 U.S.526, 536 (1963).

64. Ibid., 532–535.

65. Ibid., 532–533, 538–539.

66. Klarman, *From Jim Crow to Civil Rights,* 340–341.

67. Henry Jay Kirksey interview with Worth Long, (n.d.), SRC: Will the Circle be Unbroken?, Emory University, Box 8, Folder 18, 8–9.

68. Vollers, *Ghosts of Mississippi,* 111, and *Jackson Daily News,* "Negroes Make Little Headway With Campaign," May 31, 1963, 1, 12.

69. Salter, *Jackson, Mississippi,* 145.

70. Ibid., 148–150, and Vollers, *Ghosts of Mississippi,* 112.

71. Vollers, *Ghosts of Mississippi,* 112; Salter, *Jackson, Mississippi,* 149–150; "Police Jail Over 600: Mass Protests Will Continue; Charge Police with Brutality," *Mississippi Free Press,* June 8, 1963, 1, located in the *American Historical Newspapers* database; and "Jackson Police Jail 600 Negro Students," *New York Times,* June 1, 1963, 1, 8.

72. Salter, *Jackson, Mississippi,* 150–151.

73. NAACP Immediate Release, "Wilkins Jailed In Mississippi As NAACP Drive Is Accelerated," June 3, 1963, Papers of the NAACP: Part 20, Group III, Box A-232, microfilm reel 2; Evers-Williams and Marable, *The Autobiography of Medgar Evers,* 283.

74. Evers-Williams and Marable, *The Autobiography of Medgar Evers,* 283–284.

75. "Jackson Police Jail 600 Negro Students," *New York Times,* June 1, 1963, 8.

76. NAACP, *Crisis* 70, no. 6 (June–July 1963): 347–348; Salter, *Jackson, Mississippi,* 154–155; *NAACP Annual Report,* "In Freedom's Vanguard NAACP Report for 1963," 6–7; and A. D. Beittel, "Oral History Memoir," June 2, 1965, Mississippi Oral History Program, University of Southern Mississippi, 22.

77. *New York Times,* "Jackson Police Jail 600 Negro Students," June 1, 1963, 8.

78. Salter, *Jackson, Mississippi,* 156–157.

79. Ibid., 164–173.

80. Evers-Williams, October 25, 2006, interview.

81. Ibid.

82. Medgar Evers et al., "Reply to Mayor Allen C. Thompson from Jackson, Miss., Negro Leaders," June 3, 1963, Papers of the NAACP: Part 20, Group III, Box A-232, microfilm reel 2.

83. *NAACP Annual Report,* "In Freedom's Vanguard, NAACP Report for 1963," 108.

84. "Statement by Medgar W Evers . . . ," June 6, 1963, Papers of the NAACP: Part 20, Group III, Box A-232, microfilm reel 2.

85. "Press Conference with Robert L. Carter, General Council, NAACP," June 7, 1963, Papers of the NAACP: Part 20, Group III, Box A-232, microfilm reel 2.

86. Ibid., 2.

87. NAACP, "Excerpts from Remarks by Miss. Lena Horne," June 7, 1963; NAACP Records, LOC, Group III, Box E-9, Folder 8; NAACP, "People of the Movement" Release, June 1963, NAACP Papers, LOC, Group III, Box E-9, Folder 8; and Evers and Peters, *For Us, the Living,* 282–283.

88. Evers and Peters, *For Us, the Living,* 284–285.

89. Ibid., 285.

8.

Epigraphs. Quote inscribed on a plaque honoring Medgar Evers at the University of Mississippi Law School. Medgar Evers quoted in Adam Nossiter, *Of Long Memory,* 48. Medgar Evers to Gloster Current, May 4, 1956, NAACP Papers, LOC, Group III, Box C-243, Folder 5. Margaret Walker Alexander quoted in "Evers Symbolizes Struggle, Hope," *Clarion-Ledger,* June 6, 1993, 17A. John F. Kennedy televised Civil Rights Speech, June 11, 1963, http://www.jfklibrary.org/Historical+Resources/Archives/Reference+Desk/Speeches/JFK/003POF03CivilRights06111963.htm (accessed December 12, 2010).

1. "Jackson Police Department Offense Report, Medgar Evers Murder, 1963–1964," June 26, 1963, Evers (Medgar Wiley and Myrlie Beasley) Papers, Box 29, Folder 1.

2. Evers and Peters, *For Us, the Living,* 289–290.

3. Nossiter, *Of Long Memory,* 61, and David Gallen O'Reilly, ed., *Black Americans: The FBI Files,* 136.

4. Bryant, *The Bystander,* 23–25. For a detailed discussion of Kennedy's take on civil rights, see Theodore C. Sorensen, *Kennedy* (New York: Harper & Row, 1965), 470–506. Sorensen also served as special counsel to the president.

5. Bryant, *The Bystander,* 25–30.

6. Ibid., 33–42. For a powerful examination of the life and times of Harry T. Moore, see Ben Green, *Before His Time: The Untold Story of Harry T. Moore, America's First Civil Rights Martyr* (Gainesville: University Press of Florida, 1999).

7. Bryant, *The Bystander,* 133, and Robert Dallek, *An Unfinished Life: John F. Kennedy, 1917–1963* (Boston: Little, Brown and Company, 2003), 268.

8. Dallek, *An Unfinished Life,* 268–269.

9. Marable, *Race, Reform, and Rebellion,* 59–60; Carson, *In Struggle,* 29; Dallek, *An Unfinished Life,* 292–293; Schlesinger Jr., *A Thousand Days,* 73–74; Dallek and Golway, *Let Every Nation Know,* 52; Bryant, *The Bystander,* 180–185; and Herbert S. Parmet, *JFK: The Presidency of John F. Kennedy* (New York: Penguin Books, 1983), 54–56.

10. Marable, *Race, Reform, and Rebellion,* 59.

11. Ibid., 59–60. Marable notes that the three-fourths African American voting statistics occurred in "most cities and states."

12. Sorensen, *Kennedy,* 211–223.

13. Franklin and Moss Jr., *From Slavery to Freedom,* 528–529. Also, see Bryant, *The Bystander,* 187.

14. "NAACP Head Hails Victory of Kennedy," *State Times,* November 10, 1960, Evers (Medgar Wiley and Myrlie Beasley) Papers, Box 24, Folder 10.

15. Bryant, *The Bystander,* 189.

16. For the Inaugural Address delivered January 20, 1961, see Vito N. Silvestri,

Becoming JFK: A Profile in Communication (Connecticut: Praeger Publishers, 2000), 178–180.

17. Dallek, *An Unfinished Life*, 380, 383–388, and Bryant, *The Bystander*, 282. See also, Arsenault, *Freedom Riders*.

18. "Kennedy Plans No Rights Bills," *Jackson Daily News*, January 24, 1961, Evers (Medgar Wiley and Myrlie Beasley) Papers, Box 24, Folder, 12.

19. "When Influence Useful, JFK Would Aid Mixing," *Clarion-Ledger*, February 9, 1961, Evers (Medgar and Myrlie Beasley) Papers, Box 24, Folder 13. In regard to New Orleans, Kennedy was referring to the issue of school desegregation. Bryant also discusses Kennedy's lack of commitment to civil rights issues; see *The Bystander*, chapter 14, "Executive Inaction."

20. Dallek, *An Unfinished Life*, 388.

21. Reed Massengill, *Portrait of a Racist: The Man Who Killed Medgar Evers?* (New York: St. Martin's Press, 1994), 17–38, 41. Although listed as Jr., Massengill notes that Byron was really the third to carry the Byron De La Beckwith name. See ibid., 358 n. 2.

22. Ibid., 46. There exists a variety of works on James Kimble Vardaman and Theodore Gilmore Bilbo that provide their ideologies and the times in which they lived. For example, see William F. Holmes, *The White Chief: James Kimble Vardaman* (Baton Rouge: Louisiana State University Press, 1970); A. Wigfall Green, *The Man Bilbo* (Baton Rouge: Louisiana State University Press, 1963); and Chester L. Morgan, *Redneck Liberal: Theodore G. Bilbo and the New Deal* (Baton Rouge: Louisiana State University Press, 1985). There also exists a series of Ph.D dissertations written on Bilbo. For a few examples, see Stephen Richard Black, "The Man with a Plan: Theodore Bilbo's Adaptation of National Progressivism in Mississippi" (Ph.D. diss., University of Southern Mississippi, 2006), and Larry Thomas Balsamo, "Theodore G. Bilbo and Mississippi Politics, 1877–1932" (Ph.D. diss., University of Missouri, Columbia, 1967).

23. Evers and Szanton, *Have No Fear*, 31; Evers and Peters, *For Us, the Living*, 17; and Charles Evers, February 4, 2005, interview.

24. Massengill, *Portrait of a Racist*, 54–55 and 57.

25. Ibid., 72–73 and 75–76.

26. Dittmer, *Local People*, 18.

27. Massengill, *Portrait of a Racist*, 76, and Dittmer, *Local People*, 18. After the 1904 murder of James Eastland, his brother Woods Eastland named his son James O. in honor of his slain brother. See Moye, *Let the People Decide*, 18.

28. Massengill, *Portrait of a Racist*, 89.

29. Ibid., 90–91.

30. Vollers, *Ghosts of Mississippi*, 51.

31. Massengill, *Portrait of a Racist*, 116–117.

32. Dallek, *An Unfinished Life*, 600–601.

33. Ibid., 601–602.

34. Evers and Peters, *For Us, the Living*, 287, 290, 297.

35. Dave Dennis interview with Worth Long, February 1997, SRC: Will the Circle be Unbroken?, Emory University, Box 7, Folder 12, 9.

36. Evers and Peters, *For Us, the Living*, 297–298; Evers-Williams and Marable, *The Autobiography of Medgar Evers*, 261; and Fred Clark Sr., interview with Leesha Faulkner, June 10, 1994, Mississippi Oral History Program, University of Southern Mississippi, volume 494, 1994, 44.

37. Fred Clark Sr., interview with Leesha Faulkner, June 10, 1994, Mississippi Oral History Program, University of Mississippi, volume 494, 1994, 43, 48.

38. Henry with Curry, *Aaron Henry,* 146–147. Henry records that his meeting with Medgar took place on June 12, and he learned of the assassination the following day. However, the meeting had to have taken place on the eleventh as Medgar was assassinated during the early morning hours of June 12, 1963.

39. Evers-Williams, October 25, 2006, interview. The reference to Broadwater is a probable reference to former president of the Jackson branch Joseph Broadwater, who was an active civil rights leader in the city of Jackson.

40. Dallek, *An Unfinished Life,* 603, and Dallek and Golway, *Let Every Nation Know,* 206–208.

41. Text of John F. Kennedy televised Civil Rights Speech, June 11, 1963, http://www.jfklibrary.org/Historical+Resources/Archives/Reference+Desk/Speeches /JFK/003POF03CivilRights06111963.htm (accessed December 12, 2010); "Text of President's Message: 'This is a Problem Which Faces all—the North as well as the South,'" *Commercial Appeal,* June 12, 1963; "Kennedy Pleads for Equal Treatment for all Citizens: Asserts Race has no Place in U.S. Life," *Chicago Tribune,* June 12, 1963; and "Transcript of President's Address," *New York Times,* June 12, 1963.

42. Ibid.

43. Ibid.

44. Evers and Peters, *For Us, the Living,* 301.

45. Salter, *Jackson, Mississippi,* 182–183, and Vollers, *Ghosts of Mississippi,* 124.

46. "The Ideal," Ed King Collection, "Medgar Evers," Folder 7, University of Mississippi Department of Archives and Special Collections.

47. Ibid. and Evers-Williams, October 25, 2006, interview.

48. Henry with Curry, *Aaron Henry,* 147, and Roberts and Klibanoff, *Race Beat,* 335, 340. Medgar's prediction that "tomorrow will be a big day" taken from "N.A.A.C.P. Leader Slain in Jackson: Protests Mount," *New York Times,* June 13, 1963, 12. Although the *New York Times* did not identify the reporter Evers spoke to before leaving the church, it may well have been Shoemaker.

49. Aurelia Norris Young interview with unidentified interviewer, (n.d.), SRC: Will the Circle be Unbroken?, Emory University, Box 9, Folder 8, 8, and Vollers, *Ghosts of Mississippi,* 124–125.

50. Evers and Peters, *For Us, the Living,* 299.

51. Ibid., 302; Myrlie Evers, "'He Said He Wouldn't Mind Dying—If . . . ,'" *Life* magazine, June 28, 1963, 37; and Roberts and Klibanoff, *Race Beat,* 340 .

52. Evers and Peters, *For Us, the Living,* 302.

53. Myrlie Evers, interview by Nicholas Hordern, 4, Evers (Medgar Wiley and Myrlie Beasley) Papers, Box 3, Folder 48, 4. References to pregnancy, see Evers-Williams and Blau, *Watch Me Fly,* 76.

54. Myrlie Evers, "'He Said He Wouldn't Mind Dying—If . . . ,'" 37.

55. "M.W. Evers Shot Dead in Mississippi," *Chicago Tribune,* June 12, 1963.

56. Myrlie Evers, "'He Said He Wouldn't Mind Dying—If . . . ,'" 37.

57. Evers and Peters, *For Us, the Living,* 302–303; Evers (Medgar Wiley and Myrlie Beasley) Papers, Box 3, Folder 48; "M.W. Evers Shot Dead in Mississippi," *Chicago Tribune,* June 12, 1963, 1; and "N.A.A.C.P. Leader Slain in Jackson; Protests Mount," *New York Times,* June 13, 1963, 1.

58. Aurelia Norris Young interview with unidentified interviewer, (n.d.), SRC: Will the Circle be Unbroken?, Emory University, Box 9, Folder 8, 8.

59. "Jackson Police Department Offense Report, Medgar Evers Murder, 1963–1964," Evers (Medgar and Myrlie Beasley) Papers, Box 29, Folder 1.

60. Moody, *Coming of Age in Mississippi*, 278; O'Reilly, *Black Americans*, 136; and "Unknown Subject," Federal Bureau of Investigation Papers, Part V, June 7, 1963, http://foia.fbi.gov/evers_medgar/evers_medgar_part05.pdf (accessed December 7, 2010).

61. Henry Jay Kirksey interview with Worth W. Long, (n.d.), SRC: Will the Circle be Unbroken?, Emory University, Box 8, Folder 18, 12, 14.

62. Charles Evers, February 4, 2005, interview.

63. Evers-Williams and Blau, *Watch Me Fly*, 78.

64. "Jackson Police Department Offense Report, Medgar Evers Murder, 1963–1964," Evers (Medgar Wiley and Myrlie Beasley) Papers, Box 29, Folder 1. The children's names and ages follow: Willie Mae Bishop, (female) 16 yrs.; Harold Bishop, 12 yrs.; Sammy Bagwell, 14 yrs.; and Herbert Bishop, 15 yrs.

65. Ibid.

66. "Jackson Police Department Offense Report, Medgar Evers Murder, 1963–1964," Evers (Medgar Wiley and Myrlie Beasley) Papers, Box 29, Folder 1.

67. "A Trail of Blood—a Negro Dies," *Life* magazine, vol. 54, no. 25, June 21, 1963, 28.

68. *NAACP Annual Report,* "Martyrdom of a Crusader," 1963, 51.

69. "Reward is Posted in Evers Slaying," *New York Times,* June 13, 1963, 12.

70. The *Jackson Advocate* noted the letter from Kennedy in "Rowdy Demonstrations Mar the Solemn Funeral Rites for Medgar Evers Here Saturday: Police Quell Demonstrations; Many Notables Attend Rites," *Jackson Advocate,* June 22, 1963, 8, John F. Kennedy quoted in Evers-Williams and Marable, *The Autobiography of Medgar Evers*, 298; and Harry Truman quoted in "Truman Predicts Evers Slayer Will Be Caught," *Jackson Advocate,* June 22, 1963, 1.

71. For more on the comments of the foreign press, see "Foreign Press Condemns Murder of Medgar Evers," *Chicago Defender,* June 15–21, 1963, 7.

72. Evers-Williams and Marable, *The Autobiography of Medgar Evers*, 292; Evers and Peters, *For Us, the Living,* 326–327; and John F. Kennedy quoted in Schlesinger Jr., *A Thousand Days,* 966.

73. Salter, *Jackson, Mississippi,* 188–189. A group of thirteen ministers left Pearl Street Baptist Church at approximately 11:25 A.M. headed to City Hall in protest and were arrested. For further account, see "N.A.A.C.P. Leader Slain In Jackson; Protests Mount," *New York Times,* June 13, 1963, 1; and "Weapon Discovered Near Ambush Scene," *Jackson Daily News,* June 12, 1963, 1.

74. Moody, *Coming of Age in Mississippi,* 277.

75. Salter, *Jackson, Mississippi,* 188–190; Moody, *Coming of Age,* 278–281; "160 Arrested in Marches," *Clarion-Ledger,* June 13, 1963, 1A, 12A; *New York Times,* "N.A.A.C.P. Leader Slain in Jackson," June 13, 1963, 12; and "Martyr to an Immoral System," *Life* magazine, June 28, 1963, 4.

76. "Jackson Negroes Clubbed as Police Quell Marchers," *New York Times,* June 14, 1963, 1, and Salter, *Jackson, Mississippi,* 194–204.

77. Evers and Szanton, *Have No Fear,* 139; *NAACP Annual Report,* "Martyrdom of a Crusader," 1963, 51–53; A. D. Beittel, "Oral History Memoir,"

Mississippi Oral History Program, University of Southern Mississippi, 29–30; and "Medgar W. Evers Order of Worship," funeral program, NAACP Papers, LOC, Group III, Box C-245, Folder 3.

78. James E. Jackson, *At the Funeral of Medgar Evers in Jackson, Mississippi: A Tribute in Tears, A Thrust for Freedom,* MDAH, 7.

79. Aaron Henry interview with McMillen and Burson, Mississippi Oral History Program, University of Southern Mississippi, 71.

80. Salter, *Jackson, Mississippi,* 211.

81. Special Announcement, "Medgar W. Evers: in Memoriam, Remarks by Roy Wilkins at Funeral Services for Medgar W. Evers . . . ," June 15, 1963, NAACP Papers, LOC, Group VIII, Box 186, Folder 7, 3; Evers and Szanton, *Have No Fear,* 139.

82. Ivanhoe Donaldson and Charles Cobb interview with George King, April 16, 1996, SRC: Will the Circle be Unbroken?, Emory University, Box 7, Folder 7, 25.

83. Salter, *Jackson, Mississippi,* 209.

84. Fred Clark Sr., interview with Leesha Faulkner, June 10, 1994, Mississippi Oral History Program, University of Southern Mississippi, volume 494, 1994, 49.

85. Salter, *Jackson, Mississippi,* 213–220; Jackson, *At the Funeral of Medgar Evers,* 9; Dittmer, *Local People,* 166–167; *NAACP Annual Report,* "Martyrdom of a Crusader," 1963, 52–54; "Funeral March Finishes in White-Led Agitation," and "Minority of Mourners at Evers Rites Jailed," *Jackson Daily News,* June 16, 1963, 1, 14A, and 16A.

86. Colia Liddell Clark and Dr. Lewis Liddell interview with Worth Long, May 23, 1983, SRC: Will the Circle be Unbroken?, Emory University, Box 8, Folder 19, 4.

87. Dave Dennis interview with Worth Long, February 1997, SRC: Will the Circle be Unbroken?, Emory University, Box 7, Folder 12, 12–14; Ivanhoe Donaldson, Charles Cobb, Frank Smith, and Marion Barry interview with George King, May 1996, SRC: Will the Circle be Unbroken?, Emory University, Box 7, Folder 17, 27–28; and Dr. Robert Smith interview with George King, May 1992, SRC: Will the Circle be Unbroken?, Emory University, Box 9, Folder 5, 7.

88. "Reward is Posted in Evers Slaying," *New York Times,* June 13, 1963, 12.

89. Malcolm X, "The Oppressed Masses of the World Cry Out for Action Against the Common Oppressor," speech given at the London School of Economics, February 11, 1965, in Steve Clarke, ed., *Malcolm X Talks to Young People: Speeches in the U.S., Britain, and Africa* (New York: Pathfinder Press, 1991), 44. The hundred years Malcolm referred to was the period between 1863 and 1963 beginning with the Emancipation Proclamation.

90. "Jackson Police Department Offense Report, Medgar Evers Murder, 1963–1964," Evers (Medgar Wiley and Myrlie Beasley) Papers, Box 29, Folder 1; "But 3 'Hot' Clues May Break Case," Jackson Daily News, June 13, 1963, 1A, 14A; and "Suspect Eyed in Evers Case," Clarion-Ledger, June 13, 1963, 1; and Delaughter, Never Too Late, 48. This, however, was not the first arrest connected to the Evers murder. On June 12, the Jackson Police Department arrested Levi E. J. White, a fifty-five-year-old white male, at "Melbas Café." White confessed to "E.C. Roberts and wife and Marguet Evans," a waitress at the Café, that the murder weapon police had found belonged to him and that he had "killed the negro [*sic*]." After being detained overnight, White was released when it was discovered that he

suffered from psychiatric problems and police determined that he was not involved in the murder.

91. See "Jackson Police Department Supplementary Offense Report, Medgar Evers Murder, 1963–1964," Evers (Medgar Wiley and Myrlie Beasley) Papers, Box 29, Folder 1.

92. "Jackson Police Department Offense Report, Medgar Evers Murder, 1963–1964," Evers (Medgar Wiley and Myrlie Beasley) Papers, Box 29, Folder 1.

93. Vollers, *Ghosts of Mississippi*, 150–151; Nossiter, *Of Long Memory*, 130–131; and Delaughter, *Never Too Late*, 50. Also see, "State of Mississippi vs. Byron De La Beckwith," July 8, 1963, 1, Federal Bureau of Investigation Papers, Part I, File # 157–901, http://foia.fbi.gov/evers_medgar/evers_medgar_part01.pdf (accessed December 7, 2010).

94. "Jackson Police Department Offense Report, Medgar Evers Murder, 1963–1964," Evers (Medgar Wiley and Myrlie Beasley) Papers, Box 29, Folder 1; *State of Mississippi V. Byron De La Beckwith*, NO. 17,824 File No. JN 44–37 Volume 3, Evers (Medgar Wiley and Myrlie Beasley) Papers, Box 29, Folder 51; Federal Bureau of Investigation Papers, Part I, File # 157–901, February 1, 1964, http://foia.fbi.gov/evers_medgar/evers_medgar_part01.pdf; and Vollers, *Ghosts of Mississippi*, 175.

95. The *Commercial Appeal* newspaper clipping, November 4, 1963, *State of Mississippi V. Byron De La Beckwith*, no. 17, 824.

96. Nossiter, *Of Long Memory*, 132, and Vollers, *Ghosts of Mississippi*, 160–164.

97. Nossiter, *Of Long Memory*, 134–135, and Vollers, *Ghosts of Mississippi*, 208–209.

98. Vollers, *Ghosts of Mississippi*, 208; "Mrs. Evers Lead Off in Beckwith Trial," April 11, 1964, "Beckwith Free on Bail Bond 2nd Trial Ends in Hung Jury," April 20, 1964, Papers of the NAACP, Part 20, Group III, Series A, Administrative File, General Office File, Box A-116, microfilm reel 15; and "They don't have any idea who killed the nigger. I didn't kill Medgar Evers," *Esquire*, July 1991, Tougaloo College Archives, 62.

99. "President Phones Mayor Thompson, Allen Tells Kennedy 'You can Stop' Strife," *Jackson Daily News*, June 18, 1963, 1.

100. NAACP, "Limited Concessions Gained in Jackson," June 22, 1963, Papers of the NAACP, Part 20: Group III, Box A-232, microfilm reel 2; "Mayor Promises Jobs for Negroes," *Jackson Daily News*, June 19, 1963, 1, 14.

101. "Mayor Promises Jobs for Negroes," *Jackson Daily News*, June 19, 1963, 1, 14; "First Negro Policeman is Sworn in by Mayor," *Clarion-Ledger*, June 21, 1963, 6; and "City to Name Second Negro Officer Today," *Jackson Daily News*, June 21, 1963, 1, 5. It is important to note, however, that Joe Louis Land was not the first African American police officer to be hired in Mississippi. Because of pressure placed on Indianola officials by the Indianola NAACP branch, in February 1949 "the Indianola police force hired Nathanial "Slim" Jack, a charter member of the Indianola branch and the first African American police officer in the entire state." See Moye, *Let the People Decide*, 53.

102. "Mayor Promises Jobs for Negroes," *Jackson Daily News*, June 19, 1963, 1.

103. "City Continues Work for Racial Solution," *Clarion-Ledger*, June 20, 1963, 1.

104. Ibid., 14A, and "Progress in Race Relations Noted in Jackson," *Jackson Advocate*, June 22, 1963, 6.

105. Dr. Robert Smith interview with George King, May, 1992, SRC: Will the Circle be Unbroken?, Emory University, Box 9, Folder 5, 9.

106. "Mississippi Father Keeps Promise and Gets Fired," Papers of the NAACP, Part 20: Group III, Box A-231, microfilm reel 2.

107. Claude Ramsay interview with Orley B. Caudill, April 28, 1981, Mississippi Oral History Program, University of Southern Mississippi, Part I, 69–70.

108. Moye, *Let the People Decide,* 90–91.

109. Both Molpus and McLemore are discussed in Nadine Cohodas, *The Band Played Dixie: Race and the Liberal Conscience at Ole Miss* (New York: Free Press, 1997), 130, 133.

110. Evers and Peters, *For Us, the Living,* 226; Donald Jr., "The Civil Rights Leader as Utopianist," 220; and Sam Bailey interview with George King, May 1992, SRC: Will the Circle be Unbroken?, Emory University, Box 6, Folder 24, 5–6.

111. "North Slapped by Mrs. Evers," *Press-Scimitar* (Memphis), September 30, 1969, University of Memphis Libraries Special Collections Department, *Press-Scimitar* Morgue File # 60988, 11.

112. "Evers Was Used to Threats," *Washington Post,* June 13, 1963, A6.

113. Evers and Dr. King quotes in "Evers was Used to Threats" and "FBI Assists City Hunt for NAACP Aide's Killer," *Washington Post,* June 13, 1963, Evers (Medgar and Myrlie Beasley) Papers, Box 25, Folder 7.

114. Evers and Peters, *For Us, the Living,* 322–323; Evers and Szanton, *Have No Fear,* 140–141; and Federal Bureau of Investigation Papers, Part I, File # 157–901, http:/foia.fbi.gov/evers_medgar/evers_medgar_part01.pdf (accessed December 7, 2010). Although not reflected in the above quote, the FBI report was recorded in all capital letters. I chose not to include all caps to avoid a disruption in the narrative's flow.

115. "10,000 File by Evers' Coffin, Paying respects in Silence," *Evening Star,* Washington, D.C., June 18, 1963, Evers (Medgar and Myrlie Beasley) Papers, Box 25, Folder 7.

116. Ibid.

117. Ibid.

118. Ibid.

119. Roy Wilkins quoted in Metcalf, *Black Profiles,* 214; Schlesinger Jr., *A Thousand Days,* 966.

120. Dallek, *An Unfinished Life,* 604, Sorensen, *Kennedy,* 496–498, and Schlesinger Jr., *A Thousand Days,* 967. Charles and Barbara Whalen note that Kennedy's civil rights bill was initially comprised of eight provisions addressing the varied forms of inequality that denied the full-measure of citizenship rights although they list only seven. See Charles and Barbara Whalen, *The Longest Debate: A Legislative History of the 1964 Civil Rights Act* (Washington, DC: Seven Locks Press, 1985), 1–2.

121. Medgar Evers is buried in Arlington National Cemetery Section 36 grave number 1431.

122. Steven F. Lawson, *Running for Freedom: Civil Rights and Black Politics in America Since 1941,* 2nd ed. (New York: McGraw-Hill, 1997), 91, and Whalen and Whalen, *The Longest Debate,* 4–15.

123. Whalen and Whalen, *The Longest Debate,* 118–123.

124. Robert D. Loevy, *To End All Segregation: The Politics of the Passage of the Civil Rights Act of 1964* (Lanham, MD: University Press of America, 1990), 1–2, 277–284, and Whalen and Whalen, *The Longest Debate,* 198–200.

125. Whalen and Whalen, *The Longest Debate,* 215–216, 227–228; Lawson, *Running for Freedom,* 95; Marable, *Race Reform and Rebellion,* 82–83; and Bryant, *The Bystander,* 462.

126. Charles Evers, February 4, 2005, interview.

127. Charles Evers, interview with CBS anchorman Dan Rather, *CBS Evening News,* "A Reporter's Notebook," aired March 1, 2005.

128. "Mississippi Man" is a term used by Ethel Murrain.

129. Medgar Evers, "Why I Live in Mississippi," 70.

130. Henry Lee Moon, "The Martyrdom of Medgar W. Evers," *Crisis* (June–July 1973): 188. Moon served as the NAACP's public relations director.

131. Newspaper clipping, MDAH, Subject File, "Evers, Medgar, 1990."

132. Clarence Mitchell, "Excerpts from Remarks by Clarence Mitchell," June 13, 1965, Papers of the NAACP, Part 20: Group III, Box, A-114, microfilm reel 14, 3.

133. Charles Evers, February 4, 2005, interview.

134. Mildred Bond Roxborough, July 27, 2005, interview.

135. Sam Bailey interview with George King, May 1992, SRC: Will the Circle be Unbroken?, Emory University, Box 6, Folder 24, 5.

136. Alpha Morris, September 14, 2006, interview.

137. Ineeva May-Pittman, September 11, 2006, interview.

138. Evers-Williams, October 25, 2006, interview.

139. "Medgar W. Evers, Address," August 11, 1957, Evers-Williams and Marable, *The Autobiography of Medgar Evers,* 75.

Conclusion

Epigraphs. See Ra Un Nefer Amen, *Metu Neter,* vol. 1. W. E. B. Du Bois quoted in Payne, *I've Got the Light of Freedom,* 1. Lillie Jones interview with Michael Garvey, December 11, 1974, Mississippi Oral History Program, University of Southern Mississippi, volume 181, 1981, 26. Medgar Evers, "Mississippi Victim Lived with Peril in His Job," *New York Times,* June 13, 1963, 12. Marcus Garvey quoted in Tony Martin, *Race First: The Ideological and Organizational Struggles of Marcus Garvey and the Universal Negro Improvement Association* (Dover, MA: Majority Press, 1976), 3.

1. Jerry Mitchell, "State Checked Possible Jurors in Evers Slaying," *Clarion-Ledger,* October 1, 1989, 1, 17A; Jerry Mitchell, "Beckwith Spied on, too," *Clarion-Ledger,* January 20, 2001, 1, 6A; and Delaughter, *Never Too Late,* 19–20 and 24.

2. Delaughter, *Never Too Late,* 166, 173–175, 177, 208, 212, 217–219, 234, 283–288, and "Convicted Assassin of Medgar Evers Dies," *Oxford Eagle,* January 22, 2001, 5. The sitting jury consisted of eight African Americans (three men and five women) and four whites (two men and two women).

3. Jerry Mitchell and Thyrie Bland, "Evers' Killer Beckwith Dies," *Clarion-Ledger,* January 22, 2001, 1A, 8A; "Convicted Assassin of Medgar Evers Dies," *Oxford Eagle,* January 22, 2001, 5; Jerry Mitchell, "Younger Beckwith Angry at Officials," *Clarion-Ledger,* January 23, 2001, 1B, 7B; and "Beckwith Remembered as 'Tragic Figure,'" *Oxford Eagle,* January 23, 2001, 6.

4. Evers and Peters, *For Us, the Living,* 30.

5. Medgar Evers, "Why I live in Mississippi," 70.

6. Commercial "United-Co-Op," Ltda., a Brasilian Corporation, Evers (Medgar Wiley and Myrlie Beasley) Papers, Box 3, Folder 40. Charles noted that he and Medgar had planned to travel to South America to see the land and relax "for a month" before returning "for the NAACP convention" scheduled for July 1–6. See Evers and Halsell, *Evers,* 109. For a discussion of the Convention itself, see *NAACP Annual Report,* "In Freedom's Vanguard NAACP Report for 1963," 56–61. Evers-Williams noted, however, that they no longer own the land; Evers-Williams, October 25, 2006, interview.

7. Fairclough, *Race & Democracy,* 67.

8. Medgar Evers, "Why I live in Mississippi," 69.

9. Ibid., 70.

10. Delaughter, *Never Too Late,* 164.

11. Jacqueline Dedeaux, "The Developmental Years," Tougaloo College Archives, Medgar Wiley Evers Collection, unprocessed, 3.

12. Evers and Peters, *For Us, the Living,* 294–299, and Evers-Williams, October 25, 2006, interview.

13. Evers-Williams, October 25, 2006, interview.

14. Ibid.

15. Sitkoff, *The Struggle for Black Equality,* 211. The 1964 Civil Rights Act is important to this discussion because of its connection to Evers's assassination.

16. Sitkoff, *The Struggle for Black Equality,* 211–212.

17. Ibid., 212–213, emphasis mine.

18. Evers-Williams, October 25, 2006, interview. The italicized word "snow" was chosen by the author and not Myrlie Evers-Williams.

19. Although Obama is considered the first African American president, there are noted scholars who argue that previous presidents were part black as well and thus, if the "one drop rule" is applied, they were considered black. For further discussions along this line, see noted anthropologist and historian J. A. Rogers, *The Five Negro Presidents: According to What White People Said They Were* (St. Petersburg, FL: Helga M. Rogers, 1993), 3–18. For a deeper study of Rogers's extensive examination of people of color, see his premier work, *World's Great Men of Color,* vol. 1 (New York: A Touchstone Book, 1974), and *World's Great Men of Color,* vol. 2 (New York: Collier Books, Macmillan Publishing Company, 1972).

20. Thomas M. Shapiro, *The Hidden Cost of Being African American: How Wealth Perpetuates Inequality* (Oxford: Oxford University Press, 2004), 8.

21. Ibid.

22. Ibid., 7.

23. U.S. Department of Health and Human Services, The Office of Minority Health online, http://minorityhealth.hhs.gov/templates/browse.aspx?lvl= 3&lvlid=23 (accessed September 18, 2009).

24. Ibid.

25. Sean F. Reardon and John T. Yun, "Integrating Neighborhoods, Segregating Schools: The Retreat from School Desegregation in the South, 1990–2000," in *School Resegregation: Must the South Turn Back?* ed. John Charles Boger and Gary Orfield (Chapel Hill: University of North Carolina Press, 2005), 51.

26. Gary Orfield and John T. Yun, "Resegregation in American Schools," The Civil Rights Project, Harvard University, 1999, 3.

27. Gary Orfield, "The Southern Dilemma: Losing Brown, Fearing Plessy," 2–3, and Erwin Chemerinsky, "The Segregation and Resegregation of American Public Education: The Court's Role," in John Charles Boger and Gary Orfield, eds., *School Resegregation*, 30.

28. Orfield, "The Southern Dilemma," 11–12. Regarding the conservatism of the Rehnquist Court, see Boger, "*Brown* and the American South: Fateful Choices," John Charles Boger and Gary Orfield, eds., *School Resegregation*, 307. See also, *Board of Education of Oklahoma City Public Schools, Independent School District No. 89, Oklahoma County, Oklahoma, Petitioner, v. Robert L. Dowell*, et al., 498 U.S. 236, 111 S.Ct. 630 (1991), 630. For further clarity on the Court's position on the issue of school desegregation mandates and the key precedent it relied upon, see *Charles C. Green et al., v. County School Board of New Kent County, Virginia et al.*, 391 U.S. 430, 88 S.Ct. 1689 (1968). The issue of "unitary" status is an important basis of the *Green* decision and one that the Supreme Court relied upon in the three cases discussed here. The Court admitted, however, that "the term 'unitary' does not have fixed meaning." Quoted in *Robert R. Freeman, et al., Petitioners, v. Willie Eugene Pitts, et al.*, 503 U.S. 112 S.Ct. 1430 (1992), 1444.

29. *Oklahoma City v. Dowell*, 637.

30. *Freeman, et al., Petitioners, v. Pitts*, 1431.

31. Ibid., 1432.

32. *Missouri, et al., Petitioners v. Kalima Jenkins, et al.*, No. 93–1823, 515 U.S. 70, 115 S.Ct 2038 (1995), 2046, 2039, 2051–2052.

33. Erwin Chemerinsky, "The Segregation and Resegregation of American Public Education," Boger and Orfield, eds., *School Resegregation*, 40.

34. Glenn C. Loury, *The Anatomy of Racial Inequality* (Cambridge, MA: Harvard University Press, 2002), 3–4.

35. Evers-Williams, October 25, 2006, interview.

36. Evers-Williams and Marable, *The Autobiography of Medgar Evers*, xix, xxi.

37. John Frazier, October 23, 2010, interview.

38. Evers-Williams and Marable, *The Autobiography of Medgar Evers*, 75.

39. Ever and Peters, *For Us, the Living*, 373.

Bibliographical Essay

Medgar Wiley Evers as a
Historical "Person of Interest"

I don't think the history of the civil rights movement can be told without the indomitable courage of Medgar Evers.
　　　　　　　　　　　　—Margaret Walker Alexander

History is not everything, but it is a starting point. History is a clock that people use to tell their time of day. It is a compass they use to find themselves on the map of human geography. It tells them where they are, but more importantly, what they must be.
　　　　　　　　　　　　—John Henrik Clarke

The historian John Tosh argued in *The Pursuit of History* that historians play a more practical role in society and thus the history they teach, whether to students in schools and colleges or the public at large, "needs to be informed by an awareness of this role." Once historians integrate this knowledge into their teaching methodologies, then and only then can a historical education achieve a number of core objectives.[1] According to Tosh, a historical education "trains the mind, enlarges the sympathies *and* provides a much-needed perspective on some of the most pressing problems of our time."[2] As an historical figure, Medgar Wiley Evers's connection to the African American struggle for civil equality in Mississippi during the 1950s and early 1960s commands attention from scholars of the civil rights struggle in the Deep South.[3] As a movement leader, however, Evers has failed to maintain a position of prominence at the table of historical reflection and thus limited historical analyses of his contributions to the civil rights movement have failed to provide that "much-needed perspective" Tosh describes.

Although a variety of smaller questions concerning Evers laid the foundation for this book, two basic queries provided the primary stimulus: what factors motivated Evers to fight against oppression in Mississippi, knowing full well that he might be murdered for his efforts; and what did he consider redeemable about the political structure of Mississippi during the 1950s and

1960s? A quick answer might indicate that Evers confined his fight for social equality to the state of Mississippi primarily because of his courage and determination. A deeper analysis uncovers a much more complex individual. In essence, to understand Medgar Evers's contributions to the civil rights struggle in toto, one must address the reasons behind his commitment.

Although Evers has not yet attained the same level of reverence within the public consciousness as civil rights leaders such as Martin Luther King Jr., Malcolm X, or Fannie Lou Hamer, scholars have not entirely overlooked him as a subject of interest. The objective here is to analyze Evers as a means of understanding his political development and thus to make a better evaluation of his significance to the modern civil rights movement.[4] Both the breadth and depth of his contributions, which often went unnoticed due to his unassuming nature, have for the most part been ignored by civil rights scholars. His work, however, has received some attention over the years from researchers with varying academic interests.

Any historical discussion of Medgar Evers and his leadership role in the civil rights movement should acknowledge the works and contributions of those who have analyzed him in the context of civil rights activism. The purpose here is to chronicle and critique some of the more significant works that reference his importance to the civil rights movement, the significance of the times in which he lived, and the political opposition he faced. A discussion of contemporary works provides both a backdrop and atmosphere to the period and clears the way for an extended dialogue.

For individuals interested in Mississippi history such as Ronald Bailey, Anne Moody, and Minnie White Watson, Medgar Evers and the struggle for civil rights remain synonymous. However, many people, including many young Mississippians, have never heard of the civil rights activist. Unlike more familiar names such as Martin Luther King Jr., Stokely Carmichael (he later changed his name to Kwame Ture), Fannie Lou Hamer, or Huey P. Newton, Medgar Evers does not immediately bring to mind specific identifiable achievements. For Evers, although an active member of the NAACP, there existed no March on Washington, Black Power movement, Mississippi Freedom Democratic Party (MFDP) or Black Panther Party to catapult him into national prominence. As a consequence, the significance of his contributions to the civil rights movement have received far less attention than that of many of his contemporaries.

Although noted scholars such as John Dittmer and Charles Payne acknowledge his contributions when dealing with the political and social make up of Mississippi during the 1950s and 1960s, very few texts examine the social and political development of Evers from his birth in Decatur,

Mississippi, to his assassination in Jackson. Because so few works focused on Medgar Evers, it proved feasible to divide existing scholarship into four specific categories: sources addressing his life, works dealing with his assassination, materials examining his assassin Byron De La Beckwith, and works that describe the psychological and emotional environment of Mississippi during Evers's lifetime. The concluding section critiques the works and situates this study within the overall historical discussion. I choose to begin with the work of the one who possibly knew him best, his wife, Myrlie Evers.

Myrlie Evers and William Peters provide both a detailed and intimate look into the life and times of Medgar Evers. Throughout *For Us, the Living,* the authors present a primary account of Evers as husband, father and social/political activist. As both Evers's wife and widow, Myrlie Evers (now Evers-Williams) provides a passionate and personal analysis of the life and political development of the civil rights leader. In many ways, *For Us, the Living* serves as a memoir of both Medgar and Myrlie Evers and the sociopolitical conditions of the state of Mississippi, and thus the reader finds constant reminders of the inner strength and personal convictions behind Evers's work. *For Us, the Living* also demonstrates the importance that organized resistance played on both sides of the racial divide.

Myrlie Evers writes with candor regarding the impact that white supremacist organizations such as the White Citizens' Council and the Mississippi State Sovereignty Commission had on the struggle for civil rights in Mississippi, and she also discusses the creation of the Council of Federated Organizations (COFO) and its intrinsic value to the African American community. COFO proved a powerful political presence that Evers invariably employed in the struggle for sociopolitical parity.[5] The strength of *For Us, the Living,* however, resides in the attention placed on Evers's personal attributes like kindness, anger, frustration, determination, and the fear that gripped him on a day-to-day basis. In many ways, *For Us, the Living* exposes the desperation that the African American population internalized during the 1950s and 1960s. It also displays the inner strength and devotion that Evers and other civil rights leaders called upon to persevere and to continue the daily grind of individual and group activism.[6]

Ethel Patricia Churchill Murrain provides one of the more scholarly works on Evers in her dissertation, "The Mississippi Man and His Message." Murrain examines the impact Evers had upon the civil rights struggle through the use of rhetorical analysis. She uses a variety of primary and secondary sources to support her contentions concerning the rhetorical effectiveness of Evers's public addresses. In much the same vein as scholars examining other civil rights leaders, Murrain argues that to "understand

Medgar Evers it is important to understand his background—the economic, social and political conditions that he was born into."[7] As a result, she divides her analysis into two effective descriptors: the social and political conditions of Mississippi and the events and circumstances that both shaped and developed Evers's political maturity. For Murrain, the political growth of Evers proved directly proportional to his oratorical development.

Her focus upon the oratorical growth of Medgar Evers and his overall political and rhetorical progression makes her contribution to the scholarship of civil rights leadership significant. By examining thirty-three speeches Evers delivered between 1957 and 1963, Murrain analyzes the oratory processes Evers used to educate and to motivate African Americans to seek citizenship rights, publicize racial conflict, bring to light racialized violence, and lessen racial tensions among African Americans and their white counterparts.[8]

Murrain concludes that Evers developed his oratory power considerably between the years 1957 and 1963. The fact that his earlier speeches tended to be more formal and organized, effective but somewhat scripted and formulaic, supports her overall argument. From 1961 until his assassination, however, Evers was at the height of his oratorical power and considered himself a committed and vested member of the Jackson community. As a result, he became more comfortable with his leadership role and much more unyielding in his desire to lead others in the fight for equality and resistance to oppression. His personal development resulted in a more effective and influential oratorical exchange.

Whereas Murrain focuses on specifics, scholars such as Jennie Brown have attempted to provide a more comprehensive examination of Medgar Evers. Her *Medgar Evers Activist* stands as one of the few works that describes, although briefly, Evers's development from childhood to civil rights activist. In addition to providing a biographical synopsis of Evers, Brown describes specific instances that helped to shape his political development. Everyday acts of racism, segregation, degradation, and disrespect exhibited by whites toward African Americans fueled Evers's drive to take a stand against oppression. Brown points to these occurrences as significant to his overall development.[9] The first two chapters of my work expand on the social and cultural events that helped transform Medgar Evers into a political force to be reckoned with.

Although Brown provides a fine introduction to the life, dedication, and work of Medgar Evers, some historians may place less emphasis upon its overall contribution due to its lack of footnotes or endnotes. Yet her account holds value because of its constant attention to the everyday realities of the African American population of Mississippi. By understanding the oppressive social and political conditions African Americans experienced on a daily basis, one can appreciate the courage behind activism at both the grassroots and leadership levels. Thus Brown provides a clear synopsis of Medgar Evers that incorporates common knowledge about his life with new opportunities to expand the civil rights discussion.

As dedicated, determined, and devoted to fighting for the cause of justice in Mississippi as Medgar Evers proved to be, he was not a solo act. Grassroots activists were quite active in Mississippi, and historians argue that their actions, sacrifice, and support allowed leaders such as Evers to accomplish as much as they did and as quickly as they did. The historian John Dittmer is a proponent of this argument and his phenomenal work, *Local People: The Struggle for Civil Rights in Mississippi,* recognizes the labor and sacrifice of the many local Mississippi leaders and foot soldiers in the fight for civil equality.[10]

Dittmer uses an array of primary sources and archival collections from organizations and institutions such as SNCC, CORE, SCLC, and the Mississippi Department of Archives and History. In addition to a variety of secondary materials and oral histories, he utilizes works from civil rights leaders and advocates such as Martin Luther King Jr. Dittmer demonstrates, effectively, the extent to which whites attempted to prevent African Americans from voting and the unintended backlash their tactics engendered in the black community. In this regard, his account, though more in depth, parallels the works of Myrlie Evers, Ethel Murrain, Jennie Brown, and others. His true focus, however, is the illumination of the varied methods local people utilized in their opposition to political and public oppression.

Although Dittmer fairly criticizes, highlights, celebrates, and admonishes the work of national organizations and leaders such as Evers, his focus centers around grassroots participants and their role in the civil rights struggle. His central argument holds that local people, far from being empty ciphers awaiting the arrival and guidance of national organizations, were the driving force behind the struggle for justice in Mississippi. He argues throughout that the problem was not that local people were inactive but rather that their actions were often overshadowed by civil rights tactics employed on the national level. Dittmer points out that these tactics more often received far greater coverage by both the media and scholars. Medgar Evers also understood the power behind the local population, and although he is not a central figure in Dittmer's analysis, he has a recurring role that Dittmer presents as important to the civil rights movement.

By focusing on the actions of local leaders such as Aaron Henry, Amzie Moore, Dr. Clinton C. Battle, Dr. A. Maurice Mackel, E. W. Steptoe, and others, Dittmer argues that the civil rights movement in Mississippi and elsewhere owes its success to the sacrifices and determination of local people. It is important to note, however, that Medgar Evers proved an integral part of the local population and as such proved an intricate member of the very community Dittmer describes. Although during World War II Evers had traveled overseas as a soldier in the U.S. Army and later received a college degree from Alcorn College in Lorman, Mississippi, his commitment and selfless devotion to the welfare of Jackson and its surrounding communities led many black residents to accept him as one of their own. Their acceptance of Evers was not based upon his being an outsider offering assistance to the downtrodden from an emotional distance, but rather as a valued member of the community who triumphed when they triumphed and suffered when they suffered. This reality Dittmer fails to fully examine. Chapters 4 and 5 of this work place Evers squarely within the grassroots community working to create change from the bottom up rather than the top down.

John Dittmer is only one of many scholars who examine the significance of historical movements using a "bottom up" analysis. Sociologist Charles Payne's comprehensive book, *I've Got the Light of Freedom: The Organizing Tradition and the Mississippi Freedom Struggle,* provides wonderful insight into the Black Freedom movement in Mississippi. Like Dittmer, Payne uses a variety of primary and secondary works, including NAACP materials and interviews to examine the historical importance of the civil rights struggle in Mississippi. He focuses upon the many lesser-known individuals who struggled on the local level to bring about positive social and political change. Payne's work is an effective argument for applying understandings gained through analyzing the civil rights struggle and leadership issues at the local level, to much larger themes involving the national movement for social and political parity. Much like Dittmer, Payne asserts that the closer one examines the foundations of history, "the less comfortable one becomes with reducing the tens of thousands of people across the South who participated in local movements to faceless masses, singing, praying, and marching in the background."[11] The strength of this work is its personal attention to the grassroots and their contributions to social change.

Medgar Evers is one of the key individuals whom Payne recognizes as significant to the civil rights movement. In fact, he argues that Evers served as a living symbol of resistance for blacks across the state of Mississippi.[12] However, his section on the state field secretary serves more as a brief introduction to the life of Medgar Evers than an in-depth analysis of his role as a civil rights activist.[13] Although he points to his significance in various sections of the book, Evers is not his primary focus and thus his role in the overall struggle tends to get lost within Payne's total analysis. As a volume dealing with the birth and development of organized struggle in Mississippi, however, Payne's work captures the movement on a variety of important levels. As a consequence, his analysis of the civil rights struggle in the Delta helps illuminate the crucial reasoning behind Evers's willingness to sacrifice his financial comfort, his own life and that of his family in the struggle for equality in Mississippi.

Yet to appreciate his legacy, one has to examine every aspect of Evers's life, both before and after his assassination. A variety of monographs describe his assassination and the political and social fallout resulting from his murder. In his work *Of Long Memory: Mississippi and the Murder of Medgar Evers,* journalist Adam Nossiter analyzes the assassination of Evers and its political ramifications for the state of Mississippi. Although Nossiter focuses on De La Beckwith, his overall objective is to explain Beckwith's retrial in the context of Mississippi's changing political atmosphere.[14] In this regard, his work differs from that of then district attorney Bobby Delaughter, whose *Never Too Late* proves to be more of a tale of personal trials and demons excised in solving Evers's murder. Nossiter, however, is much more interested in the social and political mechanisms, which, by the late 1980s and early 1990s, had transformed Mississippi politically and ideologically to the point where a retrial of Byron De La Beckwith was even possible. The murder of Evers forced white Mississippians to reevaluate the existing foundation of black/white relations within the state.

The death of Medgar Evers had a profound effect upon the conscience of white Mississippians and helped to curb previous accepted behaviors regarding the treatment of African Americans. Nossiter argues that when Medgar Evers "was killed, white Mississippi, forced to look at itself, was confronted with the ultimate logic of the white supremacist state: political assassination. This logic seemed too much even for official Mississippi." Thus Nossiter argues that Evers's murder started a "long process of internal unraveling in the state that entailed nothing less than the downfall of respectability for the Beckwith worldview."[15] This study goes a bit further than Nossiter. The murder of Evers profoundly—and in many ways instantaneously—altered the political structure of Mississippi in ways that constricted chances for state-sanctioned protection of individuals engaged in a Beckwith type ideology of violence and overt racism. As a consequence, by the time slain civil rights workers James Chaney, Michael Schwerner, and Andrew Goodman were found buried in an earthen dam near Philadelphia, Mississippi, in 1964, the nation and federal government having long been aware of the extreme violence and terror blacks were subjected too in Mississippi felt pressured to provide some form of assistance to end it. In this regard, the assassination of Medgar Wiley Evers was a part of the overall tightening and eventual snapping of the nation's string of patience with overt violence and racism in Mississippi.

Another work that focuses on the death of Medgar Evers is journalist Maryanne Vollers's *Ghost of Mississippi: The Murder of Medgar Evers, the Trials of Byron De La Beckwith and the Haunting of the New South.* Vollers, however, is more concerned with the defiant culture of whites during the era in which Evers lived. She relies upon interviews, secondary works, NAACP papers, FBI files, and other materials to reconstruct the life and significance of Medgar Evers, Byron De La Beckwith, and the mentality of a segregated Mississippi. The attention she gives to events that produced greater participation in the civil rights struggle, in particular the brutal murder of fourteen-year-old Emmett Louis Till, strengthens the overall work.

Although Vollers covers much of the same materials and reaches similar conclusions as Nossiter, she adds to the discussion by presenting an in-depth analysis of both the determination and organizational structures that white conservative Mississippians put in place to uphold the status quo. For Vollers, organizations such as the Citizens' Council and the Mississippi State Sovereignty Commission played an integral role in Mississippi's civil rights woes. Vollers, much like Nossiter, provides a closer look at Mississippi during Evers's lifetime and thus highlights the significance of those who fought for justice and equality when resistance often meant death.[16] As a companion piece to Vollers, regardless of the brevity of references to Medgar Evers, *To Do Justice: The Struggle for Human Rights,* by William Paine, also provides a cursory understanding of the development and times in which civil rights leadership, public outrage, and active participation encompassed the nation. The final trial and 1994 conviction of Byron De La Beckwith, however, helped to redirect the nation's attention upon Mississippi and sparked a reexamination of the role that Evers played in its social and political development.[17]

Bobby Delaughter, in *Never Too Late: A Prosecutor's Story of Justice in the Medgar Evers Case,* chronicles the events leading up to the prosecution and eventual conviction of Byron De La Beckwith for the assassination of Medgar Evers. Throughout, he describes the problems associated with reopening a case that many people, for various reasons, wanted to remain closed. Both Delaughter and Nossiter maintain that the new social and political atmosphere, after Evers's murder, provided people with the courage to divulge information they had previously kept to themselves.[18]

Delaughter makes effective use of personal journals, letters, newspaper articles, police reports, FBI court transcripts, taped investigative interviews, and his memory of the case to reconstruct not only the death of Evers and eventual vindication for the Evers family, but his own personal reasons for wanting to solve this particular case. Despite the risks, both physical and political, Delaughter proved determined to right this specific wrong. Why? According to Delaughter, it "is never too late for that which is right, just, and brings honor to one's home state, to the human race itself."[19] Within this statement lies the central premise of the book; Delaughter saw the Evers case as the one true opportunity to combat the tarnished image of Mississippi. Thus, *Never Too Late* serves more as a recounting of the personal and professional development of Delaughter, as well as the vindication he felt after solving Medgar Evers's murder, than an account of Evers and his impact upon the movement for equality.

Never Too Late, nevertheless, is a well-researched book that provides a clear look into the problems the death of Evers created for white as well as African American communities. Of more importance, Delaughter described the amount of power exerted to keep the case quiet and the positives that came out of Beckwith's conviction. With a note of sadness, *Never Too Late* also reveals just how little the average Mississippian knew about Evers when the case came to trial in the early 1990s. The jury selection process, Delaughter recalled, revealed that many people, including African Americans, did not know who Medgar Evers was or what contributions to the freedom struggle he had made. This may have been a wonderful situation for the defense attorneys; however, it was a pitiful reality for the African American community.[20]

In the *Assassination of Medgar Evers,* Myra Ribeiro also adds to the scholarship. Ribeiro contends that Evers remains an important, yet overlooked, figure in the civil rights movement. Thus she seeks to reintroduce him to the public and demonstrate the ways in which he led a "Short but Heroic Life."[21] Ribeiro began with the assassination of Evers in detail before examining his early years and affiliations with the NAACP.

Much like Brown, Ribeiro provides a useful introduction for understanding the life and legacy of Medgar Evers. *The Assassination of Medgar Evers* is not an in-depth analysis of Evers. Ribeiro failed to provide a list of sources for her work, but her "further readings list" contains relevant source materials from Jennie Brown, Maryanne Vollers, Reed Massengill, R. W. Scott, Adam Nossiter, and others. Thus her work serves as an effective companion to other materials examining the assassination of Medgar Wiley Evers.

A variety of works address Medgar Evers's assassin. Scholars reference two works in particular: R. W. Scott's *Glory in Conflict: A Saga of Byron De La Beckwith* (Beckwith's official biography) and Reed Massengill's *Portrait of a Racist: The Man Who Killed Medgar Evers?* Massengill, the nephew of Byron De La Beckwith by marriage, provides an in-depth, although unofficial, biography of his uncle. The well-researched book uses a variety of primary and secondary source materials. In addition, Massengill provides an extensive appendix containing a number of government and FBI memorandums concerning Evers and Beckwith.[22]

Glory in Conflict provides a strong lens for peering deeper into the mindset of Byron De La Beckwith. With the assistance of Beckwith, Scott constructs a work that lends a certain level of appreciation for the ways in which Beckwith's life experiences produced the overall man. Both *Portrait of a Racist* and *Glory in Conflict* provide an inside look at the racist transformation of Medgar Evers's assassin and thus provide further detail regarding the social and political atmosphere that cost Evers his life.[23] Beckwith did not develop within a cultural vacuum. Rather, he was a product of an environment based upon racist ideologies and expressions.

To understand the significance of Evers and what he meant to the civil rights movement, one has to grasp the racial environment of Mississippi during the 1950s and 1960s. *Jackson, Mississippi: An American Chronicle of Struggle and Schism,* by sociologist John R. Salter Jr. provides a better understanding of the social psychology of Mississippi, the city of Jackson in particular, during this period. Salter provides what he argues "is a primary account—as much as one could ever be" of the racially oppressive conditions African Americans faced.[24] He presents a play-by-play analysis of the trials, triumphs, failures, and violence that occurred during the Jackson campaign. *Jackson, Mississippi* relies upon the memory of Salter, who served as both participant and observer during this volatile period in Mississippi history.

The significance of Salter's contribution, in relation to the previous materials discussed, is his focus upon the political atmosphere of Mississippi during the 1950s and 1960s and how Evers fit within that environment. His account of what happened during this period provides a real sense of the level of determination exhibited by those opposed to any change in a political structure that exclusively empowered whites. In addition, Salter addresses the role Evers's assassination played in encouraging others to unite and fight for equal rights and protection under the law. The stance conservative white leaders in Mississippi took against African Americans' desires for equal protection and social positioning, however, were not left to chance. Since the Compromise of 1877, which signaled the official end of Reconstruction and the reestablishment of southern rule, Mississippi had effectively put into place institutional mechanisms to suppress any challenge to the hegemony of white supremacy.

After Reconstruction, southern whites intensified their intimidation methods against African Americans through highly structured and politicized organizations. The Ku Klux Klan helped create an atmosphere of intimidation and violence. Groups such as the Klan produced an air of fear that permeated African American communities in the South. However, the Citizens' Council (later referred to as the White Citizens' Council) and the Mississippi State Sovereignty Commission were two of the most dominant, although less public, organizations designed to prevent African Americans from achieving true equality in Mississippi. The historian Yasuhiro Katagiri describes the Citizens' Council as "an ostensibly 'nonpolitical' and 'grassroots' private pro-segregation organization."[25] This description does not fully highlight the reach and impact of the Citizens' Council. Many of its members were prominent politicians, police officers, bankers, and other key community leaders. Thus the council, which may have began as a "private" grassroots organization, depended on public support for group activities and used its extensive political connections to further the organization's segregationist agenda. A variety of institutions and individual works deal with both the Citizens' Council and the Mississippi State Sovereignty Commission.[26]

The Department of Archives and Special Collections at the University of Mississippi houses a three-box collection containing Citizens' Council's writings, memorabilia, and propaganda material. This assortment of collected works provide a clear understanding of the type of racist ideology Evers and other civil rights activists had to contend with. In addition, *The Mississippi State Sovereignty Commission: Civil Rights and States' Rights,* by Katagiri, provides an in-depth examination of the development and central role that the Sovereignty Commission played in denying African Americans their civil rights.

Both the White Citizens' Council and the Mississippi State Sovereignty Commission were committed to controlling African Americans. The origins of both organizations and their relationship to the state's governmental structures, however, were quite different. Private citizens in Indianola, Mississippi, under the auspices of plantation manager Robert "Tut" Patterson, founded the first Citizens' Council in response to the 1954 *Brown v. Board of Education* decision. The Sovereignty Commission was a political organization that received both sanction and economic funding from the state and thus served as the state's official appendage of intimidation. Unlike the Klan, both the Citizens' Council and the Sovereignty Commission favored economic rather than violent tactics to intimidate African Americans and their supporters.

As a consequence of participating in any move to obtain political or social equality for African Americans, individuals often faced immediate and devastating economic repression. In 1957, the Commercial Credit Corporation in Hattiesburg, Mississippi, came out to repossess Reverend W. D. Ridgeway's car after he returned from testifying before the U.S. Senate Sub-Committee on Constitutional Rights in Washington, D.C. His son-in-law was also denied a home loan he had been approved for and all because of his trip to D.C.[27] African Americans who fought to change the status quo often faced instant foreclosures on mortgages, loans were suddenly demanded in full, or individuals lost their jobs without explanation. As Dittmer noted, "What it all comes down to is that in the mid-1950s white supremacists in Mississippi had a specific program: to maintain the status quo in race relations, whatever the cost."[28]

Dittmer argues that Mississippi proved a closed society that fiercely and violently protected white supremacy.[29] This symbolized the type of environment in which local people lived and operated. Although Myrlie Evers argued that the Sovereignty Commission served as "Mississippi's official guardian of segregation," the Citizens' Council also played a significant role in maintaining the status quo.[30] As organizations of intimidation and violence, the Klan, White Citizens' Council, and the Sovereignty Commission served as formidable adversaries to which civil rights leaders such as Medgar Evers worked hard to counter and whenever possible to defeat.

The historian David Chalmers, an authority on the Ku Klux Klan, has written two distinctive works on the history and development of the Klan: *Hooded Americanism: The History of the Ku Klux Klan* and *Backfire: How the Ku Klux Klan Helped the Civil Rights Movement*. The latter provides an in-depth examination of how the Klan operated in Mississippi along with the warning that as "bad as Alabama was [for African Americans], Mississippi was more intimidating."[31]

McComb represented the Ku Klux Klan stronghold in Mississippi. During the 1940s and 1950s, whites participated in bombings, beatings, and general violent acts against African Americans as a means of controlling the actions of black citizens. It was because of the actions of the Klan, as well as the inaction of those who may not have agreed with Klan tactics but desired the results, that Chalmers argued, "Mississippi had been the most resolutely white supremacist and racially repressive of the southern states, home of the Citizens' Councils and the State Sovereignty Commission, most unwilling to recognize the rights of its black citizens."[32] The unwillingness of whites to extend the hand of equality to African Americans resulted in both physical and economic reprisals against any who fought against white hegemony.

The primary argument of Chalmers in *Backfire* holds that Klan violence, combined with an ever-growing national critique of the South, played
an important role in bringing the federal government to Mississippi and
other southern states. He also argues that the intimidation and violent tactics of the Klan aided in the passage of civil rights legislation; in particular,
he cites the "1964 Public Accommodation Law" and the "Voting Rights
Law" of 1965 as support for this contention.[33] Chalmers provides a sense
of the varied social and political reactions against societal change that civil
rights activists encountered on a daily basis. Thus, he provides a deeper
understanding of the courage civil rights leaders and grassroots participants
had in the fight for equality and the problems they faced.

Today we seem quite removed from the desires of white supremacists
organizations to undercut the momentum of civil rights leadership during
the 1950s and 1960s. Yet they may not have failed entirely, at least where
the legacy and memory of Medgar Evers is concerned. In 1988, Ronald
Bailey published an article titled "Remembering Medgar Evers . . . For a
New Generation." Bailey argued that preserving the memory of Medgar
Evers must become an essential goal of present scholars and the community
at large.

He warned that to forget the contributions Evers provided the overall
struggle for equality would prove a tragic mistake. For Bailey, Evers holds
the key to understanding the civil rights movement in the South, in
Mississippi, and within the national arena. He argued that Evers epitomized
what it meant to work diligently for African Americans in Mississippi and
to unite those who also worked toward the goal of racial equality. Bailey
also maintained that Evers represented more than just a committed work
ethic:

> Medgar Evers is more than just a symbol of building Black unity. He
> is an important symbol for all Mississippians and for all freedom-lov-
> ing people in the U.S. and around the world. There are those who will
> argue that we should try and forget the turmoil of the 1950s and
> 1960s, to forget the struggle to achieve democracy, to forget Medgar
> Evers. But those who fail to remember history are doomed to repeat
> it. . . . Certainly they will not use the lessons of history to build a bet-
> ter future.[34]

Bailey was not alone in arguing for the importance of remembering the life
of Evers and his meaning to the struggle for equality.

Again, Myrlie Evers-Williams stands on the frontline of the ideological
battle to preserve the memory of her murdered husband and to acknowledge his contributions to the overall movement for equality. In 2005, she
and noted historian Manning Marable published *The Autobiography of*

Medgar Evers: A Hero's Life and Legacy Revealed Through His Writings, Letters, and Speeches. This work provides a cursory look at Evers by examining some of his NAACP correspondences and speeches. In addition, it provides primary documentation and analysis for understanding Evers and his overall commitment and sacrifice. This proves vital to comprehending the man and his time. This work, however, is neither a biographical nor comprehensive analysis of Evers.

Although an invaluable resource that adds to our overall understanding of Medgar Evers, neither Marable nor Evers-Williams intended the *Autobiography* to be the final word on Evers or the civil rights period. Regarding the completed work, Marable stated that when taken "together, the entire volume represents only one small part of the intellectual output and creative legacy of a man of uncommon courage . . . [and] cannot by any measure represent the full complexity of the Freedom Movement in Mississippi, much less that which occurred across the American South in the decade following the *Brown* decision."[35] Bailey's warnings regarding the dangers of historical forgetfulness continue to speak volumes.

Bailey holds that to forget the contributions of Medgar Evers is tantamount to forgetting all the struggles and lessons learned in the past. He reminds us:

> The almost nine years Medgar Evers served as the NAACP Field Secretary in Mississippi . . . were certainly among the most intense and important in the history of the U.S. Civil Rights Movement. This is not properly understood and chronicled by scholars or the press. It is this period of struggle in Mississippi which laid the foundation for the upsurge of the national movement which was to follow. It sparked developments such as the Montgomery Bus Boycott which brought Dr. Martin Luther King [Jr.] and others to prominence in 1955 and 1956.[36]

Mississippi (due to its violent repression against its African American citizens) proved to be an area that media outlets considered ripe for continued coverage. Tragic events such as the lynching of fourteen-year-old Emmett Till brought national attention to the problems African Americans suffered in the state. Sam Bailey, former Jackson NAACP president and close friend of Evers, "described Medgar as the 'mailman of the movement. He was always there.'"[37] Through his advocacy and organization, Evers proved essential to the success and nationalization of the civil rights movement in Mississippi.

Ronald Bailey's work adds depth to the argument for remembering and acknowledging the contributions of Evers. He also demonstrates the necessity for further study and provides an analysis of why Evers should be placed upon the mountain with King, Malcolm X, and others who have openly fought for civil and human rights. Although Bailey quotes liberally throughout the article without providing footnotes and offers only a sketchy bibliography of the civil rights movement, his argument for in-depth research and analysis of the life of Medgar Wiley Evers remains sound. It is within this academic sphere that this present work finds its place.

Each of the authors discussed provide glimpses into the life of Medgar Evers and what his death meant to the civil rights movement. The works of Myrlie Evers, Manning Marable, Ethel Murrain, Jennie Brown, John Dittmer, and Charles Payne provide insight into the life of Evers and how he fit both politically and personally within the civil rights struggle. The works of Bobby Delaughter, Adam Nossiter, Maryanne Vollers, and Myra Ribeiro help us to understand the ramifications surrounding and resulting from Medgar Evers's assassination. In addition, Reed Massengill, R. W. Scott, John Salter Jr., David Chalmers, and Yasuhiro Katagiri provide useful critiques of Byron De La Beckwith and the social and political atmosphere in which Evers and other civil rights leaders operated. Each of these works help clarify the life of Medgar Evers because each deals with an important facet of his life and the realities in which he lived and died. None of them, however, provide an in-depth biographical analysis of Evers that details his overall role in and contributions to the civil rights movement in Mississippi and the nation at large. It is within this conversational kaleidoscope that the present work adds to the historical discussion of civil rights activism and meaning.

Notes

Epigraphs. Margaret Walker Alexander quoted in *Clarion-Ledger* (Mississippi), "Evers Symbolizes Struggle, Hope," June 6, 1993, 17A. John Henrik Clarke, *My Life in Search of Africa* (Chicago: Third World Press, 1999), 106.

1. John Tosh, *The Pursuit of History: Aims, Methods and New Directions in the Study of Modern History,* rev. 3rd ed. (Pearson Education Limited, 2002), 52. For a deeper examination of the historian's role and the strengths and weaknesses related to the historical profession, see Peter Novick, *That Noble Dream: The "Objectivity Question" and the Historical Profession* (Chicago: University of Chicago Press, 1988).

2. Tosh, *The Pursuit of History,* 52.

3. The states making up the Deep South include Alabama, Georgia, Louisiana, Mississippi, and Tennessee. In some instances, Texas, Florida, Arkansas, North Carolina, and Virginia are included in this category as well.

4. For the purpose of this study, modern represents the period of civil rights struggle beginning in the 1950s, marked in particular by the 1954 *Brown v. Board of Education* decision ending racial segregation in public schools.

5. The Council of Federated Organizations represented an amalgamation of several civil rights organizations including the Student Nonviolent Coordinating Committee; National Association for the Advancement of Colored People, and the Congress of Racial Equality.

6. Myrlie Evers and William Peters, *For Us, the Living* (New York: Doubleday & Company, 1967).

7. Ethel Patricia Churchill Murrain, "The Mississippi Man and His Message: A Rhetorical Analysis of the Cultural Themes in the Oratory of Medgar Wiley Evers, 1957–1963" (Ph.D. diss., University of Southern Mississippi, 1990), 43.

8. Ibid., 8.

9. Jennie Brown, *Medgar Evers, Activist* (Los Angeles: Melrose Square Publishing Company, 1994).

10. Dittmer, *Local People.*

11. Charles M. Payne, *I've Got the Light of Freedom,* 3. For insight into other opinions regarding the importance of local people to the direction and success of the civil rights movement, see David Garrow, "Commentary," in Charles Eagles, ed., *The Civil Rights Movement in America* (Jackson: University Press of Mississippi, 1986), 55–60.

12. Payne, *I've Got the Light of Freedom,* 47.

13. Ibid., 47–56.

14. Adam Nossiter, *Of Long Memory: Mississippi and the Murder of Medgar Evers* (New York: Addison-Wesley, 1994). In 1994, Byron De La Beckwith was convicted of the murder of Medgar Evers and although he was the prime suspect in 1963, two mistrials led him to his remaining free.

15. Ibid., 20.

16. Maryanne Vollers, *Ghosts of Mississippi: The Murder of Medgar Evers, the Trials of Byron De La Beckwith, and the Haunting of the New South* (Boston: Little, Brown and Company, 1995).

17. William Paine, *To Do Justice* (New York: Pyramid Publications, 1965).

18. For a written account supporting this argument, see Carolyn Haines, *My Mother's Account: The Peggy Morgan Story* (Montgomery: River City Publishing, 2003).

19. Bobby Delaughter, *Never Too Late: A Prosecutor's Story of Justice in the Medgar Evers Case* (New York: Scribner, 2001), 63.

20. Ibid., 224–225.

21. Myra Ribeiro, *The Assassination of Medgar Evers* (New York: Rosen Publishing Group, 2002), 13.

22. Reed Massengill, *Portrait of a Racist: The Man Who Killed Medgar Evers* (New York: St. Martin's Press, 1994).

23. R. W. Scott, *Glory in Conflict: A Saga of Byron De La Beckwith* (Camden, AR: Camark Press, 1991).

24. John R. Salter Jr., *Jackson, Mississippi: An American Chronicle of Struggle and Schism* (rpt. ed., Malabar, FL: Robert E. Krieger Publishing Company, 1987), xxiv.

25. Yasuhiro Katagiri, *The Mississippi State Sovereignty Commission: Civil Rights and States' Rights* (Jackson: University Press of Mississippi, 2001), xiii.

26. For a detailed historical analysis of the White Citizens' Council, see Neil R. McMillen, *The Citizens' Council: Organized Resistance to the Second Reconstruction, 1954–64* (Urbana: University of Illinois Press, 1971). See also, Joseph Crespino, *In Search of Another Country: Mississippi and the Conservative Counterrevolution* (Princeton, NJ: Princeton University Press, 2007).

27. Medgar Evers to John A. Morsell, April 10, 1957, Papers of the NAACP: Part 20, Group III, Box A-114, microfilm reel 14.

28. Dittmer, *Local People*, 69.

29. For a detailed discussion of Mississippi's closed society ideology, see James W. Silver, *Mississippi: The Closed Society* (New York: Harcourt, 1964).

30. Evers and Peters, *For Us, the Living*, 218.

31. David Chalmers, *Backfire: How the Ku Klux Klan Helped the Civil Rights Movement* (New York: Rowman & Littlefield Publishers, 2003), 47.

32. Ibid., 87.

33. Ibid., 3. For an examination of the "backlash thesis," see Michael J. Klarman, "How *Brown* Changed Race Relations: The Backlash Thesis," *Journal of American History* 81 (June 1994): 81–118. Scholars have challenged Klarman's argument regarding the underlying importance of the *Brown* decision overall. For a scathing critique, see David Garrow, "Hopelessly Hollow History: Revisionist Devaluing of *Brown v. Board of Education*," *Virginia Law Review* 80, no. 1, Twentieth-Century Constitutional History (February 1994): 151–160, and for a less antagonistic response, see Mark Tushnet, "The Significance of *Brown v. Board of Education*," *Virginia Law Review* 80, no. 1, Twentieth-Century Constitutional History (February 1994): 173–184. For a response to his critics, see Michael J. Klarman, "Reply: *Brown v. Board of Education*: Facts and Political Correctness," *Virginia Law Review* 80, no. 1, Twentieth-Century Constitutional History (February 1994): 185–199.

34. Ronald Bailey, "Remembering Medgar Evers . . . For a New Generation," A Commemoration Developed by The Civil Rights Research And Documentation Project Afro-American Studies Program—The University of Mississippi (Distributed by Heritage Publications in cooperation with The Mississippi Network For Black History And Heritage, 1988), 17.

35. Myrlie Evers-Williams and Manning Marable, *The Autobiography of Medgar Evers: A Hero's Life and Legacy Revealed Through His Writings, Letters, and Speeches* (New York: Basic Civitas Books, 2005), 296–297.

36. Bailey, "Remembering Medgar Evers . . . For a New Generation," 8.

37. Ibid.

Bibliography

Primary Sources

Manuscript Collections

Alcorn State, Mississippi
Alcorn University Archives and Special Collections

The "Alcorn Ode"
The Alcornite (Alcorn: Junior Class, Alcorn A&M College, 1948)
The Alcornite (Alcorn: Junior Class, Alcorn A&M College, 1951)

Atlanta, Georgia
Emory University
Manuscript, Archives and Rare Book Library
Southern Regional Council: Will the Circle be Unbroken? Program Files and
    Sound Recordings, 1956–1998

Hattiesburg, Mississippi
University of Southern Mississippi Center of Oral History and Cultural Heritage

The Mississippi Oral History Program

Jackson, Mississippi
Millsaps College Archives
J. B. Cain Archives of Mississippi Methodism
Oral History Memoir of Dr. A. D. Beittel
Oral History Memoir of Five Negro High School Students

Jackson, Mississippi
Mississippi Department of Archives and History Archives & Library Division,
    Special Collections Section

Anne Romaine interviews
Evers, Medgar Homecoming, June 4–6, 1982
Evers, Medgar Memorial Festival, Subject File
Evers, Medgar Speeches, Subject Files
Evers, Medgar Subject Files, 1954–1979, 1980–1988, 1989, and 1990
Evers (Medgar Wiley and Myrlie Beasley) Papers, Manuscript Collection, no.
    Z/2231.000/S
Evers, Myrlie (Mrs. Medgar), Subject File

Congress of Federated Organizations Records (1964)
Interview with Charles Evers
Interview with John R. Salter Jr.
Interview with Reverend Robert L. T. Smith
Mississippi Institutions of Higher Learning, Minutes
Mississippi Sovereignty Commission Papers (online)
Paul B. Johnson Jr., Subject Files
Tougaloo Nine Papers

Memphis, Tennessee
University of Memphis Libraries Special Collections Department

Press-Scimitar Morgue File # 60988

New York City, New York
Schomburg Center for Research in Black Culture

Gwendolyn Brooks Collection

Starkville, Mississippi
Mississippi State University Special Collections Department

James P. Coleman Papers
John C. Stennis Oral History Project

Tougaloo, Mississippi
Tougaloo College Archives Lillian P. Benbow Room of Special Collections

Medgar Wiley Evers Collection, unprocessed

University, Mississippi
University of Mississippi Department of Archives and Special Collections

Citizens' Council Papers
Ed King Collection
James Meredith Collection
William Doyle Collection

Washington, D.C.
Library of Congress Manuscript Division

National Association for the Advancement of Colored People (NAACP) Records

Washington, D.C.
Federal Bureau of Investigation Papers, Medgar Evers (online)
Federal Bureau of Investigation Papers, Mack Charles Parker (online)

Published Primary Works

Bates, Daisy. *The Long Shadow of Little Rock: A Memoir by Daisy Bates.* Fayetteville: University of Arkansas Press, 1987.

Breitman, George, ed. *Malcolm X Speaks: Selected Speeches and Statements.* New York: Merit Publishers, 1965.

Carson, Clayborne, ed. *The Papers of Martin Luther King, Jr.* Vol. 3. Berkeley and Los Angeles: University of California Press, 1997.

Carson, Clayborne, ed. *The Papers of Martin Luther King, Jr.* Vol. 4. Berkeley and Los Angeles: University of California Press, 1997.

Carson, Clayborne, David Garrow et al., eds. *The Eyes on the Prize Civil Rights Reader: Documents, Speeches, and Firsthand Accounts from the Black Freedom Struggle, 1954–1990.* New York: Penguin Books, 1991.

Clarke, Steve, ed. *Malcolm X Talks to Young People: Speeches in the U.S., Britain, and Africa.* New York: Pathfinder Press, 1991.

Delaughter, Bobby. *Never Too Late: A Prosecutor's Story of Justice in the Medgar Evers Case.* New York: Scribner, 2001.

Evers, Charles, and Grace Hasell. *Evers.* New York: World Publishing Company, 1971.

Evers, Charles, and Andrew Szanton. *Have No Fear: The Charles Evers Story.* New York: John Wiley & Sons, 1997.

Evers, Medgar. "Why I Live in Mississippi." Interview in *Ebony* magazine, 1958.

Evers, Medgar. Address to the Los Angeles, California Branch of the NAACP. Jackson: Mississippi Department of Archives and History.

Evers, Medgar. "Quiet Integrationist: Medgar Wiley Evers." Interview in the *New York Times*, 1963.

Evers, Medgar. "The Years of Change are Upon Us." Televised Address. Jackson: Mississippi Department of Archives and History.

Evers, Myrlie. "'He Said He Wouldn't Mind Dying If . . .'" Interview in *Life* magazine, 1963.

Evers, Myrlie, and William Peters. *For Us, the Living.* New York: Doubleday & Company, 1967.

Evers-Williams, Myrlie, and Melinda Blau. *Watch Me Fly: What I Learned on the Way to Becoming the Woman I was Meant to Be.* Boston: Little, Brown and Company, 1999.

Evers-Williams, Myrlie, and Manning Marable. *The Autobiography of Medgar Evers: A Hero's Life and Legacy Revealed Through His Writings, Letters and Speeches.* New York: Basic Civitas Books, 2005.

Garrow, David, ed. *The Montgomery Bus Boycott and the Women Who Started It: The Memoir of Jo Ann Gibson Robinson.* Knoxville: University of Tennessee Press, 1987.

Gregory, Dick, and Robert Lipsyte. *Nigger: An Autobiography.* New York: Pocket Books, A Pocket Cardinal Edition, 1965.

Haines, Carolyn. *My Mother's Account: The Peggy Morgan Story.* Montgomery, AL: River City Publishing, 2003.

Hampton, Henry, and Steve Fayer, eds. *Voices of Freedom: An Oral History of the Civil Rights Movement from the 1950s to the 1980s.* New York: Bantam Books, 1990.

Henry, Aaron, with Constance Curry. *Aaron Henry: The Fire Ever Burning.*
    Jackson: University Press of Mississippi, 2000.
Hudson, Winson, and Constance Curry. *Mississippi Harmony: Memoirs of a
    Freedom Fighter.* New York: Palgrave Macmillan, 2002.
Jackson, James E. *At the Funeral of Medgar Evers in Jackson, Mississippi: A
    Tribute in Tears, A Thrust for Freedom* (MDAH). New York: Publisher's
    New Press, 1963.
Kenyatta, Jomo. *Facing Mount Kenya.* New York: AMS Press, 1978.
King, Coretta Scott. *The Words of Martin Luther King, Jr.* New York: Newmarket
    Press, 1987.
Lewis, John, with Michael D'Orso. *Walking With the Wind: A Memoir of the
    Movement.* New York: Simon & Schuster, 1998.
Mason, Gilbert R., Sr. *Beaches, Blood and Ballots: A Black Doctor's Civil Rights
    Struggle.* Jackson: University Press of Mississippi, 2000.
Meredith, James H. *Three Years in Mississippi.* Bloomington: Indiana University
    Press, 1966.
Moody, Anne. *Coming of Age in Mississippi.* New York: Dell Publishing, 1968.
National Association for the Advancement of Colored People. New York: Annual
    Report, 1917.
NAACP. Eighth and Ninth *Annual Reports,* "A Summary of Work and an
    Accounting." New York: 1917 and 1918.
NAACP. Tenth *Annual Report,* "A Summary of Work and an Accounting." New
    York: 1919.
NAACP. Eleventh *Annual Report,* "A Summary of Work and an Accounting."
    New York: 1920.
NAACP. Thirteenth *Annual Report,* "A Summary of Work and an Accounting."
    New York: 1922.
NAACP. Fourteenth *Annual Report,* "A Record of Things Accomplished for the
    Negro." New York: 1923.
NAACP. Twenty-fourth *Annual Report,* "A Summary of Work and an
    Accounting." New York: 1933.
NAACP. Twenty-seventh *Annual Report.* New York: 1936.
NAACP. Twenty-eighth *Annual Report.* New York: 1937.
NAACP. Twenty-ninth *Annual Report.* New York: 1938
NAACP. *Annual Report,* "The Treatment Accorded Negro Americans Continues
    to be the Acid Test of Democracy." New York: 1940.
NAACP. *Annual Report,* "The Association Stands on Guard for Full Democracy
    and Against Racial Discrimination." New York: 1941.
NAACP. *Annual Report,* "The Association Strives for an America of Equality,
    Justice, Freedom, and Security for All." New York: 1947.
NAACP. *Annual Report,* "The Fortieth Year in the Crusade for Civil Rights."
    New York: 1948.
NAACP. *Annual Report,* 1951–1960.
NAACP. *Annual Report,* 1961–1967.
NAACP. *Papers of the NAACP: Part 20, White Resistance and Reprisals, 1956–
    1965.* Edited by John H. Bracy Jr. and August Meier. Bethesda, MD:
    University Publications of America, 1995. Microfilm.
Parks, Rosa, and Jim Haskin. *Rosa Parks: My Story.* New York: Dial Books, 1992.

Royster, Jacqueline Jones, ed. *Southern Horrors and Other Writings; The Anti-Lynching Campaign of Ida B. Wells, 1892–1900*. Boston: Bedford Books, 1997.

Salter, John R., Jr. *Jackson, Mississippi: An American Chronicle of Struggle and Schism*. Rpt. ed., Malabar, FL: Robert E. Krieger Publishing Company, 1987.

Salter, John R., Jr. "Interview with John Salter, Jr. John C. Stennis Oral History Project. Mississippi State University, December 26, 1990."

Scott, R. W. *Glory in Conflict: A Saga of Byron De La Beckwith*. Camden, AR: Camark Press, 1991.

Silver, James W. *Mississippi: The Closed Society*. New York: Harcourt, 1964.

Sorensen, Theodore C. *Kennedy*. New York: Harper & Row, 1965.

Till-Mobley, Mamie, and Christopher Benson. *Death of Innocence: The Story of the Hate Crime that Changed America*. New York: Random House, 2003.

Thomas, Brook, ed. *Plessy v. Ferguson: Brief History with Documents*. Boston: Bedford Books, 1997.

Truman, Harry S. President's Committee. *To Secure These Rights: The Report of the President's Committee on Civil Rights*. Washington, DC: Government Printing Office, 1947.

Wamwere, Koigi Wa. *I Refuse to Die: My Journey for Freedom*. New York: Seven Stories Press, 2002.

Williams, Robert F. *Negroes With Guns*. Detroit, MI: Wayne State University Press, 1998.

Wright, Richard. *Black Boy: A Record of Childhood and Youth*. New York: Harper & Row, 1966.

X, Malcolm. *By Any Means Necessary (Malcolm X Speeches & Writings)*. New York: Pathfinder, 1992.

Zellner, Bob, with Constance Curry. *The Wrong Side of Murder Creek: A White Southerner in the Freedom Movement*. Montgomery: New South Books, 2008.

Personal Interviews

Andrews, Ponjola. Interview with the author, September 14, 2006, cassette recording, Magnolia, Mississippi. Tape in possession of the author.

Azangu, Eliakim. Interview with the author, July 11, 2006, cassette recording, Kenya National Archives, Nairobi, Kenya. Tape in possession of the author.

Bond Roxborough, Mildred. Interview with the author, July 27, 2005, cassette recording, Manhattan, New York. Tape in possession of the author.

Evers, Charles. Interview with the author, February 4, 2005, cassette recording, Jackson, Mississippi. Tape in possession of the author.

Evers-Jordan, Carrie Elizabeth. Interview with the author, June 10, 2005, cassette recording, Jackson, Mississippi. Tape in possession of the author.

Evers-Williams, Myrlie. Interview with the author, October 24–25, 2006, note and cassette recording, Bend, Oregon. Tape and notes in possession of the author.

Foster, Velvelyn, Dr. Interview with the author, December 14, 2006, cassette recording, Jackson State University, Jackson, Mississippi. Tape in possession of the author.

Frazier, John. Interview with the author, October 23, 2010, cassette recording, Hattiesburg, Mississippi. Tape in possession of the author.

Jackson, Laplose. Interview with the author, September 13, 2006, cassette recording, Alcorn State University, Lorman, Mississippi. Tape in possession of the author.

Mason, Gilbert R., Sr., Dr. Interview with the author, August 13, 2005, cassette recording, Biloxi, Mississippi. Tape in possession of the author.

May-Pittman, Ineeva. Interview with the author, September 11, 2006, cassette recording, Jackson, Mississippi. Tape in possession of the author.

Meredith, James H. Interview with the author, July 13, 2005, cassette recording, Jackson, Mississippi. Tape in possession of the author.

Morris, Alpha, Dr. Interview with the author, September 14, 2006, cassette recording, Alcorn State University, Lorman, Mississippi. Tape in possession of the author.

Phillips, Ivory, Dr. Interview with the author, December 13, 2006, cassette recording, Jackson, Mississippi. Tape in possession of the author.

Public testimonials and individual discussions by the author with persons attending the 42nd and 44th Annual Medgar Evers Gospel Memorial Celebration at St. Luther MB Church and Pearl Street AME Church in Jackson, Mississippi, June 9, 2005, and May 31, 2007, respectively.

Ranaku, James, Dr. Interview with the author, July 7, 2006, Kakamega, note recording, Western University College of Science and Technology, Kakamega, Kenya. Notes in possession of the author.

Turner, Cornelius. Interview with the author, July 12, 2005, cassette recording, Jackson, Mississippi. Tape in possession of the author.

Wamwere, Koigi Wa, Honorable. Interview with the author, July 13, 2006, cassette recording, Nairobi, Kenya. Tape in possession of the author.

Watson, Minnie White. Interview with the author, September 12, 2006, cassette recording, L. Zenobia Coleman Library, Tougaloo College, Tougaloo, Mississippi. Tape in possession of the author.

Newspapers and Periodicals

American Historical Newspapers (database)
Associated Press
Atlanta Journal
Birmingham News
Chicago Defender
Chicago Tribune
Clarion-Ledger
Commercial Appeal
Crisis: A Record of the Darker Races
Daily Journal
Delta Democrat-Times
Evening Star
Facts on Film
Greater Alcorn Herald
Hattiesburg American
Jackson Advocate
Jackson Daily News

Mississippian
Mississippi Free Press
Montgomery Advertiser
Mound Bayou Sentinel
Nashville Tennessean
New York Times
Oxford Eagle
Pittsburgh Courier
Press-Scimitar
State Times
Vicksburg Evening Post
Washington Post

Magazines

Ebony
Esquire
Jet
Life
Look

Year Books

The Alcornite

Media

Beauchamp, Keith. *The Untold Story of Emmett Louis Till.* Directed by Keith
    Beauchamp. 70 minutes. Velocity Home Entertainment, 2006. DVD.
Evers, Charles. Interview by CBS anchorman Dan Rather. *CBS Evening News,*
    "A Reporter's Notebook," aired March 1, 2005.
Hampton, Henry. *Eyes on the Prize: America's Civil Rights Movement,*
    1954–1985. Executive Producer, Henry Hampton. Approximately 14 hours.
    Blackside Productions, 1987.
Meredith News Conference, Reel # M09, item # 4262 (News conference with
    James Meredith and Medgar Evers announcing Meredith's plans to register
    for his second semester at the University of Mississippi), Mississippi
    Department of Archives and History.

Online Resources

"Geneva Tisdale–Greensboro Sit-Ins: Launch of a Civil Rights . . . ," @
    www.sitins.com/genevatisdale.shtml.
Google Maps @ http://www.maps.google.com.
Mississippi Historical Society @ http://mshistory.k12.ms.us/articles/53/
    medgar-evers-and-the-origin-of-the-civil-rights-movement-in-mississippi.

U.S. Department of Health and Human Services, The Office of Minority Health online @ http://www.omhrc.gov/templates/browse.aspx?lvl=2&lvlID=51.
U.S. Department of Health and Human Services, The Office of Minority Health online @ http://minorityhealth.hhs.gov/templates/browse.aspx?lvl=3& lvlid=23.
University of Southern Mississippi, Civil Rights Documentation Project @ www.usm.edu/crdp/html/transcripts.

Supreme Court Cases

Samuel Bailey et al. v. Joe T. Patterson et al., 369 U.S. 31, No. 643 (1961).
Brown et al. v. Board of Education of Topeka et al., United States Reports, Vol. 347 (1954).
Court of Appeals of Maryland Pearson, et al. v. Murray, 182 A. 590. 169 Md. 478, 103 A.L.R. 706 No 53 (1936).
Robert R. Freeman, et al., Petitioners, v. Willie Eugene Pitts, et al., 503 U.S. 112 S.Ct. 1430 (1992).
Charles C. Green et al., v. County School Board of New Kent County, Virginia et al., 391 U.S. 430, 88 S.Ct. 1689 (1968).
Missouri, et al., Petitioners v. Kalima Jenkins, et al., 515 U.S. 70, 115 S.Ct. 2038 (1995).
Board of Education of Oklahoma City Public Schools, Independent School District No. 89, Oklahoma County, Oklahoma, Petitioner, v. Robert L. Dowell, et al., 498 U.S. 236, 111 S.Ct. 630 (1991).
Peterson et al. v. City of Greenville, 373 U.S.244, 323 (1963).
Watson et al. v. City of Memphis, 373 U.S.526, 536 (1963).

Secondary Sources

Books

Akbar, Na'im. *Visions for Black Men*. Nashville: Winston-Derek Publishers, 1999.
Amen, Ra Un Nefer. *Metu Neter*, vol. 1: *The Great Oracle of Tehuti and the Egyptian System of Spiritual Cultivation*. Brooklyn, NY: Khamit Media Trans Visions, 1990.
Andrews, Kenneth T. *Freedom Is a Constant Struggle: The Mississippi Civil Rights Movement and Its Legacy*. Chicago: University of Chicago Press, 2004.
Arsenault, Raymond. *Freedom Riders: 1961 and the Struggle for Racial Justice*. Oxford: Oxford University Press, 2006.
Ball, Howard. *A Defiant Life: Thurgood Marshall & the Persistence of Racism in America*. New York: Crown Publishers, 1998.
Bartley, Numan V. *The Rise of Massive Resistance: Race and Politics in the South During the 1950s*. Baton Rouge: Louisiana State University Press, 1969.
Beito, David T., and Linda Royster Beito. *Black Maverick: T.R.M. Howard's Fight for Civil Rights and Economic Power*. Urbana: University of Illinois Press, 2009.

Belknap, Michael R. *Federal Laws and Southern Order: Racial Violence and Constitutional Conflict in the Post-Brown South*. Athens: University of Georgia Press, 1987.

Bel Monte, Kathryn L. *African American Heroes & Heroines: 150 True Stories of African-American Heroism*. Hollywood, FL: Lifetime Books, 1998.

Berg, Manfred. *"The Ticket to Freedom": The NAACP and the Struggle for Black Political Integration*. Gainesville: University Press of Florida, 2005.

Blauner, Bob. *Black Lives, White Lives: Three Decades of Race Relations in America*. Berkeley and Los Angeles: University of California Press, 1989.

Boger, John Charles, and Gary Orfield, eds. *School Resegregation: Must the South Turn Back?* Chapel Hill: University of North Carolina Press, 2005.

Branch, Taylor. *Parting the Waters: America in the King Years, 1954–1963*. New York: Simon and Schuster, 1988.

Brieger, James F. *Hometown Mississippi*, 2nd ed. 1980.

Bristol, Douglass Walter, Jr. *Knights of the Razor: Black Barbers in Slavery and Freedom*. Baltimore, MD: Johns Hopkins University Press, 2009.

Brooks, Jennifer. *Defining the Peace: World War II Veterans, Race, and the Remaking of Southern Political Tradition*. Chapel Hill: University of North Carolina Press, 2004.

Brown, Jennie. *Medgar Evers Activist*. Los Angeles: Melrose Square Publishing Company, 1994.

Brown, Jeremy-Murray. *Kenyatta*. London: Allen & Unwin, 1979.

Bryant, Nick. *The Bystander: John F. Kennedy and the Struggle for Black Equality*. New York: Basic Books, 2006.

Burk, Robert Fredrick. *The Eisenhower Administration and Black Civil Rights*. Knoxville: University of Tennessee Press, 1984.

Burner, Eric. *And Gently He Shall Lead Them: Robert Parris Moses and Civil Rights in Mississippi*. New York: New York University Press, 1994.

Bush, Roderick D. *The End of White Supremacy: Black Internationalism and the Problem of the Color Line*. Philadelphia: Temple University Press, 2009.

Cabaniss, Allen. *The University of Mississippi: Its First Hundred Years*. Hattiesburg: University & College Press of Mississippi, 1971.

Cagin, Seth, and Phillip Dray. *We are not Afraid: The Story of Goodman, Schwerner, and Chaney and the Civil Rights Movement*. New York: Nation Books, 2006.

Carson, Clayborne. *In Struggle: SNCC and the Black Awakening of the 1960s*. Cambridge, MA: Harvard University Press, 1981.

Carson, Clayborne, et al. *Civil Rights Chronicle: The African American Struggle for Freedom*. Lincolnwood, IL: Legacy Publishing, 2003.

Catsam, Derek Charles. *Freedom's Main Line: The Journey of Reconciliation and the Freedom Rides*. Lexington: University Press of Kentucky, 2009.

Chafe, William H. *Civilities and Civil Rights: Greensboro, North Carolina, and the Black Struggle for Freedom*. Oxford: Oxford University Press, 1981.

Chafe, William H., Raymond Gavins, and Robert Korstad, senior eds. *Remembering Jim Crow: African Americans Tell About Life in the Segregated South*. New York: New Press, 2001.

Chalmers, David. *Backfire: How the Ku Klux Klan Helped the Civil Rights Movement*. New York: Rowman & Littlefield Publishers, 2003.

Chalmers, David. *Hooded Americanism: the History of the Ku Klux Klan*. Durham, NC: Duke University Press, 1987.

Chappell, David L. *A Stone of Hope: Prophetic Religion and the Death of Jim Crow*. Chapel Hill: University of North Carolina Press, 2004.

Clark, Eric. *2004–2008 Official and Statistical Register: Mississippi Blue Book*, 2005.

Clarke, John Henrik. *My Life in Search of Africa*. Chicago: Third World Press, 1999.

Classen, Stephen D. *Watching Jim Crow: The Struggles over Mississippi TV, 1955–1969*. Durham, NC: Duke University Press, 2004.

Cobb, James C. *The Most Southern Place on Earth: The Mississippi Delta and the Roots of Regional Identity*. New York: Oxford University Press, 1992.

Cohodas, Nadine. *The Band Played Dixie: Race and the Liberal Conscience at Ole Miss*. New York: Free Press, 1997.

Colley, David. *The Road to Victory: The Untold Story of World War II's Red Ball Express*. Washington, DC: Brassey, 2000.

Cone, James H. *Black Theology and Black Power*. New York: Seabury Press, 1969.

Cotman, John Walter. *Birmingham, JFK and the Civil Rights Act of 1963: Implications for Elite Theory*. New York: Peter Lang, 1989.

Crespino, Joseph. *In Search of Another Country: Mississippi and the Conservative Counterrevolution*. Princeton, NJ: Princeton University Press, 2007.

Crosby, Emilye. *A Little Taste of Freedom: The Black Freedom Struggle in Claiborne County, Mississippi*. Chapel Hill: University of North Carolina Press, 2005.

Dallek, Robert. *An Unfinished Life: John F. Kennedy, 1917–1963*. Boston: Little, Brown and Company, 2003.

Dallek, Robert, and Terry Golway. *Let Every Nation Know: John F. Kennedy in His Own Words*. Naperville, IL: Sourcebooks MediaFusion, 2006.

Daniel, Pete. *Lost Revolutions: The South in the 1950s*. Chapel Hill: University of North Carolina Press, 2000.

David Smith, John. *Historians at Work: When Did Southern Segregation Begin*. New York: Palgrave, 2002.

Davis, Michael D., and Hunter R. Clark, eds. *Thurgood Marshall: Warrior at the Bar, Rebel on the Bench*, updated and revised ed. New York: Carol Publishing Group, 1994.

DeConde, Alexander, Richard Dean Burns, and Fredrik Logevall, eds. in chief. *Encyclopedia of American Foreign Policy*, 2nd ed., Volume I, Chronology A–D. New York: Charles Scribner's Sons, 2002.

D'Emilio, John. *The Civil Rights Struggle: Leaders in Profile*. New York: Facts On File, 1979.

DeRoche, Andrew J. *Andrew Young: Civil Rights Ambassador*. Wilmington, DE: Scholarly Resource, Imprint, 2003.

Dickerson, James. *Dixie's Dirty Secret: The True Story of How the Government, the Media, and the Mob Conspired to Combat Integration and the Vietnam Antiwar Movement*. New York: M. E. Sharpe, 1998.

Dierenfield, Bruce J. *The Civil Rights Movement*, rev. ed. London: Pearson Education Limited, 2008.

Dittmer, John. *Local People: The Struggle for Civil Rights in Mississippi*. Urbana: University of Illinois Press, 1994.

Doyle, William. *An American Insurrection: James Meredith and the Battle of Oxford, Mississippi, 1962*. New York: Anchor Books, 2001.

Drimmer, Melvin, ed. *Black History: A Reappraisal*. New York: Doubleday & Company, 1968.

Du Bois, W. E. B. *The Souls of Black Folk: Essays and Sketches*, 22nd ed. Chicago: A. C. McClurg & Co., 1938.

Dunham, Melerson Guy. *The Centennial History of Alcorn Agricultural and Mechanical College*. Hattiesburg: University and College Press of Mississippi, 1971.

Dymally, Mervyn M., ed. *The Black Politician: His Struggle for Power*. Belmont, CA: Duxbury Press, 1971.

Eagles, Charles W., ed. *The Civil Rights Movement in America*. Jackson: University Press of Mississippi, 1986.

Eagles, Charles W. *The Price of Defiance: James Meredith and the Integration of Ole Miss*. Chapel Hill: University of North Carolina Press, 2009.

Eskew, Glenn T. *But for Birmingham: The Local and National Movements in the Civil Rights Struggle*. Chapel Hill: University of North Carolina Press, 1997.

Fairclough, Adam. *Race & Democracy: The Civil Rights Struggle in Louisiana, 1915–1972*. Athens: University of Georgia Press, 1999.

Fairclough, Adam. *To Redeem the Soul of America: The Southern Christian Leadership Conference and Martin Luther King, Jr.* Athens: University of Georgia Press.

Feldman, Glenn, ed. *Before Brown: Civil Rights and White Backlash in the Modern South*. Tuscaloosa: The University of Alabama Press, 2004.

Fireside, Harvey. *Separate and Unequal: Homer Plessy and the Supreme Court Decision that Legalized Racism*. New York: Carroll & Graf Publishers, 2004.

Foner, Eric. *The Story of American Freedom*. New York: W. W. Norton & Company, 1998.

Ford, Lacy K., Jr. *Origins of Southern Radicalism: The South Carolina Upcountry 1800- 1860*. Oxford: Oxford University Press, 1988.

Fourteenth Census of the United States Taken in the Year 1920, Vol. III, Population 1920. Washington, DC: Government Printing Office, 1922.

Franklin, John Hope, and Alfred A. Moss Jr. *From Slavery to Freedom: A History of African Americans*, 8th ed. Boston: McGraw-Hill, 2000.

Franklin, John Hope, and Evelyn Brooks Higginbotham. *From Slavery to Freedom: A History of African Americans*, 9th ed. New York: McGraw Hill, 2011.

Garrow, David J., ed. *The Walking City: The Montgomery Bus Boycott, 1955– 1956*. Brooklyn, NY: Carlson Publishing, 1989.

Garrow, David, J. *Birmingham, Alabama, 1956–1963: The Black Struggle for Civil Rights*. Brooklyn, NY: Carlson Publishing, 1989.

Garrow, David J. *Bearing the Cross: Martin Luther King, Jr., and the Southern Christian Leadership Conference*. 1st Perennial Classics ed. New York: Perennial Classics, 2004.

Green, A. Wigfall. *The Man Bilbo*. Baton Rouge: Louisiana State University Press, 1963.

Green, Ben. *Before His Time: The Untold Story of Harry T. Moore, America's First Civil Rights Martyr*. Gainesville: University Press of Florida, 1999.

Gilmore, Glenda Elizabeth. *Defying Dixie: The Radical Roots of Civil Rights, 1919–1950*. New York: W. W. Norton & Company, 2008.

Gilmore, Glenda Elizabeth. *Gender and Jim Crow: Women and the Politics of White Supremacy in North Carolina, 1896–1920.* Chapel Hill: University of North Carolina Press, 1996.

Halberstam, David. *The Children.* New York: Fawcett Books, 1998.

Harding, Vincent G. *There is a River: The Black Freedom Struggle in America.* New York: Harcourt Brace Jovanovich, 1981.

Harlan, Louis. *Booker T. Washington: The Making of a Black Leader, 1856–1901.* New York: Oxford University Press, 1972.

Haskins, James. *The Life and Death of Martin Luther King, Jr.* New York: First Beech Tree edition, 1992.

Haskins, James. *Lena Horne.* New York: Coward-McCann, 1983.

Haskins, James, and Kathleen Benson. *Lena: A Personal and Professional Biography of Lena Horne.* New York: Stein and Day Publishers, 1984.

Hayes, Diana L. *And Still We Rise: An Introduction to Black Liberation Theology.* New York: Paulist Press, 1996.

Higginbotham, Evelyn Brooks. *Righteous Discontent: The Women's Movement in the Black Baptists Church, 1880–1920.* Cambridge, MA: Harvard University Press.

Hill, Lance. *The Deacons for Defense: Armed Resistance and the Civil Rights Movement.* Chapel Hill: University of North Carolina Press, 2004.

Hine, Darlene Clark, William C. Hine, and Stanley Harrold. *The African-American Odyssey,* Combined Volume, 2nd ed. Upper Saddle River, NJ: Prentice-Hall, 2003.

Hine, Darlene Clark, William C. Hine, and Stanley Harrold. *The African American Odyssey,* 3rd ed. Upper Saddle River, NJ: Pearson Education, 2006.

Hofstadter, Richard, and Michael Wallace, eds. *American Violence: A Documentary History.* New York: Alfred A. Knopf, 1970.

Holmes, William F. *The White Chief: James Kimble Vardaman.* Baton Rouge: Louisiana State University Press, 1970.

Ho, Fred, and Bill V. Mullen, eds. *Afro Asia: Revolutionary Political and Cultural Connections between African Americans and Asian Americans.* Durham, NC: Duke University Press, 2008.

Hopkins, Dwight N. *Introducing Black Theology of Liberation.* Maryknoll, NY: Orbis Books, 1999.

Hudson-Weems, Clenora. *Emmett Till: The Sacrificial Lamb of the Civil Rights Movement.* Troy, MI: Bedford Publishers, 1994.

Hughes, Langston. *Fight for Freedom: The Story of the NAACP.* New York: W. W. Norton & Company, 1962.

Jackson, David H., Jr. *A Chief Lieutenant of the Tuskegee Machine: Charles Banks of Mississippi.* Gainesville: University Press of Florida, 2002.

Jacoway, Elizabeth. *Turn Away Thy Son: Little Rock, the Crisis that Shocked the Nation.* New York: Free Press, 2007.

Jacoway, Elizabeth, and David R. Colburn, eds. *Southern Businessmen and Desegregation.* Baton Rouge: Louisiana State University Press, 1982.

Johnston, Erle. *Mississippi's Defiant Years 1953–1973: An Interpretive Documentary with Personal Experiences.* Forest, MS: Lake Harbor Publishers, 1990.

Jonas, Gilbert. *Freedom's Sword: The NAACP and the Struggle Against Racism in America, 1909–1969.* New York: Routledge, 2005.

Jong, Greta de. *A Different Day: African American Struggles for Justice in Rural Louisiana, 1900–1970*. Chapel Hill: University of North Carolina Press, 2002.

Jordan, Winthrop D. *Tumult and Silence at Second Creek: An Inquiry into a Civil War Slave Conspiracy*, rev. ed. Baton Rouge: Louisiana State University Press, 1995.

Katagiri, Yasuhiro. *The Mississippi State Sovereignty Commission: Civil Rights and States' Rights*. Jackson: University Press of Mississippi, 2001.

Kay, James Tertius de. *A Rage for Glory: The Life of Commodore Stephen Decatur, USN*. New York: Free Press, 2004.

Kirk, John A. *Redefining the Color Line: Black Activism in Little Rock, Arkansas, 1940–1970*. Gainesville: University Press of Florida, 2002.

Kirk, John A. *Beyond Little Rock: The Origins and Legacies of the Central High Crisis*. Fayetteville: University of Arkansas Press, 2007.

Klarman, Michael J. *From Jim Crow to Civil Rights: The Supreme Court and the Struggle for Racial Equality*. New York: Oxford University Press, 2004.

Kluger, Richard. *Simple Justice: The History of Brown v. Board of Education and Black America's Struggle for Equality*. New York: Alfred A. Knopf, 1976.

Krenn, Michael L ed. *Race and U.S. Foreign Policy During the Cold War*. New York: Garland Publishing, 1998.

Lambert, Frank. *The Battle of Ole Miss: Civil Rights v. States' Rights*. New York: Oxford University Press, 2010.

Lawson, Steven F. *Running for Freedom: Civil Rights and Black Politics in America Since 1941*, 2nd ed. New York: McGraw-Hill, 1997.

Lawson, Steven F. *Black Ballots: Voting Rights in the South, 1944–1969*. Lanham, MD: Lexington Books, 1999.

Lawson, Steven F., and Charles Payne. *Debating the Civil Rights Movement, 1945–1968*. Lanham, MD: Rowman & Littlefield Publishers, 1998.

Lee, Chana Kai. *For Freedom's Sake: The Life of Fannie Lou Hamer*. Urbana: University of Illinois Press, 2000.

Levine, Lawrence W. *Black Culture and Black Consciousness: Afro-American Folk Thought From Slavery to Freedom*. New York: Oxford University Press, 1977.

Lewis, David Levering. *W. E. B. Du Bois: The Fight for Equality and the American Century, 1919–1963*. New York: Henry Holt and Company, 2000.

Litwack, Leon. *Trouble in Mind: Black Southerners in the Age of Jim Crow*. New York: Alfred A. Knopf, 1998.

Loevy, Robert D. *To End All Segregation: The Politics of the Passage of the Civil Rights Act of 1964*. Lanham, MD: University Press of America, 1990.

Loury, Glenn C. *The Anatomy of Racial Inequality*. Cambridge, MA: Harvard University Press, 2002.

Lowery, Charles D., and John F. Marszalek, eds. *The Greenwood Encyclopedia of African American Civil Rights From Emancipation to the Twenty-First Century: Volume I A-R*. Westport, CT: Greenwood Press, 2003.

Lunn, Joe. *Memoirs of the Maelstrom: A Senegalese Oral History of the First World War*. Portsmouth, NH: Heinemann, 1999.

Lynch, Hollis R. *Black American Radicals and the Liberation of Africa: The Council on African Affairs, 1937–1955*. New York: Cornell University Africana Studies Research Center, 1978.

MacLean, Harry N. *The Past is Never Dead: The Trial of James Ford Seale and Mississippi's Struggle for Redemption*. New York: Basic Civitas, 2009.

Manis, Andrew M. *A Fire You Can't Put Out: The Civil Rights Life of Birmingham's Reverend Fred Shuttlesworth*. Tuscaloosa: The University of Alabama Press, 1999.

Marable, Manning. *Race, Reform, and Rebellion: The Second Reconstruction in Black America, 1945–1990*, 2nd ed. Jackson: University Press of Mississippi, 1991.

Marsh, Charles. *God's Long Summer: Stories of Faith and Civil Rights*. Princeton, NJ: Princeton University Press, 1997.

Martin, Tony. *Race First: The Ideological and Organizational Struggles of Marcus Garvey and the Universal Negro Improvement Association*. Dover, MA: Majority Press, 1976.

Massengill, Reed. *Portrait of a Racist: The Man Who Killed Medgar Evers*. New York: St. Martin's Press, 1994.

McGuire, Danielle L. *At the Dark End of the Street: Black Women, Rape, and Resistance—a New History of the Civil Rights Movement from Rosa Parks to the Rise of Black Power*. New York: Alfred A. Knopf, 2010.

McLoyd, Vonnie C., Nancy E. Hill, and Kenneth A. Dodge, eds. *African American Family Life: Ecological and Cultural Diversity*. New York: Guilford Press, 2005.

McMillen, Neil R. *The Citizens' Council: Organized Resistance to the Second Reconstruction, 1954–64*. Urbana: University of Illinois Press, 1971.

McMillen, Neil R. *Dark Journey: Black Mississippians in the Age of Jim Crow*. Urbana: University of Illinois Press, 1989.

McMurry, Linda O. *To Keep The Waters Troubled: The Life of Ida B. Wells*. Oxford: Oxford University Press, 1998.

McWhorter, Diane. *Carry Me Home, Birmingham, Alabama: The Climactic Battle of the Civil Rights Revolution*. New York: Simon & Schuster, 2002.

Meier, August, and Elliot Rudwick. *CORE: A Study in the Civil Rights Movement, 1942–1968*. New York: Oxford University Press, 1973.

Meillassoux, Claude. *The Anthropology of Slavery: The Womb of Iron and Gold*. Chicago: University of Chicago Press, 1991.

Mendelsohn, Jack. *The Martyrs: Sixteen Who Gave Their Lives for Racial Justice*. New York: Harper & Row, 1966.

Meriwether, James H. *Proudly We Can Be Africans: Black Americans and Africa, 1935–1961*. Chapel Hill: University of North Carolina Press, 2002.

Metcalf, George R. *Black Profiles*. New York: McGraw-Hill, 1968.

Middleton, Stephen, and Charlotte M. Stokes, consultants. *The African American Experience: A History*, 2nd ed. Upper Saddle River, NJ: Globe Fearon Educational Publisher, 1999.

Mills, Kay. *Changing Channels: The Civil Rights Case That Transformed Television*. Jackson: University Press of Mississippi, 2004.

Morgan, Chester L. *Redneck Liberal: Theodore G. Bilbo and the New Deal*. Baton Rouge: Louisiana State University Press, 1985.

Morris, Aldon D. *The Origins of the Civil Rights Movement: Black Communities Organizing for Change*. New York: Free Press, 1984.

Morris, Willie. *The Ghosts of Medgar Evers: A Tale of Race, Murder, Mississippi, and Hollywood*. New York: Random House, 1998.

Moses, Greg. *Revolution of Conscience: Martin Luther King, Jr., and the Philosophy of Nonviolence.* New York: Guilford Press, 1997.

Motley, Mary Penick, ed. *The Invisible Soldier: The Experience of the Black Soldier, World War II.* Detroit, MI: Wayne State University Press, 1975.

Moye, J. Todd. *Let the People Decide: Black Freedom and White Resistance Movements in Sunflower County, Mississippi, 1945–1986.* Chapel Hill: University of North Carolina Press, 2004.

Namorato, Michael V. *Have We Overcome? Race Relations Since Brown.* Jackson: University Press of Mississippi, 1979.

Newman, Richard. *African American Quotations.* New York: Oryx Press, 2000.

Niven, David. *The Politics of Injustice: The Kennedys, the Freedom Rides, and the Electoral Consequences of a Moral Compromise.* Knoxville: University of Tennessee Press, 2003.

Nossiter, Adam. *Of Long Memory: Mississippi and the Murder of Medgar Evers.* New York: Addison-Wesley, 1994.

Novick, Peter. *That Noble Dream: The "Objectivity Question" and the Historical Profession.* Chicago: University of Chicago Press, 1988.

Nunnelley, William A. *Bull Connor.* Tuscaloosa: The University of Alabama Press, 1991.

Odhiambo, E. S. Atieno, and John Lonsdale, eds. *Mau Mau & Nationhood: Arms, Authority & Narration.* Athens: Ohio University Press, 2003.

O'Reilly, Kenneth. *Black Americans: The FBI Files,* Edited by David Gallen. New York: Carroll & Graf Publishers, 1994.

Orfield, Gary, and John T. Yun. "Resegregation in American Schools." The Civil Rights Project, Harvard University, 1999.

Oshinsky, David M. *A Conspiracy So Immense: The World of Joe McCarthy.* Oxford: Oxford University Press, 2005.

Owings, Alison. *Hey, Waitress!: The USA from the Other Side of the Tray.* Berkeley and Los Angeles: University of California Press, 2002.

Packard, Jerrold M. *American Nightmare: The History of Jim Crow.* New York: St. Martins Griffin, 2002.

Paine, William. *To Do Justice.* New York: Pyramid Publications, 1965.

Parmet, Herbert S. *JFK: The Presidency of John F. Kennedy.* New York: Penguin Books, 1983.

Patterson, James T. *Brown v. Board of Education: A Civil Rights Milestone and Its Troubled Legacy.* Oxford: Oxford University Press, 2001.

Payne, Charles. *I've Got the Light of Freedom: The Organizing Tradition and the Mississippi Freedom Struggle.* Berkeley and Los Angeles: University of California Press, 1995.

Posey, Josephine McCann. *Against Great Odds: The History of Alcorn State University.* Jackson: University Press of Mississippi, 1994.

Powdermaker, Hortense. *After Freedom: A Cultural Study in the Deep South.* New York: Viking Press, 1939.

Raines, Howell. *My Soul is Rested: Movement Days in the Deep South Remembered.* New York: G. P. Putnam's Sons, 1977.

Report of the Seventeenth Decennial Census of the United States, Census of Population: 1950 Vol. II Characteristics of the Population. Washington, DC: Government Printing Office, 1952.

Ribeiro, Myra. *The Assassination of Medgar Evers.* New York: Rosen Publishing Group, 2002.

Riley, Dorothy Winbush, ed. *My Soul Looks Back "Less I Forget": A Collection of Quotations by People of Color.* New York: Harper Collins Publishers, 1991.

Roberts, Gene, and Hank Klibanoff. *The Race Beat: The Press, the Civil Rights Struggle, and the Awakening of a Nation.* New York: Alfred A. Knopf, 2006.

Robinson, Armstead L. *Bitter Fruits of Bondage: The Demise of Slavery and the Collapse of the Confederacy, 1861–1865.* Charlottesville: University of Virginia Press, 2005.

Rogers, J. A. *The Five Negro Presidents: According to What White People Said They Were.* St. Petersburg, FL: Helga M. Rogers, 1993.

Rogers J. A. *World's Great Men of Color,* vol. 1. New York: A Touchstone Book, 1974.

Rogers, J. A. *World's Great Men of Color,* vol. 2. New York: Collier Books, Macmillan Publishing Company, 1972.

Rogers, Kim Lacy. *Life and Death in the Delta: African American Narratives of Violence, Resilience, and Social Change.* New York: Palgrave Macmillan, 2006.

Romano, Renee C., and Leigh Raiford, eds. *The Civil Rights Movement in American Memory.* Athens: University of Georgia Press, 2006.

Rosenberg, Jonathan, and Zachary Karabell. *Kennedy, Johnson, and the Quest for Justice: The Civil Rights Tapes.* New York: W. W. Norton & Company, 2003.

Royce, Edward. *The Origins of Southern Sharecropping.* Philadelphia: Temple University Press.

Rummel, Jack. *A to Z of African Americans: African-American Social Leaders and Activists.* New York: Facts on File Books, 2003.

Sansing, David G. *The University of Mississippi: A Sesquicentennial History.* Jackson: University Press of Mississippi, 1999.

Sansing, David G. *Making Haste Slowly: The Troubled History of Higher Education in Mississippi.* Jackson: University Press of Mississippi, 1990.

Schlesinger, Arthur M., Jr. *A Thousand Days: John F. Kennedy in the White House.* Boston: Houghton Mifflin Company, Boston the Riverside Press, 1965.

Scott, John H., with Cleo Scott Brown. *Witness to the Truth: My Struggle for Human Rights in Louisiana.* Columbia: University of South Carolina Press, 2003.

Shapiro, Thomas M. *The Hidden Cost of Being African American: How Wealth Perpetuates Inequality.* Oxford: Oxford University Press, 2004.

Silvestri, Vito N. *Becoming JFK: A Profile in Communication.* Connecticut: Praeger Publishers, 2000.

Simmons, Charles A. *The African American Press: A History of News Coverage During National Crises with Special Reference to Four Black Newspapers, 1827–1965.* Jefferson, NC: Mcfarland & Company, 1998.

Sitkoff, Harvard. *A New Deal for Blacks: The Emergence of Civil Rights as a National Issue Volume I: The Depression Decade.* Oxford: Oxford University Press, 1978.

Sitkoff, Harvard. *A New Deal for Blacks, the Emergence of Civil Rights as a National Issue: The Depression Decade.* 30th Anniversary ed. New York: Oxford University Press, 2009.

Sitkoff, Harvard. *The Struggle for Black Equality, 1954–1992,* rev. ed. New York: Hill and Wang, 1993.

Smead, Howard. *Blood Justice: The Lynching of Mack Charles Parker.* New York: Oxford University Press, 1986.

Smith, John David. *Historians at Work: When Did Southern Segregation Begin.* New York: Palgrave, 2002.

Stampp, Kenneth M. *The Peculiar Institution: Slavery in the Ante-Bellum South.* New York: Knopf, 1956.

Stockley, Grif. *Daisy Bates: Civil Rights Crusader from Arkansas.* Jackson: University Press of Mississippi, 2005.

Sullivan, Patricia. *Lift Every Voice: The NAACP and the Making of the Civil Rights Movement.* New York: New Press, 2009.

Tertius de Kay, James. *A Rage for Glory: The Life of Commodore Stephen Decatur, USN.* New York: Free Press, 2004.

Thornton, J. Mills, III. *Dividing Lines: Municipal Politics and the Struggle for Civil Rights in Montgomery, Birmingham, and Selma.* Tuscaloosa: The University of Alabama Press, 2002.

Throup, David. *Economic Origins of Mau Mau, 1945–53.* Athens: Ohio University Press, 2003.

Torres, Sasha. *Black, White, and in Color: Television and Black Civil Rights.* Princeton, NJ: Princeton University Press, 2003.

Tosh, John. *The Pursuit of History: Aims, Methods and New Directions in the Study of Modern History,* rev. 3rd ed. Pearson Education Limited, 2002.

Tucker, Spencer. *Stephen Decatur: A Life Most Bold and Daring.* Annapolis, MD: Naval Institute Press, 2005.

Tyson, Timothy B. *Radio Free Dixie: Robert F. Williams and the Roots of Black Power.* Chapel Hill: University of North Carolina Press, 1999.

Vernell, Majorie. *History Makers: Leaders of Black Civil Rights.* San Diego, CA: Lucent Books, 2000.

Vollers, Maryanne. *Ghosts of Mississippi: The Murder of Medgar Evers, the Trials of Byron De La Beckwith, and the Haunting of the New South.* Boston: Little, Brown and Company, 1995.

Walton, Anthony. *Mississippi: An American Journey.* New York: Alfred A. Knopf, 1996.

Watson, Denton L. *Lion in the Lobby: Clarence Mitchell, Jr.'s Struggle for the Passage of Civil Rights Laws.* Lanham, MD: University Press of America, 2002.

Wendt, Simon. *The Spirit and the Shotgun: New Perspectives on the History of the South.* Gainesville: University Press of Florida, 2007.

Whalen, Charles, and Barbara Whalen. *The Longest Debate: A Legislative History of the 1964 Civil Rights Act.* Washington, DC: Seven Locks Press, 1985.

White, Deborah Gray. *Ar'n't I a Woman? Female Slaves in the Plantation South,* rev. ed. New York: W. W. Norton & Company, 1999.

White, Marjorie L., and Andrew M. Manis, eds. *Birmingham Revolutionaries: The Reverend Fred Shuttlesworth and the Alabama Christian Movement for Human Rights.* Macon, GA: Mercer University Press, 2000.

Whitfield, Stephen J. *A Death in the Delta: The Story of Emmett Till.* Baltimore, MD: Johns Hopkins University Press, 1988.

Williams, Juan. *Eyes on the Prize: America's Civil Rights Years, 1954–1965.* New York: Viking Penguin, 1987.

Williams, Nancy K. *The History of Newton, Mississippi 1860–1988*. Newton, MS: Nancy K. Williams, 1989.

Williamson, Joel. *The Crucible of Race: Black White Relations in the American South Since Emancipation*. New York: Oxford University Press, 1984.

Wilson, Bobby M. *Race and Place in Birmingham: The Civil Rights and Neighborhood Movements*. Lanham, MD: Rowman & Littlefield Publishers, 2000.

Wolff, Miles. *Lunch at the Five and Ten: The Greensboro Sit-ins, A Contemporary History*. New York: Stein and Day Publishers, 1970.

Woodruff, Nan Elizabeth. *American Congo: The African American Freedom Struggle in the Delta*. Cambridge, MA: Harvard University Press, 2003.

Woodward, C. Vann. *The Strange Career of Jim Crow: A Commemorative Edition*. New York: Oxford University Press, 2002.

Wormser, Richard. *The Rise and Fall of Jim Crow*. New York: St. Martin's Press, 2003.

Articles

Bailey, Ronald. "Remembering Medgar Evers . . . For a New Generation." A Commemoration Developed by The Civil Rights Research And Documentation Project Afro-American Studies Program—The University of Mississippi. Distributed by Heritage Publications in cooperation with The Mississippi Network For Black History And Heritage, 1988.

Butler, Michael J. "The Mississippi State Sovereignty Commission and Beach Integration, 1959–1963: A Cotton-Patch Gestapo?" *Journal of Southern History* 68, no. 1 (February 2002): 107–148.

Davis, Dernoral. "Medgar Wiley Evers and the Origin of the Civil Rights Movement in Mississippi." A part of the *Mississippi History Now* online publication of the Mississippi Historical Society. http://mshistory.k12.ms.us/features/feature45/medgar_evers.htm.

Du Bois, W. E. B. "Returning Soldiers." *Crisis*, 18, no. 1 (May 1919): 13–14.

Du Bois, W. E. B. "Three Centuries of Discrimination." *Crisis* 54 (December 1947): 362–381.

"Editorial Comment: The University of Maryland Versus Donald Gaines Murray." *Journal of Negro Education* 5, no. 2 (1936): 166–174.

Fraser, Cary. "Crossing the Color Line in Little Rock: The Eisenhower Administration and the Dilemma of Race for U.S. Foreign Policy." *Diplomatic History* 24, no. 2 (Spring 2000): 233–264.

Garrow, David. "Hopelessly Hollow History: Revisionist Devaluing of *Brown v. Board of Education*." *Virginia Law Review* 80, no. 1, Twentieth-Century Constitutional History (February 1994): 151–160.

Guzman, Jessie P. "Twenty Years of Court Decisions Affecting Higher Education in the South, 1938–1958." *Journal of Educational Sociology* 32, no. 6, Southern Higher Education Since the Gaines Decision: A Twenty Year Review (February 1959): 247–253.

Hollander, Ronald A. "One Negro Who Didn't Go To College." *The Reporter: The Magazine of Facts and Ideas* 27, no. 8 (November 8, 1962): 30–34.

Keller, Daniel T. "The Case of Lloyd Lionel Gaines: The Demise of the Separate

But Equal Doctrine." *Journal of Negro History* 56, no. 4 (October 1971): 262–271.

Klarman, Michael J. "How *Brown* Changed Race Relations: The Backlash Thesis." *Journal of American History* (June 1994): 81–118.

Klarman, Michael J. "Reply: *Brown v. Board of Education:* Facts and Political Correctness." *Virginia Law Review* 80, no. 1, Twentieth-Century Constitutional History (February 1994): 185–199.

Minchin, Timothy J., and John A. Salmond. "'The Saddest Story of the Whole Movement': The Clyde Kennard Case and the Search for Racial Reconciliation in Mississippi, 1955–2007." *Journal of Mississippi History* 71, no. 3 (Fall 2009): 191–234.

Tushnet, Mark. "The Significance of *Brown v. Board of Education.*" *Virginia Law Review* 80, no. 1, Twentieth-Century Constitutional History (February 1994): 173–184.

Umoja, Akinyele O. "The Ballot and the Bullet: A Comparative Analysis of Armed Resistance in the Civil Rights Movement." *Journal of Black Studies* 29, no. 4 (March 1999): 558–578.

Book Chapters

Beito, David T., and Linda Royster Beito. "T.R.M. Howard: Pragmatism over Strict Integrationist Ideology in the Mississippi Delta, 1942–1954." In *Before Brown: Civil Rights and White Backlash in the Modern South.* Edited by Glenn Feldman. Tuscaloosa: The University of Alabama Press, 2004.

Boger, Charles. "Brown and the American South: Fateful Choices." In *School Resegregation: Must the South Turn Back?* Edited by John Charles Boger and Gary Orfield. Chapel Hill: University of North Carolina Press, 2005.

Brady, Tomas. *Black Monday.* In *Mississippi: A Documentary History.* Edited by Bradley G. Bond. Jackson: University Press of Mississippi, 2003.

Chemerinsky, Erwin. "The Segregation and Resegregation of American Public Education: The Court's Role." In *School Resegregation: Must the South Turn Back?* Edited by John Charles Boger and Gary Orfield. Chapel Hill: University of North Carolina Press, 2005.

Coard, Stephanie I., and Robert M. Sellers. "African American Families as a Context for Racial Socialization." In *African American Family Life: Ecological and Cultural Diversity.* Edited by Vonnie C. McLoyd, Nancy E. Hill, and Kenneth A. Dodge. New York: Guilford Press, 2005.

Dittmer, John. "The Politics of the Mississippi Movement, 1954–1964." In *The Civil Rights Movement in America.* Edited by Charles W. Eagles. Jackson: University Press of Mississippi, 1986.

Donald, Cleveland, Jr. "Medgar Wiley Evers: The Civil Rights Leader as Utopianist." In *Mississippi Heroes.* Edited by Dean Faulkner Cole and Hunter Cole. Jackson: University Press of Mississippi, 1980.

Driskell, Jay. "Amzie Moore: The Biographical Roots of the Civil Rights Movement in Mississippi." In *The Human Tradition in the Civil Rights Movement.* Edited by Susan Glisson. Lanham, MD: Rowman & Littlefield, 2006.

Garrow, David. "Commentary." In *The Civil Rights Movement in America.* Edited by Charles W. Eagles. Jackson: University Press of Mississippi, 1986.

Lauren, Paul Gordon. "Seen from the Outside: The International Perspective on America's Dilemma." In *Window on Freedom: Race, Civil Rights, and Foreign Affairs 1945–1988.* Edited by Brenda Gayle Plummer. Chapel Hill: University of North Carolina Press, 2003.

Mattis, Jacqueline S. "Religion in African American Life." In *African American Family Life: Ecological and Cultural Diversity.* Edited by Vonnie C. McLoyd, Nancy E. Hill, and Kenneth A. Dodge. New York: Guilford Press, 2005.

Orfield, Gary. "The Southern Dilemma: Losing Brown, Fearing Plessy." In *School Resegregation: Must the South Turn Back?* Edited by John Charles Boger and Gary Orfield. Chapel Hill: University of North Carolina Press, 2005.

Reardon, Sean F., and John T. Yun. "Integrating Neighborhoods, Segregating Schools: The Retreat from School Desegregation in the South, 1990–2000." In *School Resegregation: Must the South Turn Back?* Edited by John Charles Boger and Gary Orfield. Chapel Hill: University of North Carolina Press, 2005.

Thomas, Joyce. "The Protest Against 'Insult': Black Soldiers, World War II, and the 'War' for 'Democracy' at Home." In *Black Resistance Movements in the United States and Africa, 1800–1933, Oppression and Resistance.* Edited by Felton O. Best. African Studies, vol. 38. New York: Edwin Mellen Press, 1995.

Unpublished Theses and Dissertations

Balsamo, Larry Thomas. "Theodore G. Bilbo and Mississippi Politics, 1877–1932." Ph.D. diss., University of Missouri, Columbia, 1967.

Black, Stephen Richard. "The Man with a Plan: Theodore Bilbo's Adaptation of National Progressivism in Mississippi." Ph.D. diss., University of Southern Mississippi, 2006.

Crofton, Gregory Charles. "Defending Segregation: Mississippi State Sovereignty Commission and the Press." MA thesis, University of Mississippi, 1985.

Murrain, Ethel Patricia Churchill. "The Mississippi Man and His Message: A Rhetorical Analysis of the Cultural Themes in the Oratory of Medgar Wiley Evers, 1957–1963." Ph.D. diss., University of Southern Mississippi, 1990.

Tisdale, John R. "Medgar Evers (1925–1963) and the Mississippi Press." Ph.D. diss., University of North Texas, 1996.

Legislative Resolutions

Mississippi Legislature, House Bill 880.

Mississippi Legislature, House Concurrent Resolution Number 94, 03/HR03/R1864.

Mississippi Legislature, Senate Concurrent Resolution No. 6.

Booklet

44th Annual Medgar Wiley Evers/B.B. King Mississippi Homecoming Booklet. May 31–June 2, 2007.

Presentations/Events

Alcorn State University National Alumni Association, 30th Annual Mid-Winter Conference, Heritage Luncheon. February 24, 2007 (Myrlie Evers-Williams, keynote speaker), Jackson, Mississippi.

Forty-fourth Annual Medgar Wiley Evers/B. B. King Mississippi Homecoming, May 31–June 2, 2007 (Myrlie Evers-Williams, inspirational speaker), Jackson, Mississippi.

Forty-second Annual Medgar Wiley Evers/B. B. King Mississippi Homecoming, June 9–11, 2005, Jackson, Mississippi.

Jackson-Evers International Airport Open House, December 12, 2006, Jackson, Mississippi.

Myrlie Evers-Williams book signing and lecture presentation, Jackson, Old Capitol Building, June 13, 2005, Jackson, Mississippi.

The Twenty-third Annual Fannie Lou Hamer Memorial Symposium Lecture Series: "Civil Rights, Social Justice, Active Citizenship." Jackson State University and Campbell College Students in the Jackson Movement, October 5, 2006, Jackson, Mississippi.

Index

gies, 232, 261, 288; Evers' funeral, 290; historical analysis, 386, 391; and Medgar Evers, 236, 248; NAACP Freedom Fund banquet, 167; NAACP statement, 241; safety concerns, 106; school desegregation, 154; sit-in demonstration, 253; as youth council advisor, 141, 230–33; and youth involvement, 259

Samuel Bailey et al. v. Joe T. Patterson et al. (1962), 238

Sanders, Fred, 9, 293

Sanders, I. S., 252, 262

Sanders, Stanney, 294, 306

San Francisco, California, 132

Sansing, David, 74

Saucier, Murray J., Jr., 184

Schlesinger, Arthur M., Jr., 287, 299

school desegregation, 69–81, 89–93, 152–54, 163–64, 176, 188, 223–25, 238–39, 313–14

school integration petition, 229, 239

Schutt, Mrs. Wallis, 193

Schwerner, Michael, 5, 383

Scott County, Mississippi, 14, 16

Scott, R. W., 385, 386, 391

Seale, James Ford, 5

self-esteem, 95

self-sufficiency, 15–16, 18–19, 57, 96

Sellers, Robert M., 95, 96

Senate Concurrent Resolution No. 6 (Mississippi), 141–42

separate but equal doctrine, 69–70, 73, 80, 91

761st Tank Battalion, 28–29

Shapiro, Thomas, 312

sharecroppers/sharecropping system, 53, 58–63, 65–66

Sharkey County, Mississippi, 53

Shaw University, 190

Shelby, Mississippi, 65

Shelton, G. V., 157

Shelton, Isacc (Ike), 119

Shevlin, John, 28

S. H. Kress store, 255–56

Shoemaker, W. C. (Dub), 283

Shriver, Sargent, 271

Shuttlesworth, Fred, 94, 215–16, 233, 249–52

Shuttleworth, Bill, 174

Sillers, Walter, 139

Sims, Harry, 215

Singleton, Edna Marie, 239

sit-in demonstrations, 176–80, 190, 192–93, 225, 250, 253–55

Sitkoff, Harvard, 311

Sitton, Claude, 289

Sixteenth Street Baptist Church, 251

Slaughter-Harvey, Constance, 228

Slaughter, Mrs., 181

Smead, Howard, 160, 161

Smith, Arthur, 161

Smithart, Ray, 199

Smith, Jerome, 277

Smith, Lamar, 118, 122–23, 127, 162, 167

Smith, Leona, 167, 168

Smith, Mack, 123

Smith, Noah, 123

Smith, R. B., Jr., 77

Smith, Robert, 103, 198, 295–96

Smith, Robert L. T., 9

Smith v. Allwright (1944), 38

Smith, William C., 207–8

social codes and boundaries, 24–25, 51–52

socialization, 95–96

social resistance efforts, 44

social responsibility, 17

socioeconomic disparities, 312–13

Solomon Islands, 275

Sorenson, Theodore, 272, 280, 299

South Carolina, 214–15, 255–56

South Carolina, Davis v. Board of Education of Prince Edward County, Virginia (1952), 77

Southern Christian Leadership Conference (SCLC), 9, 134–37, 156, 220, 232, 250

Southern Conference Educational Fund, 233

Southern grassroots resistance movements, 90–92

Sovereignty Commission, 138–43, 146–47, 174, 181–83, 193, 241–42, 252, 305–6, 387–88

Speights, H. R., 292

Spence, Howard, 125–26

Springfield riots, 332n2

Standard Oil of Kentucky, 207–8

Starr, Douglass, 166, 168

State Times, 103, 123, 166

Stennett, J. C., 263

Stennis, John, 91

Steptoe, E. W., 381

Stevens, Thaddeus, 287

*Michael Vinson Williams is assistant professor
of history and African American studies at Mississippi
State University. A lifelong resident of Mississippi,
he lives in Etta with his wife, Truly, and their
two children, Ayo and Marimba.*